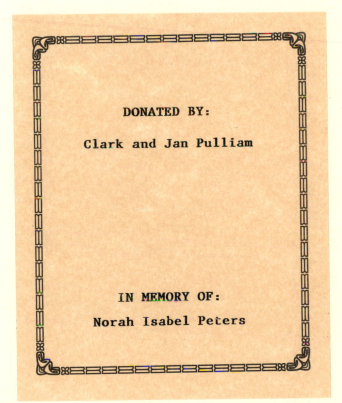

THE ARMIES
OF WELLINGTON

THE ARMIES OF WELLINGTON

Philip J. Haythornthwaite

ARMS AND
ARMOUR

Arms and Armour Press
A Cassell Imprint
Villiers House, 41-47 Strand, London WC2N 5JE.

Distributed in the USA by Sterling Publishing Co. Inc., 387 Park
Avenue South, New York, NY 10016-8810.

Distributed in Australia by Capricorn Link (Australia) Pty. Ltd,
2/13 Carrington Road, Castle Hill, New South Wales 2154.

British Library Cataloguing-in-Publication Data: a catalogue record
for this book is available from the British Library

ISBN 1-85409-175-1

Designed and edited by DAG Publications Ltd.
Designed by David Gibbons; edited by Michael Boxall;
Printed and bound in Great Britain by
Hartnolls Limited, Bodmin, Cornwall

Acknowledgements
The author would like to take this opportunity to extend
especial thanks for their assistance to the following: Thomas
E. De Voe; Dr. John A. Hall; David C. Hamilton-Williams;
and Alan Harrison.

Jacket illustrations
Main illustration: *Waterloo*, an engraving by T. Sutherland
after William Heath. Inset: Arthur Wellesley, First Duke of
Wellington, KG (1769–1852) painted in 1814 by Sir Thomas
Lawrence, PRA (1769–1830), reproduced by courtesy of the
Trustees of the Victoria and Albert Museum, London.

Contents

Introduction

OF ALL THE NATIONS THAT OPPOSED REPUBLICAN FRANCE AND THE Napoleonic Empire between the years 1793 and 1815, only Britain remained in the field during the entire period of hostilities, and Britain's efforts were instrumental in the defeat of Napoleon. In the process, the reputation of the British Army was established as superior even to that attained under Marlborough, and as the most successful campaigns were those of the Iberian peninsula and the 'Hundred Days', the army is associated inseparably with its commander, arguably the greatest ever produced by his country: Arthur Wellesley, 1st Duke of Wellington.

A number of previous works have examined the army which Wellington led, generally concentrating upon the Peninsula and Waterloo campaigns. This present study considers the British Army during the entire period, to which end individual cases and events are quoted by way of exemplification of the various aspects. Most of these are taken from contemporary sources, in which the factor of possible inaccuracy must be taken into account: writing to Robert Craufurd on 23 July 1810, Wellington himself remarked that: 'As soon as an accident happens, every man who can write, and who has a friend who can read, sits down to write his account of what he does not know, and his comments on what he does not understand.' Thus, while many such contemporary accounts can be demonstrated as being extremely accurate, at least when concerning events which fell within the writer's personal scope of vision, others tended to distort facts for a variety of reasons, from motives of personal aggrandisement to national bias. The latter was not restricted to enemy forces: for example, Jonathan Leach of the 95th complained that in the popular perception of the battle, the Highland regiments received most of the credit for the victory of Waterloo, as if 'John Bull and Pat were little better than idle spectators'.[1]

Accounts of the army's campaigns are legion, so although in this study the operations are summarized chronologically, more extensive coverage is reserved for minor actions or incidents within a battle which serve to exemplify various aspects of the army, its character and mode of operation, with the concentration upon the tactical matters which concerned the army most closely, rather than upon those of wider strategy.

Throughout the text, it has been found practical to use footnotes largely as identification of the sources of quotations; other important references are listed in the bibliography.

1
'The Land which has saved us all!'

WHEN TSAR ALEXANDER I STEPPED ASHORE AT DOVER FOR HIS state visit in 1814, he exclaimed, 'God be praised! I have set my foot upon the land which has saved us all!'[2]

Even allowing for the courtesy of diplomatic language, it is hard to discount the Tsar's sentiment, for of all the states in Europe, only Britain remained consistently opposed to the regimes which succeeded to power in France following the deposition of the monarchy, and without Britain it is difficult to imagine how Napoleon's empire could ever have been defeated. The part played by Britain's own naval and military forces was significant, but equally important was the immense financial and material support provided to the other states opposing France.

Unlike all the other major European powers, Britain never suffered a reverse so severe as to call into question the very principle of opposing France. This determination to prosecute the war was facilitated by the fact that apart from a period of barely a year, the successive British ministries were of one political complexion, Tory, presided over as prime minister by William Pitt the younger (1783–1801, 1804–6); Henry Addington, Viscount Sidmouth (18014); William Bentinck, Duke of Portland (1807–9); Spencer Perceval (1809 until his assassination by the maniac Bellingham in June 1812); and Robert Jenkinson, Earl of Liverpool (1812–27). The brief hiatus in Tory administration was the ministry of William, Baron Grenville, from February 1806 to March 1807.

The apparently unflinching determination to combat the French should not disguise the fact that there was an opposition both inside and outside parliament, although much of this was concerned more with the manner in which the war was waged than with doubts about the wisdom of waging it. Criticism was not surprisingly strongest during those periods, often protracted, when the war was perceived as either progressing aimlessly or at the expense of British interests; in December 1798, for example, the *Morning Chronicle* wondered 'whether the remaining blood and treasure of the British empire is to be wasted in an attempt merely to transfer some of the states of Europe from one set of despots to another'.[3]

Much of the political opposition came from outside parliament, in publications like William Cobbett's *Weekly Political Register*, which presented what might be termed the Radical perspective. Some of the opposition to the war was immensely ill-informed, but Cobbett wrote from the viewpoint of one who had served in the army, having been so capable a soldier as to rise to the rank of sergeant-major in the 54th Foot before obtaining his discharge in 1791. Though not lacking courage (he went to gaol over his campaign against flogging in the army), and despite his military experience, Cobbett's judgement on military affairs appears somewhat curious, especially in his preference of believing French military dispatches rather than British. French dispatches – described elsewhere as 'the tinsel web of sophistry'[4] – were not even believed in France, where a common expression was 'to lie like a Bulletin'; yet Cobbett appeared to hold that British dispatches were either invented or warped by the government. For example, he exhibited considerable naïevety by remarking that the statements in the French account of Albuera *must* be true, otherwise the Duke of Dalmatia (Soult), 'would not dare, Duke as he is, to say so'.[5] His belief in French dispatches was used to support his opinion that the Peninsular War was a hopeless undertaking, 'nothing but a drain upon this country, without the smallest chance of any ultimate benefit ... the sooner we abandon the undertaking the better. By prolonging it we do, indeed, cause some expense and some mortality to France; but we, at the same time, weaken ourselves in a degree tenfold to what we weaken her.'[6]

Cobbett was by no means a lone voice; for example, in July 1809 *The News* published a leader on 'The Deceptions of the English Press', blaming 'the corrupt administration of the late Mr Pitt' for perpetuating falsehoods relative to the progress of the war, and that following the defeat of Austria: 'We have no other resource but in peace ... if a trial was now made to procure peace, in a real pacific spirit, Europe might be relieved from the horrors of further bloodshed, and the tears which the calamities of war have occasioned, be at length wiped from our eyes', and that those who advocated any other course were in a state of 'mental imbecility'.[7]

Conversely, especially during the period when Britain was most at risk from invasion, the virulence of anti-French propaganda reached an unprecedented level, with Napoleon in particular being accused of every evil from cannibalism to bearing 'a striking similitude' to the Antichrist;[8] for example, a pamphlet published in 1803–4, *A Hint to England*, purported to *prove* that Napoleon was 'the Beast that rose out of the Earth, with Two Horns like a Lamb, and spake as a Dragon, whose Number is 666', i.e., the beast from *Revelations*, 13.[9]

Neither within parliament nor without was there sufficient pressure to deflect successive administrations from continuing to prosecute the war, even though throughout the period of almost 22 years of conflict, it took up the greater part of government expenditure. Despite the pre-eminence of the Royal Navy as the guardian both of Britain's shores (and thus the main protection against invasion) and of the sea-lanes upon which British trade and communication with the colonies depended, between the years 1800 and 1815 only rarely did naval expenditure exceed that allocated to the army; and subsidies to allied nations, enabling them to continue to fight, were also extensive. In 1800, for example, almost 7.6 per cent of the Treasury's total revenue was spent on such subsidies (£3 million out of £37,920,000), while in 1813 loans to allies actually exceeded the amount spent on the Royal Navy. Although much of what might be termed public expenditure, for example maintenance of roads and relief of the poor, was levied and spent at local level rather than by central government, the extent to which war expenses dominated the national budget can be gauged from the following statistics:

1803: total expenditure £38,956,917, of which
    Navy £10,211,378
    Army £8,935,753

Militia £2,889,976
Ordnance £1,128,913
1808: total expenditure £48,319,807, of which
Army £19,439,189
Navy £17,496,047
Ordnance £4,534,571
Subsidy £1,100,000
1812: total expenditure £97,521,371, of which
Army £24,987,362
Navy £20,500,339
Subsidies £8,204,028
Ordnance £4,252,409
1814: total expenditure £117,587,979, of which
Army £33,795,556
Navy £21,961,566
Subsidies £10,024,618
Ordnance £4,480,729
Militia and deserters' warrants £138,494
(Examples of the breakdown of such expenditure are given in the appendices.)

This level of expenditure was frequently criticized – for example the annual £306,960 for the staff of the Local Militia was decried by *The News*: 'THREE HUNDRED THOUSAND POUNDS! *Was anything so profligate ever heard of?*'[10] – but some of the economies suggested were militarily wildly impracticable. For example, in June 1809 the notorious Gwylym Wardle, MP proposed an economy of £7^1/$_2$ million by reforming the navy's Victualling Office and disbanding parts of the army, including the Life Guards, Staff Corps, foreign corps, Waggon Train and horse artillery. Even if some criticisms were valid, for example that hiring draught-horses for the artillery was uneconomic, his proposal to cut the very supporting services of which the army already had insufficient, suggests the ignorance from which such suggestions were made; government spokesmen immediately derided the scheme as futile, calculated to cause discontent, and founded upon false calculations.

Despite the dissipation of a portion of the national resources in ill-advised expeditions, the consequence of this considerable expenditure was that Britain could field an army adequate for the duties imposed upon it; but latterly this adequacy was largely the result of possessing in Wellington a general of the highest calibre, who was able to succeed despite, rather than because of, the level of financial support received by the army.

Although there were periods of grievous financial hardship which affected much of society, national prosperity was such that the economy was able to survive the stresses of decades of warfare, without there ever appearing a serious popular or ideological movement to end the conflict. Indeed, although the leaders of society for obvious reasons generally endeavoured to emphasize the 'patriotic' mood, much of the information available as to the general feelings of the nation suggests that, despite periods of civil unrest which arose at the times of greatest economic hardship, John Bull would have been receptive to the following editorial, written at a time when Britain stood alone against Napoleonic Europe, and in language which uncannily recalls that of 1940:

'What must be our emotions at the present period? How can we look backward without horror, or forward without despondency? Yet despondency never was, nor ever can be, the characteristic of Englishmen. Let us, therefore, fix our eyes, our thoughts, our hopes, on the only bright and cheering Spot which illuminates Europe – Britain stands alone, independent, intrepid, immovable! Firm as our native rocks, let us dash on their own shores the surges with which our Enemies threaten to overwhelm us ...'[11]

2

'All for King and Country bearing'
THE MILITARY SYSTEM

'Thus the soldier, all things daring,
Fearless into battle goes;
All for King and Country bearing,
Meets the fiercest of their foes.'[12]
(The Villers-en-Cauchies song of the 15th Light Dragoons)

IT WAS NOT SIMPLY TO KEEP A CHECK UPON EXPENDITURE THAT THE military system had strict political control. Although almost a century and a half had elapsed since military government was ended by the restoration of Charles II, the spectre of army oppression still cast a shadow. Although the fear that military force was by definition a threat to liberty was nothing like so strong as in the past, it was still a view expressed by Burke (who originated the term 'rapacious and licentious soldiery' in a speech in 1783), and what might be termed the radical end of British politics still had sympathies with Trenchard's expression of a century before, 'If any Man doubts whether a Standing Army is Slavery, Popery, Mahometism, Paganism, Atheism, or any thing which they please ...'[13] Apart from the minority most concerned with the concept of liberty, the middle and upper classes were not too enamoured of the army because its upkeep accounted for a considerable proportion of the taxes they paid, while elements of the labouring classes also viewed it as an instrument of repression, the army at times acting as police and periodically making itself obnoxious by causing problems when billeted on local innkeepers.

The nominal head of the army was the King. Despite the fact that all orders were issued in his name, and that he signed officers' commissions, in reality his influence was minimal, and the very existence of the army was dependent upon parliament's passing of the Mutiny Act every year. George III was the ruling monarch throughout the entire period of the French Wars, although his deteriorating state of mental health led to his eldest son, George Augustus Frederick, Prince of Wales, being appointed Prince Regent in his stead in 1811. The army formed a career for several of George III's sons, most significantly Frederick Augustus, Duke of York, although Edward Augustus, Duke of Kent, and Adolphus Frederick, Duke of Cambridge, eventually aspired to the rank of field marshal, Kent serving actively as commander-in-chief at Gibraltar for most of the period.

Undoubtedly the most colourful of George III's military offspring was his fifth son, Ernest Augustus, created Duke of Cumberland in 1799 and colonel of the 15th Hussars in 1801. His stern demeanour and dislike of publicity fostered a sinister reputation, the wilder rumours including his having fathered a son upon his sister Sophia, of having attacked the wife of the Lord Chancellor, and of being the cause of the suicide of a wronged husband. Undoubtedly he was unlucky: as a cavalry general in the Hanoverian army he lost the sight of an eye at Tournai in May 1794, and was involved in a sensational case in May 1810. Awakened in the night by what he thought was a bat landing on his head, he found it to be a murderous attack by his own sabre, hacking through the bed-curtains. After suffering six severe slashes and numerous punctures, Cumberland aroused a servant, and on investigation found his Piedmontese valet Sallis lying dead with a cut throat. No motive for the attempted assassination and suicide was ever discovered, but it gave rise to scurrilous stories that Cumberland had murdered the man. The Duke became commander of the Hanoverian army in 1813–14 and was present (though not in action) at Leipzig. Scandal continued to follow him when in 1815 he married his cousin, Princess Frederica of Mecklenburg-Strelitz, who had previously jilted his brother (the Duke of Cambridge) and was said to have murdered her two previous husbands. The marriage caused a rift in the royal family and Ernest went abroad, returning to oppose Catholic Emancipation as champion of the most reactionary elements in parliament. In 1837 he became king of Hanover.

Few members of the royal family saw active service, although the Prince Regent lost his father-in-law and brother-in-law, both Dukes of Brunswick, killed in battle by the French. The Duke of Clarence (later King William IV) had chosen the Royal Navy as a career, but after years of being denied an active command followed the army to The Netherlands in 1813–14 and at Merxem, in accompanying the advanced skirmishers, got himself surrounded by Frenchmen and had to be saved by a small party led by Lieutenant Thomas Austin of the 35th, after a sharp fight in which the Duke showed considerable courage. In addition to acknowledged members of the royal family, a number of illegitimates served in the army. George Fitzclarence of the 10th Hussars (later 1st Earl of Munster), who served in the Peninsular War, was a son of the Duke of Clarence; and First Lieutenant John Stilwell of the 95th, alias 'Scamp', who was killed at Waterloo, was believed to be a natural son of the Duke of York.[14] Charles Hesse of the 18th Hussars, a lieutenant at Waterloo, where he was wounded, was also believed to be an illegitimate son of the Duke of York; if so, there was a terrible irony about his death, for he was killed in a duel with Count Leon, an illegitimate son of Napoleon.

The curtailment of the royal family's power left control of the army not primarily with parliament but with the government, which used it as a vehicle for the exercise of patronage, and some political interference, as in the appointment of staff positions, was evident throughout the period. Commands to the army originally passed through the hands of the Secretary at War, previously the monarch's military secretary but by the late 18th century a minister responsible to parliament and with direct access to the king, who in theory still retained personal command of the Foot Guards and thus had to issue to them the orders promulgated by the Secretary at War. The Secretary, though not responsible for the army's actions, controlled the register of commissions and was responsible for ensuring that parliament's money was spent in the purposes for which it had been voted. At the time when the French war was looming, the Secretary at War was Sir George Yonge, a politician who exercised patronage for political ends and cast a somewhat malign influence over the military system, and was not above reproach in his personal dealings: having been sent to the Cape as governor in 1799, he was recalled in 1801 for having given the contract for supplying meat to undesirables, and in having shared in the profits.[15]

Prior to the outbreak of war, each of the two Secretaries of State had controlled affairs in particular parts of the globe, including military operations; but in 1794 Pitt established a third secretariat, for War, to which colonial affairs were added. The Secretary of State for War and the colonies assumed a role in the direction of military policy, which, with the creation of the post of commander-in-chief, reduced the role of the Secretary at War theoretically to that of a clerk, even when the position was held by Yonge's successor, William Windham, though the element of rivalry which could exist between the two was potentially damaging to the smooth running of the nation's military policy. The first Secretary of State for War was Pitt's friend Henry Dundas (Viscount Melville from 1802), whose only military knowledge came from a commission in the Royal Edinburgh Volunteers. This was not the most felicitous of appointments – Fortescue remarked that he was the very worst man who could have been found, which is probably somewhat harsh – and Dundas's appointment ended with the change of ministry in 1801. (He was impeached in 1806 for the misappropriation of public funds, and though acquitted never again held office.)

As government policy and the wider strategy by which Britain waged war falls outside the scope of this study, concentration should now be shifted towards the administration and composition of the army; but the political perspective should always be kept in view. Politics, however, loomed large in the minds of probably only a few officers, and those of higher rank; as John Fitzmaurice of the 95th stated, 'as to politics ... a soldier should have none',[16] which was why he always voted Conservative. (The only prejudices held by this gallant officer 'were against Napoleon, Scotchmen and "Puseyites"',[17] presumably in that order.) Indeed, the majority would probably have agreed with Francis Skelly Tidy, who commanded the 3/14th at Waterloo, of whom his daughter wrote:

'"What are you, papa?" said a young sister of mine to him one day, "Whig or Tory?". "I am a soldier," he replied, "and one of his Majesty's most devoted servants, bound to defend the crown with my life against either faction if necessary."'[18]

As for the lower ranks, political perspectives probably never entered their minds. Moyle Sherer records the nearest to a political philosophy approached by an ordinary soldier, overheard as his battalion stumbled on, weary and unfed in the Peninsula: 'Bill, the parliament and the great men at home, they do know all about the movements of the army and the grandè lord, but they don't know any thing about individuals; for instance, now, they don't know that you are damned tired, and that I had got no pong' [bread].'[19]

The regular military forces of the crown were divided into two separate organizations, the Army and the Ordnance, the troops of the latter not officially part of the army and with a different structure of command and establishment. The army's command was usually styled 'the Horse Guards', from the location in that building of the office of the Commander-in-Chief.

The position of Commander-in-Chief was normally activated only in wartime (to the detriment of the army in time of peace), but its responsibility was less than the title might suggest. The Commander-in-Chief would have led the defence of the country in case of invasion, but had no authority over foreign expeditions or the appointment of their commanders, and did not even have to be consulted on questions of wider military policy; but he was responsible for training and discipline of the army (less the Foot Guards) and for the appointment and promotion of regimental and staff officers.

The appointment of the first commander-in-chief in 1793 did little to improve Yonge's administration, as the officer selected was Jeffrey, 1st Lord Amherst, a 76-year-old veteran of the Seven Years War; he was largely incapable of the office, and even Dundas remarked that his brief tenure was productive only of mischief. In 1795, however, upon Pitt's recommendation, the Duke of York was appointed Commander-in-Chief, and it was through his reforms that the army was able to assume the character it retained throughout the Napoleonic Wars. He standardized the system of training and overhauled the process of granting commissions, reducing the grip of patronage and radically improving the calibre of officer by introducing strictures over the process of promotion. Although an uninspired field commander, the Duke was an earnest and capable man, both able and willing to devote all his energies to the reforms which were vital, and his status as a royal prince permitted few challenges from even the most influential vested interests.

It is unfortunate that the Duke's entirely beneficial effect upon the army was overshadowed by the celebrated scandal of 1809, which gave his opponents their opportunity for revenge. In 1791 the Duke had married Princess Frederica Charlotte of Prussia, but the union was not happy, and he made the acquaintance of Mrs Mary Ann Clarke, wife of a bankrupt stonemason, full-time society courtesan and part-time blackmailer, 'a very pretty, sprightly, gaily-disposed girl, being very fond of shewing herself, and attracting attention'.[20] In 1802 the Duke set her up as his mistress with an income of £1,000 per annum, but even this sum was insufficient for her extravagant lifestyle. Despite extracting more than £16,000 from the Duke in three years, she was compelled by her improvidence to swindle traders who had trusted her because of her royal connections, and finally began to take bribes in exchange for securing the Duke's patronage for military, civil and even clerical preferments. On becoming aware of her nefarious practices, the Duke broke off the relationship in 1806, but promised her a pension of £400 per annum if she conducted herself with discretion, but, besieged by creditors and with the pension withdrawn, in June 1808 Mrs Clarke threatened to publish all she knew unless the pension were restored and the arrears paid. When the Duke refused to bow to blackmail, Mrs Clarke's latest friend, Colonel Gwylym Lloyd Wardle, Radical MP for Okehampton, raised the matter in parliament. (As an ex-officer in the Ancient British Fencibles, Wardle had been denied rank in the regular army as a result of the Duke's reforms, and thus had a personal motive for agitation.)

A committee of inquiry established the payment of bribes to Mrs Clarke, but no evidence was produced to show that she had ever influenced the Duke over the disposal of commissions, save a note which he claimed was not genuine (and it was proven that she was sufficiently accomplished a forger to reproduce his handwriting). The Duke was acquitted of the charge of selling commissions, and it was stated in parliament that the House observed with pleasure that he 'regretted the existence of such a connection', and trusted that in future the Duke would 'exhibit a right example of every virtue, in imitation of his Royal Parent'.[21] However, the Duke had no option but to resign as Commander-in-Chief.

It has been suggested that Wardle and Mrs Clarke led a conspiracy to profit from the affair, and on 3 July 1809 an upholsterer, Francis Wright, won his case at King's Bench against Wardle for unpaid bills against Mrs Clarke, in which it was stated that they 'had made a kind of treaty: the Colonel was to furnish the lady's house in Westbourne-place; the lady was to assist the Colonel in the investigation'.[22] Despite Wardle's somewhat unsavoury role, he received unstinting praise from certain quarters: *The News* described him as 'a tried, disinterested Patriot' who 'having hurled a Royal Personage from his high situation ... now prepares to storm the strong holds of Corruption ... to shew how a whole People are deprived of their rights and privileges, by the venality of a few' and to attack 'that odious, inquisitorial impost' known as the Income Tax.[23] Mrs Clarke continued her career, and in February 1814 was sentenced to nine months in Marshalsea prison for blackmailing the Chancellor of the Exchequer for Ireland. She died in Boulogne in 1852.

Upon reflection, it is perhaps unfortunate that the Duke of York had not heeded the warning in the handbook *The Military Mentor*, which cautioned against those 'vile and disgraceful appetites' which delivered young officers 'into the embraces of those unhappy females, who are distinguished only for the corruption of their manners, and the depravity of their actions, and for the number of victims that have been sacrificed to their arts', to effect 'the ruin of the bravest and most courageous characters. How many officers do we every day see, who, after having been the dupes of a set of abandoned women, become incapable of an honourable passion, are discarded from well-bred society, and finish their career in misery and disgrace!'[24]

In the Duke's stead, Sir David Dundas was appointed Commander-in-Chief, 'Old Pivot', who had produced the first universal drill manual. He was not a success in his new office and was unpopular with some; George Napier described him as 'old Sir David, who had the greatest antipathy to giving any man promotion who was not as old as himself ... the crusty old fellow could not bear the idea of promotion; and, except his money, he would sooner part with anything else ... thank God, the old boy is gone, and the Lord defend us from ever seeing such another at the head of the army'.[25]

In 1811, however, the Duke of York was re-appointed and held the office until his death in 1827. Not only was he responsible for the intelligent reform of the army, but was known also for his concern for the rank and file, and was known to them as 'the Soldier's Friend', possibly the most honourable title ever bestowed upon a commander.

The two departments through which the Commander-in-Chief worked were those of the Adjutant-General and the Quartermaster-General. The former was responsible for all matters relating to discipline and equipment; its incumbents were Lieutenant-General Sir William Fawcett to 1799, and thereafter Lieutenant-General Sir Harry Calvert, Bt., who occupied the position with distinction until 1820. The Quartermaster-General was responsible for the quartering and marching of troops: Colonel George Morrison occupied this office until 1796, and was succeeded by David Dundas (1796–1803), Lieutenant-General Robert Brownrigg (1803–11) and from then until 1851 by General Sir James

Willoughby Gordon, Bt. The Commander-in-Chief was also assisted by a third officer, the Military Secretary, who attended to correspondence and liaised with other departments. Under Amherst this was a civilian appointment paid a pittance (10s. per diem); the Duke of York appointed a field officer with a salary which rose to £2,500 per annum.

A second virtual Commander-in-Chief was the Master-General of the Ordnance, who directed the artillery and engineers, was responsible for manufacture of arms and some equipment, and as a member of the Cabinet was to some degree the government's senior military adviser. The office was held by Charles, 3rd Duke of Richmond (1784–95); Charles, 1st Marquess Cornwallis (1795–1801); John, 2nd Earl of Chatham (1801–6, 1807–10); Francis, 2nd Earl of Moira (1806–7); and Henry, 1st Earl of Mulgrave (1810–18).It was not such an onerous position as that of Commander-in-Chief; Cornwallis, for example, retained it even when Lord-Lieutenant of Ireland during the critical period from 1798 to 1801.

Other offices controlled parts of the military system. The militia and volunteers were the responsibility of the Home Secretary, who had to be consulted before regular troops were sent abroad, to ensure that sufficient remained to maintain domestic tranquillity. The Treasury was responsible for the supply of food and fuel, for any hired transport, and for the commissariat department which administered these affairs on campaign; thus the army's sustenance was officially outside its own control. Medical affairs were administered by separate departments, the Paymaster-General paid the troops, camp-supplies were the responsibility of the Storekeeper-General, and the Barrackmaster-General was responsible for home barracks from 1793, taking over from the Ordnance; transport by sea was regulated by the Transport Board, an offshoot of the Admiralty. With so many organizations and so many of the senior cabinet ministers having a share of the responsibility, it is hardly surprising that some confusion arose, and that Wellington himself could complain that he had no clear idea of what he was expected to achieve in the Peninsular War.

At a lower level, all administration was based upon the regiment. The 'regimental system' has been one of the cornerstones of the British Army, especially from the perspective of morale, by which men were inculcated with a unique sense of pride in their own regiment above all others, and conscious of their predecessors and traditions. Many of the regiments of the period under review were newly formed, but others had up to a century and a half of tradition behind them, and past honours and present distinctions were emphasized, whether it was the death's-head badge of the 17th Light Dragoons, the black eagle of the 14th Light Dragoons, the ancient badges of the 'royal' regiments and so-called 'Six Old Corps' (3rd, 5th, 6th, 8th, 27th and 41st Foot), or unique battle honours like 'Mangalore' of the 73rd.

Each regiment was headed by a colonel, an administrative appointment in that the colonel did not lead his regiment in the field, and one almost always held by a general officer. Although in British service the colonel's control was less than that enjoyed by colonels in Austrian and some German armies (where they were actually styled *Inhaber*, 'owner' or 'proprietor'), the British colonel was responsible for the well-being of his regiment and for the provision of its annual clothing, for which he received a lump sum from the government (except for greatcoats or 'watch-coats', supplied by the Ordnance).

To offset this, it was possible for a colonel to make a profit on the annual clothing: the *Morning Chronicle* (26 November 1798) asserted that a battalion's clothing could yield its colonel a profit of between £400 and £800 per annum, and advocated that all uniforms be supplied by the government and the average profit added to the colonel's pay, presumably so that they would not seek other ways of defrauding the government. Some of these were stated in March 1800 when Colonel Francis Blake of the Northumberland Fencibles was court-martialled for allegedly pocketing the pay of men no longer serving, and having over-charged the government for bounties paid to recruits. He was acquitted, and it was stated in evidence that far from making a profit, he had spent £1,400 of his own money on recruiting. Indeed, colonels who made a profit were probably few; Wellington himself said that he probably lost money in his colonelcy of the 33rd, and Thomas Graham, who raised the 90th Perthshire Volunteers in 1794, expended about £10,000 of his fortune.

Other colonels, however, did cheat their men; in 1813, for example, Colonel Beaufoy of the 1st Royal Tower Hamlets Militia was court-martialled and removed from command because of misappropriation of regimental funds, a 'vulgar meanly-avaricious neglect of the soldier's comforts ... a canker at the heart's core, unseen, distributing its poison through every nerve and vein, and paralyzing every limb' according to his accuser, Lieutenant Scott of his own regiment.[26] (Beaufoy's quartermaster was also dismissed and, singularly, so was the prosecutor, Scott, perhaps for having tried the court's patience by rambling speeches, quoting Cicero and Pliny, during which the president of the court-martial ceased to listen and wrote letters while the prosecution stated its case!

Under normal circumstances, a man might hold only one colonelcy at a time, although the position of colonel-in-chief of the multi-battalion 60th and 95th were held concurrently with an ordinary colonelcy. The post was intended as a reward for long or meritorious service, although a colonelcy might be granted from patronage or 'influence'. More fairly, it arose from merit: General William Picton, uncle of Sir Thomas, held the colonelcy of the 12th Foot for more than 32 years, despite having neither powerful friends, parliamentary influence nor the manners of a courtier. When appointed, George III informed him that 'you are entirely obliged to Captain Picton, who commanded the grenadier company of the 12th Regiment in Germany',[27] an allusion to Picton's heroic behaviour in that capacity during the Seven Years War.

A colonelcy was usually held for life: for example, Charles Moore, 1st Marquess of Drogheda, was colonel of the 18th Light Dragoons for 62 years, from 1759 until the regiment was disbanded in 1821. A colonel could move from regiment to regiment, although frequent moves were unusual: Sir David Dundas, for example, held five (22nd Foot 1791–5, 7th Light Dragoons 1795–1801, 2nd Dragoons 1801–13, 1st Dragoon Guards 1813–20, plus the colonelcy-in-chief of the 95th 1809–20); Henry Seymour Conway held seven colonelcies between 1746 and 1795, although these numbers of changes were quite exceptional. Usually (but not always) a colonel would only move to a regiment senior to his own. Voluntary resignation of a colonelcy was the greatest rarity, yet was adopted by Hugh Percy, 2nd Duke of Northumberland, who resigned the colonelcy of the Royal Horse Guards (at 41s. per diem the best-paid in the army) when the Duke of York denied his request of the right of appointment and promotion of his regiment's officers; he was succeeded as colonel by the Duke of Wellington on 1 January 1813. During the period, only one colonel was forcibly dismissed, John Whitelocke of the 89th Foot, although that was for mismanagement of the Buenos Ayres expedition, not for any irregularity in his regimental duties.

Regimental pride, so much part of the ethos of the army, might find expression through regard for its colonel; on first passing Foot Guards after his appointment as colonel of the Royal Horse Guards, Wellington is said to have remarked, 'Thank God, I have got a "present" out of the Guards at last!',[28] i.e., a 'present arms', implying that they only considered him worthy of the honour after he had been appointed to a Household regiment! On other occasions regimental pride could be a threat to discipline. An element of this was probably one of the causes of a serious fracas which occurred in July 1806 at Tullaghmore, though a conflict of nationalities was perhaps equally to blame. In this affair, a serious fight erupted between a light battalion of Irish militia (the light companies of the Sligo, Derry, Monaghan and Limerick regiments) and a detachment of German Legion, after the Germans had arrested some militiamen for cudgelling a German who had objected to insults from the militia. Each side suffered a fatality, and eight militiamen and 23 Germans were wounded, eleven of the latter (and their dead man) being shot, five bayoneted and seven cudgelled. What makes the case somewhat unusual was the suggestion that militia officers actually encouraged their men to attack the Germans and release the men in custody: a Sligo officer was observed at the head of one party, sword drawn; the Sligo surgeon was heard to exclaim 'by the Holy Saviour, there shall be corpses in the street,' and another man, evidently an officer in civilian clothes, declared 'Now, my boys, play away, pursue the prisoners.'[29]

Much was written upon the unscientific subject of 'national character'. Whether or not certain nationalities exhibited recognizable or even predictable characteristics is perhaps not the question, so long as it is remembered that at the time it was commonly believed that they did. Nor was this restricted to any nation or class. The Prince de Ligne expressed the widest view in his comments on the appointment and conduct of officers:

'Whenever it falls to the lot of an individual to be entrusted with the command of an army composed of lively materials, such as are to be found among the English, the Italians, the French, and the Hungarians, it must be his study to repress his own ardour, in order to keep under the natural effervescence of his followers. When a man is put at the head of an army made up of colder elements, such as Germans, Bohemians, Russians, or Dutchmen, he must, like Prometheus, endeavour to steal a spark of celestial animation, to give them motion and activity.'[30]

In a more restricted sense, most of the Peninsular War memorialists not unnaturally expressed the view that the British Army was superior to any other (though few were stinting in their praise of the French as worthy opponents), and not a few expressed this in terms of innate national character rather than the result of leadership, training and similar factors. Whether or not there was any foundation in what might be termed national or regional stereotypes – the stolid English countryman, the apparently quicker-witted Cockney, the earnest Highlander and devil-may-care Irishman – it was believed at the time that these did exist. A typical expression of this is found in the reminiscences of William Grattan of the 88th Connaught Rangers, the archetypal regiment of Irish 'bhoys'. Grattan wrote with pride of the characteristics of his countrymen:

'An Irishman ... can live on as little nourishment as a Frenchman; give him his pipe of tobacco and he will march for two days without food and without *grumbling*; give him, in addition, a little spirits and biscuit, and he will work for a week. This will not be a task so easy of accomplishment to the English soldier; early habits have given him a relish for good eating, and plenty of it too: if he has not a regular allowance of solid food, it is certain he will not do his work well for any great length of time. But an Irish fellow has been accustomed all his life to be what an Englishman would consider half-starved; therefore quantity or quality is no great consideration with him; his stomach is like a corner cupboard – *you might throw any thing into it*! Neither do you find elsewhere the lively thought, the cheerful song, or pleasant story to be met *only* in an Irish regiment. We had a few Englishmen in my corps, and I do not remember ever to have heard one of them attempt a joke ... The English soldier is to the full as drunken as the Irish, and not half so pleasant in his liquor ...

'Some of our best regiments were English, and one, to please me, decidedly the finest in the Peninsular army, the 43rd, was principally composed of Englishmen. Then there was that first-rate battle regiment, the 45th, a parcel of Nottingham weavers, whose sedentary habits would lead you to suppose they could not be prime marchers, but the contrary was the fact ... But if it come to a hard tug, and that we had neither rations nor shoes, then, indeed, the Connaught Rangers would be in their element, and outmarch almost any battalion in the service; and for this plain reason, that scarcely one of them wore many pair of shoes prior to the date of his enlistment, and as to the rations (the most part of them at all events), a dozen times had been in all probability the *outside* of their acquaintance with such a delicacy.'[31]

Opinions on the respective worth of various groups extended beyond matters of nationality: for example, when beating-up for recruits in 1794, Rowland Hill remarked that he would rather pay fifteen guineas to obtain a Shropshire countryman than five guineas to recruit a city-dweller from Manchester or Birmingham.

It is interesting to note that Samuel Johnson's essay on 'the English Common Soldiers' was reprinted as late as 1801 in a publication intended as an officers' 'trade' journal. He mentioned the maxim that the difference between English and French was that French officers would always lead, if the soldiers would follow; whereas English soldiers would always follow if officers would lead. British military success, he thought, was less the result of discipline and training than of national character: 'Our nation may boast, beyond any other people in the world, of a kind of epidemic bravery, diffused equally through all its ranks. We can shew a peasantry of heroes, and fill our armies with clowns, whose courage may vie with that of their general.' This courage did not grow from esteem of their leaders, for 'it does not often happen that he thinks much better of his leader than of himself ... the Englishman despises such motives of courage: he was born without a master; and looks not on any man, however dignified by lace or titles, as deriving from nature any claims to his respect, or inheriting any qualities superior to his own.' Nor, thought Johnson, did the

Englishman fight better because he had more to defend: 'Liberty is, to the lowest rank of every nation, little more than the choice of working or starving.' Instead, he thought, the national character was formed by the knowledge that no man was less necessary to his employer than his employer was to him; 'From this neglect of subordination, I do not deny that some inconvenience may from time to time proceed ... but ... they who complain, in peace, of the insolence of the populace, must remember, that their insolence in peace, is bravery in war.'[32]

British characteristics were not always appreciated even by their allies; Moyle Sherer noted the British propensity to laugh at or deride foreigners: 'The English are admired ... as a free, an enlightened, and a brave people, but they cannot make themselves beloved; they are not content with being great, they must be thought so, and told so. They will not bend with good humour to the customs of other nations, nor will they condescend to soothe (flatter they never do) the harmless self-love of friendly foreigners. No: wherever they march or travel, they bear with them a haughty air of conscious superiority, and expect that their customs, habits, and opinions should supersede, or at least suspend, those of all the countries through which they pass.'[33]

Despite the contemporary opinions concerning national characteristics, those concerned with recruiting could not afford to be discriminating, so insatiable was the demand for men. Only in the rarest cases were potential recruits turned away, but the line was drawn in 1813 when Germans were being enrolled from the prison-camps around Portsmouth, when 'above 1,000 Italians offered themselves, but none were accepted'.[34]

The demand for recruits may be gauged from the following statistics concerning the rank and file of the army, including ranks up to corporal; for the total strength, to include officers and sergeants, one-eighth should be added:

Year	Cavalry	Infantry	Total
1793	4,681	34,262	38,945
1794	14,527	70,570	85,097
1795	28,810	100,452	129,262
1804	16,729	119,751	136,480
1806	23,396	142,177	165,573
1809	27,391	183,223	210,614
1813	28,931	201,538	230,469

The Ordnance troops should be added to these figures, a number rising from 14,113 in January 1804 to 25,407 in January 1813. When the militia is included, the grand total of rank and file rose from 236,112 in January 1804 to 326,931 in January 1813. As will be demonstrated, to maintain these numbers from a population which in 1812–14 was calculated to include some 2.7 million men capable of bearing arms (i.e., those aged between 15 and 60) could impose severe strains, both physically and financially. In his last great speech on 9 November 1805, William Pitt made the memorable comment that 'England has saved herself by her exertions; and will, I trust, save Europe by her example.' If the defeat of Napoleonic hegemony could be seen as the saving of Europe, Pitt's prophecy was correct; but its accomplishment exerted a heavy price upon the saviours.

3
'Trusty and Well Beloved'
OFFICERS AND GENTLEMEN

GEORGE THE THIRD BY THE GRACE OF GOD, KING OF GREAT BRITAIN France and Ireland, Defender of the Faith, &c., To Our Trusty and Well-beloved – Esq., Greeting: We reposing especial Trust and Confidence in your Loyalty, Courage and good Conduct, do by these presents, Constitute and Appoint you to be ...'

Thus ran the opening lines of the commission-document given to every officer in the army upon the attainment of every rank through which he passed. To hold the king's commission might be thought a signal honour based upon 'especial Trust and Confidence', but occasionally it depended upon influence, and frequently upon the depth of the candidate's purse.

The concept of the purchase of commissions originated in the late 17th century, to provide a retiring officer with some finance from the sale of the commission, to avoid the government having to provide a pension. The system was open to wide abuse, but for all its ills is perhaps not deserving of the criticism which has been heaped upon it, at least not after the reforms introduced by the Duke of York. During the most successful campaign of the period, the Peninsular War, only about one-fifth of commissions were obtained by purchase, and even during the period of the worst excesses of patronage and promotion by cash, it enabled gifted individuals to rise to high rank at an early age: had Arthur Wellesley been compelled to languish in the lower echelons of the army list by a system which would today be considered more acceptable, it is not inconceivable that the whole course of European history might have been different.

To emphasize this point, it is worth considering the Ordnance services, where promotion depended upon seniority, and where even junior ranks were thus occupied by comparatively elderly people. In 1818, shortly after the conclusion of a war which might have been expected to speed the course of promotion, the average service of Royal Artillery colonels was 36 years, lieutenant-colonels 24 years, first captains seventeen years and second captains eleven years; twenty years later these lengths of service had so increased that the average first captain had 30 years' service, 'a serious evil, tending to produce a very baneful effect on the efficiency of the corps'.[35]

Nevertheless, as applied at the beginning of the French Revolutionary War the purchase system was thoroughly rotten. In the rapid and at times chaotic enlargement of the army which occurred shortly after the outbreak of war (for as usual existing forces were insufficient to meet the demands imposed upon them), any rank up to lieutenant-colonel was on offer, if the applicant had the money, so that a man might command a battalion only days after entering the army. Henry Paget, the future Marquess of Anglesey, entered the army as lieutenant-colonel in command of the 80th Foot at the age of 25, with so little previous military experience (as a militia officer) as to be negligible; Thomas Graham of Balgowan, the future Lord Lynedoch, received the lieutenant-colonelcy of the 90th at the age of 45, with no military experience whatever, save for a brief period as a civilian volunteer with the Toulon expedition.

Even at the time there were critics of the system. In the House of Commons General Banastre Tarleton claimed that 'Gold and rank ... were now the only passports to preferment; and this he exemplified in the case of Lord Granard, who jumped into the rank of Lieutenant-Colonel, and in seventeen days experience found himself qualified for the command of the army'.[36] J. F. Neville, who was serving at the time, wrote that so gross was the system of the disposal of commissions that for the first two years of the war:

'It would be fulsome flattery to give the name of "AN ARMY" to an unwieldy concourse of men, necessarily ill-disciplined, from the fatal circumstance of their being ill-officered ... the most barefaced profligacy prevailed throughout every military department. Whatever was connected with the army-establishment was, more or less, a dirty job, and a public robbery. Commissions were thrown away on persons unworthy of bearing them, or incapable of performing the duties which the letter and spirit of them religiously enjoined. *Boys at school*, smarting under the wholesome application of *birch*, were field-officers in the British army, and regularly received their daily pay, as a *just* remuneration for the important services which they were rendering to the State! The brother or relative of a *petty prostitute*, was complimented with the command of a regiment, while the son of a low, but opulent *mechanic*, by the means of a bribe, saw himself at the head of a troop of horse, which he had neither the courage nor the abilities to lead ...'[37]

The most obvious abuse was the commissioning of children, even though it might have been sanctioned for the best of motives: in 1711 the then Secretary at War informed the Paymaster-General that Queen Anne had given a child an ensign's commission 'in order for the support of his mother and family, in consideration of the loss of his father and uncle, who died in the service'.[38] Such cases were exceptional; most were like that of Anthony Graves, who served in the Peninsula with the 31st Foot. Born in 1789, he was commissioned as ensign in the Somerset Militia before his fourth birthday, his father being that regiment's adjutant. He later received two commissions in the 1st and 6th West India Regiments by the influence of the lamentable Whitelocke (a friend of Graves senior), in both cases being given indefinite leave to allow him to remain at school. He finally joined the 31st in 1804, five months before his 15th birthday. Some young children actually joined their regiments on service: Sir John Floyd, one of the first to attempt to introduce a system of equitation training in the cavalry, had been praised for his courage during the charge at Emsdorf, as a cornet aged 12!

Before 1802, some 20 per cent of all new officers were aged under 15 years, and even after the Duke of York had brought in the regulation that 'no person is considered eligible for a commission until he has attained the age of sixteen years', which ended the appointment of children, half the new commissions were of youths under 18. There were still contraventions of the rule: George Keppel was said to have been flogged as a Westminster schoolboy only four months before he celebrated his 16th birthday as an ensign in the 14th Foot, five days before fighting at Waterloo.

The social background of officers who entered the army with a commission was wide. Only a relatively small number of noblemen made a career in the army, by reason of numbers, as there were probably less than 500 peers in total, upon whose junior offspring the Royal Navy and the Church had an equal call. The aristocracy might have been expected to be represented most strongly in the Household regiments and Foot Guards, and in the cavalry; yet even in these élite corps they represented a minority. For example, of 170 Foot Guards officers at Waterloo (including 23 on staff duty), there were only seven peers or those titled 'Lord', 23 sons or heirs of peers and one illegitimate son of a peer, six sons of baronets, six knights, three sons of knights, one heir to a disputed peerage, one son of a Count of the Holy Roman Empire, and apparently seven grandsons of peers not included in the previous categories. Among the 329 cavalry troop officers at Waterloo (excluding those on staff duties, and including one volunteer from the Ceylon Regiment), there were one peer, thirteen sons of peers, seventeen sons of baronets, two knights, one son of a knight, one Italian prince, one Hanoverian baron and one son of a German countess (Henry Acton, 13th Light Dragoons, whose father was a general in the Neapolitan army). The scarcity of aristocratic officers in the line regiments was regretted by some: Kincaid remarked that although they were neither better nor braver than the rest, they were more 'beloved' and respected by their men, as if possessed of some innate quality of leadership not attainable by those of lower birth.

A larger proportion was drawn from the 'old' gentry of the rural counties, but the fact that these were not very numerous would seem to be suggested by the nickname of the 34th Foot in the Peninsula, 'the Cumberland Gentlemen', 'certainly some of the most select and high-caste officers I ever met in the army – and such brave and zealous men too ...'[39] A tradition of military service existed in some of the families of the gentry, which could have terrible consequences: for example, the Nevilles of Badsworth Hall, Yorkshire, lost five sons within a short time: Lieutenant Neville of the 2nd Foot, killed aboard HMS *Queen Charlotte* at the 'Glorious First of June' (subject of Mather Brown's famous painting); Captains John and Brownlow Neville of the Foot Guards were killed in Holland; Captain Cavendish Neville, also of the Guards, was taken ill at Malta en route for Egypt, was sent home but died from the malady; and Captain Martin Neville of the Royal Navy, who died from yellow fever at Honduras.

Another class of officer were those from a military background, the sons and grandsons of officers. The concentration of influence and power in a comparatively small part of society produced many examples of distinguished officers with distinguished relatives; for example, William George Moore of the 1st Foot Guards, a Deputy Assistant Quartermaster-General at Waterloo, was the son of the Under-Secretary at War and the Countess of Eglinton, and nephew of the great Sir John Moore.

Two examples illustrate such exclusively military families. Sir John Macleod, who served in the artillery from the age of 15 until his death as lieutenant-general and Director-General of Artillery in his 82nd year (a worthy man, 'to the private soldier a benefactor, ever watching over their comfort and their welfare'),[40] had four sons. The eldest was killed commanding the 43rd at the storming of Badajoz; the second, an engineer, never ceased to suffer from a wound sustained in the same action; the third served in the Peninsula with the artillery and died with the 41st at Rangoon in 1824; and the youngest served with the artillery early in the Peninsular War and was desperately wounded at Quatre Bras when seconded from the 35th to staff duties.

Sir Harry Burrard, the unfortunate general forever associated with the disgrace of Cintra, had one son mortally wounded at Corunna when ADC to Moore; later in the same year another son, a midshipman in the Royal Navy, was drowned by the upsetting of a boat from the royal yacht *Royal Sovereign* in Weymouth harbour. A third son, ensign in the 1st Foot Guards, was mortally wounded at San Sebastian. Burrard himself died in October 1813.

It was uncommon for a father and son to serve in the same regiment, especially when both were company officers, but not unknown; perhaps the best-known example was Captain Benjamin Siborn of the 9th Foot, who from September 1813 was joined in the regiment by his son William, an ensign, though apparently they served together only in 1817. Siborn senior never fully recovered from wounds sustained at Nivelle; Siborn junior became the historian of Waterloo, his name being changed to Siborne in 1834.

Even after the Duke of York's reforms, all that was required of an aspirant officer was that he should be aged sixteen; be able to afford the price of a commission, if he were buying one; and be able to provide a letter of recommendation from someone holding the rank of major or above (or sometimes a person of social standing) which confirmed that the candidate was a fit person to hold an ensigncy of infantry or cornetcy of cavalry. Thus, it was possible for a man of humble birth or a background of 'trade' to rise to high rank: Sir Harry Calvert, the worthy Adjutant-General, was colonel of the 5th West India Regiment (1800–6) and 14th Foot (1806–26), and his regiment was nicknamed 'Calvert's Entire' from the fact that his family were brewers. Lieutenant-Colonel James Inglis Hamilton, killed at Waterloo in command of the 2nd Dragoons, was the son of Sergeant-Major William Anderson of the 21st Foot, born on campaign in America in 1777, and rose through the commissioned ranks by the patronage of his father's old commanding officer, whose name he took. Such a route to a commission was not unusual: Quartermaster Haigh of the 33rd Foot used the influence of his old commanding officer (Wellington) to secure commissions in the regiment for both his sons, Captain John and Lieutenant Thomas Haigh; both were killed at Waterloo. Even officers apparently from the lesser nobility might have humble backgrounds: Sir William Myers, Bt., lieutenant-colonel of the 7th, killed at Albuera at the age of 28, was the grandson of a builder from Whitehaven, whose son under the patronage of Lord Drogheda rose to the rank of lieutenant-general and colonelcy of the 2nd West India Regiment, 1795–1805.

Not until 1829 did the Catholic Relief Act remove virtually all strictures on Roman Catholics, prior to which there were in theory restrictions upon the holding of commissions by members of that faith, despite the relaxation of discriminatory laws by the 1791 Roman Catholic Relief Act. Such discrimination does seem to have deprived the army of some officers, especially those from prominent Catholic families. For example, the Hon. Robert Edward Clifford had served in the Régiment Dillon of the French army until 1791; wishing to serve his native country after the revolution, he was denied a commission and worked instead on intelligence matters in a largely unofficial capacity;[41] and it is stated that Henry Howard of Corby Castle, who had trained with the Austrian army, was denied a regular commission because of his religion and instead served in the militia and raised volunteer corps, the Edenside Rangers and the Cumberland Rangers. Generally, however, officers' religion was overlooked, and the Indemnifying Act passed by every session of parliament postponed the necessity of taking oaths, negating the Test Act, and thus Roman Catholics did serve as officers. For example, Colonel Edward Stack was an Irish Catholic who had served in the French army against Britain during the War of American Independence (including as a marine officer aboard John Paul Jones's ship *Bonhomme Richard*), but served later in the Irish Brigade in British pay. When in 1808 he was due to be promoted to major-general, he was questioned about his religion, which officially would have prevented the promotion; he replied that he was 'of the religion which makes general officers'[42] and was duly granted not only that rank, but became a full general four years before his death at Calais in December 1833.

The motivation for a young man to obtain a commission varied. Many joined the army simply to earn a living, especially if they were unfitted for any other occupation (even Wellington's mother condemned him as 'food for powder' and nothing more!). John Blakiston was typical: 'Out of a family of six boys it was proper that one should be devoted to the infernal gods; and, as my shoulders promised to be of the requisite breadth, and my head of a suitable thickness, I was chosen as a fit offering; or, in other words, I was selected for the military profession, as being the greatest dunce in the family.'[43] Nobler motives were often present: 'When I turned soldier it was not for the purpose of admiring myself like a peacock in gaudy plumage; no, it was to meet the enemies of my country and go wherever my duty called me, and merit the name of soldier, which I now say is the greatest pleasure I ever enjoyed'[44]

Prospects of advancement were another motive, and led officers to compete for the most hazardous tasks; 'a gold chain or a wooden leg' was a popular expression, or as Peter O'Hare of the 95th remarked before the storming of Badajoz, 'a lieutenant-colonel or cold meat in a few hours'; in his case it was the latter. Some relished the life: 'it is quite immaterial to me whether I roll myself in a blanket and sleep upon the ground ... to be living in England after this wild, romantic existence would not give me half so much satisfaction'. For others, illusions of glory soon disappeared: Joseph Dornford joined the 95th in preference to the Church, but after hard service in the Pyrenees remarked to his fellows that 'I am astonished how you can joke and pass off so lightly scenes of misery and woe such as we have gone through ... God knows how I repent ever turning soldier.'[45] He returned to his original calling and was doubtless much happier as a country parson.

Moyle Sherer believed that the army was the best refuge for those of little resources: 'Wander where he will, a regiment is ever, to a single man, the best of homes ... For him, who by the want of fortune or other controlling circumstances, is debarred the exquisite happiness of reposing his aching heart on that blessed resting-place, the bosom of a wife – for such a man there is no life, save one of travel or military occupation, which can excite feelings of interest or consolation. The hazard of losing life, which a soldier is often called on to encounter, gives to his existence, as often as it is preserved, a value, it would, otherwise, soon cease to possess ... if it is painful at a certain age, to think, that, when you fall, no widow, no child, will drop a tear over your grave – it is, on the other hand, a comfort to know, that none are dependent upon your existence; that none will be left unprotected and in misery at your death.'[46]

When lying wounded, Lieutenant Thomas Austin recalled two Irish soldiers' wives discussing him, which must have given him pause for thought: 'I wonder, so I do, why you young gentlemen come out to the wars to be murthered entirely; and get such cruel treatment, when you might live at home comfortably wid your friends ...'[47]

It was possible for a junior officer to live on his pay, but only just, and in a fashionable regiment, when stationed at home, a substantial private income was needed to supplement the salary: Sir John Moore remarked that a private income of between £50 and £100 per annum was necessary. The cost of officers' kit alone, provided at their own expense, could represent a huge financial outlay: even the plain regimental-pattern sabre of the 52nd Light Infantry, for example, at four guineas represented 16 days' pay for an ensign. Kit might be acquired cut-price (George Simmons advised his brother to buy second-hand and take cardboard with him to his regiment, for their tailor to make his hat!), but some officers spent vast sums on their uniform: Captain Hobkirk of the 43rd, for example, was reputed to spend almost £1,000 per annum on his uniform, which was so rich that when dining with Soult on the evening of his capture in November 1813 he was mistaken for a field marshal! On obtaining a lieutenancy in the 12th in April 1796, George Elers spent £300 on his uniform: 'I had six regimental jackets, besides dress-coats, great-coat, shirts about twelve dozen, and everything else in the same proportion';[48] but his colonel, Hervey Aston, bought his coats thirty at a time, owned between fifty and a hundred pairs of boots, and on lending Elers an undress jacket told him not to worry if it became dirty, as 'I have two hundred more.'[49]

Officers' pay was so meagre that General Gascoigne claimed in the House of Commons in 1811 that once income tax was deducted, they received less than they had in 1695; Palmerston replied that officers' 'chief objects in entering the army were the honours and distinctions to which merit must in due course advance them';[50] in other words, they weren't serving for the money! Similarly, an attempt made in parliament in July 1814 to increase subalterns' pay was defeated by the government on the grounds that there were sufficient applications for commissions without the need to increase their pay.

The improvidence of many subalterns hardly strengthened their case for better pay: Francis Tidy told how he went to London on leave until his money was gone, then returned to his regiment at Portsmouth, but after finding a further 10 or 12 guineas in a coat-pocket when he unpacked, he set off by the next coach back to London, determined not to return until he had spent all but his return fare. As George Wood remarked, but for foolishness when a subaltern, he would not 'have found myself pennyless; neither should I have fallen asleep on the highway from inebriety, and run the risk of being crushed to death by the wheel of a mail-coach'.[51]

Nevertheless, it was possible for officers to accumulate great wealth, but generally only those who achieved high rank. A noted example of affluence was General Charles O'Hara, who upon his death in February 1802 as commander at Gibraltar, left his personal effects and his immense collection of plate to his black servant, and about £70,000 in trust to two ladies, by each of whom he had two children.

The demand for officers was so great that, after the restrictions imposed by the Duke of York, what might be regarded as the usual sources of supply were insufficient. By the end of the Peninsular War, excluding foreign corps, veteran battalions and the units controlled by the Ordnance, there were more than 10,500 officers in the army, with a wastage of up to 800 per year, apart from those needed to complete new battalions. Illness and casualties were a constant drain, the casualty-rate among officers usually being higher than that of the other ranks, arising from their frequently more conspicuous position. The chance of becoming a casualty varied according to the intensity of the action, but the comparative danger was about the same. Taking six Peninsula actions at random: at Nivelle and Fuentes de Oñoro there was approximately a one in sixteen chance of an officer becoming a casualty, against a chance of 1:17 for other ranks; at Busaco, 1:30½ chance for officers, 1:40 for other ranks; at Salamanca, 1:7½ for officers, 1:10 for other ranks; at Barrosa, 1:4 for officers, 1:5 for other ranks; and only at Albuera was the chance equal, 1:2½ for both officers and men. Very roughly, officers were probably about one-fifth more likely to be hit than other ranks.

To help fill the requirements, more than one in twenty officers were commissioned from the ranks. It is perhaps indicative of the general standard of the rank and file that an intelligent, sober man could make his mark quickly, and some very fine officers rose from the lowest ranks. Most notable, perhaps, was Sir John Elley of the Royal Horse Guards, the son of an eating-house keeper and apprenticed to a tanner, who enlisted in the regiment as a private, became one of the army's noted 'characters', rose to the rank of lieutenant-general and was buried in St. George's Chapel, Windsor, a remarkable career considering the aristocratic background of the majority of Household Cavalry officers. However, he was no exception: John Winterbottom of the 52nd was another, who rose from private in 1799 to ensign in 1808 and lieutenant in 1810, and was never absent from the regiment from his enlistment to his death from yellow fever in Barbados in 1838, save for his period of recuperation from wounds received at Redinha, Badajoz and Waterloo. Upon his death 130 officers who had served with him entered a subscription to raise an impressive memorial in the parish church of his native Saddleworth, to commemorate 'his extraordinary talents as an officer, and his acknowledged worth as a man'; it still exists, topped by a sculpted shako, sash, sword and belt.

The routes to promotion from the ranks were varied. Some won a commission as a reward for an act of great valour, among the most notable being Sergeant Patrick Masterson of the 2/87th, commissioned in his own regiment for capturing the 'Eagle' of the French 8th *Ligne* at Barrosa. (This act secured the future of his descendants, one of whom, Lieutenant James Masterson of the 1st Battalion Devonshire Regiment won the Victoria Cross at Waggon Hill near Ladysmith in January 1900. By a curious coincidence, the 87th's commander at Barrosa, Hugh Gough, had similarly distinguished kinsmen: Major Charles Gough of the 5th Bengal European Light Cavalry, and his brother Lieutenant Hugh Gough of the 1st Bengal European Light Cavalry, both won the Victoria Cross in the Indian Mutiny, and Charles's son John won the same decoration in Somaliland in 1903.)

Some commissions were granted in the field out of necessity: after an injury to their adjutant, whose duties included much tiresome clerical work, after Waterloo the 2/73rd appointed Colour-Sergeant George Austin to the post with an ensign's commission; he performed the job wearing a sergeant's great-coat with an officer's sword and sash, not having a proper uniform. More unusual was a promotion as a reward to a battalion; for example, following especially distinguished service in March 1811, the three battalions of the Light Division (1/43rd, 1/52nd, 1/95th) were each instructed by Wellington to rec-ommend a sergeant for a commission as a tribute to their units.

Those who were commissioned from the ranks were mostly worthy men; as was said of Major James Bland, a journeyman weaver who enlisted in the 46th in about 1754 and spent 50 years and 42 engagements in the same regiment, his career was evidence 'of what may be done in a military life by a steady attention to sobriety, united with a prudent economy'.[52]

Nevertheless, some ex-'rankers' found difficulty in being accepted. To some extent this was a matter of social background, as expressed by the wife of Sergeant-Major Buffet of the 28th when he was promoted to ensign; she missed the party held to mark the occasion, but sat by the kitchen fire smoking her pipe, remarking that although the king might make her husband a gentleman, not even the Sultan of the Indies could transform her into a lady![53] Discrimina-tion probably occurred most in fashionable regiments, and a story was told of one ex-sergeant who asked to revert to his former rank as his fellow-officers would not associate with him; but he was accepted after the Duke of York deliberately walked arm-in-arm with him in front of the regiment, further testi-mony of the Duke's concern and decency.

Much of the criticism came of the practice rather than of individuals, as articulated by Lieutenant Nathaniel Hood of the 40th, author of *Elements of War; or, Rules and Regulations of the Army*, who in a section on 'Officers in gen-eral'[54] included: 'The hope of reward actuates an army, from the highest down-ward, with spirit and animation ... Let it not be understood that soldiers (some brought up as gentlemen excepted) should be rewarded with military rank. No! there should be different rewards as there are different characters. Soldiers are but soldiers, and officers are soldiers and gentlemen. Under this consideration the line of distinction is preserved, the profession, through all its tracts of hon-our, guarded ...'

Wellington was rather more blunt, remarking that commissioned rankers never turned out well, being unable to resist drink, when their low ori-gin reappeared, a most unfortunate and inaccurate condemnation. It was shared, however, by much of the rank and file, whose view was articulated by Benjamin Harris: that gentlemen were always more popular and kind, not bru-tal and overbearing like many ex-'rankers', and that the ordinary soldiers responded much better to a man 'who has authority in his face'.[55]

The regimental staff officers – paymaster and quartermaster – were often ex-NCOs. They were officially non-combatants, and would generally remain with the regimental baggage in the rear during combat. Quartermaster Matthew Stevens of the 69th summed up this practice when on the morning of Waterloo a man was killed by his side: 'Aweel, it is time for a respectable non-combatant to gang awa'!'[56] This was more evidence of his sense of humour than any faint-heartedness, for he was the same Matthew Stevens who as a private in the same regiment had accompanied Nelson in his epic boarding exploit at St. Vincent, and had broken the stern-gallery windows of the Spanish ship *San Nicolas* to allow Nelson to enter.

Officers could gain a commission, or promotion, by 'recruiting for rank', i.e., by bringing in a specified number of recruits, either from civilian life or from the militia. For example, in 1804 21 recruits were needed to receive an ensigncy, twelve to gain promotion from ensign to lieutenant, 45 from lieutenant to captain, 90 from captain to major and 82 from major to lieutenant-colonel, promotion in this case being restricted to a new battalion of the regiment in which the officer was already serving, and no more than one 'step' in rank was permitted no matter how many recruits an officer brought in, with promotions only to take effect if the new battalion had been recruited to full strength within six months.

A final route to a commission was to serve as a volunteer, by which a young gentleman would accompany a battalion on active service (at the invitation of its commander), would carry a musket and usually fight in the ranks, but would live with the officers, until a vacancy occurred and he could be appointed to an ensigncy. This route, followed by almost one in twenty new commissions, was especially useful for a youth of good family but modest means.

Perhaps a more telling difference between officers and other ranks than class or station was literacy, one of the few conditions for entry into the commissioned ranks. In many cases, however, the level of education was not high: comparatively few officers were products of the great public schools, and very few were university graduates. Some had pretensions towards learning, but usually this was not actively encouraged as being beneficial to an officer's duty: as late as 1897 the then Commander-in-Chief (Lord Wolseley) stated that he hoped the British officer would never degenerate into a bookworm!

Probably the only education thought necessary was that regarded as essential for any ordinary gentleman, but some officers exhibited considerable erudition: for example, Lieutenant-Colonel John Squire of the Royal Engineers, who died of a fever in May 1812, attributed to exertions at the siege of Badajoz, had published a paper upon an inscription on 'Pompey's Pillar' near Alexandria, which had baffled earlier archaeologists. Lieutenant-Colonel Richard Collins of the 83rd was another, an expert linguist who spoke perfect French, German, Spanish and Portuguese, was an accomplished artist and an expert in military history. He lost a leg to a cannon-ball at Albuera, and had the thigh removed as a result of gangrene, but it was said that his intellect aided him to survive, and return with a cork leg to command a brigade in the 7th Division; he died aged 38 in February 1813.

The more 'technical' services might have been expected to contain more intellectuals, and indeed the accounts of the engineer Sir Richard Fletcher for 1812[57] include considerable expenditure on reading-matter (£29 5s. 7d. for unspecified 'publications', plus a Spanish dictionary at £2 6s. 6d. and a subscription to the Lisbon Gazette at 36s. per annum). Probably very exceptional was Hon. Edward Cocks, one of the most intelligent officers of his generation; his library is known to have included not only military works and history from Saxe to Adye's *Bombardier and Pocket Gunner*, but classics, poetry, science and mathematics; with the *Sermons* and *Lectures on Rhetoric* of Hugh Blair (the Presbyterian divine known for his literary work, such as his defence of the author-ship of Ossian), and Adam Ferguson's *Lectures* on philosophy and politics (which may have appealed to a soldier like Cocks in that the author had been chaplain to the Black Watch and had actually fought at Fontenoy).[58]

Many of those who took books on campaign preferred light reading – Scott was especially popular – and the difficulty of transporting reading-matter was doubtless a significant factor in the discouragement of intellectual pursuits. This was not always viewed realistically: *The Military Mentor* noted rather unnecessarily that the 66 large volumes of the *English Universal History* were too bulky to find a place in an officer's kit, but that the *New Universal History*, in 25 pocket-sized volumes, was worth consideration! An interesting comment on the literacy of officers is provided by Moyle Sherer, who described how he found a bookshop at Vittoria with an excellent stock of cheap, pocket-sized Paris editions, the proprietor of which remarked that he had sold more books to British officers in a fortnight than he had sold to the French army in two years, even though many officers were probably like the worthy Colonel J. F. Browne who commanded the 28th in the Peninsula, who 'never had but one book, and that was the Army List'.[59]

Rise in rank might involve a transfer from one regiment to another, but this did not depend entirely upon promotion: officers wishing to change regiments (for whatever reason, such as a wish to avoid or participate in a par-ticular campaign) could 'exchange' with another of equivalent rank. It was, however, possible for an officer to spend a long career in one regiment, although this was probably more common in the militia than in the regular army: Major Ralph Grenside of the North Yorkshire Militia, who died at East-bourne Barracks in January 1808, had served 49 years in the same regiment; he was so popular that the men of his regiment offered to pull the hearse by hand the 320 miles from Eastbourne to his birthplace, where he was to be buried.

Promotion was the principal aim of most officers, which originally could be achieved with great rapidity, simply by purchasing 'step' after 'step'. George Elers, for example, had been an ensign in the 90th for less than two weeks when he decided to become a lieutenant in the 12th, and gave £100 above the regulated price for the commission. (Throughout the period, com-missions could change hands for a sum differ from the official amount: an offi-cer selling a commission in a regiment stationed in an unpopular place, such as the West Indies, might have difficulty finding a buyer at even less than the reg-ulated price. Conversely, it was said that when Robert Craufurd temporarily quit the army, he could have sold his commission for £1,000 more than the official figure, but declined as he regarded it as dishonourable to accept more than the sum decreed by the sovereign.) This system enabled a man to com-mand a battalion after only a few months' service, which could have appalling consequences: the failure to implement the Royal Warrant of 1720 which stip-ulated that no lieutenant could purchase a higher rank until he had served ten years led to Lord Craven commanding the 84th in action in Holland as a lieu-tenant-colonel at the age of 17, and indeed the Adjutant-General to the army in the Netherlands in 1793–4 reported that of 41 regiments present, 21 were commanded either by boys or idiots![60]

The Duke of York ended such absurdities, ordering that no officer could become a captain without having served two years as a subaltern, and that no captain could become a major without six years' service. A General Order was issued in December 1809 to explain one of the previous 20 March: that henceforth no officer was to be promoted to captain until he had served three years; none to major until he had served seven years, at least two as a captain; no major to lieutenant-colonel until he had served nine years; no officer to fill a staff appointment (ADC excepted) until he had served four years; and no subaltern to serve as ADC unless he had served one year on regimental duty. This elucidation may have been prompted by the case of Lord Burghersh which had been raised in parliament in May 1809, he having been promoted to lieutenant-colonel after only eight years' service: 'A more flagrant instance of injustice and undue influence never occurred in the military annals; and he could only attribute it to the Noble Lord being the son of a Cabinet Minister',[61] according to the MP Colonel Shipley, who raised the matter. Burghersh's promotion was revoked as a result.

Losses on campaign were a principal cause of promotion; George Wood records an exchange between two officers after Vimeiro, one of whom having had his hat smashed by a piece of shell: '"Oh, my dear fellow, I am very sorry to see your hat so broken!". "Thank you," replied the other, "but I suppose you would rather have seen my head, and then you would have risen a step."'[62]

Despite such opportunities, many deserving officers were overlooked, and to a man without wealth or influence promotion could be extremely slow. George Dyer purchased an ensigncy in the 65th, 'in an unlucky hour, with the consent slow and reluctant of his friends'; 'a lieutenancy, at length, after a toilsome service of many years, became the humble compensation for time, talents, and property, ingloriously wasted'. Apparently he only gained his captaincy as a result of marriage to the sister of the Duke of Northumberland's steward, but his new influence led him only to go to the East Indies, from where he soon returned 'with a shattered constitution and defeated hopes',[63] having suffered a severe sunstroke, and he died aged 39 at his brother-in-law's house in July 1813.

Another was Lieutenant-Colonel Aubrey, who died as Inspecting Field Officer for Buckinghamshire in January 1814, one of the oldest majors in the army (his lieutenant-colonelcy was only temporary, for as long as he was an inspector): he was a captain at Bunker's Hill, and had been promoted to major in June 1782, and thus had spent $31^1/_2$years in that rank. To such an officer, promotion could depend upon the merest chance. Archibald Campbell of the 29th, who had been greatly commended for keeping his men quiet and in barracks at the time of the 'Boston massacre' of 1770, which could have been worse had they been allowed on to the streets, owed his majority in the regiment to the king's fairness. When a commission to the vacant rank was handed to the king for signature, he threw it aside and ordered another to be made out in Campbell's name, saying, 'A good and deserving officer must not be passed over.'[64]

Wellington's attitude to promotion was pragmatic, though the process still infuriated him: 'It would be desirable, certainly, that the only claim to promotion should be military merit; but this is a degree of perfection to which the disposal of military patronage has never been, and cannot be, I believe, brought in any military establishment. The Commander-in-Chief must have friends, officers on the staff attached to him, etc., who will press him to pro-mote their friends and relations, all doubtless very meritorious, and no man will at all times resist these applications; but ... I, who command the largest British army that has been employed against the enemy for many years, and who have upon my hands certainly the most extensive and difficult concern that was ever imposed on any British officer, have not the power of making even a corporal!!!'[65]

One method of rewarding good conduct was by brevet rank, promo-tion without there having to be found a regimental post commensurate with it. This led to some officers having two ranks, one in his regiment which deter-mined his duties, and a largely honorary superior rank 'in the army'. This led to strange situations: in 1799, for example, the senior captain in the 1st Dra-goon Guards was a lieutenant-general in the army, and even more unusual was the case of Robert Crauford of the 73rd, a captain in his regiment and perform-ing that duty when the regiment was on its own; but when in garrison with another unit he took command of the whole, by virtue of a brevet rank of brigadier-general granted for his services in the militia in the 1798 rebellion.

Despite the Duke of York's reforms, it was still possible for very young men to attain high rank: the son of Admiral Duckworth, lieutenant-colonel of the 1/48th, who was killed at Albuera, was apparently aged only 23 when shot in the left breast in that action; he refused to leave his battalion and was killed by a shot through the throat. Extreme youth, indeed, was no hindrance to being a good officer. Edward Freer of the 43rd was an ensign at sixteen, 'So slight in person, and of such surpassing and delicate beauty that the Spaniards often thought him a girl disguised in man's clothing', and he was thus a perfect casting for the heroine Peggy in the play *Raising the Wind* performed by the officers of the Light Division at Gallegos in March 1813. Despite his youth and frail appearance he was the most intrepid of men, a veteran in his teens and with an unfailingly cheerful spirit, so that even 'the most daring and experi-enced veterans watched his looks on the field of battle, and implicitly follow-ing where he led, would like children obey his slightest sign'.[66]

Severely wounded at Badajoz, he rejoined his regiment and before the Battle of Nivelle exhibited characteristics more appropriate to his age and appearance, weeping with a premonition of imminent death and distressed at the effect it would have on his mother and sisters. On the following day, Freer was killed, 'and the sternest soldiers in the regiment wept even in the middle of the fight when they heard of his fate'.[67]

Conversely, great age was not necessarily any reason for an officer to retire. Regimental colonels generally held this appointment until their death, though this was not active duty (for example, Cyrus Trapaud of the 52nd was at the time of his death in May 1801 the oldest general in the service, aged 85, having served at Dettingen. He was of Huguenot descent and, perhaps uniquely for a British officer, was a kinsman of the great French marshal Turenne). Others, however, continued to perform active duty into extreme old age: at his death in October 1803 the oldest officer in the service was Captain Thomas Burton, who had lost an arm at Fontenoy, but was still performing active garrison duty at the age of 94. Patrick Nisbet, in service until his death at the age of 85 in September 1801, had been a Royal Artillery surgeon for 60 years and was a veteran of Carthagena (1739), Dettingen and Fontenoy. Probably the most unusual, in that he was only appointed in old age, was Captain C. A. Quist, a Hanoverian equitation expert, who was appointed Riding Master of the Ordnance Department in January 1803 at the age of 73, and commanded the Riding Troop from its formation in 1808 until his death in December 1821. His appropriately named horse 'Wonder' was equally long-lived, and was buried with ceremony and a headstone at St. John's Wood Barracks upon its death at the age of 40.

There was virtually no official training for officers in any but the Ordnance services. The Royal Military College's junior department, established in 1802 to train youths aged 13–15, accommodated only 100 cadets, of whom twenty were educated on behalf of the East India Company, into whose forces they were to be commissioned. Thirty per cent were the sons of dead or crippled officers, educated free; twenty per cent the offspring of serving officers, educated at reduced price; and the remainder paid the full fee of £90 per annum. Not even an increase of places (by 1809 there were 320 cadets under instruction) made much effect on the training of officers as a whole, the majority joining their regiments totally ignorant of any military duty, to be taught drill by the adjutant and often to learn their trade on the field of battle itself. This may explain why some subalterns were given leave to complete their education before actually joining their regiment, but few cases can have been as unusual as the ensigncy in the 3rd Foot Guards awarded to William Scott, son of the major-general of the same name, who had settled in France and was consequently interned upon the resumption of war after the Peace of Amiens. Young Scott was permitted by the French to study at Weimar, during which time he was commissioned and permitted to continue his schooling; eventually he came home, joined his regiment, but was wounded and captured at Talavera and again returned to imprisonment until 1814.

Knowledge of a foreign language was highly regarded as part of a gentleman's education, and most officers acquired some Spanish and Portuguese in the Peninsula, but as Grattan observed, a man of polished manners and fluency of language put the others in the shade in terms of charming the local señoritas! Many spoke French, but probably few were as fluent as Wellington himself: for example, one of his greatest friends and commandant at headquarters during the Waterloo campaign, Colonel Sir Colin Campbell, despite this important position spoke French so badly that when ordering his dinner spoke to it as if it were a soldier: '*Bif-teck venez ici!*'[68]

There were few aids to the education of an officer beyond the official drill manuals and some privately published simplifications, but among other learning-aids were 'Webb's Military Figures for the Practice of Tacticks', wooden blocks bearing printed pictures of infantrymen, which could be moved about to represent the manoeuvres of a battalion. Another, devised by John Charnock and advertised in 1806, was a wargame played with a map and more than 100 small figures, to teach the wider aspects of military science which could not be learned on the parade-ground.

Edward Cocks, one of the wisest and most knowledgeable officers in the army (one of the 'observing officers' used on intelligence missions) had little opinion of the conventional education provided by officers' schools, which he thought produced officers of sergeant-majors' mentality, military pedants more concerned with drill than practical operations. He believed that all a

34

young man required was a determination to do well and make the best of his situation, and a spare habit, as for every one 'who falls sick from want, a dozen die from the gross habits of eating and drinking'. Military training, he thought, should be left until the officer joined his regiment, and that all the education needed was a knowledge of history, inspirational military anecdotes, French, Latin (the foundation of the Romance languages), mathematics and the elements of fortification; tactics and strategy, he thought, could only be appreciated after experience of active service.[69]

It was quite possible for an officer to rise to high command and still remain totally inept in even the rudiments of drill. The commander of the 1st Life Guards, who joined the Peninsula army in 1812, Major Camac, was unable to perform even a simple manoeuvre when requested. A similar story was told of a colonel of the Warwickshire Militia whose stammer prevented him from giving orders clearly; on one occasion, in front of his advancing regiment, he stuttered so long that he was driven into a muddy ditch before he could stop them.

Alternatively, some were proficient on the parade-ground but not in action; a good field commander, like Sydney Beckwith of the 95th, was one who recognized the real priorities and while maintaining discipline 'was always averse to tease and torment the old soldier with more than a certain quantum of drill', knowing that to allow 'every possible indulgence compatible with the discipline of the battalion ... was the surest way to make the soldiers follow him cheerfully through fire and water, when the day of trial came'.[70]

Although officers might be dismissed for contravention of the articles of war or civil crimes, it was difficult to remove a well-meaning incompetent, although an Inspecting Officer might suggest that an officer be persuaded to retire: this occurred with the 13th Foot in 1812 when a lieutenant was reported to be a drunkard of weak intellect who was in need of constant supervision to keep him out of mischief. Others might realize their unsuitability and resign voluntarily: one who took this course was the Prince of Wales's crony George 'Beau' Brummel, who served in the Prince's 10th Light Dragoons 1795–8 and was so neglectful of duty that it was said he was unable to recognize his own troop. He resigned his captaincy when the regiment was ordered to Manchester, reputedly declaring his unwillingness to go on foreign service! A real incompetent could, however, be ejected from the army by the simple expedient of being informed that the king no longer had need of his services. This occurred with two battalion commanders in March 1814, Sir Nathaniel Peacocke of the 71st and Duncan Macdonald of the 57th, the former for cowardice at St. Pierre, although another discredited at the same action, William Bunbury of the 3rd Foot, was permitted to sell his commission rather than face a court-martial.

Throughout the period there were cases of officers behaving in an unseemly manner, which could be cause for dismissal, of which typical examples might be quoted from each end of the period under review. In April 1794 a party of officers of the Argyllshire Fencibles stormed the pit of an Edinburgh theatre to attack some 'refactory persons' who had refused to stand or remove their hats during the playing of the national anthem, resulting in 'general uproar'.[71] Altogether more reprehensible was the conduct of Captains Isherwood and Walker of the Berkshire Militia in Liverpool in April 1815, who under the influence of drink behaved like hooligans, tearing off door-knockers, breaking lamps, throwing stones through windows, rioting in the mess-room and throwing a chair at the waiter, and even when under arrest singing, dancing, hallooing and stamping their feet in order to prevent their commanding officer from sleeping. Both were dismissed from the regiment, and their commanding officer was censured for not having suppressed their *joie de vivre* earlier.

Neglect of military duty formed a clearer case for dismissal, as occurred in 1803 after 'disgraceful instances of Indiscipline' had been committed by members of the 83rd in the vicinity of Chelmsford; after investigations a lieutenant-colonel and two captains were immediately dismissed for having not only been 'most scandalously deficient' in endeavouring 'to curb the licentiousness of the Soldiers', but had obstructed the investigation to prevent discovery of the offenders.[72]

In extreme cases, a regiment might have most of its officers transferred; this occurred with the 85th Foot during a period of 'rest' during the Peninsular War, when a number of irregularities occurred. All but the lieutenant-colonel were moved, as 'a general measure of expediency, and not intended as an imputation against any individual';[73] its new officer corps transformed it into a regiment of the highest calibre when it returned to the Peninsula in 1813.

A similar case involved the 10th Hussars, when most of the officers submitted a letter of complaint concerning their commanding officer, George Quentin, an ex-member of the Hanoverian *Garde du Corps* who was a favourite of the Prince of Wales and later his ADC. He appears to have been an ineffective officer, but the resulting court-martial acquitted him of all but part of one charge of neglect of duty; he was reprimanded, but all the officers who had complained were transferred to other corps for daring to criticize their commanding officer. The execution of this order was peculiarly humiliating: Adjutant-General Calvert paraded the regiment at Romford on 9 November 1814, called forward the 25 officers involved, ordered them to sheathe their swords and addressed the regiment: 'Gentlemen – I have the Commander-in-Chief's command to signify to you his Royal Highness the Prince Regent's pleasure, that you no longer belong to the 10th Regiment of Hussars.'[74] Consequently, when the 10th fought at Waterloo, only Quentin and one other officer had commissions dating earlier than 12 November 1814. Had Quentin not been a royal favourite, the serious charge of neglect of duty in the presence of the enemy might have had a different outcome.

Officers could be removed from their regiments for other reasons. So great was the enmity between two particular subalterns that they were transferred to different corps; but on meeting again when recruiting at Nottingham, Ensign Browne of the 36th was shot through the heart by Lieutenant Butler of the 83rd in a duel on New Year's Day, 1806. Duelling was punishable by civil law, but still occurred with distressing frequency, although such 'matters of honour' were not always conducted with honour, as perhaps occurred at Stroud in August 1807 when Lieutenant Joseph Delmont of the 82nd was shot in the back by Lieutenant Heazle of the 3rd. Delmont had provoked the quarrel by making derogatory remarks about a lady of Heazle's acquaintance, and his memorial stone made an appropriate comment on the practice of duelling: '...

the inglorious victim of a practice equally abhorrent to Reason, Humanity, and Religion, opposed alike to the discipline of the Soldier, and the moral excellence of the Man. Too proud to apologize for an unwarrantable expression, and mistaking obstinacy for dignity, he improvidently staked his life, and suddenly lost it, to the great grief of those who saw in him characteristicks of a nobler exit.'[75]

When duellers were prosecuted, the verdicts varied considerably, as exemplified by two cases which occurred in Ireland in 1808. In August a major was hanged at Armagh for killing another, yet at Wexford Assizes in March Congreve Alcock was acquitted of killing John Colclough in a duel over votes in the Wexford election, in which both had been candidates; in a bizarre comment upon the legal system, the prosecution was based not upon whether Alcock had committed the act, but upon whether his putting on spectacles before the duel had given him an unfair advantage! Seconds were equally guilty if a charge of murder were proven; at Hampshire Assizes in August 1813 four subalterns of the 100th were found guilty of the murder of a fifth, in a trivial disagreement over clothes; all four were pardoned by the Prince Regent but only the man who had fired the fatal shot, Ensign McGuire, was permitted to remain in the service, the seconds presumably being thought more culpable for having urged McGuire to seek satisfaction.

The absurdities to which the concept of 'honour' could lead were demonstrated by the case of the celebrated Colonel Hervey Aston of the 12th, who was involved in a minor breach of etiquette during a brief absence from his battalion. When he returned he did not resume command immediately, and informed all his officers that he would meet them one after another if they desired, so that they could not be accused of having challenged their commanding officer. Only the second-in-command and the senior captain took him up; Aston refused to shoot after the former's pistol misfired, but the captain shot and mortally wounded him. The propriety of not challenging one's commanding officer arose again in a case involving Henry 'Orator' Hunt, later a leading Radical politician and the speaker at the 'Peterloo' affair. Hunt refused to accept his expulsion from the Wiltshire Yeomanry (presumably he was regarded as a troublemaker), and inquired of his commanding officer, Lord Bruce, whether he was still regarded as a member of the unit. When Bruce replied, 'Certainly not,' Hunt said, 'As you are no longer my Colonel, nor I your subject, you ought to give me satisfaction; and if you are a gentleman, as you ought to be, I shall expect some.'[76] Instead, Bruce prosecuted him for making a challenge contrary to law, and as Hunt refused to apologize he was fined £100 and imprisoned for six weeks.

The importance placed upon personal honour produced some strange reactions: Lieutenant-Colonel the Hon. Arthur Wolf of the 70th, a young man of promise, retired from the service after the dishonour of being reprimanded by a reviewing general over his manoeuvering of his battalion; he died in 1805, aged only 28. More serious was the sad case of Lieutenant-Colonel Charles Bevan of the 4th Foot, who was blamed for the escape of the French garrison of Almeida in May 1811, by not moving to the place Wellington had ordered. It appears that he received the order too late for it to be effectual, the sad Erskine having put it in his pocket and forgetting to send it on, and then apparently inventing a story about the 4th becoming lost to excuse his own negligence. Feeling himself hopelessly wronged, Bevan killed himself.

Not all officers were the models of propriety suggested by the term 'gentleman', and it is surprising that some retained their rank as long as they did. Even the most prestigious regiments were not immune from reprehensible characters: when the 3rd Foot Guards lost a battalion commander by suspension following 58 prosecutions for debt in five years, plus a charge of gross indecency, they received as his successor a tyrannical martinet whose answer to *his* creditors was to throw them, and the law officers who accompanied them, into the regimental guardhouse![77]

The character of the officers of even one of the most distinguished regiments was recounted in the poem *The Blueviad*, by a subaltern of the Royal Horse Guards, Edward Goulburn (or Goldbourne), for which he was prosecuted for libel at the Court of King's Bench in 1805–6. Only three of the officers bothered to prosecute, and received almost as much censure from the judge as did Goulburn, for encouraging him to publish and then prosecuting. The damages awarded, only £50, and the fact that most did not challenge him, must cast doubts upon the denials of the accuracy of the poem, which used pseudonyms indicative of the officers' characters: 'Pomposo', 'Bluster', 'Numscull', 'Slipslop', 'Macsycophant', etc. They were variously accused of fraud (selling horses known to be infirm), drunkenness, violence, even indecent exposure:

'What yields him most supreme delight
By showing parts obscene, disgust your sight.'

'Slipslop' and 'Macsycophant' are described as being the colonel's toadies, constantly attempting to ingratiate themselves; and of 'Lothario' (Sir John Elley),

'Wife, Maid or Virgin, are to him the same,
And each at his desire, must yield their fame.'

Captain Cherry (alias 'Sir Pepper Absolute') is described as beating a sick man unable to defend himself, and Captain Browne is condemned as a foul-mouthed officer who would not even stop swearing when ordered by his colonel: 'Dam – dam – I will dam dam, God dam my Soul'.

Following Goulburn's exit from the regiment, he was insulted by Captain John Horsley, whom he challenged. Horsley had been characterized in *The Blueviad* as a fraudulent spendthrift who had wasted all his wife's and sister's money and who refused to repay a loan from a brother-officer:

'With looks ill temper'd, fraught with gloomy pride,
Bluster next rears, his gross & pamper'd hide;
The face bespeaks the man, at once we see,
The bloated remnants of a Debauchee...'

The case had a curious outcome. Horsley, 'conceiving that Mr. Goulbourn's [*sic*] character did not entitle him to be met as a gentleman',[78] refused his challenge, in which he was supported by his brother officers. However, when Goulburn made the refusal public knowledge, the officers signed a paper which compelled Horsley to resign, disgraced for not having accepted the challenge. Having been first supported and then condemned by his fellows, Horsley published *The Case of John Horsley, Esq., late a Captain in the Royal Regiment of Horse Guards Blue*, in his own defence and in exasperation at what he conceived a travesty of the laws of honour.

Immoderate gambling was another passion which bedevilled some officers, as suggested by a mock epitaph on Captain Daniel Danvers of the Royal Marines:

'Yet so strong was his passion, it sleeps with his clay;
And you'll find, when he wakes in the last *busy* day,
When his neighbours around are bestirring their stumps,
The first thing he'll ask will be, Pray what is Trumps?'[79]

This could have serious consequences: for example, Captain Amos Norcott of the 33rd made one disastrous foray in gaming in India in 1797, losing more than £500 at a stroke, which would have been his ruination had not his battalion commander, Arthur Wellesley, discharged the debt by borrowing on his own account; without this, the army would have lost a valuable officer, who rose to command the 2/95th at Waterloo and became a major-general. Another case involved Henry Mellish of the 10th Hussars, later known as a brave and resourceful officer, who was so inveterate a gambler that he was given permanent leave of absence to prevent his habits rubbing off on his brother officers!

Despite the leavening of bad characters, the impression of the average regimental officer, particularly in the Peninsula army, is of a man with no especial pretensions to higher military skill, but capable of performing his regimental duty with assiduity if often with a carefree attitude to life; and very often with heroism, though in many cases this was regarded as no more than what was expected. As distinct from later memoirs, there are few recorded letters describing the emotions experienced before battle, but the following, by Lieutenant Robert Gwinn Grainger of the Royal Marines to his parents, expresses sentiments typical of many:

'I seize a moment to write these few lines to you, that, should I fall, you may have the satisfaction of saying that it was in a glorious cause, and, I hope, in a brilliant victory. To all of you, who I know so much love me, I know how great will be your satisfaction in being informed, that, to the last, I was brave and honourable ... God bless and preserve you all; and remember that by virtue and righteousness we may meet in another and a better world.'[80]

Wounded several times, Robert Grainger refused to leave his post until completely incapacitated, or to have his wounds dressed before those of his men; he died universally regretted. He was 21 years of age.

The great level of devotion which could be accorded to officers by their men is exemplified by the case of Captain Charles Douglas of the 51st, who was shot through the heart in the Pyrenees on 31 August 1813, while endeavouring to rescue a wounded man. Four of his skirmishers tried to recover his body, but after two of them had been killed and a third wounded, the fourth, unable to move the body on his own, had reluctantly to leave it in the hands of the French.

Relations between officers and rank and file were often much more free than was possible in later years. Thomas Morris recounts a story concerning the 2/73rd in Germany in 1813, in which Ensign William MacBean asked

Private Jack Smith for some of the potatoes he was roasting. MacBean, known as 'the Sick Black' from his cadaverous, dark complexion, was highly unpopular, and Smith replied that he would see him damned first. Shortly after, a popular officer, Ensign Robert Stewart, came past and asked if he could *buy* some potatoes; Smith said that he wouldn't sell any, but would give Stewart as many as he wanted, on condition that MacBean didn't receive any! This exemplifies Morris' remark that men would gladly follow and risk all for a popular officer, but would do the minimum for those they did not respect.

To demonstrate the level of respect which might be accorded by the ordinary soldier to his officer, George Napier wrote movingly about a visit he received after he had been wounded, from an Irish drunkard in his company, John Dunn, who had walked seven miles to inquire after Napier's health. Seven miles, after seeing his brother killed by his side, and after 'Why sure it's nothing, only me *arrum* was cut off a few hours ago below the elbow joint, and I couldn't come until the anguish was over a bit.' As Napier remarked, 'Could a brother have done more?'[81]

Part of the successful relationship between officers and rank and file was the fact that, on campaign at least, all shared the same tribulations. This was actively encouraged: when 'Black Bob' Craufurd saw an officer being carried across a river on the back of a private, he shouted at the man to put him down instantly, which he did, in the middle of the water; Craufurd then berated the officer and sent him back to cross the river again, to emphasize that all must share alike the rigours of the day.

Pensions granted to the dependents of a deceased officer could be generous: for example, the family of John Gaspard Le Marchant, killed at Salamanca, received annual pensions of £300 to his eldest son, £120 to each of four daughters, and £100 to each of three younger sons; his wife had died shortly after his arrival in the Peninsula, Le Marchant having had to leave her far advanced in pregnancy. Widows' pensions were normally much less generous; by the end of the Peninsular War, for example, they ranged from £120 per annum for a general officer's widow, to £50 for a captain and £36 for an ensign. Pensions for living officers were granted for the loss of a limb or eye in action, one pension per item: thus an officer who had lost an arm and an eye, for example, received a double pension. These were graded according to regimental rank at the time of the injury, or brevet rank if acting in a capacity superior to that of regimental rank, and ranged from £400 per annum for a lieutenant-general to £200 for a major, £100 for a captain and £50 for an ensign, for example; these were announced in 1812 but were retrospective to 1793. Similar pensions for commissariat officers were announced in February 1813, similarly retrospective but paid only from Christmas 1811, ranging from £350 for a Commissary-General at the head of a department to £40 for a commissariat clerk.

Officers whose units were reduced, or who in some cases resigned, went on half-pay, a system which maintained a reserve of officers, ostensibly able to be recalled to service if required, even though many were physically unfit for it. Half-pay imposed a sizeable financial burden upon the national resources, as officers might draw it for many years: in 1799 George Bell and Captain R. Browne, ex-officers of Gually's Dragoons, and Cornet Whitney Makean of Lord Windsor's Horse, were still receiving half-pay at least 86 years after their regiments were disbanded in 1712–13. Half-pay ceased when an officer received a new commission, but not if this were in the Ordnance or East India service; for example, Sir Alexander Lindsay, a general of the Royal Artillery, drew lieutenant's half-pay from the 104th Royal Manchester Volunteers for almost 80 years, from the drafting of the regiment until his death.

The half-pay system provided an avenue by which an officer's services could be dispensed with (many of those who undeservedly received commissions in the early 1790s were soon put on half-pay), but it was never sufficient to allow the worthy veteran to live in much comfort. One who was living on it in 1801 calculated that for an officer and his wife, annual living expenses were at a minimum £77 7s. (allowing only 5s. per week for rent, 3s. 6d. for bread, 5s. for meat, and no wine); against which, after tax, an infantry captain's half-pay was only £87 8s. 6d. per annum, and very much less for subalterns. Nor, the officer continued, could much have been saved when on full pay, especially in a new or militia regiment in which there were frequent changes of uniform, as if 'the Colonels think lace and feathers the sole requisites necessary to qualify the officer and soldier'; and even the half-pay officer who was physically fit 'too often sees the school-boy preferred before him; and without interest, all his past services will not entitle him to a command, so that he seems doomed ... to be literally starved in old age'.[82]

Examples might be quoted to prove the veracity of these assertions; for example, in August 1798 a half-pay lieutenant, Valentine Rudd, applied for relief to Bow Street magistrate's office, as he was a gentleman but completely destitute; he was told that by so doing he was committing an act of vagrancy and threatened with six months' imprisonment, but after a short detention was allowed to go on his way.

Another case occurred at Surrey Assizes in August 1801, when an unemployed captain was prosecuted for debt, 'a fine looking man, in the prime of life, and had the manners and appearance of the most polished gentleman'. The prosecutor asked why he had not declared his household goods when listing the resources available to discharge his debts; he replied that these 'goods' were no more than a hard bed he had used in prison, and 'I have been used to it; and I am fain to content myself, after undergoing the perils and hardships of war, and being exposed to the fire of the enemy in the East and West Indies, in America and Africa, and different parts of the Globe – I am not so fortunate as you, who perhaps sleep on a soft bed, and by your conduct to me do not know the behaviour of a gentleman: I have fought bravely, as these testimonies will shew' (handing some documents to the Bench) – 'I am an old soldier!' The prosecutor wondered why the captain had not declared his clothes as a realizable asset; 'unbuttoning an old great coat, "This", said he, "is my wardrobe, and this is the only shirt I have – I have not one shilling in the world".' He was discharged; and his situation was, it was noted, 'too often the case with Officers in the Army, who upon a small pittance are obliged to keep up an appearance of rank to which their incomes are totally inadequate'.[83]

With so many half-pay officers living in reduced circumstances, criticism was made of 'gross and scandalous abuses' when a case was brought before parliament in May 1809 concerning the appointment of the store-keeper of the Hyde Park Magazine, a situation worth more than £200 per annum.

Instead of this going to one of the 'respectable, though poor Officers on half-pay, whose lives have been spent in the service of their country, from whose bounty they barely derive sustenance', and for which a half-pay officer would have been an ideal candidate, the man chosen was a retired footman of Marquess Wellesley's, recommended by Mr. Wellesley Pole, Secretary of the Admiralty and the Marquess' brother, it was suggested to avoid having to pay the man a pension upon his retirement, 'mean, infamous parsimony, which impels an opulent Nobleman to foist his decayed menial servants on these establishments which were intended as rewards of military merit, and tokens of gratitude for wounds received in the service of their country, by aged and infirm veterans'.[84]

4
'Men of a Very Low Description'
THE RANK AND FILE

SPEAKING IN THE HOUSE OF COMMONS ON 20 NOVEMBER 1795, concerning mutinies which had occurred allegedly because the government had broken its word over the terms of enlistment, the Secretary for War stated that 'in recruiting, it was always necessary to employ men of a very low description, and that it was impossible to make Government answerable for the engagements such men entered into'.[85] This attitude to the ordinary soldier was widespread: the concept of 'a brutal and insolent soldiery' in the words of Lord Erskine, who had himself served briefly as an officer in the Royal Scots. A more balanced view was adopted by most of those who knew the soldier better:

'Let not the lac'd loungers mock their thankless toil,
Their homely meals, and toilet's thrifty plan,
Nor broider'd generals hear, with scornful smile,
The simple annals of the private man'.[86]

The demand for recruits was insatiable. The following were the published statistics of troops (excluding Ordnance units) under arms on a full-time basis on Christmas Day 1811:

	At home	Abroad
British cavalry	12,050	11,719
Foreign cavalry	1,568	2,136
Foot Guards	3,748	3,130
British infantry	45,501	99,735
Foreign infantry	2,745	36,320
Militia	77,159	–

(Of these, recruiting for the British units had in the previous twelve months brought in 7,893 men and 1,580 boys enlisted for life, and 1,639 men and 360 boys for limited service; 3,631 had deserted at home during the same period.)

The problem of maintaining such numbers, and of increasing the size of the army when necessary, was considerable. Deaths in battle were comparatively few; the numbers of men who died or were incapacitated by disease were huge. Taking the same year, 1811: fatalities and death from wounds in the Peninsular War were about 2,000, yet the total loss to the army in the year was 19,019 British and 3,441 foreign troops. This was a little over the average annual loss in the period from the resumption of war in 1803 to the end of 1813, some 20,500 per annum, ranging from 16,070 in 1803 to a peak of 25,498 in 1812. To put these figures in perspective, the total loss during this period, more than 225,000 men, represents the entire regular army of 1793 being killed more than five times over, or virtually the entire army of 1812. When set against these losses, the immense number lost in the West Indies, almost all to disease, is revealed in its true horror: from 1794 to 1797 some 80,000 men died or were permanently disabled in this pestilential posting.

Apart from militia service, there was no system that in any way resembled conscription, and the regular forces were recruited exclusively by voluntary enlistment. This had an enormous disadvantage: for a variety of reasons, not least the type of civilian who normally served in the army, and the fact that soldiers were used in crowd-control duties in the absence of any organized police, military service in general was regarded as a livelihood in which only the worst members of society participated, and was extremely unpopular in many quarters. Wellington's oft-misquoted remark that soldiers were in general 'the scum of the earth', enlisted for drink or to escape the consequences of having fathered illegitimate children, when considered in its correct context has much to support it. Wellington was not adopting a superior attitude by way of condemnation – he added how astonishing it was that they had been made into such 'fine fellows' – but used the term to indicate the social background from which they came, in course of a plea to involve the higher classes of society as did many other European armies.

Some of the motivations for joining the army were described upon a recruiting-poster for the 14th Light Dragoons, which advertised for likely candidates: 'All you who are kicking your heels behind a solitary desk with too little wages, and a pinch-gut Master – all you with too much wife, or are perplexed with obstinate and unfeeling parents...';[87] and although Wellington was scornful of the idea that men might enlist out of 'fine military feeling', undoubtedly some did, like Thomas Morris of the 73rd. He joined the St. George's Volunteers at the age of 16, not to avoid the militia ballot as many did (he was then too young), but out of a desire to participate in the 'heart-stirring accounts of sieges and battles'[88] about which he had read. At length, feeling ashamed at being only half a soldier, he enlisted for full-time service in his brother's regiment.

If the appeal of a life of adventure encouraged many men to enlist, then simple hardship would appear to have been a greater motivation, for at least in the army a man was guaranteed food, clothing and a place to lay his head. It is noticeable that in some instances the occupations of recruits correlate with depressions in their particular trade, and there were even a few cases of the genuine 'gentleman ranker' who enlisted simply out of penury. John Harcomb of the 10th Hussars was an example: a solicitor who had squandered his fortune, he enlisted as a private until he again came into money and purchased a commission. Having again wasted his resources he was forced to sell out and again enlisted as a private in his former regiment, and died in 1814 in Kingston workhouse, Portsea. The realities of soldiering in the lower ranks came as a rude shock to such people, who experienced none of the glamour suggested by the uniform. The poet Coleridge entered the 15th Light Dragoons in 1793 (under the alias of Silas Tomkyn Comberbatch), probably because of a combination of expected glamour and lack of money; he was saved from a miserable existence as a trooper by his brother, a captain, who arranged for his discharge.

One who enlisted to escape 'obstinate and unfeeling parents' was Thomas Wheatley of the 23rd Light Dragoons, who fled to the army after trying to shoot his father for breaking the strike of the stocking-weavers with whom Thomas sympathized. He survived Waterloo and returned home, and is buried beneath a monument at Cossall churchyard, Nottinghamshire, which commemorates the area's three Waterloo heroes. The others, both killed in the battle, exemplify other reasons for enlisting in the army: John Shaw, the celebrated prize-fighter, fell out with his master and forsook his apprenticeship, joining the 2nd Life Guards to further his pugilistic career (which prospered in the Household Cavalry); and Richard Waplington, who enlisted in the same regiment as a refuge from the coal-mines in which he had laboured from the age of 12 or 13.

Some entered the army as fugitives from justice, although the number was probably less than the army's critics believed, and many of these would form the hard core of 'incorrigibles' which existed in most regiments, and which caused more trouble than all the others combined. A minor element of conscription, albeit largely unofficial, did exist in the legal system; in September 1798, for example, a list was published of men 'convicted before Magistrates of the county of Cork, of being idle and disorderly persons, and ordered to serve in the army or navy'.[89] Even some of those convicted in the New Year's Day riot in Edinburgh in 1812 were similarly enrolled.

Because of the public disapproval of the army and military service, various expedients were used to attract men to the colours. The most obvious was the bounty paid to each recruit upon joining, a financial incentive irresistible to many paupers who had spent their lives at mere subsistence level. The bounty varied according to the urgency with which recruits were required, and there was often competition between the regular army, militia and navy for the recruits available; in 1796, for example, one recruiting officer gave up the unequal struggle of putting his 10-guinea bounties against the up to 40 guineas offered by the Royal Navy. In 1805 the enlistment-bounty, paid in money and in the provision of the 'necessaries' (equipment) which each soldier had to provide at his own expense, was twelve guineas; but this was not the total expense to the government of each recruit, as the person who brought the recruit to the recruiting-party received £2 12s. 6d., and the recruiting-party itself £1 11s. 6d., bringing the total expense to 16 guineas per man.

The payment to the 'bringer of the recruit' raises the question of various nefarious practices. For various reasons, recruiters sometimes were prepared to pay well over the ordinary price for a recruit (for example if 'recruiting for rank'), and some resorted to the employment of crimps. These were a species of rogue who undertook to supply a number of men at a price, by persuading the gullible to enlist (some crimps offered 25 guineas cash-in-hand), or by methods more in keeping with their ordinary occupations, which in some cases were as receivers of stolen property or even coiners, in addition to the dubious merchants and publicans who were the typical crimps. Likely recruits might be stood free drinks until they were insensible, and then handed to the army before they sobered, or in extreme cases could be literally kidnapped after being lured into the crimpers' hands by women or other means. An example of this dreadful practice was revealed in 1795, when a window in a house in St. George's Fields was smashed by a kidnapped pot-boy, who cried 'Murder'; when the building was entered eighteen men were found in chains, awaiting 'sale' to the army.

The worst excesses of the crimping trade occurred in the mid-1790s, when the demand for recruits was at its height; yet it continued despite criticism in parliament. One MP described seeing a newly raised Irish regiment 'filled up with decrepid [sic] men from 70 to 80 years, and of boys little more than 12. In the very town he represented an old man had been enlisted, and received seven guineas bounty, though ten years before he had been dismissed as wholly unfit for any service';[90] another asked 'What confidence ... could be expected to subsist between the officer and the soldier, when the former was a boy just escaped from school, and the other a victim redeemed from the dungeons of the crimps?'[91]

Most recruits were gathered by recruiting-parties sent out by a battalion or regiment on the strength of a 'Beating Order', to range about likely venues and enlist whomsoever they could. Such a recruiting-party usually consisted of an officer, one or two sergeants, a drummer (to attract the crowds), and four or five privates, selected for their smart appearance and quick wits, and decked out with ribbons and favours which were presented to each recruit. Some men would enlist at the sight of the recruiting-party, but others had to be enveigled into joining. Weavers, it was said, were the easiest to attract, simply by contrasting their damp and monotonous existence with the delights of an open-air life as extolled by the recruiting-sergeant; agricultural labourers responded best to tales of rapid promotion, and how the officer of the party had himself been a ploughboy only a few years before. A glimpse of the type of outrageous claims made by recruiters is provided by posters issued by recruiting-parties, which sometimes varied between the unrealistic and the deceitful: 'Five Shillings a Day and a Black Servant';[92] '... the men will not be allowed to hunt during the next Season, more than once a week'; 'luxurious living, an hospitable table and capacious bowl of punch'.[93] Others extolled the reputation of their corps: 'The Regiment has been one year and a half in Ireland, constantly employed in exterminating the Croppies, who are now, damn their bloods, about finished ... At the battle of Hacketstown one of the Dragoons at full speed, with a single blow of the Sabre, cut the head of a rebel clean off ...'[94]

Some unusual devices were employed to attract recruits. Recruiting-sergeants of the 33rd flourished havercakes on their swords (oatcakes characteristic of the West Riding) to represent the abundance of food they claimed was common in the army. John Heyes, a Yorkshire dwarf some 42 inches tall, was in demand to follow recruiting-parties and perform the sword-exercise to attract the crowds, presumably a more pleasant way of earning a living than being exhibited in a freak show, his previous employment.

When the Duke of Gordon was raising his regiment in 1794 (ultimately numbered the 92nd), his wife reputedly provided the biggest attraction to recruits. Though aged 46 she was outstandingly beautiful, and joined the recruiting-parties dressed in uniform and accompanied by her daughters, who danced a reel with any man prepared to enlist. Instead of handing each recruit the 'King's shilling' which sealed the bargain before the official swearing-in, it was said she placed the coin between her lips and offered to kiss every man who would take it. Two stories concerning 'Bonnie Jean' show contrasting reactions to this offer: one man was said to have taken his kiss and immediately paid his pound 'smart money' to release him from the engagement before he took the enlistment-oath, remarking that a pound was a cheap price for a kiss from the Duchess; another, said to have been offered a guinea between her lips, took the coin and flung it into the crowd, to show that it was the kiss, not the money, which had persuaded him to enlist. Even if these stories are apocryphal, they represent the methods taken to lure civilians into the army.

A good band, a distinctive uniform (like that of the 95th Rifles) or even a famous colonel could be a valuable aid to recruiting; for example, so popular was the Marquess of Huntly (the Duke of Gordon's son) that in 1812 it was reported that his regiment (42nd) was having no difficulty in obtaining recruits from even the English and Irish militia.

The number of recruiting-parties operational at any one time varied with the demand for recruits; for example, in the year July 1805–July 1806 some 405 parties were operating in Britain, but in 1806–7 the number increased to 1,113. In 1812, to reduce the reliance upon recruiting-parties from individual regiments, every recruiting district was formed into subdivisions, each commanded by an experienced officer to oversee recruiting.

Originally enlistment was for life, until the soldier became too infirm to do his duty or until his services were no longer required. When Grenville's 'Ministry of all the Talents' came to power in early 1806, William Windham took over the war department and introduced a scheme for limited service as an alternative to lifetime enlistment. It permitted recruits to engage for three successive periods of service:

	1st period	2nd period	3rd period
Infantry	7 years	7 years	7 years
Cavalry	10 years	7 years	7 years
Artillery	12 years	5 years	5 years

The stated intention was to improve the attraction of the military trade, and 'to bring it into fair competition with a sufficient portion of the habits and callings of the lower orders'.[95] It was claimed that the new conditions curbed desertion (from one man in 157 in 1805 to one in 263 in 1806–7), but in subsequent years the numbers of deserters rose again, to 6,611 in 1808 and 5,918 in 1812, for example. It involved a variation in the bounty, which by 1812 had risen to £23 17s. 6d. for lifetime service and £18 12s. 6d. for limited service, but in practice it did not make a great deal of difference, as the majority of men still enlisted for life. (Whether it reflects upon perceived national characteristics or not, it is interesting to observe that the Irish appear to have been most willing to enlist for life, and the more cautious Scots most eager to engage for limited service.)

Recruits soon discovered that the bounty was a transitory blessing, being almost always expended before the man joined his regiment, some going on drink and women and the rest squandered: 'Winchester ... has been a scene of riot, dissipation and absurd extravagance. It is supposed that nine-tenths of the bounties ... amounting to at least 20,000 £ were all spent on the spot among the public houses, milliners, watch-makers, hatters, &c. In mere wantonness, Bank notes were actually eaten between slices of bread and butter.'[96] Nor was the bounty dissipated solely by the recruit's own folly; the recruiting-parties frequently fleeced their victims. An 11th Light Dragoon wrote of 'the knavery of others', especially NCOs who gave the recruit favoured treatment only until his money was gone: 'They will first suck you dry, and then grind you to powder.'[97] It was also expected that the recruit should use his bounty to treat his fellows: in July 1809 a recruit of the 18th Light Dragoons was tossed in a blanket for choosing not to squander his money in this way, and died from a broken neck when a corner of the blanket gave way.

Some strange events occurred in recruiting: in April 1794 a man in the Grassmarket, Edinburgh, put himself up for public auction to the various recruiting-parties present, allowing no bid of less than a guinea; he was eventually knocked down for 20 guineas. Another case involved a man selling himself like butcher's meat, asking for bids of so much a pound. Disappointment with the bounty, such as the withholding of part of it to cover purchase of 'necessaries', was sometimes the cause of discontent; at Mansfield and Nottingham in January 1798, for example, recruits refused to march and the situation was exacerbated by the interference of 'some disaffected persons'.[98]

Having accepted the token 'King's shilling', the recruit was taken before a magistrate or justice of the peace (provided that this functionary was not an army officer) to swear the enlistment-oath, which was to take place within four days of enlistment, but not within 24 hours (presumably as a safeguard against recruits being sworn while drunk and incapable). On being presented to the magistrate, the recruit could withdraw his consent to enlist provided that he returned any money he had received, and twenty shillings in addition to defray other expenses; failure to produce this sum within 24 hours meant that he was regarded as properly enlisted. The magistrate read to the recruit those articles of war relating to mutiny and desertion; the recruit declared on oath his name, occupation, age, place of birth, that he was not already a member of any regiment, militia, navy or marines, 'and that he has had no Rupture, and was not troubled with Fits, and was no ways disabled by Lameness, Deafness, or otherwise, but had the perfect Use of his Limbs and Hearing, and was not an Apprentice ...' (The declaration regarding ruptures was a necessary safeguard, as manual work among the labouring classes was so arduous that it was estimated in 1814 that one in eight males in the land was affected by a rupture.)

Until the Catholic Relief Act of 1791, the English attestation form began, 'I, – do make Oath, That I am a Protestant, and by Trade a – and to the best of my Knowledge and Belief, was born in the Parish of –'; the affirmation of Protestantism was dispensed with at that date, but the corresponding Scottish Catholic Emancipation Act was not introduced into parliament until April 1793, and some old attestation-forms were still used in Scotland in that year, which cost some recruits (Sir James Grant of Grant, refusing one who was a Roman Catholic, remarked that 'I cannot desire you to do an illegal act though I am convinced many Roman Catholics are good subjects ...')[99] Such problems did not extend beyond 1793, and were probably often ignored even before.

The oath sworn by the recruit before the magistrate was:

'I swear to be true to our Sovereign Lord King George, and serve Him honestly and faithfully in Defence of his Person, Crown, and Dignity, against all His Enemies or Opposers whatsoever: And to observe and obey His Majesty's Orders, and the Orders of the Generals and Officers set over me by His Majesty.'

Medical standards were imposed, and although some poor specimens were accepted, there were probably no such outrageous exceptions allowed like that which permitted John Metcalfe to enrol as a musician in 1745 (he was captured at Falkirk); he is better-known as Blind Jack of Knaresborough, the road-builder and engineer, who had lost his sight at the age of four!

In 1806 the height-restriction was 5 feet 4 inches for 'general service', an inch more for those choosing their own regiments, and higher still for Guards and cavalry. There were also a few regimental height-restrictions; for example, in August 1812 it was reported that the 10th Hussars intended to discharge all men under 5 feet 7 inches, and in future recruit none under that height. In 1839 Henry Marshall, Deputy Inspector of Army Hospitals, described common tricks adopted by undersized men to meet the height requirement, and by those wishing to procure their discharge by making themselves appear smaller than they were: in the former case by glueing buff-leather to the soles of the feet or concealing a lump of wood in the hair, and in the latter by bending the knees imperceptibly. Marshall believed that the best way of measuring a recruit was to do so when the man was laid on his back!

During the period just after the Napoleonic Wars, an analysis of 1,000 men accepted as fit by recruiters in London recorded the following heights:

5ft 5in – 5ft 6in:	73
5ft 6in – 5ft 7in:	476
5ft 7in – 5ft 8in:	220
5ft 8in – 5ft 9in:	126
5ft 9in – 5ft 10in:	56
5ft 10in – 5ft 11in:	35
5ft 11in – 6ft:	12
over 6ft:	2

The average chest-measurement of these men was 32.66 inches, that of country recruits being ¾in greater than that of town-dwellers. More than one-third were rejected as unfit, the proportion of unfit men increasing with their height, suggesting that the smaller men were the most physically able. This confirms the opinion of some officers who believed that tall men were less hardy, though Kincaid thought that there was no difference, except that when a tall man broke down under fatigue he was noticed more than a small man, whose constitution presumably was not expected to be as robust.

Trades and occupations of recruits varied with the area from which they were drawn, and dependent upon the prosperity of each trade at each date: a depression in the textile trade, for example, would result in the recruitment of more weavers than normal, and an area with a well-developed industry would bring in a higher percentage of its employees than an area with a less-developed branch of the trade; the large numbers of weavers from Lancashire and the West Riding, or the 'framework knitters' from the Midlands are examples. The number of labourers enlisted was greater from areas without a developed manufacturing industry. Statistics for recruits enlisted in Dublin in 1825–7 show the following occupations per 1,000 men: labourers 645, servants 65, weavers 63, shoemakers 43, clerks 31, tailors 24, carpenters and blacksmiths eighteen each.[100] Conversely, of the rank and file who served with the 23rd at Waterloo, occupations numbered as follows: labourers 332, textile workers 100, metalworkers 39, shoemakers 38, clothing-makers 32 and woodworkers nineteen.[101] (An analysis of the 1811 census showed that for every 20 people, in England seven were employed in agriculture, nine in trade, manufacture or handicraft, and four lived on the rental of property or on interest from capital. In Wales agricultural workers outnumbered manufacturers by 2:1.)

An estimate of literacy in the post-Napoleonic period stated that of Scottish recruits, between 7 and 10 per cent could neither read nor write and that 20 per cent were unable to sign their name; but even in 1839 this was remarked upon as being an unusual figure, for it was thought that only one-third of soldiers were able to sign their account-books. Some men, however, did learn to read and write in the army, but although regimental schools were encouraged by the Duke of York in a General Order of 1 January 1812, not all units had them, and attendance was entirely voluntary. In 1814 it was estimated that one-ninth of the population died without having acquired any learning whatever.

Young recruits were much preferred; in 1839 it was stated that those who enlisted aged 25 or over were 'habitually dissipated and profligate characters, broken-down gentlemen, discharged soldiers, deserters, &c';[102] and that because as few as 5 per cent were still fit for service at age 40, on average the enlistment of a 20-year-old gave five years' extra service than that of a 25-year-old recruit. The average age of soldiers was indeed quite young, but although the more elderly might be left at the home depot when a unit was ordered abroad, it is interesting to note the presence of comparatively old men even on active service. For example, when the 13th Foot was inspected at Martinique in May 1812, it contained three men aged 55 and over, nine of 50–55, eight of 45–50, twenty-four of 40–45, sixty-three of 35–40, 137 of 30–35, 209 of 25–30, 240 of 20–25, sixteen of 18–20, and twelve under 18.[103]

An interesting comparison may be made with a roll of 100 men recruited for the 98th in the spring of 1794; of whom two were rejected, five deserted, and two gentlemen-rankers were sent to the Scots Brigade in Netherlands service, presumably as officers. Seventeen of these recruits were aged 15–17, thirty-one 18–24, nineteen 25–29, and thirty-three 30–35; four stood only 5 feet 2 inches tall, 60 were 5 feet 5 inches or less, only five were 5 feet 9 inches or over, and the tallest was only 5 feet 10½ inches.[104]

So desperate was the manpower shortage that from December 1797 six regiments (9th, 16th, 22nd, 34th, 55th and 65th) were authorized to be completed 'entirely of boys, from 13 to 18 years old. They are to be well fed, and for some time to be mere walking drills, after which they are to be exercised with light fusees, one hundred of which have been sent to each of the six regiments';[105] their bounty was only 1½ guineas. This was an extension of the practice by which all regiments were permitted to take boys an inch lower than the official height, if they might be expected to grow. The 4th and 52nd were also permitted to recruit boys, as were in 1800 the 32nd and 45th.

A recruit of genteel upbringing would regard the average enlistee with dismay: 'I could not associate with the common soldiers: their habits made me shudder. I feared an oath – they were never without one; I could not drink – they loved liquor; they gamed – I knew nothing of play. Thus I was a solitary individual among hundreds.'[106] Consequently, there was always difficulty in keeping newly enlisted men true to their oath, and so prevalent was the practice of enlisting and then absconding with the bounty that it even had its own slang term, 'pear-making'. Probably the most outrageous exponent of the art was Thomas Hodgson, alias 'Tom the Devil', who in 1787 was executed for robbery at the age of 26, and who admitted enlisting under various names no less than 49 times and in each case deserting within a couple of days, which had garnered him the sum of 397 guineas. The greatest proportion deserted while under the supervision of the recruiting districts rather than after induction into their regiments: in the first half of 1805, for example, one man in 202 deserted from the army at home (one in 204 in Ireland), yet during the same period one in ten deserted from the recruiting districts.

Various methods were adopted to prevent the desertion of newly enlisted men, including keeping them drunk. Benjamin Harris, for example, was enlisted by a recruiting-party which flourished two decanters of whiskey and 'danced, drank, shouted and piped' the route between Cashel and Clonmel, where they arrived all rolling drunk.[107] When Harris himself went on the recruiting service, he records handcuffing himself to a recruit overnight, to prevent the man absconding when sober. When recruiting for the 90th in 1794, one officer commented that he had to send 40 of his recruits to Altrincham, to keep them away from the temptations of Warrington races, lest they be persuaded by their friends to run off; only his most reliable dozen did he allow to attend the races, which might have been a fertile recruiting-ground. (It is an interesting comment on the practices of recruiting-parties that his two sergeants were charging the officer 35s. per week for their services, plus two guineas for each man they enrolled!)[108]

Some of those who enlisted when drunk or in a fit of anger immediately regretted their actions: in October 1807 a Lambeth wheelwright named Pearce shot himself over disagreements with his wife about his recent enlistment in the Guards, which course he had taken as a result of 'a life of idleness and extravagance'![109] Equally drastic were cases in which a wife took an axe to her husband and chopped off one or more fingers, to prevent his being accepted into the army.

Recruiters had greater difficulties in some areas than others, for reasons sometimes removed from the normal constraints of local prosperity: as late as 1805 it was reported that Carmarthenshire was especially barren, as the inhabitants had not forgotten the formation of a battalion there some three decades before, which had been sent to Goree from where not a private soldier returned.

The difficulties of providing recruits led to the utilization of the militia (which is detailed elsewhere in this work), to provide a reservoir of men used to military discipline and already conversant with drill and weapon-handling. In 1798 parliament passed an Act which enabled militiamen to volunteer for regular service, but it was not a success because of fears of the plague-ridden West Indies; but a revised Act of 1799, which stipulated that those who volunteered from the militia would not be required to serve outside Europe, produced the required 10,000 recruits. That this plan was not an unqualified success was due more to the manner of its implementation than to the quality of the recruits: instead of sending small drafts of militia volunteers to many units, they were incorporated *en masse* into a number of battalions. The result was that 'the officers and men were unacquainted with each other; numbers of the latter embarked with the clothing and equipment of the militia regiments to which they had belonged; and the instances were not a few in which, when questioned to what corps they belonged, and who were their commanding officers, they gave the names of their respective militia regiments, not those with which, and under whom, they were serving'.[110] Nevertheless, in general the militia recruits were a most valuable asset in the 1799 campaign in North Holland: John Colborne recalled how Abercromby called for forty or fifty volunteers to charge with him, whereupon the whole of the 20th stepped forward, including many so newly joined that they still wore their militia uniform. Recognizing this, Abercromby called 'Come along! You are as safe here as if you were in Norfolk!'[111]

When recruiting by ordinary methods again failed to fill the ranks as required by the resumption of the war, a further Act was passed in 1805 to permit another round of volunteering from the militia, and between 10 April and 26 June about 11,000 volunteered for regular service.[112] Good though these men were, they were extremely expensive, because in addition to the ten-guinea bounty given to militiamen entering the regular army, many had already received the equivalent of a bounty upon joining the militia. When a renewed release of militiamen was authorized in 1807, the cost of those recruited from the Irish militia caused some public comment, because instead of twelve guineas for a recruit from civilian life, a militiaman received ten guineas on joining the regulars after having mostly already received fourteen guineas for entering the militia, thus making the price of these recruits exactly double those recruited by ordinary means.

From 1809 an Act permitted the regular volunteering of militia into the line, and although some cases of heavy 'persuasion' are recorded, the militiamen mostly came forward not only willingly but eagerly: for example, the 11,450 militiamen who volunteered in 1811 represented more than 1,100 in excess of the number required, and some militia regiments provided so many willing men that recruiters could select the best. Indeed, regiments that tried to enlist militiamen sometimes had to compete with one another to win the best recruits. George Napier of the 52nd and his brother William of the 43rd, both recruiting in Limerick, were on one occasion confronted by ten of the best militiamen possible, all six-footers, who said they would enlist with whichever line officer could beat them at running and jumping. Both Napiers were athletic men, but only William could beat the ten Irishmen, so they all joined the 43rd.

As the war drew to a close, the number of militia recruits declined (in 1813 the number obtained was some 900 short of the 10,000 required), and additional incentives had to be offered, such as the grants of land in North America proffered to eighteen militia regiments if their men enrolled in the 49th Foot in that part of the world. Nevertheless, from 1805 until the end of the war the regular army received some 100,000 men from the militia, a fact probably related to the marked improvement in standards which led to the excellence of the Peninsula army, such recruits being on average so superior to those enlisted from civilian life.

Apart from those who latterly opted for limited service, a soldier remained in the army until his services were no longer required (by the reduction of the army at the conclusion of a war) or until he became disabled by wounds or sickness, or became too old or feeble to do his duty ('worn out' was the term applied, which could involve men as young as their late twenties, dependent upon their constitution). Those no longer able to withstand the rigours of campaign might be transferred to a garrison or veteran battalion, or to sedentary garrison or invalid companies which manned fortifications at home. In the latter units, men often served until they died: John Urquhart, late of the 42nd, who had been wounded at Fontenoy, was stationed in garrison at Hull for 56 years until the day of his death, aged 84, in 1801; barrack-sergeant Durham of Plymouth, who died in 1812 aged 88, had been 70 years in the army and was probably one of the last Culloden veterans still in the service. Even older was Bombardier R. James of the Royal Artillery, part of the garrison of Carlisle Castle, and a veteran of 65 years' service when he died in March 1812 at the age of 92; his son, a sergeant in the Royal Artillery, was present at his funeral.

Long-serving veterans were not restricted to such corps: Quartermasters Thomas Page of the 4th Dragoons, who died in January 1800, and Richard Barnes of the Royal Horse Guards, who died aged 67 in 1811, had both spent fifty years in their regiments. Drum-major J. Lyster of the Staffordshire Militia, who was pictured c. 1804 as appearing very elderly, died in 1811 at Windsor (where the regiment was in garrison) at the age of 79.

Further proof that age was no inhibitor of service is the fact that fathers and sons sometimes served together; for example, a father and son served as privates in the 2/7th at Albuera, both named Robert Baily, distinguished in the regimental records by the numbers '1st' and '2nd'. This was the usual way of differentiating men of the same name, a problem especially prevalent in some Scottish regiments. Although the concept of 'clan' regiments was by this date largely archaic, units recruited from particular areas might have many men with a similar surname and distantly related. In the Strathspey or Grant Fencibles, for example, the original establishment included 41 rank-and-file named Fraser, 80 named Grant, and 94 named McDonald or McDonell, including no less than sixteen named John McDonald. (Of the officers who served in this regiment, raised and commanded by Sir James Grant of Grant, no less than 38 bore his name.)

One of the most important elements of a regiment was its non-commissioned officers, the link between officers and privates. Promotion to NCO rank was not hard to achieve for a man whose personal habits and intelligence made him stand out from his fellows. A steady and sober man might expect to come to the attention of his superiors, and be promoted to corporal and sergeant, the two NCO ranks which existed before July 1813, when the appointment of colour-sergeant was created to reward deserving individuals (despite the title and the depiction of a flag as part of its badge of rank, this appointment did not signify that those who held it acted as escort to the regimental Colours). A unit's senior sergeant was usually styled the sergeant-major, and other appointments might include the drum-major and fife-major, though to some extent the status of these individuals varied between corps.

Literacy was essential for promotion to sergeant, a sergeant being required to keep the company's clerical records, but to judge from some extant order-books, the definition of literacy was sometimes wide! By no means were all sergeants the models of propriety which their rank might have implied: court-martial records include the frequent demotion of NCOs for misdemeanours, and some men were promoted and 'broken' with regularity. (Out of 97 men court-martialled in the 10th Hussars in 1813, for example, during the malign command of Quentin, sixteen were NCOs, for crimes mostly involving intoxication and conduct unbecoming their rank, such as 'having a disorderly woman in barracks'; most were reduced to the ranks and some were flogged into the bargain.)

The men selected for promotion were not always the best qualified, however; when in 1799 Captain Aylmer Haly of the 4th Foot wrote to the Duke of York's secretary with suggestions for improvements, he remarked: 'If commanding officers paid more attention in the choice of non-commissioned officers, we would see the interior discipline of our infantry superior to its actual state; and, instead of having the husbands of officers' washer-women corporals and serjeants, we would have men capable of regulating the interior oeconomy of their squads – they should always be selected from the veterans.'[113]

Wellington himself acknowledged the failings of many NCOs ('... they are as bad as the men, and too near them, in point of pay and situation ... for us to expect them to do anything to keep the men in order');[114] yet he recognized their importance in performing duties which officers would have undertaken had they not been constrained by being 'gentlemen': '... all that work is done by the non-commissioned officers of the Guards. It is true that they regularly get drunk once a day – by eight in the evening – and go to bed soon after, but then they always take care to do first whatever they were bid'; and, speaking of sergeants, he remarked 'I am convinced that there would be nothing so intelligent, so valuable, as English soldiers of that rank, if you could get them sober, which is impossible.'[115]

With the aim of preserving discipline, NCOs were forbidden to become too familiar with those under their command, and their relationship with their officers reflected the wide gap in society. This was demonstrated never more clearly than in 1809, when the sergeants of the 1/7th Fuzileers presented a testimonial of their great regard for him to Captain J. Orr of that battalion, upon his translation from adjutancy to command of a company. This gesture of genuine esteem brought down such wrath that it was made the subject of a condemnatory General Order: 'in presuming to meet, in order to deliberate on the conduct of their superior officer, they have, in fact, however unintentionally, been guilty of an act of great insubordination ... If the non-commissioned officers of a regiment are permitted to express their approbation of the conduct of the Adjutant ... what reason can be given why they should not be equally entitled to express their disapprobation? Indeed, should the practice become general, the merely withholding of the former would imply the latter.'[116] Their commanding officer received even greater criticism for not forbidding their action, and so sensitive was the issue that this General Order was repeated in 1839.

In desperate circumstances, junior NCOs or even private soldiers might assume command of their unit. A case which received some celebrity, and was adverted to as late as 1834 upon the presentation of new Colours to the 35th, concerned the action at Bunker's Hill during the War of American Independence, when the officers and NCOs of the 35th's flank company were all disabled; 'when at this crisis it was said, "Fall back, there is no one to command", the oldest soldier present, a man who sought no other name, here stepped forth, exclaiming – "Never retreat, boys, for want of a leader, while I have a musket to point the way to go."'[117]

Next to promotion to NCO, the most favoured appointment in the army was probably that of officer's servant, which originally excused a soldier from ordinary duty and paid an extra shilling a week. Later regulations were tightened so that servants had to attend drills and parades like the rest. Care was often taken that only men from the officer's own company could be considered as a servant, and generally only the less-impressive in appearance: 'In Future no Officer will be Allowed a Front Rank Man for a servt. & every Officer who has a front Rank man at Present for his Servt. will be so Good as Change him';[118] 'an officer Servant from the Ranks most [sic] be from the Compy. in which he himself does duty and with approbation of the capt. or officer commanding that Compy.; officers servants are never to ware thire Regementals but when on duty thire Masters is Exspecked will see this obeded ['obeyed'].'[119] The above instruction that officers' servants were to wear uniform only when actually on military duty would seem to be confirmed by an incident in February 1807: when a sentry of the 3/1st Royal Scots was murdered while standing guard at Culverscroft battery, Sussex, his assailant was described as 'dressed in a great coat, round hat, and cockade, who appeared to be an officer's servant'.[120]

The position of officer's servant was so much esteemed that when in May 1806 Leonard Sprotsom, servant to Colonel Carey of the 3rd Foot Guards, was told to return to the ranks, he shot himself as a result of this decision having 'preyed on his spirits'.[121]

In addition to a soldier-servant, an affluent officer might also employ one or more civilians: for example, the accounts of the engineer Sir Richard Fletcher for the years 1812–13 in the Peninsula include payments to two named English servants, a Portuguese servant Joan Rodriguez, and to Domingues the cook and his wife.[122] Such civilian servants were not bound by military discipline: one general officer received a note from an ex-servant in February 1807 in which the eminent person was referred to as 'you Dam'd Old Scoundrel ... you Savage ... Rascal and Old Negro driver ... you Old Vagabond in spite of all you have done or can do I am as happy as a Man can be as Captns. Steward on board one of the finest Frigates in is [sic] Majesties Service ...'[123]

Perhaps surprisingly, given the dubious background of some recruits and their often unpleasant living conditions, there was little evidence of political disaffection in the army. Outbreaks of civil violence were not uncommon, and there was mutiny and rioting among some troops, but these could be ascribed largely to more immediate concerns such as hunger or unemployment, rather than primarily to political agitation in emulation of what had occurred in France during the Revolution. There was, however, some disquiet in certain sections of society over the level of public support for the war, resulting in the publication of such addresses as *Advice to English Day Labourers*, which appeared at the height of the invasion threat in August 1803, to answer the feared reaction of 'Let Buonaparte come ... *we* cannot be worse off than we are at present'. This demonstrated that nothing less than genocide was proposed by the French, or so the authors would have their audience believe: '... he gives his soldiers leave to ravish every woman or girl who comes their way, and then to cut her throat. The *little children* perish (of course) by hunger and cold, unless some *compassionate* soldier shortens their misery with his bayonet ... Now *Labourers*! honest, brave fellows! who love your children, and your good country-women ... take your choice – Enrol yourselves instantly; be trained to arms, and be ready to fight Buonaparte; or else, within two months, he will murder you, and all who are dear to you.'[124]

> The same theme was even taken up in verse:
> 'Because I'm but poor,
> And slender my store,
> That I've nothing to lose is the cry;
> Let who will declare it,
> I vow I can't bear it,
> I give all such praters the lie.
>
> 'Tho' my house is but small,
> Yet to have none at all,
> Would sure be a greater distress, Sir;
> Shall my garden so sweet,
> And my orchard so neat,
> Be the pride of a foreign oppressor?'[125]

So far as the army was concerned, the general attitude of the rank and file was probably that expressed by Stephen Morley of the 5th: 'The British soldier fortunately for himself is a dunce in politics; it is a subject which he heartily despises. To keep his arms in serviceable condition, as well as clothing and appointments; to be patient under privations; cool and steady in dangers; brave and daring in action; to be obedient to orders and to have an honest and cheerful heart form the perfection of his character.'[126]

This seems proven by incidents such as occurred in the Craven Head Inn, Drury Lane, in October 1798. A corporal and private of the 3rd Foot Guards were drinking there when a journeyman currier, John Glass, remarked, 'there is one of the Duke of York's crew'. During the altercation which followed, Glass damned the Duke of York, the army and the king, 'and spoke in the most indecent manner of all the Royal Family'; one guardsman apprehended him and the other brought a constable, and Glass was arraigned at Bow Street for 'uttering certain treasonable expressions against the King and Royal Family'. He pleaded intoxication and was bound over to behave well in future;[127] similar reactions by ordinary soldiers were by no means uncommon.

At the beginning of the period there was some disquiet over the circulation of radical pamphlets and copies of Paine's *Rights of Man*, but these appear to have had very little effect. A few officers were involved in radical political societies, but apparently only three were considered as suitable candidates for dismissal from the army, among them Lord Edward Fitzgerald, later a leader of the Irish rebellion. Although a number of regiments were reported as having members who were reading political tracts of dubious nature, only the 2nd Dragoons had an organized political club, the existence of which was blamed on dissenters in the ranks and its station in Manchester, where radical ideas were circulating; but it was not inherently disloyal and seems to have faded away when the regiment was moved. It was reported that some members of the 73rd circulated radical ideas as a result of the political leanings of their commanding officer, Lieutenant-Colonel Norman Macleod, a government opponent as MP for Inverness-shire, but who, despite membership of some radical political clubs, was permitted to pursue his military career.[128] The only officers' club with any political overtones seems to have been the Loyal and Friendly Society of the Blew and Orange, which existed in the 4th Foot, apparently from 1727, a 'True Blue' association commemorating the accession of William III and in support of the House of Hanover; it included a medal worn by members on the anniversaries of the Battles of the Boyne and Culloden, and held its last recorded dinner in 1801.

Within the army there seems to have been more reaction against radical political literature than there were those sufficiently interested to read it. The rank and file of a number of regiments spontaneously opened subscriptions or offered money to combat the circulation of seditious material: for example, the Norfolk Fencible Cavalry, stationed at Carlisle, offered three days' pay from every NCO and private for the conviction of anyone who used rebellious language or distributed seditious literature. The 6th Dragoons went a stage further and set out to find a man in Norwich who had been making political speeches calculated to inflame the audience. Fortunately for his own safety the culprit hid, and after a few inns were turned-over the dragoons' officers persuaded them to return to barracks. More eloquent rebuttals of seditious handbills were made by some units, such as the marines at Chatham who answered one such paper with one of their own: 'You ask, are we not men? We are men, we know it, and should the enemies of our King, our Country or Constitution ever oppose us, we will prove ourselves.'[129] Indeed, one of the few disciplinary measures taken against a suspected radical (the court-martial of Private Thomas Atkinson of the 76th for possessing a copy of *Rights of Man*) collapsed when it was proved that he was only using it to write a rebuttal in defence of the existing constitution. A few soldiers were said to have become involved with the 'United Englishmen' movement in 1798, but there was little proof, and when members of that organization went to Woolwich to suborn artillerymen there, they were told in no uncertain terms to go away.[130]

Excluding Ireland, the most serious case of incipient rebellion involving the military was that of Colonel Edward Marcus Despard, who after treatment which he perceived as unfair, relating to his governorship of Honduras, he conceived an absurd plan to seize the Bank of England and the Tower and assassinate the king. He and some confederates were executed in February 1803, and soldiers questioned at his trial deposed that some soldiers had been present at societies named 'Free and Easy', the purpose of which was to overthrow the government. Of the six men executed with Despard, John Wood and John Francis (the only soldiers) were dressed in Foot Guards uniform, Francis even wearing his regimental dress cap. Even this drastic act was insufficient to damage the career of his elder brother, John Despard (one of five of the six brothers who made the army or navy a career), who became a general in 1814.

Actions 'in support of civil power' were never popular, and some murmurings were heard, especially among the auxiliary forces, when compelled to perform such duty, but these were not serious. For example, when the South Hants Militia was sent to Manchester in the spring of 1812, some of their members were heard to remark in Wells that 'in case of their being employed against rioters, they have formed the resolution not to direct their fire against them, but in the event of their receiving orders to such effect they will fire in the air over the heads of the offenders'.[131] This prompted the adjutant of the West Mendip Local Militia to report these conversations to the Home Secretary.

Desertion was a constant problem, usually arising from dissatisfaction with the army, or simply from foolishness and the influence of alcohol. The numbers of deserters were considerable: even during the Peninsular War about 500 deserted per year (about half of them foreigners), and not unnaturally many more deserted at home (one man in 202 in the first half of 1805, for example), and its effects may be gauged by the increase in the reward offered for the apprehension of deserters, rising in July 1812 from 20s. to £3.

Some found the experience of military service so unbearable as to take inordinate lengths to avoid capture. Richard Andrews, who deserted at Chatham, lived rough around Whittlesea in the winter of 1807–8 and when apprehended was found to be suffering from frostbite. Despite being hand-cuffed, he stole away from his guard during the night and when found four days later was dying of exposure ('died of a mortification brought on by the cold').[132] Even the most unlikely were not immune from desertion: at Edinburgh in 1812 a private named Macroy was drummed out of the 9th Veteran Battalion for deserting twice, losing the pension due to him for 30 years' good service. Those who attempted to desert ran a considerable risk, not only of a flogging or capital punishment for deserting in the face of the enemy: for example, when James Snowden, a multiple deserter from several regiments, was shot when trying to escape arrest in December 1806, a verdict of justifiable homicide was recorded because he and his fellows 'had laid plans for their escape; one of which was on the point of being executed when the deceased lost his life'.[133]

Occasionally, guards who killed deserters were themselves prosecuted (for example, in April 1806 a Sergeant Hugh Mack was convicted of manslaughter for killing Thomas Kirby, a deserter from the 56th, by a blow on the head from his spontoon), but more often summary justice was accepted. In May 1800 William Jackson, an apprehended deserter from the Cornish Fencibles, slipped his handcuffs in Covent Garden and attempted to escape; he had run only six yards when one of his guards shot him through the back of the neck, narrowly missing a passing baker. No warning was given before the shot, and Jackson's body was left in the street for a considerable time, presumably *pour encourager les autres*.

5
'The Simple Annals of the Private Man[134]
EVERYDAY LIFE

TROOPS QUARTERED AT HOME WERE KEPT EITHER UNDER CANVAS (IN summer, at one of the large camps established for the accommodation of several regiments), or were billeted upon innkeepers. Neither was an ideal situation, which led to a programme of barrack-building, of the type which existed already in a few locations.

The establishment of barracks was not popular, largely because of the fear among those of 'liberal' views that they implied a use of the army as a tool of repression; there were also more practical objections from landowners who feared a depreciation in property values, but whilst many publicans objected to the billeting of troops in inns, others doubtless profited from the custom of the soldiers. In 1793 an independent member brought before parliament a resolution that barrack-building was unconstitutional, which was supported by both Fox and Grey on the grounds that the mixing of soldiers and civilians in billets ensured the security of the constitution. Pitt demolished the opposition by stating that quartering soldiers in barracks would remove the danger of conflict with civilians, and would help protect the army from the spread of seditious ideas.

Barracks were controlled by the Ordnance Department, until in June 1792 a Barrackmaster-General's Office was instituted, without parliamentary sanction but nominally under the control of the Secretary at War. The first Barrackmaster-General was Colonel (later General) Oliver De Lancey (1749–1822), scion of the influential New York family of that name and son of the loyalist leader of the same name. The unusual status of the barrack department meant that its expenditure only came before parliament after the fact, so that funds were employed in a somewhat reckless manner. In 1796 it was estimated that £10 million had been spent (actually a gross over-estimate, £9 million having been the actual expenditure by November 1804), but such guesses were inevitable because it appears that no one really knew how much had been spent. The cost of barrack-building was indeed considerable: for example, Brighton Cavalry Barracks cost £49,574 9s. 8d. to build (completed June 1795), Weymouth Cavalry Barracks £59,089 11s., and Totnes Barracks (1794) £8,110 13s. 8d. Additional expenses included rents (for Colchester Cavalry Barracks, for example, the annual ground-rent was £41 18s.) and other charges, such as that levied annually on Piershill Barracks, Edinburgh, of £2 18s. 8$^{10}/_{12}$d. towards the stipend of the Minister of Leith, and 7s. 6d. for the same for the Minister of Lesswade.

From an initial salary of 30s. per diem plus travelling expenses, De Lancey drew more than £135,000 between his appointment and his resignation in November 1804 (his salary increasing to £8 per diem), plus £8,000 spent on his house, more than £6,000 travelling expenses over eight years (though no receipts were presented) and a contingency allowance of almost £89,000. Eventually the drain on the public purse was such that action had to be taken, and the Barrackmaster-General's Department was abolished. Barrack-masters were transferred to Treasury supervision, a board of three commissioners running affairs until 1817. De Lancey was accorded a pension of £6 per diem; but perhaps to satisfy those who questioned the expenditure, an agent for barrack supplies was prosecuted. This was none other than Alexander Davison, Nelson's prize-agent and now most famous for his private issue of medals for Aboukir Bay and Trafalgar. He had been responsible for buying barrack supplies, on which he made 2½ per cent commission; but being a merchant, instead of justifying his 2½ per cent by working to obtain goods at the cheapest price, had in fact been selling his own wares to himself, making his usual profit and taking his agent's commission. He was fined £8,883 (the amount of the commission) and imprisoned in Newgate for 21 months. It is, perhaps, surprising that such expenditure should have been overlooked, but it was probably because the army required barracks which the Ordnance Department would not have sanctioned nor parliament funded, that led to the removal of superintendence from the responsibility of the Ordnance. More than 200 barracks were built and maintained, but the ultimate value for money is questionable.[135]

Typical of the objections to barracks were heated debates in parliament in the spring of 1812, prompted by the annual barrack estimates (£554,411 for the year) and a proposal to build new barracks for the Life Guards in London (they having been evicted from their rented property in King Street, which had been re-let for a short period at exorbitant cost), a barracks for 1,000 men at Liverpool (£82,000), for 800 at Bristol (£60,000) and a new stable at Brighton (£26,000). Upon the suggestion that an empty warehouse in Liverpool be converted, Samuel Whitbread launched a vituperative attack, claiming that the government's economic policy had caused the warehouse to be empty, so that it was appropriate that after 'inducing starvation [which] had filled the people with discontent, [they] should now fill the vacant warehouses with soldiers, to repress the murmurs of discontent, and control those whom [their] measures had irritated to madness ... Were barracks to become fortresses for controlling the citizens?'[136]

Later an opposition member described barracks as 'a praetorian camp to overawe the city',[137] and Sir Francis Burdett declared that all barracks were unconstitutional, and 'that the object of Government in erecting barracks all over the country was, that they might use the troops paid by the people to subdue the people'. So vehement was Burdett's attack that it even alienated some of the anti-barrack members: Mr Barham declared that he 'was an enemy to barracks, but if any thing could convince him to think them necessary, it would be the prevalence of such doctrines as he had heard with disgust that night';[138] thus the plan was approved with a majority of 22.

The barracks which resulted were thoroughly unpleasant. Care was taken that the dormitories were kept clean: 'the Barrack Gaurd to Mount at 9 a clock and the Old Gaurd is to asist the Cooks in Sweeping out the Barracks when the Men is Out at Drill; A Capn. will in future visit the Barracks Every Forenoon & see that they Cleand and when the Weather will Permot that the Beds are Put out to Air'.[139] Nevertheless, there was no sanitation save open tubs in the dormitories, in which beds often had to be shared, and in which the privacy accorded to married soldiers was no more than that afforded by a parti-tion made of a blanket slung upon a piece of string. There was no form of orga-nized recreation, which led to the men drinking or gambling what small amounts of money they possessed.

Pay varied according to rank and corps; the highest was the 2s. 4d. per diem accorded to sergeants of the Royal Horse Artillery (and 3s. 4d. to sergeant-majors), but the generally accepted military pay was the 1s. per diem of infantry privates. The same rank received 1s. 1d. in the Foot Guards, 1s. 3d. in the cavalry and 1s. 11¼d. per diem in the Life Guards; infantry corporals received 1s. 2¼d. per diem and sergeants 1s. 6¾d. In addition, the soldier received free clothing and quartering. On the march he received 6d. per diem, which with 4d. out of his subsistence, went to the innkeeper for three meals. In quarters there was an allowance of 2d. per diem paid to the innkeeper to cover bed, five pints of small beer or cider, salt, vinegar, fire and cooking utensils; if the commanding officer agreed, 2d. could be paid to the individual soldier if he wished to make his own lodging arrangements. In barracks there was no cash allowance, but bed, coal, candles, cooking utensils and five pints of small beer per diem were provided. In camp there was no beer ration, but instead bread was provided at reduced prices and a cash allowance of ¾d. per diem (Varia-tions are recorded: Adye[140] notes that from March 1800 innkeepers' revenue for troops on the march was 1s. 4d., of which cavalrymen contributed 6d. and infantrymen 4d. out of their pay, with 1d. allowed for beer.)

When deductions were made (for 'necessaries', laundry, etc.) very little was left from the soldier's wage, virtually nothing if he decided to supplement the meagre rations. The official daily ration was 1½ pounds bread, 1 pound beef or ½-pound pork, ¼-pint pease, 1 ounce butter or cheese and 1 ounce rice. Many variations were permitted according to circumstances: to simplify the number of ingredients, a complete daily ration could be 1½ pounds flour or bread, and 1½ pounds beef or 10 ounces pork; or 3 pounds beef; or 2 pounds cheese; or ½-pound rice.

Different rations were allocated for troops being transported by sea, when for each 'mess' of six men the following was issued: 4 pounds bread every day; 4 gallons beer, or 4 pints wine, or 2 pints spirits every day; on Tuesday and Saturday, 8 pounds beef or ½-pound suet and 1 pound raisins; on Sunday and Thursday, 4 pounds pork; on Sunday, Wednesday, Thursday and Friday, 2 pints pease; on Monday, Wednesday and Friday, 4 pints oatmeal, ½-pound butter and 1 pound cheese; and one quart vinegar per week. Among permitted substi-tutions were 1 pound rice for 1 pound cheese or 2 pints oatmeal; 1 pound sugar or 1 pint oil for 1 pound butter; 1 pint wine, or ½-pint brandy, rum or arrack for 1 gallon beer; and 1½-pounds fresh beef for 1 pound pork. Women were allowed one-half of a soldier's ration, and children one-quarter, but neither were allowed rum.

There were many variations: at Madeira in 1801, for example, the fol-lowing was ordered per week for each mess of six men of the 85th Foot: 42 pounds bread, 28 pounds meat, 7 quarts spirits, 6 quarts oatmeal, 4 quarts pease, and 1 pint molasses.

'Messing' was general practice, i.e., several soldiers pooling rations and cooking them together, which prevented some soldiers starving themselves to save money, and others from gambling or drinking instead of spending their allowance on food; it also allowed the purchase of larger lumps of meat, so that some of the best cuts went to each mess, which soldiers could not afford if each bought individually. Beef and mutton was regarded as more nutritious than pork, and boiling more healthy and less thirst-inducing than roast or baked meat, besides providing broth. Meat was considered best boiled with oatmeal and potatoes, with cabbage, pease or beans being cooked separately. The use of fish was discouraged from its propensity soon to become rotten, and like pork, its frequent use was thought to cause fluxes. A soldier could exist well, it was said, upon 8½d. per diem, paying 2d. for breakfast and supper (butter, milk, tea or saloop), 3¼d. for dinner (meat, vegetables and salt), and 1¼d. for the bread eaten with all three meals.

Superintendence of the men's meals was required: 'In Highland regiments it is essential to make the men live better than they are commonly inclined to do. I found that some of the soldiers in my first battalion had actually reduced their strength, and almost starved themselves, in order to send money home to their friends; one man in particular, not for his parents, nor for his family, which was very common, but for his sister.'[141] Soldiers took turns in cooking for their mess, for 'a soldier capable of doing his duty, would never agree to it but in turn',[142] i.e., being a cook!

Quality of rations was often more important than quantity. Weights of meat were inclusive of bone, so that the edible quantity was generally less than the specified amount, and often the rations were bad or adulterated. For example, it was apparently common in Cork and Limerick to prepare a mixture including alum, magnesia, oil of vitriol and rock-salt in lime water, to pour on to wheat as it was being ground in proportion of five pints per 20 stones of grain, to increase its bulk. Cork and Limerick flour was thus renowned for not keeping well, would not endure a sea voyage and, it was claimed, was not even fed to cattle by the millers of those areas!

Occasionally the adulteration was so bad that legal action was taken against the perpetrators: for example, in 1814 a baker named Dixon was fined £100 and imprisoned for six weeks for supplying bread to the Royal Military Asylum at Chelsea (an institution which educated the children of 'other ranks') which contained 'divers noxious and unwholesome ingredients, not fit for the food of men'.[143] As a Quaker, Dixon refused to be sworn to give evidence, but it was proven that alum and potatoes had been used to economize on flour. In another case concerning the contractor for the Royal Artillery, who had used inferior grain or 'middlings', it was stated that army bread 'ought to be of a superior quality, such as is usually eat [sic] at farm-houses, and often at gentlemen's tables, and very different from the nauseous compositions that have hitherto been too frequently forced down the throats of his Majesty's soldiers'.[144]

Rations on campaign were often much worse, despite earnest efforts in Wellington's forces to ensure that food was delivered on time. John Cooper of the 7th wrote that 'When a man entered upon a soldier's life ... he should have parted with half his stomach ... Picking of teeth was not at that time much practised, or wanted. In the Peninsula we were allowed a pound and a half of soft bread, or one pound of biscuit; one pound of beef or mutton; one pint of wine, or one-third of a pint of rum; but no vegetables. Sometimes we were reduced to half rations, and once, for a whole week, we had nothing but one pound of bad beef daily. When bread could not be obtained, we got a pint of unground wheat, or a sheaf of wheat out of the fields, or else two pounds of potatoes. No breakfasts, no suppers, no coffee, no sugar, in those days.'[145]

Little attempt was made to experiment with foreign food or methods of preparation even on campaign, as these were generally regarded with disdain, as exemplified in a verse against 'Ragouts and Kickshaws':

'The Turks they chew opium – your Hindoos eat rice, Sir,
But of Westmorland ham – give me a stout slice, Sir'.[146]

This point was made rather more crudely by Tom Crawley of the 95th, when seized by violent indigestion after gorging on pork and Spanish cuisine. The regiment's Dr. Burke exclaimed, 'You cannibal, what garbage have you been swallowing?' Crawley replied, 'By the mother of God, Sir, this infernal country will kill the whole of us – may a curse fall on it; arrah, Doctor dear, when I came into it I had a stomach like any other Christian; but now, oh God have mercy on me poor stomach, that for the want of Christian food is turned into a scavenger's cart, obliged to take in every rubbage.'[147]

Examples of virtual starvation on campaign are legion. Leach of the 95th recommended a holiday at Almaraz for anyone wishing to lose weight, for in a fortnight there in 1809 all that was available to eat was a little unsalted goat-meat and pancakes made of bran and chopped straw. Even that was better than meals he had in November 1812, when rain prevented any cook-fires and the only things to eat were acorns. Under such conditions, even nauseating fare could be welcome; Kincaid records begging a bowl of soup from General Alten, and found it was just water in which beef had been boiled: 'and, though it would have been enough to have physicked a dromedary at any other time, yet, as I could then have made a good hole in the dromedary himself, it sufficiently satisfied my cravings to make me equal to anything for the remainder of the day.'[148] Just before Vittoria, Cooper of the 7th was given some unsifted barley which had been intended to feed French horses, which he made into dumplings 'like little frightened hedgehogs. To get a mouthful, I had to pick lots of prickles from the mass.'[149] The only food George Wood received in two days after Talavera was some wheat, which he made into gruel with chocolate or mixed with mulberries; even this was a bounteous repast compared to four days in the Pyrenees, when his battalion had nothing but leaves plucked off the trees they marched past. Experiences like these made the arrival of ordinary beef and biscuit seem luxury, 'which gave us such spirits, that, woe to the enemy who should dare oppose us!'[150]

Conversely, the consumption of alcohol was prodigious in the extreme, which reflected the habits of civilian society, of which countless examples are recorded in the contemporary press; for example, a man named Joyce, of Limehouse, who died in September 1805, was estimated to have consumed 32,054 gallons of porter in 62 years, more than eleven pints per day. Burrows' History of the Essex Yeomanry[151] records the feat of three men at Harwich who in 1796 drank 57 quarts of 'upright' (a quart of beer to which a quartern of gin had been added) in 6½ hours; upon breaking up the session, one declared that he was still thirsty and drank another pint.

It was not quantity as much as strength which counted, however, for according to a petition from brewers in 1799 soldiers generally chose three pints of strong beer in place of five of small beer, and the strength of the former was awesome: 'not the beastliness of these days, that will make a fellow's inside like a shaking bog, and as rotten; but barleycorn, such as would put the souls of three butchers into one weaver. Ale that would flare like turpentine ... good, unsophisticated, John Bull stuff – stark! – that would stand on end – punch that would make a cat speak.'[152]

The culture of hard drinking was just as entrenched in what might be termed the officer class: for example, a calculation concerning a London merchant published in 1801 stated that in his daily visits to the Bull Inn in Bishopsgate-street, in a period of 23 years he had consumed 35,688 bottles of port, in addition to what he drank at home and elsewhere. A glimpse of the stupidity which could overtake the officers is provided by the mess-book of the North York Militia, in which is recorded: 'Lieut. Westlake bets Ensign Allen one pound that he (Ensign Allen) falls from the effects of liquor the first this night'; not surprisingly, the consequence was that West-lake was fined a bottle of port on two occasions that night, for 'singing without being called upon to do so, and at the same time making a very improper noise'.[153] Few took the business so far as Ensign George Adney of the 60th, however, who died in January 1806 after drinking a quart of rum straight off for a bet.

Over-indulgence in alcohol is not difficult to understand in the case of the rank-and-file, for with virtually no organized recreation and little opportunity to obtain books even for those who could read, drinking was one of the few off-duty occupations available to the majority. Its most severe consequence was not the trouble caused off-duty, but when it impinged upon active duty, in which it was by far the most common cause of misbehaviour: of the 97 men of the 10th Hussars court-martialled in 1813, for example, 48 were for crimes directly involving drunkenness, and others involving 'conduct unbecoming a soldier' or being absent without leave may well also have arisen from alcohol.

Wellington's sweeping remark that the British Army was composed of 'the scum of the earth ... fellows who have enlisted for drink. That is the plain fact – they have *all* enlisted for drink'[154] was undoubtedly an exaggeration, but the origin of this opinion is not difficult to ascertain. When the Foot Guards were dispatched to The Netherlands at the very outbreak of war, they were described as 'Primed with Whitbread's entire and their bosom friend gin By driblets our men joined their ranks, to fall in.'[155]

Such scenes, of men 'hissing hot from the bung'[156] were repeated in countless campaigns. On the retreat to Corunna hundreds drank themselves into stupefaction at Bembibre and had to be left lying senseless in the streets, to be captured or killed by the French, and even when casks of spirits and wine were smashed to deny them to the French, the soldiers scooped up the drink in their hands or caps, or even lay down to lap it up from the gutters. Surtees of the 95th witnessed this unedifying spectacle and remarked, 'What noble soldiers would our country produce, were not that detestable vice of drunken-ness so common among us; but to it how many have I seen deliberately sacrifice their own and country's honour, nay their very life itself, rather than forego the beastly gratification!'[157]

If there were some excuse for the drunken orgies which followed the storming of fortresses like Cuidad Rodrigo and Badajoz, there was none at all for dereliction of duty by immoderate imbibing: men lay senseless in the streets of Buenos Ayres while the fighting was still raging around them, abandoning comrades in favour of their own excesses, and there were even worse examples. Perhaps most notable was the case of a lost dispatch which Sir David Baird had sent to General Fraser's Division in the retreat to Corunna, which ordered the latter to rest for two days to reorganize. Baird gave the order to his orderly dragoon from the 15th Hussars, but Fraser continued to trudge on, and on the next day had to trudge back again, a forced march which cost about 400 casualties; the cause, in Baird's words: 'By God, the rascal of a dragoon by whom I sent those dispatches this morning, has got drunk and lost them.'[158]

Immoderate drinking was not the sole cause of bad behaviour; as Cooper of the 7th admitted, 'It has frequently been stated that the Duke of Wellington was severe. In answer to this I would say, he could not be otherwise. His army was composed of the lowest orders. Many, if not most of them, were ignorant, idle and drunken.'[159] They included a relatively small proportion of what one officer termed 'incorrigibles', who were capable of committing virtually any crime and who were genuinely a menace to society. Their crimes were as varied as those encountered in civil life, sometimes magnified by the fact that gangs of soldiers could act in concert. For example, Garrison Orders at Cork (17 November 1798) noted that since the troops had been prevented from ill-using traders in the market, gangs had taken to roaming outside the city, stopping incoming 'Country People' and compelling them to sell their potatoes at whatever small price the soldiers imposed, necessitating a permanent cavalry patrol on all roads, parties under arms to protect traders in the market, and a roll-call of each regiment every two hours.[160]

Deserters roaming the country were always a problem: for example, in September 1814 three, still wearing the uniform of the 45th, robbed a carpenter from Staines whom they encountered on the road, taking his clothes, watch, umbrella and a £10 Staines bank-note, and leaving him tied up in a gravel-pit. Two of the deserters were convicted, one sentenced to death. Soldiers still in the service on occasion might behave like footpads, as for example in a notorious incident concerning the Tarbert Fencibles in 1800. At Botley, a poor pedlar in wooden ware, Thomas Webb, was brutally done to death with a bayonet by two of Tarbert Fencibles, one of whom, John Diggens, was hanged and gibbeted for the crime, although the man who appears to have struck the fatal blows, Prendergrass, was acquitted but flogged and drummed out of the regiment for disobeying orders. The deed caused such outrage that the NCOs and men of the regiment subscribed half a day's pay for Webb's widow and family, and advertised in the press their detestation of the act of their fellow-soldiers.

Although courts-martial were used for all crimes committed on active service, at home the civil law applied and prosecutions were made in civil courts: for example, in November 1809 a guardsman and another man were pilloried at Charing Cross for attempting to commit 'unnatural offences': 'the morning being wet, the streets afforded mud to the women, who attended in great numbers, and were so highly exasperated at the enormity of the offence, that they assailed them therewith in such quantities that in a few minutes scarce a vestige of their faces was to be seen ... The crowd at the extremity of the ring, being well provided with eggs, also made some *palpable hits* ...'[161] They were then taken to Tothill Fields Bridewell for a year's imprisonment.

The need for civil restraint on soldiers was articulated by the City of London's Common Serjeant in November 1802, adverting to the number of discharged servicemen in the city following the reductions brought about by the peace: 'He meant not to insinuate any thing to the prejudice of those brave defenders of the country; but it was a fact too notorious to escape observation, that they were too apt to indulge in excesses which required the coercive arm of the law to repress.'[162] A measure of the nature of this 'coercive arm' was provided by the case of a drummer-boy of the 1st Foot Guards, who was shot while stealing turnips 'and other garden stuff' from Mr Merrick's land at the rear of Windsor Barracks in November 1797. He and the guardsman who accompanied him were the ones arrested, not the firer of the shot.[163]

Few with actual experience of the army doubted the necessity of the strictest discipline, if only to control the small number of genuine bad characters. Moyle Sherer commented that too many such men had been 'honoured by admission into her [the army's] ranks. We must not look to all who have fought our battles, in the vain hope of meeting heroes; we shall find *but men*. *No*. Scars and decorations can only effectually ennoble men of virtue, of sense, and of courage.'[164] However, he also stated (perhaps with an unduly uncritical eye) that soldiers in general were 'charitable and generous, kind to children, and fond of dumb animals: add to this, a frequent exposure to hardship, privation and danger, makes them friendly, and ready to assist each other. Nor are they without a just and laudable pride. The worthless characters who are to be met with in every regiment (and society) are generally shunned; nor have I seen an expression of discontent on their countenance at the just punishment of a moral offender.'[165]

The harsh enforcement of discipline was criticized at the time and has been pilloried since by images of 'a brutal and insolent soldiery' brutalized further by the infliction of the lash. However, Wellington's own comments provide an account of its necessity:

'It is not by ... native gallantry, it is not by the exertion of bodily strength ... that bodies ... can contend effectually ... bodies of men ... must get into confusion unless regulated by discipline; unless accustomed to subordination, and obedient to command. I am afraid that panic is the usual attendance upon such confusion. It is then by the enforcement of rules of discipline, subordination, and good order, that such bodies can render efficient service to their King and Country; and can be otherwise than a terror to their friends, contemptible to their enemies, and a burthen to the State. The rules of discipline, subordination, and good order teach the Officers their duties towards the soldiers; and how to render them efficient, and to preserve them in a state of efficiency to serve the State. They teach the soldiers to respect their superiors the non-commissioned Officers and the Officers; and to consider them as their best friends and protectors. The enforcement of these rules will enable the officers to conduct with kindness towards the soldiers those duties with which he is charged; and to preserve him in a state of health and strength; and in a state of efficiency as regards his arms, ammunition, clothing, and equipments, to perform the service required from him, without undue severity, or unnecessary restraint or interference with his habits ... There may be some whose youth, indiscretion, or bad habits may lead into irregularities. These must be restrained: discipline, subordination, and good order must be established among all.'[166]

It was said that the regiments with the best officers generally had the fewest men punished, and enlightened officers endeavoured to spare corporal punishment. Alternatives to corporal punishment were not new: for example, on the Quebec expedition two men were punished for firing and screaming with fear on sentry-duty by having to stand for an hour 'at ye necessary house, each with a woman's cap upon his head'.[167] Attempts to relax the often barbaric means by which discipline was enforced were not always appreciated: as Wellington wrote in 1813, 'It is quite impossible for me or any other man to command a British army under the existing system. We have in the service the scum of the earth as common soldiers; and of late years we have been doing every thing in our power, both by law and by publications, to relax the discipline by which alone such men can be kept in order. The officers of the lower ranks will not perform the duty required from them for the purpose of keeping their soldiers in order; and it is next to impossible to punish an officer for neglects of this description ... It is really a disgrace to have any thing to say to such men as some of our soldiers are.[168]

Punishments in the army, however, should be considered in the context of those imposed by the civil law, which could be barbaric in the extreme: for example, in June 1798 a man named O'Coigley, evidently a Catholic priest, was executed at Pennenden Heath, near Maidstone, for High Treason, having been convicted of sending letters to France and being a member of a Corresponding Society, both charges he denied, claiming persecution by the government of Ireland. In a scene more applicable to the 17th century, he was dragged to the place of execution on a hurdle, hanged for some twelve minutes, then cut down and beheaded so that the executioner could announce 'This is the head of a traitor.'[169] This must have been the most distasteful service ever performed by the Maidstone Volunteers, who provided the military escort.

Nor were some of the punishments imposed by civilian courts available to the military, as soldiers generally had no money to be taken from them in fines, and the military equivalent of transportation, the sending of malefactors to the more unhealthy colonies to what were virtually penal corps, could only be applied in a few cases. To compare military with civilian crimes, it is instructive to consider a typical year's civil legal activity. In 1803 some 4,605 persons in England and Wales were committed to gaol for trial, including 3,555 for larceny, receiving stolen property 137, burglary 136, uttering base money 123, fraud 94, sheep-stealing 71, horse-stealing 65, highway robbery 63, manslaughter 56, murder 53, rape and cow-stealing 38 each, forgery 36, forging bank-notes 28, bigamy 23, cutting and maining 21, sodomy and bestiality 15, returning from transportation 15, shooting at others 14, arson 13, piracy 7 and sedition 4. Of these, 350 were sentenced to death (but only 68 were executed, including 15 for burglary, 10 for murder and 7 each for horse-stealing and forging bank-notes), 877 were transported, 1,680 were imprisoned (the maximum sentence being three years, imposed upon five individuals), 105 were whipped and fined, and 53 were sent to the army or navy; the remainder were acquitted.[170]

Military corporal punishment was by flogging with a cat-o-nine-tails, upon the bare back of the offender, who was tied to a 'triangle' formed of sergeants' spontoons, the flogging performed by a relay of drummers, either striking as quickly as they could, or in an even more fearful practice, 'flogging by beat of drum', in which ten taps were beaten on a drum between each blow. (The story was told of a drummer who refused this duty, having heard that it was 'corporal punishment' and thus should be carried out by a corporal!) Flogging was performed in the presence of the offender's regiment, to serve as a warning to others, and was stopped only when the regimental surgeon judged that to continue would endanger life, when the man would be untied from the triangle and sent to recuperate. Before the practice was stopped, once his back had healed he would then be returned to the triangle for the balance of the sentence to be completed.

Many were flogged into unconsciousness, and occasionally into insanity. The injuries caused were horrific; Cooper's remark that 'it required strong nerves to look on' is a considerable understatement. The blows of the 'cat' often cut to the bone, and Cooper saw the results of a man who had been flogged for stealing some silver candlesticks: 'I saw the poor fellow brought in to have his back dressed. He was laid upon the floor, and a large poultice taken off the wound. O! what a sickening sight! The wound was perhaps eight inches by six, full of matter, in which were a number of black-headed maggots striving to hide themselves. At this scene those who looked on were horrified.'[171]

Although there were restrictions upon the number of lashes could be ordered, up to 1,200, the average punishment was still appalling, 5-600 lashes being in no way uncommon. For example, in 136 punishments given to the 10th Hussars between December 1812 and July 1814 (most of that time on campaign), some 34,300 lashes were ordered, and 21,895 actually administered, ranging from 600 for plundering to 20 (out of 200 ordered) for being absent without leave for five weeks, and 50 for killing a fowl. This produced an average punishment of more than 250 lashes, of which 160 were actually inflicted. It is surprising to remark what might be considered leniency: for striking an officer when being apprehended for riotous behaviour (doubtless when drunk), in November 1798 Elias Horsfield of the 7th Light Dragoons was sentenced to 'only' 1,000 lashes, because of previous good character![172]

Sentences could be remitted, even when a man was actually at the triangle, in the case of those with previous good records, and occasionally distinguished men might receive favoured treatment: for example, when Sergeant Levi Grisdale of the 10th Hussars was convicted of being drunk and absent on 17 February 1813, he was not even permanently demoted, a singular case of leniency in this regiment doubtless because of his reputation as the man who had captured the French General Lefebvre-Desnouettes at Benevente, for which he had received a regimental medal.

The practice of flogging attracted much opprobrium, the most vehement of its critics probably being William Cobbett, who (presumably influenced by his own military career) described flogging as 'that most heart-rending of all exhibitions on this side hell'. He observed that not even Bonaparte inflicted upon a soldier an ordeal in which 'his back [was] torn to the bone by the merciless cutting whipcord ... Bonaparte's soldiers have never yet with tingling ears listened to the piercing screams of a human creature so tortured; they have never seen the blood ooozing from his rent flesh; they never beheld a surgeon with dubious look, pressing the agonized victim's pulse, and calmly calculating to an odd blow, how far suffering may be extended, until in its extremity it encroach upon life.'[173]

Cobbett was imprisoned in Newgate for two years and fined £1,000 for libel after he had written critically of the flogging of Local Militiamen at Ely in 1809; he continued to edit his *Weekly Political Register* from gaol. (In contrast, L. and J. Hunt, proprietors of *The Examiner* newspaper, were acquitted of libel for a similar attack on flogging despite instructions to the jury by Lord Ellenborough that they should be found guilty.)

In a parliamentary debate on corporal punishment (18 June 1811) Sir Francis Burdett described the lash as a 'dreadful instrument of torture ... Every lash inflicted by it was, more properly speaking, nine lashes. These were pieces of whipcord, not such as Gentlemen used to their horse-whips, but each of them as thick as a quill, and knotted.' He quoted dreadful cases: of a young soldier with defective eyesight who was flogged as a malingerer, and when a surgeon proved that his sight really *was* defective, an officer was said to have remarked, 'Well! what signifies a hundred lashes to a man of his description?' Two soldiers in Gibraltar were said to have found the prospect of the lash so dreadful that each chopped off a hand to escape (but were punished for self-mutilation!); and finally a 70-year-old veteran with more than 50 years' service was flogged for drunkenness. Burdett stated that the French army maintained discipline with only the threat of imprisonment or execution, to which Palmerston replied that he was sure many of the men brought to the halberds (i.e., the 'triangle') for flogging would be much obliged to the Honourable Baronet if they were told that as a result of his personal intercession they were not to be flogged, but shot![174]

The agitation of Cobbett and Burdett was said to have prompted the Judge Advocate General to declare it unlawful to flog a man twice for the same offence, in respect of those cases in which a man was made to endure the full sentence, the punishment having been stopped by the surgeon before it could be completed, and recommenced after his recovery.[175]

In March 1812 the Duke of York issued a circular entreating officers to reduce the incidence of flogging: 'When Officers are earnest and zealous in the discharge of their duty, and competent to their respective stations, a frequent recurrence to punishment will not be necessary.'[176] In praising the Duke, Cobbett repeated the belief of many officers that a regiment with good commanders would not need much use of the lash: 'It requires neither talents nor virtue of any sort to govern by *mere force*. Any fool can be *a despot* or tyrant ... but, to govern with gentleness, requires *wisdom* as well as a just mind ... he who governs solely by the principle of *fear*, shall cease to govern the moment that that fear is overcome by any one of those who are under his tyranny.'[177] (Similarly, desertion was often more prevalent under a martinet colonel: as an example, see *The Soldier Who Walked Away*, A. Pearson, ed. A. H. Haley, Liverpool 1987, a new edition of *The Autobiography of Andrew Pearson, A Peninsular Veteran*, Edinburgh 1865. Pearson deserted from the 61st after being victimized by a tyrannical commanding officer, W. C. Royall; he maintained that he had *not* deserted when he walked out on his regiment, never having been attested nor having accepted a bounty, after being kidnapped into the army at the age of 14.)

Among officers who spoke out against flogging was Sir John Stuart, who thought it 'tends strongly to debase the minds and destroy the high spirit of the soldiery ... deprives discipline of the influence of honour, and destroys the subordination of the heart, which can alone add voluntary zeal to the cold

obligations of duty ...'[178] Conversely, corporal punishment had many support-
ers, most of whom pointed to that proportion of the army which could only be
made obedient by the threat of physical violence. For example, in 1834 the editor of the *United Service Journal* stated that until the army became a conscripted
force, drawing recruits from all levels of society, harsh discipline would always
be necessary; and until military service came to be regarded as a respectable
profession, the inherent prejudice against the army would continue it 'to be
recruited from a class for whose coercion that punishment has been found necessary ... nor can we ... conceive any material worse suited for the composition
of a Soldier than a pert, half-educated, turbulent Cockney ...'[179]

One defence of flogging recalled the Burdett-Palmerston argument in
parliament, by quoting as a contrast the so-called 'enlightened' French system
which had no flogging, but by which a French soldier was sentenced to death
for the same offence punishable in British service by 300 lashes. The anti-flog-
ging movement was dismissed as 'mob orators and factious disputants, who
with the cant of patriotism on their lips, but utter want of principle in their
hearts, would unhesitatingly sacrifice both the honour and discipline of the
Army, as well as the interests of their country, to their own selfish views', and
'those *really* philanthropic persons whose well-meaning but meddling interference in military affairs, of which their knowledge must be superficial in the
extreme, may one day be productive of the most serious mischief ... let the
question be asked of the veteran, whether officer or private, and what will be
his reply, "That the total abolition of corporal punishment, *must* be followed
by a far greater and much more extensive authority to shoot."'[180]

Where recorded, the opinions of the lower ranks were curiously mixed:
Morris of the 73rd believed that flogging only made a good man bad, and a bad
man worse, by degrading him in his own esteem; but probably most would
have agreed with Benjamin Harris of the 95th: 'I detest the sight of the lash;
but I am convinced the British army can never go on without it',[181] believing
that only Craufurd's savage and instantaneous punishment of offenders had
kept the Light Brigade together during the retreat to Vigo. William Lawrence of
the 40th, who received 175 of the 400 lashes awarded for a trivial first misde-
meanour, described the fear and degradation he felt on hearing the sentence: 'I
felt ten times worse on hearing this sentence than I ever did on entering any
battle-field; in fact, if I had been sentenced to be shot, I could not have been
more in despair, for my life at that time seemed of very little consequence to
me.' As he did not cry out at any time during the flogging, 'though the blood
ran down my trousers from top to bottom', his colonel called him a 'sulky rascal'! Yet Lawrence believed that his flogging was perhaps 'as good a thing for
me as could then have occurred, as it prevented me from committing any
greater crimes which might have gained me other severer punishments and at
last brought me to my ruin; but for all that it was great trial for me, and I think
that a good deal of that kind of punishment might have been abandoned with
great credit to those who ruled our army.'[182]

Certainly, the 'cat' was dreaded by all but the most desperate of malefactors: for example, it led a corporal of the 48th to kill himself by swallowing
four ounces of vitriol in January 1809, rather than suffer the sentence of a
court-martial, and Morris records a member of his battalion who shot himself
rather than receive 300 lashes.

Whereas on campaign civil crimes like murder or looting could be punished by hanging, serious military offences such as desertion to the enemy drew the ultimate sanction of death by firing-squad. Such executions were carried out in full view of all troops available, who were then marched past and made to look at the corpses, 'a good and wholesome practice'[183] according to Grattan, in that it made a good soldier determined not to meet such a disgraceful end, and the bad soldier to fear for his life. These spectacles were horrific: Grattan recounts the execution for desertion of one Curtis of the 88th who was not killed by the firing-squad but sprang up terribly disfigured, until the provost-marshal virtually blew his head off with a huge gun almost the size of a blunderbuss. A second 88th deserter scheduled for execution at the same time was pardoned at the last moment, but went mad as a result and shortly after died in convulsions. Such scenes were invariably affecting and presumably had the intended salutary effect: the report of the firing-squad's muskets 'was followed by a sound as if every man in the division had been stifled for the last five minutes, and now at length drew in his breath. It was not a groan, nor a sigh, but a sob ...'[184]

Officers were reprimanded frequently for neglect of duty, as in Wellington's order of 17 August 1812 (Madrid): '... officers must recollect, that to perform their duty well in the field is but a small part of what is required of them; and that obedience to order, regularity, and accuracy in the performance of duties and discipline, are necessary to keep any military body together, and to enable them to perform any military operation with advantage to their country, or service to themselves'. In their maintenance of discipline, however, probably most would have agreed with Lieutenant Nathaniel Hood of the 40th, who in his *Elements of War; or, Rules and Regulations of the Army*, included in his section on 'Officers in general' (pp. 116-23) some perceptive comments on discipline as exercised by the more enlightened officers:

'Discipline is the very life and soul of an army ... Subordination is the foundation and support of discipline; but ... it was never intended that an instrument should be made of it in the English army to suppress the affability of politeness, civility, and good manners; it is not to cover and sanction unwarranted passions ... if it is sported with where it ought not, it falls off, it loses every virtue which itself proposes ... Discipline is not to be promoted, however zealous the intent may be, by exercising the stern and haughty power of distinction out of place; nor will extreme, unnecessary severity favour the attempt. If a deportment founded on such principles is held out to enforce obedience, obedience comes without respect ...'

Nevertheless, there are many accounts of officers who behaved with undue brutality or unfairness in their efforts to enforce obedience and discipline, but apparently only one officer was actually dismissed for unauthorized use of the lash (Lieutenant-Colonel Richard Archdall of the 40th, court-martialled at Lamego in February 1813). Those who truly exceeded their authority faced severe punishment: in January 1802 Joseph Wall, governor of Goree, was executed after a trial at the Old Bailey, for having flogged to death a sergeant by the infliction of 800 lashes. (One of his defence witnesses, Major Winter of the Royal Artillery, dropped dead on the steps of the court on his way to give evidence.) So severely was Wall's crime regarded that his body was ordered to be sent for dissection, but upon payment of 50 guineas to the Philanthropic Society his relatives were allowed to give it a Christian burial.

Physical assaults on malefactors was rare, unlike in some European armies, notably those of Russia and Prussia, where the beating of soldiers was commonplace. One exception was noted on the retreat to Vigo, when 'Black Bob' Craufurd (doing his utmost to maintain morale and discipline amid atrocious conditions) personally felled a man with a rifle-butt, whom he suspected of muttering 'Damn his eyes' over Craufurd's Draconian discipline. Nevertheless, although on one level Craufurd was hated for his savagery, on another he engendered a rare level of respect; Benjamin Harris said that if he lived a hundred years he would never forget this perfect example of a soldier; and of how he would stop frequently, deliver one of his tirades against a group of exhausted, shoeless and scowling riflemen, but as he galloped away they would pick up their rifles and hobble after him. (Not all harsh disciplinarians were admired for their soldierly conduct: John Green of the 68th recalled how his battalion with difficulty refrained from cheering when at Ostiz on 30 July 1813 their unpopular and cruel major, G. C. Crespigny, was killed!)

In camp or on campaign, NCOs would be appointed as temporary provost-marshals, to assist in the maintenance of discipline. Thomas Morris of the 73rd remarked that they were regarded by the army in much the same way as the hangman Jack Ketch would have been, and so unpopular was their duty that at the conclusion of their appointment they rarely returned to their own regiment, but were promoted into other corps.

Under a reasonable commanding officer, there were more lenient modes of punishment for minor crimes, such as extra duties, confinement to barracks, or being made to stand guard with a log of wood or roundshot chained to the leg. In the 95th, minor misdemeanours could be tried by a 'court' of NCOs and privates, which had the power to impose minor fines, confinement to barracks or 'cobbing' (smacks on the buttocks), and in this regiment one defaulter was made to wear a smock with a green cross painted on it as a mark of shame; but he turned it to his advantage by extracting sympathy from gullible civilians, by telling them that it was a new regulation to identify Roman Catholics! A tyrannical commander of the 94th, who punished good men unfairly, introduced a system of black-and-yellow patches to be sewn to the sleeve to identify those who had been punished, which so degraded the unjustly punished good men that they felt at one with the genuine bad elements, to the cost of all as the battalion's behaviour declined accordingly. Even comparatively light punishment could have a serious effect: in July 1807, Paymaster-Sergeant Miller of the 3rd Foot Guards, a reliable old soldier, was ordered extra drill for being accidentally late on parade; unable to bear the humiliation, he hanged himself at the Golden Cross Inn, Charing Cross.

A temporary escape from military discipline, and a supplement to the meagre wage, was provided by the practice of 'working-out'; when in camp or garrison soldiers might be permitted to follow a trade, provided that it did not interfere with duty. Although the products of this labour might be of national benefit, it was held that discipline could suffer: 'it is observable that the taylors in a regiment, who are annually employed to make up the clothing, are very inferior in discipline and appearance'.[185] Care was taken that regimental duty did not suffer ('No Work to be permitted to be Done for the Officers by the

Taylors untill the Regimental Clothing be finished'),[186] or that soldiers did not abuse the privilege of being allowed out: in May 1804, for example, a Coldstream Guardsman received 300 lashes for begging in the streets disguised as a cripple! A tradesman in the army might be burdened by extra duty, but could make a tidy sum: Benjamin Harris of the 95th accumulated the huge amount of £200 from his cobbling, most of which he spent on private medical treatment for Walcheren fever. The practice also caused the loss of some men by industrial injury: a typical case was that of Samuel Barnes of the 3rd Foot Guards who was drowned repairing while the brick-work of a Pimlico sewer in July 1806.

If the monetary rewards for military service were meagre, other recognition was even worse. Apart from the orders of chivalry (restricted to the higher commissioned ranks), the Army Gold Medal and even rarer Army Gold Cross (awarded for actions between 1806 and 1814, to ranks not lower than an officer who had commanded his battalion or regiment), there was no official method of rewarding brave or meritorious conduct other than by promotion. A few medals were presented by their regiments to deserving soldiers, of which few were governed by any system, with exceptions like the 'Order of Merit' of the 5th Foot, instituted 1767, and the long-service medal of the 71st, instituted probably before 1808. Some of the better-known regimental awards, like those of the 42nd, 48th and 88th, although commemorating Peninsula service, were established only after the end of the Napoleonic Wars. Regimental badges of distinction were few, for example the crowns and stars worn over the rank-chevrons by the 28th Foot, the long-service stripes worn above the cuff by the 72nd, or the 52nd's 'VS' badge ('Valiant Stormer', awarded to survivors of the 'forlorn hope' of Ciudad Rodrigo and Badajoz). Indeed, the very concept of awards was discouraged: in November 1811 the proprietor of *The Independent Whig* was tried for libel for asking why ordinary soldiers were not awarded medals as were general officers; it was claimed that this article was intended to excite disaffection, but he was found not guilty after it was revealed that at the time of publication he was in Dorchester Gaol, and thus had no control over what appeared in his newspaper!

The award of the Waterloo Medal to all ranks, and the two years' extra service awarded to survivors, was much resented by Peninsula men who regarded their service as infinitely more protracted and arduous, but without any mark of distinction; one writer complained that while it was bad enough for Waterloo men to parade wearing their medal, what was unbearable was for officers seconded to Portuguese service to wear medals awarded by that country, when British Peninsula men had only 'more kicks than ha'pence' and were doomed to 'range the streets or saunter in the ball-room, undecorated, nay almost unregarded'.[187] Not until 1848 was Peninsula service recognized by the issue of the Military General Service Medal, by which time many of those eligible for the award were dead.

Ex-soldiers, however, might be eligible for a government pension. Although there was even a set table of compensation for the loss of officers' pocket-watches on service (40 guineas for a general officer's watch, 20 for a field officer, ten for a captain and six for a subaltern), there was only limited generosity towards the rank and file. A few became in-pensioners of the Royal Hospital at Chelsea:

'Valour's just meed for those who fought or bled,
In laurel'd peace to eat their well-earn'd bread ...
Hail'd by their country, many a battle won,
The veterans boast a palace of their own;
In sacred leisure here their lives shall close,
By friends remember'd, nor forgot by foes.'[188]

The remainder were 'out-pensioners' of Chelsea or the Irish equivalent, Kilmainham hospital, near Dublin.

In 1814 soldiers' pension-scales were published so that the public could be aware of the support given to discharged soldiers who were then 'traversing the country in all directions':[189] for out-pensioners of Chelsea Hospital, a 1st class pension was £18 5s. per annum; 2nd class thirteen guineas; 3rd class £7 12s. For blindness or the loss of a limb, a sergeant's pension was 1s. 6d. per diem, a corporal's 1s. 2d., and a drummer's or private's 1s. Soldiers discharged from Veteran Battalions received 9d. per diem, or if totally incapacitated 1s. Pensions established in October 1806 had been extended in August 1812, so that those who had lost more than one limb, or were so incapacitated as to be unable to earn a living, should receive not exceeding 3s. 6d. per diem for sergeants, 3s. for corporals, and 2s. 6d. for privates. Pensions might be withdrawn or forfeited, and in most cases were inadequate; in the post-Waterloo period, for example, when a textile worker might earn more than a guinea a week, almost a quarter of Chelsea pensions were only 3s. 6d. per week. This was a useful supplement for men able to work, but for those in bad health even the average pension of 9s. 11d. per week provided only meagre support.

The number of army pensions rose from only 20,150 in 1792 to more than 61,000 by 1819; more than 85,000 were drawing pensions from Chelsea Hospital by 1828, which in 1822 had taken over responsibility for the 15,000 Kilmainham pensioners. There was no automatic right to a pension, discharged soldiers having to apply, and many of the most deserving cases either never applied, or received a pension only in advanced old age. John Cooper of the 7th, having twice been rejected, received the princely sum of 1s. per diem exactly fifty years after his discharge. John McKay of the 42nd, who was born aboard HMS *Victory*, in which his father was a marine, was discharged after being wounded three times at Waterloo. He applied for a pension only at the age of 90, when it was reported that his livelihood was to wander the country, begging. Such tragic cases were legion, including some who applied for a pension only when no longer able to work for a living, having reached the age of 100. Nor were there many other means of financial assistance for ex-soldiers, although as early as 1805 the 4th Dragoon Guards had their regimental St. Patrick's Fund, a kind of savings-bank to pay out gratuities to soldiers upon their discharge. Although he may have been 'his country's stay, In day and hour of danger', in most cases Burns' *The Soldier's Return* was only too true:

'For gold the merchant ploughs the main,
The farmer ploughs the manor;
But glory is the sodger's prize,
The sodger's wealth is honour ...'

6

'That Article'
THE INFANTRY

O N THE EVE OF THE WATERLOO CAMPAIGN, THOMAS CREEVEY asked the Duke of Wellington about the approaching conflict. Wellington pointed to a British infantryman and said: 'There, it all depends upon that article whether we do the business or not. Give me enough of it, and I am sure.'[190]

The infantry was not only the most numerous element of the army, but was also that without which it was impossible to undertake any operation. Although divided into Foot Guards, line and light infantry and rifle corps, the organization was basically standard for all, and centred upon the regiment, which consisted of one or more battalions. Unlike the common continental practice, each battalion was virtually an independent entity, so that it was unusual for any two battalions of a regiment to serve together.

The regiments of foot were numbered consecutively according to seniority; the 1st Foot or Royal Scots, for example, the senior line regiment, dated its precedence in the British Army to 1661, although its origins extended to Hepburn's Regiment, formed for French service in 1633, and tenuously to the Scottish regiment raised by Sir Andrew Gray in 1620 for Frederick V, Elector Palatine, and which served subsequently as part of the Scottish 'Green Brigade' in the army of Gustavus Adolphus.

Almost invariably regiments were known by their numbers, which were borne with considerable pride and only relinquished with the greatest reluctance in 1881, but a few bore titles of some antiquity which were commonly used in place of the number, for example the 'Queen's Own' of the 2nd Foot. From 1782 almost all regiments received a 'county' designation intended to increase the *esprit de corps* by associating the regiment with the area from which it drew many of its recruits; nevertheless the actual composition of units frequently bore little resemblance to the county title. For example, in 1799 it was noted that while the 5th Foot bore the title 'Northumberland' as a compliment to the Duke of Northumberland, most of its recruits came from Lincolnshire. Of more than 250 members of the 68th Durham Light Infantry who were awarded pensions subsequent to their service during the period, only nine appear to have been from the county; when inspected in May 1812 at Castello Branco, the 68th mustered 252 Englishmen, 247 Irishmen and 109 Scots. (It is interesting to observe that in contemporary argot 'a Durham man' was not necessarily a native of that county, as the term was also applied to one who was knock-kneed; mustard being popular in Durham, it was said that a knock-kneed man could grind mustard between his knees.) Territorial identity was even more distorted by the large drafts of volunteers from county militia regiments; for example, in the 23rd Royal Welsh Fuziliers at Waterloo, only about 29 per cent were actually Welshmen (and but 13 per cent of NCOs), more than one-tenth were Lancastrians (and 25 per cent of the NCOs), and almost one-tenth were Irish (and more than 17 per cent of NCOs).

Thus, in a few cases regiments changed their territorial title without affecting their recruiting, as no recruiting-grounds were exclusive to any particular regiment (for example, in 1809 the 14th Bedfordshire and 16th Buckinghamshire Regiments exchanged titles; the 35th Dorsetshire became Sussex in 1805, the 39th East Middlesex became Dorsetshire in 1807, and the 70th Surrey became Glasgow Lowland in 1812). The most bizarre regimental title was that of the 76th, called 'the Hindoostan Regiment' 1807–12; and although the 60th retained its traditional title 'Royal American', its recruits were no longer enrolled from that continent. Other regimental designations were concerned more with *esprit de corps* and tradition than any distinction of composition or employment, hence the three Fuzileer regiments (7th, 21st and 23rd) and the Highland regiments (42nd, 71st-75th, 78th, 79th, 91st-93rd and the ephemeral 97th, 109th, 116th, 132nd and 133rd), of which the 71st-75th and 91st were ordered to relinquish Highland dress in 1809 as it was believed that the kilt, an undoubted attraction for Highland recruits, discouraged the enlistment of lowlanders and Englishmen.

At the outbreak of war, regiments existed up to the 77th, that corps having been formed in 1787; regiments with higher numbers had existed in previous wars, but in the usual way had been disbanded upon the conclusion of peace. In the early stages of the French Revolutionary War there was a somewhat unwise flurry of raising new regiments instead of adding new battalions to existing corps; one of the evils of the sale of commissions which found expression in 1793–4 was the calculation that the government could actually make a profit by raising new regiments, the sale of commissions outweighing the expense of recruiting by some £250, whereas only £150 profit would be made by adding a new battalion to an existing regiment.

Some of the new corps were 'recruiting regiments', intended to be broken up and the men drafted elsewhere; and some were so ephemeral as to never even receive a number, but were known by their colonel's name during their brief existence. The numbers rose to the 135th Foot, some new regiments having unusual titles such as the 105th Borough of Leeds or the 129th Gentlemen of Coventry; others had only a title, like Podmore's City of Chester Regiment or Pringle's Jedburgh Burghs Regiment, a system open to confusion as between (for example) D. Cameron's 132nd Wakefield Regiment and D. J. Cameron's (un-numbered) Loyal Sheffield Regiment. Many new regiments were disbanded rapidly, and others consequently re-numbered; for example, the 91st Argyllshire Highlanders bore the number 98 from 1794 to 1798. In a few cases this resulted in the same number being borne by two different regiments during the period; the 92nd Highlanders, for example, had been the 100th until 1798, a corps having no connection with the previous 100th Regiment (a Highland corps of 1761–3 and Mackenzie's Regiment of 1780–4), nor with the 100th County of Dublin Regiment raised in 1804 and re-numbered the 99th in 1816, when the previous 101st Duke of York's Irish Regiment became the 100th. To ensure that the subject of regimental lineage be truly labyrinthine, none of these had any connection with the 100th Royal Canadians formed in 1857, although that corps ultimately assumed the Prince of Wales's crest and battle-honour 'Niagara' awarded originally to the County of Dublin Regiment.

Regiments raised during the war, and which endured throughout, included those ultimately numbered 77 to 96, all formed during the Revolutionary Wars, including the 94th (Scotch Brigade) brought into the line in 1802; the 97th brought into the line in 1804, when the 98th to 100th were raised; the 101st raised in 1806, the 102nd and 103rd (previously the New South Wales Corps and 9th Garrison Battalion respectively) taken into the line in 1808, and the 104th ex-New Brunswick Fencibles taken into the line in 1810.

Generally a more effective way of increasing the infantry was by adding battalions to existing regiments, although the creation of a Second Battalion was by no means universal: at the commencement of the Peninsular War, for example, of the 103 regiments then existing, 37 had but one battalion, 61 had two, the 1st had four and the 14th and 17th three each (the remaining two, the 60th and 95th, are covered later). Subsequently seven of the single-battalion regiments raised a second, and the 56th a third. The 1st Foot Guards had three battalions, and the 2nd and 3rd, two each.

Battalion organization was standard, but strength was not regulated as in many continental armies to a fixed 'establishment' in terms of numbers of men of each rank. A battalion comprised ten companies, eight 'battalion companies' (sometimes termed 'centre companies' for their position when the battalion was assembled in line), and two 'flank companies', one of grenadiers (which stood on the right flank, supposedly the largest and most stalwart men), and one of light infantry (which stood on the left, the most nimble men best-suited for skirmishing and scouting). Each company was intended to comprise about 100 other ranks, but while in a few corps this number was at times exceeded, usually the actual strength was much less. Each company was supposedly commanded by a captain, with two or more subalterns, but in practice it might well be led by a lieutenant or, on rare occasions in a very attritional campaign, by a sergeant.

It was intended originally that one battalion of a regiment should go on active service while the other (if the regiment had more than one) remained at home, to act in part as regimental depot; and that before a battalion embarked on service it should exchange its 'ineffective' personnel (sick and headquarters staff) for men from the 'home' battalion, to field the maximum strength on active service. Consequently, if the 2nd Battalion were then ordered abroad, it had to leave behind not only its own 'ineffectives' but also those of the 1st Battalion, so that 2nd Battalions (and single-battalion regiments) were usually weaker than 1st Battalions, and were lucky to embark with more than about 750 men. The respective strengths and values of 1st and 2nd Battalions depended upon circumstances, however; for example, in 1799 the 5th Foot's 1st Battalion, recently returned from Canada, numbered 327 other ranks, whereas the newly formed 2nd Battalion was 1,268 strong. When it was proposed to replace the supposedly weaker 2nd Battalions by new 1st Battalions in the Peninsula in 1812, Wellington commented that 'some of the best and most experienced soldiers in this army, the most healthy and capable of bearing fatigue, are in the 2nd battalions. The 2nd batts. 53rd, 31st, and 66th, for instance, are much more efficient, and have always more men for duty in proportion to their gross numbers, and fewer sick, than any of the 1st battalions recently arrived which had been in Walcheren; and it is certain that this army will not be so strong by the exchange of new for old soldiers.'[191]

On campaign, strength could dwindle alarmingly. At the commencement of the Vittoria campaign, for example, the 2nd to 7th Divisions each fielded seven British or 'foreign corps' battalions (save the 2nd Division with nine, the 5th with six), of which the average battalion-strength was about 650 (just under 800 for the 2nd Division). When the existence of Provisional Battalions in the 2nd, 4th and 7th Divisions is taken into account (each composed of two battalions too weak to operate on their own), average battalion-strength in those divisions drops to about 575 (about 700 in the 2nd Division). Of the army at Salamanca, only three battalions out of 44 numbered more than 900 strong (two of these being Foot Guard battalions, habitually stronger than those of the line), and twelve had less than 400 men, the 2/44th having just 231 rank and file. A specific example of the diminution in numbers on campaign is provided by a return of the 7th Division in January 1814: one brigade comprised the 1/6th (709 rank and file), 3rd Provisional Battalion (2/24th 271 men, 2/58th 184), and nine companies of Brunswick Oels Corps (250); another brigade comprised the 51st (268), 68th (238), 82nd (489) and *Chasseurs Britanniques* (288); and the third comprised the 7th (684) and 19th Portuguese Line (854) and 2nd *Caçadores* (374); with some 1,707 men of the division (more than 22 per cent of the total of all ranks) absent sick. Of the six British battalions, four had a strength of less than three full companies.

The Provisional Battalions mentioned above were temporary amalgamations of two ordinary battalions which had so shrunk in numbers as to prevent them from serving alone. A similar expedient were the 'Battalions of Detachments' which served at Talavera, *ad hoc* formations of stragglers and recovered invalids able to take their place in the line of battle before being returned to their own corps. Different temporary formations were the 'flank battalions' formed of grenadier and light companies detached from their parent battalions, an expedient by which it was possible to increase the number of battalions available for a particular service by, in effect, weakening by one-fifth each of the others. This was not simply a campaign expedient: in 1800, for example, even the Foot Guards in London had separate field-days for their composite Grenadier Battalion and Light Infantry Battalion, and such formations were not even limited to one type of unit. For example, in May 1798 a brigade of two flank battalions was formed in the Yorkshire District, one of grenadiers and one of light infantry, in which regulars were mixed with militiamen (31st Foot, North York and Nottinghamshire Militias, and 1st-3rd West York Supplementary Militias). Presumably because of the need to retain light companies with their parent battalions, the practice was not applied in larger formations such as the main Peninsular army, but was most suitable for smaller expeditions.

For tactical purposes, each company was styled a platoon, within which were two subdivisions of two sections each, though a weak company might form three sections instead of four. Two companies formed a 'grand division', and a battalion might be divided into two 'wings', but these terms were often applied only loosely.

Reinforcements on campaign were provided by drafts sent from the home depot, or by the return of convalescents from hospital. In extreme cases a corps on foreign service might be so weakened that a cadre of officers and NCOs would be sent home to recruit, the remaining rank and file being transferred to the regiment's other battalion (if it were in the same campaign), or if so far from home as the West or East Indies, for example, to another regiment. Years of hard campaigning could involve a considerable turnover of men: in 1814 it was remarked, for example, that of the entire 1/61st which had begun their Peninsula service in 1809, only three officers and seven other ranks were still serving.

Because of the turnover of men, it is sometimes difficult to assess the level of experience of a battalion. At the time, some battalions might be described as especially 'young', although the distinction was rarely clear-cut and obviously changed from year to year. Even units not regarded as particularly 'young' can be seen to have contained a number of comparatively inexperienced men (even when ex-militiamen were present, as there was considerable difference between militia service and active campaigning). In the 2/95th at Waterloo, for example, only some 15 per cent of the corporals and privates had ten years' previous service, and almost one-third had enlisted in 1813 or later. To judge from their Peninsula service, the 23rd Fuzileers at Waterloo might have been thought to be truly a veteran regiment: yet of the men present at the battle, half had enlisted in 1813 or later, with only about 28 per cent having joined before 1809.[192]

The value of reliable and experienced men cannot be over-stated, for no matter how willing and well trained were volunteers from the militia, it took some time to become used to the conditions of active service. This was demonstrated graphically in the Netherlands in 1799, when during a particularly arduous march at night by two flank battalions, huge numbers of newly enrolled militiamen fell out from exhaustion. One company of 110, which included only fifteen old soldiers, had only twenty men left at the end of the march; fourteen of these were the old soldiers, and the remaining six were Irish rebels who had been enlisted following their capture at Vinegar Hill! Thus, an experienced unit was a priceless asset: 'the intelligence of several campaigns stamped on each daring, bronzed countenance, which looked you boldly in the face, in the fullness of vigour and confidence, as if it cared neither for man nor devil'.[193]

A battalion's most precious possession was its Colours, originally flags to mark the position of each company but by this period reduced to two per battalion; they had the character of holy relics, symbolizing the almost mystical attachment of the men to their regiment, and through it to their sovereign and nation. Each battalion possessed a King's Colour (a large Union Flag) and a Regimental Colour (of the shade of the regimental facings, with a small Union in the upper corner nearest the pole, with a large St. George's cross upon it for regiments with white or black facings, lest the former be mistaken for a flag of surrender and the latter rendered invisible in the smoke of battle). Both bore the regimental number and identity, any badges to which the regiment had a right, and ultimately battle-honours, although the majority of these were granted only after the conclusion of the war (the most common exception being the sphinx and 'Egypt' inscription awarded to regiments that had served in that campaign). Foot Guards' Colours were dark red for the King's, and of the Union pattern for the Regimental. When a battalion was arrayed in line, the Colours, each generally borne by an ensign, were positioned with an escort of sergeants between the two central companies, immediately behind the battalion-commander.

The mystique of the Colours was enforced by their religious consecration, although this practice was criticized at the time by a number of sources: 'We have borrowed this relict from the Romish Church, which enjoins the consecration not only of *banners* and *swords*, but of *bells*, *beeds*, &c. How Protestantism came to stand in need of Popery as a *buttress*, we leave to be determined by those who have introduced this *consistent* novelty.'[194]

Unwieldy pieces of silk some two yards square, Colours were difficult to handle: John Cooke, who joined the 43rd in 1805, a month before his 14th birthday, recalled how at that age he was swept off his feet at a field-day when the wind blew on to the flag. Nevertheless, their loss was the greatest disgrace which could befall a battalion; when the 2/69th lost their King's Colour at Quatre Bras, they felt the loss so keenly that they endeavoured to conceal the fact, and had another made by their tailors.

Apart from acting as a symbol of the regiment's honour, Colours had a very practical value in serving as a rallying-point in action, and in marking a battalion's position; at Buenos Ayres, for example, the 5th raised their Colours on a rooftop and in a church tower to mark their position in the confused street-fighting. They also restored flagging morale: at Talavera the 7th Fuzileers staggered under French musketry until their commander, Sir William Myers, jumped from his horse, seized one of the Colours and brandished it, crying 'Come on, Fuzileers!'

Given the significance of the Colours, they were often a focal point of an action; fire was often directed upon them, so that the task of escorting them was hazardous in the extreme. William Lawrence of the 40th recalled that during the afternoon of Waterloo, 'I was ordered to the colours. This, although I was used to warfare as much as any, was a job I did not at all like; but still I went as boldly to work as I could. There had been before me that day fourteen sergeants already killed and wounded while in charge of those colours, with officers in proportion, and the staff and colours were almost cut to pieces. This job will never be blotted from my memory: although I am now an old man, I remember it as if it had been yesterday. I had not been there more than a quarter of an hour when a cannon-shot came and took the captain's head clean off ...'[195]

Some of the most desperate acts of valour were performed in defence of Colours, perhaps most famously around those of the 3rd Buffs at Albuera, when the corps was cut to pieces by lancers. Ensign Thomas, aged 16, held up the Regimental Colour to act as a rallying-point; he was cut down and the Colour taken from him (it was recovered later in the day). Ensign Walsh was wounded, so Lieutenant Matthew Latham took the King's Colour from him, then was surrounded by cavalry. A sabre destroyed part of his face, another severed an arm, but with the remaining arm he clung to his burden as the cavalry slashed, lanced and trampled him. At the end of the day he was found with the Colour concealed beneath his body; astonishingly Latham survived his appalling injuries and continued to serve one-armed, having received treatment for his disfigurement at the Prince Regent's expense. He was promoted to captain in the regiment on 13 May 1813, and the officers of the regiment subscribed £100 to purchase a gold medal bearing a representation of the event and the legend 'I will surrender it only with my life.' A Royal Warrant was issued to permit Latham to wear it in uniform.

Musicians formed another important part of the battalion. The company drummers not only beat time to keep the battalion in step, but transmitted orders on the battlefield, when drum-beats were more audible than spoken commands. Among the calls used in the field were 'To Arms' (to assemble in line), 'March' and 'Quick March' to advance, the 'Grenadier's March' to form column, 'the Preparative' to prepare to fire, two short drum-rolls to fire from the flanks, 'the general' to cease fire, and, doubtless the most alarming of all, a continual drum-roll to order square to be formed in preparation for cavalry attack. It is perhaps significant that this call was the most unmistakable, and also that performed in situations of greatest urgency, when confusion could have fatal consequences. 'Halt' was signalled simply by the drums ceasing to beat. Drums could even have an effect on morale: in the Netherlands in 1799 Lieutenant-Colonel Montgomery of the 9th took up the drum of a dead drummer, and personally beat it until his men steadied and rallied to him. (This gallant officer was killed in a duel in April 1803 by Captain Macnamara of the Royal Navy, in consequence of a fight between their pet dogs in Hyde Park. After Lord Nelson had given evidence as a character witness, Macnamara was acquitted of manslaughter.)

Although drummers could be enlisted at an early age (some contemporary pictures show tiny children), the popular concept of the boy drummer is not accurate, as many were mature men. Of those in the 23rd at Waterloo whose ages are known, for example, only one was under 18 but two were over 50 (the oldest 62), with the average age 28. Only 42 per cent were under 18 when enlisted, the youngest aged 12.

Regimental bands might range from about eight players to very large assemblies, such as the 25-strong band of the 21st in 1798. A good band was useful as a boost for morale, and could even be used in action: when the 28th came under fire at Geldermalsen in 1795, Lord Cathcart is said to have called, 'Where is your band, sir? Now is the time for it to play.'[196] At Tarifa the band of the 87th struck up the rousing *Garryowen* as a French attack was repelled, and as the 52nd assaulted the breach of Savandroog in 1791, its band played them into action with *Britons Strike Home*. The 43rd was heartened by its band playing *The Downfall of Paris* at the storm of Ciudad Rodrigo, but when the 88th's band played mournful Irish airs before the attack on Badajoz, they engendered only a feeling of the deepest melancholy (despite being such bad musicians that the discordant racket they made once made General Sontag's horse to fall flat, with him on it, according to Grattan!). On rare occasions, musicians had to fight, like the 48th's band at Talavera; and at the conclusion of an action they laid aside their instruments and took the role of stretcher-bearers and medical orderlies.

Many regiments spent considerable sums upon their band, and hired professional musicians; in 1788, for example, only two of the 29th's bandsmen were enrolled soldiers. Many of the best were foreigners, sometimes hired *en masse*: in 1785, for example, the 2nd Foot Guards had hired their band in Hanover; in 1804 Major-General Alexander Mackenzie-Fraser received permission to enlist German prisoners of war from the prison-hulk

HMS *Sultan*, to form the band of the 2nd Battalion of his 78th Foot; and in 1805 General the Hon. Chapple Norton was told that he could employ Swiss, Germans and Italians to form the band of his 56th Foot, but no Frenchmen. Of the foreign bandsmen who received pensions subsequent to their service in the 10th Light Dragoons, seven were Germans, two Hungarians, two Dutchmen, one an Austrian, one a Frenchmen, one an African and one a Negro from St. Kitts.

The popularity of 'Turkish music' (cymbals, tambourine, 'Jingling Johnny', etc.) led to an increasing use of Negro percussionists, many dressed in outlandish pseudo-oriental costumes. These were so fashionable that even the West Middlesex Militia in 1793 aspired to include in their band two mulattoes with tambourines and a 'real blackamoor' playing the 'clash-pans' (cymbals). (This exemplifies the composition of a typical infantry band of the period: in addition to the above it comprised nine clarionets, two French horns, two bassoons, a bugle-horn, a trumpet, a base drum, and two triangles played by nine-year-old boys.) An older tradition was the use by the 29th of Negroes as ordinary company drummers, originating in 1759 when Admiral Boscawen acquired ten West Indians at the surrender of Guadeloupe and brought them home as a gift for his brother, the Hon. George Boscawen, colonel of the 29th. The tradition only ended with the death of the last Negro drummer in 1843, but apparently was not universally popular: in 1807 one such was reported to have been set upon by a party of soldiers in a 'house of bad fame' in Aberdeen, and murdered.[197]

Foreign musicians introduced a number of continental tunes into the British Army: for example, French deserters enrolled in the 31st's band in 1813 taught them the tune known as *Bonaparte's March*. *Le Sentinel* was another example, written by an Austrian, popular with the French and copied from them in the Peninsula. The most famous adoption of a foreign tune, however, was the violent *Ça Ira* of the French Revolution, which was actually banned by Napoleon. Traditionally, it was adopted by the 14th Foot after the Battle of Famars (1793), when their commanding officer, Lieutenant-Colonel Doyle, ordered his band to copy the music being played by the French, traditionally to 'beat them to their own damned tune'. Whether or not it was intended to cause confusion in the French ranks, it did, and the 14th adopted *Ça Ira* as their quickstep. However, the tune was heard much more often than just as the march of one regiment: under its British name it was known as *The Downfall of Paris*, and may have been even more popular than *The British Grenadiers*. The tune caused offence to the French: for example, when the Royal Scots led the army into Paris after Waterloo, they were told to stop playing it, so changed to the anti-Irish rebel tune, *Croppies Lie Down*; and *Ça Ira* caused consternation in Nivelles when the 14th marched through on the morning after Waterloo, especially as the men were dressed in captured French head-dress and accoutrements![198]

The choral singing of the German Legion both on the march and in camp was greatly admired, being very different from the raucous noise made by British troops, and although martial music was of immense value in raising spirits, it was not universally popular. At least one writer railed against the evil of educating the lower classes (reading and writing making them 'proud, idle and discontented', and encouraging them to carry on amorous correspondences 'or what is worse, to commit forgery'), stating that 'Spelling-books and pens are not the only implements of evil in the hands of the vulgar ... the number of military bands established in the kingdom, have so much extended a degree of knowledge in musick, that either some discarded soldier, servant, or player, scrapes a fiddle in every parish, and promotes drunkenness, lewdness, and idleness ... our people seem to be becoming, like the German vulgar, all fidlers [sic] and soldiers.'[199]

The inordinate concern taken over the minutiae of uniform was far in excess of that required for identification on the battlefield or even *esprit de corps*:

'Can kerseymere or scarlet, bought on trust,
Compel the lungs to stay the fleeting breath?
Can funeral volleys wake the slumb'ring dust?
Or gleamy gorget ward the dart of Death?'[200]

The uniform caused the soldier untold labour in cleaning, piepclaying and polishing, but on campaign deteriorated into a state scarcely recognizable; against the traditional British scarlet coats of the officers and sergeants, those of the lower ranks were a duller shade even when new, and on campaign changed from the colour of brick-dust to russet-brown, enlivened by patches of whatever material was to hand, until they became 'as ragged as sheep and as black as rooks'.[201] Even officers' fine uniforms became almost unrecognizable: '... my cap, which had served me both for pillow and nightcap, crushed into different forms ... my shoes without a sole, my sword, from having been drawn all day and sheathed in a wet scabbard at night, covered with rust, my belt of a deep brown, my epaulette very blue, my shirt very black, and my coat any colour but red, and in the most wet and miry condition';[202] and many must have followed this officer's example at the end of the campaign, and thrown the whole lot out of a window!

Wellington took a relaxed and sensible attitude over the deterioration of uniformity on campaign, expressed most famously by Grattan: 'Lord Wellington was a most indulgent commander; he never harassed us with reviews, or petty annoyances, which so far from promoting discipline, or doing good in any way, have a contrary effect ... Provided we brought our men into the field well appointed, and with sixty rounds of good ammunition each, he never looked to see whether their trousers were black, blue or grey; and as to ourselves, we might be rigged out in all the colours of the rainbow if we fancied it. The consequence was, that scarcely any two officers were dressed alike! Some with grey braided coats, others with brown; some again liked blue; while many from choice, or perhaps necessity, stuck to the "old red rag".'[203]

Wellington expressed his thoughts on the subject to Henry Torrens in November 1811, in a fruitless attempt to prevent the adoption of French-style uniforms:

'I hear that measures are in contemplation to alter the clothing, caps, &c. of the army.

'There is no subject of which I understand so little; and, abstractedly speaking, I think it is indifferent how a soldier is clothed, providing it is in a uniform manner; and that he is forced to keep himself clean and smart, as a soldier ought to be. But there is one thing I deprecate, and that is any imitation of the French, in any manner.

'It is impossible to form an idea of the inconvenience and injury which result from having any thing like them, either on horseback or on foot. Lutyens and his piquet were taken in June because the 3rd Hussars had the same caps as the French *Chasseurs à Cheval* and some of their hussars; and I was near being taken on the 25th September from the same cause.

'At a distance, or in action, colours are nothing: the profile, and shape of a man's cap, and his general appearance, are what guide us; and why should we make our people look like the French? A *cock-tailed* horse is a good mark for a dragoon, if you can get a side view of him; but there is no such mark as the English helmet, and, as far as I can judge, it is the best cover a dragoon can have for his head ... I only beg that *we* may be as different as possible from the French in every thing. The narrow top caps of our infantry, as opposed to their broad top caps, are a great advantage to those who are to look at long lines of posts opposed to each other.'[204]

Although, as Harry Ross-Lewin of the 32nd remarked, a unit on campaign might compare poorly with Falstaffe's 'ragged regiment', the truth was that expressed by Frederick Mainwaring of the 51st: 'No one thought about the cut of a coat, or the fashion of a boot, or looked coldly on his neighbour because his ragged garment was less fashionable than his own; sufficient was it that he had a coat on his back.'[205]

Although scales of issue sometimes varied with unit and circumstances, as decreed in 1800 a soldier usually received annually a coat, a waistcoat, a pair of unlined breeches with one pocket, and two pairs of shoes; a shako every two years, with a new crown, cockade and tuft annually. Other items of clothing, known as half-mountings, were part of the 'necessaries', the cost of which was deducted from the soldier's pay. Annually, these included two pairs of black cloth gaiters at 4s. each; a second pair of breeches, 6s. 6d.; a hair-leather (for securing the 'queue') 2½d.; an extra pair of shoes, 6s.; spare shoe-soles and cost of fixing, 6s.; three pairs socks, 8d. each; three shirts, 5s. 6d. each; a forage-cap, 1s. 3d.; a knapsack every six years, 6s. (1s. deducted per annum); pipe-clay 4s. 4d.; a clothes-brush every two years, 2s. (1s. deducted per annum); three shoe-brushes, 5d. each; black-ball, 2s.; worsted mittens, 9d.; a black stock, 9d.; a hair-ribbon, 9d.; two combs, 6d. each; and a weekly deduction of 4d. for washing. In place of the shako and legwear, Highland regiments received a bonnet and four pairs of hose annually, six yards of plaid every two years, and a sporran every seven years; and instead of the legwear in the necessaries, a kilt at 5s. 6d., feather at 6s. and extra hose at 3s. were to be provided annually. Units in the West Indies received unlined coats, a pair of linen trousers and a sleeved waistcoat (often worn in hot weather instead of the coat), of which the cost of the body was defrayed by the coat having no lining, and the sleeves paid for out of the soldier's necessaries money. Greatcoats were issued by the Ordnance, but the cost of the leather straps which fastened them to the knapsack was deducted from the necessaries money; but the cost of altering clothing to fit, and materials to clean weapons, were provided from the public purse, not exceeding 2s. 6d. and 2s. 9d. respectively per man per annum.

The supply of 'necessaries' was open to fraud: for example, in October 1812 Quartermaster William Weir of the 2nd Dragoons was cashiered for charging the men exorbitant prices. The sums involved could be considerable:

in July 1813 Captain Robert Gilmour of the 1st West India Regiment was cashiered for embezzling the necessaries money of his own company and ordered to make reparation of the sum of £111 12s. 1½d.

One burden of which the soldier was relieved during the period was the 'queue', the hair grown long and pulled back into a pigtail, or folded back upon itself to form a 'club', which was powdered for dress occasions. This useless appendage, which had caused the soldier much time and effort, was abolished by a General Order of 20 July 1808, and in future commanding officers were to 'take care that the men's hair is cut close in their necks in the neatest and most uniform manner, and that their heads are kept perfectly clean by combing, brushing, and frequently washing them'. This order was received with such joy by the 28th Foot, aboard ship at Spithead, that they collected all the severed queues and ceremonially threw them overboard with three cheers. Facial hair was permitted officially only for pioneers (beards) and later some cavalry (moustaches worn by hussars and the 2nd Dragoons), but moustaches and even beards were popular among officers on campaign (but not at home), an unofficial practice which gave rise to this repartee:

'The son of a Scots Marquis, who had seen much service on the Continent, was lately accosted by a friend in Bond-street, who facetiously desired, "that as hostilities were over, his *whiskers* might be put upon a *Peace Establishment!*" – "To that I have no objection," was the answer, "but I desire that at the same time your *tongue* be put on the *Civil List!*"'[206]

The infantryman's equipment was an immense burden, including a knapsack containing everything but food (which was in his haversack), cartridge-box of ammunition, rolled greatcoat or blanket atop the knapsack, and a drum-shaped wooden water-canteen, with pipeclayed, thick leather belts crossing the breast, and with the chest further constricted by the cross-strap of the knapsack. (Greatcoat and blanket were apparently not often carried simultaneously, being 'more than [a man] can carry. The Duke of Wellington tried it the year that his army entered France, but it distressed the troops greatly.')[207] Benjamin Harris of the 95th thought the load so great that the soldier was bent under it and half-beaten before he began, and far from the design being improved as a result of the experience of campaigning, the knapsack was made even worse when the original, unstiffened, canvas bag-like design was replaced from 1805 by a wooden-framed pattern (known from its designer as 'Mr Trotter's'), which so pressured the lower spine that with the constricting belts it produced a medical condition known as 'pack palsy'. The design was amended over the years but it was not replaced until 1871.

Cooper of the 7th wrote that 'The government should also have sent us new backbones' to bear the weight of kit, as carried in the Peninsular War. He itemized the ordinary load, with weight (in pounds) in parentheses: musket and bayonet (14), pouch and sixty rounds (6), full canteen (4), mess-tin (1), knapsack (3), blanket (4), greatcoat (4), dress coat (3), white undress jacket (½), two shirts and three ruffles (2½), 2 pairs shoes (3), trousers (2), gaiters (¼), 2 pairs stockings (1), 2 tent-pegs (½), pipe-clay (1), pen, ink and paper (¼), three days' bread (3), two days' beef (2); in addition, the orderly sergeant of each company had to carry the orderly book (2), and in turn had to bear the regimental Colours.[208] Even this was not the most that the infantryman might have to bear: Sergeant-Major Murray of the 3rd Foot Guards calculated the weight carried by a private of that regiment in Spain in 1812 at 75¾ pounds, inclusive of the shared duty of carrying camp-kettle and bill-hook.[209]

The tactics of the infantry were determined by its musket, a muzzle-loading, smoothbored flintlock existing in a number of patterns, known by the generic term 'Brown Bess' ('brown' from the colour of rustproofing on the barrel, and 'Bess' perhaps from the German *buchse* (gun) or simply an alliterative term of endearment). The pattern in general use at the outbreak of war was the 'Short Land Service' musket with 42-inch barrel, but as there were insufficient arms for the rapid increase in the size of the army, huge quantities were purchased from the East India Company, weapons so good that from 1797 gunsmiths were ordered to produce only 'India Pattern' muskets with 39-inch barrels, which became the standard infantry weapon for the remainder of the period.

Loading via the muzzle was a ponderous business, by inserting the propellant gunpowder, projectile and 'wadding' which held it in place (the paper wrapping in which the powder and ball were contained, opened by the soldier biting off the end of this cartridge: the raging thirst experienced in battle was caused partly by the gunpowder thus introduced into the mouth). Rates of fire, even under ideal conditions, were consequently low. The Duke of York sanctioned trials in Hyde Park in 1802 and Jersey in 1805 to test foreign drill against British, the Prussians claiming to fire five rounds a minute; British practice was three per minute, and the best attained in 1802 was three rounds in 49 seconds and five in 90 seconds. Three sergeants of the 2nd Foot Guards claimed they could beat the three rounds per minute, but when tested were unable to manage it. It should be emphasized that such 'trial data' refers to ideal, not battlefield conditions, and thus is only a rough guide to what happened in combat.

A short-cut to loading was to insert powder and ball but instead of tamping them down with the ram-rod, to bang the butt upon the ground in the hope that it would shake enough of the propellant gunpowder through the touch-hole and into the priming-pan, to eliminate both the ramming and the separate filling of the priming-pan. This substantially increased the number of misfires, but British commanders had been bemoaning the impossibility of eliminating such lazy behaviour since at least the time of Earl of Orrery's *The Art of War* (1677); General Henry Hawley remarked in 1726 that although German and Dutch troops might be compelled to load properly, 'by the nature of our men, I believe it impossible to bring them to it'.[210] Edward Cotton remarked his surprise at the ineffectiveness of the British musketry during the French cavalry charges at Waterloo, which 'might be attributed to many of our infantry, when hard pressed, adopting the French skirmisher's method of loading, viz., giving the butt a rap or two on the ground, which, from the rain, was quite soft. The ball, in consequence, not being rammed down to confine the powder, came out at times nearly harmless'.[211]

The ordinary projectile was a lead ball of about an ounce in weight, which could inflict appalling injury, but such was the construction of the musket that all kinds of projectiles could be fired from it. At Vimeiro, Rifleman Brotherwood of the 95th, having used all his ammunition, fired his razor at the French, and even more bizarre projectiles are recorded: during the celebrations to mark the Peace of Amiens, a London tin-plate worker named Edward Thurmood was killed when accidentally shot by a wooden ruler; in November 1803 James Aldred, a farmer of Urmston, was murdered by footpads near Throstlenest bridge, who shot him with a pewter spoon; and in June 1795 a Mr Knox of Edinburgh was shot through the breast and killed by a piece of chewed tobacco fired at him as a joke. Even blank cartridges could be lethal: in November 1802 an actor named James Bannerman received a mortal wound on stage at Preston when struck by the wadding of a blank round fired as part of the play.

Even the method of igniting the charge, by a flint held in the 'hammer' or 'cock' of the musket-lock, striking sparks against a hinged metal plate or 'frizzen', which then ignited gunpowder in the priming-pan to communicate a flame to the powder in the barrel via the touch-hole, was fraught with danger, especially when firing in the ranks: at a field-day of the Foot Guards in Hyde Park in April 1796, for example, one man 'had his eye nearly blown out' by the blast of his neighbour's musket.[212] At close range the discharge of a musket could set alight anything it touched; in April 1811 about 24 cottages in the village of Merriott, near Crewkerne, were destroyed by a fire started by a man shooting rats in a thatched building, the musket-flash setting it afire; and *The News* of 3 August 1806 carried the story of a thief shot at while robbing an orchard, whose breeches were set alight by the wadding of the cartridge: 'being very *hotly* pursued, he darted across the fields like a blazing meteor, every now and then striking his hands behind him ...'

On the battlefield this had a particularly dreadful consequence, as at Talavera: '... the intermediate space of ground between the lines was covered partly with standing corn & high stubble which from the incessant firing kept up on both sides, was set in a blaze several times during the day, & Lines of running fire half a mile in length were frequent & fatal to many a Soldier, some by their pouches blowing up in passing the fire, other Wounded unable to reach their respective Armies lying weltering in their gore with the devouring element approaching & death most horrid staring them in the face!'[213] The explosion of ammunition by stray sparks was a constant danger: General Sir James Murray Pulteney, Bt., Colonel of the 18th Foot, was killed in April 1811 when his gunpowder flask blew up. Indeed, loaded muskets were always hazardous and not always handled with care: for example, in September 1807 a Corporal Andrew Bazell was shot and killed near Ashford by one of his companions, whose musket went off accidentally as he was laying it down at an inn; and at a field-day in Hyde Park in May 1800 one of the guardsmen inadvertently loaded with ball instead of blank cartridge and shot a spectator, Mr Ongley of the Navy Office, the ball only narrowly missing the King (Ongley was attended by the battalion surgeon and his wound through the thigh was pronounced as not dangerous!).

In addition to a belch of flame, the discharge of a musket produced clouds of dense smoke, hence the 'fog of war' which settled over a battlefield, obscuring from sight everything more than a few yards, distant, and often creating immense confusion. An example of this was the expenditure of considerable energy by the French troops attacking Hougoumont, by shooting at a red brick wall which when glimpsed through the dense smoke was thought to be a line of British redcoats!

Despite the dreadful injuries which could be caused by the ounce lead ball (actually 14 to the pound was the standard weight), the chances of it striking an individual were slim, due mainly to the bad quality of the muskets. Colonel George Hanger described the usual standard:

'A soldier's musket, if not exceedingly ill bored and very crooked, as many are, will strike the figure of a man at 80 yards; it may even at a hundred; but a soldier *must be very unfortunate indeed* who shall be wounded by a *common musket* at 150 yards, PROVIDED HIS ANTAGONIST AIMS AT HIM; and, as to firing at a man at 200 yards with a common musket, you may just as well fire at the moon and have the same hope of hitting your object. I do maintain, and will prove, whenever called on, that NO MAN WAS EVER KILLED, AT TWO HUNDRED YARDS, by a common soldier's musket, BY THE PERSON WHO AIMED AT HIM.'[214]

In *Reflections on the Menaced Invasion* (London 1804), Hanger stated that a reasonable expectation in combat was as few as one hit per 200 shots, mainly because most barrels were bent when the fixing-loops were soldered on. Tests in 1841 showed a range of 100–700 yards (dependent upon elevation), but at every elevation there could be a variation of 100–300 yards. Against a target twice as high and twice as broad as a man, at 150 yards three-quarters of the shots registered; but not one at longer range, and not one at a target twice as wide at 250 yards. Even these results could not normally be attained in combat, when volley-firing prevented men taking individual aim, when the target was often obscured by smoke and when the misfire-rate might rise from 15 to 25 per cent in damp weather. A further complication resulted from carelessness or panic: men might accidentally fire away their ramrods, or might over-load the musket. For example, at Blackheath in August 1804 a member of the Tower Hamlets Militia continued to load despite his musket misfiring; after four misfires the fifth attempt ignited all five charges, blew the musket in pieces, killed him and severely injured seven of his comrades.

The head of the Field Train Department in the Peninsula calculated that in all Peninsula actions save Barrosa, if all French casualties had been caused by musketry (i.e., not taking into account that many would have been hit by artillery fire), only one hit was registered per 459 shots, which seems to confirm the contemporary view that each casualty required the expenditure of seven times the man's weight of shot. Other statistics suggest greater effectiveness: the artillerist Müller recorded tests in which 53 per cent of shots from well-trained soldiers hit a target representing a line of cavalry at 100 yards, 40 per cent from 'ordinary' soldiers, a rate which fell to 23 and 15 per cent respectively at 300 yards. Taking into account combat conditions, and the fact that in close formation men at the front would be hit more than once, a reasonable casualty-rate might have been 3 or 4 per cent at 200 yards, rising to about 5 per cent at 100 yards or less. Such statistics, however, are to some extent academic, as are opinions regarding the ability to hit a single man; for with the prevailing tactics, it was not necessary to hit single men or small groups, but only to register a hit somewhere upon a densely-packed mass at very short range, making the volley delivered at short range a terrible weapon; and indeed, it is unlikely that tactics would have changed even had a more accurate musket been available.

Although columnar formations were used for manoeuvring, the basis of the system of combat was the infantry's battle-formation in line. Until 1788 each regiment was drilled and trained according to its colonel's preference, but in that year Sir David Dundas published his *Principles of Military Movements*, which was amended and re-issued with official sanction in 1792 as *Rules and Regulations for the Movements of His Majesty's Infantry*, the first universal system of operation. Often styled 'the Eighteen Manoeuvres', this work had imperfections but was of immense value in standardizing infantry drill and manoeuvres, and won for its author the appellation 'Old Pivot', from the 'pivots' upon which the manoeuvres were based. (Bunbury recalled Moore remarking to Dundas that the drill-book would have done even more good but for 'those damned eighteen manoeuvres'. '"Why-ay," says Sir David, slowly, "ay, people don't understand what was meant. Blockheads don't understand!"')[215]

Dundas decreed the three-deep infantry line as the ideal formation, the third able to fill the gaps in the first two ranks caused by casualties, and the formation solid enough to withstand a charge. The third rank, however, could fire only with difficulty (between the second and over the heads of the first, kneeling, rank), and as early as 1801 a two-deep line was given official approval, and was probably in common use even earlier. When formed two deep, a battalion had a wider frontage (though would shrink towards the centre in battle, as the gaps caused by casualties were closed), and by being able to bring all muskets to bear simultaneously, the formation was immeasurably superior to the columnar formations usually adopted by the French, in which only the front two or three ranks could use their muskets. The longer two-deep line could even edge forward on the flanks, catching the enemy within a crescent of musketry.

Especially with inexperienced troops, it was difficult to maintain fire-discipline, men being tempted to fire without orders, or to break ranks and charge. As late as 1799 an experienced officer advocated a return to the old plug-bayonet, which was inserted directly into the muzzle, making firing impossible, as a way of imposing fire-discipline: 'by which means you become master of the men's fire; you will never be so without it'.[216] A more practical method was reported by Roderick Murchison, later the eminent geologist, who bore the Colours of the 36th at Vimeiro: 'up we rose, old Burne (our Colonel) crying out, as he shook his yellow cane, that he "would knock down any man who fired a shot"!'[217] Benjamin Harris noted that when he first came under fire he felt such exhilaration that his captain had to call on him by name to keep steady, and in his first Peninsula action the unit became so excited that one man jumped up, crying, '"Over, Boys! Over! Over!" when instantly the whole line responded ... They ran along the grass like wildfire ... fixing their sword-bayonets as they ran. The French light bobs could not stand the sight, but turned about and fled ...'[218] Similarly, at Ciudad Rodrigo Kincaid asked a rifleman who was shooting aimlessly, 'What, sir, are you firing at?' 'I don't know, sir! I am firing because everybody else is!'[219]

Much has been made of the 'typical' Anglo-French infantry conflict of the later Napoleonic period, particularly in the Peninsular War; what Wellington termed as the French coming on in the old style, and being beaten off in the old style. This has been interpreted as a simple contrast between the superior firepower of the line against the column, and while this is partially true, the actual process was considerably more complicated.

In the early Revolutionary Wars, the French achieved great success by rapid attack in column, adopted originally because their largely raw troops lacked the training to manoeuvre conventionally. Later, however, although advances could be made more rapidly in column, probably only rarely did French generals intend to use their columnar attacks in the old battering-ram style; rather, they intended to advance rapidly and then deploy into line before contact with the enemy was made. That this happened rarely against the British was due to the tactic, devised probably by Wellington, of keeping his infantry on the reverse slope of rising ground until the French had advanced almost to the crest; whereupon the British line would advance and appear over the crest in the face of the French, who not knowing their whereabouts would still be in column, and would be assailed before they had a chance to deploy. After receiving one or more devastating volleys, the French would be thrown into momentary confusion; then the British would cheer (itself a terrifying sound) and rush upon the shaken enemy with the bayonet; whereupon the French would break before contact was made. This was repeated throughout the period, and the French never overcame the tactic; but, strangely, neither was the 'reverse slope' manoeuvre adopted by any other army, despite its success.

A number of writers have described the damaging effect on morale of advancing upon a British line which remained totally immobile and silent until the close range at which fire was opened; even worse was when a British line appeared over a crest shortly before the French has reached it. The Marquis de Chambray described it from the viewpoint of one upon the receiving end:

'... the French infantry ... charges the infantry of the enemy with shouldered arms. This manoeuvre is executed ... deployed or in close columns of divisions: it has often succeeded against the Austrians and other troops, who begin firing at too great a distance; but it has always failed against the English, who only open their fire within a short distance. When the English infantry is near the enemy ... it generally executes its movements in close columns of divisions, but it always deploys to fight ...

'In order to defend a height, the English infantry does not crown the crest, as practised by the infantry of other armies; it is placed about fifty yards behind the crest, a position in which it is not seen if the ascent be at all steep; it has almost always some skirmishers along the slope, which must be climbed in order to attack it. The musketry and the retreat of the skirmishers inform it of the enemy's arrival; at the moment that they appear it gives them a discharge of musketry, the effect of which must be terrible at so short a distance, and charges them immediately. If it succeeds in overthrowing them, which is very probable, it is satisfied with following with its skirmishers, does not pass the crest, and resumes its position ... It can easily be imagined that a body which charges another, and which is itself charged, after having received a fire which has carried destruction and disorder into its ranks, must necessarily be overthrown.

'I now give an instance of a fact, which ... offers at once an example of the force of military discipline, of the influence of officers and non-commissioned officers, and of the excellence of the manoeuvres employed by the English against the French ... [at Talavera] the troops were deployed on both sides. The French charged with shouldered arms, according to their custom. Being arrived at a short distance, and the English line remaining immobile, the soldiers hesitated to advance. The officers and non-commissioned officers cried to the soldiers: "Forward – march – do not fire!" – some of them even exclaimed "They surrender!" They then continued their forward movement, and were very near the English line, when it opened a fire of two ranks, which carried destruction into the French line, stopped its progress, and produced some disorder. While the officers cried to the soldiers, "Forward, do not fire!" and the fire had commenced notwithstanding their efforts, the English, leaving off firing, charged with the bayonet. Every circumstance was favourable to them – good order – the impulse given – the determination to fight with the bayonet: among the French, on the contrary, no longer an impulse – the surprise occasioned by the unexpected resolution of the enemy – disorder – they had no alternative but flight. This flight, however, was not the result of fear, but necessity ...

'Similar occurrences will always be attended with the same results, for the most impetuous courage can be of no avail when it is not accompanied by a good system of war. At the commencement of the wars of the French revolution, the English infantry did not enjoy much reputation; and during the war in Spain it appeared to the French to be the best of all the infantries against which they had successively fought.'[220]

The infantry's second weapon was the bayonet, which was claimed by a number of nations as their own traditional arm; but excepting fights between skirmishers or small groups, its use was almost entirely psychological. Charges were generally only made when the enemy was already in confusion after being raked by musketry, so that the sight of a line of levelled bayonets approaching apace would cause them to give way before contact was made. Bayonet-fights were so rare that one writer commented, 'no shock or contact takes place, *or can take place*, with modern infantry arms'.[221]

Many discussions took place in the post-war period concerning the efficacy of the bayonet, in which Napier commented succinctly that 'the moral influence of that weapon is great. Men know *psychologically* and *physiologically*, that whether it be called a *"rickety zigzag"*, or any other name, it will prick their flesh and let out life, and, therefore, they eschew it. Many persons will stand fire, who will not stand a charge, and for this plain *psychological* reason, that there is great hope of escape in the first case, very little in the second, and hope is the great sustainer of courage.'[222] ('Rickety zigzag' was the name given to the weapon by one of the anti-bayonet faction, Colonel John Mitchell.) Rifleman Benjamin Harris noted that although he had seen many charges, he had never seen bayonets cross or men slain in such actions. When he did recall seeing men killed with bayonets, a soldier of the 43rd and a French grenadier who had apparently killed each other, it was a sight so unusual that 'our Riflemen looked at these bodies with much curiosity, and remarked the circumstance as well as myself.'[223]

So effective was the bayonet-charge that some writers went too far and suggested that on occasion fire could be dispensed with entirely: 'The fire of troops advancing in a line, is not worthy of notice, and if they find that it has no effect on the countenance of the enemy, they themselves will be the first to give way; on the other hand, we have seen armies firing at each other from sun-rise till dark, without either of them gaining three acres of ground. Whenever the nature of the country will admit of it, the line that advances without firing is sure to carry the day, which is still long enough to allow it to pursue its advantages';[224] or, as Graham is reported to have remarked to the 87th and others, upon the appearance of the French at Barrosa, 'Now, my lads, there they are – spare your powder, but give them steel enough.'[225]

One writer, quoting Suvarov's opinion of the bayonet ('lead often misses, steel never; steel is a hero, lead but a fool') even attributed the defeat at New Orleans simply to over-reliance on musketry, claiming that this 'most calamitous defeat [was] occasioned solely by the infantry halting to fire, instead of dashing forwards with the steel';[226] which demonstrates the often unreasonable support given by advocates of the bayonet.

Another emphasized the effect of morale in close combat, citing not only Napoleonic actions but the so-called 'battle of Bossenden Wood' between the 45th Foot and the rebel gang of 'Mad Tom' Courteney in 1838: 'The fight at Bosenden [sic] Wood has shown that men determined to close will close in spite of the hottest fire of infantry, who at the utmost can but fire twice before being closed upon; that at close quarters the men are as ignorant as when first levied ... Soldiers cannot with any result fire above three shots a minute. No prudent officer will open his fire on a rush till within a hundred yards; but men rushing forward without packs will perform a hundred yards in twenty seconds.' He advocated the use of the bayonet in street-fighting instead of musketry, the smoke of which in such close confines blinded those who fired, and stated that to clear a street with musketry 'you might as well seek to put out a fire with a watering-pot'. Finally, he repeated a view probably held widely in Britain, that 'Mêlées with steel can ... occur only between races of equal firmness. The French people never closed on the Saxon-English, *and never will*. The men who stood at Maida were all Poles. The old French *noblesse* on the other hand never refused ... The Swedes, the Americans, the Turks, if un-Italianized, and our own mutinous population, are the only enemies now who will wait a bayonet shock ...'[227]

Equally destructive of enemy morale was the British cheer which accompanied a charge, especially after a period of complete silence. It was always given in concert, unlike French cheers, which as Gleig of the 85th remarked, were not half so intimidating, being only 'discordant yells ... in which every man halloos for himself, without regard to the tone or time of those about him'.[228]

Most important was the timing of a charge, to ensure that it was not delivered before the enemy was disordered. For example, at Barrosa Lieutenant-Colonel Charles Belson of the 1/28th ordered his men to fire by platoons from the centre to the flanks upon a body of French attempting to deploy from column, and to 'fire at their legs and spoil their dancing' according to Charles Cadell, who was present. After some time of this, two British charges were attempted, but the French only withdrew a short way before each, and the charges were halted when it became obvious that the French were not breaking. Only after the third charge did they run away, confirming that a charge would only be pressed home when the enemy was observed to be on the point of breaking.

This demanded great discipline in pursuit, so that charges could be halted before they got out of hand, and the line re-formed. Indeed, when the 3/27th and 1/48th charged downhill into a milling body of disordered French at Sorauren, one of the French officers noted that although they came on at a run they held formation so well that from a distance it looked like cavalry galloping at a set stride, and the order and discipline was such that they were able to attack three French forces in turn, putting each to flight. The ability to maintain such order was doubtless aided by the fact that serious hand-to-hand combat occurred so rarely; as G. J. Guthrie, Deputy Inspector of Hospitals in the Peninsula, remarked, this was 'for the best possible reason, that one side turns and runs away as soon as the other comes close enough to do mischief'.[229]

Skirmishing was another important duty performed by infantry. Light infantry tactics had developed in the later 18th century, but from the proficiency attained by the British Army in the War of American Independence, they had been so neglected that in the French Revolutionary Wars it was found necessary to employ foreign troops (especially Germans, who were traditionally most adept at skirmishing) to enable the British to counter the French, the skirmishers *par excellence*.

French skirmishing (by *tirailleurs* or sharpshooters) had developed apace in the early Revolutionary Wars, huge masses of marksmen preceding advances or covering retreats, harassing the enemy line with skirmish-fire. Volley-firing against skirmishers, who would throw themselves down as the volley was fired, being ineffective, light troops could only be opposed by light troops, so that armies unable to match the French were at an immense disadvantage, to the extent that troops in line might be so galled by the fire of *tirailleurs* that they were ready to break even before the main attack came at them. As late as the campaign in the Netherlands in 1799, the British Army was unable to respond in kind:

'Though perfectly unacquainted with the system of sharp-shooting (and it is impossible not to lament the want of that species of warfare in our army), though galled on all sides by offensive weapons that did their mischief, partly unseen, and always at a distance; though momentarily deprived of the encouraging presence of numbers of their officers, by the wounds they received; and although they themselves were neither equipped for light service ... our brave countrymen persevered and fought their way forward for four miles ... the imposing aspect of a charge of bayonets, could not be injurious to troops that were scattered over an immense surface ... and almost always protected by the long and mischievous shots of dispersed and lurking Riflemen'.[230]

Regimental light companies were unable to provide the number of skirmishers required, and even their training had been severely neglected (Dundas's *Rules and Regulations* devoted nine out of 458 pages to light infantry service!). The creation of the expert light infantry, which by the middle of the Peninsular War was at least as good as the best of the French, is often attributed to Sir John Moore's training at his camp at Shorncliffe. Even though he had experimented with light infantry tactics in Ireland as early as 1798–9, however, he was not the originator: probably the first light infantry school was that established in the West Indies by General Grey, who sought to restore the skills perfected in the American War. Most influential was a book on rifle tactics written by the commander of the 5/60th under Moore in Ireland, Francis de Rottenburg, and by combining elements of his theories with parts of Dundas', Moore produced a system of training by which troops were able to fight both in the conventional manner, or to skirmish as light infantry, making them doubly valuable, a considerable advance on many continental light corps which were not suited for ordinary infantry service and fighting in line. Entire regiments were converted to light infantry: the 90th Foot was raised as such in 1794, the 43rd and 52nd were converted in 1803 (although the latter received the appellation only in 1809), the 68th and 85th in 1808, and the 51st and 71st in 1809. Although they were normally used in the same manner as ordinary line infantry, the concentration of several battalions into the Light Brigade, later Light Division, of the Peninsula army produced a force ideally suited as a vanguard, exceptionally adept at 'outpost' duty (maintaining the army's forward positions), and deservedly regarded as the élite of the army.

The second element of the light corps were the rifle regiments. Rifling the inside of a musket-barrel imparted a spin to the projectile, permitting a greatly enhanced degree of accuracy in the hands of a trained rifleman, although it was very much a specialist calling and there was never any suggestion that rifles be introduced more widely: often regarded as being slower to load, it was thought that rifles were less suitable for volley-firing. Rifle-shooting was especially prevalent in Germany, where there existed a reservoir of huntsmen and foresters who used rifles in their civilian life; in Britain there was no such resource, so rifle-shooting had to be taught to the recruits. (However, it was proposed in 1807 that the South Hampshire Militia could be converted to a rifle corps, as 'a great proportion of our men coming from the New Forest and the Forest of Bere ... are mostly expert marksmen, and from their early habits feel a partiality to that kind of service'.)[231]

Although individual rifle companies had existed earlier, the first rifle battalion in the regular army was the 5th Battalion, 60th Royal Americans, a regiment already used as the receptacle for many of the foreigners enlisted in the army, and particularly suited for a rifle corps given the expertise in shooting possessed by many Germans. Raised in 1797, the 5/60th was also the first green-coated regular infantry unit, although this colour had been used a short time before by the rifle company of the North York Militia. The original four battalions of the 60th remained as ordinary line infantry, but the battalions they raised subsequently were all riflemen, and such was the composition of the regiment that even at the end of the Peninsular War almost half its members were German, and about 25 per cent of the officers were foreigners.

To exploit this comparatively new tactic, in 1800 the Duke of York ordered the formation of the 'Experimental Corps of Riflemen', drawn from fourteen line regiments, to be instructed in rifle-shooting and then to be returned to their regiments, as the first step in providing each battalion with a rifle detachment. After training under Colonel Coote Manningham (41st) and Lieutenant-Colonel William Stewart (67th), the unit was employed in the operation against Ferrol. The scheme of giving each battalion a rifle detachment was not pursued, but the Experimental Corps was reinforced by drafts from 26 Fencible regiments and taken into the line as the 95th Foot. Two further battalions were formed (1805 and 1809), and all three served with such distinction in the Peninsular and Waterloo campaigns that at the end of the war the unit was taken out of the line and established as an independent entity, the Rifle Brigade.

The 95th enjoyed an *esprit de corps* probably higher than that of any other unit, as befitted those who 'fired the first and last shot in almost every battle, siege and skirmish in which the army was engaged during the war'.[232] Their sombre, dark ('rifle') green uniform with black facings emphasized their individuality, and also acted as a form of camouflage. (Although tests conducted by Hamilton Smith in 1800 suggested that the least-noticeable colour, and thus the best for skirmishers, was the light iron-grey of the Austrian *Jägers*; but in tests involving rifles at 150 yards' range, he proved that the green uniform was less noticeable than the red of the line.)

The rifle chosen for use by the British Army was designed by Ezekiel Baker, and was probably the most accurate mass-produced firearm of the entire period: in a test, Baker fired 34 shots at 100 yards and 24 at 200 yards at a man-sized target, and hit it every time, a feat unimaginable with a smoothbore musket. This enabled riflemen to have a potentially devastating effect in action: for example, at Badajoz, George Simmons of the 95th silenced the fire of a French battery by the sharpshooting of 'forty as prime fellows as ever pulled a trigger',[233] and to prove this was no exception, John Kincaid did the same thing at Waterloo. Such was the expertise in marksmanship of the rifle corps that it became a matter of routine to single-out the enemy's officers and NCOs, the most famous example of which was the killing of the French General Auguste-Marie-François Colbert near Cacabellos on 3 January 1809, by one of the 95th's 'characters', rifleman Tom Plunket. To perform this feat Plunket lay on his back with his rifle-sling looped over his right foot, one of the positions recommended for rifle-shooting; the short length of the barrel of the Baker rifle made loading in a prone position feasible, unlike the ordinary musket which was too unwieldy to allow of prone shooting.

Although the 95th usually served in battalion-sized units, the rifle battalions of the 60th were deployed as individual companies, so that each brigade of the Peninsula army had a 'rifle' capability, although to find enough troops of this nature it was necessary also to employ the Brunswick Oels riflemen and Portuguese *Caçadores* in a similar manner. The 1st and 2nd Light Battalions of the King's German Legion were also excellent rifle-armed troops.

Light infantry and rifle tactics introduced an entirely new form of warfare, demanding not the drill of automaton-like close formations, but superior intelligence and self-reliance, as skirmishers had to act on their own initiative and take advantage of natural cover:

'Vigilance, activity, and intelligence, are particularly requisite ... The intelligence chiefly required in a light infantry man is, that he should know how to take advantage of every circumstance of ground which can enable him to harass and annoy an enemy, without exposing himself ... In some situations they must conceal themselves by stooping, in others they must kneel, or lie flat ... Against regular infantry ... they must hover round these continually ... In such a situation light infantry can be opposed not otherwise than by men acting in the same manner with themselves ... *To fire seldom and always with effect* should be their chief study ... Noise and smoke is not sufficient to stop the advance of soldiers accustomed to war ... a considerable proportion of their force should at all times be kept in reserve. The men who are scattered in front ought to be supported by small parties a little way in the rear; and these again should depend upon, and communicate with stronger bodies, further removed from the point of attack ... In advancing the reserves must not be too eager to press forward ... In retiring, the skirmishers must keep a good countenance, and avoid hurry. They must endeavour to gall the enemy from every favourable situation, and make him pay dearly for the ground he acquires ...'[234]

One reason for the success of the 'reverse slope' tactic was the screen of skirmishers thrown out in front of the British position, which engaged the French skirmishers and concealed from them the actual position of the British main body. Such skirmish-screens could be so dense that occasionally they were actually mistaken for the main line; for example, at both Barrosa and Busaco the French believed they had penetrated the British 'first line' when in fact they had only driven back the skirmishers.

Skirmishers normally worked in pairs, firing alternately, so that one would always be loaded and ready to fire. They were normally deployed in two ranks, the rear-rank men moving through the gaps in the front rank when advancing, and vice versa in retiring, the man of each pair who was loading sometimes being shielded by his comrade. Although skirmishers took advantage of natural cover, the official deployment was either in 'open order' with two feet between files, or 'extended order', two paces. All movements were carried out in quick time, with orders transmitted by bugle or by the whistles carried by officers and sergeants.

When engaging enemy skirmishers it was common for light troops to engage in personal duels ('for 10 or 15 minutes we were amusing ourselves shooting at one another as deliberately as if we had been Pigeon Shooting'),[235] of which a number were recounted by witnesses. For example, a British officer recalled of the later Peninsular War, 'after a trifling skirmish, when the firing had ceased on both sides ... we observed a Portuguese ... amusing himself by fighting a sort of duel with the French sentry in his front. After they had exchanged three or four shots, down dropped the Portuguese to all appearance dead; and the Frenchman, without waiting to reload his musket, ran up in the hope of securing the dead man's knapsack before any one could reach the spot from our side. But the Portuguese proved too cunning a fellow for "Johnny Crapaud"! He allowed him to come within a few yards of him, when, jumping up, he shot him dead, and then quietly resumed his duty.'[236]

Despite the remarkable feats of the light infantry and rifle corps in the Peninsular War, the commonest reputation of the infantry was probably its stolid nature and imperturbability under fire. This led a French engineer (no doubt reflecting upon the *élan* which supposedly marked the French army's advances) to remark that 'It is well known that agility is not the distinctive quality of British troops. Their movement is, in general, sluggish and difficult; steady, but too precise; or, at least, more suitable for a pitched battle, or behind entrenchments, than for an assault', and claimed the attack on New Orleans as evidence that the enormous load they had to carry deprived them of the agility necessary for such an undertaking.[237]

This reputation was presumably greatly enhanced by the events at Waterloo, a somewhat untypical action in which the infantry remained in position, often under heavy fire, for much of the day. Certainly, it was this action which made the square famous.

Formation of square was the universal defence against cavalry. Infantry in line or column had vulnerable flanks, and if assailed in this formation by cavalry could be destroyed literally in moments; the most famous example was Colborne's brigade at Albuera, which was routed when attacked

Right: The Duke: Wellington as he appeared in 1814, wearing the dress uniform of a field marshal and the honours bestowed by the Allied sovereigns, including the Orders of the Garter and Golden Fleece, the Austrian Order of Maria Theresa, and the Swedish Order of the Sword. The Peninsular Gold Cross is worn on a ribbon around the neck, before the bestowal of the unique gold collar bearing the name of his final victory, Waterloo. (Engraving by W. Say after Thomas Phillips)

Below: King George III, wearing staff uniform and the star of the Order of the Garter. (Engraving by W. Skelton)

Below right: 'The Grand Old Duke of York': Frederick Augustus, Duke of York, and commander-in-chief during most of the Napoleonic Wars, wearing the uniform of a field marshal. (Engraving after Mais)

Left: Mary Anne Clarke, whose liaison with the Duke of York was the cause not only of a scandal of monumental proportions, but the reason for his removal from the post of commander-in-chief.

Below left: Sir Ralph Abercromby: one of Britain's best-loved soldiers shown in a caricature by John Kay, the pyramids in the background adverting to the Egyptian campaign of 1801 in which Abercromby received his mortal wound.

Below: Sir Arthur Wellesley as a major-general; this engraving after Robert Home, *c.* 1804, shows the future Duke of Wellington as he probably appeared at the beginning of the Peninsular War.

Right: Sir John Moore; to many, the *beau idéal* of a military officer: as George Napier commented, 'the obedient soldier, the persevering, firm, and skilful general; the inflexible and real patriot . . . the truly virtuous and honourable man; the high-minded, finished, and accomplished gentleman'. (George Napier, pp. 77-8)

Below: William Carr Beresford, 1st Viscount Beresford, in the uniform of Marshal of the Portuguese Army. The ornate collar is that for the Army Gold Cross, composed of alternate lions and enamelled 'Union' shields, of which only two awards were made, to Beresford and Wellington. (Engraving after Sir William Beechey)

Below right: Rowland, 1st Viscount Hill. Wellington's great friend, Hill was probably the best subordinate commander in the British Army and one of the few whom Wellington trusted in semi-independent command. Commander-in-chief from 1828 to 1842, he was worshipped by the soldiers for his unfailing attention to their welfare and was known, appropriately, as 'Daddy' Hill.

Far left: Sir Thomas Picton, one of the ablest and most fearless of Wellington's subordinates. (Engraving after M. A. Shee)

Near left: An excellent depiction of hussar costume is provided by this portrait of Henry William Paget, Earl of Uxbridge and 1st Marquess of Anglesey, in the uniform of a general officer of hussars. (Print after Henry Edridge, 1808)

Bottom, far left: Stapleton Cotton, Lord Combermere, Wellington's best cavalry commander. This early portrait presumably depicts the uniform of the 25th Light Dragoons, with whom he served in the Netherlands in 1794, at the Cape, and in India until after the fall of Seringapatam.

Bottom, near left: John Cameron of Fassiefern in the uniform of his 92nd Highlanders, a man admired throughout the army for his soldierly qualities, though a harsh disciplinarian. This portrait includes the Waterloo Medal which he did not live to receive, being killed at Quatre Bras.

Top right: Few colonels both raised and commanded their own regiments during this period. One who assumed almost the status of a continental-style 'colonel-proprietor' was Sir James Grant of Grant, Bt., who raised a regiment in 1793 which, singularly for British service, even bore his name, the Strathspey or Grant Regiment of Fencibles, in whose uniform he was portrayed by John Kay in 1798. The major, two captains, nine lieutenants, 22 ensigns, two surgeons, the chaplain and 80 of the original 'other ranks' also bore the name of Grant. Sir James also raised the 97th Highlanders in 1794, in which nineteen other officers, the chaplain and two surgeon's mates were Grants.

Right: The infantry uniform worn prior to the adoption of the closed jacket and 'stovepipe' shako was characterized by a lapelled, open-fronted coat and cocked hat. This print (by John Kay, 1795) shows James, 3rd Earl of Hopetoun, as colonel of the Hopetoun Fencibles; illustrated in the background are the different head-dress worn within a battalion, bicorn hats for the 'battalion companies' (left) and fur caps for the grenadiers (right).

Left: A symbol of commissioned rank, the gorget was worn at the throat by infantry officers to signify that the wearer was on duty. From 1797 they were gilt, bearing a crowned royal cipher; prior to that date they were gilt or silver according to a regiment's lace-colour, and generally bore the royal arms. Many variations included some bearing regimental numbers or insignia.

Below left: Captain John Rose of Holme, pictured by John Kay in the uniform of the Strathspey Fencibles, including the 'round hat' popular among officers at the turn of the century. An active physique was not a prerequisite for officers: William Stuart told of his uncle, five feet four and seventeen stone, who when asked why he did not lie down and take cover like the rest of his light company, stuttered that 'if-if-if I once l-l-lie down, by G-God, I'd never get up again'! (*Reminiscences of a Soldier*, London 1874, I, p. 55)

Opposite page, top left: Few officers who served in the storming-parties at both Ciudad Rodrigo and Badajoz can have survived into the age of photography. This is one: Lieutenant-Colonel Benjamin Geale Humfrey, who was a lieutenant in the 45th's light company in both actions, was wounded by falling off a scaling-ladder at Rodrigo and virtually lost the use of his right hand at Pampelona.

Opposite page, top right: The Hon. George Thomas Keppel, later 6th Earl of Albemarle, was almost the last survivor of the British officers who had fought at Waterloo. He joined the 3/14th as an ensign in 1815 and spent his 16th birthday on campaign. He died on 21 February 1891, aged 91, and appears to have been outlived by only one other Waterloo officer, who by a strange coincidence was a member of the same battalion, William Hewitt, a captain at Waterloo, who died on 26 October 1891, aged 96.

Above left: Recruiting: despite the entreaties of his wife, a countryman, under the influence of ale and the illusion of military glory, is persuaded to enlist by a sergeant and the drummer from his recruiting-party. (Engraving by G. Keating after George Morland)

Above right: Recruiting: a sergeant of the 33rd entices civilians into taking the King's shilling; the recruiting-notice on the wall, headed 'Heroes' and 'Wellington', promises 'Honor', 'Wealth' and 'Fame'. Alcohol supports the sergeant's exhortations; the ribbons worn by the recruiting-party and given to enlistees were usual, but the oatcake impaled upon the sergeant's sword was a practice unique to the 33rd, this West Riding delicacy giving rise to the regimental nickname, 'The Havercake Lads'. (Engraving by R. and D. Havell after George Walker, published 1814)

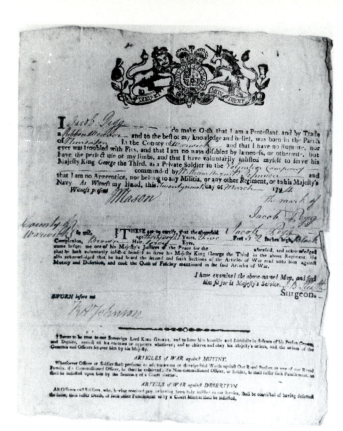

Left: An attestation for a recruit, a document completed for every man enlisted. Jacob Pegg, a 38-year-old, 5-foot 2-inch ribbon-weaver from Nuneaton, enrolled in an independent company in March 1794; he signed his name with a cross. Despite the lapse of time since the passing of the Catholic Relief Act of 1791, an old form was used which retained the affirmation that the recruit was a Protestant.

Below: The 'breastplate' or shoulder-belt plate was the most prominent place to display regimental insignia; it was universal in the infantry, but was worn only rarely by cavalry. Officers' plates were frequently of fine workmanship, such as the gilt plate illustrated here, of the Berkshire Yeomanry, with engraved lettering and applied decoration; other ranks' brass plates were more rudimentary, with incised decoration, like that of the Strathspey Fencibles illustrated.

Right: Drilling 'the awkward squad' *c.* 1801: a contemporary cartoon which depicts a party of recruits attempting drill, a scene which must have been commonplace and not at all exaggerated in their 'hubbledeshuff' appearance. The officer may be intended to be a member of the 23rd Fuzileers, from the apparent presence of the Prince of Wales's feathers upon his hat, scale epaulettes and blue facings. (Dr. John Hall)

Centre right: 'A Field Day in Hyde Park'; aquatint by T. Malton after Thomas Rowlandson. Such confusion among the spectators was not unknown, especially when the troops fired a volley.

Below: 'John Bull going to the Wars': a cartoon by James Gillray symbolizing Britain's entry into the war. 'John Bull' himself bears a resemblance to the king.

Left: Punishment at the 'triangle': this critical engraving exaggerates the evil of the process in that the victim was only unclothed to the waist (unless he had been flogged so often that his back could take no more, when the lash might be applied to the calves). The common punishment of 300 lashes was hardly feared by some men; one commissioned ex-ranker ended a discussion on the subject by remarking, 'Well, gentlemen, you may all say this, or say that, but I was never worth a damn as a soldier until I got three hundred' (W. K. Stuart, *Reminiscences of a Soldier*, London 1874, I, p. 73). The shakos with diced band identify the unit as the 71st Highland Light Infantry.

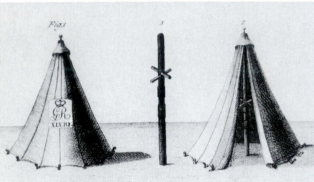

Left: A military bell-tent, bearing the regimental identification of the 19th Foot; the central illustration shows the internal tent-pole, with pegs on which equipment could be hung or against which muskets could be stacked.

Left: A camp-kitchen, with a soldier's wife wearing a typical quasi-uniform made from a cut-down military hat and coat. Uncovered cooking-pots and earthen ovens were not conducive to hygiene, but the prevailing attitude was that expressed by an Edinburgh landlady in response to complaints over the cleanliness of her cuisine: 'It tak's a deal o' dirt to poison sodgers'! (Anton, J. *Retrospect of a Military Life*, Edinburgh 1841, p. 29)

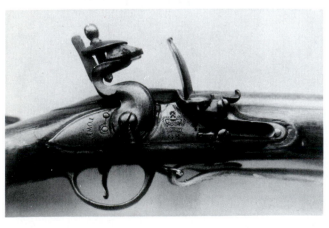

Left: The foundation of tactics in the Napoleonic era: the flintlock mechanism. The British 'Brown Bess' with Tower-marked lockplate shows the mechanism in the firing position, the 'cock' or hammer holding the flint drawn back to its fullest extent, and the pan-cover closed.

Right: The ordinary soldier of the Napoleonic Wars: John Gilbert of the 40th Foot, photographed in old age, presumably with his wife; he wears his Waterloo Medal and Military General Service Medal with clasps for nine Peninsular actions. (Dr John Hall)

Right: The infantry uniform of 1800, characterized by the Austrian-style short jacket closed to the waist, and the 'stovepipe' shako; this print, after P. W. Reynolds, depicts a private and officer of a light company of the 60th Royal American Regiment, their company identified by the shoulder-wings, green plume, bugle shako-badge and the officer's corded sash.

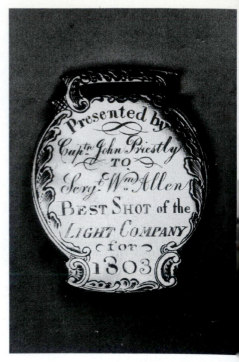

Above: An officer of light infantry, 1815, showing the cylindrical cap with bugle-badge which remained in use with the light infantry even after the ordinary infantry had adopted the false-fronted 1812-pattern shako. (Print after Genty)

Above right: Target-shooting - or 'firing ball at a mark' - was not much practised in the regular army, but appears to have been more prevalent in the auxiliary forces. Comparatively few shooting awards exist for line regiments, of which this is a fine example, of the 32nd Foot. John Priestly (or Priestley) was gazetted captain in the regiment in October 1795.

Left: French artists produced many illustrations of British troops during the occupation of France after Waterloo, many bearing only a superficial resemblance to the actual appearance of their uniforms. Doubtless because of their unusual costume, Scottish soldiers were favourite subjects; this print shows what may be a sergeant of the 92nd's light company (left) and a piper of the 42nd, although the uniform-detail is poor, especially the rendering of tartans and bagpipes.

Above: Coote Manningham, ultimately a major-general, colonel and one of the founders of the 95th Rifles, whose uniform he wears in this illustration. Considerably responsible for the excellent quality of the Rifles, he did not live to see the full fruits of his creation: he commanded a brigade of Baird's Division in the Corunna campaign, but died at Maidstone in August 1809, probably as a result of the exertions it had entailed.

Above right: Green uniform with black facings was the peculiar distinction of the 95th, but this was not the first regiment to adopt this colour: the rifle companies of the North York Militia wore green from 1795, as shown in this 1814 print by R. and D. Havell after George Walker. A typical 'rifle' uniform is depicted, with the Baker rifle as used by the 95th; in the background are men in typical skirmishing poses.

Right: A battalion's 'stand' of Colours: the King's Colour (top) and Regimental Colour of the 1st Battalion, 60th (Royal American) Regiment, 1802-16, of the regulation pattern: the former a large Union bearing a regimental device and number, the latter consisting of a facing-coloured field with Union canton, with the same device in the centre surrounded by a 'union wreath' of rose, thistle and shamrock.

Left: 'The Sharpshooters in Ambush': a rare depiction of the tactics of rifle corps in a print of the Duke of Cumberland's Sharpshooters on exercise, sheltering in woodland to fire at their 'enemy'. In the foreground is the adjutant, Charles Random de Berenger, a noted rifle expert, artist and one of the perpetrators of the Stock Exchange fraud of 1814. (Aquatint by Reinagle after Berenger)

Left: 'The Cumberland Triumph': a print by Fores depicting a rare view of rifle practice, showing the style of target used. The men in 'round hats' are the team from the Nottingham Riflemen, the man in the foreground is presumably a *Jäger* of the Honourable Artillery Company, while the others are the team from the Duke of Cumberland's Sharpshooters, which won this competition at Stamford in August 1811.

Left: A damaged but unique relic illustrated here for the first time: a rare example of 'camp-' or 'company-Colour', the marker-flag used by each infantry company. These were of the regimental facing-colour (in this case brownish-green) and bore the regimental number, here that of the 97th Inverness-shire Highlanders. Twelve such Colours were received by the regiment in 1794, and used until its disbandment in 1796.

Above: The heroes of the moment always provided subjects for popular prints and paintings. This depiction of Sergeant Charles Ewart of the 2nd (Royal North British) Dragoons shows the exploit which made him famous, the capture of the 'Eagle' of the French 45th *Ligne* at Waterloo, but presumably was painted so soon after the event that although the uniform is largely accurate (even to the 'R.N.B.D.' inscription on the valise), the design of the flag is entirely fictitious, the artist obviously not having had the opportunity of observing an example of the actual pattern.

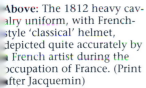

Above: The 1812 heavy cavalry uniform, with French-style 'classical' helmet, depicted quite accurately by a French artist during the occupation of France. (Print after Jacquemin)

Right: Facets of military life extended throughout British society, even to the coinage, some unofficial token-coins bearing martial symbols. This halfpenny, celebrating the 1st Troop of Loyal Suffolk Yeomanry and emblazoned with a galloping light dragoon, was issued by the Troop's commander, Sir John Rous, Bt., in Blything Hundred, Suffolk, in 1794.

Above, left and right: The silver regimental medal awarded to Corporal William Hanley of the 14th Light Dragoons for his great exploit while on 'outpost' duty, at Blascho Sancho, 26 July 1812.

Below: Royal Foot Artillery in action at Waterloo, showing the block-trail carriage which became almost universal for all fieldpieces except howitzers. (Engraving after Captain George Jones)

without warning out of a hail-storm, the cavalry including lancers whose weapon was especially lethal against broken infantry. The battalion farthest from this charge (1/31st) had just time to form square; the others (1/3rd, 2/48th and 2/66th) lost 1,258 men from 1,648, the 1/3rd no less than 643 out of 755.

Squares were formed from column or line upon any company, to present a square or oblong formation with each side facing outwards, normally four deep, with the front rank kneeling with musket-butts grounded and the barrel angled upwards so that the bayonet pointed forwards at horse-breast height; with a hedgehog of bayonets levelled on each face of the square, the formation was virtually impenetrable by cavalry. Lancers might poke at the square from outside bayonet-range, but musketry from the square could clear its immediate vicinity of horsemen, and though vulnerable to any artillery which might have accompanied the cavalry, in all other circumstances it was inviolable, provided the troops kept their nerve, which was where the British excelled.

The term 'square' is somewhat deceptive, as it could actually be an oblong, with three companies on two opposite faces and two on the others (for a ten-company battalion); Dundas, in fact, referred to 'the square or oblong' throughout his manual. Sir James Shaw Kennedy, who was responsible for the array of the 3rd Division at Waterloo, claimed that oblongs could be formed in half the time of a true square, and that his preferred formation was to have just one company at each end and four on each of the front and rear faces.[238] The angles of a square were always the most vulnerable, and the most hazardous point; Cotton recalled how amusing it was to see some of the foreign troops running away from the angles of squares, and equally how surprising it was when they returned after British officers pursued and drove them back! One square might be formed by two battalions, individually too weak to form a practicable square on their own (this was a tactic used by Shaw Kennedy at Waterloo, for example), and where more than one square was formed, the ideal configuration was in chequerboard array, so that the squares were mutually supporting, with less chance of hitting friendly troops when they fired.

The importance of retaining order and discipline was commented on by William Tomkinson, who wrote of squares from the cavalryman's viewpoint. He noted that the breaking of a square by cavalry was 'A thing never heard of. The infantry either break before the cavalry come close up, or they drive them back with their fire. It is an awful thing for infantry to see a body of cavalry riding at them full gallop. The men in the square frequently begin to shuffle, and so create some unsteadiness. This causes them to neglect their fire. The cavalry seeing them waver, have an inducement for riding close up, and in all probability succeed in getting into the square, when all is over. When once broken, the infantry, of course, have no chance. If steady, it is almost impossible to succeed against infantry.' He noted that of all troops, 'where great steadiness, coolness, and obedience to orders is required, I should select the Scotch'[239] (yet he thought them inferior to all others in outpost duty).

The necessity to remain steady and stay in formation was always impressed upon the troops. Francis Skelly Tidy remarked to his young battalion (3/14th) at Waterloo: 'Now, my young tinkers, stand firm! While you remain in your present position, old Harry himself can't touch you; but if *one* of you give way, *he* will have every mother's son of you, as sure as you are born!'[240] Alexander Wallace made a similar speech to his 88th, warning them that if ever they had to form square, they should expect to be in 'a damned ugly way, and have plenty of noise about you'; and 'by God, if you are once broken, you'll be running here and there like a parcel of *frightened pullets!*'[241] Such warnings were heeded, and the coolness with which British infantry usually formed square is demonstrated by an anecdote concerning the 40th at Waterloo, recounted by their Major Fielding Browne, that as repeated French attacks were driven off, the French 'would encompass us with fierce gesticulations and angry scowls, in which a display of incisors became very apparent to all'. These scowls 'became so remarkable towards the end of the day, consequent on defeat' that as each charge came on, instead of ordering 'Prepare for cavalry', the 40th's officers ordered their men to meet the French on even terms: 'Now men, make faces'![242]

Ordinary squares were hollow, which permitted the officers, Colours and drummers to shelter inside; but in extreme emergency, when a unit was scattered, an officer or NCO could cry 'Form rallying square!', when the nearest men would run to him and form a tightly-packed, solid mass. The need to keep their nerve applied to this as much as to an ordinary square: 'There was no time to collect or form a square, so we threw ourselves as best we could into compact circles, and stood to receive them. They came on with the noise of thunder. One circle wavered – some of the men abandoned their ranks – the cavalry rode through it in an instant. That in which I was stood more firm. We permitted them to approach till the breasts of the horses almost touched our bayonets, when a close and well-directed volley was poured in, and numbers fell beneath it ...'[243]

Ordinary manoeuvres on the battlefield were generally conducted in a variety of columnar formations, deployment into line or square occurring only when necessitated tactically; thus even in a 'static' battle units might be moving almost constantly, changing formation or position as required. When movement was not imminent, it was common to permit the men to lie or sit down, not just to allow them to rest but to present a smaller target for longer-range fire. Musketry was customarily delivered by all except skirmishers in volley-fire, which could be by rank or by a 'rolling volley' which progressed up and down the line, one platoon firing after another.

The most archaic weapon used by the infantry was the spontoon, a half-pike carried by sergeants of line regiments from 1792 (light infantry sergeants carried muskets). It was useful not only as a weapon but as a marker for rallying the men and even, when held horizontally, for pushing the ranks into place: a rare account of this use was recorded by a sergeant of the 3/1st Foot Guards, concerning Waterloo: 'The fight, at one time, was so desperate with our battalion, that files upon files were carried out to the rear from the carnage, and the line *was held up by the serjeants' pikes against the rear* – not for want of courage on the men's parts (for they were desperate), only for the moment our *loss so unsteadied the line*.'[244]

Despite the generally stalwart demeanour of the British infantry, there were of course occasions when they became unsteady and even broke; as Wellington once remarked, *any* troops might run away, but he was not especially concerned provided that they came back again! There were awkward moments, such as the confusion at Quatre Bras when Colin Halkett's brigade retreated into the cover of woods after suffering quite severely, and had to withdraw through woodland to reorganize. In such situations, the leadership and confidence of officers was paramount. This was exemplified during the débâcle at Ostend in 1798, in which a party on the left of the 11th Foot gave way and retired. All the officers of the 11th who were present followed this party to rally them; whereupon their remaining men, left without officers, 'rose up and caused confusion';[245] they also retired and only returned when their officers came back. (Major Andrew Armstrong of the 11th was court-martialled for this incident, for leaving his post. Eyre Coote testified that he had had to rally the regiment in Armstrong's absence – saying something like 'For shame, 11th regiment, have you no regard for your King and country?',[246] but Armstrong was acquitted.)

Conversely, it usually took exceptional circumstances to disturb a battalion's composure. The infantry's usual stolid nature seems to be typified by a remark overheard by Francis Skelly Tidy of the 3/14th at Waterloo, when one of his young soldiers reported seeing some British cavalry retiring. 'What of that?' replied another. 'They must blow off the froth before they come to the porter.'![247]

7
'Galloping at everything'
THE CAVALRY

GEORGE GLEIG RECORDED THE MUTUAL OPINIONS OF THE INFANTRY and cavalry: 'The former ... regarding the latter as more ornamental than useful, the latter regarding the former as extremely ungenteel.'[248] Such opinions were probably widespread, and while it is true that numerically the cavalry formed only the minor part of the army, it does them less than justice.

The cavalry was divided into three basic types: Household, heavy and light dragoons, the 'heavies' theoretically intended for shock action and the light especially adept at skirmishing and 'outpost' duty, but unlike the cavalry in many European armies, the distinction was blurred. Indeed, writing of the action at Genappe prior to Waterloo, one commentator noted that 'to be either light or strong, [cavalry] must be mounted on horses fully equal to the weight they have to carry ... heavy cavalry and heavy infantry are terms for heavy heads to amuse themselves with; in modern war, cavalry and infantry, if they are to be strong, must be light also'.[249] On the battlefield, therefore, there was no difference in the tactical use of heavy and light dragoons; and while 'outpost' duties were performed by light cavalry where possible, the comparatively small numbers of cavalry employed in the Peninsula meant that heavy dragoons had to be used in this role on occasion, with no diminution in effectiveness.

The Householders, however, were heavy cavalry who did not generally perform outpost duty and, being the royal bodyguard, were not even sent on active service until 1812. The two regiments of Life Guards were of comparatively recent creation, having been reorganized in 1788 from the previous troops of Horse Guards (or 'Life Guard of Horse'), membership of which had become merely a recognized step on the social ladder for the offspring of London merchants, hence the regimental nickname 'Cheesemongers'. The Duke of York had described them as 'the most useless and most unmilitary Troops that ever were seen ... nothing but a collection of London Tradespeople',[250] so their reorganization into the regularly recruited 1st and 2nd Life Guards was entirely beneficial. So bad was their original reputation that it was recalled twenty years later: 'When Lord NORTH was Minister ... his Lordship wittily remarked in the House of Commons that "the only service I knew them to perform, was kissing the Nursery-maids, and drinking the Children's milk in the Park!"'[251] The third Household regiment, although its status as such was not confirmed until March 1820, was the Royal Horse Guards or 'Blues', a suffix added to the regimental title as early as 1750, derived from the regiment's blue coat, a colour unique among the heavy cavalry.

The heavy dragoons comprised seven regiments of Dragoon Guards (numbered separately) and six of Dragoons, the only difference in the two being in the minutiae of uniforms. The light dragoons were numbered consecutively after the 6th Dragoons, the number rising briefly to 33, but settling at 25 from 1802. From April 1799 there was a vacant number in the list, caused by the disbandment of the 5th Dragoons following a plot in which some members of the regiment planned to mutiny and murder their officers. The 5th had been stationed in Ireland for about half a century, and following the 1798 rebellion had enrolled some Irish rebels, the leader of the intended insurrection being a notorious malcontent, James M'Nassar, who turned king's evidence and implicated two other dragoons, the Feney brothers. It was stated at the time that 'almost every regiment belonging to the Irish establishment, was more or less tainted by the admission of disaffected persons',[252] and despite the small number of men involved it was thought necessary to make an example and disband the regiment, even though it was recognized at the time that this punishment was unduly harsh.

The 7th, 10th, 15th and 18th Light Dragoons were converted to Hussars in 1806–7, but this involved nothing more than an adoption of Hungarian-style uniform, a fashion popular in many European armies, though often decried in Britain ('a mere gee-gaw ... subject, by its intrinsic frivolity, to public ridicule').[253] The hussar regiments even retained their original title of Light Dragoons.

The organization of cavalry regiments was based upon a number of squadrons of two troops each, this being the principal formation for manoeuvre. At the beginning of the Revolutionary Wars establishments were increased from six to nine troops, totalling about 530 men, but in the 1794 campaign all but the 1st Dragoon Guards retained the old six-troop establishment, of which two were left at home as a depot squadron. In 1800 establishment was increased to ten troops (two forming the depot), reduced in 1811 to six 'service' and two depot troops. In September 1813 the light regiments, which had maintained ten troops, were increased to twelve, two continuing to act as the depot. When the Householders were sent to the Peninsula in 1812, and to the Waterloo campaign, only two squadrons of each regiment were sent abroad so as to leave sufficient troops for ceremonial duties at home.

Strength on campaign was often frequently less than establishment, average regimental strength being only about 400. At the start of the Corunna campaign, for example, the average of the units involved was 615; at the start of the 1809 campaign 385; at Salamanca 354; at the start of the Vittoria campaign 412; and at Waterloo 441. Generally, the British mounted forces formed a much smaller proportion of the army than the vast cavalry forces of some European states, partially a reflection upon the unsuitability of much of the Peninsula terrain for massed cavalry formations.

Although pay and reputation were higher than those of the infantry, recruits were drawn from the same background, and probably few men had had experience of horses before their enlistment. A purely random sample of 50 recruits whose occupations are recorded reveals the same proportion of trades as for infantry recruits, only four having possible previous experience at managing horses, a farrier, a waggoner, a farm servant and a farm labourer; the remainder were industrial workers and a sailor (an escaped Negro slave from North Carolina!). Officers were also drawn from the same background as those of the infantry, with a higher proportion of aristocrats in the more fashionable regiments.

The supply of horses was a considerable problem on campaign, as their casualties were usually greater than those among their riders. An example of comparative casualty-figures are those of the 3rd Hussars of the King's German Legion in the action at Göhrde, 16 September 1813, where they made repeated but costly charges against French squares:

	Officers	ORs	Horses
Killed	2	11	47
Wounded	5	64	76
Missing	-	16	15[254]

The introduction of light cavalry in the middle of the 18th century caused a considerable change in the type of cavalry horse. The previous heavy 'black horse' (referring not just to colour but as a generic name for a heavy charger) had been replaced by lighter hunters and carriage-horses bred originally for civilian use, and capable of moving at greater speeds, so that heavy cavalry horses were about 15 hands high and those of the light cavalry slightly smaller. Most were bred and purchased in Britain, and when sent abroad cavalry regiments took their horses with them; the 20th Light Dragoons went to the Peninsula without horses as an experiment in 1808, but this was not repeated when it was found almost impossible to procure suitable mounts abroad. The ideal troop-horse was reckoned to be a 5- or 6-year-old costing about £40 or £45; in 1813 Wellington commented that if such remounts were too expensive, older horses should be sent to the Peninsula from regiments at home, and be replaced with younger mounts costing about £25, which were adequate for home service. Nevertheless, some very poor material was sent on active service, such as the 61 remounts received by the 14th Light Dragoons in July 1809, a batch from the Irish Commissariat Corps already rejected as unfit for heavy cavalry.

Horses were purchased by or on behalf of the regimental colonel, a system open to abuse. In 1799, for example, the colonel (Sir George Thomas, Bt.) and lieutenant-colonel (Christopher Teesdale) of the Sussex Fencible Cavalry were court-martialled for having allegedly bought inferior mounts cheaper than the price allowed by the government, but receiving full reimbursement and pocketing the difference. Both were acquitted, but the Duke of York found the verdict 'so extraordinary' that he said had he seen the evidence before the trial he would have dismissed Thomas immediately. After the verdict, all he could do was to order that neither officer should ever again be entrusted with the purchase of horses.

Veterinary surgeons were regularly commissioned from 1796, indicative of an increased awareness of the need to take care of the health of the horses. Instructions concerning feeding were published in 1795, but were so neglected that they had to be repeated in 1801, to prevent horses being badly attended: 'Many horses grow broken winded every year, owing to the troopers being allowed to fill them with water, and giving them as much hay in one day, as would nearly be sufficient for three.'[255] Care for horses was never the highest priority with British troopers, and vigilance was needed to supervise their proper maintenance, and to prevent an unscrupulous minority from selling the horses' forage to buy alcohol. The attitude was quite different in the

German Legion, whose mounts were generally held to be invariably in the best condition, in accordance with the care lavished on them. Gleig was one of those who compared British and German troopers: 'The latter dreams not under any circumstances of attending to his own comfort till after he had provided for the comfort of his steed. He will frequently sleep beside it, through choice; and the noble animal seldom fails to return the affection of his master, whose voice he knows, and whom he will generally follow like a dog.'[256]

The cavalry's principal weapon was the sabre, and although it was widely accepted that the most effective blow was a thrust, the slash was the tactic preferred officially, which dictated the design of sword-blades. Until 1788 the patterns of cavalry swords were not standardized, each colonel purchasing privately for his regiment, but in that year a curved sabre for light dragoons and a straight, basket-hilted weapon for heavy cavalry were approved. These had not become universal by the 1794 campaign, when the various designs compared very unfavourably with those of Britain's Austrian allies, and were so ill-balanced that many men and horses were injured in trying to slash at the enemy. Consequently, John Gaspard Le Marchant, the most forward-thinking of British cavalry officers, re-designed both heavy and light cavalry sabres and introduced the first universal system of swordsmanship, his *Rules and Regulations for the Sword Exercise of Cavalry*.

The resulting 1796 patterns were used for the remainder of the period, but even these were somewhat clumsy and designed only to deliver a cut akin to a blow from a meat-cleaver. A Peninsula veteran condemned the curved light cavalry sabre by remarking that 'We can answer for its utility in making billets for the fire,' and the straight-bladed heavy cavalry sabre as 'a lumbering, clumsy, ill-contrived machine. It is too heavy, too short, too broad, too much like the sort of weapon with which we have seen Grimaldi cut off the heads of a line of urchins on the stage.'[257] Nevertheless, the cut remained the approved tactic despite the fact that it was acknowledged that thrusts caused a greater number of fatal injuries, though some concession was made to this prior to the Waterloo campaign when heavy regiments were ordered to grind the hatchet-points of their sabres into a spear-shape, making the thrust possible.

Nevertheless, the cut was a horrific blow in the hands of a trained man, as described by an 11th Light Dragoon who witnessed the following while lying wounded:

'... a French officer ... delivered a thrust at poor Harry Wilson's body; and delivered it effectually. I firmly believe that Wilson died on the instant; yet, though he felt the sword in its progress, he, with characteristic self-command, kept his eye still on the enemy in his front; and, raising himself in his stirrups, let fall upon the Frenchman's helmet such a blow, that brass and skull parted before it, and the man's head was cloven asunder to the chin. It was the most tremendous blow I ever beheld struck; and both he who gave, and his opponent who received it, dropped dead together. The brass helmet was afterwards examined by order of a French officer, who, as well as myself, was astonished at the exploit; and the cut was found to be as clean as if the sword had gone through a turnip, not so much as a dint being left on either side of it.' (This witness believed that the cut was more damaging to morale than the thrust: referring to cuts on the Frenchmen's heads and faces, he observed that 'the appearance presented by these mangled wretches was hideous ... as far as appearances can be said to operate in rendering men timid, or the reverse, the wounded among the French were thus far more revolting than the wounded among ourselves'.)[258]

With the exception of an ephemeral corps of emigrant cavalry, the *Uhlans Britanniques*, unlike many European armies the British never adopted the lance during the period, and while recognizing its use in attacking infantry, had no opinion of it for cavalry combat: 'the long unwieldy two-handed lance, at all times ridiculous on horseback, is totally useless the moment you close with the gewgaw champion who bears it'.[259] It was remarked after Albuera, however, that the fluttering pennons on lances terrified the opposing British cavalry horses, 'and rendered every effort impractical to make them meet the charge'.[260]

Cavalry firearms were almost equally disregarded. Carbines and pistols were carried by almost all cavalry, the former used for skirmishing and 'out-post' duty, but its shorter barrel so retricted the range as to make the 'little pop-gun of a carbine ... almost useless'.[261] Indeed, long-range hits were so unknown that in August 1813 Thomas Moon of the 9th Light Dragoons fired at a farm labourer on Finchley Common, at a range of more than 200 yards, presumably as a joke; the target, Joseph Lemon, was killed, and Moon was convicted of manslaughter. A small number of rifled carbines were issued to a few regiments from 1803 (most notably to the 10th Hussars), and were reported as 'little, if at all, inferior to the long, infantry fusil'.[262] Pistols, however, were of little or no use whatever: 'We never saw a pistol made use of except to shoot a glandered horse.'[263]

Tuition in riding was generally the responsibility of each regiment's riding-master and rough-riders (at least one corporal per troop, who were excused guards and stable duty). There was no universal system of tuition, although recruits might be trained at central establishments such as the Cavalry Depot at Maidstone, or that established in India at Arcot in April 1807 (the latter was abolished after less than a year). The first system of universal training was attempted in India by Sir John Floyd, who instructed regimental riding-masters at Trinchinopoly in 1808. Perhaps from this lack of central direction, the standard of equitation was at times not high, whether from badly-schooled horses or incompetent riders. In 1798, for example, it was reported that even among regiments considered 'the élite of the British Cavalry', the horses 'are not well broke to fire. When *feux de joye* were fired on the birthdays of the Prince of Wales and Duke of York, a great number of horses were so scared by the report of the pistols, as to run out of the ranks, in spite of all the efforts of their riders.'[264] Bad management of horses even existed in royal bodyguards: an especially unfortunate incident in November 1809 involved the Royal Horse Guards escort for the king's journey from Windsor to London, when an ill-trained horse (which had hospitalized its previous rider) threw its new incumbent, who was 'very much hurt'; another of the escort was so out of control that it ran off and bowled over one of the king's mounted outriders![265]

Even officers' horses, which were privately purchased, often suffered from severe indiscipline, and there were countless examples of officers begin killed or injured simply from being unable to control their mounts; for example, in 1806 the 6th Dragoon Guards lost their Lieutenant-Colonel Bagwell, killed on the spot when thrown by a horse which had run away with him.

Manoeuvres were normally conducted in column, but attacks in line, generally two deep (a third rank might be used, but added little to the impetus of the charge and would suffer unduly if a horse were brought down in front of it). The term 'attack in line' is deceptive, however, as it was generally conducted in echelon of squadrons, the first to move off (150 paces ahead of the next, and so on) attracting the enemy's fire, thus protecting the succeeding units; and when one squadron had breached the enemy's line, the rest would aim towards that spot, only a little to one or other side of it. Against cavalry, where no musketry would disorder the ranks, three or four ranks were recommended, but depth had to be sacrificed to ensure that the frontage was at least equal to that of the enemy, thus preventing any overlapping to strike the flank. The cavalry regulations instructed that charges should begin at a walk, increase to a brisk trot until 250 yards from the target, then increase to a gallop and only begin an all-out charge 80 yards from the enemy, to avoid horses arriving at the target already 'blown'. Movements were often carried out with the men very close together, which in itself was hazardous; for example, at a field-day in Hyde Park in April 1794, a Life Guard 'had his thigh broke, by being jammed between his own horse and that of his comrade'.[266]

The cavalry's greatest problem was in preservation of order and an inability to rally at the conclusion of a successful charge, the cause of a number of disasters throughout the period. Part of the problem was in the training: William Tomkinson complained of the habit of 'each regiment estimating its merit by the celerity of movement'; 'We do everything so quickly that it is impossible men can understand what they are about ... Before the enemy, except in charging, I never saw troops go beyond a trot ... In England I never saw or heard of cavalry taught to charge, disperse, and form, which, if I only taught a regiment one thing, I think it should be that.'[267]

Another failing was in leadership, for among cavalry officers were some who were quite incapable, despite having achieved high rank. For example, Major Camac, who joined the Peninsula army with his 1st Life Guards in 1812, was unable to perform a simple manoeuvre when requested by his general, and was told in public to report to his own adjutant to be taught his business; in a temper he then attempted to manoeuvre his regiment and almost drowned the man at the end of the line when he rode them accidentally into the sea![268] Another was George Quentin of the 10th Hussars, whose behaviour caused a revolt among his officers, as previously mentioned. A typical incident occurred at Toulouse, when Quentin disappeared and left his regiment without orders, under fire and only 80 yards from the enemy. Lack of decision apparently paralysed the other officers, for in this situation the senior officer present, Major Howard, asked *his* subordinate, Captain Fitzclarence, 'What shall we do now?'![269]

The combination of these factors produced an inevitable sequence of events: a charge would overthrow its target, but then career on until the horses were exhausted and the formation completely scattered; when they would be counter-charged by the enemy's reserve, driven back, and the previous success undone. The failure to keep a reserve (to second the initial charge and guard against a counter-attack) was largely the failure of the commanders; and, the troopers rarely having been trained to rally, this depended upon the good sense of officers who realized the dangers. For example, in the pursuit at Sahagun,

Alexander Gordon of the 15th Hussars wrote of his difficulty in curbing the pursuit: 'Having rode together nearly a mile, pell-mell, cutting and slashing each other, it appeared to me indispensable that order should be re-established, as the men were quite wild and the horses blown; therefore, seeing no superior officer near, I pressed through the throng until I overtook and halted those who were farthest advanced in pursuit.'[270]

The best comments on the failings of the cavalry, and upon their best tactics, were made by Wellington himself: 'I considered our cavalry so inferior to the French from want of order, although I consider one squadron a match for two French squadrons, that I should not have liked to see four British squadrons opposed to four French; and, as the numbers increased, and order of course became more necessary, I was more unwilling to risk our cavalry without having a great superiority of numbers ... Mine would gallop, but could not preserve their order.'[271] In the wake of the débâcle at Maguilla, in which a successful charge had blundered on and been routed, he raged:

'It is occasioned entirely by the trick our officers of cavalry have acquired of galloping at every thing, and their galloping back as fast as they gallop on the enemy. They never consider their situation, and never think of manoeuvering before an enemy – so little that one would think they cannot manoeuvre, excepting on Wimbledon Common; and when they use their arm as it ought to be used, viz., offensively, they never keep nor provide for a reserve. All cavalry should charge in two lines, of which one should be in reserve; if obliged to charge in one line, part of the line, at least one-third, should be ordered beforehand to pull up, and form in second line, as soon as the charge should be given, and the enemy has been broken and has retired.'[272]

Finally, after more uncontrolled charges at Waterloo, Wellington issued detailed instructions concerning the tactics to be utilized in a charge, which may be summarized thus: a reserve should always be kept, never less than half, and even up to two-thirds of the strength. A cavalry force should deploy in three bodies, the first two in line but the third in column and able to deploy rapidly. When opposed to cavalry the three bodies should be 400–500 yards behind each other, a space sufficient for a defeated first line to retire without disordering the second, but close enough to support the first; when attacking infantry, the second line should be only 200 yards behind the first, so as to support a charge so rapidly that the infantry would not have time to reload after firing on the initial charge. Finally, when the first line charged, the supports should follow at a walk, and on no account become carried away with the advance and thus lose their formation or control.

Skirmishing, both on the battlefield and in scouting and patrolling on 'outpost' duty, was another skill totally neglected in training at home, 'which, like Chinese puzzles, only engross time and labour to the unprofitable end of forming useless combinations'[273] according to Ludlow Beamish of the King's German Legion. In action, skirmishers might be thrown out some 200 yards in advance of the main body, firing with carbines from the saddle, in two thin skirmish-lines (shooting alternately as for infantry skirmishers), with a formed reserve between them and the main body. The regard paid officially to skirmishing may be judged from the fact that in the 1801 revised edition of *Instructions and Regulations for the Formations and Movements of the Cavalry*, skirmishing occupied only some four of 374 pages. Tactics of the 'outpost' were even more disregarded; as Tomkinson remarked, 'To attempt giving men or officers any idea in England of outpost duty was considered absurd, and when they came abroad, they had all this to learn. The fact was, there was no one to teach them. Sir Stapleton Cotton tried, at Woodbridge in Suffolk, with the 14th and 16th Light Dragoons, and got the enemy's vedettes and his own looking the same way.'[274]

Consequently, regiments had to learn their business actually on campaign, so that until each unit became acclimatized, the outpost and scouting facility depended upon previously arrived regiments, and the cavalry of the German Legion, who were by far the most proficient at this service, doubtless benefiting from the continental experience of many of their officers and other ranks.

8
'The effect is Hardly Conceivable'
THE ORDNANCE

AVALIÉ MERCER DESCRIBED FIRING HIS GUNS AT CLOSE RANGE into a frantic mass of French cavalry at Waterloo: '... that part next to us became a complete mob, into which we kept a steady fire of case-shot from our six pieces. The effect is hardly conceivable, and to paint this scene of slaughter and confusion impossible. Every discharge was followed by the fall of numbers, whilst the survivors struggled with each other, and I actually saw them using the pommels of their swords to fight their way out of the mêlée ...'[275] This most graphic picture of the effect of artillery-fire emphasizes the significance of the army's gunnery element.

The Royal Regiment of Artillery was not officially part of the army, but a department of the Ordnance, superintended by the Master-General and distinctive in its practices and organization. Officers were promoted strictly by seniority, and thus the occupants of the higher ranks were often superannuated and unenthusiastic. The imperfections of this system compared to that of the army are exemplified by the trouble Wellington experienced with his artillery commanders in the Peninsula; he only achieved the energetic and capable man he needed by appointing Lieutenant-Colonel Alexander Dickson over the heads of more senior colleagues, by virtue of Dickson's also holding a Portuguese commission. Artillery officers were well trained (they had to be professionally competent to qualify for a commission, unlike the army system) but were comparatively few in number, one of the causes why Britain's artillery arm remained small compared to the huge numbers of guns fielded by some other nations.

The Royal Artillery was organized into battalions of ten companies (eight battalions in 1803, with a 9th formed in 1806 and a 10th in 1808). These did not serve as units, but each company formed an autonomous artillery 'brigade', including a detachment of drivers. Before 1802, guns were grouped for administrative purposes into 'brigades' of about twelve pieces; after that date, each 'brigade' normally consisted of six pieces of ordnance. (In artillery terminology, a 'brigade' had no connection with the same term used to describe a tactical unit of several battalions, but referred to what is now termed an artillery battery, although at the time 'battery' was used more often to indicate a fixed gun-position). In 1799 an artillery company comprised five officers, eight NCOs, seven bombardiers, 98 gunners and three drummers, commanded by a captain (field officers and staff were restricted to battalion headquarters). This strength was increased by two bombardiers and eighteen gunners in 1808. These dismounted companies were often styled Royal Foot Artillery, indicating that the crews generally accompanied the ordnance on foot.

Horse artillery was formed in 1793 as a support for cavalry, all gunners riding on horses or upon the artillery carriages; although part of the same regiment, they were distinguished by a light dragoon uniform and by the title Royal Horse Artillery. In 1801 there were seven troops or 'brigades' of horse artillery, rising to twelve by 1806.

The thoroughly unsatisfactory system of using hired civilian carters and teams to transport artillery vehicles was replaced by the formation of the artillery's own Corps of Drivers in September 1794. By 1808 the corps consisted of eight troops (ultimately eleven), each of five sections of 90 drivers, plus craftsmen, totalling 554 men per troop. Theoretically this was a great improvement, at least putting them under regular military discipline, but as the troops were split up as required among the artillery companies, they were frequently outside the supervision of their own officers, who often were neglectful in any case. As a result, the Corps of Drivers became notorious for various types of ill-discipline and criminality; William Swabey of the RHA described it as 'that nest of infamy',[276] which seems a not unreasonable assessment. Integration of the drivers into the artillery proper would have prevented these problems, but this was not accomplished until after the Napoleonic Wars, the Corps of Drivers being disbanded only in 1822.

The variety of ordnance was immense, but comparatively few were used for field service: for example, Adye's *Bombardier and Pocket Gunner*, 2nd edn. 1802, the gunner's *vade mecum* of the period, lists some 64 different types of ordnance. Excluding mortars, used exclusively for siege work, the ordnance was divided into two categories, guns and howitzers, guns classified into 'natures' according to the weight of shot they fired, and howitzers according to the calibre (bore-diameter). The gun was a muzzle-loading, smoothbored cannon capable only of direct fire (i.e., with an uninterrupted track between gun and target); the howitzer was a short-barrelled weapon with chambered bore, which projected its missiles with a high trajectory, and was thus the only artillery capable of indirect fire, i.e., over obstacles or over the heads of friendly troops.

The principal projectile of guns was the 'roundshot', a solid iron ball discharged with low elevation, which would strike down anything in its path, and unless hitting very boggy ground would then rebound and bounce onwards, continuing to ricochet until its impulsion was spent. Roundshot at the end of their career would roll along the ground like a bowl, leading one officer to compare Waterloo to a giant cricket-match, the rolling balls tempting a steady player to drive them back with his bat! Even at this stage they were lethal: for example, in Holland in 1814 one rolled towards Lieutenant Stowards and Ensign Chapman of the 37th, who were walking arm-in-arm; it carried off a foot from each man. It was claimed that even the wind of a roundshot could cause severe injury: for example, Lieutenant John Winterbottom of the 52nd claimed to have been wounded at Redinha in March 1811 by the wind of a shot, which although it never touched him caused an extensive bruise on the hip which turned into a deep wound when the flesh sloughed away.

Howitzers fired explosive projectiles. 'Common shell' was a hollow iron casing with a bursting-charge inside, ignited by a fuze which protruded through the casing, itself being ignited by the belch of flame from the propellant charge. Shells could splutter and fizz after landing, sometimes for several moments before exploding, causing consternation all around, and were deadly in the hands of the untrained even when unexploded or when the fuze had gone out, : for example, one man was killed and another lost an arm at

Sevenoaks in June 1809 when they foolishly applied a lighted brand to a shell which an old woman had stolen from gunners practising in the area. More effective was the British 'secret weapon', 'spherical case-shot' or Shrapnel shell, named after its inventor, Henry Shrapnel of the Royal Artillery. This was similar to 'common shell' but with a thinner casing filled with musket-balls, so that by careful trimming of the fuze it could be made to explode in the air, raining balls and shell-casing on to the heads of the enemy. After its first use in 1804 it represented some 15 per cent of all artillery ammunition, and 50 per cent of howitzer ammunition.

For close ranges, case-shot or canister was used, a tin container packed with small balls, which ruptured as it left the gun-barrel, turning the cannon into a huge shotgun and spreading its missiles in a circle of some 32 feet in diameter per 100 yards of range. Two varieties existed, light and heavy case (for a 6pdr gun, for example, the former consisted of 85 1½oz. balls, for the latter 41 3½oz. balls); heavy case was sometimes styled 'grapeshot', although this term was applied correctly only to a munition consisting of a number of larger balls, used almost exclusively at sea.

Range of artillery varied according to factors such as elevation and the quantity of propellant gunpowder, but as accuracy decreased markedly at longer ranges, it was usual to conserve ammunition by opening fire at ranges sufficiently close for shots to take effect. Artillery officers were guided by published tables which gave exact distances for each 'nature' of piece and elevation; for example, the 'first graze' (i.e., where the roundshot first pitched before it ricocheted) varied between 1,745 yards with a medium 24pdr at 5° elevation, to 628 yards with a short 6pdr at 1° elevation, according to tests conducted with brass guns in 1793.[277] Light case was effective only to about 250 yards, and in British practice it was usual to restrict the firing of heavy case to no more than 350 yards.

It was often possible to follow the course of an approaching cannon-ball with the naked eye, but it was regarded as bad form to move or duck; as Sergeant-Major William Ballam of the 2/73rd remarked to Private William Dent, 'Damn you, sir, what do you stoop for? You should not stoop if your head was off!' Almost immediately Ballam was struck dead by a ball which hit him in the middle of the face, whereupon Dent turned to the mangled remains and said, 'Damn it, sir, what do you lie there for? You should not lie down if your head was off!'; which, of course, it was.[278] It was also possible to distinguish the flatter trajectory of a roundshot from the arching course of a shell, and at Badajoz Kincaid records a Portuguese being posted to call out whenever a shot or shell approached, 'bomba, bomba', or 'balla, balla' as appropriate; 'but, sometimes he would see a general discharge from all arms, when he threw himself down, screaming out, "Jesus, todos, todos!", meaning "everything".'[279]

The propellant charge of gunpowder was packed into a fabric or paper bag, known as a 'prepared cartridge', which was rammed down the barrel via the muzzle of the gun before the projectile followed it; a further development was 'fixed ammunition' in which the projectile had a wooden 'sabot' or shoe affixed, which rested upon the propellant charge. When these were in place, one of the gunners pierced the cartridge with a 'pricker' inserted into the touch-hole of the gun, which was then filled with a length of 'quick-match' (cotton soaked in saltpetre and spirits of wine) or, after about 1800, a quill or paper tube of milled gunpowder, which communicated to the propellant charge the spark of ignition from the exterior of the barrel, as a piece of smouldering 'slow-match' held in a portfire was applied to the touch-hole. After each shot, the gun-barrel was swabbed-out with a wet 'sponge' (a fleece or similar material nailed to the reverse end of the rammer) in order to clear the barrel of any smouldering embers, to prevent the premature ignition of the next shot. This could happen in the confusion of battle, and an especially tragic example occurred during the firing of guns celebrating the peace of 1814 at Lude, Perthshire, when a volunteer gunner named Macpherson was killed, and another lost an arm, by the gun discharging itself during loading drill. Macpherson left a wife and eight children.

In 1800 the *British Military Library* described an acceptable rate of fire in action as six shots per minute; a faster rate was certainly possible, but in practice two roundshot or three canister per minute (less with heavier guns) was probably nearer the average. The time taken to re-position a gun after the recoil of each shot slowed as the crew became more tired; for example, by the end of the Battle of Waterloo Cavalié Mercer recalled that his gunners were so exhausted as to be unable to keep their guns in position, so that the recoil entangled them with each other. In an emergency guns could be fire almost non-stop, but on other occasions the clouds of smoke they produced might obscure the target and cause a cessation in fire; although in especially desperate affairs a battery might fire 'blind' (at Waterloo, for example, Lieutenant John Wilson of Sinclair's battery noted that 'The smoke was so dense that I could not see distinctly the position of the French, being at that time ordered to direct my fire over the dead bodies of some horses in front.')[280]

Each 'brigade' or battery usually consisted of five guns and one howitzer (though all-gun or all-howitzer batteries were not unknown), the guns almost always of one 'nature' to facilitate ammunition-supply. Foot batteries originally had light 6pdrs and 3pdrs, which proved greatly inferior to the French ordnance and were replaced as soon as possible by the much superior 9pdr; the original 8in and 10in howitzers were replaced similarly by the superior 5½in model. Some horse batteries retained 6pdrs: at Waterloo, for example, three troops had 9pdrs, four light 6pdrs and one was armed exclusively with 5½in howitzers; and not until the Waterloo campaign had all the foot batteries received 9pdrs. Compared with that of some European armies, the field strength of artillery was generally low, even though it was increased during the Peninsular War. In August 1808, for example, it was in such short supply that it had to be deployed in three-gun batteries; in May 1809 the artillery in the Peninsula comprised only three batteries of light 6pdrs and three of 3pdrs, and even in the Vittoria campaign there were only seven batteries of 9pdrs, two of heavy 6pdrs and four of light 6pdrs, the small numbers of guns making it doubly important that none was lost to the enemy.

Each battery or troop could be divided into three divisions of two subdivisions each, each subdivision consisting of one gun, crew, and ammunition-wagon; they could also be divided into two half-brigades of three subdivisions each. In action it was common for guns to act in pairs (i.e., divisions), firing alternately. After unlimbering for action, deployed ideally in a staggered line to reduce damage from enfilade fire, some ammunition would be kept in proximity of the gun, usually that carried in the limber; ammunition-wagons (one per gun plus one extra per division) would be positioned in two lines, about 50 and 100 yards respectively behind the gun-line, with the other battery vehicles (baggage-wagons, etc.) a further 100 yards in the rear. To minimize the danger to ammunition-wagons, it was not usual for each gun to be serviced by its own wagon, but one wagon at a time would distribute its ammunition to the entire battery, and when empty would retire to the third line, being replaced in the second by one of the reserve wagons. This constant shuttle of ammunition exposed only one wagon at a time to enemy fire, for an exploding wagon could cause immense havoc.

The ideal artillery position was just over the crest of gently rising ground, allowing the guns to sweep the slope but without 'dead ground' in which enemy troops could be shielded by folds in the terrain; with the battery vehicles protected from enemy fire by the reverse slope. Very elevated positions caused difficulty in depressing the gun-barrels sufficiently; Adye thought that 'the greatest effects may be produced from a height of 30 or 40 yards at a distance of about 600; and about 16 yards of height to 200 of distance'.[281] The best ground on which to site artillery was boggy, to absorb enemy shot; the best to fire upon, stony, so that ricocheting shot would throw up rocks upon the enemy. As indirect fire was impossible with guns, they had to be sited in front of or among infantry, or behind cavalry which could act as a 'blind', concealing the artillery until they moved aside to allow the guns to shoot unhindered.

A change occurred in the theory of artillery deployment during the Napoleonic Wars. Initially, it was common for guns to be attached to infantry, these 'battalion guns' to provide them with immediate fire-support; but as the guns were necessarily light they lacked hitting-power, and were more likely to hinder than help, as the troops had to advance at a pace slow enough for the manhandled guns to keep up. Consequently, they were soon withdrawn from the infantry although two light fieldpieces or 'galloper guns' were issued to cavalry regiments serving in India. Even these were not always accepted: Thomas 'Black Jack' Vandeleur, commanding officer of the 8th Light Dragoons, repeatedly refused them, saying that 'the 8th must depend on their good swords and their own innate bravery'.[282]

It came to be held that the effect of a concentration of fire was greater than the sum of its parts: 'In order to strike terror into the enemy, and put him to flight, something uncommon must be effected; whole platoons and ranks must be swept away at once. This terrifies the troops; whichever way they look, death stares them full in the face, and it becomes a very arduous task for the officers to keep the men steady and in order.'[283] This could only be achieved by concentrating fire against specific sections of enemy line, rather than deploying guns piecemeal along the entire battle-front. Unlike some European armies, Britain never fielded sufficient guns to exploit fully the offensive potential of 'massed battery' fire, to destroy part of an enemy line as a preparation for an attack, but care was taken to maximize the artillery's potential by judicious selection of targets. Adye's suggestions on artillery deployment articulated the best practice:

'... guns must be positioned as to produce a cross-fire upon the position of the enemy, and upon all the ground which he must pass over in an attack ... [it may] be united to produce a decided effect against any particular points ... the *débouchés* of the enemy, the heads of their columns, and the weakest points in the front ... the cross-fire of the guns must become *direct*, before it can impede the advance of the troops; and must annoy the enemy's positions nearest to the point attacked, when it is no longer safe to continue the fire upon that point itself. The shot from artillery should always take an enemy in the direction of its greatest dimension; it should therefore take a line obliquely or in flank; but a column in front.'[284]

Counter-battery fire (i.e., against enemy artillery) was regarded as wasteful of shot, and was not normally employed except against enemy guns that were proving a particular nuisance.

Heavier ordnance was used almost exclusively in the defence or assault of fortifications. The travelling siege-train employed 18pdrs and the more effective 24pdrs, but more cumbersome pieces might also be used, such as iron or brass 42- and 32pdrs, and such was the shortage of ordnance in the early Peninsular War that Spanish and Portuguese guns dating from the early 17th century had to be pressed into service. Latterly in the Peninsula naval guns and crews were landed from British ships, a considerable improvement. Often using oxen to drag the guns, siege-trains were exceptionally slow-moving, and had to transport enormous quantities of powder and shot (in the second siege of Badajoz in 1812, for example, more than 400 tons of powder and roundshot were used, excluding shells and case-shot). Mortars were even less mobile (the 13in iron 'land service' mortar weighed more than 36 cwt., for example), and were used exclusively for bombardment; they projected explosive shells with a very high trajectory, and instead of using the normal, wheeled artillery carriage, were affixed to flat wooden 'beds', which absorbed their recoil.

A more unusual weapon was the Congreve rocket, named after its designer, Sir William Congreve. It consisted of a stick (up to 24 feet long) and a body comprising the propellant charge and the head, either explosive shell, case-shot or incendiary. Originally they were heavy rockets used for bombardment (40,000 were fired at Copenhagen in 1807, for example), but mobile rocket troops for field service were established as a separate branch of the Royal Horse Artillery in January 1813. The heaviest field (and lightest bombardment) rocket was the 32pdr, but the 12pdr was that recommended for use on campaign; launching could be from a rocket-cart, but an iron tripod launcher was used in the field. The concept was so unusual that it attracted considerable attention; there was even *The Sky-Rocket Waltz*, composed by Samuel Wesley and dedicated to Congreve (but it seems to have fallen to earth faster than the weapon, a reviewer lamenting that so eminent a musician 'should not find it more advantageous to employ his distinguished talents on their proper objects than on unmeaning trifles, like the present, that do him no credit').[285]

Wellington was most dismissive of rockets, claiming that he only accepted a rocket troop in the Peninsula in order to get their horses, as he had no wish to set any town alight and knew of no other use for them; and insisted that Whinyates' rocket troop at Waterloo should also be equipped with 6pdr guns. The moral objection to the use of rockets was articulated by an officer writing of the suggestion that Bayonne should be bombarded with them in January 1814: 'The demolition of so many buildings, the properties of the unoffending and distressed *bourgeois*, is certainly a measure greatly to be deprecated. It is hoped that the idea of moral conquest ... will not be inconsiderably abandoned, if any other means are adoptible, by which the troops of the despot can be forced from this position.'[286]

The effect of rockets upon the enemy, however, could be devastating. Gleig of the 85th called them 'diabolical engines', creating confusion which 'beggars all description. I saw and conversed with a French sergeant who ... assured me that he had been personally engaged in twenty battles, and that he had never known the sensation of fear till that day. But a rocket ... had passed harmlessly through his knapsack; and such was the violence with which it flew, that he fell upon his face, not stunned, but stupefied – so frightful was the hissing sound which the missile sends forth in its progress. Nor is it the least appalling incident in a rocket's eccentricities that you see it coming yet know not how to avoid it. It skips and starts about from place to place in so strange a manner, that the chances are, when you are running to the right or left to get out of the way, that you run directly against it; and hence the absolute rout which a fire of ten or twelve rockets can create, provided they take effect. But it is a very uncertain weapon. It may indeed spread havoc among the enemy, but it may also turn back upon the people who use it ...'[287]

The rocket troop of Captain Richard Bogue was the British contribution to the Allied army at the 'Battle of the Nations' at Leipzig (where Bogue was killed); their rockets were witnessed by the Russian general Wittgenstein, who made the apt comment on their infernal appearance: 'They look as if they were made in hell, and surely are the devil's own artillery.'[288]

The carriage of munitions was the responsibility of the Field Train Department, whose services were so overlooked that Sir Richard Henegan, head of the department in the Peninsula, complained publicly that although its personnel wore Royal Artillery uniform, its half-pay officers were even omitted from the Army List, and his own name was never listed with the army holders of the Guelphic Order. The services of the department were not only vital to the operation of the artillery, but also dangerous, due to the instability of gunpowder, the handling of which, even when making-up cartridges, was always hazardous. The consequences of an accident were exemplified by the explosion of a magazine in Malta in July 1806, when 370 barrels of powder and more than 1,600 shells blew up. Immense devastation was caused, stones were flung some two miles, and one estimate put the dead and injured at about 1,000; among the sufferers was the band of the 39th which was playing 'God Save the King' at the moment of explosion: two members of the band were killed and the rest injured.

The second of the principal Ordnance services was the Corps of Royal Engineers. This was composed exclusively of officers, and although highly trained was very small, the number of engineer officers rising from 73 in 1792 to 262 in 1813, and as the senior ranks were generally old and inactive, field service devolved upon an even smaller number of junior officers. That so few had received specialist training (the engineers maintained their own training establishment at Woolwich) meant that those with a field army tended to be consulted only on major projects such as siege-work, bridge-building or surveying, were very over-worked and suffered heavy losses: 102 served in the Peninsula, of whom 24 fell in action and one died from over-work. So severe were their casualties that Wellington, who appreciated in full the difficulties caused by an inadequate engineer service, actually remarked that so many had been killed or wounded that he could hardly request any more, lest the same fate befall them. Consequently, 'assistant engineers' were appointed temporarily from other units, many of them not fully trained.

The rank-and-file of the engineer service existed in the Royal Military Artificers and Labourers (titled Royal Military Artificers from 1798), twelve companies of artisans each commanded by a sub-lieutenant (always a retired NCO) and a staff-sergeant seconded from the Royal Artillery. They were stationed in fortresses to perform carpentry and building work (two companies were in Gibraltar, one in Nova Scotia and one in the West Indies). For campaigns, small detachments were seconded from these companies, but as their commanders usually retained their best men, only the most useless were normally sent on campaign, making their presence almost an irrelevance; in November 1809, for example, the entire strength with the Peninsula army was two sergeants and 23 other ranks, of whom two had gone missing and four were ill. Consequently, the manual work of military engineering was performed by infantrymen, few of whom had received specialist training.

The deficiencies in the engineer service were such that in 1798 the Horse Guards established the Royal Staff Corps, to provide engineers who were part of the army rather than under the control of the Master-General of Ordnance. Initially of four companies and a headquarters, the unit was expanded to a battalion in 1809, and its members were also fully trained as infantrymen as well as in engineering skills. They were employed piecemeal as overseers or foremen for gangs of infantry labourers; singularly, their privates were divided into three classes, 1st class privates to act as sergeants, 2nd class as corporals and 3rd class as lance-corporals, to instruct the infantry labourers. The officers were also employed on detached duties, overlapping the responsibilities of the Royal Engineers and the Quartermaster-General's Department; for example, perhaps their most famous officer, Robert Henry Sturgeon, was responsible for two remarkable feats of engineering, the repair of the bridge at Alcantara in 1812, and for the bridge of boats over the Adour in 1813. (To demonstrate that despite their 'technical' qualifications, Staff Corps officers were not restricted to the middle classes from which they might have been expected to draw their members, it is worth remarking that Sturgeon was nephew to the Marquess of Rockingham; nor does his career appear to have suffered from the fact that his wife, whom he married in November 1805, was the same Sarah Curran who had been involved romantically with the Irish rebel Robert Emmet.)

Even including the Staff Corps personnel, the engineer service was quite inadequate for the tasks it had to undertake, despite the universal bravery and capability of its members who included such men of talent and energy as Sir Richard Fletcher, Wellington's most capable engineer (who, like so many, failed to survive the war: he was killed at San Sebastian). The problem is exemplified by the unsuccessful siege of Badajoz in 1811, when the besiegers were so devoid of *matériel* that the battering-train included ordnance dating from the era of the Spanish Armada, six Portuguese naval guns and makeshift mortars made from howitzers with the wheels removed from their carriages. The scale of such an undertaking is shown by calculations of Lieutenant-Colonel John T. Jones (brigade-major of engineers at this siege), which stated that for a fortress with a garrison of 5,000 men, 8,000 men would be needed to work in the trenches, in four shifts; 11,250 to guard the trenches from counter-attack, in three shifts; and 7,700 men in support, in four shifts, not including cover for any casualties.[289] When the French had successfully besieged Badajoz earlier in the year, they had employed in addition to infantry labourers some 25 officers and 649 *specialist* sappers and miners;[290] yet when Britain attempted the same task, their engineer service comprised 21 officers of the Royal Engineers, 25 artificers from the Staff Corps, eleven volunteers from the line serving as assistant engineers, and some 265 infantrymen who possessed some few manual skills.

Napier's condemnation of the events of this siege is a reflection upon the engineer service of much of the period: '... it is most strange and culpable that a government, which had been so long engaged in war as the British, should have left the engineer department, with respect to organization and equipment, in such a state as to make it, in despite of the officers' experience, bravery, and zeal, a very inefficient arm of war. The skill displayed belonged to particular persons, rather than to the corps at large; and the very tools with which they worked ... were so shamefully bad that the work required could scarcely be performed; the captured French cutting-tools were eagerly sought for by the engineers as being infinitely better than the British; and when the soldiers' lives and the honour of England's arms, were at stake, the English cutlery was found worse than the French.'[291]

Finally, after the carnage of the second (successful) siege of Badajoz, Wellington's demands for trained artificers were heeded, and in April 1812 the Royal Military Artificers or Sappers and Miners was formed (titled Royal Sappers and Miners from 1813), 2,800 rank and file trained in engineering at Chatham, organized in regular companies, with Royal Engineer officers. For the 1813 campaign, 300 were present with the Peninsula army, and from San Sebastian made a considerable difference to the conduct of sieges. For the Waterloo campaign each division had a Sapper and Miner company attached, with sufficient wagons and drivers to transport their own equipment and entrenching-tools for 500 infantrymen. Until that date the engineer service had no transport, but was entirely dependent upon whatever vehicles the artillery could spare. Even the pontoon train had no wagons of its own, and indeed it was stated that some of the very pontoons used by Marlborough were still in service with the Peninsular army, perhaps accounting for their poor design, 'constructed on erroneous principles, being without decks, and much too short in proportion to their breadth, and to the breadth of the superstructure to be supported; and, presenting great resistance to a current, they were in constant danger of being swept below the water and sunk, when great floods or gales of wind occurred'.[292] (The use of such old equipment was not unique; for example, the wooden bridge thrown over the river Barrow at New Ross during the 1798 rebellion was a veteran of the American War, having been shipped home for further use.)

The process of besieging a fortress began by establishing a 'covering force' to intercept any attempted relief expedition. The siege-works commenced (styled 'breaking ground') with the construction of 'parallels', circuits of trenches connected by zigzag saps, which were pushed ever nearer to the outer defences of the fortress. Breaching-batteries were constructed, and the siege-train generally bombarded a particular section of the wall (*enceinte*) deemed most suitable for an assault. The trenches were bolstered by gabions (tubular wicker baskets packed with earth), and any ditches filled with fascines (bundles of brushwood), all extremely labour-intensive, demanding much effort from the infantry who performed the manual work. This was not only tiresome but hazardous, as in addition to occasional sallies from the besieged fortress, the defenders would maintain a counter-bombardment and, when the parallels had approached within range, a fusillade of sharpshooting.

Consequently, trench-duty was most unpopular, and as Moyle Sherer remarked, 'I know not how it is, death in the trenches never carries with it that stamp of glory, which seals the memory of those who perish in a well-fought field.'[293] William Grattan thought that this was because the British soldier preferred a fair, stand-up fight to one conducted amid holes in the ground. Nevertheless, the work was usually undertaken with good spirits and often a fatalistic attitude which led to an ignoring of the enemy's fire. For example, Edmond Man of the 88th sat calmly outside a gun-embrasure, weaving a fascine, during the first siege of Badajoz. Sir Richard Fletcher urged him to get under cover, but Man replied, 'I'm almost finished, Colonel, and it isn't worth while to move now; those fellows can't hit me, for they've been trying these fifteen minutes.'[294] As he finished speaking a roundshot cut him in two, and hurled half his body across the gun. Under such circumstances, Kincaid's remark is doubly apt: 'One day's trench-work is as like another as the days themselves; and like nothing better than serving an apprenticeship to the double calling of gravedigger and gamekeeper, for we found ample employment both for the spade and the rifle.'[295]

As soon as a breach in the fortress-wall was adjudged 'practicable' (i.e., sufficient to allow an assault to succeed, by the old courtesy of war the garrison could surrender without impugning its honour. Because of the slaughter which could be inflicted upon the attackers during an assault, a garrison which did not surrender at such a time traditionally forfeited any rights to mercy, and conferred upon the besiegers an unwritten right to plunder the place once it was captured. In theory this was the justification for what happened after an assault (notably those of Ciudad Rodrigo, Badajoz and San Sebastian), although by any standards the appalling scenes which resulted were truly inexcusable.

Assaults were usually led by a 'forlorn hope' of volunteers, as near to a suicide mission as anything experienced in the warfare of the period. There were, however, never any shortages of volunteers: officers would go on the implicit understanding (not always carried into fact) that they would receive promotion if they survived, but the other ranks seem to have volunteered simply for the honour of the business. Usually conducted at night, assaults were the most sanguinary events that could be experienced, to the effect that some observers or participants were simply stunned by the carnage. As at Badajoz, a well-defended breach (filled by the defenders with rubble and such horrors as *chevaux de frise*, beams studded with spikes or sword-blades) was often impenetrable, so that the attackers would mill about in the ditches in front of the breach simply being slaughtered, unable to proceed yet unwilling to abandon the attack. Occasionally there might occur an event so dreadful as to cause fighting to cease momentarily: when the French exploded a mine as the British stormed San Sebastian, accidentally blowing up part of their own garrison, the flash and noise was so profound that both sides stood as if paralysed for half a minute, 'insomuch that a whisper might have caught your ear for a distance of several yards'.[296]

Consequently, after such uncontrolled butchery, when the attackers did get inside the fortress they might run wild, and presumably arising from trauma induced by the slaughter of the assault, and compounded by intoxication, would wreak not only upon the garrison but also the civilian inhabitants such scenes of rapine, murder and destruction that disgraced not only the army but very humanity itself. It was virtually impossible to restore order until the perpetrators were sated; officers who tried were sometimes murdered, and generally all they could do was to stand guard over civilians or prisoners of war in an attempt to save at least a few from the depravity of the mob. Only after days of horror was it possible to restore order in Badajoz, for example, by the threat of a gallows and by the exhaustion of the guilty.

William Surtees of the 95th, an experienced and unemotional campaigner, wrote of Badajoz in a manner typical of all who witnessed the scenes of havoc, which he attributed to the soldiers' passion to 'sacrifice every thing to drink; and when once in a state of intoxication, with all the bad passions set loose at the same time, I know not what they will hesitate to perpetrate ... At this time I think I was fairly tired of life, so disgusting and so sickening were the scenes the last few days had presented.'[297] It is probable that such experiences caused in him what would now be recognized as a form of mental collapse, involving a delirium of fears of damnation and the belief that Satan was endeavouring to persuade him to commit suicide. The utter revulsion he felt was shared by all those who wrote of such scenes, undoubtedly the worst of all experiences of campaigning.

9

'The great engine in the hands of the Commissariat'[298]
THE SUPPORTING SERVICES

THE ARMY'S SUPPORTING SERVICES INCLUDED COMMISSARIAT AND transport, to which might be added comforts spiritual and physical, as dispensed by the chaplains and camp-followers respectively.

The commissariat was administered by the Treasury, so its personnel were officially civilians, outside military discipline. Responsible for the supply of provisions in the field, Assistant-Commissaries, their Deputies and clerks were attached to each infantry brigade and cavalry regiment, but many were little more than half-trained clerks, totally unprepared for campaigning. Many owed their appointments to the patronage of Treasury officials, and not until 1810 were any qualifications imposed (and then only that candidates should be aged 16 years and have a year's clerical experience); only in 1812 were examinations in arithmetic and English introduced. Their superiors were the Commissary-General and his Deputies and Assistants, but even these ranks were not immune from the incompetence and dishonesty prevalent elsewhere: for example, at Vittoria in 1814, Deputy Assistant Commissary-General Thomas Jolly was court-martialled and cashiered for embezzling £738.

Even after improvements during the Peninsular War, Wellington's complaints illustrate the imperfections of the commissariat service. Of one senior commissariat official he wrote: 'He appears to me but little calculated to do the business I require from him. I want him to assist me in obtaining a knowledge of the mode in which the connection between the troops and the several civil departments is regulated; to know how all that business is now going on here; and to see how we can make the matter work better than it does under the existing regulations. He thinks of nothing but new regulations and establishments ... but it is not his business to propose them, nor mine to carry them into execution ... You will hardly believe that we were obliged to pick up the French shot in our camp to make up ammunition for Arentschild's guns, his reserves having been left behind at Saragoça, and there being no Portuguese means of transport to carry on the ammunition ... I have reported the state of things to the British Government, and they will do as they please ...'[299]

On one occasion Wellington noted that he thought the commissariat staff incapable of managing anything outside a counting-house, a belief exemplified in a reply to a Deputy Commissary-General who had complained at being dismissed, which Wellington had done:

'... because the service had suffered, and is now suffering, the greatest inconvenience, owing to delays in that part of the department of which you were the head; and from which post I ordered that you might be removed, from a thorough conviction, which has since proved to be well founded, that the service would be still further embarrassed if you continued to conduct it ... His Majesty's Government, and the British public, will not hear excuses for failures in this country: and it is my business to take care where there is any failure in any department, not to employ again the person who is the cause of it; and in instances in which the officer who fails is of high rank and standing in respect to others, as you are, there is no remedy excepting to remove him from the country to one in the service of which he may be better acquainted, and in which failure may be less critical than it is in this ...'[300]

In fairness, the commissariat officials were beset by many tedious and probably unnecessary clerical regulations, and despite the criticisms many performed their duties diligently; Thomas Brooke, for example, was mortally wounded at Talavera when conducting a convoy to the front line, 'not limiting his exertions to the bare discharge of his professional duty'.[301] In general, however, they were regarded with disdain by those in authority, as perhaps suggested by the fact that commissaries were unique in having their pay of 15s. per diem reduced to 5s. when on active service! The story attributed to both Picton and Craufurd, that they had threatened to hang a commissary if he did not provide rations on time, may not be an exaggeration, as this message from Wellington to Lieutenant-General Sherbrooke suggests:

'I am not astonished that you and the General Officers should feel indignant at the neglect and incapacity of some of the Officers of the Commissariat, by which we have suffered and are still suffering so much; but what I have to observe, and wish to impress upon you, is, that they are gentlemen appointed to their office by the King's authority, although not holding his commission; and that it would be infinitely better, and more proper, if all neglects and faults of theirs were reported to me, by whom they can be dismissed, rather than that they should be abused by the General Officers of the army. Indeed, it cannot be expected that they will bear the kind of abuse they have received, however well deserved we may deem it to be; and they will either resign their situations, and put the army to still greater inconvenience, or complain to higher authorities, and thereby draw those who abuse them into discussions, which will take up, hereafter, much of their time and attention...'[302]

The unsuitability of some commissariat officials is exemplified by a letter Wellington wrote to the Commissary-in-Chief in April 1810, regarding the Deputy Commissary-General commanding at Cadiz, whom Wellington remembered from his service in India, when the man had been dismissed by the East India Company under unusual circumstances: 'An officer of the army accused him of having robbed him; that is to say, he literally stole his purse from him ... other persons recollected having lost their purses in company with him; and I understand that he had once been accused of taking a purse out of an officer's writing box ... I think that a person who has an itch for taking purses is not a fit person to be a Deputy Commissary-General, in charge of a department ...'[303]

The level of fraud which could be perpetrated by commissariat officials was spectacular. Inquiries into the supply of provisions revealed examples; in the West Indies, for example, new rum could be bought cheaply by a commissary, coloured to resemble more expensive old rum, the government charged for the latter and the difference pocketed by the commissary; Commissary-General Valentine Jones in Dominica in 1796 was calculated to have made £9,789 17s. 9d. on one transaction. Assistant-Commissary Fretwell Philips in Barbados auctioned 100 tierces of damaged flour from government stores but persuaded the auctioneer to give a receipt for 250 tierces, leaving him 150 in hand; Valentine Jones bought provisions for the West Indies from his father in Belfast, when the same could have been purchased cheaper in Martinique; and purchased 300 pipes of wine via an intermediary at £59 18s. per pipe, sold it to government stores at £90 per pipe, and presumably divided the resulting £9,030 profit with his associate. Michael Sutton, Assistant-Commissary at St. Vincent in 1804, merely by appropriating empty provision-barrels, in one transaction received £1,580. (To put these figures into perspective, the sum garnered by Jones on the rum transaction would have paid the officers and men of a battalion of 750 rank and file for about six months.)

Until 1794 the army's transport service, with which the commissariat officials co-operated, was dependent upon wagons and teams hired from civilian contractors, but in that year the Corps of Royal Waggoners was formed, with horses and carts purchased by the government. The selection of personnel clearly demonstrated their low priority: 'Withdraw from several Regts. such men as the Board of General officers and surgeons declared unfit for field service, 100 of those men will be piggd [sic: 'picked'] out to compleat one of the waggon compys.'[304] Consequently, the unit was little better than useless, Commissary-General Havilland Le Mesurier writing that its miserable state became proverbial in the army. Its replacement was the Royal Waggon Train, formed in August 1799 for service in Holland, with personnel mostly drafted from the cavalry, with NCOs commissioned as officers. Initially composed of five troops, it was enlarged by the incorporation of the two troops of the Irish Commissariat Corps of Waggoners, and by 1814 numbered fourteen troops with some 1,903 other ranks. When compared to the size of the army, these numbers were negligible, and the quality not impressive: Commissary Schaumann described them as 'Fat General Hamilton ... with his useless waggon corps'.[305] Their nickname 'Newgate Blues' is probably sufficient testimony of the regard in which they were held.

As the Treasury refused to establish a regular transport service run by the commissariat following the failure of the Royal Waggoners, the army had to continue to rely upon hired civilians, which in the Peninsula meant Spanish and Portuguese muleteers and ox-cart drivers, renowned neither for their honesty nor energy, and not regulated by military discipline. The Iberian carts, with fixed wheels and ungreased, rotating axles, were universally execrated for 'making the most horrible creaking that can be imagined ... almost sufficient to make anyone within reach of the sounds pray to be divested of the sense of hearing'.[306] They were also desperately slow, and not only did the transportation and commissariat difficulties cause problems for the troops by non-delivery of rations, but had a serious effect upon the conduct of war, exemplified by this from Wellington to Lord Liverpool:

'The contents of my last letters will have inclined you to expect that by this time I should have invested Ciudad Rodrigo. I thought that I should, after a fair calculation of the work to be done ... but after every allowance is made, we must expect disappointments when we have to deal with Portuguese and Spanish carters and muleteers ... What do you think of empty carts taking two days to go ten miles on a good road? After all, I am obliged to appear satisfied, or they would all desert! ... depending upon Portuguese and Spaniards for means of having what is required, I can scarcely venture to calculate the time which this operation will take ...'[307]

The incapacity of the organizers of the transport and commissariat, which because of Treasury parsimony Wellington was unable to reform, meant that he had to oversee even the most trivial arrangements:

'The ninety cars unemployed ... and the sixty-six expected to arrive this day, are to be sent on the 2nd to Almeida; fifty of them are to be loaded with the small stores required by Major Dickson, 106 must be loaded with what is required by Colonel Fletcher, and to move on the 3rd to Gallegos ... The mules (fifty) in the engineers' department to be sent on the 2nd to Almeida, to be loaded with engineers' tools, and to proceed on the 3rd to Gallegos, on the 4th to return to Almeida for the remainder of the tools, on the 5th to Gallegos, and on the 6th to Ciudad Rodrigo ... The gun bullocks now grazing at and in the neighbourhood of Celorico to go to Almeida as soon as possible to draw the guns from Almeida to Gallegos ...'[308]

That the commander of the entire army should have to arrange for the movements of each cart and virtually each mule demonstrates not only Wellington's energy and conscientiousness, but also the failings of the system.

Each battalion or regiment maintained its own transport, usually hired civilian wagons, to carry the heavy baggage. Presumably enough were rarely provided, so that (as shown by contemporary illustrations) the transport-wagons were often so overloaded as to be rendered unsafe: for example, one of the Royal Horse Guards' wagons overturned descending a hill near Wellingborough in June 1801, killing one of the women riding on it and injuring two others. Overloaded wagons made for precarious seats: a member of the 43rd fell off one en route to Harwich in May 1809 and was killed when the wheels went over him.

Units often carried quantities of their own munitions, supervision of which was sometimes lamentable. In June 1808, for example, a baggage-cart of the Usk Volunteers exploded on the road between Cardiff and Newport, the two soldiers in charge having allowed a sailor to sit on a cask of ammunition while smoking his pipe; the resulting tragedy killed the sailor and the two careless volunteers were 'dreadfully scorched'.[309] Very much worse was the devastation caused in Portsmouth in June 1809 when the 2nd Battalion, 8th Foot piled their baggage and seventeen barrels of powder on the beach, prior to embarkation for Walcheren. One barrel blew up when an old woman knocked out her pipe against it. Two taverns and a store were set on fire, and 'the effect was most dreadful. About 30 men, women and children were literally blown to atoms, and the remains of their bodies, limbs, and heads, are strewed in all directions. One poor fellow was blown over the whole of the buildings in Point-street; another against the wall of the Union Tavern, as high as the garret-window; the thigh of a third was blown as far as Broad-street point. Numbers of legs, arms, &c. have been seen, taken from the tops of the houses; and the whole presented a scene shocking beyond description.'[310] The other barrels were covered by burning debris, but this was extinguished by some sailors and a company of the Worcestershire Militia before an even more catastrophic explosion could occur.

However, the transportation of powder and shot was essential and only in rare cases did troops run out of ammunition, usually in situations where re-supply was difficult; although with contemporary tactics, volley-firing was not expected to be so protracted as to exhaust the ammunition carried by each man within a short period. Defensive actions were different: probably the most famous incident was the loss of La Haye Sainte at Waterloo, when the defenders were unable to hold the post at bayonet-point after running out of ammunition. Quite possibly this was due to their being armed largely with the Baker rifle, of a smaller calibre than the ordinary musket, so that the ammunition-wagons within reach (such as that driven into the beleaguered Hougoumont at the same action) might not have included rifle ammunition. Indeed, when Amos Norcott (who had commanded 2/95th at Waterloo) submitted a memorandum to the Horse Guards in 1816 relative to improvements in the equipment of rifle corps, he noted that existing pouches containing 52 rounds was 'a number infinitely too small for Riflemen to have in their possession'.[311] A less-celebrated incident concerned isolated companies of the 82nd and 92nd at Maya (25 July 1813), who held a knoll by pelting their attackers with stones after expending their ammunition.[312]

If the soldiers on campaign were often deprived by the commissariat of their few bodily comforts, they received hardly any of the spiritual variety. Until they were abolished in 1796, each regiment was supposed to have a regimental chaplain, but few clergymen paid to do the job actually served; in 1796, for example, the Revd. Peter Vataas (or Vatas) of the 14th Light Dragoons had been on paid leave for 52 years. At his death he was an octogenarian[313] and one of the oldest on the list of army chaplains, but his non-attendance on army duty was not unusual according to the ecclesiastical practices of the time: from 1747 he was minister of Caversham, Oxfordshire, and from 1780 was also rector of Warley Parva, Essex, to which parish he made only an annual visit!

Regimental chaplains were replaced by general chaplains for troops abroad, who were paid 10s. per diem; at home, civilian clergymen in the vicinity of barracks acted for the troops, for £25 per annum. The Duke of York established the Army Chaplains' Department in 1796, with John Gamble as Chaplain-General (the same man who devised the Gamble system of semaphore), but great difficulty was experienced in obtaining suitable clergymen prepared to accompany the army on active service. Some of them were extremely unimpressive, like the Light Division chaplain Parker in the Peninsula, 'with his tall, lank, ungainly figure, mounted on a starved, untrimmed, unfurnished horse ... the least calculated of any one I ever saw to excite devotion';[314] this wretched man was captured by the French when he failed to notice that the army had marched, but after keeping him for a couple of days the French realized how useless he was, and sent him back to the British minus his property and with a kick in the breeches.

From 1810 Wellington attempted to organize brigade or divisional chaplains to perform regular services for the Peninsula army, but few met with his approval, notable exceptions being Mr Denis at Lisbon and Samuel Briscall, chaplain at headquarters, of whom Wellington had so high an opinion that he appointed him his domestic chaplain in 1814. Briscall played almost a lone hand because of the lack of support he received and the failings of some of the other chaplains who did venture to join the field army. The strength of the Chaplains' Department at the conclusion of the Peninsular War illustrates the paucity of spiritual comfort available to the army: headed by the Chaplain-General, the Revd. Archdeacon John Owen (Gamble's successor, and like Briscall a brave and worthy man who performed his duty regardless of the dangers of enemy fire), the department comprised only 36 other clergymen. Of these, Briscall and fifteen others were with the Peninsula army, two were at Gibraltar, five in Sicily, and one each in Malta, Ceylon, Martinique, Guadeloupe and the Cape, among other overseas postings. Briscall and five others accompanied the army to Belgium for the 1815 campaign.

Some military chaplains seem to have tailored their preaching to their audience; for example, when the commander-in-chief's chaplain, the Revd. William Dakins, preached to the 2nd Foot Guards in Westminster Hall in February 1807, he took as his text 2 Chr.: xv.2: 'The Lord is with you, while ye be with Him; and if ye seek Him, he will be found of you; but if ye forsake Him, he will forsake you', perhaps an appropriate sentiment to express to soldiers. The Revd. William Pratt, rector of Jonesborough, County Armagh, published a booklet on the subject of military chaplaincy (*Divine Service for the Camp or Garrison...*) which noted that a military chaplain 'on parade ... must use common (I had almost said vulgar) language, intelligible to the meanest capacity', and emphasize morality, preparation for death, and discourage swearing: for 'God sees in the dark every bad action as well as every good one ... for every idle word you must give an account ... the smallest theft or the slightest falsehood will be entered in the everlasting book against you.' A chaplain should not, said Pratt, preach so as to be understood only by officers; anything suitable to their higher intellect should be reserved for the 'social hours'. When preaching to the 8th Foot he advanced a secular argument: that regimental pride should be such as to prevent any soldier from tarnishing its honour, or his own.

Although many of the army's Irish soldiers were Roman Catholics, and although most of their campaigning was in Catholic countries, they seem to have been concerned little with religion; as Wellington remarked, he had not seen a single act of worship performed by them, except in making the sign of the cross to induce the local people to give them wine! Presumably the 9th Foot were especially successful in this regard, as the inhabitants of the Peninsula mistook the regiment's badge of Britannia for a representation of the Virgin Mary, hence their nickname 'the Holy Boys'.

Perhaps because of the abolition of regimental chaplains, and the general neglect of things spiritual, nonconformism appealed to some rank and file, a few of whom even became lay preachers; John Wells of the 1st Foot Guards, for example, converted by hearing preaching at the Tottenham Court Road chapel, became a Baptist preacher and even published a sermon in 1807. Nonconformism was not universally popular; in 1794, for example, the first two toasts at a meeting of the Halifax Volunteers were 'Damnation to all dissenters and Methodists' and 'Down with all their meeting-houses, chapels and conventicles';[315] but those who were converted found the effect beneficial. For example, Sergeant John Stevenson of the 3rd Foot Guards, who described himself in the title of his memoirs 'sixteen years a Non-commissioned Officer, forty years a Wesleyan class leader',[316] recorded that he was greatly comforted in times of trial by the thought that, as at Talavera, the Lord could save them; and that even if the worst happened, it was better to be with Christ in Heaven than on earth. Such sentiments were not unique; Christopher Ludlam of the 59th, for example, who lost an arm at San Sebastian, stated that after his conversion he no longer feared going into battle, because 'sudden death would be sudden glory'.[317]

Wellington tolerated the spread of nonconformity, stating that prayer-meetings and sermons were a better way for the men to spend their time than indulging in the vices of the majority, but was not entirely easy with the idea of Methodist congregations in the army, lest they undermine discipline, and used the existence of such meetings as evidence to press for more efficient clergymen to be sent to the army. Indeed, nonconformist preachers could have dire effects upon their congregations: 'An itinerant preacher in the vicinity of Kensington told his congregation on Sunday last that all the great guns of Heaven were charged up to their muzzles and would shortly be fired off by the Angel Gabriel against the Devil's heir-at-law, Napoleon Bonaparte. All the old ladies fainted.'[318] For such reasons, attempts at evangelism among the military were sometimes regarded with suspicion. In 1821 a public meeting at the Goat Tavern, Pimlico, was called to establish 'a Friendly Society and Bethel Union for the purpose of promoting Religion and Morality among Soldiers', chaired by the Revd. Smith of Penzance and addressed by two Life Guards. This seemingly worthwhile enterprise was attacked in the press for being intent on overthrowing church and state, fomenting disaffection in the army and raising the 17th-century spectre of 'a praying army, and a synod of military saints'![319]

A similar attitude was taken by Captain Richard Drewe of the 73rd, who ordered one of his company to burn the Bible he carried, saying, 'Damn you, Sir, I'll let you know that your firelock is your Bible, and I am your God Almighty.'[320] Indeed, excessive religious feeling could have consequences as dire as having none at all: Sergeant Joseph Donaldson of the 94th told of a foul-tempered soldier who became a religious convert, and so despaired of his inability to control his violent outbursts that he took literally the message of Matt. 5: 30: 'And if thy right hand offend thee, cut it off, and cast it from thee; for it is profitable for thee that one of thy members should perish, and not that thy whole body should be cast into hell.' He borrowed a pioneer's axe and chopped off his right hand to prevent him sinning again in the same way.

To attend soldiers' physical comforts, most armies were accompanied by camp-followers. Officers were allowed to hire servants in the countries in which they campaigned, and the sliding scale of rations allowed them to be fed at government expense (subalterns received only one ration, but captains three – five in the Peninsula from September 1809 – majors seven, and so on). In addition to servants and grooms, many itinerants trailed behind an army, selling provisions and other services, often disruptive of discipline and composed of thieves and vagabonds. Regularly-appointed sutlers, who opened booths for the sale of provisions and small items, were common in camps at home, but rarely were present on campaign, and even home service was not without hazard: in July 1800, for example, Mr Cantrell, chief sutler at Swinley Camp, dropped dead from heatstroke and over-work.

Many of the hangers-on were a pestilential presence, plundering the army if they got the chance, stripping bodies in battle, and quite capable of murdering enemy wounded or indeed any unfortunate who tried to prevent their nefarious activities: 'Nothing, indeed, has ever astonished me more than the celerity with which these body-strippers execute their task. A man falls by your side, and the very next moment, if you chance to look round, he is as naked as when he came into the world, without your being able to guess by whom his garments have been taken.'[321] Not all the barbarities inflicted upon the helpless could be ascribed to camp-followers and muleteers, however (although the latter in the Peninsular War were renowned for their bad habits): Roderick Murchison of the 36th recorded a Portuguese volunteer who 'coolly unfolded before myself and others a large piece of brown paper, in which he had carefully folded up like a sandwich several pairs of *Frenchmen's ears* ...'[322]

Many of the rank and file were married, and when stationed at home it was usual for wives to live in the same barrack-rooms as the men, or in rarer cases in rented accommodation nearby. The number of married women allowed in a company was calculated for practical purposes: 'there never ought to be above three or four women in a company, that number is necessary to keep the linen, &c. in order, but more become a burthen'.[323] A soldier required his commanding officer's permission before he married, and some officers found the whole concept of married soldiers insupportable. Arthur Hill Trevor, who fought at Waterloo with the 33rd and rose to the rank of major-general, commented:

'... Soldiers' wives in Barracks, *poor things*! ... the evil begins ... where these wretched creatures are allowed to crowd into Barracks, with their starving children – some with families of 5, 6, 7 & 8 (I have this last number in the depot) taking up the room, bedding, tables, fires of the men – destroying their comfort, and all attempts at cleanliness – making the Soldiers discontented & driving them to the Canteen or Beer Shop and frequently to Desertion. Soldiers wives, are generally the greatest nuisances – and I have had more trouble to control their conduct & behaviour than I can describe – altogether the system of admitting them into the men's rooms is revolting to decency – and certainly demoralizing – there have been too many inducements held out for marriage among Soldiers and what is the consequence – the man is starved – his children are naked & starved – and the wife – she is not to be described – it is a sad case – and to keep up any thing like propriety I am obliged to appear hardhearted & stern – not allowing a woman of the Regiment to come near me. If she has any thing to say she must make her husband her attorney ...'[324]

When a unit went upon active service, only a few women were permitted to accompany then, often six per company but sometimes as few as four; for example, when the 1/1st Foot Guards departed for the Peninsula in September 1812, only four women per company were allowed to go with them, and only those without children. Those who went were usually selected by drawing lots, or as described by 'Flexible Grummet', by casting dice upon a drum-head prior to embarkation:

'... the soldiers had formed a circle, in the centre of which stood their officers round a drum, whilst outside the circle, at a short distance, a number of women were assembled in distinct groups, and all seemed eagerly watching the proceedings that were going on ... there was an unusual decorum, and silence almost approaching to melancholy ... and the women kept approaching stealthily towards the circle, and endeavouring to get a glimpse of what was passing within its bounds. some of them were old and withered, as if inured to hard service; others were younger, and their apparel was more gay ... the circle continued unbroken, except by the soldiers, who in turn quitted the ranks to advance to the centre; and I was surprised to hear the rattling of dice which were thrown on the drum-head, and the throws were frequently followed by a long drawing of the breath as if it had been held for several minutes, and sometimes by a hysterical laugh of joyous certainty. Some had returned to their stations with a smile upon their faces; others sad and dejected, and every moment seemed to produce an increased excitement ... By some it was treated as a matter of indifference, but those were generally the successful parties; but to others it seemed the issue between life and death.'[325]

Those who had to stay at home went to their native parishes, which supported them financially, although their plight was often sad, perhaps bereft of news of their husbands for years on end:

> 'Fond Mary, the while, in her spirits quite broken,
> Disturb'd in her sleep, and perplex'd in her mind,
> No letters from William, no tidings, no token ...'[326]

The women who did accompany the troops on campaign 'stuck to the army like bricks: averse to all military discipline, they impeded our progress at times very much'.[327] By any standards, they showed remarkable fortitude; Alexander Gordon wrote with admiration of the camp-followers on the retreat to Corunna: 'The women who followed the army displayed astonishing energy, but the sufferings they endured beggar all description. This night proved fatal to many of these unfortunate creatures. One of them, who had been delivered of twins only three days before, and another with an infant at her breast, were among the victims. The children were in both instances alive when discovered, and owed their preservation to the humanity of some infantry soldiers.'[328]

George Gleig found soldiers' wives as hard as the lives they led, which 'after they have for any length of time followed an army in the field, sadly unsexes them ... I recollect but one instance in which any symptoms of real sorrow were shown even by those whom the fate of a battle had rendered widows. Sixty women only being permitted to accompany a battalion, they are, of course, perfectly sure of getting as many husbands as they may choose; and hence few widows of soldiers continue in a state of widowhood for any unreasonable length of time ...'[329] Indeed, most bereaved widows married again, sometimes within hours of their loss, to prevent being returned home.

On campaign the wives became expert foragers, attended to laundry and cooking, and helped with the wounded, but despite the practical help they provided, at times the presence of families must have had a somewhat unsettling influence, as a witness of the troops' departure from Brussels before Waterloo described: 'Numbers were taking leave of their wives and children, perhaps for the last time, and many a veteran's rough cheek was wet with the tears of sorrow. One poor fellow, immediately under our windows, turned back again and again to bid his wife farewell, and take his baby once more in his arms; and I saw him hastily brush away a tear with the sleeve of his coat, as he gave her back the child for the last time, wrung her hand, and ran off to join his company ...'[330]

In addition to the 'official' wives, every unit on campaign accumulated a number of camp-followers or common-law wives. (Among the more usual ways of acquiring a companion was that adopted by the 4th Foot's mulatto big-drummer, who in March 1805, for the sum of 6d., purchased the wife of one of the men employed on the Shorncliffe canal. The low price is even more remarkable when it is considered that the lady in question was only about twenty years of age, and possessed of a good figure!) Such women acquired on campaign had no official status or support, and thus no rights to accompany their men at the conclusion of a campaign. At the end of the Peninsular War, these poor creatures were simply abandoned, mostly without money as the army's pay was months in arrears, although a small subscription was raised to assist them in returning the hundreds of miles to their homes, if homes they had. As Grattan remarked, those who had followed their menfolk through battlefields, staunched their wounds and shared all the rigours of campaign with fidelity and heroism, were now left on the beaches, staring at the disappearing ships which were bearing away their partners and only means of support. There was surely no more affecting scene at any time during the period, and 'there was much weeping and wailing on the part of the signoras'.[331]

Even the legally married were sometimes conveniently forgotten: in March 1803 James Hoskisson, a light dragoon sergeant, was transported for seven years for bigamy, having been absent from his wife for ten years on overseas service, and having then married a new wife on his return. The seriousness of the case may be gauged from the fact that the constable of Croydon was sent from there to Newcastle to ascertain if the original wife was who she was supposed to be! The plight of children was sometimes even worse: for example, in 1821 a girl pauper requested assistance from the Lord Mayor of London, being the child of a soldier of the 35th who, his wife having died from the hardships of following the regiment, had abandoned the child in Naples and returned home. As the man died shortly after, the girl found neither family nor resources at the end of her quest.

Some officers took their wives on campaign; the French officer and artist Baron Lejeune recorded a typical scene while a prisoner of the British in the Peninsula:

'It amused me to see the English officers riding about in uniform holding parasols above their heads ... I was surprised and amused to see several groups of officers, on the way back to their quarters, followed by a very picturesque though unusual suite. First came the captain in his scarlet uniform, mounted on a very fine horse, and carrying a big open parasol; then came his wife, in a pretty costume, with a very small straw hat, seated on a mule, holding up an umbrella and caressing a little black and tan King Charles spaniel on her knee, whilst she led by a blue ribbon a tame goat, which was to supply her night and morning with cream for her cup of tea. Beside Madame walked an Irish nurse, carrying slung across her shoulders a bassinet made of green silk, in which reposed an infant, the hope of the family. Behind Madame's mule stalked a huge grenadier, the faithful servant of the captain, with his musket over his shoulder, urging on with a stick the long-eared steed of his mistress. Behind him again came a donkey laden with the voluminous baggage of the family, surmounted by a tea-kettle and cage full of canaries, whilst a jockey or groom in livery brought up the rear, mounted on a sturdy English horse, with its hide gleaming like polished steel. The groom held a huge posting whip in one hand, the cracking of the lash of which made the donkey mend its pace, and at the same time kept order amongst the four or five spaniels and greyhounds which served as scouts to the captain during the march of his small cavalcade.'[332]

On many occasions, however, officers' wives shared the privations of those of the rank and file. One of the best-known was Eleanor, wife of Lieutenant-Colonel James Dalbiac of the 4th Dragoons, who followed him throughout the Peninsular War, sharing his tent when he had one, and at other times lying in the rain under a blanket. After Salamanca she went in search of her husband, wandering alone among the dead and wounded; 'I cannot conceive a more unpleasant situation for a woman to be in, particularly at night', according to Tomkinson.[333] Napier even mentioned her in his history, as 'an English lady of a gentle disposition and possessing a very delicate frame, [who] had braved the dangers, and endured the privations of two campaigns, with the patient fortitude which belongs only to her sex; and in this battle, forgetful of every thing but that strong affection which had so long supported her, she rode deep amidst the enemy's fire, trembling yet irresistibly impelled forwards by feelings more imperious than horror, more piercing than the fear of death.'[334]

Not all were so fortunate as to find their husbands unscathed after a battle: after Salamanca, the wife of Captain G. Prescott of the 7th, with her two children, searched for him among the wounded and slain. Not even her military background – she was the daughter of Colonel Skinner of the Newfoundland Fencibles – can have prepared her for finding him dead with a ball through the head. Ensign Thomas Deacon of the 2/73rd had his pregnant wife Martha and their three children with him in the Waterloo campaign. He was wounded at Quatre Bras, and Mrs Deacon, having searched the convoys of wounded, walked the entire distance to Brussels, in pouring rain and wearing only a black silk dress and shawl, with her three small children; having found her husband there, recovering from his injury, she gave birth to a girl on the day after Waterloo, the child being christened 'Waterloo Deacon'.

Officers' children were treated as befitted their status, but could be nuisances none the less: Francis Tidy's little daughter once cut open a drum to discover the source of the noise, and recalled vividly how ever after the drum-major would scowl and shake his stick at her. (A member of the regiment was once caught plying this tiny child with port wine in an effort to make her shout 'God save the King and down with the French'!)[335]

In the same way that many other ranks accumulated 'unofficial wives', a number of officers were accompanied by women to whom they were not married, although not surprisingly this is rarely mentioned in contemporary memoirs. Such ladies could be the cause of friction: George Sulivan of the 1st Life Guards, for example, seriously fell out with his commanding officer (Major Camac) when he took with him to the Peninsula a woman who had previously refused to accompany Camac![336]

During the Peninsular War, a number of Iberian ladies eloped with British officers, sometimes causing considerable trouble. For example, Lieutenant William Kelly of the 40th ran off with one Anna Ludovina Teixeira de Aguilar in 1813, and being pursued by her family's servants cut two fingers off one of them, 'which was an unfortunate circumstance'(!).[337] The girl's mother complained to Wellington, who wrote to Lowry Cole: 'I beg that you call upon Lieut. Kelly to restore the young lady to her family. If he should decline to do so upon your order, I beg you put him in close arrest, and then to take measures to remove the young lady from his power into that of her family ... as I cannot allow any officer of this army to be guilty of such a breach of the laws of Portugal as to carry away a young lady, and retain her in the cantonments of the army.'[338] Kelly, however, was legally married to Anna by the regimental priest of the 7th *Caçadores*, and she followed him throughout the remainder of the war.

The most celebrated Peninsula marriage was probably that of Harry Smith of the 95th with the girl he saved from the rampaging hordes after the fall of Badajoz, Juana Maria de Los Dolores de Leon, a descendant of Ponce de Leon, the discoverer of Florida. Although Juana was barely fourteen, the pair remained blissfully happy throughout Harry Smith's entire military service, proving Smith's friends wrong: 'Every day was an increase of joy ... both intoxicated in happiness. All my dearest friends ... were saying to themselves, "Alas! poor Harry Smith is lost, who was the example of a duty-officer previously. It is only natural he must neglect duty now".'[339] In the event, Juana became an invaluable support throughout Harry's distinguished career, and gave her name to the town of Ladysmith, the site of a siege as famous as that which had brought them together.

An elopement without such a felicitous ending was that of Jacintha Cherito, daughter of a prominent citizen of Campo Mayor, with Drum-Major Thorp of the 88th, a 'gentleman-ranker' from a wealthy Lancashire family. They were married against her family's wishes, and when her father went to the regiment to demand her return, they disguised her with a uniform and blackened face as a Negro cymbal-player in the band. Thorp was promoted to sergeant-major for heroism at Busaco, and set his heart on a commission so that his Jacintha would have a husband of social standing equal to her own. Consequently he set out to distinguish himself in every action, surviving four wounds, until after Orthes he was recommended for an ensigncy. Determined to prove himself worthy of it, at Toulouse he deliberately stood in the open, in full view of the French, waving his cap, until a roundshot cut him in two and hurled his remains into the air. On the following day the confirmation of his commission was received, and although Thorp never saw it, it enabled his wife to return to her family with the dignity of a widow of an officer and gentleman; and, in the eyes of all who knew him, of a hero.

Some of the army's women assumed a status higher than that of simple camp-followers. One was the remarkable Mrs Maguire, who saved the Colours of the King's Own from capture. A genuine 'daughter of the regiment', born within the sound of gunfire at Bunker's Hill, she was the wife of the 4th Foot's surgeon, and was aboard the transport *The Three Sisters* when it was captured by a French privateer off Land's End, en route from North America in 1797. To prevent the Colours from falling into French hands, Mrs Maguire wrapped them around her flat-irons and dropped them into the sea. Until an exchange of prisoners she was the only woman in the prison-camp at Brest, with her young son Francis, where she gave birth to a daughter. Surgeon Maguire transferred to the 69th before the Peninsular War, but the family connection with the 4th was maintained because in due course the child Francis was commissioned into it, and was killed in circumstances of great gallantry at the storming of San Sebastian. Mrs Maguire lived until 1857, the recipient of three pensions, one for her husband who died of yellow fever on service, one for Francis, and one for her son Peter who was lost at sea.

Officially, women were not employed in any military capacity, though at the height of the invasion danger at least two proposals were made to form units of women volunteers: in 1803 two hundred women from Neath, who stated that they were used to hard work such as coal-mining and road-repairing, requested light pikes to enable them to fight in the event of invasion, and in the same year a proposal was made to form 'a Corps of Ladies, in the present exigency of the country; and the Duchess of Gordon, it is said, has offered to command it'.[340] It is possible that a few women served in the army in the guise of men – there were known cases in the navy during this period, and it was reported that a woman served as a private in the Berkshire Militia for six years before she admitted her sex, having remained undiscovered by always sleeping in her clothes – but the most celebrated cases were before and after the Napoleonic Wars (Christian Davies, alias 'Mother Ross', of the Scots Greys in the late 17th and early 18th centuries, Hannah Snell in the mid-18th century, and the even more famous Dr James Barry, who became Inspector-General of Army Hospitals but who was revealed upon 'his' death in 1865 to have been a woman.) More unusual was a woman serving in a combat capacity when her sex was known, and probably the only example in British service was that of Madame de Bennes, from a genteel Norman family, who followed her husband into French royalist service in 1792, and after he was killed in 1793 had an additional motive for continuing the fight. Serving in the Damas Legion, which transferred from Dutch to British service in January 1795, she fought through The Netherlands campaign, much admired for 'the decency and propriety of her conduct, and ... for the intrepid courage which always led her to the most dangerous post'. Captured with the remnant of the unit at Quiberon, she was sentenced to be shot but escaped and reached London in December 1795, 'having no cloaths but a drummer's jacket, and two coarse woollen petticoats'.[341]

Few soldiers' dependants recorded their thoughts or emotions, and none perhaps with the same effect as Magdalene De Lancey, who recalled taking her final leave of her husband in July 1815:

'I had a stone placed, with simply his name and the circumstances of his death ... The burying-ground is in a sweet, quiet, retired spot ... quite out of sight among the fields, and no house but the grave-digger's cottage is near. Seeing my interest in that grave, he begged me to let him plant roses round it, and promised I should see it nicely kept when I returned ... At eleven o'clock that same day, I set out for England. That day, three months before, I was married.'[342]

10
'The Butcher's Bill'
THE MEDICAL SERVICES

SOLDIERS WHO WERE INJURED OR FELL ILL HAD TO RELY UPON THE mercies, rarely tender, of an inadequate medical service administering the often crude treatments of the period.

Primarily at the instigation of the Duke of York, in 1794 an Army Medical Board was formed for the better superintendence of the army's medical affairs. It consisted of the Surgeon-General, the Physician-General, and the Inspector-General of Hospitals; beneath them were the senior medical officers who served on campaign, the Inspectors and Deputy Inspectors of Hospitals. Next in the tier of command were the hospital staffs, physicians (the most senior), surgeons, their assistants and hospital mates. At the sharpest end of the trade were the regimental medical officers, each battalion or regiment having a surgeon (ranking as a captain) and two assistant surgeons (ranking as lieutenants); there were no trained orderlies or ambulance personnel.

Between the Physician-, Surgeon- and Inspector-Generals there was some duplication of responsibility, each selecting the personnel for his own department, and the latter choosing the regimental medical officers. There was in addition the Apothecary-General (whose office had been hereditary since 1747!), responsible for purchase and supply of medicines; although prior to 1796 regimental surgeons had been allowed a cash sum to buy their own medical supplies, which enabled them to make a profit. The purchase of non-medical supplies for use by the medical services was the responsibility of yet another department, that of the Purveyor-General.

Within the limits of contemporary medical knowledge, which saw amputation as the universal cure for an injured limb, and had little conception of the importance of hygiene, the system could have worked adequately had all its members been both capable and conscientious; which was not always the case. The higher echelons were occupied by many who were also civilian practitioners; John Rush, for example, inspector-general of regimental hospitals from 1798 until his death in 1801, had served in the American War and was then appointed surgeon to one of the troops of horse grenadiers, pay for which he drew until his appointment as inspector-general, even though the corps had been disbanded for a decade. Almost all his time after his return from America was spent in civilian practice in London, where he became one of the most eminent in his profession. Even regimental surgeons could maintain a private practice, if based in one location: John Leslie of the 3rd Foot Guards, for example, only resigned his appointment with the onset of old age and the increase of an extensive private practice which had grown as a result of his renowned skill. Private practices were presumably so much more lucrative than military service that those who possessed them might be tempted to concentrate on that part of their occupation; indeed, when the Physician-General was asked to investigate 'Walcheren fever', he declined on the grounds that he was unacquainted with the diseases of soldiers in camp and quarters!

There was often a shortage of competent medical officers. Dr Hugh Moises of the West Middlesex Militia wrote a devastating criticism of the training of assistant surgeons in 1799, remarking that before a tailor, shoemaker or carpenter could establish a business they had to undergo an apprenticeship, but only the most passing acquaintance with medical matters was needed for a man to be appointed as assistant-surgeon, via family connections or patronage, for example men who had served behind the counter of a country apothecary for a few months, or in a chemist's laboratory, or in one case a private soldier who had been a surgeon's servant. Such men, wrote Moises, would 'deal out his poisons to the aggravation of disease; and ... too frequently, deprive us of our dearest friends'.[343]

Such was the shortage of medical officers in the earlier stages of the French War that for the raid on Ostend a Mr Jarvis, a surgeon from Margate, volunteered to accompany the expedition and was mentioned in Eyre Coote's dispatch: 'His great attention was unremitting, and his conduct on this occasion is highly praiseworthy.'[344] Semi-trained junior medical officers were allowed to practise throughout the period: Thomas Austin of the 35th, who lost a leg in the Netherlands in February 1814, encountered many assistant-surgeons who were entirely inexperienced and were known by the nickname 'butchers' boys'.

Conversely, probably the huge majority of surgeons worked conscientiously within the bounds of what by later standards seems a most neglectful and inefficient system. One of the most important influences upon that system was the great humanitarian Dr James McGrigor, who was appointed Inspector-General of Hospitals in the Peninsula in 1811. He made constant attempts to better the condition of the infirm, and some idea of the controversies and acrimony which existed in the medical establishment can be gauged by an extract from a pamphlet written by McGrigor when Deputy Inspector of Army Hospitals, in reply to claims by the Surgeon-General's Deputy, Dr Nathaniel Bancroft, that only physicians were capable of supervising hospitals and that regimental surgeons were not, contrary to McGrigor's advocacy of regimental hospitals. McGrigor's passion for reform resulted in his use of language which could hardly be described as scientific: 'Away with such dark and assassin-like insinuations. Speak out like a man – I am full prepared to meet you. I challenge you to state any one circumstance, which can occasion me the least pain on recollection. And to compel you, if possible, to accept this challenge, I thus publicly declare, that, unless you do speak out, I shall regard you in no better light than that of a malignant and dastardly assassin.'[345]

Treatment of battle-casualties was only a minor part of the duties of medical officers, disease being a far greater scourge. As a comparison between casualties caused by disease and those incurred in combat, in the 7th Fuzileers during the Peninsular and New Orleans campaigns, 264 other ranks were killed in battle and 1,138 wounded; but 1,720 died in, or in transportation between, hospitals. As a background to the diseases to which soldiers succumbed, it is interesting to note that for the year beginning 15 December 1801, the following were the most common causes of death in London: consumption 4,078; convulsions 3,503; fevers 2,201; smallpox 1,579; old age 1,452; cough and whooping-cough 1,004; dropsy 845; asthma 639. (Out of 19,918 deaths, 8,304 were of children aged under five years; there were but ten deaths attributed to excessive drinking, one to fighting, one each killed by a bull and by a madman, but 112 drownings and 41 suicides.)

The most devastating sicknesses that ravaged the army were tropical fevers in the West Indies, which caused mortality of a huge degree, and 'Walcheren fever', apparently a malarial infection which recurred to such a degree that Wellington requested that no further ex-Walcheren battalions be sent to the Peninsula if their members were to fall ill so regularly. There were also ordinary 'camp fevers' which might originate on campaign but be brought home; for example, on their return from the Corunna campaign, the 10th Hussars brought typhus with them, which struck at Truro barracks and killed the venerable Sergeant Abraham McCrow of the 13th Light Dragoons, who had survived 33 years in the army only to be struck dead by disease at home. Conditions associated with such fevers could also be fatal: for example, Thomas Green of the 43rd cut his throat with a razor in September 1809, while in the grip of delirium which accompanied Walcheren fever. Such maladies were no respecters of rank, so it was presumably not a difference in care between the treatment of officers and other ranks which made them so fatal: for example, Walcheren fever killed Lieutenant-General Alexander Mackenzie Fraser, commander of the left wing of the expedition to the Scheldt.

Treatments for such illnesses were sometimes unusual: for example, the cure for 'putrid fever' was recorded as an infusion of rue, sage, mint, rosemary and wormwood in strong vinegar, with the addition of camphor dissolved in spirits of wine, this mixture to be wiped over the face and loins, with a bag of camphor to be carried near the stomach. Jonathan Leach of the 70th cured himself of yellow fever in Antigua by drinking a jug of boiling Madeira, 'a kill or cure business, and worthy only of a wild youth, who, in after-years, has often looked back with astonishment at his folly, and at the success which attended his mad-brained remedy'.[346]

Some ailments were generally peculiar to foreign service, such as the opthalmia (inflammation of the eyes) prevalent in Egypt. Another curious malady involved the 13th Foot, whose members were reported as becoming bald after an epidemic of fever at Gibraltar in 1805, for which the treatment was a daily application of rum and oil rubbed into the scalp (under strict supervision, presumably to prevent the sufferers from drinking the mixture instead). Many of the illnesses afflicting the army were brought on by ravaged constitutions and exhaustion, so that fatigue became an acknowledged cause of death; as was noted of Sergeant William Cheetham of the 2nd Foot Guards, who died at Badajoz in October 1809, they 'escaped destructive warfare only to engage that more formidable enemy disease, brought on by excessive marching and uncommon fatigue'.[347] Indeed, the rigours of active service were such as to ruin all but the most robust constitutions; many were like Captain Thomas Williams of the 24th, who died at home, worn out from active service, aged 22, whose 'zeal for the service proved too powerful for his constitution'.[348]

Some recommendations were made to prevent illness; for example; 'The Lieutenant-colonel earnestly recommends that no gentleman shall liee down to sleep while warm, or with wet feet; but, however fatigued, always to take time to cool gradually, and to put on his dry stockings and shoes. In case of being very wet, it is highly useful to rub the body and limbs with spirits, warm if possible, taking at the same time a mouthful, and not more, inwardly, diluted with warm water, if to be had.'[349] In addition to such advice on clothing and diet – an avoidance of green vegetables, for example, lest they occasion fluxes – more concrete measures included the Duke of York's instruction in November 1803 that commanding officers should ensure that serving soldiers or recruits who did not bear scars of smallpox or cowpox should be inoculated against the disease.

Tobacco was also recommended as a guard against illness: 'Smoking tobacco ought to be encouraged, particularly in cold, raw, and damp weather: It has a tendency to prevent infectious diseases; it kills the vermin with which camps are apt to be inflected, and it is almost the only way in which warmth can be admitted into a tent. The Dutch pipe, however, ought to be used, which prevents any risk of fire.'[350] Its morale value was described by Jonathan Leach, who wrote that only a campaigner could appreciate it fully: 'He must rise, wet to the skin and numbed with cold, from the lee side of a tree or hedge, where he has been shivering all night under a flood of rain – then let him light his cigar, and the warmth and comfort which it imparts is incredible ... or if he is marching on foot, rolling about in the ranks in a state between sleeping and waking – let him then apply his cigar, and he is awake again.'[351]

Malingering was another problem for medical officers. Feigning illness to get a medical discharge was apparently quite common, although recorded measures adopted were so appalling that they demonstrate the desperation of some individuals to escape from the army. The commonest practices included putting lime or snuff into the eye to fake opthalmia, jabbing a table-fork into the cornea to fake cataract, inserting silver nitrate into the eye to give the appearance of partial blindness, or a mixture of snuff and belladona to produce the effect of amaurosis (total blindness). Consumption could be feigned by drinking vinegar and lacerating the mouth to simulate the spitting of blood; varicose veins and swollen legs by tying a ligature around the limb; physconia or 'enlarged belly' by drinking mixtures of vinegar and chalk, or in India a mixture of fermenting toddy, rice-water and soap; and heart disease by inserting tobacco or garlic into the anus. One of the easiest conditions to aggravate was an external ulcer, by the application of nitric acid, copper acetate, yellow arsenic or quick-lime, and an unusual means of frustrating such malingering was adopted in the 7th Fuzileers in 1808. One W. Reginauld had suffered from an ulcerated leg for 3½ years until the limb was locked in a boot-shaped iron box, to prevent his administering the corrosive substance which had kept the ulcer open; once locked inside the iron boot the sore healed in twelve days, and the man received 500 lashes for malingering.[352] Another 'abominable conspiracy'[353] was reported in the 28th in July 1807, of opthalmia faked by the application of ointment in an attempt to gain a discharge and pension. Such endeavours even extended to self-mutilation: for example, in 1813 Thomas Beckwith of the 45th cut the tendons of his heel to make himself unfit for service; he was sentenced to 1,000 lashes for self-maiming but received only 550 before the punishment was stopped on a surgeon's instruction.

Accidental deaths and injuries were a constant drain upon the army, many from understandable causes, such as falling off, or being kicked or bitten by horses, having feet crushed by carts or artillery pieces, stumbles and falls, and even from being gored by a bullock when escorting ration-beef on the hoof. To such expected injuries as ruptures when manhandling artillery or wounds from exploding firearms, there could be added a catalogue of more bizarre occurrences, some arising from wilful stupidity, such as the killing of Corporal William Askew of the 85th in July 1810, in a prize-fight with another member of his regiment, Nathaniel French (a verdict of manslaughter was brought in, perhaps because the fight was not for sport but arose from a quarrel between the two); or the death of Cornet Bateson of the 12th Light Dragoons in September 1809 as a result of eating 'an immoderate quantity of nuts'[354] on his 21st birthday. Examples of other peculiar fatalities, all dating from 1807, include the deaths of Privates John Hodge and William Stock of the 3rd Dragoons, overcome by fumes in a foul well at Canterbury barracks; of Captain George Sargent of the 9th, shot by a highwayman near Petworth; and of Corporal Davis of the 2nd Dragoons, killed by the collapse of a whim-wham (merry-go-round) at Albrighton in Warwickshire. Another most singular accident killed Lieutenant Joseph Strachan of the 2/73rd on the march from Quatre Bras to Waterloo, when a whisp of standing corn became entangled in the musket-trigger of Private Jeremiah Bates. The musket fired and the officer was shot through the heart.

Lack of medical supervision must also have caused casualties: a most tragic example occurred in December 1807 when Drummer Joseph Holdham of the 77th obtained medicine from the military hospital at Lincoln, but not understanding the instructions gave the dose to his child instead of to his wife, for whom it was intended, with fatal results.

Medical officers were required most obviously in battle, where units might establish their own dressing-stations some distance in their rear, to which casualties had to make their own way, in the absence of ambulances or orderlies. The surgeons, however, usually followed their units closely, often risking their own lives: for example, Dr George Fryer charged with the 8th Light Dragoons at Laswaree, until in the midst of the fight he was told to get out of the way. Being short-sighted, he asked which way to go, then proceeded in the wrong direction and was almost captured.

Regimental bandsmen might be employed as stretcher-bearers, but in most cases those injured too severely to shift for themselves had to lie where they fell, often remaining for hours or even days before they were found by the parties usually sent out by each regiment after an action, to see who among the dead and dying could be helped. Otherwise, removal from the scene of action usually depended upon the goodwill of those in the immediate vicinity. George Simmons of the 95th was shot in the thigh at the Coa, and was saved from bleeding to death by William Napier (the historian), who used his neckerchief and a ramrod as a tourniquet, the sergeant who assisted him being shot through the head and killed as he worked. Some of Simmons' men placed him in a blanket and carried him away, defying 'Black Bob' Craufurd, who said that a battle was no time to be carrying off wounded officers; but they replied to the general, 'This is an officer of ours, and we must see him to safety before we leave him.' Such concern for their officers was in no way exceptional: Simmons was subsequently laid on the floor of a church, where a dying soldier of the 43rd insisted that he share his palliasse, as the man's 'noble nature would not allow him to die in peace when he saw an officer so humbled as to be laid near him on the bare stones. I have experienced many such kindnesses from soldiers, and indeed if I had not, I should not be alive to tell the tale.'[355]

The scenes in the rear areas of a battlefield were invariably confused and horrific, thronged with wounded staggering to the rear, surgeons performing first-aid, baggage-details, shirkers trying to appear busy so as to stay out of the firing-line, and the air as thick with rumours of victory and disaster as it was with powder-smoke at the front: 'In short, while everything is going on in front with the order and precision of a field-day, in rear everything is confusion worse confounded.'[356]

Many of the stragglers were a consequence of the haphazard nature of casualty-evacuation. A criticism made by a number of British writers of the Netherlandish and other 'foreign' troops at Waterloo was that they 'attended a wounded comrade in whole bands; one man carried the sufferer's cap, another his musket, a third his knapsack, and the bleeding invalid himself was often supported by as many friends as could possibly lay hands on him; most of these compassionate persons forgot to return to the field'. Contrary to what most of these critics imply, to a lesser degree this also occurred in British service, as the same writer continues of them, 'That, as usual, many of the men who escorted wounded officers and comrades to the rear stayed away, is true; others, however, returned; and numbers of officers and soldiers who had been wounded came back to the ranks after getting their wounds dressed. Those who, with the Belgians and other fugitives, hurried to the rear, carrying panic ... were men of the baggage-guards that had been stationed behind the army, and had never come within miles of the field of battle, but were frightened away by the absurd reports which the runaways spread in their flight.'[357]

Some unfortunates had to make long journeys before they received even first-aid. Colonel William Gooday Strutt of the 54th was wounded three times in an action in the West Indies, the most severe being a shot which broke his thigh in eleven places. He was carried more than twenty miles before any medical treatment could be obtained, seventeen hours after the injury, and was said to have been the only man to survive such an amputation in that part of the world. Ironically, some would have suffered less had they not been moved immediately after being wounded; hit in the neck by a musket-ball at Talavera, Colonel Alexander Gordon of the 83rd was being carried away for treatment when a shell fell on him and killed him on the spot. Even more tragic was the case of Sir Robert Macara, when commanding the 42nd at Quatre Bras; as he was being carried away, wounded, by four of his men, a party of Frenchmen made them prisoner, and recognizing Macara as an important officer by his decorations (he was a KCB), they immediately killed him and cut down his attendants.

Medical treatment near the battlefield was generally crude and totally unhygienic, dressing-stations consisting of little more than amputation-tables made from doors or boards, usually with piles of severed limbs lying about to sicken the senses of those observing or awaiting treatment. If performed competently, however, amputation could be the means of saving life, and some surgeons were so skilful that they could complete the task in moments, to lessen shock. George Napier was not so lucky when hit in the arm by a grapeshot at Ciudad Rodrigo:

'... I must confess that I did not bear the amputation of my arm as well as I ought to have done, for I made noise enough when the knife cut through my skin and flesh. It is no joke I assure you, but still it was a shame to say a word, as it is of no use ... Staff Surgeon Guthrie cut it off. However, for want of light, and from the number of amputations he had already performed, and other circumstances, his instruments were blunted, so it was a long time before the thing was finished, at least twenty minutes, and the pain was great. I then thanked him for his kindness, having sworn at him like a trooper while he was at it, to his great amusement, and I proceeded to find some place to lie down and rest, and after wandering and stumbling about the suburbs for upwards of an hour, I saw a light in a house, and on entering I found it full of soldiers, and a good fire blazing in the kitchen. As I went towards the fire I saw a figure wrapped up in a cloak sitting in the corner of the chimney place apparently in great pain. Upon nearer inspection I found this was my friend John Colborne, who had received a severe wound in the shoulder. Upon asking me if I was wounded, I showed him the stump of my arm, which so affected him, poor fellow, that he burst into tears. He was in such horrid pain, his spirits were quite sunk, and he could not stand the sight of my loss. How often afterwards did he wish *his* arm had been taken off, for the sufferings he went through for two years afterwards were very great. His arm was broken close up to the joint of the shoulder, which, and the scapula itself, were split. The ball remained in the joint for two years...'[358]

The fortitude of many wounded men was scarcely credible, especially those who suffered amputations without making a sound or gesture of pain. Edward Costello observed an operation after Waterloo which led him to remark that 'The French I have ever found to be brave, yet I cannot say they will undergo a surgical operation with that cool unflinching spirit of a British soldier. An incident which here came under my notice, may in some measure show the difference of the two nations. An English soldier belonging to the 1st Royal Dragoons, evidently an old weather-beaten warfarer, while undergoing the amputation of an arm below the elbow, held the injured limb with his other hand, without betraying the slightest emotion; near to him was a Frenchman bellowing most lustily while a surgeon was probing for a ball near his shoulder. When the Englishman's arm was amputated, he struck the bawling Frenchman a smart blow across his cheek with the bloody part of the lost limb, holding it at the handwrist, then said, "Take it, and make soup with it, and stop your damned bellowing."'[359]

Such fortitude, though scarcely credible, was by no means uncommon, and throughout the period there are countless records of wounded soldiers bearing surgical operations without flinching and without even groaning; Thomas Austin, for example, deliberately suppressed even a sigh as his leg was amputated, to give an example to the wounded around him. At times such bravery exceeded good sense: at Seringapatam, for example, Lieutenant-Colonel Edward Montagu of the Bengal Artillery was hit by a roundshot which shattered his arm; he left the trenches long enough for the limb to be amputated an inch from the shoulder, then immediately returned to his men. He died eight days later from an injury to the chest sustained at the same time.

Some of the injuries sustained in battle were so appalling that it is little short of miraculous that the victims survived both wounds and medical treatment. This was especially true in the case of multiple injuries: one Royal Horse Guard at Waterloo survived sixteen sabre and lance-wounds, including a fractured skull. Some injuries were truly bizarre: Captain Rawdon McCrea of the 87th's light company, for example, was wounded at Talavera when a musket-ball smashed his watch and carried part of the works into his groin. He was taken prisoner but after receiving great attention from the French, was returned to the British on the following day. He died from parts of the watch-mechanism having lodged deeper in the wound than had been thought. Conversely, miraculous escapes feature in some contemporary accounts, but perhaps few as remarkable as two at the same instant at Sorauren, when Captain Sempronius Stretton, commanding the 1/40th, was conversing with one of his sergeants. A roundshot hit the sergeant's knapsack and spun him around like a top, tearing the knapsack from his back and showering its contents in the air, yet leaving the man startled but unhurt. At the same moment a musket-ball struck Stretton's throat, tore his cravat, passed under the collar of his coat and out at the back, astonishingly without doing any damage.

After immediate first-aid, casualties might be carried to a nearby building nominated as a temporary hospital. George Gleig wandered into one such before New Orleans, where 'war loses its grandeur and show, and presents only a real picture of its effects. Every room ... was crowded with mangled wretches, and apparently in the most excruciating agonies. Prayers, groans, and, I grieve to add, the most horrid exclamations, smote upon the ear wherever I turned. Some lay at length upon straw, with eyes half closed and limbs motionless; some endeavouring to start up, shrieking with pain, while the wandering eye and incoherent speech of others indicated the loss of reason, and usually foretold the approach of death.' The officers lay in a separate room, where 'little better accommodation could be provided than to their inferiors'; Gleig found this especially distressing as all were his friends, including one with a musket-ball lodged in the spine, 'in the most dreadful agony, screaming out, and gnawing the covering under which he lay'.[360]

If a camp had been established before a battle, a fortunate officer might be carried to his own bed to save him lying in the open field. When William Grattan was shot through the body at Badajoz, two faithful men of his regiment bore him away and laid him on his own camp-bed, in which they found Nelly Carsons, his batman's wife, lying dead drunk. They laid the bleeding man alongside her, to keep him warm (!), and gave him a pig-skin of wine for use as a pillow, so that he would have refreshment at hand.

Transportation of casualties from the battlefield, and to more distant hospitals, was haphazard at best, and utilized any conveyance available, even if only unsprung bullock-carts whose jolting caused greater torture than the initial wounds, and served to kill many of the wounded. In the Peninsula the worthy James McGrigor badgered Wellington to improve the quality of casualty-evacuation, and was told that 'The only mode that I know of removing sick to the rear is in spring waggons, which are all applied to this service, and in aid of them bullock carts. I am aware that the drivers of the spring waggons are very irregular, and take but little care of their horses; but this, like many other evils in the service ... and, among others, the irregularities of the soldiers themselves, it is impossible for me to remedy, till the Mutiny Law and the whole system of the service is altered.'[361] However, McGrigor's establishment of prefabricated, portable hospitals, which accompanied the army, saved many thousands of wounded the long and often fatal trips to reach hospital in unsuitable vehicles.

Often casualties were unattended until they reached their destination: when George Simmons was moved after being wounded at the Coa, the only treatment he received was a bread poultice which he prepared himself from his own food, and he had to use his medical knowledge to dress his fellow-sufferers. Lack of medical supervision caused another horror: 'Soldiers in general are like children, and must be directed as such; although they were frequently told if they exposed their wounds, the flies would deposit their eggs upon them, still they took no notice ... so their wounds became completely alive with myriads of large maggots, the sight of which made me really shudder.'[362] Sergeant Cooper of the 7th was once ordered to take six fever patients to hospital, but, unable to find transport, 'I grew desperate. An empty car came up; I ordered my men to get into it, but the driver would not stop. I threw their knapsacks into the car; he threw them out again. Enraged, I drew my bayonet, took it by the small end, and swinging round, gave him such a blow on the mouth with the heavy end as stunned him. Then I got them into the car, and he drove on, holding his mouth as if he had got the *tic*.'[363]

Convoys of wounded were terrible to encounter. An 11th Light Dragoon recalled meeting a convoy of 700 wounded from Albuera, 'whose plight was as pitiable – I might have used a stronger expression and said horrible – as it is easy for the human imagination to conceive'. After their initial treatment they had been carried in carts under broiling sun, with no cover and no further dressing of their wounds, which 'were now in such a state as to defy description'. The dragoons helped them under cover, but the stench from the suppurating wounds was such that 'over and over again we were forced to quit the miserable patients in a hurry, and run out into the open air, in order to save ourselves from fainting'. For weeks afterwards the writer had no appetite, as all food 'seemed to be tainted with effluvia from these cankered wounds, and my dreams were all such as to make sleep a burden'.[364]

Medical treatment was often seriously delayed: after William Tomkinson had been wounded on 11 May 1809, the dried blood was not washed off his arm until 18 June, after the injury had been probed anew and a jacket-button extracted. Scarcity of dressings had caused his injuries to be bound up with tallow, and the bandages were only changed when the smell became too offensive. Indeed, to some extent life or death depended upon the willingness of a surgeon to pursue what others considered a hopeless case; for example, Charles Ward, barrack-master of Lewes, who died in February 1806, owed his last almost thirty years to the perseverance of surgeon Ramsey of the 16th, who treated Ward after he had been grievously wounded in the head at Pensacola, when other surgeons said he should be left to die in peace. A similar sentiment was expressed as Sir William DeLancey lay dying from the impact of a round-shot on his back after Waterloo, the treatment for his broken ribs being an application of leeches and a fomentation on the opposite side. DeLancey's young wife 'said, was it not a great pity to torment him. He[the surgeon] said he would not pretend to say that he thought it could be of much consequence', but that it would make her feel better after her husband's death to think that something had been done: 'It does no harm to be trying something'![365]

The horrors of military hospitals were recounted by John Cooper, who suffered from recurrent ague during his Peninsula service. At Elvas the ward had a door and a chimney but no ventilation, with twenty patients, of whom eighteen died, and orderlies mere 'brutes' who did not even treat the suppurating sores on his back, caused by the application of blisters having become infected. The convalescent ward, which could accommodate 1,700 men, was simply a huge, paved room with straw on the floor for those able to gather it. At Celorico the hospital was two small rooms containing twelve patients, most bawling with delirium, without a single chamber-pot, a blanket on the floor serving for that purpose, although some patients used the window instead. At Villa Viciosa the hospital was established in the corridors of a convent, with hardly any ventilation and logs burning in the corners of the building, almost stifling the patients with smoke; and with large tubs for sanitary use, apparently never emptied because the stench was overpowering.

Wounded officers were usually billeted in civilian houses or hotels, altogether more conducive to recuperation than the foul hospitals; unless, like Jonathan Leach of the 95th, they experienced 'The intolerable stench of the small fish called Sardinias, frying in villanously [sic] bad oil under the windows of the hotel [in Lisbon] where I lingered some weeks in a sad plight, called forth maledictions on the miscreants so employed which need not be committed to paper, but which will be fully understood by those whose olefactory nerves have been put to a similar test, by inhaling that detestable odour whilst on the bed of sickness.'[366] A billet in a civilian household could have compensations: George Simmons, shot through the liver at Waterloo, was put in the house of an English-speaking Protestant named Overman in Brussels, whose family showed him every kindness, including 'My dear little nurse [who] has never been ten minutes from me since I came to the house ... for ten nights together she never went to bed, but laid her head on my pillow ... I am with the best people in the world ...'[367]

Until the later stages of the Peninsular War, however, officers were not provided with free medical treatment: for example, George Wood of the 82nd, ill with a high fever and having no money with him, had to sell his shirts for a trifle to pay for the food to keep him alive. The consequences of leaving the wounded to shift for themselves could be extremely harsh. Ensign Gardner of the 1/4th was desperately wounded at the Nive on 11 December 1813, having been on active service only some three weeks and thus presumably scarcely familiar with routine. Following this wound he left the army to recoup his health, but immediately upon rejoining his battalion in early April 1814 was court-martialled for absenting himself without leave, even though in his injured state he could have been of no use to his battalion, and indeed his absence presumably actually reduced the demands on the medical department. Despite recommendations for clemency on account of his 'youth and inexperience',[368] he was cashiered.

Despite their tribulations, morale among the injured was often astonishingly high. For example, in February 1814 some 200 invalids disembarked at Plymouth Dock from the Peninsula: 'Many of the brave fellows were dreadfully mutilated, yet evinced a cheerfulness truly astonishing ... One fine fellow, a serjeant, who had both his legs shot away, facetiously desired those who carried him out of the boat not to *wet his feet*. Besides this, many were the jibes and jokes that occurred on their again touching British ground; and the whole party hobbled off to the Royal Military Hospital, with a gaiety of heart that surprised the spectators.'[369]

Despite the appalling nature of the wounds that the weaponry of the time could inflict, many men continued to serve after a terrible catalogue of injuries. For example, John Cowley of 48th, a labourer from Ravensthorpe, Northamptonshire, was wounded in the back by a shell-splinter at Badajoz, shot in the right leg and wounded by a splinter near the left eye at Salamanca, shot in the side at Vittoria, had his right forefinger shot off at Pampelona, and was shot through the left side of the neck at Toulouse. Officers could continue to serve though effectively crippled: for example, Captain John McCullock of the 95th lost the use of an arm by a shoulder injury at Foz de Arouce in March 1811, but rejoined the army in time to lose his good arm at Waterloo. He rejoined again and presented himself to Wellington with the words, 'Here I am, my lord; I have no longer an arm left to wield for my country, but I still wish to be allowed to serve it as best I can.'[370] He survived his subsequent promotion to major by only a short time, dying in 1818.

The decrepit state of a unit whose officers continued to serve despite injury is best conveyed by Kincaid's description of the company-commanders of his battalion at the end of the Peninsular War: 'Beckwith with a cork-leg – Pemberton and Manners with a shot each in the knee, making them as stiff as the other's tree one – Loftus Gray with a gash in the lip, and minus a portion of one heel, which made him march to the tune of dot and go one – Smith with a shot in the ankle – Eeles minus a thumb – Johnston, in addition to other shot holes, a stiff elbow, which deprived him of the power of disturbing his friends as a scratcher of Scotch reels upon the violin – Percival with a shot through his lungs. Hope with a grape-shot lacerated leg – and George Simmons with his riddled body held together by a pair of stays ... lest the burst of a sigh should snap it asunder ...'[371]

Even desperate head injuries would not necessarily cause an officer to retire: for example, Major-General Johnson, who commanded at New Ross, had been so severely wounded during the American War that even in 1798 he still wore a bandage across the forehead; and Lieutenant Purefoy Lockwood of the 30th, terribly wounded at Waterloo, had a silver plate engraved 'Bomb Proof' inset in his skull.

Mental illness afflicted some soldiers, but it is difficult to be certain how many cases could be attributed directly to the experiences of active service. Some were stated as having gone mad on campaign, such as Lieutenant Charles Baldock of the Royal Artillery, who in October 1812 was in such a state that 'nothing contented him but strutting about in my pelisse, and overturning all the apples etc. that he met with in the streets'.[372]

The army's suicides were usually ascribed to mental illness, for example that of Colonel Smith of the 3rd Garrison Battalion in September 1809, who had been recognized as insane and was excluded from all weapons, until he found a carving-knife with which he all but severed his head. Others were simply inexplicable, like that of Sergeant Welsh of the 77th in June of the same year, who after paying his company wedged a musket under his chin and pulled the trigger with a piece of string tied to his foot, 'and by the explosion his brains were blown up to the cieling [sic]. He was found a shocking spectacle.'[373] Such incidents could have bizarre consequences: when in October 1809 Private T. Tomlinson of the 6th Carabiniers killed himself with a pistol-shot through the head (presumably in fear of some unspecified disgrace), the Leeds coroner's jury decreed that it was suicide and he was ordered to be buried in a lane outside the town. His comrades objected that a man distinguished for bravery in action should be buried in unhallowed ground, interrupted the ceremony and jumped into the grave. Finding difficulty in removing the coffin, they broke it open, hauled out the body, and carried it to be interred in the grounds of the parish church.

Some cases of insanity were definitely attributed to the experiences of military service. One such was that of James Hadfield, who fired a shot at the king at Drury Lane Theatre in May 1800. Hadfield had no political motive (he was a member of no society save the Oddfellows), but was simply deranged as a result of receiving eight sabre-cuts to his head at Lincelles, when a member of the 15th Light Dragoons. At his trial his ex-officers testified in his defence, declaring that before his discharge he had been a good soldier, but unstable since his injury (at Croydon in 1796 he had attempted to stab one of his officers with a bayonet in a 'paroxysm of madness'). His delusions were proven (among others, he believed a cobbler named Truelock to be God), and his only stated wish was for an opportunity 'to have another cut at the French'. His loyalty was proven when interviewed by the Duke of York immediately after his apprehension at Drury Lane, when Hadfield exclaimed, on seeing the Duke, 'God bless him! he is the soldier's friend, and I love him';[374] amazingly, the Duke recognized him, Hadfield having once served as the Duke's orderly dragoon in the Netherlands. He was found not guilty by reason of his Lincelles injuries, but he was not the only victim of this sad and alarming case: a Mrs. Gunn, who sold fruit at the theatre, died of shock when the incident occurred. Altogether it was a bad day for the royal family: the shooting upset the king not at all, but three of the princesses were much distressed and Princess Amelia had fits; earlier in the day the king had narrowly escaped being shot at a field-day when a guardsman mistakenly loaded with a live instead of a blank cartridge; and on their return from Drury Lane the royal party was accosted by a shoemaker who 'hooted and hissed his Majesty in the most impudent and audacious manner'.[375]

A suspicion of insanity caused by military service must have been considered also in the case of Philip Nicholson, who shortly after his discharge from the 12th Light Dragoons 1812 (because of a broken wrist), for a motive neither he nor anyone else could explain, beat to death with a poker his employer, Thomson Bonar (father of the colonel of the Kent Local Militia) and his wife, at Chiselhurst on 30 May 1813. He was hanged on Pinenden Heath on 23 August. Equally sad were deaths like those of James Poole, a captain of the 2nd Dragoons, who in 1817 killed himself with a dose of opium; in this case his derangement was the direct result of a sabre-cut in the head which he received at Waterloo.

In addition to treating battle-casualties and the illnesses associated with active service, regimental surgeons had to contend with a host of other problems, such as the plague of poisonous centipedes encountered by the 88th in Portugal. On the march from Niza to Portalegre their assistant-surgeon was accosted by 'Mrs. Howley, the black cymbal-man's wife ... "Och! Doctor Jewel,

what will become of me? a *great baste of a santepetre* (the woman meant a cen-
tipede!) has bit my poor infant in the ——". The screams of young Sambo effectually drowned the last word delivered by Mrs. Howley; but it was too evident,
from appearances, that the part she alluded to was high up on the back of the
thigh, where a large protuberance was visible. The colour of the skin was much
altered; it could scarcely be said to be for the *worse*; but black as the little creature's hide was, it was manifest that Mrs. Howley, as well as her "infant", had
ample cause for complaint.'[376]

11
'These Unhappy Men'
THE FOREIGN CORPS

IN THE HOUSE OF LORDS DEBATE UPON THE EMIGRANT CORPS BILL ON 5 May 1794, the Duke of Bedford described the foreign refugees as 'these unhappy men',[377] and indeed foreigners were in general not especially well-regarded in Britain; many would have agreed with J. F. Neville, who upon seeing the head of the Princesse de Lamballe carried past on a pike in Paris, remarked, 'How grateful should I not be to the Almighty, for not having made me a Frenchman.'[378] To a certain extent such attitudes were encouraged by examples from the past:

> 'Since our Harrys and Neds three to one, we are told,
> Beat the Frenchmen upon their own Dunghill of old,
> Why should we not now, boys, be brave and as bold,
> Sing, A Fig for the Grand Buonaparte.'[379]

Nevertheless, large numbers of refugees from the French republican regime were given refuge in Britain, despite fears of espionage, which were usually unfounded. In 1807, for example, a Belgian dentist, M. Faleur of Woburn Place, was reported to be a French agent; upon investigation it was discovered that he was the victim of a plot hatched by another dentist, who thought that Faleur had stolen his formula for 'Artificial Mineral Teeth'. Another facet of the subject was revealed in July 1809 when a confidence trickster named Heath, under the pretence of belonging to the Alien Office, extorted £6 from a French milliner by pretending he could suppress a non-existent complaint against her; he was arrested when the lady became suspicious and sent for a law officer. Often the treatment of foreign refugees was more sympathetic than the law required: for example, one Francis Matthew was arraigned in August 1812 for sending threatening letters to members of the government. Matthew claimed to be of British parentage, but born in Spain, and to be an ex-officer of the Spanish army, in which he had fought against Britain. The magistrate explained that if this were true, he could be prosecuted for treason; but took the most lenient course instead, committing Matthew to Tothill-Fields Bridewell for six months, for being an alien without a licence to reside in Britain!

The concept of employing foreign troops was well-established, as testified by the large numbers of Germans who had fought under British command in the War of American Independence, hired by contract from the states which supplied them. In the early French Revolutionary Wars the practice was copied, to remedy shortages of numbers in the British Army, and more than 40,000 were paid by Britain in 1793–4, drawn from Hanover, Hesse-Cassel, Hesse-Darmstadt, Brunswick and Baden; although the Hanoverians were a different case in that they shared with Britain the same king and royal house. The Peace of Basel (5 April 1795) removed these troops from the war, and there was no further hiring of troops in this way.

An Act was passed in May 1794 which legalized the creation of regiments of foreigners, generally known by the term 'emigrant corps' or *émigrés;* it was hoped that refugees from the French Revolution would have a burning desire for revenge, which could be utilized productively. Some of these corps were of splendid calibre, including ex-members of the French royal army, with middle- and even upper-class men serving in the ranks; examples included the Comte de la Châtre's Loyal Emigrants, raised in England in 1793; and the Legions of Damas and Béon. There was no definite demarkation between the status of the various types of unit: most officers received commissions from the king or commander-in-chief, even those in units styled 'white cockade corps', from the white French royalist cockade they continued to wear, instead of the British black cockade. (These corps were organized mostly in 1794, but generally failed to reach their establishment and were disbanded in 1795.) Some foreign units were not regarded as emigrants, but were taken fully into the British Army (which permitted British officers in such units to receive half-pay, not normally accorded to ordinary foreign corps); examples of such 'British' foreign units were the Royal York Fusiliers (Hardy's), the York Rangers (Ramsey's), and the York Hussars (Irwin's).

All too many units, however, were the product of giving letters of service to foreign officers or minor nobles whose main objective was to make a profit, and who thus filled their units with unreliable mercenaries or prisoners of war, many of whom wished only to desert at the first opportunity. Such unreliable men were also enrolled in the good units because of the decline in numbers of genuine refugees, which resulted in a general lowering of standards. It would be a mistake, however, to regard all the mercenaries as having been unreliable: some were stalwart men who loyally served their paymaster despite an often bewildering series of changes of allegiance; for example, Corporal James Aldenrath of the 24th Foot, who died in March 1804, had served six foreign monarchs (Dutch, French and Austrian), but still served loyally in the British Army for more than 28 years.

Difficulties of recruiting on the continent multiplied after early reverses in the war, and as early as June 1795 recruiters in Hamburg had their headquarters attacked by a mob which thought they were trying to enveigle Hamburg residents into enlisting. Some recruiting had to be done in an almost covert manner, and an odd case occurred in January 1798 when a French emigrant was arrested in Britain after a journeyman bootmaker reported that his master, a foreigner, had made the emigrant a pair of boots with false soles, in which documents could be concealed. It was found that the emigrant was in fact carrying messages to aid British recruiting abroad; but the foreign bootmaker, having made boots obviously designed for espionage without reporting the case, was considered to be disaffected and was expelled from the country under the Alien Act!

Some of the emigrant corps fought with great distinction in the Netherlands, and suffered a peculiar handicap in that they risked execution if wounded or captured by the French republicans; this happened to some of the Loyal Emigrants in the Netherlands in 1794. The landing at Quiberon in 1795, an expedition undertaken almost exclusively by emigrant corps in the hope of instigating a royalist counter-revolution, ended in a similar manner: some units had been debased by the enlistment of ex-prisoners, the expedition was thoroughly mis-handled, and some 750 of the survivors were executed after they had surrendered.

This operation marked the end of the emigrant corps as a major resource, although many foreign units remained in existence. Before the evacuation of The Netherlands some Franco-Dutch corps were taken into British pay, and many Germans were enlisted, some of whom eventually passed into the British line's own foreign regiment, the 60th Royal Americans. Some foreign units were sent to the West Indies, where most were annihilated by disease; the remainder were permitted to fade away by the turn of the century, one of the best and among the last to survive being the York Hussars, disbanded in June 1802. The emigrants certainly brought a touch of the exotic to the British military establishment: for example, at a royal entertainment at Frogmore in July 1800, six Hungarians in the York Hussars performed for the royal party, 'two of them playing on the violin, while the other four performed the Pyrthical [Pyrrhic] Dance, agreeable to their own dancing, in boots and spurs. Their manner excited much pleasantry; their steps, in the *adagio* movements, were from heel to toe, and vice versa, with their hands placed to their sides; but, when the time changes, they jump and turn about with great activity, clapping their knees with their hands, and putting themselves in a hundred different attitudes'.[380]

They were not, however, welcomed universally. Some opposition in parliament criticized the expense involved, and others doubted their loyalty (hardly surprising when ex-prisoners were being enrolled). Suggestions that they had already betrayed one cause and country by entering British service were countered by *The True Briton* (17 April 1794) which questioned 'whether *usurpation* can be the Cause of any honest man, or whether the *Guillotine* may be called a man's *Country*? ... firm reliance may be placed in men who had virtue enough to abandon a set of wretches that murdered their Sovereign ... and who no longer considered that part of the earth as their Country, when disgraced by ravage, barbarity and despotism'. Others believed that the emigrants' desire for revenge would 'give rise to every thing sanguinary and cruel',[381] as stated by the Duke of Bedford in the House of Lords, and that the war would not be conducted in a civilized manner. In a parliamentary debate in May 1796, which resulted in the grant of a further £435,000 to support the foreign corps, Windham remarked that paying refugees as soldiers actually saved money, considering 'their former rank in life' and that military pay 'was not even equal to what they were entitled to from the liberality of this country'. Sheridan replied that he 'saw myself the foreign troops that were encamped near Southampton, dancing the carmagnol, and singing Ça ira [both expressions of republican sympathies]. If these were to experience our liberalities, let it be in a different manner from that of marshalling and keeping them as an army, which could answer no purpose.'[382]

Even though most foreign troops were permitted to be stationed only in the Isle of Wight and Channel Islands, not the mainland, relations between them and British units were not always cordial: for example, in April 1800 a violent row in an alehouse in Newport, Isle of Wight, between members of the Dutch Brigade and the North Hampshire Militia, led to two of the latter's grenadiers being stabbed to death. It was remarked especially that after this 'foul and unprovoked assassination', the officers of the North Hants were so vigilant that 'no symptoms of revengeful inclination, or riot, have appeared on the part of the British troops',[383] as if this were only to be expected.

Following the renewal of the war after the Peace of Amiens, foreign corps were again created (*The True Briton* remarked that they appeared so popular that the government would 'not hesitate to employ any foreign weapons that present themselves, from a *French Musquet* down to *an American Tomohawk'*!)[384]

Most notable was the King's German Legion, an integral part of the British Army. The Hanoverian army was disbanded after France overran the state in June 1803, and its personnel formed an important resource, motivated by loyalty to the royal house shared by both Britain and Hanover, and by revenge on the French. Authority was given to form a corps of Hanoverians styled 'The King's Germans', re-titled as the King's German Legion when the number of recruits from Hanover and other German states necessitated the expansion of the force. More recruits were gathered during the brief expedition to Hanover (November 1805-February 1806), and the Legion expanded ultimately to ten line and two light battalions, five cavalry regiments (originally light and heavy dragoons, later reorganized as light dragoons and hussars), and foot and horse artillery. The difficulty of finding German recruits led to the enlistment of other nationalities, but despite this the Legion maintained its splendid quality, with the cavalry in particular superior in most respects to all but the very best British units. Some 28,000 men served in its ranks, with a peak strength of more than 14,000 in mid-1812. Officers were mainly German, with a considerable leavening of British; in July 1815, for example, there were some 689 with German (or conceivably Dutch) names, 81 apparently British, 31 French and seven Italian, although in a number of cases the nationality is not certain from the name alone. The non-Hanoverians were discharged in 1814, so the KGL units at Waterloo were weaker than they had been.

Switzerland was another source of excellent recruits, a number of units being recruited by the British Minister in Berne, from the Swiss who had vainly tried to resist the French invasion. The regiments Roverea, Salis, Courten and Bachmann were amalgamated in 1801 under the colonel of Roverea's, Frederick de Watteville, who gave his name to the new regiment, which maintained its largely Swiss character throughout. The first Swiss regiment, De Roll's, was formed in 1794-5 by Baron de Roll who, like many of his original recruits, was an ex-Swiss guardsman of the French royal army; subsequently numbers of French and Germans were enlisted, but the unit retained its good reputation. A third Swiss corps was De Meuron's, raised for Dutch service in 1781, transferring to British pay in October 1795 upon the capture of Ceylon. Although latterly it enrolled many Germans, its essentially Swiss character was maintained, and like the others it served with considerable credit.

A few corps were relics of the period of the emigrants, notably the *Chasseurs Britanniques*, formed in 1801 and ultimately including not only Frenchmen but many other nationalities, including Italians, Poles, Croats and Swiss. Its combat record was good (especially distinguished at Fuentes de Oñoro), but its desertion record was so abysmal in the Peninsula that Wellington ordered that it should never be trusted with outpost duty. (Its members were not universally popular: William Hay encountered one of its officers, originally a deserter from the French army, who 'was a regular brute, and on more than one occasion, having shown a disposition to use a large clasp knife, he was not liked ...'[385] Dillon's Regiment was another, raised in northern Italy in 1795 by Edward Dillon, an officer of the French Irish brigade, its men originally French and Italian, but during its Mediterranean service it was largely re-formed from some 22 nationalities, mainly Italians and Spaniards but including even Turks and Albanians. Its conduct was good, but its desertion record much worse than that of the Swiss regiments.

The Mediterranean region provided a number of corps, including the Corsican Rangers, one of the best foreign regiments; the Sicilian regiment, which had as many British as foreign officers; the Calabrian Free Corps, formed in Sicily in 1809 from Italian insurgent refugees; and the two battalions of Greek Light Infantry, formed 1809 and 1812, for service in the Ionian islands and which also served in Montenegro and at Genoa in 1814. Another was one of the worst of all units in British service, Froberg's Regiment, raised in 1806 by the self-styled Count Froberg (his name was actually Montjoye), a rabble of 'foreigners of all sorts ... drawn together by the most criminal and disgraceful means; inveigled, crimped, pressed, deceived. Most of them were Greeks or wild Albanians...'[386] This wretched assembly was disbanded after a mutiny in Malta in April 1807, during which they shelled Valletta. In terms of wretchedness, however, they were perhaps even exceeded by the two 'Independent Companies of Foreigners' formed in 1812 from French prisoners of war, which ran riot at Hampton, Virginia, in 1813, committing virtually every excess known to man.

Another noted unit was the 'Black Legion' raised by Friedrich Wilhelm, Duke of Brunswick, for Austrian service in 1809, following the death of his father at Auerstädt when commanding the Prussian army, and after the incorporation of his state into Napoleon's Kingdom of Westphalia. To symbolize their desire for revenge and hatred of the French, the 'Black Legion' was dressed in that colour, with a death's head as their badge. After the collapse of Austria in 1809, the Legion made a remarkable march across Germany and joined the British fleet at the mouth of the Weser, entering British service to continue the fight: 'English and Brunswickers shook each other by the hand as if they had been long acquainted; the difference of language prevented indeed mutual explanations, but so much at least was understood, that all united in the common cause for the support of liberty and independence.'[387]

Unfortunately it was not possible to maintain this standard of recruit, and other nationalities were enrolled during the Peninsular War; even the Germans they obtained were not always of the best quality, as the King's German Legion normally got the cream. The Brunswickers continued to perform well in action, but had a dreadful record of desertion, so that Leach of the 95th remarked 'we had a lease of them but for a few weeks',[388] and Craufurd announced: 'If any of those gentlemen have a wish to go over to the enemy, let them express it, and I give them my word of honour I will grant them a pass to that effect instantly, for we are better without such.'[389] The Legion formed the basis for the new national army after the liberation of Brunswick, and as such served in the Waterloo campaign, the Duke being killed at Quatre Bras.

The standard of foreign recruit obtained latterly was criticized by Wellington, who complained at the lack of success in enticing reliable French troops to turn their coats: 'The desertion is terrible, and is quite unaccountable, particularly among the British troops. I am not astonished that the foreigners should go, as those who enlisted the foreigners for Government have taken them in general from the prisons ... Then we treat deserters in such a manner, that we have for the last three years got none from the enemy. There are at this moment from 800 to 900 in confinement at Lisbon, who have been there, I believe, two years ... This, and enlisting them at Lisbon for General Campbell's West India corps, have cured the French army of deserting to us.'[390]

The numbers of foreigners employed remained considerable, however: about one in ten of the army in 1804 and about one in eight as late as 1813, although the figure of 27 per cent which has been quoted for the latter year is very deceptive, as it includes the Portuguese army, never part of the British establishment. It is also deceptive to include colonial corps in such statistics: in the calculation for 25 May 1809, for example, the total of 30,397 foreigners falls to 19,467 when West Indian, Canadian and Manx units are deducted; of which 8,691 were members of the German Legion, but not included are foreigners serving in British regiments.

Other than problems with desertion, employment of the foreign corps involved few practical problems (although it was stated in 1796 that foreign soldiers would need more bread, being bigger eaters than Britons!), but there were slight difficulties with language. Officers' reports were usually comprehensible, though sometimes expressed in unusual terms ('He ordered the infantry into the digs, and the cavalry to make everlasting skirmish',[391]) but some confusion was inevitable. Typical was the story of the Corsican Ranger who took over a guard-post at Florian, Malta. Upon the guard-report for this fly-infested position some wag had entered in the column 'in charge of the guard' the words '10,000 musquitos'; upon reading this the Ranger inquired of the location of the magazine containing the 10,000 muskets he had to guard!

In addition to the foreigners in the 60th Foot, in 1805 another foreign regiment was taken into the line as the 97th Foot, originally Stuart's Minorca Regiment, composed of Germans and Swiss who had formed the Spanish garrison of Minorca, mostly ex-Austrian prisoners of war given to Spain by France. Despite their unusual origin, the regiment performed with great credit, as testified by the grant of the title 'The Queen's Germans'. Foreigners might also be enlisted in any British regiment, not just as musicians (of whom a large proportion were foreign), and not restricted just to those nationalities regarded as the most reliable (like Germans): for example, in 1812 a scheme was devised whereby each British company in the Peninsula might enrol ten Spaniards, provided that these were men not already under arms.

A number of officers were foreign, although it is difficult to establish nationality from the name alone: some with French names were the descendants of Huguenot refugees whose families had been British for several generations, and the considerable number of American birth were of British descent. They included members of prominent loyalist families, most notably perhaps Sir William DeLancey, but including others like Frederick Robinson, who commanded a brigade of the 5th Division in the Peninsular War, the son of Beverley Robinson who raised the Loyal Americans (in which Frederick received a commission at age 14), from a long-established Virginia family. Another was Sir John Stuart, born in Georgia while his father was superintendent of Indian affairs. Others were genuinely foreign, such as Captain Saint-

Pol of the 7th Fuzileers, who was killed at Badajoz, son of the Duke of Orléans; or Lieutenant Paul Ruffo of the 6th Dragoons, wounded at Waterloo, who was the Neapolitan Prince Castelcicala. Louis William de Rohan Chabot, Vicomte de Chabot, was the son of the Comte de Tarnac and an officer in the 9th Light Dragoons (he rose to the rank of major-general and married a sister of the Duke of Leinster); George Henry Nolcken, who as a godson of the king received a commission in the 3rd Foot Guards from the monarch, and who served as a captain in the 83rd at Talavera, was the son of the Swedish Minister at the British court.

None of these appear to have experienced any difficulties in serving in a foreign army, even though their relatives might be on the opposing side: George Napier recalled at Busaco a German officer in the French army who came to inquire about his brother who was serving in the 60th, only to find his dead body. A less melancholy anecdote concerned the Comte de Gramont, who as a captain in the 10th Hussars in southern France in 1814 commanded a picquet based in the ruins of his ancestral château at Bidache, where he was seen 'rambling around the premises, and among the debris, where, I doubt not, he found ample scope for meditation, and to ruminate on the caprice and instability of fortune'.[392] (This writer took care to remark in the Comte's defence that he was not 'a pure Frenchman', but one with a British mother!)

Despite the useful contribution made by the foreign members of the British army, their employment was regarded with circumspection in certain quarters, presumably from a perception of dubious military value and in some cases from fears of their use as a tool of repression; the infamous Wardle, for example, claimed in parliament in 1809 that their very existence was unconstitutional. This was the substance of an editorial comment in *The News* on 25 June 1809, following the deployment of German troopers in Ely in quelling a riot among local militiamen: 'We are amazed at the continual blindness of Government, in making use of foreign troops to quell any little disturbance in our own Army. We are astonished it does not strike Ministers as employing these in a most hateful, invidious office ...' Similarly, in February 1812 Lord Folkestone complained in the House of Commons of the number of foreigners in British regiments, drawing attention to the 108 foreigners he said were enrolled in the 10th Hussars.

Although the quality of the foreign corps was mixed, the reputation of the whole suffered from that of the very worst, and some British observers were unfairly dismissive: 'Dillon's regiment gained great honour in Egypt; if that can be called honour which is won by fighting against their own countrymen in a foreign land ... I never heard anything very particular about the Hompesch Hussars, except that they were fond of eating mice, and rather prone to desertion. They tell a story of one of the men of this corps, who deserted in Ireland, with his horse and arms; when stopped, and made prisoner, he was asked where he meant to go – he said he was riding to the frontier.'[393] George Simmons recalled that the sterling conduct of the *Chasseurs Britanniques* (whom he dismissed as 'renegade Frenchmen'!) at Fuentes de Oñoro was the cause of much amusement among the British: 'When Greek meets Greek then comes the tug of war'![394] (a slight misquotation from *The Rival Queens* by Nathaniel Lee, 1655-92).

Although never part of the British army, a brief mention should be made of the Portuguese, which troops represented a considerable proportion of Wellington's Peninsula army.

At the beginning of the Peninsular War, the Portuguese army was in a lamentable state after years of neglect, with uninterested officers and ill-equipped rank and file cowed into submission by beatings, hangings and shootings. The raw material, however, was promising, and as early as 1799 it was said that given competent leadership the Portuguese could make good soldiers, being 'robust, alert, and active ... They are exceedingly patient, sober ... and as capable as any of supporting the fatigue of war. On the other hand, they are lazy, dirty, and little accustomed to obey command ...'[395] For them to be able to contribute usefully to the British efforts in the Iberian peninsula, it was obvious that a complete reorganization was necessary, and equally that this could not be undertaken by the Portuguese alone, which necessitated the introduction of British officers and administration. Foreign leadership was quite usual in Portugal: noted commanders-in-chief had included Count Frederick of Lippe-Bückeburg who led the Portuguese in the war with Spain in 1762, and the Duke of Schomberg (from the Palatinate) a century earlier. More recent foreign commanders had been of little use, the Prince of Waldeck, the Prussian Count de Golz, and the French *émigrés* de la Rosière and the Comte de Viomenil, who had transferred from British service. At the time of the French invasion in 1807, the senior general officer of the Portuguese army, who accompanied the monarchy when it fled to Rio de Janeiro, where he died in April 1808, was General John Forbes of Skellater (Aberdeenshire), who had entered Portuguese service at the end of the Seven Years' War.

On 9 March 1809 a new commander-in-chief was installed, as Marshal of the Portuguese army: William Carr Beresford, illegitimate son of the 1st Marquess of Waterford, who had served in the British army from 1785 and had commanded the 88th Foot. He was an uninspired field commander, but an administrator of the highest calibre, which was exactly what the Portuguese army needed. His qualities were acknowledged by Wellington, who stated that after himself, Beresford would make the best commander of the Peninsula army: 'the ablest man I have yet seen with the army ... if it was a question of handling troops, some of you fellows might do as well, nay, better than he; but what we want now is some one to feed our troops, and I know no one fitter for the purpose than Beresford.'[396] Although the army was officially controlled by the Council of War (established 1643), with Wellington as supreme commander as Marshal-General of Portugal, all organization and administration resided in Beresford's hands.

While retaining the original regimental framework, Beresford instituted a complete overhaul of the Portuguese army; useless Portuguese officers were retired and numbers of British officers were given Portuguese commissions, being integrated at all levels, so that a Portuguese field officer had British above and below him in the chain of command, and vice versa: thus a British major would have a Portuguese colonel above him and a Portuguese senior captain below him, and a Portuguese brigade-commander would have British colonels under his control, and so on. From the beginning, there was evidence that martial spirit was not lacking among the rank and file, despite the wretched treatment they had received. In March 1809 the Portuguese General

Bernardino Freire, a somewhat timid man, depressed at the lack of support he had received from the Portuguese authorities, upon the appearance of the French quit his army in the face of threats against his person from his own troops. He was apprehended and flung into Braga gaol by his own second-in-command, the Prussian Baron Eben; from where Freire was dragged by a mob of angry militia and piked to death, together with his chief of engineers, his ADC and one of his secretaries. Stories were circulated that the latter provided evidence that Freire had been planning to collaborate with the French, although conceivably this was an attempt to excuse the unprecedented murder of a commanding general for being insufficiently zealous to hazard a contest with the enemy. (The rout of the Portuguese which followed at Braga tends to support Freire's opinions of the worthlessness of the force at his disposal, however!)

The qualities of the Portuguese troops were accentuated once they received regular pay, food, clothing and the comparatively decent treatment introduced by the British reforms. An Anglo-Portuguese staff officer, William Warre, wrote of the unreformed system as 'Portuguese cowards, who won't fight a 1/16th of a Frenchman with arms, but murder and plunder the wounded'; but by April 1809 was writing that 'The Portuguese troops immediately under the instruction of British officers are coming on very well ... The men may be made anything we please of, with proper management.' In September 1809 he commented that 'The men, poor fellows, are well enough, very obedient, willing, and patient, but also naturally dirty and careless of their persons, dreadfully sickly, and they have a natural softness, or want of fortitude ... The Officers, for the most part, are detestable, mean, ignorant ... It is incredible the mean little intrigues, the apathy, the want of military sentiment, Marshal Beresford has had to work against'; but by that December reported 'now there are really many very promising young Officers, and the old ones have in great measure been got rid of ... I am inclined to think that had [the rank and file] justice done unto them in the common comforts, I may say necessaries of life, clothing and food, they would make as good soldiers as any in the world. None are certainly more intelligent or willing, or bear hardships and privation more humbly.'[397]

This last point was confirmed by Wellington in 1813, writing that '... a system of order ... can be founded only on regular pay and food, and good care and clothing ... notwithstanding that the Portuguese are now the *fighting cocks* of the army, I believe we owe their merits more to the care we have taken of their pockets and bellies than to the instruction we have given them. In the end of the last campaign they behaved in many instances extremely ill, because they were in extreme misery, the Portuguese Government having neglected to pay them. I have forced the Portuguese Government to make arrangements to pay them regularly this year, and every body knows how they behave.'[398]

The regular army was backed by a militia, the greatest value of which was to release more reliable regular troops for field service. Wellington noted of the militia that 'the greater number of this description of men we have, the greater number of the better description we should have to dispose of',[399] and the Torres Vedras fortifications were designed to be held by militia alone, who 'being possessed of innate courage, were equal to defend a redoubt',[400] as the British engineer John Jones commented. Their efficiency in open combat was a different matter, however: in a General Order of 7 May 1812 Beresford was unreserved in his criticism of some militia, especially that of Oporto, which instead of defending the heights of Guarda threw away their arms and fled; two or three hundred were captured, some drowned in the Mondego, and about 1,600 deserted. Beresford instructed that the Colours should be taken from the guilty units and not restored until they had distinguished themselves in the presence of the enemy. Conversely, he was unstinting in his praise of those units that had behaved well; as, for example, was Brigadier-General Blunt in October 1810, after 150 militia and recruits had driven off a larger party of French marauders who were 'committing dreadful outrages on the few peasants that fell into their hands'; the officer in command, a Major Fenwick, commented 'in the warmest terms of the ardour of the recruits and militia ... but what, under circumstances, he has considered equally worthy of admiration, was to see resentments stifled, and the soldiers, alive only to the feelings of humanity, anxious to spare the enemy they had subdued'.[401] This was markedly different from the atrocities perpetrated by Spanish irregulars upon French troops in similar circumstances.

Conversely, the Portuguese *ordenanca* or *levée en masse* were criticized for being little more than brigands, armed with agricultural implements or bayonets on vine-poles, who massacred any unfortunate Frenchmen who fell into their hands. However, there was mitigation, as described by Andrew Halliday, Assistant Inspector of Hospitals of the Portuguese Army, in his book *The Present State of Portugal, and of the Portuguese Army* (1813): 'If we consider for a moment the sufferings which they have undergone, the ruin which has been heaped upon them by the invading army, their conduct must cease to appear as cruel. Can a father see his house burnt, his goods pillaged, and his daughters violated, and not sigh for revenge? Indeed, I am more astonished at the very moderation of the Portuguese peasantry, than at the cruelties I have heard recounted.'

The result of the re-organization, and the inherent characteristics of the Portuguese, was to produce an army infinitely superior to that which had existed before, especially in the calibre of infantry and artillery (the cavalry remained weak, and the commissariat 'infamous beyond all description'![402]) It also introduced light troops, almost totally lacking before, including the formation of the highly effective *Caçadore* or light battalions. Three of the twelve battalions formed were taken from British service in 1811, these originally part of the Loyal Lusitanian Legion, raised partly in Britain as a 'foreign corps' in 1808; it included originally light cavalry and artillery and was commanded by one of the period's more colourful and eccentric characters, Sir Robert Wilson, who was described by Wellington as being unable to speak the truth on any subject!

Portuguese troops comprised about one-third of the Peninsula field army, for example, 35 per cent in the Vittoria campaign, and almost the same proportion at Salamanca (18,017 as against 30,562 British and 3,360 Spaniards). They were integrated into the army at divisional level, the nationalities not usually mixed at brigade level (although exceptions were not unknown); thus a division usually comprised two or three British brigades and one of Portuguese. The British influence in the Portuguese army remained vital throughout: for example, Beresford's General Order of 25 December 1813, congratulating his troops on their conduct at the Nive and announcing that 'their comportment and valour are always superior to every trial however arduous and severe', mentioned by name 37 officers deserving of especial credit, of whom no less than 21 were Britons in Portuguese service.

Despite glowing tributes to the excellence of the Portuguese troops from many sources, some British observers remained unimpressed; Grattan, for example, believed that such remarks were made simply out of political necessity, and that as troops the Portuguese were inferior not only to the British but also to the French. Blakiston remarked that 'however they may have improved in discipline and confidence by their connection with the British army, yet they still require the presence of British troops to inspire them with sufficient courage to withstand the tried legions of France. The Portuguese are a patient good-tempered people, therefore very susceptible of discipline under good officers; and when so are very steady under arms, often presenting a more imposing appearance than our battalions ... but they are, in fact, a timid people, and to make them effective as soldiers, they should be brought into such a state of discipline that they will be more afraid of their officers than of the enemy.'[403] Some were even less charitable: Leach claimed that those who described the Portuguese as equal to the British and superior to the French 'must have been well aware of their absurdity'![404]

Characteristics often remarked upon were idleness and lack of cleanliness: 'dirty in their persons, filthy in their habits, obscene in their language, and vindictive in their tempers'.[405] Kincaid, who remarked that going from Portugal into Spain was like passing from the coal-hole into the parlour, claimed that any Portuguese fatigue-party consisted of one man working, one watching for the approach of an officer, and the remainder playing cards. Altogether more charitable, and probably more accurate, was William Warre, who wrote of Badajoz: 'The conduct of the Portuguese Troops during the whole Siege, and under very trying circumstances, has been most exemplary ... It is difficult to say which troops, the British or Portuguese, are most indifferent to danger. In both it is quite remarkable. But John goes to work more steadily and sullenly, while the Portuguese must be well led, and have his joke. They are great wits in their way, and, without the resolution and impenetrable sang froid of the British, which no danger can disturb, they have more patience and subordination under greater privations and hardship. But the Portuguese has not the bodily strength of the former, is naturally lazy, and is not used to our pickaxes and shovels. Therefore on the working-parties the British do their work better in half the time. But both seem equally careless of danger ...'[406]

12
'More than we can well dispose of'
COMMAND AND STAFF

ALTHOUGH IN 1811 WELLINGTON COULD WRITE IN REFERENCE TO generals with the Peninsula army that he had 'more than we can well dispose of',[407] by comparison with the large and sophisticated staff maintained by some armies, that of the British was both tiny and virtually untrained, despite the existence of a form of staff college in the Senior Department of the Royal Military College. Excluding general officers and commandants of garrisons, the only full-time staff officers were the ten Permanent Assistants of the Quartermaster-General's Department; all other posts were filled by officers on attachment from their regiments. No unit was expected to provide more than four officers for staff duty, but this was sometimes exceeded: at Waterloo, for example, the three regiments of Foot Guards had 28 officers thus employed. Such appointments were not always made from regiments engaged in the particular campaign: Sir James Lyon's brigade-major in the Waterloo campaign, for example, was Captain George Richter of the 1st Ceylon Regiment.

Most regular staff duties were divided between the departments of the Adjutant-General and Quartermaster-General. Officially, the former was responsible for equipment and discipline, and the latter for quarters, conveyance of troops and marches, but otherwise the tasks performed by each department were dependent largely upon the circumstances prevailing in any particular operation. In Wellington's Peninsula army, for example, the Quartermaster-General's department came to predominate for no better reason than its head, Sir George Murray, was more efficient than William Stewart, his equivalent in the Adjutant-General's Department. Even the highest-ranking members of these departments were listed under their regimental affiliations: in 1814, for example, the Adjutant-General (Lieutenant-General Harry Calvert) was listed as belonging to the 14th Foot (of which he was colonel), and the Quartermaster-General (Major-General J. W. Gordon) as belonging to the Royal African Corps, with his deputy from the Royal Staff Corps. On campaign and overseas, both departments were staffed by officers detached from their regiments, as Assistant- or Deputy-Assistant Adjutant- or Quartermaster-Generals (AAGs, DAAGs, AQMGs and DAQMGs).

The headquarters of an army on campaign would also include the commanders of Royal Artillery and Royal Engineers, Commissary-General, Deputy Paymaster-General, Judge-Advocate and head of medical services, each with a small staff; and the commanding general maintained a military secretary to assist with correspondence. Connecting headquarters and each brigade-commander were the brigade-majors, again officers detached from regimental duty.

Each general officer who had a command maintained a small personal staff or 'family', principally of aides-de-camp, generally young officers for use as couriers, to transmit his orders and reports, a duty requiring little experience, but courage and horsemanship. Each general officer was allowed at least one ADC at government expense (9s. 6d. per diem for subsistence), lieutenant-generals two and the commander of the forces three; subsistence for additional ADCs had to be paid from the general's pocket. ADCs were usually chosen by the general officer, not infrequently being relatives or offspring of friends; for example, Lord Hill's senior ADC in the Waterloo campaign was his brother, Lieutenant-Colonel Clement Hill, a captain in the Royal Horse Guards (as he had been in the Peninsula); and Sir Henry Clinton's senior ADC at the same time was his nephew, Captain Francis Dawkins of the 1st Foot Guards.

Messages were also carried by dragoon couriers, and in the later Peninsular War by a locally raised Corps of Guides, but it is surprising to note that even on campaign some communications were entrusted to the civilian postal services. This could be hazardous; for example, Wellington raged to Graham about an officer who 'is really too bad; this is the eighth day since he received the orders to collect the pontoon trains ... He put his letter into the Spanish post office, I conclude, directed in English, and without knowing whether the officer in charge of the pontoons is in communication with that post office; and there he left the matter. This is the way in which all our arrangements fail. The officers charged to send an order will not attend to that essential part of their duty, the mode of transmitting it.'[408]

Intelligence and reconnaissance were undertaken by officers operating as members of the Adjutant-General's or Quartermaster-General's departments, or under the personal orders of the army commander; although there was no single department responsible for these matters, at least in the Peninsular War, under Wellington's direction, the system worked so well that an officer could write that had the French army 'been in the bowels of the earth Lord Wellington would have found them out'.[409]

Short-range reconnaissance was undertaken by the light cavalry screen which shielded the army from the enemy, and at longer range by 'observing officers' who penetrated enemy lines. Four of these had a marked effect in the Peninsular War, most notably Colquhoun Grant of the 11th Foot, whom Wellington claimed was worth a brigade, and even when captured had such a network of contacts that he still returned his reports to headquarters; he escaped after four months. More intelligence was gleaned from deserters, from friendly 'correspondents' behind enemy lines (during the Peninsular War the rector of the Irish College in Salamanca, Dr Patrick Curtis, was especially valuable in reporting on the French army), and from captured dispatches. Wellington received many of these from Spanish guerrilla bands that had intercepted the French couriers, and although many were in code only a few were indecipherable, Major George Scovell of the Quartermaster-General's Department even breaking the 'Great Paris' cipher. All such reports were normally collated by members of the commander's personal staff (in Wellington's case, often by the commander himself), there being no specific department allocated to or trained in the evaluation of intelligence.

Without adequate maps, any general's movements were akin to stumbling in the dark; yet provision of these was accorded the lowest of priorities among all except the commanders who found themselves thus severely disadvantaged. Only civilian maps were available, many of mediocre quality (Graham remarked that Faden's map of the Iberian peninsula was fit only for burning), and the consequent ignorance of topography could have a serious effect upon a general's strategy; for example, Wellington stated that in the Vimeiro campaign his movements were dictated by the fact that he had to move over the only terrain of which he had a decent map.

The official neglect of the subject becomes evident from the fact that in August 1813 Wellington had to write personally to the Secretary at War: 'I write to Mr Smith by this occasion, to beg him to buy for me Cassini's Map of France, and likewise a map which it is said he has published of the Pyrenees. As I understand these maps are very scarce, I shall be obliged to your Lordship if you will assist him with the influence of Government in procuring them, as it is very desirable that I should have them.'[410] The lack of official concern on such matters is even more evident when it is realized that 'Mr Smith' was presumably Charles Culling Smith, husband of Wellington's sister Anne, showing that acquisition of the map was a private purchase on Wellington's own behalf! However, it must have been sent through official channels as Wellington later reported to Colonel Bunbury, Under-Secretary of State: 'I am very much obliged to you for the map of France, which, however, is of a shape that I cannot conveniently carry ... I have therefore had cut out the sheets, of which I enclose the numbers, containing the maps of the country immediately in my front, which I have had pasted upon linen by the Staff corps, and made to fold up according to the size enclosed. I shall be obliged to you if you will send me out, first, the numbers containing the maps of the country bordering on the Upper and Eastern Pyrenees ... I wish I may not require them; but it is as well to have them at all events. I beg pardon for giving you so much trouble; and I do it only because I am apprehensive that Mr Smith may not be in town; and it is desirable that no time should be lost.'[411]

An attempt was made to remedy the shortage of maps in the Peninsula by Sir George Murray, who employed 'sketching officers' to survey and map terrain to a constant scale of 3 inches to a mile, but as they could only map a fraction of the total area it only gave the British army a distinct advantage when operating in central Portugal.

Inadequacies in the staff system meant that generals might be troubled with trivia that could have been delegated had the personnel been available. After Maida, for example, Sir John Stuart was bothered by a query concerning 'a Sum of Money ... that was taken by your Order from the French by the 20th Regiment under the idea that the French soldiers had taken it out of the Military Chest that was found broken open at Monteleone ... there may be some Misrepresentation made of the Transaction on the Continent, that may perhaps make against the high Character of the British Troops ... what would you now wish to have done with it ...'[412] Such trivia was bearable for commanders of small armies, but with larger concerns it required the determination and industry of a Wellington to 'do the business of the day in the day' as he expressed it. For example, among four letters he wrote to Earl Bathurst (Secretary of State for War) on 19 September 1813 was one concerning the tin camp kettles of the 76th and 84th Foot, in which 'I beg leave to remark that there ought to be a canvass bag with each kettle', and another complaining about the delivery of parcels to the peninsula, in which 'I, among others, am suffering for it, not having even a second saddle'.[413]

Despite the imperfections of the staff system, one commodity of which there was no shortage was generals. In August 1814, for example, there were five field marshals, 116 generals, 223 lieutenant-generals, and 224 major-generals, of whom no more than a small number could be employed at any one time. Promotion to the rank of general officer might be made upon merit, though seniority was an equal factor, so that many only achieved the rank of major-general after their active career had ended. For example, in the 'blanket' promotions of 4 June 1814 (the king's birthday), at least 22 of the newly created lieutenant-generals were half-pay officers, many for regiments as diverse as the Angus Fencibles or York Hussars which had ceased to exist more than a decade, and at least twelve of the new major-generals, including two on half-pay before of the Horse Grenadier Guards which had been disbanded 26 years earlier. Nevertheless, general officers remained available for active duty despite their age: in 1814, for example, the senior general (Charles, 1st Marquess of Drogheda) was aged 84 and had held the rank for 21 years; William, 5th Marquess of Lothian, third in the list of generals, was aged 77 and had held that rank for seventeen years. Both the senior major-generals, George Morgan and James Hugonin, had held their ranks for 24 years. Many of these ancient warriors were prepared to serve even if unfit: at the height of the invasion-alarm in 1803, General John Reid wrote to the Adjutant-General to the effect that although he was in his 82nd year, deaf and infirm, he was ready to exercise his feeble arm if required, against the king's perfidious enemies on whom, he thanked God, he had never turned his back! (He was a noted musicologist, composer, and 'esteemed best gentleman German flute performer in England'!)[414]

Promotion above the rank of lieutenant-colonel was largely a matter of seniority, to some extent coming as a matter of course provided the officer lived long enough. The importance of the rule of seniority was demonstrated in 1814, when it was decided that Charles Stewart should be promoted to lieutenant-general after but four years as major-general (perhaps the fact that he was Castlereagh's brother was not entirely unconnected with this decision); to permit this promotion, it was necessary also to promote the 62 major-generals who were his seniors. Fortunately this could be achieved without expense, as general officers received no pay for their rank but subsisted upon the pay of their regimental rank or half-pay, and upon various offices which provided an income, such as the governorship of an overseas colony or garrison (for those on active service), or sinecure positions awarded at home, as unimportant as (for example) the deputy-governorship of Stirling Castle (in 1814 held by Lieutenant-General Samuel Graham, 27th Foot) or the governorship of Carlisle (held in 1814 by Major-General Robert Burne of the 36th Foot).

General officers were selected for active service by a mixture of seniority, influence or patronage, and talent; although the latter commodity would seem to have been somewhat irrelevant when the qualities of some generals are considered. In fairness, failings or merits obvious in retrospect may not have been so at the time, and to a degree this did give rise to criticisms over the question of patronage. For example, for all his successes in India (where warfare was perceived to be of a different nature), prior to his appointment to the Peninsula, Wellington's European command experience was limited only to the 1807 expedition to Copenhagen. At a meeting in Winchester in 1808, Cob-

bett claimed that this appointment had been made only because of family connections, as if the whole purpose were simply to increase the amount of public
money paid to the Wellesley family; and, casting his net wider, claimed that
not only did the Duke of York receive £50,700 per annum from various public
sources, but also enjoyed immense patronage; adding, somewhat maliciously,
'we all know but too well what patronage is worth'.[415]

A brief review of the commanders of the principal expeditions during
the period perhaps underlines the calibre of leadership experienced until the
advent of Wellington.

The expedition to the Netherlands in 1793 was led by the Duke of
York, then aged 28. He had studied in Prussia, but his lack of combat or command experience, or any apparent tactical talent was hardly compensated by
his undoubted bravery and the organizational ability he displayed later as commander-in-chief. However, he was meant to operate under an overall Allied
commander, and to redress any deficiences was given as his adjutant-general
(in effect chief of staff and adviser) Sir James Murray (better-known as Sir James
Pulteney, the name he assumed later). Murray was widely experienced, intelligent and knowledgeable, but lacked self-confidence and the energy to press his
case, had no grace or skill in handling subordinates, and concealed his abilities
under an uncouth manner and 'a grotesque and somewhat repulsive exterior'.[416] It is perhaps not coincidental that this was the campaign which taught
Wellington 'how not to do it', as he said.

Command in India was complicated by the influence of the East India
Company, and even successful commanders could be overlooked no matter
how brilliant their victories. Wellington went to India as a battalion-commander and was fortunate to demonstrate his developing talents under the aegis of
his brother, Richard Wellesley, Lord Mornington, the Governor-General. His
successes, however, garnered him less repute than similar victories in Europe
would have done, and other commanders experienced worse. General George
Harris, who commanded the force which defeated Tippoo of Mysore and captured Seringapatam, was recommended by Mornington for a peerage; instead,
he had a six-year legal battle over the amount of the Seringapatam prize-
money, and having declined an Irish peerage had to wait until 1815 before he
was given a barony. Although aged only 53 at the time of Seringapatam, he
returned home in 1800 and commanded in no further campaigns. Sir David
Baird, who led the storming of Seringapatam, was similarly denied the KB recommended by Mornington, and believed himself to be greatly slighted when
Arthur Wellesley was given the governorship of Seringapatam instead of himself. Thus he left India under something of a cloud, was dismissed as governor
of the Cape after being partly responsible for the South American débâcle, and
having succeeded to command at Corunna upon Moore's injury, lost it almost
immediately when he had an arm shot off. He received no further campaign
employment, probably due in part to personal and political enmities.

The Duke of York was again in command for the expedition to North
Holland in 1799, but the government insisted that all important decisions be
taken with reference to a Council of War, which perhaps served to compound
the Duke's failings. (Bunbury remarked that he was so brave that he would
have stood all day to be shot at, but lacked the other attributes of a good field
commander, was too good-natured to refuse advice and too prone to loose talk

after dinner in criticizing others, probably one reason for the lack of co-operation he received from the Russian commanders with whom he was supposed to act.) The Council of War included the sterling Sir Ralph Abercromby, one of the most worthy and well-liked commanders of the period, experienced, capable and a great humanitarian: he had refused to fight against the American colonists in a war he regarded as fratricide, and had attempted to suppress agitation in Ireland without instituting repression. He was, however, 65 years of age and extremely near-sighted, his shaggy eyebrows giving the impression of a good-natured lion; he was beloved by all who served under him, according to Bunbury. The remainder of the Council of War was undistinguished. The best was David Dundas, 'Old Pivot' of the drill-book, skilled if somewhat hidebound, as austere and dry as his thin, aged frame suggested (he was aged 64). The others were Sir James Murray Pulteney; the Russian commander (one of whom was captured at the start of the campaign, the other not inclined to co-operate with the Duke); and Major-General Lord Chatham, son of the Elder Pitt and brother of the prime minister, a member of the cabinet (as Lord President of the Council), 'a very gentleman-like man ... but he was excessively indolent and had no military experience whatever'.[417] With the conduct of the campaign dependent upon the deliberations of such a committee, it is perhaps hardly surprising that little was achieved.

Abercromby led the expedition to Egypt in 1801, undeniably the best man for the task, but handicapped by the conflicting directions he received from the government, in the person of Henry Dundas. Political direction, even incapacity, is a different subject from matters of military leadership, but Abercromby's own remark reflects appropriately on much political direction throughout the period: 'There are risks in a British warfare unknown in any other service'![418] After Abercromby's death, and upon his recommendation, command passed to Major-General Hely Hutchinson, brave and knowledgeable but virtually unknown to the army, suffering from poor health and with extremely defective eyesight. He became disliked for an ungracious manner and violent temper, was not respected because of his slovenly dress, and his conduct of the campaign provoked such vehement unrest among his subordinates that a plan was hatched to deprive him of command, which apparently failed only because John Moore would have none of it.

For operations in the Mediterranean in 1805, Sir James Craig was selected to command. Previously the Duke of York's chief of staff in the Netherlands in 1794, he had led the successful expedition to the Cape in 1795. He was, as described by Bunbury, experienced and skilled, short but a muscular 'pocket Hercules',[419] unpopular for his quick temper and pomposity, but a kind and generous friend. The forces in the Mediterranean were to co-operate with their allies, the overall commander being the Russian General Lacy, a septuagenarian of Irish descent who spoke in an almost impenetrable brogue, showed no signs of ever having possessed much in the way of intellect, and who attended councils of war with his nightcap, which he would put on and go to sleep while others discussed strategy. Unfortunately, Craig had only been sent to the Mediterranean in the hope that the climate would allow him to recover his health; and in this unpromising atmosphere it duly broke down, and he returned home in April 1806. During the resulting hiatus in command, the British commander in Calabria, Sir John Stuart, won his victory at Maida. He was not without talent but excessively vain and appeared possessed of little idea of the requisites of command: he did little at Maida and as the French retired became paralysed with joy, perhaps concentrating on visions of fame, so that his staff had to manage as best they could. Stuart was disappointed by the arrival of Craig's successor, Lieutenant-General Henry Fox, brother of Charles James Fox (who served as Grenville's foreign secretary for a short time before his death in that year); Henry Fox was a kindly old man but neither on grounds of age, health nor talent was he truly fitted for the post of commander-in-chief in the Mediterranean, and the government sent out Sir John Moore as his deputy. As Moore was obviously a rival to Stuart, and incomparably more talented, Stuart went home to a hero's reception. He returned to the Mediterranean later, and served there until 1810, without a perceptible change in his abilities.

The South American foray was perhaps the most absurd operation undertaken during the period, begun without government sanction and continued when temporary success concealed its essential folly. The first reinforcement for the unauthorized expedition was commanded by Sir Samuel Auchmuty, who was considered too junior to command the whole affair. As commander, Windham favoured either Sir John Stuart or Robert Craufurd, but the Duke of York objected to the former on account of character and the latter as being junior to Auchmuty; so a true incompetent was selected instead, the ex-Inspector-General of Recruiting, Lieutenant-General John Whitelocke. He had served effectively in the West Indies but was arrogant, over-confident and rude, and earned the contempt not only of his officers but also the rank and file, with whom he tried to ingratiate himself by the use of coarse language. After the attack on Buenos Ayres had failed so disastrously, he was court-martialled and found 'totally unfit and unworthy to serve His Majesty in any military capacity whatever', a singular fate for a general officer during the period. He was execrated within the army – a popular toast was 'Grey hairs but no White Locks' – and so odious was his reputation that when the New Orleans expedition called to provision at São Miguel in the Azores in 1814, where it was rumoured that Whitelocke was living under an assumed name, the entire landing-party (soldiers and sailors) chased an unfortunate inhabitant who happened to resemble Whitelocke, who in fear of his life just managed to outdistance his pursuers!

For the expedition to Denmark, the 1st Earl Cathcart was chosen for command; he had led the brief expedition to Hanover, and his Danish duty had interrupted his period as commander-in-chief in Scotland. His greatest aid during the Danish expedition was Sir Arthur Wellesley, returned home from his triumphs in India; and Cathcart's next important service was not in a military capacity but as ambassador to Russia.

There was conflict between government and Horse Guards over the choice of commander for the expedition to the Iberian peninsula. The government appears to have favoured Wellesley from the outset (his military talents were obvious and he was a supporter of the administration), whereas the Duke of York seems to have favoured Sir John Moore, who was regarded by the government as a capable officer but a somewhat troublesome man and, as a Whig, a political opponent. An inspirational leader with a fine service record, and regarded almost with idolatry by those under his command, Moore was selected to command an expedition to Sweden. This was abandoned when it became obvious that the Swedish king was insane and impossible to co-operate with, but when the expedition was directed to the Peninsula instead, Moore could not be removed from command. To limit his power, two superannuated officers were appointed over both him and Wellesley (who had landed in Portugal in August 1808). Neither of these two, Sir Hew Dalrymple (governor of Gibraltar) and his deputy Sir Harry Burrard, were totally incompetent, but they could not in any way compare with Wellesley or Moore. Wellesley won a significant victory at Vimeiro before 'Dowager' Dalrymple and 'Betty' Burrard arrived, but these then threw away the success by allowing the French to escape by the shameful Convention of Cintra. All three were recalled for an inquiry (from which Wellesley alone was exonerated), leaving Moore in command in the Peninsula. Wellesley would have been sent back there even had Moore not been killed at Corunna, a tragic loss of a thoroughly decent man and a very considerable soldier; and it is a mark of the affection in which he was held that even as tough an old soldier as Thomas Graham burst into tears when speaking of him, as long as 25 years afterwards.

Thereafter, command of the Peninsula army was vested in the most capable hands of Sir Arthur Wellesley, soon to be known as Wellington. It is, perhaps, a reflection upon his talent, dedication and tireless energy that from the period of his command British military fortunes scarcely ever took a backward step, in great contrast to previous campaigns distinguished mainly by the performance in adversity of the ordinary soldier. Even later, success was frequently dependent upon Wellington's personal control, although the only major reverse during the later period was the failure of the Walcheren expedition. Its military head was the Earl of Chatham, mentioned previously, whose appointment was as much for political reasons as military. He was a sound head in cabinet and had been a capable administrator as Master-General of the Ordnance, but showed no great tactical ability and was renowned for his indolence and bad time-keeping (which led to his nickname 'the late Lord Chatham'). Nevertheless, the failure of the Walcheren expedition cannot be ascribed to him: he was given an impossible task.

An important factor in the success of a commander was the confidence in which he was held by his men. In this regard, probably no commander since Marlborough had been so trusted as Wellington. He was not 'loved', for his nature was perceived as somewhat aloof, even cold; but admiration for him was boundless, as was the certainty that he would hazard no lives unnecessarily, and would see his men well-fed and equipped wherever possible. Kincaid probably best articulated the sentiments of almost the entire army:

'The destinies not only of England but of Europe ... all hinged on the shoulders of one man: that man was Wellington! I believe there were few even of those who served under him capable of knowing, still less of appreciating, the nature of the master-mind which there, with God's assistance, ruled all things; for he was not only the head of the army but obliged to descend to the responsibility of every department in it. In the different branches of their various duties, he received the officers in charge, as ignorant as schoolboys, and, by his energy and unwearied perseverance, he made them what they became – the most renowned army that Europe ever saw. Wherever he went at its head, glory followed its steps – wherever he was not – I will not say disgrace, but something akin to it ensued ... in all his battles Lord Wellington appeared to us never to leave anything to chance. However desperate the undertaking – whether suffering from momentary defeat, or imprudently hurried on by partial success – we ever felt confident that a redeeming power was at hand, nor were we ever deceived. Those only, too, who have served under such a mastermind and one of inferior calibre can appreciate the difference in a physical as well as a moral point of view – for when in the presence of the enemy, under him, we were never deprived of our personal comforts until prudence rendered it necessary, and they were always restored to us again at the earliest possible moment. Under the temporary command of others we have been deprived of our baggage for weeks through the timidity of our chief, and without the shadow of necessity; and it is astonishing in what a degree the vacillation and want of confidence in a commander descends into the different ranks.'[420]

Wellington's demeanour was important in this regard; Moyle Sherer mentioned particularly his simplicity of manner when giving orders, exuding confidence which was transmitted to those who heard him: 'He has nothing of the truncheon about him; nothing full-mouthed, important, or fussy: his orders, on the field, are all short, quick, clear, and to the purpose ... "If they attempt this point again, Hill, you will give them a volley, and charge bayonets; but don't let your people follow them too far down the hill"...'[421]

That the confidence extended to the lowest ranks is confirmed in countless testimonies. When George Gleig first saw Wellington, it was not his bearing or plain dress which attracted him, but the shouts of 'Douro!, Douro!' from veterans who recognized him; to which Wellington took off his hat and bowed! Tomkinson overheard two privates of the Light Division referring to their commander as 'that long-nosed beggar that licks the French';[422] and his reputation was exemplified by John Cooper, who writing of Albuera remarked that the army's confidence would have improved had Wellington been there: as Fusilier Horsefall remarked to Cooper as they marched to the attack, 'Whore's ar Arthur? Aw wish he wor here.'[423] More moving was the account of Wellington's visit to a hospital at Elvas in 1812, 'when at that moment a poor soldier was undergoing the ceremony of amputation. The operation upon his leg not having been finished, so soon as he had recognized the commander, he cried out to the surgeon, "Stop! stop your duty for a minute!" and the poor fellow, with all the rest of the wounded, cheered his Lordship three times, who, pulling out his pocket handkerchief, ran out of the hospital with a feeling that does him more honour than if he had been stiled the conqueror of the world.'[424] In truth, Kincaid's famous phrase would have been echoed throughout the army: 'We would rather see his long nose in the fight than a reinforcement of ten thousand men any day.'[425]

Even after many victories, however, Wellington's popularity was not universal at home, the political opponents of the Wellesley family being disinclined to recognize his achievements. For example, when in the House of Lords in January 1810, Liverpool moved a vote of thanks to Wellington and his army for Talavera, Lords Grosvenor, Grey and Grenville opposed it, the latter declaring that he would vote for any expression of approbation to the officers and troops, except to Wellington. Similar ingratitude was observed in May 1811 when the Court of Common Council in London voted Wellington a sword worth 200 guineas; several members objected, saying that 'the Wellesley family had been sufficiently paid'.[426] Such ungenerosity attracted opprobrium:

'Though foul-mouth'd Faction thy fair fame abuse,
And squinting Envy at thy merit sneer;
Candour and Truth disdain their sordid views –
To every friend of Freedom thou art dear.'[427]

If Wellington suffered for his kinship with his brother Richard, Marquess Wellesley, the reverse was not the case: on the day when news of the victory of Salamanca was received in London, a crowd in the Strand recognized the Marquess in his carriage; they took out the horses and manually dragged the carriage to Apsley House in a fervour of reflected glory.

As successes multiplied, so the criticism diminished. When in February 1812 it was proposed in parliament to vote an annuity of £2,000 to Wellington, Sir Francis Burdett declared that, although he 'professed himself to be uninformed on military matters', he thought that not enough had been achieved for the resources deployed. Canning put him firmly in his place by stating that Wellington's services represented 'to the Portuguese the salvation of their country, and to the Spaniards a source of hope'; and to the suggestion that some other means should be found to reward him, he said that 'the reward of Lord Wellington ought to be like his services, clear as the day, and open to the eyes of the nation and the world'.[428] The motion was carried with but one dissenting vote, Burdett's. In May 1814 the government proposed to grant Wellington £300,000 to purchase an estate, and an annuity of £13,000, the latter to cease when the annual income began to flow from the estate. That inveterate critic of the government, Samuel Whitbread, duly objected – but on the grounds that it was not enough! Another stated that half a million pounds would not be too much, but when the Chancellor of the Exchequer reminded members that 'they were giving away the money of their constituents' the proposal was amended to £400,000. (Annuities of £2,000 to Lords Hill, Beresford and Lynedoch were also criticized as too small, Sir Charles Monck remarking that if only £2,000 per annum were awarded, it must be because the House 'wished that he descendants of these heroes should be exposed to the temptations of corruption'![429]

Despite his successes, Wellington had some restrictions on his freedom of action, not least the knowledge that he commanded Britain's only major army and thus resources had to be husbanded carefully. For example, in dismissing a proffered plan, he noted that it would only work 'if I could afford, or the British Government or nation would allow of my being as prodigal of men as every French general is. They forget, however, that we have but one army, and that the same men who fought at Vimeiro and Talavera fought the other day at Sorauren; and that, if I am to preserve the army, I must proceed with caution ...'[430]

Equally significantly, while enjoying operational independence, in other matters he was fettered by the government and Horse Guards; when in April 1812 he protested at the replacement of experienced men with raw battalions from home, it is easy to appreciate the irony in his opening line, addressed to Lord Liverpool and mentioning the Duke of York: 'Your Lordship and His Royal Highness are the best judges of what description of troops it is expedient that this army should be composed ...'.[431] Similarly, he had little control over the selection of subordinates, whose appointments were made under the aegis of the government or Horse Guards irrespective of the wishes of the commander in the field, open to the abuse of patronage or favouritism as well as the straightjacket of seniority. Wellington's indignation is clear from this comment of May 1815: 'I am not very well pleased with the manner in which the Horse Guards have conducted themselves towards me. It will be admitted that the army is not a very good one, and, being composed as it is, I might have expected that the Generals and Staff formed by me in the last war would have been allowed to come to me again; but instead of that, I am overloaded with people I have never seen before; and it appears to be purposely intended to keep those out of my way whom I wished to have. However, I'll do the best I can with the instruments which have been sent to assist me.'[432]

The problem of seniority made it difficult for Wellington to employ generals as he wished. Thus when Craufurd asked for leave in 1810, he replied: 'I would beg you to reflect whether, considering the situation in which you stand in the army, it is desirable that you should go home upon leave. Adverting to the number of General Officers senior to you in the army, it has not been an easy task to keep you in your command; and if you should go, I fear that I should not be able to appoint you to it again, or to one that would be so agreeable to you, or in which you could be so useful.'[433]

The necessity of having to employ whomever was sent to him was another of Wellington's problems, but one over which he had no control. All he could do was to plead with the government, for example: 'I wrote to you the other day about General Officers. I only beg you do not send me any violent party men. We must keep the spirit of party out of the army, or we shall be in a bad way indeed.'[434] Perhaps the most extreme example was the dispatch to the army of Sir William Erskine, whose appointment Wellington queried on the grounds that Erskine was a lunatic. The reply he received was hardly reassuring: 'No doubt he is sometimes a little mad, but in his lucid intervals he is an uncommonly clever fellow; and I trust he may have no fit during the campaign, though he looked a little wild before he embarked.'[435] (His insanity appeared to be confirmed when he died in Lisbon in 1813, having thrown himself out of a window.)

The supply of general officers to the Peninsula fluctuated: at times there were too many, at others so few that colonels had to fill in temporarily. Requests for home leave deprived the army of some valuable commanders, but it was a convenient way of dispensing with useless or unenthusiastic generals. Wellington showed considerable compassion towards some mediocrities, as shown in this letter of December 1811: 'I am obliged to you for attending to our wants of General Officers ... We have now more than we can well dispose of ... and there are two with whom we could dispense with advantage ... They are both respectable officers as commanders of regiments, but they are neither very fit to take charge of a large body'; one 'wishes to return home, to unite himself with a lady of *easy virtue*'; the other 'has been very ill lately, and I think might be induced to go. I shall try if I can get them away in this manner, as I would not on any account hurt the feelings of either.'[436] This toleration did not extend to officers suspected of dishonesty: 'he has been guilty of many little improprieties which render him a discreditable person with the army; and before I had received ... the official letter announcing his recall ... I had determined to send him word that he had my leave to quit the army ...'[437]

Nevertheless, many incompetents continued to be employed, often for the want of anyone better. The cavalry was especially badly served, for although there was one good commander, Stapleton Cotton, Viscount Combermere, who from 1810 was in overall command of the cavalry, except during periods of leave, the rest were undistinguished. Henry William Paget, later Earl of Uxbridge and Marquess of Anglesey, was competent if too brave for his own good, hazarding capture at Quatre Bras and charging with his first line at Waterloo, depriving the remainder of his leadership. He commanded the cavalry well in the Corunna campaign, but was ineligible for the later Peninsular War because of mutual antipathy with Wellington, caused by Paget having eloped with Wellington's sister-in-law. He was appointed to command the cavalry in 1815 against Wellington's wishes, he having asked for Combermere but being overruled by the Duke of York. Another potentially great leader, John Gaspard Le Marchant, was cut off before he had reached his prime, killed leading his charge at Salamanca.

For the remainder, the brigade-commanders included some of considerable foolishness or even cowardice: for example, Robert Ballard Long was a well-meaning if inept general who admitted, perhaps only half in joke, that he would have been better employed planting cabbages; Baron George von Bock, who executed the charge at Garcia Hernandez, was a stalwart man but so short-sighted that he had to be pointed in the general direction of the enemy. Probably the worst was Sir John ('Jack') Slade, who in 1811 briefly commanded the entire cavalry by virtue of seniority, during Combermere's absence. A blustering incompetent, incapable even of dealing with his paperwork, he was generally regarded as a coward. At Sahagun he delayed his command so long with a harangue ending in 'Blood and slaughter! March!'[438] that the action had finished before he arrived; at Mayorga he halted so long, ostensibly to adjust his stirrups, that Paget ordered the 10th Hussars' commander to take over and lead the charge. On another occasion in the same campaign he left the scene of likely action to inform Moore of the approach of the French, whereupon Moore inquired why he was doing the duty of a junior officer instead of leading his command. Despite his repeated failures, he continued to be employed, and was responsible for the reverse at Maguilla. His reputation with the army was deservedly wretched: Paget once called to an ADC to 'ride after that damned stupid fellow' to ensure he committed no blunder,[439] which being heard by all around can hardly have enhanced Slade's reputation; and Tomkinson remarked that 'The things said of him by different officers were so gross, that I am certain they would not have been allowed to pass unnoticed had they been applied to any other man in the army.'[440] So low had the reputation of the cavalry sunk by late 1812 that surgeon Charles Boutflower of the 40th remarked that 'this lamentable dereliction from what they were is not attributed to any degeneracy in the Men, but to the incapacity, not to add, want of courage, of many of the Generals ... it has become so notorious, that there is scarcely a Dinner party, or assemblage ... where the conduct of our Cavalry Generals is not spoken of with disgust & contempt.'[441]

Similar calumnies were heaped upon other general officers of mediocre competence. Andrew Hay, one of the few generals killed in action (at Bayonne), was typical of the worst type: Frederick Robinson, who held an equivalent command, described him as 'a fool and I verily believe, with many others on my side, an arrant Coward. That he is a paltry, plundering old wretch is established beyond doubt. That he is no Officer is clear, and that he wants spirit is firmly believed, ergo, he ought not to be a General ...'[442]

Most of the others were brave enough, if not suitable for much more than leading a battalion. John Skerrett was probably typical, 'by nature a gallant Grenadier and no Light Troop officer, which requires the eye of a hawk and the power of anticipating the enemy's intention – who was always to be found off his horse, standing in the most exposed spot under the enemy's fire while our Riflemen were well concealed, as stupidly composed for himself as inactive for the welfare of his command'.[443] The bravery so essential for a battalion-commander was less important than intelligence in a general. Wellington raged on this topic in 1814 after an idiot general had appointed another idiot to superintend the telegraph system: 'When I call upon a General Officer to recommend an officer to fill a station in the public service, I mean that he should recommend one fit to perform some duty, and not one so stupid as to be unable to comprehend that which he is to perform; who is recommended only because he is a favourite with such General Officer. We have not yet been able to pass one message from the right to the left of the army, on account of the stupidity of the officer at Arcangues ...'[444]

Fortunately, Wellington had a number of reliable deputies upon whom he could depend. Chief among these was Rowland Hill, probably the only man upon whom Wellington could rely upon in independent command, when in the later stages of the Peninsular War he operated virtually as a corps commander. Possessed of considerable tactical ability, Hill was also one of the best-loved men in the army for his kindness and concern for the welfare of the rank and file, hence his nickname, 'Daddy' Hill. Beresford, as mentioned already, was a most capable organizer if not especially distinguished as a field commander. A handful of divisional generals gave sterling service, chief among them being Sir Thomas Picton. This bluff and uncompromising Welshman was requested by Wellington and perhaps sent to the Peninsula as a way of removing an embarrassment, Picton having been tried, found guilty but later acquitted of torturing a mulatto woman accused of theft, during his tenure as governor of Trinidad. Leading the Third Division in the later Peninsular War, he emulated their nickname 'The Fighting Division', and never failed his chief. A noted eccentric, who habitually wore a battered round hat and greatcoat (except at Busaco where he wore his nightcap), he was rough and foulmouthed, and his laxity in dress was copied by his aides to such an extent that they were known as 'the bear and ragged staff'.

Robert 'Black Bob' Craufurd was another specifically requested by Wellington, and allowed to go perhaps because he was the opposition's most effective military spokesman in parliament. A rough and hot-tempered Scot, he made the Light Division into the élite of the army; admired and feared by his men, whom he punished without mercy, he took care to share every hardship they endured. Despite a tendency to rush in without considering the consequences, his death at Ciudad Rodrigo was a severe loss. Edward Paget, Henry Paget's brother, probably had the potential of being a considerable commander, but was dogged by ill-fortune: he lost an arm at Oporto and was captured on the retreat from Burgos within five weeks of rejoining the army. Galbraith Lowry Cole (previously a suitor for the hand of Wellington's wife), was another capable divisional commander but probably unfitted for higher authority; which perhaps might also be said of Wellington's brother-in-law, Edward Pakenham, who conducted the vital attack at Salamanca with great skill, only for his reputation to be blighted by the defeat at New Orleans, where he was killed.

One of the most remarkable of Wellington's subordinates was Sir Thomas Graham, Lord Lynedoch, who entered the army late in life, partly from a desire for revenge after the coffin of his wife ('the beautiful Mrs. Graham', a description confirmed by Gainsborough's portrait) was desecrated by French republicans en route for burial at home. He was a capable subordinate and won one of the few Peninsula battles on which Wellington had no influence, Barrosa, though he was considerably less successful in the Netherlands in 1814. As a Whig, he was one of those critical of Wellington whom many thought owed his position to Tory connections; but when he actually served under the Duke he became one of his greatest admirers. Like Hill, he was greatly beloved by those under his command (he received an address after Barrosa from the Guards in which they called him 'our Father and our Friend'); and was, incidentally, probably the best batsman of all the Peninsula generals, having made most runs in one of the earliest recorded cricket matches played in Scotland.

Wellington commented to Liverpool in 1811 that 'I certainly feel, every day, more and more the difficulty of the situation in which I am placed. I am obliged to be every where, and if absent from any operation, something goes wrong. It is to be hoped that the General and other officers of the army will at last acquire that experience which will teach them that success can be attained only by attention to the most minute details; and by tracing every part of every operation from its origin to its conclusion, point by point, and ascertaining that the whole is understood by those who are to execute it.'[445] Another letter of the same day described the 'quality which I wish to see the officers possess, who are at the head of the troops ... a cool, discriminating judgement in action, which will enable them to decide with promptitude how far they can, and ought to go, with propriety; and to convey their orders, and act with such vigour and decision, that the soldiers will look up to them with confidence, in the moment of action, and obey them with alacrity'.[446] Apart from this being a remarkable enumeration of many of the characteristics he himself possessed, the remark about things going awry when he was absent was generally true.

Despite Graham's success at Barrosa, others operating independently made lamentable errors. The expedition from Gibraltar which landed at Fuengirola in October 1810 was commanded by Lord Blayney, who was only 'distinguished by extreme good nature; and he was a most convivial companion';[447] he was duly surprised and captured with half a battalion of the 89th. A much larger expedition was landed on the eastern coast of Spain in 1813 under Sir John Murray, a woeful general who withdrew when faced by forces (commanded by Marshal Suchet) which he should have been able to defeat, and he even abandoned eighteen siege-guns in the process. Wellington's comment was scathing: '... what I cannot bear is his leaving his guns and stores; and strange to say, not only does he not think he was wrong in so doing, but he writes of it

169

as being rather meritorious, and says he did it before ... The best of the story is, that all parties ran away ... Sir John Murray ran away; and so did Suchet ...'[448] Murray was court-martialled after the war but acquitted of all charges save that of abandoning his guns, for which he received only a reprimand.

When the abilities of many of the general officers are considered, Wellington's achievements appear the more remarkable, though personally he seems to have attributed his success as much to hard work as talent: just before the last French attack at Waterloo, he remarked that he had twice saved the day by perseverance. That was a characteristic equally important when dealing with his political masters. He wrote of his own predicament in the Peninsular War: 'I cannot expect mercy ... whether I succeed or fail; and if I should fail, they will not inquire whether the failure is owing to my own incapacity, to the blameless errors to which we are all liable, to the faults or mistakes of others, to the deficiency of our means, to the serious difficulties of our situation, or to the great power and abilities of our enemy. In any of these cases, I shall become their victim; but I am not to be alarmed by this additional risk, and whatever may be the consequences, I shall continue to do my best in this country.'[449]

Of many tributes, one of the most appropriate Wellington received was that given by Castlereagh in parliament on 27 June 1814, in which he compared Marlborough's six votes of thanks with the twelve accorded to Wellington by parliament; and concluded that 'nothing occurred in the whole course of his conduct, military or political, that could cast the slightest shade to cloud the splendour of his fame, and even when his great task was ended, and he arrived in the capital of that enemy with whom he had formerly contended, it was his peculiar glory to be received by the people of that capital, with the most signal marks of ardent admiration and applause'.[450] The testimonials continued to flow, in the highest terms: 'As Britons, we owe the Duke of Wellington all that makes life worth having, we honour and venerate his name; and shall never cease to contemplate with gratitude his wonderful history, as exhibiting a combination of qualities and virtues which entails him to be placed in the first rank of those illustrious men who, in successive ages, have gained renown as the special benefactors of mankind.'[451] (The adulation, however, was not universal: when in 1814 a man in Dundalk wished to call a newly built row of houses Wellington Place, the local priest objected on the grounds that as a Protestant, Wellington was an enemy to their religion. Taking no notice, the builder erected an inscribed stone bearing the name; but as the priest had threatened, on the following night it was torn down!)

Perhaps most remarkably, Wellington was seemingly unaffected by the plaudits he received. When in 1836 Lady Salisbury remarked that Waterloo had raised his fame above that of any other person, he replied, without false modesty, that he had never considered it, for that would be 'a feeling of vanity; one's *first* thought is for the public service ... I come constantly into contact with other persons on equal or inferior terms. Perhaps there is no man now existing who would like to meet me on a field of battle; in that line I am superior. But when the war is over and the troops disbanded, what is your great general more than anybody else? I am necessarily inferior to every man in his own line, though I may excel him in others. I cannot saw and plane like a carpenter, or make shoes like a shoemaker, or understand cultivation like a farmer.

170

Each of these, on his own ground, meets me on terms of superiority. I feel I am but a man.'[452]

A somewhat similar remark was said to have been made at the closing stages of the Battle of Waterloo, when the Duke rode forward in pursuit of the French. An aide begged him not to risk his life unnecessarily; 'Let them fire away,' he replied. 'The battle's won; my life is of no consequence now.'[453] His was an accurate sobriquet: 'the Great Duke'.

13

'We to preserve our liberty contend, Our altars, homes, and families defend.'[454] THE HOME FRONT

THE EFFECTS OF THE WAR AGAINST FRANCE PERMEATED EVERY FACET of civilian life, from the taxation levied on the rich to the hardships borne by the poor. On the one hand, such was the effect of the war that almost nothing was regarded as unlikely: in 1803 local justices of the peace searched a convent in Dorset to confirm the untruth of a report that Bonaparte's brother was in residence, preparing the way for invasion, and in the same year a petition for relief presented to the mayor of Leeds by a pregnant girl named Applegarth claimed that Bonaparte was the expectant father, a story evidently given some credence. Conversely, excluding those periods when invasion was expected to be imminent, public concern for the war should not be over-estimated: for many it was probably just an ordinary fact of life, hardly surprising when it is considered that a whole generation could not remember a time when Britain was not at war with France. Thus, even momentous events might be unconsidered by those not personally involved, as suggested by the experience of Thomas Austin who, having been deprived of news at a critical time in the war in 1814, while lying wounded in the Netherlands, inquired of the latest news as soon as he returned home. He received the reply, 'Corn be mortal dear, and old Dame Jobson be dead at last.'[455]

Thus, although the war was not necessarily uppermost in the minds of the population, there was constant evidence of military activity, especially in certain areas. Soldiers in units, small groups or individually were constantly on the march, on duty or furlough, which in itself could be a cause of some disquiet to civilians, remembering the often dubious reputation of those in uniform. In December 1801, for example, Dorothy Wordsworth recorded her anxiety at meeting two soldiers on the road from Rydal to Grasmere, especially as one was rolling drunk; her fears were groundless as the soldiers proved to be very civil and honest-looking!

When not quartered in barracks, troops were billeted upon landlords in the areas in which they were stationed, or were passing through on the march. This was not always a popular arrangement as both believed the other party was likely to cheat them, and it sometimes involved hazards, for example that experienced by a party of the German Legion billeted at the Black Boy Inn, Chelmsford, in October 1804, for a night's rest on a march. During the night the stables caught fire, it was thought from the Hanoverians' habit of smoking pipes continually; twelve bodies were raked from the ashes next morning, and one of those who escaped died from his injuries.

In addition to regular marches around the country during the frequent changes of garrison, especially in times of the greatest invasion threat, many troops spent the summer under canvas in large camps on the coast or at strategic points inland, to provide forces already concentrated to oppose any enemy landing. In fine weather life in such camps was not unpleasant, as suggested by this parody of Gray's *Elegy*:

'The moon slow-setting sends a parting ray,
The topers to the mess-room march with glee;
To bed the sober shape their quiet way,
And leave the lines to pensiveness and me.
Now scarce a candle glimmers to the sight,
And o'er the tented field soft stillness reigns;
Save where the dice are dash'd with desperate might,
Or braying asses wake the distant plains;
Save that from younder tempest-sheltering box
The centry's rough voice does the ear assail
Of such, as trusting to the gloom of Nox
Steal to the well-known booth to tipple ale.'[456]

Although the army's principal task was the defence of Britain, the regular forces were relieved of much of this duty by various auxiliary forces, the principal value of which was to release regular troops for active service. Among these were the fencible regiments (a term derived from 'de-fencible'), which had existed in smaller numbers during the Seven Years' and American Wars. They were virtually regular regiments, recruited in the ordinary manner, but with the proviso that they were not liable to be sent out of the country in which they were raised except with their own consent. They included both infantry and cavalry, for which 'letters of service' were issued from February 1793, the first being the Royal Manx Fencibles and the last (in June 1799) the Ancient Irish; some 36 were issued for fencible cavalry regiments and 69 for infantry battalions, some of which appear not to have been formed. Of the 30 cavalry regiments still extant in 1799, ten were Scottish, two Welsh and two Irish (a further six regiments were formed in 1799 by conversion of the Provisional Cavalry, an abortive attempt to establish a cavalry version of the militia); and of the 41 infantry battalions existing in 1801, 23 were Scottish, two Manx and one Welsh (plus the Newfoundland Regiment).

A number of fencible regiments did offer to extend their services (in 1799 twelve regiments volunteered to serve in Europe, and the 1st Fencible Cavalry to serve in any part of the world, in recognition of which they were authorized to wear a blue ribbon in their helmets!); a number of corps served well in Ireland during the rebellion, the Cambrian Fencibles apparently went to Portugal in 1800, and the Ancient Irish served in Egypt. The terms of enlistment, however, caused some unrest among certain of the Highland fencible corps, who had enrolled on the understanding that they would only be sent to England in event of invasion, or upon their volunteering to leave Scotland; and that they would not be drafted (i.e., transferred to another regiment, an important consideration for those who spoke only Gaelic and needed to serve among their friends and kin). Unfounded rumours that they were to be sent to the West Indies, encouraged by disaffected civilian agitators in the areas in which they were billeted, caused a number of protests and disturbances.

The worst troubles were those that affected the Strathspey Fencibles, demonstrating the fears that could arise among men who clearly did not have complete confidence in their officers. In March 1794 Sir James Grant of Grant, who had raised the Strathspeys, appealed to his men to volunteer for service in England; some agreed, but others ran off and began to fortify the old palace of Linlithgow. Negotiation soon returned them to their duty, once assured that they would not be compelled to act outside their terms of enlistment; blame for the unrest was placed upon the influence of disaffected civilians, and the presence of a company of Roman Catholic Macdonells in the regiment, a body regarded as known troublemakers. A worse outbreak of mutiny occurred at Dumfries in June 1795, however, when a gang of about 60 of the most disorderly Strathspeys rescued from custody some men who had been imprisoned for attempting to free one of their number who was under guard for insubordination. After three officers were jostled the protesters must have realized the enormity of what they were doing, and meekly fell into ranks; but five 'mutineers' were court-martialled, four sentenced to death, and two (Alexander Fraser and Charles McIntosh) were actually shot, on Gullane Links on 17 July 1795, in the presence of six infantry battalions, the 4th Dragoons, and a detachment of Royal Artillery.

After this harsh punishment of what was never a true mutiny, there was not much further trouble among the fencible corps, although there was an unfortunate incident in Aberdeen in June 1802 when a mob insulted some officers of the Ross and Cromarty Rangers. In defence of their officers some members of the unit 'run among the people in the street with their arms in their hands, and began firing upon them with ball, indiscriminately and in every direction';[457] two people were reported killed and three mortally wounded. Two officers and some other ranks were prosecuted, but acquitted.

The fencibles attracted some largely unwarranted criticism in parliament; General McLeod, for example, described them as 'a useless body of men ... raised for the purpose of patronage, more than for any service they could be to the country'.[458] Their reputation suffered from the various 'mutinies' like that which afflicted the Strathspeys (all apparently arising from fears, perhaps not entirely unfounded, that their terms of enlistment were to be reneged upon), and from the brutal behaviour of a few units, notably the Ancient British Fencible Cavalry in Ireland, and the Cinque Ports and Pembrokeshire cavalry regiments which were involved in the violent suppression of the Tranent riot in August 1797. In general, however, the fencibles performed much good service, notably during the 1798 rebellion in Ireland where they formed an important and reliable part of the army; but all had been disbanded by the time of the Peace of Amiens, and only the Manx corps was re-formed, existing from 1803 to 1811.

The principal home-defence force was the militia, embodied for full-time service in time of war, and consisting exclusively of infantry battalions. Each county formed one or more battalions according to its population; they were controlled by the county's lord-lieutenant and almost invariably served outside the county in which they were raised, to eliminate any conflict of loyalty if required to suppress public disorder.

The militia was unique in being the only service to employ a measure of compulsion in its recruitment. Its ranks were filled by voluntary enlistment as for the regular army, including payment of a bounty, but if this attracted insufficient numbers the balance was selected by ballot from among the able-bodied inhabitants, each county and sub-area being allocated a quota of men which had to be supplied. It was not conscription in the conventional sense, however, because there were many exemptions from the ballot (ranging from apprentices and dissenters to members of volunteer corps and any poor man with more than one legitimate child), and even those chosen by ballot could avoid having to serve by paying a fine (which rose to £20 in 1807), or providing a 'substitute' to take their place. The term of service was five years.

'Substitution' caused a number of problems, chiefly in creating competition for men who might otherwise have joined the regular army, thus diverting likely recruits from the regulars. Because heavy fines were levied upon counties which fell short of their quota of militiamen, the fees or bounties paid to substitutes rose as demand tended to exceed supply, so that militia bounties actually exceeded those for the regular army, in effect offering more for less dangerous service. As payment of the fine gave exemption for only five years, but provision of a substitute exemption for life, the latter was the preferred method of avoiding service; but as the price of substitutes rose beyond the reach of many ordinary individuals, many took out an insurance policy, whereby in return for a regular premium, the insurers guaranteed to find a substitute for any of their clients who was selected by the ballot. By one of the quirks of the system, physical disability gave no exemption for men worth £100, which in theory imposed the heaviest burden upon the more affluent members of society.

As the demand for substitutes grew, the old practice of crimping was revived. Price of substitutes varied from county to county, so that (for example) in 1803 a substitute might be procured in Anglesey for £12, but cost more than twenty guineas in Middlesex. By the following year prices ranged from £20 in Aberdeen to £50 in Sussex and up to £60 in Middlesex, and in some cases the price went as high as £100; the effect on recruiting for the regular army may be gauged from the fact that at this time their enlistment-bounty was £7 12s. 6d. So desperate were the demands to fulfil personal obligations and parish quotas that crimping even developed into a trade in men: in one case concerning the Warwickshire Militia, a man was hired by a corporal for £10; the corporal sold him to a sergeant for £18, who sold him to a publican, who finally sold the man for £27 6s. to a parish to make up its quota. It was said that an individual in Rochdale put himself up for sale as a substitute, declaring 'that he was sixty-three inches high, and his price was a guinea an inch';[459] he got his money. One result of the trade was to limit the number of 'principals' in the militia (i.e., those who served in person, without providing a substitute); for example, of more than 26,000 militiamen enrolled in 1807, only 3,129 were 'principals', and in the Middlesex Militia, whose quota was more than 4,500 (including the augmentation of the Supplementary Militia, by which some counties formed additional regiments), only one man was a 'principal' (when his term of service expired, his lord-lieutenant tried to keep him in the regiment as a curio!). With the militia having already taken up so many men who might otherwise have joined the regular army, when volunteering from the militia to the regulars was permitted, with a bounty paid to those who transferred, it had the effect of giving a double bounty to each man, thus costing more than if such men had enlisted into the regulars directly from civilian life. Nevertheless, the acquisition by the regular army of men already used to military discipline and trained in the use of arms was a great advantage.

Despite the degree of conscription involved, public protest against the militia was limited, presumably because the system had been enacted in England and Wales in previous wars. In Scotland, however, the militia ballot was not applied until 1797, and was the cause of considerable unrest, most notably in the riot at Tranent in East Lothian, already mentioned, which was suppressed with undue severity and at the cost of twelve fatalities. Nevertheless, the system produced an efficient force perfectly able to perform the domestic duties which would otherwise have required regular troops. The strength of the militia was considerable: for example, from January 1804 to January 1813 the number of militiamen never fell below 67,600, and on 1 January 1805 the strength was as high as 89,809.

Although not obliged to serve abroad, latterly regiments from mainland Britain were permitted to serve in Ireland, and vice versa, a duty performed with good grace:

'Away, brave boys to Dublin jig,
The girls to kiss, the whiskey swig,
And each as merry as a grig – sing, one and all.'[460]

Some regiments volunteered for foreign service, but not until 1814 were three Provisional Battalions formed, from volunteers from fifteen militia regiments. The 1st Battalion, commanded by the Marquess of Buckingham, drew almost half its men from his Buckinghamshire Militia; the 2nd, under Lieutenant-Colonel Edward Bayly of the West Middlesex, drew almost half from his regiment; and the 3rd, under Sir Watkin Williams Wynn, Bt. of the Denbighshire Militia, had most of its personnel from the 2nd West York (Wynn had to be given command because the 135 men of his own regiment who completed the battalion refused to go without him!). They formed a brigade under Bayly's brother, Major-General Sir Henry Bayly, but arrived in southern France only after the cessation of hostilities. Thus, the only militia regiments to see action during the period were those Irish corps engaged in the 1798 rebellion, some of whom served with distinction while others proved to be lamentably ineffective.

An attempt to recruit an additional 34,000 men in England, 6,000 from Scotland and 10,000 from Ireland was made by the Act passed in 1803, which created the Army of Reserve. Each battalion so formed was to comprise 500 men in ten companies, raised by ballot under the militia laws, recruits to serve for five years and not be sent out of the United Kingdom. By the spring of 1804 its failure had become apparent: less than 46,000 men had been enrolled, of whom 10 per cent had deserted, and when the unfit men and under-age boys were deducted, barely 30,000 were left. Only sixteen numbered battalions were actually formed, of which three were Irish, two Scottish and one Welsh. These Battalions of Reserve were placed on the establishment on Christmas Day 1803, and in October 1804 were re-titled Garrison Battalions. All were disbanded in February 1805 and the personnel used to form three new Garrison Battalions, with the same terms of service; and six new battalions were added in December 1806, from men raised by the same Reserve and Additional Forces Acts, as had been used to create 2nd Battalions of some line regiments, whose men were available only for home service. The 7th and 8th of these Garrison Battalions were disbanded in 1810, and the 9th was taken into the line as the 103rd Foot in December 1808, as the result of the expiry of the original term of limited service and the fact that many of the men had re-enlisted for general service. Two battalions remained in existence from 1814, when the rest were disbanded, and a new 3rd Garrison Battalion was formed from invalids in May 1815.

The original seven Garrison Battalions, not to be confused with the above, were formed in December 1802 from the various corps of Invalids, which performed garrison duty in various forts and posts at home, and out-pensioners of Chelsea Hospital unfit for campaign service. In July 1804 they were re-titled Royal Veteran Battalions, recognizing their composition of old soldiers of good character; the 1st served at Gibraltar 1805-10 and in Holland 1813-14; the 2nd at Madeira 1809-14; and the 4th and 7th at Gibraltar, 1808-14 and 1810-14 respectively. The 8th Battalion was formed in December 1804, the 9th in April 1805, the 10th in December 1806 for service in Canada, the 11th in April 1807 and the 12th in June 1808; the 13th (renumbered 7th in June 1815) was formed at Lisbon in March 1813, from invalids of the Peninsular army, and served in the Netherlands in 1815.

The third category of home-defence force were the volunteers, units of locally formed 'home guard' which drilled for a few hours per week and were available to perform a variety of services from fire-fighting to peace-keeping as well as the more obvious role as a defence against invasion. These units originated from 1794, were almost all disbanded at the Peace of Amiens, and were re-created in a much expanded and altered form.

Generally the first to be formed were corps of 'Gentlemen and Yeomanry Cavalry', composed of landowners and their outdoor servants, created as much as a guard against civil disturbance (in the absence of any organized police force) as against invasion; by 1801 there were almost 24,000 members of the Yeomanry (including Ireland). The infantry equivalent, often styled 'Loyal Associations' or 'Armed Associations', were generally the urban version of the rural yeomanry, and were principally middle-class in composition ('respectable tradesmen and honest workmen' as the Clerkenwell Association was described).[461] The social exclusivity of many corps is exemplified by the conditions of enrolment in the Highland Armed Association of London: 'before a Candidate become a Member he should be recommended, and his address be given the Secretary, who is to inquire his Character and Station in Life; of which the Committee being acquainted, they are to decide, with delicacy and feeling towards the Candidate, but with lively and tenacious attention for the respectability and honour of the Highland Association'.[462] As the conventional methods of enforcing military discipline were unacceptable to 'gentlemen', it was usual for such corps to enforce discipline by the levying of fines. For example, the Loyal Loughborough Volunteers (which upon formation in October 1794 had declared 'our determination to provoke no one by insult, but in every situation to demean ourselves as peaceable Inhabitants and good Subjects, and to prove to all the World the purity of our intentions') determined the level of fines most democratically, by a panel of the eight men who stood nearest to the offender in the ranks; and reserved a special punishment for those who resigned from the unit without a convincing reason: 'he shall be deemed a Coward and voted to Coventry'.[463]

The governance of most corps arose from a similar factor: the affairs of each unit were run by an elected committee, less likely to cause protests from the members than if decisions were taken by the officers alone, who were in many cases the social equals of the rank and file.

Appropriately, the constitutions of many corps emphasized their determination to suppress civil disorder and protect their property; the Brentford Association, for example, declared its purpose was 'to defend the District against Depredators'.[464] Among the most comprehensive statements of intent was that of the Union Volunteers of Wapping: 'not only to protect our Liberties and Properties, but also to defend our invaluable Constitution (consisting of King, Lords, and Commons) under which we live, and from all attacks of its avowed and secret enemies; and in case of Invasion, be ready to assist in protecting ... the Eastern Division of the Tower Hamlets ...'[465] Most of these corps were self-supporting, each member equipping himself or being financed by a local public subscription, which could raise huge sums: for example, the Bishopsgate Volunteers raised £1,752 10s. 10d. on their first formation. The high social composition of many corps was exemplified by the common use of a dark-blue uniform, which was regarded as a far more genteel colour than the red coat associated with the regular army.

Upon the renewal of the war in 1803, the government decided that a larger volunteer force was required, supported by public funds (although some corps refused pay and continued to find their own clothing and equipment); and financial support permitted the government to impose a degree of control upon units which accepted it. Accordingly, the 'June Allowances' were established in that month in 1803, by which volunteers would receive pay for 85 days' training per year, in return agreeing to serve anywhere within their Military District. As this brought in an insufficient number of volunteers (no less than fourteen counties formed no corps under the 'June Allowances'), in July the Levy en Masse Act was passed, which gave the government the power to train every able-bodied man, whether willing or not, unless sufficient corps were raised voluntarily, for which the 'August Allowances' were provided. These granted pay for 20 days' training per year, in return for which the recipients 'shall agree to march to any part of Great Britain for the defence thereof, in case of actual invasion or the appearance of any enemy in force upon the coast, and for the suppression of such rebellion or insurrection arising or existing at the time of such invasion';[466] in effect, by giving less and expecting more than from 'June Allowance' corps, the 'August Allowances' penalized reluctance in not having volunteered earlier.

Taken unprepared by the number of volunteers enrolled under threat of the Levy en Masse Act, on 18 August 1803 the government limited the number of volunteers in any county to six times the number of its 'Old Militia' (i.e., not including the augmentation of the Supplementary Militia). This provoked such uproar that on 31 August it was decreed that *all* volunteers would be accepted, but those in excess of the 18 August quota would rank as 'supernumeraries', without pay or allowances, and without the exemption from the militia ballot which was the major perquisite accorded to volunteers. Corps having more than 300 privates were allowed a paid adjutant and sergeant-major.

By the end of 1803 no less than 604 cavalry troops, 3,976 infantry companies and 102 artillery companies had been enrolled, of which 742 units were of single troop or company strength. Artillery units mostly manned existing garrisons, few being entrusted with mobile guns, although a few corps had fieldpieces purchased privately. Strengths of corps varied from the 2,484 rank and file of the South Regiment of Devon Volunteers to the 24 men of the Norfolk Mounted Rifles, although the latter was attached to another unit, the Lynn and Freebridge Cavalry. The smallest independent corps was the Harristown Infantry of Kildare, with one officer, one sergeant, one drummer and 20 rank and file; conversely, forty-two units exceeded 1,000 in strength. The total number of enrolled volunteers in December 1803 was 380,193 in Great Britain (against a county quota of 309,908), which represents some 3.6 per cent of the entire population recorded by the 1801 census; with 82,941 in Ireland. The number in each county naturally varied with population and the proximity to envisaged landing-points for invasion; thus the southern coastal counties were especially strongly represented. Devon, with 15,212 rank and file, had the most of any county; next were Lancashire and the West Riding, between fourteen and fifteen thousand; London 12,735; Kent and Westminster between ten and eleven thousand; Hampshire and Somerset between nine and ten thousand. Six counties had more than 2,000 men in excess of quota (Edinburgh City, Hampshire and Isle of Wight, Cornwall, Devon, Kent and London), of which the first two had more than double the quota. Bute had not only the lowest number of volunteers (90) but the greatest shortage, about 75 per cent in arrears of the quota.[467]

As evident from the numbers enrolled in 1803, a major change in composition occurred, as the volunteer force now included men from all social backgrounds. This was expressed by an observer who compared the Birmingham Loyal Association of 1797-1802 with the Loyal Birmingham Volunteers of 1803: 'The Birmingham Association ... was composed of master drapers, grocers, and such gentlemen tradesmen as could afford time to play at soldiers. Their principal employment was to keep the potato rioters in proper order ... At that period the French flotilla was in preparation, and it was deemed expedient to have a more working body of men. The Volunteers were established, and a more active and earnest body was nowhere formed ... The uniform of the Association was blue trimmed with white, and a very gentlemanly cocked hat, so that the costume would either do for the battlefield or the drawing-room. The Volunteers were a different body. Their uniform was red trimmed with yellow, and a regular military cap. They looked like what they were – working men.'[468]

The combination of various social classes within a unit reveals the difficulties which might have been experienced had such a composition been possible in the regular army: when the North Pevensey Legion paraded, the light company (formed of smugglers and poachers, 'whom it may be necessary thus to occupy that they may not take a worse course'!) was ordered to stand on one flank, together with a company of 'unsightly men', to avoid embarrassing the middle-class farmers who formed the remainder of the unit.[469] Nevertheless, many of the earlier practices were continued, including the maintenance of discipline by fines, which were enforceable in law: an extreme case occurred in August 1805 when Thomas Johnson of the 2nd Royal Liverpool Volunteers was compelled by law to pay his fines for non-attendance at drill, which amounted to £274 4s.[470] Some corps emphasized the equality of officers and other ranks, as in the instructions issued by Lieutenant-Colonel Charles Hope to his 1st

Royal Edinburgh Volunteers: 'In this regiment, the officers cannot be permitted to have any indulgences or accommodation beyond the privates. They must, therefore, march with their whole baggage on their backs, of which the Lieutenant-colonel will set the example, never mounting his horse but for the purpose of command. In camp or quarters, no distinction of rooms or tents will be permitted. Officers and privates must fare alike; but the officers will mess together, as it will give opportunities, not otherwise to be easily obtained, of conversing on many points of regimental duty.'[471]

As they could be called out in any emergency, the volunteers performed many public services in addition to assisting the magistrates in keeping the peace. Countless examples of fire-fighting are recorded (indeed, one of the stated aims of the Pimlico Association was 'to work the engines, and assist otherwise in case of fire',[472] the corps maintaining an auxiliary body of 200 artificers and 50 special constables), and hardly any public service fell outside the scope of volunteer involvement, from the Portsdown Yeomanry and 1st Gosport Fusiliers maintaining soup-kitchens to feed 2,300 poor people in Gosport in 1800, to the apprehension by the Pontefract Volunteers in May 1800 of a madman who had all but decapitated his wife, and who being 'armed with two or three brace of pistols, beside his sword'[473] could not be arrested by any but armed soldiers.

In the event of invasion, volunteers were to march to alarm-posts throughout the country, to assemble in large bodies. These movements were triggered by the lighting of beacons which ran along the coast and inland, and when false alarms occurred the volunteers responded with alacrity. A typical case was that of the Rotherham Volunteers in August 1805, when a straw-burning was mistaken for the invasion-beacons: within twelve hours the entire corps had mustered, missing not a man and complete with baggage-wagons, and had marched 22 miles towards the expected invaders. The determination of such men may be glimpsed in the comments recorded by parish constables compiling lists of available men, such as those of James Sykes of Cophill, who was 'determined to kill a Frenchman, if possible',[474] or J. Broom of Exeter who 'Will crip the wings of the French Frog Eaters';[475] or, as suggested in the song of the Gateshead Volunteers:

> 'Some think Billy Pitt's hummin,
> When he tells about Bonnepart cummin;
> But come when he may,
> He'll lang rue the day
> He first meets wi' the Bonny Geatsiders
> Like an anchor shank, smash! how they'll clatter 'im,
> And turn 'im, and skelp 'im, and batter 'im,
> His banes sall by pring
> Like a fryin pan ring,
> When he mets wi' the Bonny Geatsiders.'[476]

In some areas the level of enthusiasm was remarkable: in Gisburn township in 1803, for example, only six eligible men were not enrolled in the volunteers, and three of them were infirm (although the status of Gisburn as perhaps the most loyal community in the country may not be unconnected with the fact that the local landowner, Lord Ribblesdale, was commandant of the volunteer unit in the area, the Craven Legion).[477]

180

Nevertheless, both at the time and since, the military value of the volunteer force has been questioned. Despite the small size of many units, most were trained as line infantry, only the most forward-thinking advocating that their real combat value would be as riflemen: as General Money remarked, twenty-four days' drill could not turn civilians into line troops, but ten days could produce a good sharpshooter. However, much more attention was paid in the volunteers to marksmanship than in the regular army, and a considerable proportion were trained as light infantry, intended to harass an invader rather than meet him in the open field, which would have been the duty of the regulars and militia. Marksmanship was even emphasized in corps organized as line regiments; for example, Lieutenant-Colonel Hope instructed his 1st Royal Edinburgh that 'the Regiment will see the folly and danger of firing at random. If their fire is ineffectual, they may as well stand to be shot at with ordered arms. Every individual must take a steady aim ... If the smoke prevents the Regiment from seeing the Enemy's line distinctly, they will always see the flash from the muzzles of their muskets, by which the Regiment can direct its own fire. In short, let the object rather be to keep up a well directed fire, than a very quick fire.'[478] Many volunteer corps used the award of medals as incentives for proficiency at drill or target-practice, and even the latter was made more interesting by expedients such as that adopted by the Wells Volunteers (Somerset), whose target was an effigy of Napoleon with a star on his breast as the 'bull'. The Edinburgh Light Dragoons adopted a similar idea for sabre-drill, having turnips on top of poles to represent Frenchmen; Lord Cockburn recalled Sir Walter Scott lashing out at the turnips, mumbling to himself, 'Cut them down. The villains, cut the down.' (Scott, an ardent volunteer, apparently derived considerable benefit from his service, composing much of *Marmion* while drilling and taking inspiration from the sight of the soldiers.)

Some units benefited greatly from the presence in their ranks of experienced old soldiers; for example, the adjutant of the Evesham Volunteers, Jeremiah Martin, was an active man of 52 years' regular service, in which he had risen from private to officer. The unsuitability of other officers, however, is exemplified by the publican and half-pay officer who was a captain in this corps, and challenged old Martin to a duel after he had been prevented from parading his company in front of his own inn, thus encouraging them to buy liquor from him! Other officers of little military aptitude had difficulty performing their duties; Thomas Erskine, the future Chancellor, commanding the Law Association Volunteers, found it impossible to remember his commands without use of a crib-card, and Lord Ellenborough, later Lord Chief Justice, could not even master marching in step despite chalk-marks on his boots. Some gentlemen in the ranks proved equally inept, perhaps due to the fact that their upbringing had not accustomed them to obeying orders; the redoubtable Patrick Gould, sergeant-major of the Royal Edinburgh Volunteers, once remarked (doubtless with feeling) that 'he would rather drill five fools than one philosopher'![479] To ensure maximum proficiency, inspecting officers were appointed to monitor their progress, and inefficient volunteer corps were rooted out. Some inspectors applied themselves assiduously: Joseph Hardy, late of the 93rd, for example, awarded medals at his own expense to units he inspected. Others perhaps took advantage of opportunities that presented themselves: in 1804, Colonel Charles Miller, Inspecting Officer for Derbyshire, wrote to Joseph Strutt, who commanded the Belper, Shottle and Holbrooke Volunteers, that he had recently entered into a partnership with a clothier, Mr Ross of Leicester Square, and that orders for uniforms 'will be executed expeditiously and in the best manner possible'.[480]

Despite assiduous supervision, the training and discipline of some units remained undistinguished. A story was told, for example, of the Sunderland Volunteers' target-practice shooting at a moored boat, which was so ineffective that some sailors nearby remarked that the safest place for them was if 'We'll gan an' sit i' the boat!'[481] Inter-unit rivalry was sometimes just as keen as among some regular corps, and the cause of some dissent. For example, a perceived insult by the Severn Volunteer Rifles against the neighbouring Kings Stanley corps (Gloucestershire) culminated in a legal case and a challenge to a duel; and the question of seniority of the two Preston corps caused a pamphlet war in 1805, in which the commandant of one, Nicholas Grimshaw, accused the other unit of 'disunion and jealousy' and declared that his corps would seek 'to obviate, as far as possible, the radical defects of the Preston Volunteer Establishment, by gentlemanly and soldierlike conduct', a scarcely veiled criticism of the others.[482]

Dissent within units was similarly not uncommon; for example, reference has already been made to 'Orator' Hunt's attempt to fight his commanding officer. Upsets in the Norwich Riflemen in 1804 caused their commander, Major R. M. Bacon, to publish a speech which stated that their uniform was the 'source of almost all our vexations ... There are some in finer feathers, some in finer caps, and some in finer cloth than their comrades. It is not for me to enquire whether this comes from a judicious economy or a ludicrous vanity ...';[483] obviously some of the more affluent members had been preening themselves in front of their less wealthy comrades. A measure of the independence of the ordinary volunteer is demonstrated by the case of John Mockett of the Thanet Yeomanry, who suspected his commanding officer, Captain Thomas Garrett, of misdeeds over the corps accounts, and when Garrett refused to produce the relevant documents, Mockett wrote directly to the Secretary at War. Garrett responded by discharging Mockett from the troop, and attempted to pressure Mockett's landlord; which was, said Mockett, 'ungenerous and unbecoming; not the conduct, Sir, that *you* as a *Yeoman* ought to have shewn to me as a *Yeoman*. Indeed, the Captain of the Thanet Troop should *not* have acted thus. Fortunately for me, Sir, I am Tenant to a man of such nice honour, such conscientious inflexible integrity that instead of having done me a mischief, you may have unintentionally produced the reverse...'[484]

However well motivated, such cases were inevitably prejudicial to discipline; but more serious to the aim of providing a defence against invasion were the differing terms of service under which the volunteers were enrolled. Especially difficult were corps with some members on 'June Allowances' and others on 'August Allowances', so that some had undertaken to perform wider service than others. Many corps imposed their own restrictions on service, from the 1st Reading Infantry which undertook to go anywhere ('Where Wanted') to the Somerset Place Infantry of Westminster, enrolled 'Solely for the Defence of Somerset House'; and between the two, offers of service from anywhere in the United Kingdom to the confines of a single parish. The seven troops of the Eastern Regiment of Norfolk Yeomanry illustrate the problem:

two were prepared to serve anywhere in Great Britain at any time, and one in the case of invasion; one in the Military District, and Great Britain in case of invasion; one in the Eastern District only, irrespective of circumstances; and one according to 'August Allowances' conditions. Although many restricted-service units would probably have abandoned their limitations in an emergency, it was a considerable problem to the military planners that they could not be compelled so to do; the Duke of York commented on this in 1804 when he reported that of 25,000 rank and file in the capital, only 13,400 could be ordered on extended service.

The solution, also intended to make better use of the huge amount of revenue expended on the volunteers as well as improving efficiency, was to create a new force of Local Militia, legislation for which was passed in June 1808. This provided for a force six times the 1802 militia quota (300,000 men), of infantry battalions formed from volunteers, with the balance raised by a ballot of men aged 18-30 if insufficient enrolled voluntarily, for a four-year enlistment during which, and for two years after, exemption was given from the militia ballot. Substitution was not allowed, and although exemption could be purchased by a substantial sum, service was enforced upon balloted men by the threat of imprisonment. Battalions had a paid, full-time cadre, and a property qualification was imposed upon officers: captains, for example, had to possess an estate of annual value of £150, or personal property worth £250 per annum. Corps were to train for 28 days per year and in case of invasion could be sent anywhere in Great Britain; they could be called out by the lord-lieutenant in cases of civil disorder, but such assembly was limited to fourteen days, which counted as part of the annual training; thus if disorder lasted longer than this period, county units had to be used in rotation. Volunteers received a two-guinea bounty to transfer to the Local Militia (the majority did, often *en bloc*), with officers retaining the ranks they held in the volunteer force.

The Local Militia was unpopular with many volunteers, and caused a sharp decline in the volunteer force; from 336,404 rank and file in January 1808, the number had fallen to 68,643 by January 1812, of whom 19,207 were yeomanry cavalry unaffected by the creation of the Local Militia. Within a year some 125,000 volunteers had transferred to the Local Militia, which by 1812 was about 215,000 strong. The change was probably not as beneficial as intended, as even the periods of annual training were not a marked improvement, in that many of the volunteer corps had undertaken periods of annual 'permanent duty', usually in garrison some considerable distance from their homes.

It was noted that the Local Militia were not as readily available for service as the volunteers had been, one critic claiming that they were not 'competent to cope even with a Mob, although they had ... attained the degree of perfection allowed by the present regulations ... we train just enough to give the Local-Militiaman a distaste to a military life, and that we might, therefore, recruit with better success from the plough-tail than from the ranks of the Local Militia. If then this body is not fit to oppose a mob, and obstructs recruiting, what is it good for?'[485] Not surprisingly, Sir Francis Burdett opposed the Local Militia Bill on the grounds that 'it exposed the young men of the country to be flogged'[486] while others questioned not only the efficiency of the force but the motivation of its members, as in some cases evidence existed that malcontents had joined the Local Militia simply to receive training in the use of arms. Representing those who doubted the wisdom of involving the labouring classes in military activity, as late as 1840 the editor of the *United Service Journal* wrote that a French-style National Guard, embracing all classes, was not inherently trustworthy: 'we prefer simple local associations of the gentry and respectable middle classes'.[487]

Such views were probably influenced by incidents of unrest among the Local Militia, notably that at Ely in June 1809, attributed to bad bread and charging men for their knapsacks, the cost of which was withheld from their 'marching guinea' so that some had no money to buy food and starved for two days during their period of training. The resulting riot necessitated the deployment of German Legion cavalry from Ipswich to restore order, and it was for criticizing the flogging of five ringleaders over which Cobbett was prosecuted and imprisoned. In the same month some of the Archenfield Local Militia (Herefordshire) attempted to release some of their fellows from the guardhouse, leading to a confrontation with the same regiment's flank companies, which remained loyal and whose presence quelled the disturbance. Nevertheless, despite such breaches of discipline, much of the Local Militia retained the general spirit of the earlier volunteers, and the loyalty of the majority is exemplified by the fact that when several Local Militiamen were implicated in a food riot at Loughborough in 1812, it was their own comrades who restored order. Some units even volunteered for extended service: in 1811, for example, the 4th Cornwall offered to do permanent duty for as long as the county's regular militia was in Ireland, the Berkshire Local Militia volunteered to go to the Peninsula, and the Banff offered to serve in any part of the world.

The unpopularity of the military in certain quarters was largely a result of the use of troops in support of the magistracy in the suppression of civil disorder. Such actions should be viewed in the context of a society in which violence was not uncommon, and on occasion even condoned. A revealing comment was made in 1806 when a costermonger brought an action for damages after being horse-whipped by Lieutenant-Colonel Sir John Eamer of the London Militia: the costermonger's own council stated in court that his client 'was but a dung-hearted fellow, for if he had the true spirit of an Englishman, which he hoped most Englishmen possessed, he would have given the City Knight and Colonel a good drubbing, and have saved the circuitry of an action to obtain redress'![488]

In most cases, the military was the only force available to magistrates to assist in upholding the law, for the very concept of a police force was regarded by some as a potential tool of oppression. A telling comment upon the attitude of some arose after London was horrified in December 1811 by the atrocious murder of two families during separate burglaries; the presumed perpetrator, a sailor named John Williams, alias Murphy, hanged himself in Cold Bath Fields gaol rather than stand trial. Such was the public fear that 'many persons, in their moment of panic, seemed disposed to surrender their liberties, with a view to secure the protection of their persons. Under such impressions, a cry was raised for the establishment of an armed police; but the rashness of this proposal was soon detected ...'[489] Consequently, the army assisted the civil authorities in many other duties than those involving public order: in March

1812, for example, a detachment of the 2nd Dragoons provided the force which enabled two constables to apprehend the notorious Booth gang of coiners and banknote-forgers in Birmingham. Such duties were potentially hazardous for the troops: for example, when the notorious robbers Bill Brennan and Paddy Hogan were caught by a detachment of the 11th Light Dragoons and Sligo Militia, Hogan climbed up the inside of a chimney and used the top of it as a parapet, firing at the soldiers until his ammunition was exhausted. (Both bandits were hanged at Clonmel).

Relations between civilians and military were not infrequently strained, and sometimes violent. Unusual trouble occurred in Jersey in 1795, apparently the result of the French tongue of some of the locals: 'It is particularly recommended to the officers of the 29th Rt. to enjoin their men not to quarrel or make any disturbance with any of the inhabitants which might probably arise from their not understanding the language ...'[490] Alcohol and indiscipline were the causes of some conflict, for example a most unpleasant incident at Leeds in 1812, when a landlord was ordered by the quartermaster of the Carlow Militia not to serve four drunken privates of the regiment. These four drew their bayonets, chased away the quartermaster, stabbed the landlord and another customer, but were driven from the public house by a 15th Hussar who was present; a woman who witnessed the affair died of fright. Trouble with civilians was not always the result of indiscipline, however: for example, when in February 1811 some townsmen of Arundel were beaten with cudgels in a nocturnal foray by a party of the 68th, following insults delivered on some of their officers, the avenging gang of soldiers was led by a captain and two subalterns.

A number of violent outbreaks occurred within the army, notably in the 1790s, which could only have lowered the reputation of the military in the opinions of the populace. For example, at Exeter in August 1795 the Londonderry Regiment objected to being drafted into the 43rd, during which 'one of the privates was very rude to Colonel Dennison, and he in consequence struck him with his sword';[491] the protesters had to be disarmed by a troop of 25th Light Dragoons. In the previous month a similar outbreak among the Loyal Irish Fencibles had been quelled at Bristol only by the intervention of the Northamptonshire Militia and 10th Light Dragoons, which involved some casualties.

Several militia regiments were involved in severe disturbances in 1795. In December, as a consequence of depredations committed by militiamen upon civilians, Colonel Sibthorpe of the South Lincoln Militia ordered a curfew for the troops under his command at Yarmouth; he was a martinet but his regiment was notoriously ill-disciplined, poisoned by the proximity of their own homes and friends, and by the 'low alehouses' of Yarmouth.[492] The Huntingdonshire Militia, also part of the garrison, was also badly disciplined and in response to the curfew they rioted and almost destroyed their barracks. Having been quietened by the arrival of cavalry and artillery, the Huntingdons were transferred and replaced by the Cambridgeshire Militia, who resented inheriting devastated quarters, believing that the Huntingdons had wrecked them simply to get a better posting; whereas the Huntingdons claimed to have been seduced by the wretched South Lincolns. Even more serious was a two-day riot of the Oxfordshire Militia at Seaford and Newhaven in April 1795, which began as a food riot, the militiamen seizing grain and selling it cheaply to the poor. The disturbance was suppressed by the threat of force from horse artillery and the Lancashire Fencible Cavalry; thirteen men were court-martialled, six were flogged and three executed.

Less serious disturbances were not uncommon, some arising from simple criminal behaviour among the troops and others from regimental rivalries, which sometimes spilled over to involve civilians, for example the inhabitants of Newcastle injured in a fight between the Cheshire Militia and West Lowland Fencibles in September 1797, which was only quelled by the intervention of the Dumfries Fencible Cavalry.

Some believed that most civil unrest was politically motivated: 'It is melancholy to reflect how the lower Orders of People are led away. Could they but compare their lot with those of other Countries, they would be sensible of the numerous Blessings and Privileges they enjoy. This clamour for reform is made by designing men a cloak for the most pernicious and iniquitous Intentions.'[493] Some of the disturbances which caused the military to be deployed 'in aid of civil power' were apparently political in origin, for example those in London over the weekend of 6-9 April 1810 (about which the foregoing quotation was made). On this occasion mobs assembled to protest against the arrest of Sir Francis Burdett for a breach of parliamentary privilege (by writing an article for Cobbett's newspaper). Household Cavalrymen were deployed outside his house, resisting an attack by the mob on the Saturday night (in which Horse Guardsmen galloped through Piccadilly, firing their pistols), and an artillery park of sixteen guns was ordered from Woolwich to St. James's Park, with a howitzer and 6pdr at Soho Square. On the Monday parliamentary officers forced the kitchen window of Burdett's house, seized him and took him to the Tower; his escort was pelted with stones and mud until they charged the mob, and a running fight progressed up Fenchurch Street. Three people were killed by carbine-shots; a verdict of justifiable homicide was returned on one man who had attacked the troops, but of wilful murder by unknown Life Guardsmen on the other victims, shot by accident.

Some of the peacekeeping duties of the military were distinctly bizarre; for example, in August 1800 a detachment of Foot Guards was summoned from Knightsbridge barracks to St. George's Hospital to protect the body of Thomas Flynn, a suicide who had murdered his wife, from begin seized by the mob. After escorting the corpse to the grave they formed a defensive circle until the ceremonies had been completed, and then marched away to 'the praises of the respectable part of the neighbourhood, and the execrations of the misguided mob'.[494]

The majority of unrest, however, emanated from the very genuine social ills which prevailed, especially in the 1790s and in about 1812, when the rising price of provisions and scarcity of employment led to great hardship. Many viewed the protesters with sympathy, but only on rare occasions did the military make such sentiments evident, for example in a food riot in March 1801 which apparently was actually directed by officers of the Brixham Volunteers. Some believed that the appearance of troops served only to exacerbate the situation: Lord John Russell in parliament in November 1795 quoted the case of a troop of fencible cavalry being sent to Odiham, which 'threw the whole town into consternation';[495] they had been sent, he said, to quell a riot, when there was no sign of one. Pitt replied that they had conducted themselves quietly, and suggested that their presence might have *prevented* a riot!

Many of the provision-riots, initiated by hunger, involved the seizure of victuals, which were either distributed among the crowd or sold at reduced prices. A typical example occurred at Hemstall in December 1795:

'... a number of people assembled and boarded a vessel that was waiting with the tide, bound for Bristol, laden with wheat and flour; on discovering the flour they gave three cheers, the banks were instantly covered with their comrades, who proceeded to unload and distribute the flour ... men, women and children, with sacks and bags, carried as much as they were able on their shoulders. A party of the Essex fencible cavalry, headed by Mr Pyrke, a Magistrate, arrived at the scene of depredation, when the freebooters fled in every direction; five of the most active were secured and sent to Gloucester Castle for trial at the Spring Assizes. Since the above some villain fired a piece loaded with slugs into the bed-room of Mr Pyrke, but fortunately did not effect their intended purpose. The serjeant of the military on that occasion has been violently bruised on the head, by a stone thrown at him ...'[496]

Not all such incidents ended without serious injury. Another example occurred at Rochdale in August 1795, when a mob, led by an old woman named Fenton, alias 'Sparey Springer's wife', rioted over the price of flour and potatoes. The Rochdale Volunteers assembled to help the magistrates restore order and, it was said, misunderstood an order given them by their unit chaplain, the Revd. Thomas Drake, who said, 'shoot o'er 'em'. As a manufacturer named Oram had just ridden up, they fired in his direction; but whatever the actual cause, the volley killed two innocent bystanders. The resulting inquest decided that 'they were killed of necessity in defence of his majesty's subjects',[497] but the corps henceforward enjoyed a bad reputation locally, and at least three members were persuaded by their wives and neighbours to resign.

Further tragic incidents occurred in the same month, August 1795. Only three days after the Rochdale riot an equally serious incident occurred in Sheffield, when men of the Loyal Sheffield Regiment (a regular unit) refused to dismiss in protest over arrears of pay and withholding of bounties. Sheffield was noted for its republican sentiments, and a crowd gathered in Norfolk Street to support the protesting troops. The Loyal Independent Sheffield Volunteers were called, a corps already unpopular with the republicans and satirized as 'Ruddle-neck'd tups'.[498] Their commandant was Robert Athorpe who, somewhat unusually, acted as the magistrate in the events which followed. He, 'in a peremptory tone commanded the people instantaneously to disperse, which not being immediately complied with, the Riot Act was read' (which gave the military the legal right to open fire if the crowd had not dispersed in an hour); 'when an hour was expired, the volunteers fired upon the townsmen with bullets, and killed two persons upon the spot; several others were wounded, and the rest fled on every side in consternation'.[499] Even worse was an event in the same month when the Leicester troop was called to Barrow-upon-Soar, where a mob had seized a wagon-load of corn and taken it to the churchyard for distribution. The magistrates offered to leave eight quarters of grain with the crowd if they released the rest, but as the wagon began to move the yeomen were pelted with brick-bats and shots were fired at them, wounding one of their number; they fired back, killing three and wounding eight of the crowd. Indeed, the military did not escape unscathed in these affairs: for example, at a food-riot in Halstead in Essex, also in the same month, a member of the Surrey Fencible Cavalry was knocked from his horse and pitchforked, and the riot was only quelled by the arrival of reinforcements, the flank companies of the Wilt-shire Militia.

Although there were examples of the misuse of force, as at Tranent, in many cases the troops were reluctant to harm their fellow-countrymen. An example was quoted at the trial of one Michael Sidebottom for rioting at Castleford, the judge remarking that 'he could not help testifying his satisfaction upon finding the great utility of the volunteer corps ... and giving his applause to the cool and determined conduct ... particularly to that gentleman of the cavalry, who, though his own life was in danger from the violence of Sidebottom, who endeavoured to force him and his horse into the River Aire, had declined the making use of his sword'.[500] Sidebottom was gaoled for a month.

Another outbreak of disorder occurred in northern England and the Midlands in 1812, the 'Luddite' troubles, named after the probably mythical 'General Ludd', a title used by more than one of the leaders of the unrest (for example, one William Walker, convicted at Chester in May 1812, while two women who led a mob against provision-dealers in September 1812 were known as Madam Ludd and Lady Ludd). Originating from economic depression, many of these disturbances were directed towards machine-breaking, as automation was seen as depriving textile-workers and others of their livelihood; and instead of the spontaneity of earlier riots, the Luddite movement involved some pre-meditation and even the administration of oaths to bind the conspirators together (known by the textile term 'twisting in'). In some areas the planning included the production of seditious handbills and even military organization. In Yorkshire, for example, large bodies of men were reported as drilling at night, and the theft of weapons was regarded as particularly alarming. In May 1812 it was reported that a major plot had been foiled, a simultaneous rising to be signalled by the stopping of mail-coaches; after attempts to enlist soldiers in the plot, a sergeant of the Bolton Local Militia was infiltrated as an agent to enter the conspiracy, learn their oaths and attend clandestine meetings, and when he had discovered all he could, the ringleaders were arrested.

The machine-breakers were not without sympathizers: Byron made his maiden speech in the House of Lords on their behalf; subscriptions opened at Leeds and Nottingham in the spring of 1812 enabled provisions to be retailed at a price affordable by even the poorest, and in the Commons on 13 April 1812 Samuel Whitbread described measures to keep order as attempting 'to stifle the cries of hunger by the point of the bayonet'.[501] Nevertheless, most energies were directed towards the forceful suppression of disorder rather than to alleviation of the causes; for example, in the trial of rioters at Chester in May 1812, the judge rejected the mitigation of hunger and distress but blamed 'the intrigues of wicked and designing men'.[502] Consequently, sentences were Draconian: eight rioters hanged at Lancaster in June 1812 included a woman, Hannah Smith, who had been convicted of stealing potatoes.

Disturbances confronted by the military during this period assumed a more serious nature: for example, in March 1812 a mob fired muskets into Burton's calico-printing works at Middleton, the defenders of which shot back, and further casualties were incurred in an assault on the proprietor's house. With the decline in the volunteers, who had been able to assemble in a very short time, in many cases the regular troops and Local Militia were not close enough on hand to prevent looting and destruction: for example, when in April 1812 a mob armed with guns and pitchforks broke into the warehouses of Messrs. Richardson and Dugsdale at Dalston, near Carlisle, they carried off £500-worth of bacon, hams and flour before military assistance could arrive, and all the soldiers were able to arrest were some forty girls. Two desperate tactics were employed by the Luddites at this period: premeditated and organized attacks on property, and assassination.

Probably the most famous skirmish during the Luddite unrest was the attack made by a large armed gang upon Rawfolds Mill, between Heckmondwyke and Cleckheaton, near Huddersfield, whose owner, William Cartwright, was a captain in the Halifax Local Militia and who had installed shearing-frames two or three years earlier. He had fortified the mill with spiked barricades and seven tubs of vitriol, had taken to sleeping there in person with six armed men, and on the night of 11 April 1812 five men of the Cumberland Militia were stationed there in addition. The need to protect so many properties meant that despite the number of troops deployed – in September 1812, for example, 1,000 were billeted in the inns of Huddersfield – they were spread thinly; a short distance from Rawfolds was a detachment of Queen's Bays, but they were conspicuous by their absence until after the attack. On that night, 11 April, Rawfolds was stormed by Luddites, organized with military precision into companies with specific tasks; they overpowered the two sentries whom Cartwright had posted at the gate and began to axe and hammer the mill-doors, while another company started to break the windows with stones. Cartwright roused his defenders and rang his alarm-bell, and both sides began to shoot; the defenders calculated that they fired about 140 shots, despite the fact that two of the militiamen had been very reluctant to open fire, and a third flatly refused. After about twenty minutes' shooting, the Luddites withdrew, carrying away all their wounded but two, one of whom, Samuel Hartley, was a member of Cartwright's own Local Militia; the attackers returned home to Huddersfield, buying muffins for breakfast on the way, and leaving trails of blood for four miles. Both the captured Luddites died from their wounds (Cartwright's medical treatment, the cauterization of wounds with vitriol, may have been a dubious benefit), and it was reported that two more also died of wounds, one at Halifax on 14 May, having not dared consult a doctor lest he be identified as one of the attackers. After a number of suspects were rounded up, seventeen were hanged at York in January 1813; the recalcitrant militiaman was sentenced to 300 lashes, to be administered at Rawfolds on 21 April, but Cartwright had the sentence suspended after the infliction of 25 lashes. A subscription was opened in recognition of Cartwright's defence of the mill, which by September 1813 had reached £2,700, but he was still wrangling for government compensation in 1815.

The events at Rawfolds discouraged this form of protest, and the most desperate turned to the attempted assassination of prominent personalities. Most famous was the shooting of William Horsfall, who had been a lieutenant in the Huddersfield Volunteers, was a prominent woollen manufacturer at Marsden, near Huddersfield, and was so active in his attempts to combat the Luddites that his quest to discover the Rawfolds attackers had 'rendered him obnoxious, in a high degree, to the machine-destroyers'.[503] On 28 April he was shot twice by four men from a wall loopholed for the purpose; one of the wounds proved fatal, and a friend named Eastwood who went to procure medical assistance was twice thrown from his horse during the errand, and died from his injuries. A reward of £2,000 was offered for the conviction of his killers, and lesser rewards for the perpetrators of similar attacks on other manufacturers and even upon the Huddersfield deputy constable. One of the assassins turned king's evidence which convicted the others, who were hanged in January 1813.

The use of the military in the suppression of such civil unrest served to increase their unpopularity among a section of the population, which was manifested in many minor incidents. For example, in October 1798 two Guards officers (including Captain Duncan, son of the admiral) were walking by Horse Guards when they were pelted with mud by a mob, and were so threatened that they drew their swords; one of the leading mud-throwers, Charles Collins, received six months in Cold Bath Fields prison for riot and assault. Attempts to apprehend deserters were often fraught with danger, if a mob took the part of the accused. For example, in July 1795 two 12th Light Dragoons grabbed a deserter in Holborn, and such a crowd gathered that the soldiers drew their swords, with which one of them cut off the nose of a member of the crowd, 'which so irritated them, that the lives of the two men became seriously endangered. They were knocked down, and beat very severely; and the populace had proceeded so far as to have laid one of them down in the street that a cart might run over his neck; but, fortunately, the high constable, with proper assistance, coming up, the unfortunate soldier was rescued from immediate death, though he suffered so much while in the power of the mob, that it was reported that he died last night ...'[504] This was not an isolated incident; for example, in September 1804 six men were convicted at Middlesex Sessions for riot and assault upon Captain Shaw and a party of the 23rd, in attempting to rescue a deserter; and another dreadful affray occurred in Canterbury in August 1810 when members of the Queen's Bays attempted to apprehend a suspected deserter, in which two of the dragoons were knifed severely when the crowd turned on them.

Even the mere presence of the army could be inflammatory: when a party of the 10th Light Dragoons began to perform their sword-exercise at Leatherhead Fair in October 1803, the crowd took it as provocation and a severe fight ensued in which serious injuries were sustained on both sides. Occasionally, public resentment of the military even ended in murder; an example occurred in July 1795 when Thomas Purvis was beaten to death for no other reason than that he was wearing the uniform of the Newcastle Volunteers. In May 1812 a revenge attack by Luddites was reported upon Sergeant Moore of the Local Militia in Manchester, who had refused to take a Luddite oath. He was set upon when walking down Ancoats Street with a young woman, a cry of 'murder!' was heard and a gang of men was seen to hurry away; next day both Moore and the woman were taken dead from the river where, it was presumed, they had been thrown.

As remarked upon by many contemporary observers, it was fortunate that the British army had to meet enemy troops on British soil only on the rarest of occasions, briefly during the 1798 rebellion in Ireland and in the farcical French landing at Fishguard in 1797. Otherwise, their only domestic contact was with enemy prisoners of war, the superintendence of whom occupied considerable military resources.

Initially, provision for French prisoners was the responsibility of the Navy's Sick and Hurt Board, and contrary to some accusations, prisoners received an adequate daily ration of a quart of beer, 1½ pounds bread, ¾-pound beef (4 oz. butter or 6 oz. cheese on Saturdays instead), ⅓-oz. salt, plus ½-pint pease four days a week, or 1 pound cabbage (off the stalk). The sick received extra rations, and so careful were the authorities to ensure that prisoners received their due that a fraudulent contractor at Falmouth was fined £300 and gaoled for six months. From 1798 each state maintained an Agent in the enemy country, to superintend the prisoners and be responsible for provisioning them, at the cost of the respective countries. Following the renewal of the war in 1803 it was proposed that each government defray the cost of its own prisoners, but it was claimed that Napoleon had refused to acceed to this in the belief that there were so many French prisoners in Britain (almost 30,000 by 1808, against almost 8,000 Britons in France) that their maintenance would embarrass British finances.

Ordinary prisoners were accommodated in large prison-camps like Dartmoor or Norman Cross, which were of reasonable standards; others were placed in floating prisons or hulks, generally decrepit, dismasted warships where living conditions were often very bad. The use of such places was necessary because of the numbers of prisoners accumulated: at the peace in 1814 there were 72,000 French prisoners in Britain. Officer prisoners who gave their parole (word of honour not to escape) were permitted to take private lodgings among the community, provided that they did not stray outside territorial limits set by the terms of their parole, under which conditions they could live in reasonable comfort.

Treatment of prisoners, even those captured invading Britain, was supposed to be scrupulously honourable. When French prisoners arrived in Dublin in 1798, amid huge crowds, 'there was found only one man who betrayed any other feeling than curiosity ... [who] walked up to a French Officer and spit in his face! The Frenchman drew his sword (the officers were suffered to wear their swords) and aimed a blow at the wretch who insulted him, which would have proved fatal, but for the interposition of the halbert of an English Serjeant. A member of the Merchants Cavalry, who witnessed the transaction, rode up and apologized to the Frenchman, and then turning to the mean offender, dealt him such a blow with the flat of his sword as set him reeling, at the same time damning the scoundrel for daring to treat a captive enemy in such a manner. The honest indignation of the army, yeomanry, and the people, was loudly and strongly expressed on the occasion, and the rascal slunk away amidst the hootings and execrations of the crowd.'[505]

The treatment of officers on parole was generally very good, but when the French General Boyer attended the Harmonic Concert at Bath in February 1804, a heated discussion arose about the wisdom of admitting him, as stories were circulating that he had murdered some Turks. However, 'the whole of his conduct on that evening proved that the polite attentions which he has received at Bath have not been improperly bestowed';[506] he laughed at comic songs defaming Napoleon and said that only propriety prevented him from joining in the three cheers for the king which concluded the entertainment! So comfortable was his captivity that when on parole in Derby in the following year he was described as resembling an English gentleman, and with his fellows 'vivacity beamed in every countenance'.[507] Not a few prisoners on parole married British ladies, but their mixing with the civilian population was not without problems; for example, John Gibson, a nail-maker of Hawick and late of the 94th Foot, suspected his wife of conducting an affair with a French officer who visited their house, and became convinced that she was poisoning his tea to allow her to run off with the Frenchman. Gibson was sentenced to death for cutting her throat while, he claimed, she was attempting to choke him.

Most prisoners were well behaved and those in camps developed a thriving industry in the manufacture of models or trinkets from bone or straw, which they sold to supplement their rations. At times they were even useful to their hosts: for example, French and other prisoners were commended in August 1812 for helping fight a severe fire in Oxfordshire, and in May 1813 a prisoner named Morand jumped off the hulk *Crown* at Portsmouth to save from drowning an officer of the Inverness Militia, following the sinking of a pleasure-boat.

Their very presence, however, necessitated the deployment of considerable numbers of troops, the need for which was emphasized by periodic outbreaks of unrest or attempted escapes. For example, in September 1812 there was a riot at Dartmoor after a temporary reduction of bread to 1 pound per diem after the bakehouse burned down; it was quelled only after the arrival of three fieldpieces from Plymouth to reinforce the Cheshire Militia. Among many attempted escapes, in September 1807 about 500 prisoners broke down one of the inner palisades at Norman Cross, but were bayonet-charged by the guards (and 40 wounded) before they could reach the outer wall.

Despite it being a violation of personal honour, the attempted escape of parolees was not uncommon. The most famous of the parole-violators was General Charles Lefebvre-Desnouëttes, who had been captured at Benevente. He absconded from Cheltenham, posing as a German count, with his wife disguised as his son, and his ADC as his valet; he crossed the Channel by means of a smuggling boat. General Armand Philippon, governor of Badajos, broke his parole with another general (Garnier) and ran off from Oswestry; he was aided by a miller named Robinson, landlord Hughes of the Lion Inn at Rye, and two smugglers, Hutter and Turner, who conveyed them over the Channel. Many others were less successful: General Simon, captured at Busaco, absconded from parole at Odiham but was recaptured by the Bow Street officer Vickery, hiding in a coal-hole in Camden Town.

A more legitimate method of gaining freedom was by 'exchange', by which prisoners of equivalent rank were exchanged between the combatant powers. This was generally of benefit to both sides, although the reason ascribed to the rapid exchange of General Joseph Humbert (captured in Ireland in 1798) was unusual, reported as the result of the voracious appetite shown by him and his staff at Congleton: 'it is surely a matter of rejoicing that they should have been so soon sent out of the country – for we could not have more efficacious allies to co-operate with us in our attempts to produce a famine among the enemy ... being deprived of every other offensive weapon, they were determined at least to *shew* their teeth ... wonderful was the skill in *trencher-tactics*, and *knife* and *fork-evolutions* ...'[508]

14
'White powder exchanged for black'
THE EXPERIENCE OF CAMPAIGNING

GEORGE WOOD DESCRIBED THE PROCESS OF CAMPAIGNING IN terms of exchanging white powder for black,[509] an apt comparison between gunpowder and the white powder worn on the hair in full dress. Although each campaign had its own characteristics, certain features were almost universal.

All campaigns began with the conveyance by ship to the theatre of war, in which, as with the re-supply of armies on campaign, the dominance of the Royal Navy was of crucial importance. Troopships were controlled by the Transport Board, a panel of five naval captains and a secretary. The difficulty of finding sufficient ships to hire for all the army's requirements led to the use of many unsuitable vessels, making sea voyages scarcely bearable; for example, Alexander Gordon described the ship which evacuated him from Corunna as 'my floating dungeon'![510] The conditions were markedly superior when Royal Navy ships or East India Company transports were used, but all too many hired merchantmen were insanitary hulks with incompetent crews. A notable voyage which exemplifies this fact was that of the transport *Betsy*, which carried the fever-ravaged remnant of the 88th home from Grenada in 1796. This unseaworthy tub was hit by 'Yellow Jack' (yellow fever) as it left the Caribbean, which killed its captain and first mate, leaving in command the second mate who was a hopeless drunkard, totally ignorant of navigation even in his few lucid moments. After weeks of lurching around the Atlantic, the army officers on board finally removed him from command and appointed one of their own as master, Captain Richard Vandeleur, who before joining the army had been a naval midshipman. Using the half-remembered skills of his youth, he set a course and eventually announced that they had arrived in the English Channel, but on hailing a passing ship was told that they were about to enter the Mersey. Nevertheless, it was a considerable feat to take the ship safely to harbour, and doubly fortunate that it survived, for aboard *Betsy* was James McGrigor, surgeon of the 88th, who was thus spared to make so great a contribution to the army's medical establishment.

Transportation by sea was always hazardous, and many casualties were incurred by shipwreck. For example, when some 234 bodies were washed up on the beach after the sinking of the 63rd's transport off Portland in November 1795, 'no celebrated field of carnage ever presented, in proportion to its size, a more awful sight ... Either the sea or the merciless wreckers had stripped the sufferers of the clothes worn at the fatal moment. The remains of a military stock, the collar or wristband of a shirt, or a piece of blue pantaloons, were all the fragments of their apparel that remained. The only mode of distinguishing the officers was the different appearance of their hands from those of men accustomed to hard labour ...'[511] Many other examples included the loss of the transport *Dispatch*, carrying part of the 7th Light Dragoons from Corunna, which sank near the Manacle Rocks, near Helston, in which three officers, 65 men, five women and 32 horses were lost, and only seven dragoons saved; and in November 1807 the loss of the Dublin packet *Prince of Wales*, en route to Liverpool, and the *Rochdale*, together cost about 385 lives, mostly members of the 48th and 97th and their families.

Upon landing in the theatre of campaigning, the first encounter was with the indigenous inhabitants, which was usually a friendly affair, even if the British attitude was often one of disdain for foreign customs. The inhabitants of the Iberian peninsula were most frequently criticized for their lack of cleanliness, for example: '... The Portuguese are a filthy race, no doubt, but they have one merit, and it is the only one I can give them – namely – that they feel and seem to know themselves to be a dirty race, and do not pretend to do what their neighbours do, by any affectation of false pride in a manner in which both are equally involved – dirt.'[512] Foreign religious practices were often equally criticized, although several writers remarked upon the desirability of being billeted upon priests, who seemed to enjoy the best of living; and convents remained a source of endless fascination for British subalterns. Notwithstanding the iron gratings which usually separated them, the inhabitants of these institutions were often most receptive to the attentions they received; for example, when a troopship called at the Azores in 1814, the cloistered girls waltzed in view of their admirers, 'in which the light and elegant forms of these captivating sirens were exhibited to the greatest possible advantage', with 'their lustrous eyes beaming unutterable things'.[513] (George Gleig of the 85th was less impressed on this occasion, describing the nuns as 'licensed beggars'!)[514] Most troubles with the civilian population arising from these or similar reasons were resolved reasonably amicably, although the Hon. Captain Gore of the 94th, brother of the Earl of Arran, was shot and killed in 1814 when a party of Spanish troops stormed his billet, intent on re-possessing a lady from Vittoria with whom he had eloped.

Although campaigning involved much hard labour and moments of terror, there were also long periods of intense boredom. Edward Charles Cocks emphasized the importance of the ability to fill empty hours when recommending the education for young officers: 'When first a soldier becomes a prey to *ennui* it is all over with him. He is first sorrowful and then sick. But a man will always get *ennui* unless he has the power of amusing himself, for we cannot think for ever, especially at nineteen ... If he can sing and dance ... he passes his evenings pleasantly ... and gets up in the morning with a light heart and a clear head ready to set to work at his duty, while his unharmonious comrade ... collects a quantity of black bile and turns out in the morning with a gloomy face and grumbling air sufficient to frighten the sun behind a cloud ... there is nothing we really dread, except having nothing to do. On these occasions especially the new hands from England give the matter up, go to bed and report themselves sick, others call literature and fiddling, mathematics and dancing, in a word sense and nonsense, to their aid, and get through the business pretty well.'[515]

Many contemporary accounts describe off-duty pastimes conducted with relentless good-humour, in even the most difficult of circumstances. Amateur theatricals were especially popular among the officers (those of the Light

Division in the Peninsula gained considerable renown), and the officers of the 4th Foot even put on *The Rivals* aboard their troopship (HMS *Weser*, a recently captured French frigate) en route to America in 1814: '... a very ambitious undertaking, inasmuch as there were no ladies to represent the female characters, and those in "The Rivals" are by no means such as old campaigners are likely to personate with grace and fidelity ... The romantic Lydia Languish found a meet representative in Lieutenant M., a delicate creature, standing somewhere about six feet, in what an Irishman would call "his stocking vamps". The fond and faithful Julia was "done" by Lieutenant G., who responded to the querulous sentiment of Falkland in a voice whose deep rough tones would be accurately described by Sir Anthony Absolute's neat and expressive simile of "the croakings of a frog in a quinsey", and the effect of Mrs. Malaprop's appearance, with a face and figure "made up" for the occasion, may be surmised, from an exclamation from one of the audience – "My eyes! What a brimstone!"'[516]

Unfortunately, little attention was paid to diverting the spare time of the rank and file to harmless pursuits.

A vital factor at the outset of every campaign was the higher organization of the army, the sophistication of which reflected upon the ability of the army to operate. Originally the largest unit was the brigade, an association of two or more infantry battalions or cavalry regiments, commanded by a brigadier (an appointment, not a rank: a brigade-commander could be a general officer, or the commanding officer of one of the component battalions or regiments, in which case his regimental second in command would lead the unit). No permanent structure for higher combinations existed, although there were *ad hoc* arrangements: in the Netherlands the Duke of York formed 'columns' of several brigades, and in Egypt Abercromby reverted to the 18th-century practice of referring to 'lines', which implied the old battle-array of two or more lines of infantry, cavalry on the flanks and artillery interspersed along the front.

Organization of divisions of two or more brigades, each with integral artillery and commissariat, did not occur until the Danish expedition. Moore organized his army into four divisions of two infantry brigades each, and one of Wellington's first acts upon landing in the Peninsula in supreme command was to introduce a divisional system (18 June 1809), which was maintained throughout the war and ensured the smoothest possible running of the army, supply and transmission of orders. Each division comprised two to four infantry brigades and their commissariat; artillery was initially not sufficiently plentiful to make permanent allocations, but batteries became associated with particular formations. Staffs were small (formation-commander, his ADCs and a small number of administrative officers); supporting services (engineers, etc.) could be deployed either at divisional level or in a general reserve for temporary allocation where required. Such organization enabled a judicious commander (notably Wellington) to combine strong or veteran units with weak or untried corps, hopefully raising the calibre of the whole rather than reducing the best to the level of the poorest. Integration of Portuguese troops at brigade level was not successful, so they formed their own brigades which were integrated at divisional level; and the process was of especial use in 1815, when much of Wellington's army was inexperienced or unreliable. Unlike the practice adopted by (much larger) foreign armies, there was no permanent institution of a 'corps' system, although reference was made to certain formations as 'corps' in the later Peninsular War, for example that under Hill's command. In effect, each British division resembled a French corps in miniature, in that it was a self-supporting entity including all necessary staff, support, reconnaissance and a commissariat facility.

One of the most important attributes of an army was the ability to march, although rates of movement were dependent on such variable factors as weather, condition of roads and the ponderous progress of transport vehicles. There were three 'steps' for infantry: 'ordinary time' of 75 paces to the minute, 'quick time' of 108, and 'wheeling step', used for manoeuvre, of 120; each pace of 30 inches. It was stated in 1800 that infantry in line could advance and maintain formation at 100–120 paces per minute, without running; by which, even under combat conditions, an advance would not be made with any greater urgency than a modern parade quick-march. It was estimated that cavalry could cover 400 yards in 4½ minutes at a walk, in 123 seconds at a trot, and about one minute at a gallop. The cavalry's usual rate of march was about seventeen miles in six hours, 'but this may be extended to 21, or even 28 miles in that time',[517] although the speed attainable by couriers or small parties, using relays of horses, was prodigious: Wellington rode from Ciudad Rodrigo to Badajoz (174 miles) in 76 hours, and Sir Charles Vaughan rode from the Tudela to Corunna, via Madrid and Salamanca (595 miles) in nine days (although he calculated the distance as 790 miles).

On campaign a good daily march might be fifteen miles, although brief forced marches could be very much faster. The famous march of the Light Brigade to Talavera was not unprecedented: it was said that the 10th Foot marched from near Kilkenny to Dublin in February 1760, despite winter weather, in 24 hours (more than 71 miles); and in 1798 the North Gloucestershire Militia, hurrying to Ireland at the time of the French landing, marched from Portsea to Bristol, about 100 miles, in 48 hours, using impressed civilian transport (presumably for their baggage). Only on rare occasions were troops conveyed by vehicle on campaign, for example the use of Irish jaunting-cars and carriages by the Dumbarton Fencibles en route to the Battle of Arklow in 1798.

On a day of marching, the quartermasters and camp-Colour-men would depart early, to establish each unit's camping-ground for the next night. The 'general' drum-call would beat, upon which the guard-parties would rejoin their units and baggage be packed; an hour later the 'assembly' would be beaten, when any remaining tents were struck and loaded on to those baggage-wagons not already sent ahead to the new camp-site. Twenty minutes later the march would commence, each brigade staff having received its route and time of departure from headquarters, transmitted by the brigade-major to each unit. In hot weather in the Peninsula marches usually began an hour or two before daylight, with a halt of twenty minutes every three or four miles, so that the rear might close up; but over bad roads the rear might get little or no rest.

Marches could be wearisome and damaging in the extreme: 'Men and horses were exhausted: many of the former are consequently very ill, and twenty of the latter lie dead upon the road: not a drop of wine or spirits to be had to recruit our strength; not have we tasted bread or vegetables for many days! "You gentlemen of England, who live at home at ease", little do you reflect upon the sufferings we experience, and the privations we endure. But I am getting into the Penseroso strain, and that being quite out of my way, I must close the book, and look forward with hope for to-morrow. "To-morrow, and to-morrow, and to-morrow!" "Hope deferred maketh the heart sick". This is worse and worse: hill upon hill incessant rising; more men exhausted; more horses killed; and but two leagues gained.'[518] (The quotations in this passage demonstrate a level of literary knowledge perhaps not common at the time: respectively from *The Valiant Sailors* by Martin Parker, best known for *When the King Enjoys his Own Again*; *Macbeth*; and Proverbs 13, 12).

Under such conditions, men would fall out exhausted, or even die; for example, the extraordinary heat of midsummer 1808 had dire consequences even in Britain, when three men of the 2nd Foot were reported to have died of heatstroke on their march from Ipswich to Harwich. An associated hazard was that which supposedly killed Captain Joseph Venables of the 83rd at Tarbes in 1814, by drinking a draught of cold water when hot. It was especially noted that an inexperienced regiment always lost more stragglers on a march, the men not being inured to hard service; indeed, the 1/82nd lost so many stragglers in the retreat from Burgos that the officers were accused of neglect and the colonel was put under arrest, until the true state of its infirmity was shown: for a time they were unable to parade a single man, and had not even enough convalescents to attend the sick, racked with fever, rheumatism and gangrenous and blistered feet.

The attentions of the officers were required in such circumstances, to maintain morale. Lord Blayney found a unique way of raising the spirits of his exhausted 89th Foot when making a distressing forced march in South Africa: a Hottentot woman crossed their line of march, 'whose *derrière* projected to such an excess, that Lord Blayney placed his hat upon it, and the motion of the feather, added to that of the woman, created such incessant laughter, that the men proceeded cheerfully on their march'.[519] Among the 95th in the Peninsula, 'hunting a *Caçadore*' was a similar prank, in which any mounted Portuguese officer would be chased by every British officer as he rode past; the Portuguese never saw it, but 'the soldiers enjoyed the joke, which, though trifling, helped to keep up that larking spirit among them, which contributed so much towards the superiority and the glory of our arms. In times of hardship and privation the officer cannot be too much alive to the seizing of every opportunity, no matter how ridiculous, if it serves to beguile the soldier of his cares.'[520] Clearly, the British sense of humour, so apparent in more recent wars, was equally present in earlier days.

Even a beautiful view could lift spirits depressed by a tedious march, as with the Ebro valley: 'The influence of such a scene on the mind can scarcely be believed. Five minutes before we were all as *lively* as stones. In a moment we were all fruits and flowers; and many a pair of legs that one would have thought had not a kick left in them, were, in five minutes after, seen dancing across the bridge, to the tune of "The Downfall of Paris", which struck up from the bands of the different regiments.'[521]

At the nightly camp an experienced regiment would immediately make itself at home, building shelters from brushwood, lighting fires to boil tea and cook supper, and no matter how tired put their accoutrements in order for the morrow, involving 'a complete state of gipsyfication'.[522] As the heavier items were often trailing in the rear with the regimental baggage, camp-equipment was frequently sparse: 'A haversack on service is a sort of dumb waiter ... a well regulated one ought never to be without ... a couple of biscuit, a sausage, a little tea and sugar, a knife, fork, and spoon, a tin cup (which answers to the names of *tea-cup*, *soup-plate*, *wine-glass* and *tumbler*), a pair of socks, a piece of soap, a tooth-brush, towel, and comb, and half a dozen cigars.'[523] Officers often made sleeping-bags from blankets sewn up at the sides like a sack, and Cooper of the 7th recorded the common method of sleeping in the open air: the greatcoat was inverted, the legs thrust into the sleeves, the coat wrapped around the body, the forage cap pulled over the ears, and the knapsack used as a pillow. 'When tents were issued to us in May, 1813, at the rate of three tents to a company, a great change was felt in the way of comfort. The number in each tent was generally about twenty. When these were all laid, none could turn without general consent, and the word "turn" given.'[524]

The sight of twinkling camp-fires impressed those of a poetic disposition, as before Busaco: 'The appearance of the numberless fires which both armies had kept up throughout the night, and which were still burning when we stood to our arms in the dark, was a sight indescribably grand, and far exceeding the illuminations that were ever got up at Vauxhall ...'[525] Moyle Sherer thought that a man interested in nature and the beauty of the world could actually prefer bivouacking in the open, 'with men I both liked and esteemed, [and] a coarse but wholesome meal, seasoned by hunger and cheerfulness'[526] to civilized life in cities. Certainly it was preferable to the verminous billets often encountered in the Peninsula: '... we again broke ground, and proceeded to a village, called Lobon ... my billet (the first house I have had to sleep in for many weeks) abounds with mosquitos and bugs, "Who, hush'd in grim repose, expect their evening prey."'[527]

On campaign, all camps posted sentries to prevent surprises, though nocturnal panics were not unknown. For example, on the withdrawal from Burgos, the camp of the 3rd Division was thrown into confusion when some pigs knocked over a pile of arms; the clatter caused a Portuguese regiment to begin to fire all around them, and as Pakenham (the divisional commander) endeavoured to restore order his orderly dragoon was shot dead at his side. By the time the division had assembled in battle formation, with amazing speed and lack of panic despite sustaining some casualties from the Portuguese, the pigs had escaped unscathed.

The posting of sentries was undertaken with care. George Gleig of the 85th believed that on old battlefields they should be placed in pairs, lest superstition play upon the mind of the solitary sentry and cause him to desert his post: 'I don't care for living men, but for Godsake, sir, don't keep me beside *him*',[528] referring to a dead body. One of his sentries he found unconscious, having fainted at his post, and despite the risk of ridicule swore that a creature in white had crawled towards him, moaning, and as he was about to challenge it a dead body beside him sat up! Such things do not seem to have affected the composure of the Foot Guards: even the reported nocturnal appearance of the spectre of a headless woman in January 1804 caused no more consternation among Coldstream sentries than to cause them to make a report of the incident. On being assured that the sentries had not been reading 'dismal stories',[529] the officers accepted the report as merely routine!

The greatest vigilance was required by the army's forward outposts. Throughout the Peninsular War these troops (usually the Light Division) slept fully dressed and with horses saddled, ready for action the instant they awoke; hence Kincaid's remark that 'a soldier can nowhere sleep so soundly, nor is he anywhere so secure from surprise, as when within musket-shot of the enemy'.[530] In the half-light of dawn, which could obscure the enemy, the troops stood to arms until 'you can see a white horse a mile off',[531] and only then relaxed and removed their accoutrements. The commander of the 1st Hussars of the German Legion, the outpost troops *par excellence*, once greeted Beckwith of the 95th with, 'Well, Colonel, how you do?'; Beckwith replied, 'O, tolerably well, thank you, considering that I am obliged to sleep with one eye open.' 'By ———', said the German, 'I never sleeps at all.' Such was the care taken by this officer that he was seen preparing to sleep fully dressed even after the end of the war. A staff officer remarked, 'You surely don't mean to sleep in your clothes tonight, when you know there is an armistice?'. 'Air mistress or no air mistress,' replied the hussar, 'I sleeps in my breeches!'[532]

George Gleig regarded his spaniel Juno as the best sentry he ever met: 'A well-trained dog is no bad helpmate to an officer who has charge of an outpost; indeed I was never greatly alarmed, notwithstanding the communications of my vedettes, unless my four-footed patrol confirmed their statements.'[533] (So attached was Gleig to his dog that he ended his book *The Subaltern* with a touching poem about it, rather than one about the comrades he had lost; but as the dog had saved his life, it is perhaps not surprising.)

Before considering various aspects of battle, some comment is necessary on the prevailing views as to the morality of war, which to modern eyes can appear surprising. Although not shared by people whose homelands had been devastated (the guerrilla war in Spain, for example, was pursued with revolting barbarity on both sides), among nations regarded as 'honourable' there was a widespread belief that lives should only be risked, or taken, when there was a definite advantage to be gained: the *Morning Chronicle* commented that 'The lives of men are not to be thrown away upon attempts, the success of which is inadequate to compensate the loss of a single life. We had imagined, too, that it was not justifiable to take the lives of our enemies but for some object by which we should be in a better situation, and our enemy in a worse. Mere killing is not the purpose of war, and operations that terminate in mere unavailing slaughter, have been reprobated by all Moralists and Publicists. It is probable enough, however, that these principles are antiquated, and it is natural that they should be so among those who would make war merciless and destructive, in proportion as they make it contemptible and inglorious.'[534]

Such sentiments were echoed by those involved in war: as Leach remarked of the French commander at the Coa, who ordered a hopeless attack, 'It was a piece of unpardonable and unjustifiable butchery on the part of the man who ordered those brave grenadiers to be sacrificed, without the most remote prospect of success. They deserved a better fate, for no men could have behaved with more intrepidity.'[535] And such views extended to many of the lower ranks. Moyle Sherer overheard two British soldiers mourning the death of a brave French officer: '"I was sorry to see him drop, poor fellow," said one.

"Ah!" said another, "He came so close there was no missing him; I did for him!" "Did you!" rejoined the first speaker; "By God, I could not have pulled a trigger at him. No; damn me, I like fair fighting and hot fighting; but I could not single out such a man in cold blood.'"[536]

The general revulsion towards wanton ill-treatment of the enemy was articulated by Alexander Gordon, who at Sahagun saw a member of his squadron cut down a surrendering Frenchman: 'I hallooed to the fellow to spare him, but before I could reach the spot the villain had split the French-man's skull ... It was fortunate for him that he got out of my reach, for, in the indignation I felt at his conduct, I should certainly have treated him in the same manner.'[537] The man later explained that he could not let the day pass without killing a Frenchman, and could not waste such an opportunity; but to their credit, he was reviled by his comrades. Indeed, there was little hatred of the French, and many recorded their respect for a bold enemy; Moyle Sherer thought that in the French army, 'the good hearts far outnumber the bad', and his somewhat idealized view of the military trade led him to remark of one surly, captured *chasseur* who was shunned by his comrades as a barbarian from some Austrian province whose dialect was barely comprehensible: 'I shuddered at the very thought that such a man should be a soldier. To such a wretch, thought I, the weeping female would kneel in vain: the smile of the helpless babe, the groan of the wounded warrior, would never stay that uplifted arm.'[538]

Such feelings of respect towards an enemy who generally behaved in a chivalrous manner towards the British led to much fraternization in the Penin-sula; as George Napier commented after the commander of the opposing French outpost had been entertained to supper by the British; 'There is never any personal animosity between soldiers opposed to each other in war ... and I hope always will be the case. I should hate to fight out of personal malice or revenge, but have no objection to fight for "fun and glory".'[539]

In addition to off-duty civility and the exchange of rations, cordial relations extended to duty; as one British officer commented, 'I never knew an advanced sentry of either army to be *wantonly* shot at the out-posts; and I have often myself, when strolling too far in advance of my own piquet, been waved back by the French, but in no one instance was I fired upon.' He recorded an incident which epitomized the 'live-and-let-live' system which obtained: 'One fine moonlight night our advanced sentry called the attention of Colonel Alexander to the French sentry in his front, who was distinctly seen in the moonlight leaning against a tree, and fast asleep with his musket by his side. Alexander went quietly up to him, and took possession of the musket, and then awoke him. The man at first was much frightened upon finding himself disarmed, and in the hands of an English officer. Alexander gave him back his firelock, merely remarking, that it was fortunate for him that he had found him asleep on his post, instead of one of his own officers. The poor fellow expressed the greatest gratitude; and, by way of excuse for such an unsoldierlike act, said ... he had been marching for many hours ... and, having been immediately put upon out-post duty, he was overcome with fatigue.'[540]

Kincaid tells of a case in which a French sentry did fire on a British outpost, an action so unprecedented that next morning they sent an apology under a flag of truce. Henry King told how he wandered too near the French sentries, who fired wide to discourage him; he and his companion bowed to the sentries, who called back, *'Bon soir, messieurs – allez-vous-en.'*[541] Jonathan Leach recorded how a British vedette rode too near the French lines in a fog, and in his hurry to retire dropped his cloak; a French dragoon rode after him to return it, which was 'carrying on the war as it should be'![542] George Gleig noted that so long as he wore his red jacket (to confirm his nationality) he could approach the French lines so closely and in such safety that they helped him fish for trout, but that by the end of the war Wellington had to forbid communication, as the British and French were taking turns to entertain the other's picquets every night, which, Gleig admitted, was perhaps taking friendship too far; but by merely being civil, and in his case bartering English tea for French brandy, it made it 'extremely agreeable in carrying on hostilities after this fashion'.[543] Such civility was not restricted to the outposts: the French general Maximilien Foy regularly borrowed British newspapers from the defenders of the lines of Torres Vedras to check the value of his investments in British government stock.

William Grattan described how the opposing armies encamped on opposite sides of the Douro, when 'the French and British lived upon the most amicable terms. If we wanted wood for the construction of huts, our men were allowed to pass without molestation to the French side of the river to cut it. Each day the soldiers of both armies used to bathe together in the same stream, and an exchange of rations, such as biscuit and rum, between the French and our men was by no means uncommon ... The French officers said to us on parting, "We have met, and have been for some time friends. We are about to separate, and may meet as enemies. As 'friends' we received each other warmly – as 'enemies' we shall do the same."'[544] Such Gallic bonhomie was sometimes misunderstood, however; George Landmann once had to separate two sentries who after sharing a drink had almost come to blows after the Frenchman had kissed the Englishman, who not understanding the meaning of this gesture had cuffed the Frenchman and demanded to know 'what sort of pranks would you be after?'![545]

Throughout the Peninsular War, however, the Spanish never understood this 'gentlemanly' manner of waging war, 'nor did they ever let slip an opportunity of shooting an unfortunate sentry at his post. Much as such a practice is to be deprecated between the armies of civilized nations, it cannot be denied that the Spanish soldiers had a thousand causes of irritation and hatred toward their invaders.'[546] George Simmons understood, and expressed a view common to many British memorialists: 'I looked with sorrow at the poor inhabitants, heaving a sigh, expressing at the same time delight and confidence that the happy shores of Britain would never be cursed with these detestable monsters ... May England ever fight her battles in a foreign land!' He also remarked that civility towards the enemy did not imply any unwillingness to fight, 'if for the good of old England, I do not care how soon we have another [battle]. I go with the determination of doing all the injury in my power to the enemies of the human race, of which the French certainly merit the appellation.'[547] It is noteworthy that sentiments of civility were restricted to the army; visiting naval officers, who at sea would attack any Frenchman immediately, would remark, 'Who is that fellow there?', and on being told it was a French sentry, would immediately rejoin, 'Then why the devil don't you shoot him?'[548]

Despite the friendly behaviour between outposts, sentries remained suitably vigilant: for example, on the night of Salamanca Stapleton Cotton failed to answer a challenge and was shot in the arm by a sentry, and his orderly was also hit. Similarly, when the French on Mariegalante prepared to surrender on 3 September 1808, they sent as envoy a captured Irish merchant, John Brown. Overjoyed by his release from French captivity, he neglected to take with him a flag of truce, and on approaching the British position was shot dead by a sentry of the 1st West India Regiment (an incident not described in the official dispatch, which stated only that Brown had been killed in an action with the French picquet).

When action was imminent, the influence and calm of the officers was paramount, but unlike the practice in many European armies, theatrical gestures and patriotic exhortations to the men were neither made nor wanted; as Thomas Brotherton of the 14th Light Dragoons remarked, if harangues of the type made by Napoleon had been addressed to British troops, they would have replied 'Fudge!'[549] Instead, they received only the most unemotional statements from their leaders, such as that delivered to the 88th at Busaco by Lieutenant-Colonel Alexander Wallace: 'Now, Connaught Rangers, mind what you are going to do; pay attention to what I have so often told you, and when I bring you face to face with those French rascals, drive them down the hill – don't give the false touch, but push home to the muzzle! I have nothing more to say, and if I had it would be of no use, for in a *minit* or two there'll be such an infernal noise about your ears that you won't be able to hear yourselves.'[550] Major O'Hare of the 95th offered this advice to new recruits: 'Do you see those men on the plain? Well, then, those are the French, and our enemies. You must kill those fellows, and not allow them to kill you ... Recollect, recruits, you come here to kill, and not be killed. Bear this in mind: if you don't kill the French they'll kill you.'[551] Even blunter was Lieutenant-Colonel John Browne (who had sung *Heart of Oak* when leading his battalion at Barrosa!), when ordering his 56th to charge some guns in the Netherlands: he asked if they could see the rascals ahead, and declared, 'Let's take a run at them!'[552] (They did, with success.) Despite the lack of exhortation, however, the most effective officers were those characterized by Edward Costello as the 'come on' sort, to whom the men would respond better than to those who said 'go on'.

The sensation of coming under fire, or worse of anticipating it, were described by a number of writers. Rarely was action entered in completely cold blood, although Captain William Hay of the 52nd and 12th Light Dragoons said that for his part, having said a quiet prayer, asking for strength to do his duty, 'I do myself nothing but justice when I declare I never knew what it was to feel nervous in my life at the idea of a fight.'[553] Conversely, Moyle Sherer recalled that in his first action, when he overheard a staff officer remark, 'Be prepared, sir; they are certainly coming on', 'My bosom beat very, very quick; it was possible, that the few minutes of my existence were already numbered. Such a thought, however, though it will, it must, arise, in the first awful moment of expectation, to the mind of him who has never been engaged, is not either dangerous or despicable, and will rather strengthen than stagger the resolution of a manly heart.'[554]

George Gleig wrote memorably upon the period of apprehension before an action, and the 'feeling which takes possession of a man waiting for the commencement of a battle. In the first place, time appears to move upon leaden wings; every minute seems an hour, and every hour a day. Then there is a strange commingling of levity and seriousness within himself – a levity which prompts him to laugh he scarce knows why, and a seriousness which urges him from time to time to lift up a mental prayer to the Throne of Grace. On such occasions little or no conversation passes. The privates generally lean upon their firelocks, the officers upon their swords; and few words, except monosyllables, at least in answer to questions put, are wasted. On these occasions, too, the faces of the bravest often change colour, and the limbs of the most resolute tremble, not with fear, but with anxiety; while watches are consulted, till the individuals who consult them grow weary of the employment. On the whole, it is a situation of higher excitement, and darker and deeper feeling, than any other in human life; nor can he be said to have felt all which man is capable of feeling who has not gone through it.'[555]

Others, like George Wood of the 82nd, covered their anxiety with relentless good humour, until their chattering and joking aroused the displeasure of their more serious friends. He recalled the advice of a veteran colonel, who told his officers that even when bullets were flying they should neither duck nor flinch, 'for that is unsoldier-like, and may cause a panic in the troops; but always keep the head up, the body erect, and even in danger show a pleasing and determined aspect, which may command respect and admiration in your men, and animate them to that glory which Britons have a right to anticipate'.[556] A degree of fatalism suffused the experienced campaigner: '... meeting the enemy never costs me a second thought. It of course makes one gloomy to see so many fine fellows fall round one, but one day or other we must all go. The difference is very immaterial in the long-run whether a bullet or the hand of time does your business.'[557] This view was perhaps best expressed by Lieutenant-Colonel Vassall of the 38th at Montevideo, who called to his men not to flinch as 'every bullet has its billet!' (When he fell mortally wounded by a grapeshot which smashed his leg, he told them to push on and 'never mind me ... it's only the loss of a leg in the service!')[558]

There was a tendency, both at the time and later, to discount the significance of the individual in battle. Given the employment of close formations, composed apparently of almost featureless automata that marched and fired on command, this is understandable; and it is interesting that a noted refutation of the irrelevancy of the individual was written by a member of the 95th, a corps which demanded more initiative from its members than almost any other. John Kincaid noted that soldiers in battle 'are apt to have a feeling ... that they are but insignificant characters – only a humble individual out of many thousands, and that his conduct, be it good or bad, can have little influence over the fate of the day. This is a monstrous mistake ... for in battle, as elsewhere, no man is insignificant unless he chooses to make himself so ... men in battle may be classed under the disproportionate heads – a very small class who consider themselves insignificant – a very large class who content themselves with doing their duty, without going beyond it – and a tolerably large class who do their best, many of which are great men without knowing it.'

He then gave an example of the significance of the individual: 'We were engaged in a very hot skirmish ... when we were at length stopped by [enemy] regiments in line, which opened such a terrific fire within a few yards that it obliged every one to shelter himself as best he could among the inequalities of the ground and the sprinkling of trees which the place afforded. We remained inactive for about ten minutes amidst a shower of balls that seemed to be almost like a hail-storm, and when at the very worst, when it appeared to me to be certain death to quit the cover, a young scampish fellow of the name of Priestly, at the adjoining tree, started out from behind it, saying, "Well! I'll be hanged if I'll be bothered any longer behind a tree, so here's at you", and with that he banged off his rifle in the face of his foes, reloading very deliberately, while every one right and left followed his example, and the enemy, panic-struck, took to their heels without firing another shot. The action required no comment, the individual did not seem to be aware that he had any merit in what he did, but it is nevertheless a valuable example for those who are disposed to study causes and effects in the art of war.'[559]

The outcome of actions could, indeed hinge upon minor circumstances. Bunbury recounts a story from the 1799 campaign in north Holland, in which he asked Colonel Maitland, commanding a battalion of the 1st Foot Guards, to advance. Maitland hesitated as his men were on the edge of total exhaustion and almost out of ammunition; whereupon an exhausted grenadier lifted his chin from where it was leaning on the muzzle of his musket and said in a loud voice, 'Give us some more cartridges and we will see what can be done.' The regiment responded and Maitland ordered them forward again.[560] A similar incident turned the course of the action at New Ross, when having withdrawn, General Johnson asked the survivors of his mauled command whether they would follow him back into the attack. There was silence until the quartermaster commanding the nine men of the 5th Dragoons who were all that remained of the squadron that had been engaged, rode forward and exclaimed that the ten of them at least 'were willing to shed the last drop of their blood in support of their General, and to revenge their fallen comrades'. This brought forth a spontaneous shout of 'God save the King, and success to General Johnson', three cheers, and an immediate advance which turned defeat into victory.[561]

A factor that confuses accounts of battles was the general lack of interest about the exact identity of enemy troops; the following sarcastic comment about Waterloo is typical: 'We regret, exceedingly, that we are not informed ... as to the name or quality of our opponents. They might have been the Old Guard – Young Guard – or no Guard at all; but certain it is, that they were, looking fierce enough, and ugly enough to be anything'.[562] This extended to the inability to tell friend from foe: an old Peninsula officer of the 3/14th at Waterloo mistook Belgian uniforms and remarked, 'Och, murder thin! Thim's French safe enough!'; the battalion-commander reproved him with, 'Hush, Pat, you foolish fellow, don't frighten my boys!'[563] Such confusion in action was by no means uncommon, but it was noted that enemy formations often showed less caution when attacking troops amongst whom red coats were not visible, such was the reputation of, and respect for, the British army.

Once battle was joined, participants could have no clear idea of what was happening once their field of vision was restricted to yards by blankets of powder-smoke, reducing the sensations of action to a combination of 'firing, shouting, running, swearing, sweating, and huzzaing'.[564] Kincaid remarked prosaically that one battle was much like another, 'inasmuch as they always conclude with one or both sides running away', and another officer's description of Waterloo was typical: 'I'll be hanged if I know anything at all about the matter, for I was all day trodden in the mud and galloped over by every scoundrel who had a horse.'[565]

Moyle Sherer's description of Albuera exemplifies the sensations and confusion of a close-range fight: '... a heavy atmosphere of smoke again enveloped us, and few objects could be discerned at all, none distinctly. The coolest and bravest soldier, if he be in the heat of it, can make no calculation of time during an engagement ... We were the whole time advancing upon and shaking the enemy. At the distance of about twenty yards from them, we received orders to charge; we had ceased firing, cheered, and had our bayonets in the charging position ... Already, however, had the French infantry, alarmed by our preparatory cheers, which always indicate the charge, broken and fled ... To describe my feelings throughout this wild scene with fidelity, would be impossible: at intervals, a shriek or groan told that men were falling around me; but it was not always that the tumult of the contest suffered me to catch these sounds. A constant feeling towards the centre of the line, and the gradual diminution of our front, more truly bespoke the havock of death ... how shall I picture the *British soldier* going into action? He is neither heated by brandy, stimulated by the hope of plunder, nor inflamed by the deadly feelings of revenge; he does not even indulge in expressions of animosity against his foes; he moves forward, confident of victory, never dreams of the possibility of defeat, and braves death with all the accompanying horrors of laceration and torture, with the most cheerful intrepidity.'[566]

Under such stress and confusion, the true value of instilled discipline could be appreciated fully, as could the importance of co-ordinated action with other units, if only for self-preservation; as the Foot Guards shouted to the 7th and 15th Light Dragoons on going into action at Mouveaux, 17 May 1794: 'If you lather, we'll shave them.'[567]

A unit could sustain appalling casualties in battle and still remain 'effective'; the concept of withdrawing mauled regiments from the order-of-battle was virtually unknown. In percentage terms, the worst casualties were not always incurred in the major battles; a case was quoted concerning the 54th in the West Indies, entering an action with a strength of thirteen officers and 167 other ranks; at the end of the fight two officers and 30 other ranks remained fit for duty, a casualty-rate of more than 82 per cent.[568] Much was made of the casualties sustained by the 27th at Waterloo – 'lying dead in square' – and Jonathan Leach claimed that tourists could discern their position by the dark patch of earth where they had stood. At the start of the action they had 21 officers and 729 other ranks; they lost two officers and 103 other ranks killed, thirteen officers and 358 other ranks wounded, a casualty-rate of 63.4 per cent. Yet this was not the isolated case which might be imagined from references to the fate of the 27th; reference has already been made to Colborne's brigade at Albuera, which suffered percentage losses of 85.1 (1/3rd), 75.9 (2/48th) and 61.6 (2/66th), for example. Even under these rather unique circumstances – caught in line by cavalry – such figures were not unprecedented: in the same action the 29th lost 66.2 per cent, the 1/57th 66.1, and the 2/7th 61.4. Similar statistics occurred even in actions not especially renowned for the enormity of the butchery: the 1/61st at Salamanca, for example, from 29 officers and 517 other ranks, had five officers and 175 men unwounded at the end, a casualty-rate of more than 67 per cent.

Official casualty-figures often do not give an accurate picture of the actual effective strength of a unit at the conclusion of an action, for they do not include the stragglers, lightly wounded or lost men who would rejoin in the hours following the cessation of fighting. This was probably especially true in the cavalry, in which men would cease to be 'effective' if their mounts were lost, even though not themselves casualties. This explains accounts such as that of Captain William Hay of the 12th Light Dragoons, who before Waterloo noted his regiment as comprising three squadrons of 54, 53 and 48 files each; but at the end of the battle they could form only two squadrons of 24 and 23 files, implying a casualty-rate of almost 70 per cent. In fact, the regiment fielded 430 of all ranks and reported 111 casualties, a rate of less than 26 per cent, the difference presumably begin men who had become separated from the regiment but who later rejoined.

The first sight of a battlefield was a most profound shock: '... the plains were covered with the wounded and dead; whilst, horrible to relate, the stubble caught fire, and many disabled wretches were burnt to death! ... we applied ourselves to searching out, and carrying off, the wounded. But such scenes as the field and town presented on this, and the two succeeding days, exceeds human credibility; as much as it overpowered the most unfeeling amongst us. The God of mercy grant "I ne'er may look upon the like again" ... The enemy plundered such of our officers as they laid hold of, of their watches, epaulets, and money; but in other respects, they observed the dictates of humanity: to some they administered wine, to others water, and placed others out of the battle's heat. To one friend of mine ... severely wounded, and covered with blood, they asked him, if they should terminate his sufferings? This favour he declined, and is now doing well. My poor friend E——, indeed complained, that to him they behaved otherwise, having kicked and pushed him in an unfeeling manner; yet he spoke not of them with rancour: but having lingered for two days, he died the death of a Hero, with the resignation of a Christian.'[569]

Moyle Sherer wrote with sensitivity on the appearance of a battlefield, and ended with a universal truth: '... thousands of slain, thousands of wounded, writhing with anguish, and groaning with agony and despair. Move a little this way, here lie four officers of the French hundredth, all corpses. Why, that boy cannot have numbered eighteen years! ... Perhaps, on the banks of the murmuring and peaceful Loire, some mother thinks anxiously of this her darling child ... Most of the bodies are already stripped; rank is no longer distinguished. Yes: this must have been an officer; look at the delicate whiteness of his hands, and observe on his finger the mark of his ring. What manly beauty! What a smile still plays upon his lip! He fell, perhaps, beneath his colours; died easily; he is to be envied ... Look at the contraction of this body, and the anguish of these features; eight times has some lance pierced this frame. Here again lie headless trunks, and bodies torn and struck down by cannon shot; such death is sudden, horrid, but' 'tis merciful. Who are these that catch every moment at our coats, and cling to our feet, in such a humble attitude? The wounded soldiers of the enemy, who are imploring British protection from the exasperated and revengeful Spaniards. What a proud compliment to our country! Some readers will call this scene romantic, others disgusting: no matter; it is faithful; and it would be well for kings, politicians, and generals, if, while they talk of victories and exultation, and of defeats with philosophical indifference, they would allow their fancies to wander to the theatre of war, and the field of carnage.'[570]

Robbing the dead on the battlefield was a universal practice, and quite accepted by those in authority: having killed a Frenchman at Vimeiro, Benjamin Harris searched his body without success until an officer of the 60th suggested he rip open the lining of the dead man's coat, where he found his purse. However, a dim view was taken of stealing from one's own officers: a rifleman named Orr was sentenced to 500 lashes for stealing a jewelled ring from the body of Captain Daniel Cadoux of the 95th, who was killed in circumstances of the greatest gallantry at Vera in 1813, a man whose effeminate appearance belied his great courage; Orr hacked off the finger to get the ring and was stupid enough to attempt to sell it to Cadoux's fellow-officers.

Bodies lying on the battlefield were usually shovelled into pits dug by troops or local civilians, a process fearful to see, as a sightseer wrote of Waterloo: 'The general burying was truly horrible; large square holes were dug about six feet deep, and thirty or forty fine young fellows, stripped to their skins, were thrown into each, pell mell, and then covered over in so slovenly a manner, that sometimes a hand or foot peeped through the earth. One of these holes was preparing as I passed, and the followers of the army were stripping the bodies before throwing them into it, whilst some Russian Jews were assisting in the spoliation of the dead by chiselling out their teeth, an operation which they performed with the most brutal indifference. The clinking hammers of these wretches jarred horribly on my ears.'[571]

Those taken prisoner might expect some ill-treatment in the immediate stress and rage of battle; but when tempers cooled both British and French generally treated their captives with humanity. For example, Major Charles Napier was bayoneted as he lay wounded at Corunna, and would have been murdered had he not been saved by a French drummer; but after the action, Marshal Soult sent his own surgeon to dress his wounds, gave him money and fed him from his own table; and Marshal Ney arranged for Napier to go home even before an official exchange of prisoners had been agreed. As his brother George Napier remarked; 'To treat your enemy when in your power with every respect and kindness is the true characteristic of a brave man. None but the worthless coward insults or maltreats his prisoner; and, as the French officers are as brave as any men upon earth, so their conduct was humane and generous.'[572]

Such treatment depended upon the mutual respect of the combatants, however, and on occasion British prisoners suffered appallingly, if rarely in quite so vile a manner as the detachment captured by the Turks at El Hamet during the 1807 expedition to Egypt: '... we were put into a small apartment, and had nothing but a little straw and bread thrown to us. The smell was intolerable from the number of wounded men, and, to add to our distress, they had upwards of 100 *heads* (those of our brother-soldiers) piled immediately underneath our windows, which they made the Arabs skin and stuff with straw ...'[573] One of the captured officers, Ensign Joshua Gregory of the 78th, was put up for sale as a slave at Cairo; he was ransomed by the *French* consul there, and thus secured his freedom, but never fully recovered from his injury and maltreatment (a ball in his side could never be extracted). He emigrated to Australia to find a beneficial climate, but died as a half-pay lieutenant and magistrate of the Swan River colony, aged 48.

Support for the British prisoners in French hands was channelled through the Agent appointed for the purpose, as described earlier; following his capture at Fuengirola, Lord Blayney acted in this capacity. The conditions in which British prisoners were kept were often very poor, but perhaps not a great deal worse than those endured by some French prisoners in Britain. The behaviour of British prisoners was generally good; indeed, a story concerning some 300 en route to repatriation in 1814 told how they complained to the French authorities about being billetted upon French civilians, not because the French begrudged them food, but because the provision of such food left the civilians and their children short which, according to one of the prisoners, 'we take to be a greater hardship than any we found in prison'.[574] The billeting order was revoked and the poor French people relieved of their burden.

A serious breakdown in the normal civilized manner of treating prisoners occurred in 1813 when 23 Americans captured at Queenston were sent to Britain for trial, being allegedly British subjects. The Americans retaliated by putting 23 British prisoners of war in close confinement as hostages for the safety of their prisoners; whereupon Britain placed 23 American officers and 23 NCOs into close confinement, and stated that should any of the British hostages suffer death in retaliation for any death sentences placed upon the 'traitors', then double that number of American hostages would similarly be executed.

In the same way that Britain recruited from foreign prisoners of war, attempts were made to enlist British prisoners in French service. Sergeant Nicol of the 92nd, wounded and captured in the Peninsula, wrote of the inducements offered to those who turned their coat: 'An Irish captain had charge of us. He told us his name was Hussey from Sligo. He said he had been out with the "Boys" in the United Cause and his heart warmed to see us; he gave us a dollar to buy wine, and said he liked the French service very well ... we were beset with those harpies of the Irish Brigade, Captain Reilly and Sergeant-Major Dwyer, offering us brandy and telling us all the evils of a French prison; they got three of our party to join them ...'[575]

Only a few such prisoners did join the French, however, as did a few deserters who ran off on campaign to try their luck under different colours. Such men faced trial and the death sentence if they subsequently fell into British hands, but if taken in action were lucky to survive to face a court-martial, as turncoats were shown little mercy. For example, when a French cavalry officer was captured in September 1811 and revealed his name as O'Flyn, a private Fitz-Patrick of the 16th Light Dragoons shot him dead, as 'The fellow said he was an Irishman, which the dragoon could not hear and allow him to escape alive.'[576]

A series of trials for high treason took place in February 1812 upon ex-prisoners who had enlisted in French service at Isle de France. Some of those convicted were recommended for mercy, like William Cundell, who claimed to have entered French service simply to escape a verminous prison, had attempted to desert from the French and been imprisoned again; or Joseph

Worth, who had enlisted when drunk and was too frightened to recant when sober as the French 'would have done something not right to him'; a third had enlisted in the hope of thus getting a woman to live with him, and burst into tears when first meeting his old comrades after receiving his new French uniform. Another man, C. Bird, was acquitted when he proved that he had escaped from prison and subsequently disguised himself in French uniform to enable him to take comforts to his imprisoned comrades; in his case the chief prosecution witness, Elizabeth Westlake, apparently the wife of one of the other prisoners, had given perjured evidence because Bird had discovered her 'in a situation not to be described with a French officer'! One man was sentenced to death without recommendation for mercy, John Tweedle, who had not only enlisted in the French army but had been heard to 'damn King George and all his subjects, and declare his intention to fight for Bonaparte until he died'. Not even pleas from two of his former officers, adverting to his previous good behaviour and suggesting that he was simple-minded, could mitigate the sentence passed on his conviction.[577]

Enlistment in the French army did not necessarily result in the severe punishment generally given to those taken in arms against the British, however. For example, William Fisher was captured on the retreat to Corunna and endured the hardship of a French prison for some years before he agreed to enlist in French service. Having survived the retreat from Moscow, he refused to take the field against the British, and at the conclusion of the war rejoined his British regiment. Upon describing the circumstances of his enlistment in the French army he received a pardon. (Upon his discharge from the army he became a most skilful police detective in Edinburgh and later Falkirk, and was the officer who arrested Burke and Hare. It is interesting to note that before commencing his trade as supplier of corpses to the medical profession and part-time murderer, William Burke had also been a professional soldier, serving seven years in the Donegal Militia.) A rather different mode of escaping punishment was adopted by George Adams of the 42nd, a noted bad character, who was captured or perhaps deserted in the Peninsula in 1813, and upon rejoining his regiment chose to conceal the fact that he had fought in the 1814 campaign with the French 9th Dragoons![578]

Despite the advantage of a common language, attempts to persuade British troops to desert to the Americans in the War of 1812 had little effect. Surtees overheard an American officer declaiming to some of the 95th, promising them promotion and grants of land if they joined the US forces. 'Our people listened to this harangue for some time, and then began, I regret to say, to give him some bad language; telling him, at the same time, that they would rather be privates in the British Army, than officers among such a set of ragamuffins as the Americans, and told him to sheer off or they would fire on him.'[579] Even the 'foreigners' of De Watteville's Regiment declined to enter US service: 'True to the oath they had taken, and the cause in which they had fought, not one of them accepted the offer. They all, to a man, treated it with the greatest contempt.'[580]

Although the realities of warfare were never far removed, and although the British Army was often acutely aware of the misery caused to civilians by the actions of the French, the full enormity of war only struck home in those rare cases in which it was possible to observe the consequences upon the dependents of those whom the British had engaged in the field, and for which the British realized that they were personally responsible. After a landing on the Virginia side of the Potomac in October 1814, to disperse some American militia in a brief skirmish, a British officer entered a small dwelling near Northumberland Court House to buy a cup of tea. Within he found two pretty young women who, when they realized that the British were not the 'savage and ruthless desperadoes' which they had been told to expect, willingly prepared a meal of fried pork, eggs, cakes and tea for the officer and his companions. As they shared this meal in great good humour, the younger of the women explained that the other was her newly married sister, who was concerned at her husband's failure to return after being called out with the American militia on the previous night. '... Ere we had concluded the repast to which we sat down with such overflowing glee, the young bridegroom (the unfortunate pair had been only a week married) was carried into the house, by some of his comrades, a disfigured and stiffened corpse! The frantic screams of the agonized and widowed bride, as she clung to the lifeless form of him in whom it was evident her whole heart and soul had been centred, long rung in the ears of those who had heard them ... we hastened to quit the scene of such hopeless anguish, and, having first left with a neighbour ample payment for our meal (to be handed to the widow's sister), with saddened thoughts rejoined our regiment.'

Not only did this graphic exemplification of the real effects of war make such an impression upon those used only to observing the consequences of conflict upon soldiers, but the writer ended by condemning the whole expedition as 'an ill-managed, unmeaning and unnecessary affair' of neither strategic nor tactical significance; further evidence of the belief that conflict was only morally justified if a definite goal were in view, and that killing men just because they wore the enemy's uniform was unjustifiable.[581] Witnessing in person the heartbreak caused to the relatives of their victims, which usually could only be imagined, must have been the most powerful vindication of this belief.

15
'Wild War's Deadly Blast[582]
THE CAMPAIGNS

THE CAMPAIGNS UPON WHICH THE BRITISH ARMY WAS ENGAGED between 1793 and 1815 have been recounted in numerous sources. This chapter is intended, therefore, to be little more than an expanded chronology, but including the use of some contemporary writings to exemplify certain aspects of the British military establishment, the characteristics of the troops of which it was composed, or their mode of operation. Thus in some cases small actions or episodes are highlighted instead of conventional accounts of battles, and to avoid duplication with the multiplicity of available sources, many of the contemporary statements are taken from the more obscure material.

The First Campaigns, 1793–5

The initial operations undertaken enjoyed little success. An expedition was sent to Holland in 1793 primarily to put heart into the Dutch, and was only increased and given permission to take offensive action when it became obvious that the Austrian forces in the Netherlands required assistance in opposing the invading French. In these operations the failings of the British military system were thrown sharply into focus, especially when compared to the Austrian troops with whom they were collaborating; as John Gaspard Le Marchant remarked, the Austrians appeared 'as superior to us as we are to the train-bands in the city'.[583] This remark is best understood in the light of the wretched reputation of the London Militia at this period:

> 'Bold daring old Watchmen and wooden legg'd Sailors,
> Butchers, Barbers, and Tinkers, Tomturdmen and Taylors ...
> Some Smoaking and drinking their Spirits to keep,
> Some running away and some fast-asleep.'[584]

The campaign also provided the first instance in the period of collaboration with allies regarded as less zealous than might have been expected: 'Our brave countrymen, whilst spilling their blood in defence of that country, were not considered as friends and protectors, but as enemies ... every inch of ground was bravely defended by the British army. The Dutch sat quietly by the fireside smoking their pipes, and venting their rage against the English; the roaring of the enemy's cannon would not rouse them ...'[585]

The first British contingent (three battalions of Foot Guards, three of infantry, and a cavalry contingent drawn from eleven weak regiments) formed part of the Duke of York's Anglo-Hanoverian army which collaborated with the Austrians of Prince Friedrich Josias of Saxe-Coburg. The British engaged in a number of successful actions including Famars (23 May 1793), the capture of Valenciennes (29 July) and Lincelles (18 August), but without a decisive battle the campaign was suspended for the winter, during which the expedition was kept short of supplies and reinforcements as the available resources were directed towards the West Indies and Mediterranean (an early example of the government's inability to concentrate its attention effectively on one theatre). There were few successes in the following year, although the British cavalry won considerable renown at Villers-en-Cauchies (24 April 1794, where the 15th Light Dragoons made a celebrated charge, saving the Emperor Francis II in the process), and at Beaumont (26 April). In June the expedition was reinforced by Lord Moira and some 7,000 more troops (including the 33rd Foot, commanded by Lieutenant-Colonel Arthur Wellesley), but after another appalling winter the Allies withdrew into Germany, the British being evacuated from Bremen in April 1795, having suffered severe losses in the retreat. The ineptitude of the commissariat and administration showed Wellesley 'what one ought not to do, and that is always something'.[586]

Other operations met with similar lack of success. An Allied expedition to Toulon landed on 28 August 1793, intended to form the nucleus of a French royalist counter-revolution. Again the best efforts of the small British force (something over 2,100 rank and file) were frustrated by unreliable allies: despite the good quality of the small Piedmontese contingent, the bulk of the force, Neapolitans and Spanish, were little better than a rabble. Their flight caused the collapse of the Allied defences, and they sailed away to leave those who remained to shift for themselves; the evacuation of Toulon was completed by 19 December. An interesting sidelight upon the affair is the fact that in an action apparently involving the 11th Foot, Major Napoleon Bonaparte received a bayonet-wound in the thigh; had the blow been directed at a slightly different angle, the course of European history could have been changed completely. Slightly more successful were the operations in Corsica, from where the French were expelled, and where the sterling resistance to the British attack on Mortella Tower (8-10 February 1794) caused it to be used as a model for the series of defensive works raised along the south coast of England (and elsewhere) under the mis-spelled name of 'Martello towers'.

Another disaster occurred in the expedition to Quiberon in June-July 1795, in which a force of French emigrants (in British service) landed to support the royalist counter-revolution. This injudicious operation was ill-starred from the outset, with two commanders at odds (the Comtes de Puisaye and d'Hervilly, the latter holding a British commission as commander of the troops in British pay); the expedition was virtually annihilated, a few escaping but at least 700 of those captured by the French were shot out of hand. The British force intended to support the royalists landed at Isle d'Yeu on 29 September and withdrew in early December, having fought no action, which, considering the state of the units involved, and their lack of provisions, was doubtless just as well.

The only real success during this period was the occupation of the Cape in 1795, taken from the French-satellite Batavian Republic, whose forces in South Africa were insufficient to prevent its capture by the British expedition.

The West Indies

Compared to those in Europe, operations in the West Indies were of minor significance in terms of battles, but extremely important in other respects. British colonies in the Caribbean included principally Jamaica and Barbados, and others in the Leeward Islands (Antigua, Dominica, St. Kitts, Nevis) and Windward Islands (St. Vincent, Grenada); other territories were shared between France, Spain and the Netherlands. As the source of sugar, spices and other commodities, the commercial importance of the area was great, and the political influence of the 'West India lobby' ensured that every government had to ensure the safety of the British colonies, to channel their resources from the enemy and towards Britain. Whether the economic advantages warranted the cost in lives is another matter, for the operations in the West Indies during a short period cost the army more men than the entire disposable force committed in Europe: between 1794 and 1796, as many as 80,000 died or were invalided from West Indian service, of whom as many as half were fatalities.

Operations to sweep up the foreign colonies involved some hard fighting and casualties, but some were to little purpose: for example, St. Lucia and Tobago were restored to their original owners by the Peace of Amiens and had to be re-taken in 1803, Guadeloupe could not be held, and the futility of attempting to hold on to San Domingo (Haiti) was ultimately recognized by both Britain and France, both withdrawing to leave that lawless island to its civil war and anarchy. Enemy attempts to re-possess some of the colonies were generally resisted successfully, and rebellions by the native populations, most notably the 'Maroon revolt' in Jamaica, were suppressed.

It was not the casualties of these operations which so ravaged the British army, however: the grim reaper of the West Indies was disease, tropical fevers having few known remedies and being the cause of the almost literal annihiliation of regiment after regiment. So severe were the losses by sickness that some could explain them only as divine retribution, as punishment for the practice of slavery: one writer described the West Indies as 'the theatre of the crimes of Europeans ... and they are at the same time the theatre of their punishment. The yellow fever avenges the cause of the injured African. This destroying angel, while it mows down squadrons of Europeans as it were at one stroke, passes his hut and does him no injury. Our West Indian colonies cause a greater waste of life than they are worth ...'[587]

In 1839 Henry Marshall, Deputy Inspector-General of Army Hospitals, published statistics which demonstrate the ravages of disease. In the Leeward and Windward Islands between 1796 and 1805, for example, 24,916 troops *died* (the following statistics do not include all those who were invalided with broken health), which was akin to wiping out the entire garrison twice over (on 1 January 1805, 11,558 men were stationed there, for example). In bad years more than one-third of the garrison died (6,585 in 1796, 41.3 per cent of the whole), and even in the best year (1803, when 1,173 men died) the annual mortality rate was 9.7 per cent. The annual ratio of mortality in these stations between 1796 and 1828 averaged 13.4 per cent. Even this was not the worst: Jamaica and Honduras, taken together were even more fatal, with an average loss by death of 15.5 per cent between 1810 and 1828. A comparison was made between troops in these stations and in Ireland, the rate of mortality in the Windwards and Leewards being nine times greater than that in Ireland, and in Jamaica ten times.[588]

The effect upon regiments and individuals is more telling than an enumeration of statistics. For example, it was remarked in 1802 that the high state of the 13th Light Dragoons reflected well upon their commanding officer, Lieutenant-Colonel Bolton, who had taken only 3½ years to reconstruct the unit, which had arrived from the West Indies in 1798 with a strength of only 35 'worn-out' men. Some officers were reluctant to serve in such unhealthy places (so that those wishing to sell their commissions might not be able to obtain the full price while their unit was in the West Indies), but others did their duty in full knowledge of the risks. For example, Lieutenant-Colonel John Irving of the 1st West India Regiment, after 33 years active service, refused to sell out when ordered to return to Jamaica, which had almost proved fatal to him before and had killed his nephew: 'I am a soldier; and it shall never be said that John Irving sold out, because ordered to a climate where I have suffered so much, and which may be fatal to me.' He sailed for Jamaica in July 1807, and returned to Bath at the end of the year, 'a mere skeleton, in a chaise ... "I am all that remains of Colonel Irving."' He died on 4 February 1808.[589] A similar case was that of Lieutenant-General William-Anne Villettes, a distinguished officer of Huguenot descent who was born in Berne while his father was British ambassador there. When appointed to Jamaica in late 1807 he remarked that his health was not up to it, 'but I would not object to going there on that account; for if I were ordered to march up to a battery, I should do it, though I might be of opinion that I should be killed before my troop could carry it; and, in like manner, I think I ought not to hesitate as to going to Jamaica, if his Majesty's service requires it, though I ... shall fall a victim to the climate'. He died of fever on 13 July 1808.[590]

When the commander-in-chief in the Leeward Islands, Sir William Myers, Bt., died in July 1805, he was the fourteenth member of his family of eighteen who had died in the West Indies since their arrival. A measure of the impression made by such a toll of disease is the fact that when Jonathan Leach wrote his *Rough Sketches*, after a career in the hottest actions in the Peninsula and Waterloo campaigns, he ended his book with a recollection of his earliest service: 'All the friends of my early life are entombed in Antigua.'[591]

To combat the effects of disease, 'native' units were formed in the West Indies. Originally these were small, independent corps like Malcolm's Royal Rangers (formed in Martinique in 1794 under Lieutenant Malcolm of the 41st, an early exponent of light infantry tactics), but in 1795 some were reorganized as infantry regiments: the 1st West India Regiment, for example, was formed from Malcolm's Rangers and the Carolina Black Corps, the 2nd from the St. Vincent's Black Rangers, and so on. By 1800 there were twelve numbered West India Regiments, but the 9th-12th were disbanded at the Peace of Amiens. Their rank and file were drawn partly from the West Indian colonies, but many Africans were enlisted: in the 5th Regiment, for example, between 1798 and 1807, 87.4 per cent of recruits were Africans, 10.8 per cent West Indian Negroes, and less than one per cent Europeans and East Indian lascars.[592] The resistance of these men to tropical diseases was remarkable: against the 15.5 per cent annual mortality quoted above for Jamaica and Honduras, the Negro troops in the same station and period suffered only 5.5 per cent mortality, and in 1839 it was reported that although the annual mortality for European troops in St. Lucia, Dominica, Tobago and Jamaica was between 12.3 and 15.3, for Negroes it was between 3 and 4 per cent.[593] Conversely, the West Indians suffered in other climates, as in the lines before New Orleans:

'many of the poor blacks being frost-bitten, and quite incapable of doing duty'.[594]

Recruiting originally involved that most vile of trades, the traffic in slaves, the government taking upon itself the right of taking first pick from slave-ships arriving in the West Indies, for which men the market price was paid, which might be between £60 and £120. From 1795 to 1808 some 13,400 recruits were purchased at a cost approaching a million pounds, and the practice of buying slave recruits seems to have continued for a short while even after the abolition of the trade in March 1807.[595] The newly purchased soldiers were given new names (often of cities, rivers or fortresses) which were inscribed on labels hung around their necks, as it was remarked that they all looked alike to the Europeans who officered the West India Regiments, and it took some time for them to be recognized. A happier source of recruits were the Negro slaves who voluntarily accompanied the British forces upon their withdrawal from Washington, and who upon the conclusion of the war received free land-grants in Canada in return for their excellent services (mostly in the Royal Marines), having found the 'perfect freedom – that freedom which the vaunted "Land of Liberty" denied them'[596] during their servitude in the United States.

Despite being issued with old weapons and equipment, and housed in mediocre accommodation, the West India Regiments proved to be good troops, of great value in the Caribbean and elsewhere (the 5th Regiment was that present at New Orleans). The service was not without problems, however: in April 1802 the 8th Regiment mutinied in Dominica and murdered some of its officers in a most revolting manner. Their colonel, the Hon. Andrew Cochrane-Johnstone (who was also governor of Dominica) marched to confront the mutineers with a force comprising men of the 68th, marines, seamen and militia. He found them drawn up regularly on parade, and when they refused to ground their arms the Europeans fired and pursued them as they tried to escape; the mutineers suffered about 100 casualties, and about 130 were apprehended; the governor's force lost four killed and 24 wounded, eighteen of these casualties falling among the 68th.

The career of this colonel exemplifies some of the problems with officers stationed away from close supervision. The twelfth son of the 8th Earl of Dundonald, Andrew Cochrane (who added his wife's surname to his own in 1793) was an unprincipled rogue whose governorship of Dominica was marked by corruption and tyranny; he used the 8th Regiment to build his estate, traded in slaves, and kept a harem. He was recalled in 1803 under suspicion of corruption (it was even said he did some slave-trading on the way home), and although the prosecution failed to convict him at his court-martial (in which he unsuccessfully tried to shift the blame for misappropriation of funds on to his second in command), he was passed over for promotion and resigned his commission in disgust. Cochrane-Johnstone purchased the parliamentary seat of Grampound (a 'rotten borough' so rotten that it was disenfranchised in 1821, so blatant was the electoral corruption), which gave him immunity from arrest for debt, most useful as he habitually avoided paying his creditors. He embarked on a series of fraudulent business deals, using the all too common contemporary expedient of nepotism (his brother, Admiral Sir Alexander Cochrane, was naval commander-in-chief in the Leeward Islands), for example attempting to smuggle contraband into Spanish America in one of his brother's warships, and contracting to supply Spain with muskets at three guineas each, for which he supplied 17-shilling rubbish. Most notoriously, Cochrane-Johnstone's implication in the great Stock Exchange fraud of 1814 wrecked the career of his nephew, Thomas, Lord Cochrane, one of the greatest naval heroes of the age, the rogue never revealing that Thomas was totally innocent. He was finally expelled from the House of Commons and fled abroad to escape imprisonment.[597]

In addition to the regular forces, the West Indian colonies had their own militia, some of long standing. In Bermuda, for example (though not part of the West Indies in the narrowest definition), a militia had been formed as early as 1690-1, in which every man between the ages of 15 and 60 was to participate, and to bring with them to muster all slaves over the age of 15, armed as their masters thought fit. From an early period the force included cavalry, and small artillery detachments were added from 1789, although the latter were dispensed with by the 1802 Militia Act, as there was a regular artillery detachment stationed on the island. Similar organizations existed on the other islands: in Jamaica, for example, the 1802 Militia Act established four battalions formed of 'every male person of free condition, from the age of sixteen to that of sixty years, save only the members of his majesty's council, the speaker of the assembly, and the chief justice of the island ... and persons who have borne commissions and have not been degraded by sentence of a court-martial';[598] the latter condition doubtless to avoid ex-officers having to bear the indignity of serving in the ranks of the militia.

Africa

The West Indies were not unique in being pestilential stations: for example, in West Africa between 1810 and 1819, one-quarter of the garrison died every year. So unhealthy were the African colonies that penal corps were used as their garrison, existing under various titles such as the Royal African Corps or Royal York Rangers, to which men were sent as a punishment. So appalling was this posting that in 1810 a detachment of the Royal African Corps in Senegal planned a mutiny, because 'they did not like to be detained in Africa all their lives'; of those implicated, 25 were exiled to Sierra Leone and 25 shot, 'all, with the exception of one man, suffered the dreadful sentence, in penitence and prayer'.[599] The minor skirmishes in these colonies attracted little publicity, even though they involved the European settlers as well as the military: in November 1801, for example, a force of the Timmany tribe of 'King Tom' broke into the fort at Sierra Leone and killed a number of Europeans, until they were ejected by a bayonet-charge mounted by both soldiers and civilians, and led by the governor.

India

Although the campaigns in India formed the basis of Wellington's reputation and experience, they did not attract the same degree of attention as operations in Europe. One reason, perhaps, was that the majority of troops employed belonged to the private armies of the three presidencies (Bombay, Bengal and Madras) of the Honourable East India Company, alias 'John Company', which evolved from its original mercantile character into virtually a sovereign state, maintaining its own administration and military force, and having the right to declare war on any of the 'native' Indian states. Its forces were composed largely of native regiments, organized on European lines, with European officers, with a few units of Europeans forming the élite of the army. From the mid-18th century a small number of British units were stationed in the subcontinent, under command of the Governor-General, but the division of effort between Royal and Company forces may be gauged from the numbers of troops serving in India on 25 May 1809: British 19,843 (plus 5,115 in Ceylon); Company troops, 4,051 Europeans and 128,418 natives. The maintenance of such comparatively small numbers of British troops in India was not an excessive burden upon the treasury since Pitt's East India Declaratory Bill of 1787 compelled the (reluctant) East India Company to guarantee the defrayment of 'the expense of raising, transporting and maintaining such troops as may be deemed necessary to the security of the British possessions and territories in the East Indies', thus ensuring the maintenance of an adequate garrison.

Despite the indigenous methods of warfare, the Company's native troops were equipped and trained in European style (excluding some of the wilder elements of the irregular cavalry). The cornerstone of the Company forces were the European officers, who were mostly drawn from the same background as the king's officers, although it was noted that British officers in India tended to make friends more easily, and be more ready to assist their fellow-countrymen, according to Captain Joseph Budworth, late of the 72nd Royal Manchester Volunteers, in his *A Fortnight's Ramble to the Lakes in Westmorland, Lancashire and Cumberland* (3rd edn., 1810): 'the heart expands in proportion to the distance from their native country, and the frequent warfare they are engaged in; and war ever brings home the soldier's feelings to the noblest effects. A systematic cold-blooded Indian is almost a phenomenon in their armies.'

Some of the recipients for East India commissions were perhaps like the son recommended by the Revd. Thomas Jones: 'My eldest son I intended for a pillar of the Church: with this view I gave him a suitable education at school, and afterwards entered him at Cambridge, where he has resided the usual time, and last Christmas took his degree with some reputation to himself; but I must at the same time add, that he is more likely to kick a church down, than to support one ... when rebuked by his master, tutor, &c ... he treated them in the contemptible light of not being gentlemen, and seemed to intimate, that he should call them to an account, as an affair of honour ... He is now about 20, near 6 feet high, well made, stout, and very active, and is as bold and intrepid as a lion ... If you like him, I will equip him.'[600] This unusual testimonial was successful!

The Company also found room for characters like Claude Martin, a French mercenary who rose to the rank of major-general, and as superintendent of the arsenal at Lucknow was the Nawab of Oudh's ordnance expert. He amassed immense wealth (his will disposed of 33 *lakhs* of rupees, £330,000), and maintained a zenana. He died in 1800, leaving provision for the establishment of charitable institutions in India and his native Lyons, of which one was the Martinière at Lucknow, of Indian Mutiny fame.

Reorganizations of the Company forces in 1796 reduced the influence of the native officers and increased that of the British, making it increasingly important that the British officers should be sensitive to the peculiar nature of Indian regiments. In a report rebutting the suggestion that Company troops should be transferred to the king, in effect merging the British and Indian establishments, the Company stated the case for an independent officer corps which emphasized the importance of a long connection with and deep understanding of the sepoy: 'The constitution and character which this Indian army has acquired have been the subject of just admiration. These have been owing, essentially, to the happy mixture of bravery and generosity, of firmness and kindness, exercised towards the sepoys by their European officers. The superior lights and energy of the European character have directed the powers, and conciliated the prejudices, of the native troops, but it was because the officers knew the people and their prejudices well. These officers had been trained up among them from an early age; the nature, the usages, and the language of the natives, were become familiar to them; and the natives, remarkably the creatures of habit, in return, from being accustomed, became attached to them. Without such knowledge, however, on the part of the officers, they might every day have revolted the minds of so peculiar a race, and have alienated them from our service and Government.'[601] Also noted was the fact that to facilitate operations between British and Company forces, it was the Company practice to appoint the British commander-in-chief as theirs as well, even though this caused some discontent among Company officers who suspected that the king's officers were treated with more favour.

Although the tactics and drill adopted in India were based upon those of Europe, campaigning in India involved many unique facets (not least the enormous trains of camp-followers which accompanied an army), and hazards unimagined in European warfare. For example, in the operations before Seringapatam in 1799, the 1st Native Cavalry lost a grass-cutter who was carried off by a tiger, his shrieks being audible to the whole camp, and five days later another man was eaten by another tiger. The climate caused some divergence from European practice, for example nocturnal marches to avoid the heat of the day: 'A European soldier might smile, bet let him try the sun – the Indian sun. It is really wonderful what an hour's difference makes: those who are marching cheerfully and strongly along will, in one hour's time, be completely done men, not having scarcely the strength of children.'[602]

A characteristic of Indian warfare was the importance of rapid offence; as British and Company forces were usually heavily outnumbered by vast arrays of often ill-disciplined Indian armies, the most effective counter to the disparity of numbers was to profit from British discipline and attack immediately, routing the enemy before their weight of numbers could count. Wellington himself recommended this policy: '... the best thing you can do is ... dash at the first party ... If you ... succeed in cutting up, or in driving to a distance, one good party, the campaign will be our own. A long defensive war will ruin us, and will answer to no purpose whatever ...'[603]

The most significant operations in India took place during the period that Wellington was there in person, initially as commander of the 33rd Foot (arriving in India in 1796) and later elevated to general officer's rank, under the aegis of the new governor-general, his elder brother Richard, Lord Mornington, later Marquess Wellesley. The Third Mysore War, against the ruler of that state, Tippoo Sahib, had ended in 1792, but as he was canvassing French support, it was decided to eradicate their influence. The British forces in the Fourth Mysore War, commanded by General George Harris with Arthur Wellesley in subordinate command, besieged and stormed Tippoo's capital of Seringapatam (4 May 1799), when Tippoo was killed. Wellesley was appointed governor of the captured city to the chagrin of Sir David Baird, who had led the assault, and who doubtless thought the governorship no more than his due, having previously endured four years in Mysore captivity.

In May 1800 Arthur Wellesley was given his first independent command, a campaign to hunt the bandit Doondia Wao, which provided valuable experience and emphasized the importance of an adequate supply system. His reputation was enhanced further in the Second Maratha War (1803-5), waged in support of the Maratha ruler allied to the British, the Peshwa Baji Rao II, who had been deposed by Holkar of Indore. The governor-general planned one offensive in the Deccan under Arthur Wellesley, and a second in Hindustan, under General Gerard Lake. Wellesley restored the Peshwa and pressed on against the leader of the Maratha Confederacy, Doulut Rao Scindia, capturing his fortress of Ahmednuggur (11 August 1803). With his small force of British and Company troops (including only three European regiments) and a host of Mysore and Maratha irregular horse, Wellesley inflicted a crushing defeat upon Scindia's immense army at Assaye (23 September 1803), a desperately fought contest against native troops trained and led by French adventurers. Wellesley finally dispersed Scindia's army at Argaum (29 November 1803) and ended the campaign with the storming of Gawilghur (15 December).

Lake also faced Maratha forces under French command. He stormed and captured the fortress of Aligarh (4 September 1803) and, advancing towards Delhi, met the Maratha army on 10 September. This action, against overwhelming numbers (about 19,000 against Lake's 4,500), including the powerful and well-served Maratha artillery, demonstrated the advantages of operating aggressively against such an enemy, which despite the quantity of its artillery could not stand against a disciplined infantry attack, with cavalry making an effective pursuit. Lake's report makes these points forcibly:

'When the length of our march (upwards of eighteen miles) is considered, the fatigue the whole army underwent, and that we were exposed to a most galling fire from the enemy of grape and chain shot while advancing in line, the operations of yesterday must ever reflect the highest credit on all descriptions of the troops engaged, and cannot fail of striking the enemy with a dread of our army, and prove to them that opposition to such superior discipline and courage is useless. The steadiness and gallantry of the whole corps, both Europeans and Natives, under a formidable fire of artillery, does them infinite honour. After the gallant and steady charge of his Majesty's 76th regiment, led by Capt. Boyce, and the whole of the infantry line, who advanced to within 100 paces of the enemy without taking their firelocks from their shoulder, when they fired a volley, and rushed on with the bayonet with a determination nothing could resist, had forced the enemy to abandon their formidable artillery, Colonel St. Leger, with the cavalry under his command, moved rapidly forward, when a dreadful slaughter ensued; by a well-timed manoeuvre of the Colonel's, in intercepting their retreat to the Jumna, much execution was done; the enemy's confusion was such, that many were drowned in attempting to cross the river.'[604]

Lake pursued the Marathas and defeated them again at Laswaree (1 November 1803), which with Wellesley's successes caused Scindia to submit. Almost a year later Holkar again took the field, and in August 1804 almost annihilated a small British force under Colonel William Monson. This success was fleeting; Lake defeated Holkar at Furruckabad (17 November 1804) after which the pursuit, led by the 8th Light Dragoons, demonstrated the effectiveness of disciplined cavalry against broken fugitives: some 3,000 of Holkar's army were killed, against two British fatalities and 26 wounded. Lake captured Deig (25 December), but the British were unable to take the fortress of Bhurtpore, a siege which continued until its ruler made peace in April 1805; Holkar was pursued until he surrendered at Amritsar on 24 December 1805. Lake's talents and accomplishments were considerable and he was adored by his army, yet his reputation suffered from not having been made in Europe, testimony to the way some 'sepoy officers' could be somewhat overlooked. He returned to Britain in 1807, but died in February 1808, thus begin spared the knowledge of the fate of his gallant son, his aide in India, who had been severely wounded by his side at Laswaree. Lieutenant-Colonel the Hon. G. A. F. Lake was killed leading the 29th at Rolica.

There were no other major campaigns in the subcontinent until the Nepal War of 1814-16, although intermittent hostilities continued in Ceylon against the kingdom of Kandy, which included the annihilation of a detachment in 1803 which surrendered to the natives and was then massacred. One man – Corporal Barnsley of the 19th Foot – survived to carry news of the disaster to the nearest garrison, and the detachment's commander, Major Adam Davie of the Malay Regiment, was held in captivity until his death, probably in late 1811, the British being unable to negotiate his freedom or defeat the Kandians for lack of resources. Such events, with disease periodically as destructive as that in the West Indies, exemplify the trials of serving in such stations; the 19th, for example, which served in Ceylon from 1796 to 1820, lost some 10 per cent of its strength every year to disease and the occasional skirmish, a toll greater than that of some regiments whose casualties were sustained performing famous deeds in Europe, whereas tribulations in the colonies were scarcely known.

One of the most remarkable incidents from this period was the mutiny at Vellore on 10 July 1806, adumbrating the 'great mutiny' of 1857 and arising from not dissimilar causes. Discipline in the Indian regiments was not always what it might have been: for example, in July 1802 a detachment of Bengal Volunteers (formed for, and recently returned from, the Egyptian campaign) was detailed as the guard of honour to the Persian ambassador to the governor-general, Khuleel Khan. The Volunteers got into a row with his retinue, and when the ambassador himself tried to mediate the Volunteers began to shoot, killing him and four of his staff and wounding four others.

The mutiny at Vellore involved three Madras battalions (1st/1st, 2nd/1st and 2nd/23rd), which shared the garrison with four companies of the 69th Foot. There appear to have been two causes of discontent, one of which appeared ridiculous to those unaware of the peculiar religious and cultural sensitivities of the Indian troops, and which were ignored by the British at their peril. In November 1805 the commander-in-chief of the Madras Army, Sir John Cradock, ordered that round hats were to replace turbans, beards to be removed, and face-painting and 'joys' (jewellery) to be banned. Caste-marks, ornaments and beards were often of religious significance, and hats were synonymous in Indian eyes with Christianity, and thus the new regulations could have been regarded as an attack upon the troops' religion, as would have been obvious to officers properly knowledgeable about the country and its inhabitants. It was also believed that as the new head-dress 'had never in the slightest degree been objected to by the native officers, and others of the highest castes, to whom it had been submitted prior to adoption', such objections were used as an excuse to raise rebellion by the retainers and sons of Tippoo, who lived on East India Company pensions in their palace at Vellore. 'A rumour was at the same time circulated that the Government had caused the blood of swine to be mixed with the salt sold at the public sales, for the purpose of offending the religious prejudices both of Mussulman and Hindoo. The mendicant friars (Fakeers) were the most active in propagating this mischievous report, which had much more influence over the minds of the native soldiers than the introduction of the turban.'[605] The parallels with the 1857 mutiny are remarkable.

Whatever the immediate cause, on the night of 10 July the sepoys rose, murdered officers, fired into the 69th's barracks and massacred the sick in their hospital. They then began to ransack the fort, allowing the surviving British troops to gather on the ramparts; and an officer who was outside the fort when the rising occurred went for help to the nearest military post, Arcot, the station of the 19th Light Dragoons and some Madras cavalry. The 19th's commander, Sir Rollo Gillespie, was one of the most capable and energetic officers in India, and had a relief-force on the road within a quarter of an hour.

Gillespie's own account of the rescue shows how desperate was the situation of the surviving Europeans, about 60 men of the 69th, commanded by NCOs and with assistant-surgeons Jones and Dean, holding out on the ramparts but with their ammunition expended. Gillespie raced ahead of his column with Captain Wilson and about twenty men of the 19th Light Dragoons, and finding the gates barred attempted to penetrate a wicket-gate, but found it impregnable. Sergeant Brady of the 69th, who had served with Gillespie in San Domingo, seeing the tiny relief-party, cried out that 'If Colonel Gillespie be alive, he is now at the head of the 19th Dragoons, and God Almighty has sent him from the West Indies to save our lives in the East.'[606] Gillespie had a rope thrown up to the rampart, and Brady lowered his sash to help him climb. Upon the rampart, Gillespie found a pair of Colours (despite the desperation of the moment, the officer-less men of the 69th must have ensured that these prized symbols were saved); waving these and uttering a 'loud shriek', Gillespie led the 69th in a bayonet-charge along the ramparts and captured a battery of three guns, which he turned upon the mass of sepoys preparing to storm the position. Even though he had no ammunition, it scared the attackers sufficiently to hesitate until the rest of the 19th Light Dragoons arrived outside the walls. Still carrying the Colours over his shoulder, Gillespie returned to the wall by the gate and called down to an engineer officer, John Blakiston, to blow in the gates with the 19th's two galloper guns. With this accomplished, as the gateway was narrow, Gillespie led his group of 69th to clear a space at bayonet-point to permit the cavalry to enter and deploy; they then charged and slaughtered any sepoy who stood in their way. By 10 a.m. all was over and the fortress back in control of the British, although Gillespie himself admitted that so tight was the situation that even a delay of a further five minutes would have caused all to be lost.[607]

Following the massacre of the helpless hospital patients, no mercy was shown to the mutineers: '"Revenge! revenge!" was the cry, and many a sword drank deep of the cowardly blood which flowed from hearts that could have prompted such a deed. For my own part ... nothing like pity entered my breast during the day. Upwards of a hundred sepoys, who had sought refuge in the palace, were brought out, and, by Colonel Gillespie's order, placed under a wall, and fired at with canister-shot from the guns till they were all dispatched. Even this appalling sight I could look upon, I may almost say, with composure. It was an act of summary justice, and in every respect a most proper one; yet, at this distance of time, I find it a difficult matter to approve the deed, or to account for the feeling under which I then viewed it.'[608]

Evidently the normal tenets of 'civilized' warfare were not thought appropriate under such conditions, perhaps a mark of the difference between European and colonial warfare. There was, however, little difference in the nature of the troops. One of the few officers to escape the massacre passed a sentry of the 69th outside the magazine, 'and, seeing him walking up and down with the utmost composure, hastily asked if he knew that the sepoys were murdering all the Europeans. "I thought as much," he replied. "Why don't you fly for your life then?" exclaimed the officer. "I was posted here," he said, "and it is my duty to remain. I've six rounds in my pouch, and I'll sell my life dearly." The noble fellow was afterwards found dead at his post.'[609]

Ireland, 1798

The only serious campaigning to occur within the United Kingdom during the period was in the Irish rebellion of 1798, a sad chapter in the history of that country. It was the culmination of years of political and religious grievances, and the more radical elements in organizations like the Society of United Irishmen saw French intervention as the solution to Ireland's problems, encouraged by the French who realized that a rebellion in Ireland would occupy much of Britain's military resources. To this end the United Irishmen prepared a military organization, while the Irish loyalists organized yeomanry to guard against such insurrection or invasion, which forces being identified with the Protestant Orange Society virtually assured that any conflict would be a civil war. The British forces in Ireland were few in number, the Irish militia had been infiltrated by United Irishmen, and Sir Ralph Abercromby, who resigned as commanding general in Ireland shortly before the outbreak of the rising, issued a general order which stated that 'The very disgraceful frequency of courts-martial and the many complaints of irregularities in the conduct of the troops in this kingdom have too unfortunately proved the army to be in a state of licentiousness which must render it formidable to every one but the enemy.'[610] The succeeding lord-lieutenant and commander-in-chief, Charles, Marquess Cornwallis, described the Irish militia as undisciplined, contemptible in action but 'cruel in the extreme' to unarmed prisoners who fell into their hands,[611] perhaps an unduly critical view but confirmed by some of the events of the rebellion.

The rising was somewhat unco-ordinated, and only in Wexford was it truly threatening. The United Irish plans were thrown awry by the arrest of their leader, Lord Edward Fitzgerald, who had previously served in the British army and is still remembered by the Green Howards as a gallant officer of the 19th Foot. He was severely wounded at Eutaw Springs (8 September 1781) and later transferred to the 54th, where Cobbett, at that time their sergeant-major, described Fitzgerald as the only truly sober, honest, conscientious and humane officer he had encountered.

On both sides the rebellion was marked by revolting brutality, as the combatants took the opportunity to settle old scores, and some of the action was of semi-guerrilla nature, with raiding parties from both sides terrorizing both their opponents and the innocent. Although the rebels were largely unorganized and many armed with nothing more than home-made pikes and their own courage, they managed to inflict some reverses upon the government forces, especially where these were composed largely of militia. Against better-disciplined regulars, however (including fencibles who usually performed well in action), the rebels had little chance, although some actions were contested bitterly despite the wretched nature of the rebels' armaments, for example in the rebel defeats at New Ross (5 June 1798) and Arklow, four days later. The defeat of the most significant rebel army occurred at Vinegar Hill (12 June 1798) before the arrival of the promised French expedition under General Joseph Humbert, which landed at Killala Bay, County Mayo, on 22 August.

The new lord-lieutenant and commander-in-chief, Charles, 1st Marquess Cornwallis, had landed at Dublin on 20 June, and now sent Gerard Lake to take command of the forces assembled at Castlebar in opposition to Humbert; but on 27 August Humbert attacked and dispersed Lake's mediocre collection of militia, fencibles and regulars, some of whom behaved very badly (the flight of the militia was such that the action became known as 'the Castlebar races'). Not all the Irish militia was of such quality, however: the Limerick City Militia put up a sufficiently good fight at Coloony on 5 September to prevent the French from entering Sligo. Meanwhile, Cornwallis marched with reinforcements to Athlone, when his amiable nature and sharing of their hardships despite his 60 years endeared him to his men: '... the attention and kindness extended by the Marquis Cornwallis to the troops under his command, completely won their hearts; like a true soldier, he sought no comfort or refreshment for himself while one of his men remained unsupplied, and even then shewed himself content with the coarsest fare and meanest accommodation. Inspired by the example of their veteran Leader, the troops made rapid marches, and arrived in the highest spirits at Athlone ...'[612]

The forces of Cornwallis and Lake encountered Humbert at Ballinamuck on 8 September, the French surrendering after a short action, which effectively ended the 1798 rebellion. Its legacy, however, was not easily dispelled, and the bitterness it engendered is exemplified by the story of a traveller in 1799, who found the ordinary people hardened by the war. Over the gate of Carlow prison he saw displayed the heads of some of those executed for rebellion, one badly damaged by the local boys throwing stones at it, a sight which horrified the traveller. At dinner that evening another traveller remarked that not only would such a display brutalize the people, but would keep alive the memory of the recent conflict, which could only damage future relations. One of the 'gentlemen of the town' to whom this remark was addressed then declared that 'I wish we had more heads up if it were likely they could again

Top: A fieldpiece with horse-team harnessed to it directly, a form of *'prolonge'* which permitted the gun to be moved without the use of a limber, thus saving time when advancing on the battlefield. Note the handspike inserted into the double-bracket trail, the design of carriage used before the introduction of the single-piece or 'block' trail. (Print after W. H. Pyne, 1802)

Above: Early mobile artillery: fieldpieces with mounted gunners but still dependent upon the speed of movement of a dismounted driver; these were soon replaced by true horse artillery, with mounted drivers and gunners. (Print after W. H. Pyne, 1802)

Below: The siege of Badajoz: a typical siege-battery, with guns shielded by earthworks and gabions. The vehicle in the foreground is an ammunition-wagon.

Left: The use of artillery in a bombardment role: the attack on Copenhagen on 2-4 September 1807. The bombardment of such a civilian target was acceded to only with reluctance by the British commander, Cathcart, and was loathed by the besiegers. Some 30 guns, 40 mortars and ten howitzers were employed, and the unfortunate city was ablaze within five minutes of the commencement of the bombardment. This view may be intended to represent the two 24pdrs which fired towards the city's West Gate.

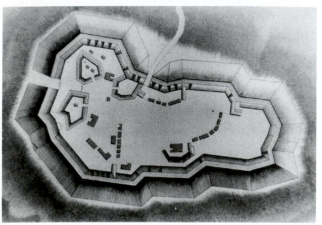

Left: Military engineering: a plan of one of the main works comprising the Lines of Torres Vedras, the fortification at Monte Agraça, which mounted fourteen 12pdrs, six 9pdrs, four 6pdrs and one $5^1/2$ in howitzer, with accommodation for 1,590 men. (Engraving after Lieutenant George Hotham, RE)

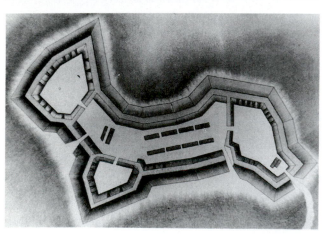

Left: The main work of Torres Vedras, showing how three separate strongpoints were connected by entrenchments; this position mounted ten 12pdrs, two 9pdrs, eleven 6pdrs and three $5^1/2$ in howitzers, and was manned by a garrison 1,720 strong. (Engraving after Lieutenant George Hotham, RE)

Right: Defensible posts could attain considerable significance. This engraving by Whitehead shows the shattered ruins of Hougoumont, possession of which secured the right of Wellington's line at Waterloo; shown here is the rear gate, which the French penetrated briefly. At the right are the ruins of the barn; the building with a spire is the chapel.

Right: Strategy was not infrequently dictated by the possession of geographical features. This print after Robert Ker Porter shows the bridge over the Tagus at Alcántara (in Arabic, 'the bridge', named from the famous Roman bridge built *c.* AD 105 in honour of Trajan). It was partially destroyed by the British in 1809, but in 1812 was made usable by Colonel Sturgeon and Major Todd of the Royal Staff Corps, who in an amazing feat of military engineering threw a suspension-bridge of planks and ropes over the shattered span, capable of supporting even heavy artillery, and of being temporarily rolled up and moved if threatened by the enemy.

Right: A regimental baggage-wagon, typically piled high with camp-equipage, soldiers and their dependants. (Print after W. H. Pyne)

Left: A Portuguese ox-cart, upon which slow and excruciatingly noisy contraptions much of the Peninsular army's transport depended. (Print after Revd. William Bradford)

Lower left: 'Over the hills and far away': a regiment and its baggage on the march. (Print after W. H. Pyne).

Below: Casualty-evacuation was often dependent upon the willingness of individuals to carry off a friend or officer, as in this depiction of three grenadiers bearing away Lieutenant-Colonel the Hon. Sir Alexander Gordon of the 3rd Foot Guards, one of Wellington's ADCs, mortally wounded at Waterloo. In the absence of stretchers, blankets were a common substitute. An anecdote characteristic of Abercromby was his insistence that the blanket in which he was carried from the field of Alexandria should be returned to its owner, lest the soldier be charged with its loss.

Right: 'The Supplementary Militia turning out for Twenty Days Amusement', a cartoon by James Gillray, 1796, which pokes fun at the local defence forces. The men in the front rank carry tools which represent their occupations, from left to right a shoemaker, brick-layer, artist, tailor and hair-dresser; the officer with the flag wears a carpenter's apron and carries a chisel. In the following ranks are coun-trymen with straw hats and presumably a sailor with a 'thrum cap'; the only profes-sional soldier among them is the drummer, a retired invalid with one eye and two wooden legs!

Below: Even the loss of a limb did not necessarily dis-qualify an officer from ser-vice. George Webb Derenzy lost his right arm as a lieu-tenant in the 82nd at Vitto-ria, but continued to serve

despite his disability, and later transferred to the 4th Dragoons. He became bar-rack-master at Exeter. An interesting feature of this engraving by Turner after I. G. Strutt is that Derenzy is wearing his jacket fastened in the 'feminine' style, presum-ably being easier for him to fasten with his left hand.

Below: A private of the 5th Loyal London Volunteers, *c.* 1804. The uniform is of infantry style, but with the 'Tarleton' light dragoon hel-met favoured by some volun-teer corps. (Aquatint by Mitan after W. M. Craig)

At a Court of Emergency of the Hon. Artillery-Company, held at the Mansion-House, on Thursday, August 21, 1794, at Three o'Clock in the Morning:

On a Requisition from the Right Hon. the Lord-Mayor, for the Purpose of assisting the Civil Power,

RESOLVED,

THAT the Company do appear completely armed and accoutred, with Two spare Flints, in the Artillery-Ground this Evening, at Five o'Clock precisely, and that every Member be required to assign substantial Reason for Absence.

By Order of the said Court of Assistants,

William White, *Clerk.*

To all whom it may Concern.

THIS is to certify, that ~~John Buck~~ was duly sworn and enrolled to serve as a Substitute for ~~Mr. John Scarborough~~ in the County of Middlesex, who was allotted to serve in the Militia for the said Parish, on

And I further certify, that the said ~~John Buck~~ is actually now serving in the Eastern Regiment of Militia, for the County of Middlesex, under my Command.

Given under my Hand, and Seal of the Regiment, at Head Quarters.

Williams, Printer, Queen Street, Perism

Above left: A call to arms: an emergency handbill to summon members of the Honourable Artillery Company to the support of the 'civil power'.

Above: Confirmation-document that a ballotted militia-man had provided a substitute to serve in his place; in this case, John Buck was serving in the East Middlesex Militia in place of Mr. John Scarborough of Marylebone.

Left: In the absence of any official decorations, deserving soldiers sometimes received medals from their regiments or, as in this singular case, from the officer who performed the annual inspection. Lieutenant-Colonel Joseph Hardy had previously served in the 93rd Foot.

Above: The effects of the war touched even those who would not otherwise have been involved in public life. This silver-gilt medal is one of the earliest British awards to a female recipient. Presented in 1794 by the Tenterden Volunteers as 'a Grateful Tribute to a Work of Patriotism' to a Miss Sawyer, probably a relative of the mayor of Tenterden in that year, John Sawyer, it was awarded for helping to embroider the unit's Colours.

Above right: To commemorate 309 French prisoners of war who died in the camp at Penhycuick, this monument was erected by a local paper-manufacturer, Alexander Cowan. The Latin verse was suggested by Sir Walter Scott who translated it thus:

'Rest in fair France 'twas vain for them to crave;

A cold and hostile climate affords their grave'.

Right: Insignia of the King's German Legion: an officer's shoulder-belt plate.

Left: Such was the impact of the war upon society that for a time it was fashionable for ladies to wear costumes styled on those of their military relatives. This print by John Kay, 1795, is typical, depicting General Francis Dundas of the 94th (left) and the Earl of Eglinton of the West Lowland Fencibles (right), with the two Misses Maxwell in costume styled after the uniform of the latter. (The officers in the background are Sir Henry Jardine and Sir Robert Dundas of Beechwood, both of the Royal Edinburgh Volunteers.)

Centre left: 'The Heroine of Matagorda': exemplifying the qualities of many of the army's women, the wife of Sergeant Reston of the 94th not only helped the surgeon during the siege of Matagorda fort at Cadiz in 1810, but braved enemy fire to bring water to the wounded; and carried ammunition and supplies to the defenders. Despite her bravery and renown 'the services she rendered . . . have been entirely overlooked'* – and although even the commander-in-chief supported her request for a pension, it was denied and she died in a Glasgow workhouse. (* Donaldson, J., *Recollection of an Eventful Life*, London 1825, p. 74)

Bottom left: The military system and institutions of Britain were extended to the colonies: this engraving of 1802 shows the Calcutta Militia Cavalry, which existed from 1798 to 1805, 'for the defence and protection of that metropolis . . . justly celebrated for its loyalty, zeal, and perfection' (*Gentleman's Magazine*, June 1802, p. 489). The uniform made few concessions to the climate, but was in British light dragoon style, red with yellow facings. The dismounted figures show other orders of dress.

Above left: 'Sepoy general': Sir Arthur Wellesley in India, in a print after Robert Home. Native gunners are manhandling a fieldpiece in the background.

Above right: Although under the command of the East India Company, the Indian native regiments wore a costume styled on that of the British Army, with the addition of *jangeers* (shorts) and a turban-like head-dress. This aquatint by I. C. Stadler after Charles Hamilton Smith shows a *havildar* (sergeant) of a light company and *sepoy* (private) of a battalion company of Madras Infantry.

Below: Abercromby mortally wounded at Alexandria; he was struck in the leg by a ball and died a week later, his whole career 'worthy the imitation of all who desire . . . a life of heroism and a death of glory', according to the Duke of York. In this print by Rogers after Stothard, the so-called 'Invincible Standard' lies as a trophy at his feet.

Above: The Highland Society's medal for Egypt, intended for presentation to the 42nd, but not issued in the manner envisaged. The Gaelic inscription reads 'These are the heroes who won victory in Egypt'.

Above right: Anton (or Antoine) Lutz of the Minorca Regiment, in 1801 the Queen's Germans and in 1804 the 97th Foot, with the Colour captured from the French 21ème *Demi-Brigade Légère* at Alexandria, after it had been re-possessed from its original captors of the 42nd. Lutz wears the 1800 infantry uniform with 'stovepipe' shako, and the distinctive badge, showing the captured flag, on the left breast; originally it was worn upon the right arm. (Engraving after Reinagle)

Below: Buenos Ayres: although this is a later engraving, it provides a graphic depiction of the chaos which ensued in attempting to capture a city in which almost every building was fortified.

Right: Maida: British infantry rush upon the French, who are depicted, correctly, as deployed, not in column. Contrary to some later analyses, the French generally seem to have intended to deploy before engaging the British line, so that it was especially remarked when they remained in column; an officer of the 87th noted especially that at Barossa, 'we came within about twenty paces of them before they broke, and as they were in column, when they did they could not get away it was therefore a scene of most dreadful carnage. They appeared so frightened and confounded . . .' (*The Courier*, 9 April 1811)

Right: The square in action was generally impervious to attack by cavalry: only on rare occasions did cavalry approach so near as to engage the infantry with sabres, as in this print after A. Dupray.

Right: British infantry tactics: this print of Busaco exemplifies the classic British tactic of occupying rising ground and counter-attacking with the bayonet once the French advance had been halted by a British volley. (Print after T. S. St. Clair)

Above: The morality of war: when a French officer was seen reconnoitring the British position at Alba de Tormes in November 1812, prior to the French attack, Lieutenant-Colonel John Cameron of Fassiefern of the 92nd specifically ordered his men not to fire, as deliberately shooting at an individual was considered dishonourable. Tradition asserts that the Frenchman thus saved was Marshal Soult himself.

Below: Storming a breach: ostensibly depicting Ciudad Rodrigo (but incorrectly depicting the 1812 shako which had not been introduced by this date), this engraving accurately reflects the dangers of this most hazardous of enterprises.

Right: The hardships of the retreat to Corunna are exemplified by this print of Robert Ker Porter's depiction of the army stumbling along a snow-covered, precipitous and winding mountain track.

Right: An assault by escalade: a graphic representation of the carnage and confusion in the ditches during such an attack.

Right: Infantry tactics: a battalion advances with skirmishers thrown forward to harass the enemy; this print after A. Dupray shows the bridge over the river at Toulouse.

Top: Toulouse: this engraving by T. Sutherland after William Heath shows the immense amount of smoke generated by firearms using black powder, the 'fog of war' which often restricted vision to a few yards and concealed from commanders events which otherwise would have been in their vision.

Above: Bergen-op-Zoom, 1814: confusion is evident among the attackers in this engraving of a sadly-mismanaged enterprise.

Right: Irrespective of artistic merit, the unreliability of some contemporary prints is exemplified by this engraving by Freeman after W. H. Brooke, depicting the closing stages of the Battle of Waterloo. It runs together various incidents, including (left background) the 42nd attacked by French lancers which occurred at Quatre Bras), the charge of the 'Union' Brigade (right midground) and Cameron of Fassiefern, who had been killed at Quatre Bras leading the 92nd (right foreground); and it depicts the 1st Foot Guards on the left wing of the Allied army, instead of the right (left foreground) and shows (centre) a fight for an 'Eagle' of the Old Guard, which never occurred!

Right: 'I left the lines and tented field/Where lang I'd been a lodger/My humble knapsack a' my wealth/A poor but honest sodger.' (Burns, *The Soldier's Return*). Those soldiers were lucky who found employment after their discharge from the army; this man, wearing his old jacket apparently of the 33rd Foot, was seen working in a ruddle-pit at Micklebring, near Doncaster. (Print by R. and D. Havell after George Walker, published 1814).

Right: The only medals awarded officially to commemorate the service of the ordinary soldier were those for Waterloo (left) and the Military General Service Medal, with clasps for 29 actions. The former was suggested by Wellington, who remarked, only ten days after the battle, that it should be awarded to all ranks, for 'if that battle should settle our concerns, they will well deserve it' (*Dispatches* XII p. 20). The latter was awarded only in 1848, by which time many of those qualified were dead.

Above: The memorial to the Water-loo heroes at Cossall: John Shaw, Richard Waplington and Thomas Wheatley.

Right, top and bottom: A few of Wellington's soldiers are commem-orated by monuments, mostly to deserving officers, such as the memorial obelisk at Kilmallie to John Cameron of Fassiefern, killed at Quatre Bras. (Print after J. M. Joass.) Very few of the largely anonymous 'other ranks' are distin-guished by similar monuments; one exception was Private Thomas Gard-ner of the 1st Life Guards, a Water-loo veteran killed by a fall from his horse when drill-sergeant of the Fur-ness Cuirassiers, whose memorial is at the church of Great Urswick.

rouse the villains to insurrection; for we are fully able to put them down, and the more of them we dispatch the better!', which seemed to be the opinion of all present.[613]

Rebellion flared again, very briefly, in July 1803, when a badly organized attempt led by Robert Emmet miscarried and was suppressed with some minor skirmishing. Emmet was hanged, and among the victims of the disturbance in Dublin on 23 July was Lieutenant-Colonel Lyde Browne of the 21st Foot, who was killed by the rebels, a second terrible blow for his widow whose brother, the famous Captain Edward Riou, had been killed at Copenhagen. However, despite the lingering memories of 'the "98"', Ireland continued to provide an ample supply of recruits of unquestioned loyalty, to the extent that the following could be written in 1803:

> 'With lies, and with many a Gallican wile,
> They spread their dire poison o'er Erin's green Isle;
> But now each *shillalah* is ready to thwack,
> And baste the lean ribs of the Gallican Quack.'[614]

Ostend, 1798

Other operations in 1798 included the maintenance of a small force of regulars and *émigrés* in Portugal, commanded by Sir Charles Stuart, serving under Portuguese control and, in response to an appeal for assistance, which had been dispatched to little effect in the previous year. Most notable, however, was an operation both futile and ill-managed, a raid to destroy the locks on the Bruges-Ostend Canal, which was believed to be strategically important in the preparations for an invasion of England. The locks being only a mile from Ostend, the raid would have best been performed by the crew of a naval frigate; but perhaps for political reasons, a military expedition was planned. The raid was delayed considerably as a result of Admiralty objections (presumably they realized the hazards, or were rightly mistrustful of the abilities of the plan's instigator, Captain Home Popham, RN), so that when it was finally mounted it was during a period of bad weather. The expedition was commanded by Major-General Sir Eyre Coote and comprised the 11th Foot, the flank companies of the 23rd and 49th, the light companies of the 2nd and 3rd Foot Guards, and detachments of artillery and 17th Light Dragoons; the four light companies of the 1st Foot Guards should also have participated but got lost en route to Ostend. Landing on 19 May, the expedition destroyed the lock with ease; but found the weather too bad to allow them to re-embark. Coote entrenched in the sandhills and waited for the weather to improve, but was attacked on the following day. After about two hours' fighting Coote was wounded in the thigh while attempting to rally part of the 11th, which had given way, and after consulting his deputy, Harry Burrard, reasoned that 'we could not hold out for Ten Minutes longer', so surrendered to avoid having 'their Fate ... decided by the Bayonet'.

The entire force was lost: 45 killed, 69 wounded, 47 missing, and 1,134 captured. The opening lines of the dispatches sent on 19 and 20 May exhibit the most remarkable reversal of fortune and suggest a lack of appreciation of the hazards of the position when Coote wrote the first dispatch:

'19 May: I have the most sincere Satisfaction to acquaint you of the complete and brilliant success attending the expedition ...'

'20 May: Major-General Coote, in his Dispatch Yesterday, had the Honor to inform you of the brilliant Success of the Enterprize ... The General having been severely wounded this Morning, I have the painful Task of detailing our unavoidable Surrender ...'

A professional criticism of the affair was more realistic: that once it had become obvious that re-embarkation was impossible, Coote should have occupied a position sufficiently strong to enable him to surrender with the honours of war, rather than to attempt a hopeless defence which would only cause unnecessary casualties. Indeed, among the most praised was Captain Knight of the 11th's grenadier company, who had his men lie under cover and not fire a shot, rather than engage and suffer losses in a hopeless cause, a significant reflection upon the contemporary morality of war.

The Netherlands, 1799

The expedition to north Holland in 1799 was part of a concerted Allied strategy, the Duke of York's forces collaborating with a Russian expeditionary force. It was notable for its use of militiamen, an Act of July 1799 permitting them to enrol in the regular army on unusually advantageous terms (not to be sent out of Europe or be drafted into other regiments), as a solution to the problem of finding sufficient numbers. The assembly of the militia volunteers was pursued with speed: 'The press, or requisition of carriages to convey the militia to the head-quarters of the troops, destined for the secret expedition against Holland, &c. was peculiarly felt at Bath. All coaches, carriages, waggons, carts, &c. public and private, appear to have been pressed for this service in every part of the kingdom. A serious riot was apprehended at Bath from the state of intoxication of the privates.'[615]

On 27 August Sir Ralph Abercromby landed in Holland with some 12,000 infantry, 600 gunners and 218 18th Light Dragoons, and three days later the Dutch fleet surrendered. From then on, however, the expedition faltered: the commissariat arrangements were wretched, the anticipated rising in support of the House of Orange never occurred, and co-operation with the Russians was poor. The Duke of York's reinforced Anglo-Russian army was defeated at Bergen on 19 September, due largely to the unreliability of the Russians who paid more attention to looting and intoxication than fighting; the Duke defeated the Franco-Batavian forces at Bergen on 2 October, but on 6 October the reverse at Castricum was proof of the hopelessness of the campaign, and by the Convention of Alkmaar (18 October) hostilities ended and the Allies withdrew.

Abercromby declared that the newly enrolled militiamen were a very superior class of recruit, which was a significant pointer to future methods of recruiting; yet even though they were already disciplined and trained in the use of arms, this campaign demonstrated the difference between veterans and those who had seen no active service. William Surtees had enlisted in the 56th Foot from the Northumberland Militia, and wrote of the naïvety of such people as himself who believed a rumour that the Duke of York had given permission for them to throw away their knapsacks to lighten their load; as night came on and the rain began to pour, 'then I plainly perceived that I had played the young soldier'. With neither knapsack nor blanket, by morning they were almost dead from exposure, with shoulder and trigger-finger bruised and swollen from the hitherto unexperienced previous day's fighting. He remarked on the steady conduct of the 23rd, all stalwart old soldiers, when compared to the newly recruited battalions, 'who had as little idea of service in the field, as if newly taken from the plough ... I should never be inclined to put very much confidence in raw troops of whatever nation, or of what stuff soever they may be composed, for it is certain, that without being at all deficient in point of courage, they have not that confidence in their own powers which soldiers who are inured to service possess; and if hastily or hotly set upon, while without the aid and example of others more experienced than themselves, it is many chances to one I think that they will give way. So it was on this occasion. Nothing could exceed the materials of which these two battalions were composed, had they the advantage of a little more experience; and no troops could fight better than they did, after gaining the support and countenance of the old regiments which were sent to reinforce them. But I confess with shame, we showed a great want of nerve in the early part of the day ... the retreat ... degenerated into a flight, and every one seemed intent only on making the best of his way to the rear ...'[616]

This 'experience' factor was appreciated by the best commanders (hence some of Wellington's system of brigading), but is sometimes overlooked, although the presence or absence of nearby reliable troops would seem to be one explanation of some of the anomalies regarding units which behaved well on some occasions and badly on others.

Egypt, 1801

The expedition to Egypt, in which Britain's first real laurels of the period were won, was conceived as a joint Anglo-Ottoman venture against the French invaders of the Middle East, who had been marooned there by the destruction of the French fleet at Aboukir Bay. (Bonaparte's invasion, it was said, was a greater plague on Egypt than anything chronicled in scripture:

> 'Th' infernal French! whose infamy and vice
> Surpass blains, locusts, boils, and flies, and lice.')[617]

Even the ministry's aims were somewhat obscure; the campaign was ill-planned and had to be conducted without the envisaged co-operation of the Turks, but its commander, Sir Ralph Abercromby, could hardly have been better selected. Overcoming the ignorance of the government (for example, he was expected to land with only the water which could be supplied by the navy, as there was believed to be no natural water in the area of the landing), he ensured that the troops were trained in the techniques of disembarkation from longboats, to avoid the chaos he had witnessed in the Netherlands in 1799. He also had the benefit of a most capable subordinate in Sir John Moore, with whom he had served in the West Indies.

Despite being opposed, the landing was made successfully on 8 March 1801; an action was fought on 13 March, but the decisive battle took place at Alexandria on 21 March when, after a desperate fight, a French attack was beaten off; it was in this action that the rear rank of the 28th faced-about to repel an attack from the rear, commemorated by the unique badge worn ever since on the back of the regiment's head-dress. Abercromby was wounded in the thigh in this engagement, and died of gangrene on 28 March. His successor, Hutchinson, conceived the plan of a march on Cairo which almost caused his subordinates to revolt, but the French surrendered before any further major action was necessary.

An incident much celebrated at the time was the capture at Alexandria of the French 'Invincible Standard', a term of uncertain origin, perhaps invented by the British to convey even greater honour upon its captors. The flag taken at Alexandria was actually that of the 3rd Battalion of the French 21st *Demi-Brigade Légère*, captured by Major Stirling and Sergeant Sinclair of the 42nd. In commemoration, the Highland Society of London commissioned a medal to be presented to each member of the regiment present on that day, and to the relatives of those killed, 'as an inestimable inheritance of glory, carrying down the tide of time, to ages yet unknown, the illustrious deed of that day'.[618] Later in the action Sinclair, guarding the trophy, was knocked senseless by a cut from a French cavalryman, being saved from decapitation by his 'clubbed' hair and two neck-cloths, which absorbed the force of the sabre-cut. When he regained consciousness he saw a member of Stuart's Minorca Regiment carrying off the Standard, and as this man was presumed merely to have picked it up, it was Sinclair who was credited with its capture.

William Cobbett investigaged the circumstances, and for all his political bias appears to have uncovered the true facts. After Sinclair dropped the flag, it was evidently re-possessed by a French officer, who was later shot by Antoine Lutz, a young Alsatian in the Minorca Regiment (later the Queen's Germans). Lutz took the flag and defended it successfully against two French dragoons, and received a dollar for his bravery from his officer, Lieutenant Moncrieff, who later confirmed Lutz's story. The deed was acknowledged immediately within his regiment, Lutz being awarded an honorary badge to be sewn to his jacket-breast, and was promoted to corporal; and when later charged with murder after a fight in which his drunken antagonist accidentally fell on a bayonet, his innocence was supported by his officers' testimony of his heroism at Alexandria. Cobbett suspected that the exploit of a foreigner was concealed deliberately in order that a Briton should take the credit, and supported his view by stating that another deed in the same action, the killing of the French General Roize, was not done by the Highlander to whom it was attributed but by Corporal Karabaum of the Minorca Regiment, who proved it by bringing home the general's gold watch and some lace off his coat. (He sold the watch for so large a sum that he returned home to Germany a rich man.)

Lutz was somewhat put out by the version of the story which became popular, and when shown the trophy in London 'he snatched hold of the staff, and, stamping it upon the floor, while his face reddened with anger, "now," said he, in German, "let that serjeant come, and claim this standard if he dares!"' Cobbett used the case to complain about bias against foreigners in British service: 'shall the man who took this standard, be rewarded with a worsted shoulder-knot [corporal's insignia], and two-pence a day added to his pay? Shall he, because he is a *foreigner*, waste his life in penury and obscurity, and finally, perhaps, drop into the grave from the wards of an hospital or a poor-house? Forbid it justice! Forbid it British justice and British honour!'[619]

Following this investigation, the Highland Society abandoned the issue of the medal to those whom it had been intended, officially because only the sovereign could bestow medals for war service (a convenient excuse which did not prevent the awarding of numerous regimental medals during the period), and used them for other purposes (an example was presented by the Society at least as late as 1881). Sinclair, however, was commissioned in 1803, and despite the doubts over the circumstances of the capture of the flag, Thomas Campbell could still write in *Ode composed for the 21st of March 1809, the Anniversary of the Highland Society*:

> 'Health to the band, this day, on Egypt's coast
> Whose valour foil'd proud France's Tricolor,
> And wrench'd the banner from her bravest host,
> Baptiz'd "Invincible" in Austria's gore!'[620]

(Antoine Lutz's career demonstrates the number of armies in which such an individual could serve: originally an unwilling conscript in the French army, he deserted to join the royalist *Armée de Condé*, went with them into Russian service, transferred to the Austrian army, was captured by the French in Italy and conscripted into Spanish service, was then captured by the Royal Navy and joined the Minorca Regiment; proving that it was quite possible for a man to serve five nations in as many years, and still remain a brave and reliable professional soldier.)

A contingent from India under Sir David Baird was sent to join the army in Egypt, which although it only arrived after the cessation of hostilities performed one of the most remarkable of marches, 'crossing 130 miles of a barren desart [sic], where human nature was put to the shifts to support us on our march; yet every individual bore it with the greatest resignation. At Cossier we dug wells, the waters of which were bitter, and gave our men bowel complaints; yet we were obliged to sew ox hides together, to carry some of it on camels for our use, over the desart ... our skins leaked the water; and but for our camels, we should never have survived the march over burning sands, as by their assistance we made forced marches of 30 miles a day; when the men dropped from fatigue and want of that necessary, and here invaluable article, we put them on the camels and pushed forward. After each day's march we dug for water, but could only succeed in three places, on our way to Upper Egypt. I have seen a dollar paid for one draught of water. Some few of the corps, who could not keep up, were lost in the parching sands. After 14 days march across the desart of Thebais, we congratulated each other on seeing the long-wished for waters of the Nile ...'[621]

The Mediterranean

British forces had been engaged in minor actions in the Mediterranean from the early French Revolutionary Wars, and such operations continued, often revolving around support for the royal family of the Kingdom of the Two Sicilies, who for much of the period were excluded from Naples and, with British support, resided in Sicily. The Mediterranean also provided the scene for the first British victory on land since the resumption of the war in 1803, in Sir John Stuart's expedition to Calabria, where on 6 July 1806 he defeated Reynier's French army at Maida. This battle has been held as a classic example of the superiority of the firepower of the British line over the French column, as was to be experienced many times during the Peninsular War; but in fact such calculations in regard to 'line v. column' would seem to be based upon an incorrect premise, as the French deployed into line before battle was joined, an interpretation seemingly proven by Reynier's official report.[622]

Just after the battle there occurred a most singular incident, which if chiefly remarkable for its unusual aspect is also indicative of the morale and state of discipline of the troops. Each brigade in turn was permitted to refresh itself by bathing in the sea, including Cole's brigade of eight companies of 1/27th and a 'flank battalion' of the grenadier companies of the 20th, 1/27th, 1/36th, 1/58th, 1/81st and de Watteville's Regiment, all the 27th and most of the grenadiers 'hard-biting fellows of long standing'.[623] While they were bathing, a staff officer (described as a 'noodle' by his superior, Bunbury!) was deceived by a dust-cloud stirred up by a herd of cattle, and rode up, shouting frantically that French cavalry were coming; whereupon the two battalions dashed out of the sea, caught up their muskets and pouches and fell in, without a stitch of clothing among them. Although it served to amuse the rest of the army, the incident was a remarkable demonstration of the discipline and spirit of the men.

Stuart received great acclaim for his victory, but was negligent in exploiting it; John Colborne led the 20th's light company in pursuit of the French but was amazed to find no one was following him and, according to Bunbury, Stuart occupied two days honing the phrases of his dispatch, while his command 'remained kicking their heels and eating grapes'.[624]

Minor actions took place in the Mediterranean during the period, for example a raid on the coast of Naples in late October 1811, when 250 men of the 62nd, and 50 marines landed from the frigates *Imperieuse* and *Thames*, put to flight some 900 enemy troops, destroyed their batteries and three gunboats, captured six gunboats and twenty merchantmen, and after a lodgement on the coast lasting two days, returned to Milazzo (Sicily) with their prizes. There was also a 'military flotilla', a fleet of coastal gunboats operating from Sicily and crewed by army personnel; in July 1810, commanded by Captain Thomas Reade of the 27th, it even captured an enemy convoy.

The Ionian Islands were occupied in 1809-10 (save Corfu, which remained French until 1814), the principal forces involved, commanded by Sir John Oswald, being the 35th Foot, naval landing parties and locally raised corps, some of which were of limited use. Among them were the Greek Light Infantry, who participated in the attack on Santa Maura fort (22 March 1810): 'The Greeks, to whom the advance had been given, no sooner came within the smell of powder than they assumed the attitude of adoration used by Mussulmans to the Prophet; they remained prone on their faces until the 35th passed them. This attachment to the soil, although an amiable feeling in some instances, is rather inconvenient in the case of storming a fort. The title of this regiment was evidently a misnomer; no troops could better deserve the name of *heavy* infantry than those who became altogether immovable ... The commander of the expedition, who had most likely some reasons for not denouncing his Greeks, took the means of extenuating their conduct in this manoeuvre by stating in his despatch, when accounting for the delay, that it was in great measure owing "to the peculiar mode of fighting of the Greeks".'[625] (To be fair to Oswald, he described it as a 'trying occasion'[626] and admitted that nothing would induce the Greeks to advance; the position was carried by two companies of Royal Marines with two companies each of De Roll's and the Calabrian Free Corps in support; the fort finally surrendered on 16 April.)

South America

Other operations during this period enjoyed little success; an Anglo-Russian force attempting to recover Hanover landed on the Elbe in late 1805, but withdrew with nothing achieved. The search for success perhaps influenced ministers to support the wildest and most impractical scheme devised during the period. In January 1806 an expedition under Sir David Baird, and the fleet of Sir Home Popham, re-possessed the Cape; after which Popham persuaded Baird to lend him the 71st Highlanders under William Beresford to launch an unauthorized expedition to South America, to assist the colonies to throw off the Spanish yoke and to deprive Spain of her New World revenue. Presumably Popham's conversations with members of the government led him to believe that they were in favour of the plan, but the expedition was wholly without sanction.

Beresford captured Buenos Ayres in June 1806 and sent home a huge quantity of treasure, which on 20 September was conveyed in ceremony through London to the Bank, in eight wagons, each with a sailor on top bearing a flag inscribed 'Treasure' and 'R.M.' ('Royal Money'), escorted by the Loyal Britons and the Clapham Volunteers, under command of Alexander Davison of the former, himself Nelson's prize agent. Deposited at the bank was the sum of 1,086,203 dollars and a box of jewels.

Doubtless not unaffected by the sight of this treasure and by Popham's circularization of London merchants concerning the new markets awaiting exploitation, the ministry determined to support the enterprise. This involved impractical plans (fortunately aborted) for the capture of Chile and the invasion of Mexico; and before Beresford could be reinforced the Spanish colonists had gathered and forced him to surrender. Nevertheless, reinforcements were sent, and Sir Samuel Auchmuty captured Montevideo on 3 February 1807. Most ill-advisedly, Lieutenant-General John Whitelocke was appointed to supreme command, a man quite unfit for the task; leaving his best elements at Montevideo, he made a wretchedly planned attack on Buenos Ayres on 5 July 1807, in which the assaulting troops became so bogged-down in confused street-fighting that they were compelled to sue for a truce, the conclusion of which led to the British evacuation of South America and drew a curtain over the whole, ill-conceived affair.

The experiences of Buenos Ayres provide an insight into street-fighting against a determined enemy, for where such combat occurred following the storming of a fortress, the strength of opposition was probably influenced by the fact of their imminent capitulation. It is an interesting reflection upon the contemporary view concerning the morality of war that street-fighting was viewed by some as unworthy of a true soldier: Henry Kennett, whose brother Captain George Kennett of the Royal Engineers was killed in Beresford's fight at Buenos Ayres by a sniper firing from a window, wrote of the defenders that 'their ignoble souls preferred the despicable and dishonourable warfare of firing from windows and tops of houses' to a fair fight in the open![627]

In the confusion of Whitelocke's attack, individual officers and small parties acted virtually independently. The experiences of Major Henry King of the 5th Foot exemplify the confusion of such an action, even to the extent of deliberately disobeying orders by exercising his own discretion, which 'every officer in danger has a right to do'. Although his account attempts to detail his movements, it is clear that he had no idea of how to proceed short of attacking any enemy who revealed himself, losing men all the time, detaching parties to storm known enemy strongpoints and rallying men from other units who had become separated from their officers. Only by raising the Colours on the top of buildings could any idea be gained of the positions of the British and their enemies. Typical of the confusion was an incident in which King's small party was confronted by a body of Spaniards bearing a white flag; King presumed that they were attempting to surrender, whereas they were probably calling upon *him* to yield, though King thought later that it was probably a subterfuge to allow the Spaniards to surround him. After a scuffle between King and the Spaniards, 'Mr. Harvey, who carried the colour, called out they were trying to seize it; and some men said they were taking their arms; on which I hesitated no longer, but gave the order to charge, when the scoundrels immediately turned and ran, and galloped off as fast as possible ... The above-mentioned officer, and about twelve of his men paid the forfeit of their lives for this treachery.'[628]

Despite such difficulties, King described Whitelocke's surrender as 'a most disgraceful and ignominious convention', a 'scandalous business' concluded 'to the grief and astonishment of the Army, who were eager for action'.[629] The same opinion was held by the court-martial which adjudged Whitelocke 'totally unfit and unworthy to serve His Majesty in any military capacity whatever'. Even the court-martial was marred by tragedy, when one of its members, Gerard, Lord Lake, was taken ill and died before the verdict was announced.

Operations of 1807

Another small expedition was mounted to Egypt in 1807, interfering in the virtual civil war taking place in that country, and to frustrate perceived French intentions. Ill-planned and under-strength, the expedition came to a somewhat ignominious end, British forces withdrawing in September 1807 after suffering considerable losses to no useful purpose.

In the same year Lord Cathcart's expedition went to Denmark, to prevent that country's fleet from falling into French hands; the brave resistance of the Danes was unsuccessful, and the campaign is remarkable chiefly for the bombardment of Copenhagen and Sir Arthur Wellesley's first European victory, at Kjöge (or Roskilde) on 29 August. A further Scandinavian expedition, led by Sir John Moore, to support Sweden, failed because of the impossibility of collaborating with the mad King Gustavus IV of that country.

The Peninsular War, 1808-9

British determination to oppose the French invasion of Portugal and the deposition of the Spanish royal family in favour of Napoleon's brother led to their most significant campaign of the period, the Peninsular War, Napoleon's 'Spanish ulcer' which consumed vast amounts of his resources over the succeeding five and a half years. Sir Arthur Wellesley was appointed to command the British expedition, but as his original force was deemed insufficient, Moore was detailed to lead a reinforcement. Because Moore was a political opponent of the ministry, supreme command was vested in Sir Hew Dalrymple, governor of Gibraltar, with Sir Harry Burrard as his deputy.

Wellesley departed for Portugal in a pensive mood, but made a remarkable prediction: '... they may overwhelm me, but I don't think they will outmanoeuvre me. First, because I am not afraid of them, as everybody else seems to be; and secondly, because if what I hear of their system of manoeuvre is true, I think it a false one against steady troops. I suspect all the continental armies were more than half beaten before the battle was begun – I, at least, will not be frightened beforehand.'[630]

Wellesley disembarked at Mondego Bay in August 1808 and advanced on Lisbon, defeating a French force at Rolica on 17 August, but was superseded in chief command by Burrard's arrival, who ordered him to suspend the advance on Lisbon. On 21 August Wellesley was attacked at Vimeiro by General Andoche Junot's French army, sallying out from Lisbon; still aboard ship on the preceding night, Burrard left Wellesley in command. Junot made two attacks on Wellesley's army, drawn up on the Vimeiro ridge, and was beaten off, a precursor of many such actions in the following years. Benjamin Harris of the 95th, skirmishing in front of the British position, recalled what might be seen as a typical sequence of events: a French advance halted by a brief burst of fire, and then repelled by a violent counter-charge:

'The French were very saucy, and firing upon us uncommon sharp; they greatly outnumbered us, and shewed so much ambition that they appeared inclined to drive us off the face of the earth ... most gallantly did they come upon us, seeming to be in a hurry to put us out of the way ... I heard the whole line (as if affronted at the Frenchmen's impudence) crying out, "D—n them, charge them, charge them." They did indeed much outnumber us in skirmishers, and we were giving ground (firing and retiring), but at the same time most wickedly inclined, and desirous of doing all the mischief we possibly could. I noticed General Fane to call out to the regiments in rear to restrain them, telling them he wished them to keep their ground ... At last he gave the word, and down they came, through a tremendous fire opened upon them, of cannon and musketry, and dreadful was the slaughter as they rushed on. I think I never beheld anything more terrible than the charge of these regiments; and as they came up with us we sprung up, gave one hearty cheer, and charged along with them, treading upon our dead and wounded comrades, who lay thick in our front. The 50th were next to me as we went, and I recollect the firmness with which they rushed on that charge, appearing like a wall of iron. The enemy could not stand the sight, and before we encountered they turned and ran for it ...'[631] So impressive was this sight that more than thirty years later Harris remarked, 'Methinks I can hear at this moment the clatter of the Frenchmen's accoutrements, when they turned in an instant to the right-about, and went off as hard as men could run for it.'[632]

A rapid pursuit would have captured Lisbon, but Burrard forbade Wellesley to follow; upon which, according to a story told by Moyle Sherer, Wellesley 'turned his horse's head, and with a cold and contemptuous bitterness, said aloud to his aide-de-camp, "You may think about dinner, for there is nothing more for soldiers to do this day."'[633] Worse followed upon Dalrymple's arrival next day; instead of evicting the French from Lisbon, he and Burrard concluded the Convention of Cintra, by which the French were to be sent home in British ships, keeping the plunder they had taken in Portugal. With reluctance Wellesley added his signature to the document. Outrage in Britain was widespread; as Byron wrote,

> 'Here Folly dash'd to earth the victor's plume,
> And Policy regain'd what arms had lost;
> For chiefs like ours in vain may laurels bloom!
> Woe to the conqu'ring, not the conquer'd host ...'

Public meetings were held to petition the king to hold an inquiry, to 'lead to the discovery of all those causes which will have produced an event so Injurious to the honour of this country' according to a plea from the county of Southampton,[634] 'in justice to the outraged feelings of a brave, injured, and indignant people ... and to remove from its character so foul a stain', as stated by the City of London's petition.[635] (The reply to the latter was somewhat dismissive, in effect stating that the king didn't need to be told his duty!) All three generals were recalled to face a court of inquiry, from which only Wellesley was exonerated. He received some criticism arising from his family connections; *The News* deplored his being given a dinner by the Duke of Richmond, stating that 'every patriotic and honest heart in this empire felt almost as much indignation on reading this account of the dinner ... as it did on reading the articles of the armistice which he signed and negociated', and suggested that any acquittal would owe less to his innocence than to 'the sinister efforts of his friends' at the expense of the other two 'unbefriended' generals.[636]

During Wellesley's absence, command of the expeditionary forces devolved upon Moore, who was instructed to support the Spanish armies in opposing the French, temporarily led by Napoleon himself. The Spanish administration, having broken down into local juntas, compounded the awful standard of their armed forces, which had suffered years of neglect; so that Moore found it impossible to collaborate effectively. From this period originated the dismissive comments on the Spanish recorded by most British observers: 'in their best days ... more like an armed mob than regularly organized soldiers';[637] 'We always know when the French are near – the Spaniards run away in every direction.'[638] (In fairness, this is a reflection upon some of the appalling units encountered by the British; when inspired with patriotic fervour, the Spanish could act with great heroism, as in the defence of Saragossa, or with considerable if barbaric efficiency, as in the guerrilla war which proved so costly to the French occupation forces.)

Moore advanced to Salamanca, to deflect the French advance on Madrid; but that city surrendered without even informing Moore, and the outnumbered and isolated British were compelled to retreat over mountainous terrain through the bitter winter weather of December 1808-January 1809, towards Corunna and Vigo. Discipline collapsed in the frozen and starving army, looting and drunkenness became endemic, causing Moore to issue his harsh order of 27 December 1808: 'The Commander of the forces has observed, with concern, the extreme bad conduct of the troops of late ... The misbehaviour of the troops in the column which marched by Valderas ... exceeds what he would have believed of British soldiers – it is disgraceful to their Officers, as it strongly marks their negligence and inattention ... he can feel no mercy towards Officers who neglect, in times like these, essential duties; or towards soldiers who disgrace their country by acts of villainy towards the country they are sent to protect.'

His succeeding remarks make it clear that he attributed this behaviour to the army's disgust at retreating: 'It is impossible for the General to explain to his army the motives of the movements he directs ... When it is proper to fight a battle, he will do it, and he will chuse the time and place ... he begs officers and men of the army to attend diligently to discharge their parts, and to leave him, with the other General Officers, the decision on measures which belong to them alone. The soldiers may rest assured, that he has nothing more at heart than their honour ...'

Some units held together well, notably the Foot Guards (as expected), Highland regiments and the rearguard; one of the army's best elements, Craufurd's Light Brigade, was detached to march to Vigo, depriving the army of an irreplaceable resource. Their march was an almost insuperable trial of endurance, but they held together largely by the force of Craufurd's iron will. The remainder staggered along their line of retreat, leaving in their wake hellish scenes like those witnessed by Alexander Gordon at Villafranca, 'the most dreadful scenes of riot and distress. Parties of drunken soldiers were committing all kinds of enormities; several houses were in flames, [streets] were flowing with rum, a number of puncheons having been staved in the streets, and a promiscuous rabble were drinking and filling bottles and canteens from the stream.'[639]

In the early stages of the retreat, Paget's cavalry won two significant actions at Sahagun (21 December 1808) and Benevente (29 December), and it was noted that even amid the chaos of the retreat, the appearance of the enemy brought about an immediate restoration of order. This was observed not only by the British: 'I have heard many French officers assert that ... when all order and discipline appeared to be lost in the British ranks, the slightest prospect of an engagement produced, as if by magic, the immediate restoration of both; the officers, who the moment before appeared wholly without the slightest authority or control, being obeyed upon the instant, as if upon the parade.'[640] Not even the presence of officers was necessary to inspire this behaviour: a party of stragglers fell-in spontaneously near Betanzos upon the approach of French cavalry and beat them off; Sergeant William Newman of the 43rd took command and led them out of danger, for which he was rewarded with an ensigncy in the 1st West India Regiment.

The same thing was observed after the weary, barefoot and starving army had struggled to Corunna, where ships were waiting to evacuate them; but the French pursuit came up so quickly that a battle was necessary before the army could get away. Basil Hall of the Royal Navy, recently in contact with Spanish forces, observed the British when the French attacked on 16 January: 'instead of listening to a set of boastful Spaniards, fighting with the air, and vapouring from morning to night about their own prowess, we beheld the actual tug of war between Greek and Greek'. He toured the army, over which an uncanny silence had settled, some asleep, some apparently in the last stages of exhaustion, gazing longingly at the ships in which they were to embark. He asked an army officer if anything could rouse so disheartened a body; 'You'll see by-and-by, sir, if the French there choose to come over.' At that moment, the French artillery opened fire:

'At the first discharge from the French battery, the whole of the British troops, from one end of the position to the other, started on their feet, snatched up their arms, and formed in line with as much regularity and apparent coolness as if they had been exercising on the parade in Hyde Park. I really could scarcely believe my eyes when I beheld these men spring from the ground, full of life and vigour, though but one minute before they had all been stretched out listlessly in the sun. I have already noticed the silence which reigned over the field; now, however, there could be heard a loud hum, and occasionally a jolly shout, and many a peal of laughter, along the distance of nearly a mile ... Not a single face could now be seen turning towards the ships ... All had become animation and cheerfulness in minds from which, but a short time before, it seemed as if every particle of spirit had fled.'[641]

The French attack was beaten off, and the army embarked for home; but without Moore, who was mortally wounded by a roundshot which almost severed his left arm. He was buried on the ramparts of Corunna,

'We carved not a line, and we raised not a stone –
But we left him alone with his glory.' as Wolfe expressed it.

Walcheren

Despite a commitment to pursue the war in the Iberian Peninsula, in the summer of 1809 the government diverted some 40,000 men to occupy the island of Walcheren in the Scheldt estuary, in an attempt to frustrate Napoleon's plans for using that area as a launching-point for operations against Britain. The secondary purpose of the expedition, to occupy French resources needed elsewhere, was reduced to nothing by Napoleon's defeat of Austria by the middle of July. Command was given to the Earl of Chatham, with Sir Eyre Coote as his deputy, and the Quartermaster-General, Sir Robert Brownrigg, as chief of staff; the expedition's naval commander was Sir Richard Strachan, and, surprisingly given his recent discredit over the South American venture, Sir Home Popham was his Captain of the Fleet.

Although Flushing was captured, the military operations were not extensive; but what marked this ill-conceived expedition was 'Walcheren fever', a recurrent malarial infection which caused more damage than several pitched battles. Walcheren had a reputation as an unhealthy region:

'Ah! wretched spot, by Nature's hand unblest,
Where fell Disease high rears her spotted crest,
Where horrid fogs eternally prevail,
And fatal damps from poisonous floods exhale,
Where blasts pestiferous taint the sullen air,
And spread contagion and despair.'[642]

The sickness devastated the army; in early September, for example, the 2/23rd were unable to furnish a single man fit for duty, and on 6 October no less than 9,514 men were incapacitated by illness. The sickness, as well as the obvious hopelessness of the operation once it was decided that Antwerp could not easily be taken, caused the expedition to be withdrawn in early December. In February 1810 a return was made of the units which had served at Walcheren (less the 2/59th, which had not submitted its statistics): embarked, 39,219 men; killed in action 106; deserted 84; discharged 25; died on the expedition or since their return, 3,960; still sick, 11,513. What made the malady so damaging was its continual recurrence, to the effect that Wellington requested that no more Walcheren battalions be sent to the Peninsula, as their members were continually falling ill.

An inquiry into the expedition revealed many of the inadequacies of the medical establishment. Surgeon-General Thomas Keate said that he had made no special preparations because he had not been informed of the expedition's destination, despite its unhealthy reputation; thus when 1,000 pounds of bark were requested, he found that only 50 pounds were in store, plus 400 pounds 'found' aboard a ship. Although the Medical Board was convened to discuss the contagion, the Inspector-General of Hospitals never attended, and although the latter, Francis Knight, said he knew of the unhealthy reputation of the region, he claimed that he had never been consulted. Keate said that none of the Medical Board had any jurisdiction over the Foot Guards, whose medical officers were entirely independent, and that even in the face of great want, he had no power to send out port wine or other 'medical comforts'; and Knight claimed that such was the reputation of the area that he could find only few hospital mates willing to go for fear of falling ill themselves.

The Peninsular War, 1809–10

For the remainder of the Peninsular War, Portugal, and especially the area around Lisbon, became the base for the British forces, permitting their easy re-supply from Britain thanks to the control of the sea maintained by the Royal Navy. Portugal became a second home for the British troops involved in the war, who maintained a generally most cordial relationship with its people.

Upon returning to command the Peninsula army, Sir Arthur Wellesley manoeuvred the French Marshal Soult out of Oporto for few casualties (12 May 1809) and advanced into Spain to co-operate with the Spanish army of the Captain-General of Estremadura, Don Gregorio García de la Cuesta, an immobile and unco-operative ally with a largely worthless army. British observers had scarcely a good word to say for either: Edward Costello, for example, described him as 'that deformed-looking lump of pride, ignorance and treachery ... the most murderous-looking old man I ever saw';[643] William Warre wrote of the 'old brute'; 'obstinate surly old ignorant fellow ... quite superannuated, and so violent and obstinate that everybody feared him but his enemies';[644] John Colborne contented himself with dismissing Cuesta as 'a perverse, stupid old blockhead'.[645] His army was little better:

'We were treated with a sight of the Spanish army, who marched through the village, headed by Cuesta, and a respectable-looking priest; they comprised a very large force, both of cavalry and infantry, and were dressed in every colour the rainbow itself can boast:

> Blue jackets and green,
> Yellow jackets and grey,
> Mingle, mingle, mingle,
> Mingle as they may,

forming, *en masse*, a most irregular set, not to be compared, even in appearance, to our rawest volunteers ... *Risum teneatis*!!! [could you keep from laughing?] ... As for his excellentissimo, the general, he has much more the appearance of a parish beadle, or a twopenny-postman, than of a military commander.' Evidently the French held the same opinion: 'An English officer of engineers, whilst employed upon his duty, was observed by a Frenchman, who immediately applied his hand to his hat, and made a respectful bow: two Spanish officers just afterwards came in sight, when the same hand was instantaneously and contemptuously applied to his most ignoble part.'[646]

It became obvious that effective collaboration with such an ally was impossible, and when the combined army was attacked by the French forces of Joseph Bonaparte and Marshal Victor at Talavera (28 July 1809), the British had to fight desperately until the French were beaten off, while the Spaniards remained immobile. The victory was most hard-won, and gained for Wellesley the title of Viscount Wellington.

Talavera was also notable for one of the greatest feats of endurance in the period, the forced march of Craufurd's Light Brigade to join the army, even though they arrived too late for the battle. Traditionally this involved a distance of 62 miles in 26 hours, but apparently this is a mis-calculation probably arising from the use in Spain of four different measurements of a league, ranging from *Legales castellana* at 2.63 miles, to *Legales España* at 4.21 miles. The actual distance covered was apparently 42 miles in 26 hours, with an additional four or five miles to forward positions beyond Talavera, which in the height of summer, over bad roads, with very few falling out, was a prodigious enough feat.[647] The noise of battle actually encouraged the brigade on its march: 'The constant cannonade in front was a stimulus which had a most beneficial effect, and made them forget, for a time, their extraordinary fatigue.'[648]

A particularly horrifying aspect of Talavera – sadly not unique – was the burning to death of many of the helpless wounded when dry grass and crops were set alight by the flashes of musketry, as described in an earlier section: '... Lines of running fire half a mile in length were frequent & fatal to many a Soldier ... lying weltering in their gore with the devouring element approaching & death most horrid staring them in the face! Thus perished many & among the rest our Major of Brigade, one of the most gallant & at the same time useful Officers in his Majesty's service when in the act of rallying the Brigade after retiring in disorder, he was knocked off his horse & fell a victim to the flames before assistance could be given ...'[649] (This officer was Captain Richard Beckett of the 2nd Foot Guards, a notably tall man for the time, six feet two or three inches, which height had been of advantage in Egypt when he waded across a lake with water up to his chin, bearing the Colours, but presumably made him a vulnerable target.) The retirement in disorder mentioned in this account was caused by an injudicious pursuit of a retreating French attack, when the pursuers were counter-attacked by French reserves and bundled back in quick time. What was remarkable about this was the fact that after having lost almost a third of their number (but not a single prisoner) and being completely disordered, the Foot Guards passed through the British reserve and reformed at the rear with amazing speed and resolution, giving a loud cheer to prove that their morale was entirely unaffected.

With communications with Portugal threatened, and having abandoned all hopes of co-operating with the Spanish (who even refused to supply food to his army), Wellington retired, leaving his wounded in Spanish care. These were immediately abandoned to the French, which 'I look upon as a fortunate circumstance; since, for myself, I had rather trust to the humanity of a Gallic foe, than to the gratitude of a Spanish friend.'[650]

To ensure the security of Lisbon, Wellington designed a double line of fortifications, the Lines of Torres Vedras, running from the Atlantic to the Tagus estuary, some 152 mutually supportive strongpoints. The work was directed by Lieutenant-Colonel Richard Fletcher of the Royal Engineers with a small staff (no more than seventeen engineer officers worked at any one time), with eighteen artificers and 150 infantrymen to supervise the 5-7,000-strong gangs of uncomplaining Portuguese peasants who performed the labouring. The forts and posts varied in size from accommodating 50 men and three 9pdrs to 1,720 men and 26 guns. By taking advantage of the terrain, the lines were virtually impregnable, and designed to be garrisoned by 18,000 Portuguese militia (14,000 for the inner line), so that the field army could remain safely in reserve, its security assured without any exertion on its part. It was the most effective piece of military engineering of the era, and of greater consequence than many of Wellington's victories in the field. As Fletcher's chief assistant, Major John Jones, remarked, it was an example of 'the foresight and skill of the general, and the exertion of the engineer ... in happy unison', so that 'a defensive army well posted shall have its front covered with works constructed on just principles, its force will be incalculably augmented, and its defeat rendered almost impracticable'.[651] By the time the lines were ready for occupation, the whole system had cost less than £100,000; even though the workers had been paid a fair wage, this represents a wonderful example of efficiency and value for money, when compared to the £59,089 11s. spent on the construction of the cavalry barracks at Weymouth, for example.

Minor skirmishing continued throughout this period. The affair at Barba del Puerco in March 1810 is a typical example of an 'outpost' action, involving a company of 95th Rifles holding a bridge over the River Agueda, with three companies in reserve.

Two sentries were placed at the bridge, with an 'alarm post' of an NCO and twelve men some 50 yards away, and the remainder of the forward company withdrawn further. About 600 French infantry approached unseen during a dark and stormy night, and although one of the sentries managed to fire a shot, they were bayoneted and the French were across the bridge before the alarm-post was roused, the NCO (Sergeant Betts) being shot through the mouth before he could properly raise the alarm. Alerted by the shots, the remainder of the forward company reached the alarm-post to find the French deploying. The company commander, Captain Peter O'Hare, had felt ill earlier in the night and had gone off to bed; so until he returned command devolved upon Lieutenant Mercer, who was shot through the head and killed while putting on his spectacles, and then upon 2nd Lieutenant George Simmons, in his first action. A furious fight raged at a range of about fifteen yards, the 43 riflemen crouching behind rocks and firing at the crossed white belts on the French uniforms as they were illuminated by occasional gleams of moonlight, while the French officers beat their men with swords to force them onward. So close-quarter was the firing that Simmons saw a rifleman shoot a French officer by placing the muzzle of his rifle against the Frenchman's throat, crying 'Revenge the death of Mr Mercer!'; whereupon the rifleman himself fell, shot seven times. After a desperate half hour, Colonel Beckwith and the remaining three companies of 95th came up at the charge, and the French fled back across the bridge.

The British loss was one officer and seven men killed, and fifteen wounded; two French officers and twelve men were left dead on the field, with eight prisoners, and almost 100 more French casualties were carried away on their retreat. One of the prisoners, a very young Frenchman, was captured with his musket, and in such a state that he was unaware that his finger was on the trigger. The gun went off and sent a ball through Beckwith's cap, and as a rifleman prepared to shoot the terrified lad, Beckwith called, 'Let him alone; I daresay the boy has a mother. Knock the thing out of his hand, that he may do no more mischief with it, and give him a kick on the bottom and send him to the rear.'[652] Beckwith followed this typical gesture of humanity by sharing his breakfast with the young Frenchman next morning. The action brought a divisional order of praise from Craufurd, noting that it proved that a rifle was just as efficient as a musket at close-quarters, contrary to a belief in other armies that rifle-armed troops were only of use at longer ranges.

Wellington's next victory was on 27 September 1810, in opposition to a French advance on Portugal under Marshal André Massena. Wellington met them on a strong position along the ridge at Busaco, involving the usual tactic of sheltering behind the ridge, appearing to deliver a crushing volley before the French could deploy, and throwing them back by a controlled counter-charge, which in this case was spectacularly successful. Wellington wrote that one reason he stood at Busaco was to boost the confidence of the rapidly improving Portuguese, giving them 'a taste for an amusement to which they were not before accustomed, and which they would not have acquired if I had not put them in a very strong position'.[653] Their improvement was confirmed by an officer of the Loyal Lusitanian Legion:

'... the Portuguese vied with the British in spirit and bravery ... I had a good deal of conversation with a French Major of Brigade, who was taken prisoner after being wounded, and who spoke most handsomely of the British, as one of our serjeants saved his life from the bayonet of a Portuguese, who was in the act of stabbing him while lying on the ground. He said, that the behaviour of the Portuguese troops had astonished them all, as their spies had made them form a different opinion of them, assuring them that they would not fight against the French. One French Colonel, who was opposed to a Portuguese regiment, before the firing on either side commenced, called out to his men not to fire on their friends, the Portuguese, and invited them to lay down their arms. He was answered by a volley.'[654]

Following Busaco, Wellington retired behind the Lines of Torres Vedras, evacuating much of the area in which the French would have to live. Finding the Lines impenetrable, the French sat outside during the winter and starved, while the Anglo-Portuguese rested in comfort, and even maintained friendly relations with their enemies: 'Our advanced lines and piquets [sic] and his are close together. The 92nd Highlanders are about a mile in front of headquarters, and so close to the enemy that they could (if they understood each other's language) speak to each other. The Highlanders and French are so near and courteous, that they salute each other, when going on or coming off duty; and, a few days ago, a bullock run from the enemy into the 92d's lines, which was immediately shot by one of the Highlanders. Two of the enemy, who were in chase of it, came over, waving white handkerchiefs, who expressed the great want they would be in for food, if the Highlanders kept the bullock from them;

on which the Highlanders, with the hospitality which characterises their county, sent half of the bullock, with a bottle of whiskey over to them.'[655]

The Peninsular War, 1811

The first major action of 1811 involved the British forces helping to defend Cadiz, the capital of free Spain. Sir Thomas Graham commanded the British contingent of the Allied army, but in repelling a French attack at Barrosa on 5 March 1811, they were largely abandoned by the Spanish and consequently had a desperate fight; after which, with Wellington's concurrence, Graham withdrew his forces from Spanish control.

There occurred at Barrosa an incident which provides an example of the resilience of a battalion, and an almost unique account of how an attack might founder. On the right of the Allied position was a hill, the Cerro del Puerco, held by five Spanish battalions and a British 'flank battalion' under Colonel Browne of the 28th, composed of two companies each of the 1/9th, 1/28th and 2/82nd, in all 22 officers and 514 men, of whom only about 470 were available for action. The Spaniards bolted upon the appearance of the French and Browne followed reluctantly, leaving the Cerro to be occupied by six French battalions and an artillery battery. Graham's orders from the Spanish commander, La Peña, were to retire, but realizing the perils of so doing he resolved to advance with his British contingent; but to buy time until it came up, a demonstration was necessary, for which only Browne's battalion was available. Graham asked Browne why he had left the Cerro; 'you would not have me fight the whole French army with four hundred and seventy men?'. On being told that the Spaniards had bolted, Graham remarked that it was a bad business, but there was nothing else for it but for Browne to attack in skirmish-order, then changed his mind and said that something more was necessary than skirmishers, and that Browne must attack in close formation; 'That I will, with pleasure,' replied Browne, 'for it is more in my way than light bobbing.'

Browne rode to the front of his battalion, removed his hat and declared, 'Gentlemen, I am happy to be the bearer of good news: General Graham has done you the honour of being the first to attack those fellows. Now follow me, you rascals!' and, pointing towards the French, began to sing *Heart of Oak*: 'Now, cheer up, my lads, 'tis to glory we steer ...' This must have been the most hopeless endeavour ever mounted by the British Army during the period. At the commencement of the attack – made with bayonets alone, with orders not to fire – no other British troops were within sight, as Dilkes' supporting brigade of Foot Guards had not yet emerged from the woods in the rear of the British position. The entire French force opened fire, including eight guns firing canister, as Browne's battalion began to ascend the Cerro; more than half the officers and almost 200 men went down to this first discharge. As the gaps closed in towards the centre, another fifty men and more officers fell; and in the words of Robert Blakeney, Browne's adjutant, 'We had by this time lost upwards of two hundred and fifty men and fourteen officers ... the remainder of the battalion now scattered.'

Unusually, and perhaps unlike what might have happened with troops of another nation, the broken battalion did not retreat; for although the men 'could not be got together', the survivors 'commenced firing from behind trees, mounds or any other cover which presented'. Only Browne and Blakeney stood in the battalion's original position, and as Dilkes' Guards were now in sight, Browne said, 'I shall go and join the Guards; will you come?' Blakeney was unsteady from a wound in the thigh, so 'told him that so long as three men of the battalion stood together and I was able to stand with them, I should not separate from them'.

The destruction of Browne's battalion had bought Graham the time he needed to push Dilkes' Guards into action, who emerged from the woods in a muddle and rushed on without hesitation. As they ascended the Cerro, over terrain with more cover than that attacked by Browne, four of the French battalions charged them in column. These 2,000 fresh troops, charging downhill in formation against an unformed and tired body of 1,400, should by all logic have swept the Guards away; but the ragged formation of Dilkes' brigade, now aided by part of the 2/67th on their right, opened such a fire that the French stopped in their tracks. Both sides stood and fired, a murderous duel at close range, until the French began to waver. At this juncture the interference of the two remaining French battalions could have been decisive, had it not been for Blakeney, still standing alone amid the dead and wounded of Browne's flank battalion.

As the French fire concentrated against Dilkes' Guards, Blakeney 'contrived to get eight or ten of the men together, principally 9th Grenadiers and 28th Light Infantry; to this little force I proposed charging a howitzer, which was pouring forth destruction immediately to our front. The proposition being well received, I seized a firelock (there were many spare ones), and on this a drummer named Adams, of the 28th Grenadiers' Company, said that were he not afraid of being obliged to pay for his drum, he also would take a musket. Upon my telling the boy that I would pay for his drum, he flung it away and armed. I have always thought Adams the bravest man, or rather boy, whom I ever met – not for seizing a musket and gallantly charging, for in the excitement that was natural enough; but that he should stand calmly calculating the price of a drum when hundreds of balls were passing close to his body is scarcely credible; but so it was.' Blakeney's party rushed the howitzer, bayoneted two of the gunners and chased away the others, and finding a piece of chalky earth, Blakeney wrote '28th Regiment' on the gun. This, he said, had 'a magic effect', for within moments he was joined by more than a hundred survivors of his battalion, who 'darted forth from behind trees, briars, brakes and out of hollows ... we now confidently advanced up the hill, and unlike most advances against a heavy fire, our numbers increased as we proceeded, soldiers of the flank battalion joining at every step'. The effect was to complete the rout of the French, leaving the mauled remnant of the British units in possession of the hill.[656]

Both sides lost heavily, about one-third of those engaged, and although it represented only a portion of the Battle of Barrosa, the disputed position was of vital significance, and is perhaps equally important in demonstrating the morale of quite ordinary British soldiers. If good sense and self-preservation prevented Browne's battalion from marching to total annihiliation, the unwillingness of the individuals to accept defeat and run away was remarkable; even more the determination to join a single officer in a charge uphill when the enemy fire had slackened sufficiently for such a movement to be no longer inevitable suicide.

Having starved all winter, Massena's army retired in the spring of 1811, followed by Wellington, whose pursuing army came upon scenes of devastation which chilled the blood: 'On passing through a small village ... the streets presented a scene of the most horrible nature – a scene that was at once calculated to harrow up every good feeling, and to make the blood run cold at the barbarities to which an unprincipled enemy is capable of having recourse, for the purpose of spreading terror and desolation over an innocent but bravely resisting people. Men, women and children were found lying dead in the middle of the streets ... some without ears, and with gashes deep and mortal in many parts of their bodies; others, with their mouths ripped open, and their heads otherwise disfigured, presented their expiring remains to the view of our soldiers ... Horror and indignation at the appalling sight filled the bosoms of the allied troops with the desire of revenge ...'[657]

During the pursuit of Massena an action occurred which demonstrated that infantry could fight successfully unaided. Wellington planned to destroy Reynier's French 2nd Corps near Sabugal, pinning it with frontal attacks by the 3rd and 5th Divisions, while William Erskine crossed the River Coa and blocked its retreat with the Light Division and two cavalry brigades. Unfortunately, the fog was so dense on the morning of 3 April 1811 that the commanders of the 3rd and 5th Divisions postponed their advance and sent to Wellington for orders; but lacking such circumspection, Erskine ordered Sidney Beckwith's leading brigade of the Light Division to cross the river as planned. The fog was so thick that Beckwith crossed at the wrong ford, and instead of encountering the French flank he ran straight into Reynier's main body. Beckwith advanced with four companies of 1/95th and three of Colonel Elder's 3rd *Caçadores* in skirmish order, with the remainder of the brigade (1/43rd and the other half of the *Caçadores*) behind them.

Beckwith pushed back the French picquet-line and the first regiment he encountered (the weak 4ème *Léger*), but then a see-saw battle developed as he engaged battalion after battalion, the British using stone walls as shelters and counter-charging with the bayonet each French attack: 'We fixed bayonets, and charged them, determined to clear the way before us; their columns were routed, and fell back in great confusion. We found them, as we advanced, forming fresh bodies still stronger, and a wall in front lined with a battalion. We fell back to the ground we charged from, and again formed under a heavy fire of grape, canister, and musketry. They again advanced upon us, and we again charged them, gained the heights they possessed, and took a howitzer that had very much annoyed us; it was posted in the rear of the battalion that was formed under cover of the wall. Our people advanced with so much impetuosity that our front was rather scattered. Their cavalry took advantage of it, and charged us. The wall we had before taken was near us, and we fell back upon it in full run. They took about 30 or 40 of our people. We gave them a volley, tumbled some of them, and the others retired with precipitation. We again pushed on, secured the howitzer we had before taken, and which their cavalry made a charge to recover: we were so hard pushed at first that our right was actually surrounded. Our second charge cleared the way and saved our gun ...'[658]

Beckwith won great fame here, directing and encouraging his men, oblivious to blood pouring from an injury to his forehead. His demeanour was perfect for the circumstances, exuding calm: 'Now, my lads, we'll just go back a little if you please', and when they began to run, 'No, no, I don't mean that – we are in no hurry – we'll just walk quietly back, and you can give them a shot as you go along … Now, my men, this will do – let us show them our teeth again!'; and to the French, with a shake of his fist, 'Now, you rascals, come on here if you dare!'[659] This was in marked contrast to the behaviour of Erskine, who, with the exception of a single squadron of 16th Light Dragoons, kept his cavalry counter-marching in the rear, bereft of any idea what to do, and actually forbade Drummond's 2nd Brigade of the Light Division to go to Beckwith's aid. Fortunately, Drummond disregarded the order, marched towards the sound of fighting, and advanced firing on Beckwith's right, helping to repel yet another heavy assault. As the fog lifted to reveal the 3rd and 5th Divisions preparing to ford the river, Reynier broke off the action, but lost much of his rearguard in the retreat. The success of the battle was due to the resolution of Beckwith's brigade, and its powers of re-forming after several charges and retreats, holding its ground without support and against overwhelming odds; never was a sorry commander (Erskine) more rescued by the excellence of the officers and men under his command.

The surrender to the French of one of the fortresses on the Spanish-Portuguese border, Badajoz, on 9 March, compelled Wellington to divide his forces, retaining command in the north and detailing Beresford to operate against Soult's French army in the south. Massena attacked Wellington on 3-5 May at Fuentes de Oñoro, and withdrew after a bitter contest. On 16 May 1811 Beresford's army, including a large Spanish contingent, fought one of the bloodiest actions of the period at Albuera, memorable for the destruction of most of Colborne's brigade, as mentioned before (ridden down by lancers before they had a chance to form square), and for the subsequent counter-attack by Myers' Fusilier Brigade of Lowry Cole's division, into a veritable tempest of shot and shell, one of the great epics of the British army and immortalized by William Napier in perhaps the most celebrated passage of military writing:

'Myers was killed; Cole and the three colonels, Ellis, Blakeney, and Hawkshawe, fell wounded, and the fuzileer battalions, struck by the iron tempest, reeled, and staggered like sinking ships. Suddenly and sternly recovering, they closed on their terrible enemies, and then was seen with what a strength and majesty the British soldier fights … Nothing could stop that astonishing infantry. No sudden burst of undisciplined valour, no nervous enthusiasm, weakened the stability of their order … In vain did the French reserves, joining with the struggling multitude, endeavour to sustain the fight; their efforts only increased the irremediable confusion, and the mighty mass giving way like a loosened cliff, went headlong down the ascent. The rain flowed after in streams discoloured with blood, and fifteen hundred unwounded men, the remnant of six thousand unconquerable British soldiers, stood triumphant on that fatal hill!'[660] The cost, however, was the shattering of Beresford's army; as Wellington remarked, another such victory would ruin them.

Albuera also produced an example of the manipulation of dispatches, although in general British dispatches were immeasurably more honest than those of some other nations. Wellington recalled that he received Beresford's first report with dismay: 'He wrote me to the effect that he was delighted I was coming; that he could not stand the slaughter about him nor the vast responsibility. His letter was quite in a desponding tone. It was brought to me next day ... and I said directly, "This won't do; write me down a victory." The dispatch was altered accordingly.'[661]

Before Albuera there occurred a classic example of the failings in discipline and leadership of the cavalry, when Robert Long, commanding Beresford's cavalry, was pursuing French forces withdrawing to Badajoz. Near Campo Mayor he engaged a French detachment covering the retirement of their siege-train; the 13th Light Dragoons duly routed the French 26th Dragoons, but instead of rallying to capitalize on their success, pursued pell-mell; Portuguese squadrons sent as their reserve merely joined in the chase. They overtook and captured the siege-train, but even then did not stop, but careered on towards the very gates of Badajoz, were chased back by French reinforcements, lost the captured artillery, and thus sacrificed all their success. Wellington's fury was intense ('If the 13th Dragoons are again guilty of this conduct, I shall take their horses from them, and send the officers and men to do duty at Lisbon'),[662] yet it is a measure of the lack of tactical awareness among most of the cavalry that this fiasco was regarded as a triumph:

'The French manoeuvred most beautifully ... and sustained three charges of our cavalry without breaking. The 13th behaved most nobly. I saw so many instances of individual bravery, as raised my opinion of mankind in general many degrees. The French certainly are fine and brave soldiers, but the superiority of our English horses, and more particularly the superiority of swordsmanship our fellows showed, decided every contest in our favour; it was absolutely like a game at *prison bars*, which you must have seen at school, except the three charges. The whole way across the plain was a succession of individual contests, here and there, as the cavalry all dispersed ... it was certainly most beautiful.'

This account records in detail the celebrated episode in which Corporal Logan of the 13th Light Dragoons killed the French Colonel Chamorin of the 26th Dragoons, which exemplifies both the brutality of cavalry combat and the scenes that succeeded a battle: 'Yesterday a French Captain of Dragoons brought over a trumpet, demanding permission to search among the dead for his Colonel; his regiment was a fine one, with bright brass helmets, and black horse hair, exactly like what the old Romans are depicted with: the Captain was a fine young man, and had his arm in a sling. Many of us went out with him – it was truly a bloody scene, being almost all sabre wounds, the slain were all naked, the peasants having stripped them in the night; it was long before we could find the French Colonel – he was lying on his face, his naked body weltering in blood, and as soon as he was turned up, the Officer knew him, he gave a sort of scream, and sprung off his horse, dashed his helmet on the ground, took the bloody hand and kissed it many times in an agony of grief; it was an affecting and awful scene. I suppose there were about 600 naked bodies lying on the ground at one view ... the French Colonel ... was killed by a corporal of the 13th; this corporal had killed one of his men, and he was so enraged, that he sallied out himself and attacked the corporal – the corporal was well mounted and a good swordsman, as was also the Colonel – both defended for some time, the corporal cut him twice in the face, his helmet came off at the second, when the corporal slew him by a cut which nearly cleft his skull asunder, it cut in as deep as the nose through the brain.'[663]

(The sight of this body, bearing a 'deep and frightful cleft ... on which the flies were already settling, which lay, all spurned and blood-stained, on the rude and prickly heath', had a profound effect upon Moyle Sherer, who mused that it had been, 'but one short hour before, a man of rank, perhaps also of talent, fortune, courage, whose voice breathed command, whose eye glanced fire, whose arm shook defiance; even so, such is war!')[664]

Albuera was the last major action of 1811, although there were considerable minor successes for Wellington's deputies, by Lumley at Usagre (25 May), Picton at El Bodon (25 September) and Hill at Arroyo dos Molinos (28 October).

The Peninsular War, 1812

Having made Portugal secure, in 1812 Wellington prepared to drive the French from Spain. His first task was to besiege and capture the two border fortresses of Ciudad Rodrigo and Badajoz, which were taken on 19 January and 6 April respectively, after short sieges involving the breaching of the defences and a storm. In both cases, especially at Badajoz, this was appallingly costly, and such was the slaughter in the breaches at Badajoz that access could not be gained, the fortress falling to a secondary assault by escalade. The capture of both, especially Badajoz, was followed by a ransacking that disgraced the army, even if the traumas of the assault might be advanced as some kind of explanation for the way in which the troops ran wild. The attack had been bad enough – like a number of writers, Kincaid compared it to the infernal regions ('as respectable a representation of hell itself as fire, and sword, and human sacrifices could make it')[665] – but the drunken orgies of murder, looting and rapine which followed exceeded even this, and left observers sickened or in a profound state of shock; Grattan's remark that 'every insult, every infamy that human invention could torture into practice was committed' was nothing more than the literal truth,[666] against which all the efforts of the officers were quite without effect. Only the exhaustion of the pillagers and the erection of gallows restored the army to order.

Wellington pressed on against the army of the French Marshal Marmont, leaving Hill to prevent Soult from moving north to reinforce him. During these operations occurred yet another example of the cavalry's old evil of charging without control or providing a reserve. On 11 June the lamentable Slade with the 3rd Dragoon Guards and 1st Dragoons engaged a French brigade of approximately equal strength at Maguilla; after a reckless pursuit following initial victory, the British were so disorganized that the French reserve cut them up severely and chased them away. This action aroused Wellington's fury, as already mentioned; and it was compounded by Slade's attempt to obscure what had happened, or at least revealing a total lack of appreciation of what was required of cavalry: '... our misfortunes arose from too great eagerness and zeal in the pursuit ... each regiment vying with each other who should most distinguish itself ... It is a satisfaction to me to be able to add, that the enemy lost in killed and wounded full as many as ourselves, and considered himself completely routed.'[667] (In actual fact, the French reported 51 casualties, whereas Slade lost 166, almost a quarter of the troops involved.)

Having secured the border fortresses, Wellington marched to defeat Marmont before he could be reinforced by King Joseph Bonaparte, and in one of his most impressive victories, smashed Marmont's army at Salamanca on 22 July 1812:

'Don Joseph and Marmont were fill'd with desires,
To place my Lord Wellington 'twixt their two fires;
But after much wonderful racket and rout
When his Lordship appear'd, both their fires went out.
No Artillery roar'd, thro' their lines not a puff:
Yet though cannon was silent, King Joseph *went off*.'[668]

This battle contradicted the perception of Wellington as a defensive general, in that he attacked the French army while it marched across his front; it gained Wellington a further step in the peerage (to Marquess) and enhanced even more his reputation among his army, as described by an officer, presumably of Leith's 5th Division:

'Lord Wellington, with the eye of an eagle, and the rapidity of lightning, changed his defence into an attack, and each division of the British, formed in two lines, advanced to the heights occupied by the enemy. Then came the tug. Lord Wellington had shown us generalship. It was now the turn of the troops. They did not fire, but with a slow, but steady pace ascended the hills, broke through the enemy's centre, and, in less than three hours, destroyed their army ... General Leith had his division in two lines ... It was beautiful, like a review – the General in front of the centre, with his hat off, as at a general salute. The enemy kept their ground, and threw in their fire, which was only answered with a shout at the top of the hill. When within five yards of their columns the General brought the division to the charge, and successively walked over their different lots of columns, taking guns, eagles, and colours ... The regularity of a parade was preserved throughout; the cannonade only made them more steady; had the hills been made of red hot iron, they would have been carried ...'[669]

The advance, which Wellington timed to perfection, was initiated by Pakenham's 3rd Division, involving an infantry combat that provides an example of the offensive power of the line, and demonstrates a variation on what might be regarded as the typical Anglo-French infantry duel, in that the British advanced in line uphill against a French division initially marching in column and which only deployed upon sighting the British.

Initially, Sir Edward Pakenham ordered into line the brigade of Colonel Alexander Wallace of the 88th, to ascend a slope against Thomières' French division; unusually, all the British officers were in front of their men, as were the French, 'but their relative duties were widely different: the latter, encouraging their men into the heat of the battle; the former, keeping their devoted soldiers back! – what a splendid national contrast!'[670] In front of Wallace's men were Portuguese *Caçadores* under a British officer, Major Haddock, and the advancing British witnessed the unedifying spectacle of Haddock beating his men with the flat of his sabre in an attempt to get them to stand and reply to the French fire; but as Grattan remarked, he might as well have attempted to animate Salamanca cathedral.

Thomières' division fired a fusillade which brought down much of Wallace's front rank, and stopped the brigade in its tracks; Wallace, in front, turned to face his men and pointed towards the French. Striding over the bodies of the fallen, the brigade continued its advance uphill, a sight which shook the French, their musketry becoming irregular and aimed high, a sure sign of approaching panic. The three British battalions cheered as they advanced: 'The effect was electric; Thomières' troops were seized with a panic ... Their mustachioed faces, one and all, presented the same ghastly hue, a horrid family likeness throughout; and as they stood to receive the shock ... they reeled to and fro like men intoxicated. The French officers did all that was possible, by voice, gesture, and example, to rouse their men to a proper sense of their situation, but in vain.'

The colonel of the leading French regiment (22éme *Ligne*), endeavouring to hearten his men, seized a musket and ran forward towards the advancing 88th Foot, led by Major Barnaby Murphy and the adjutant, Captain William Mackie, both mounted, and the Colour-party, the King's Colour borne by Lieutenant John D'Arcy and the Regimental Colour by Lieutenant T. Moriarty. As the French colonel dashed forward, Moriarty remarked, 'That fellow is aiming at me!'; 'I hope so', said D'Arcy, 'for I thought he had *me* covered.' Instead, the French officer fired at Murphy, killing him on the spot, the ball passing through him, hitting the pole of the King's Colour and ricocheting to strike off part of D'Arcy's epaulette. At the same moment someone from the 88th shot the French colonel through the head, who threw up his arms and fell forward; as Murphy, his foot caught in a stirrup, was dragged by his frightened horse along the front of the battalion, a sight which threw the 88th into a frenzy of rage. Pakenham rode up at this moment and called to Wallace, 'Let them loose'; the brigade charged and the French, astonished at the sight of a two-deep line running uphill towards superior numbers, broke and fled. After some bloody bayonet-work among the bolting Frenchmen, the brigade rallied in a state of near exhaustion; except Adjutant Mackie who, seeing the infantry fight had ended, joined a cavalry charge from which he returned covered in dust, with only the hilt of his sword left, and that reeking with blood.

This cavalry charge exemplified the confusion common on the battlefield, for so thick was smoke from musketry and from the grass having been set alight that when Wallace's brigade rallied, they could see nothing about them; and hearing a cheer in their rear began to form square in case it heralded the approach of French cavalry. Actually, it was Le Marchant's British cavalry which erupted out of the smoke and passed Wallace's men; and such was the effect of their charge that Wallace's brigade was soon surrounded by French soldiers, running to the British infantry to protect them from the sabres of the cavalry. Thus, as Grattan remarked, not only did Wallace's men defeat the French, but actually covered their retreat and saved their lives, for not one of the French fugitives was harmed once they had flung themselves into the safety of the British positions. This was, on the part of the British infantry, a remarkable example of fellow-feeling towards a defeated enemy facing annihilation; appreciating the helplessness of broken infantry attacked by cavalry, it was perhaps a case of 'there but for the grace of God go I'.

In the aftermath of Salamanca, two cavalry exploits are worthy of note, countering the damage to that arm's reputation caused by the affair at Maguilla. On the day after the Battle of Salamanca, there occurred at Garcia Hernandez that rarest of exploits, the breaking of infantry in square. In the pursuit of the French, Bock's brigade (1st and 2nd King's German Legion Dragoons) came upon a body of French infantry, the forward elements in square. The Dragoons advanced in echelon, and after the French musketry had disordered the first squadron, Captain von der Decken led his following squadron straight at the square. He was mortally wounded by the next volley, but a wounded horse crashed into the side of the square, crushing six or eight files, and through this gap the following dragoons poured; the square dissolved in disorder and most of the French surrendered on the spot. The other French battalions attempted to retire, but had not time to form square properly before they were ridden down by succeeding KGL squadrons, and the pursuit only halted when, having destroyed or captured this infantry, some of the dragoons attempted to engage another formation, which held firm and the disordered cavalry was forced to draw away. This action was greatly celebrated as an almost unique exploit, and was a testimony to the resolution and endeavour of the regimental officers who led the charge.

Three days after Salamanca a demonstration was given of the excellence which could be achieved in even that most neglected part of cavalry service, the 'outpost', and of the skill and intelligence of an ordinary non-commissioned officer. Corporal William Hanley of the 14th Light Dragoons was ordered to reconnoitre in front of his brigade and ascertain the position of the French; his patrol comprised four men of the 1st KGL Hussars and four of the 14th, reduced to three after Private Luke Billingham accidentally shot his horse in the shoulder when checking his pistol. After two leagues on his march, Hanley entered a village whose inhabitants revealed the presence of French troops at Blascho Sancho (or Blanchez Sanchez), some two leagues further on. Posting a look-out on the church tower, Hanley unbridled and fed his horses, then pressed on, sending one vedette 100 yards ahead and others 200 yards to each flank. Dismounting at the foot of a hill, Hanley climbed its brow and, observing from behind a stone cross, saw a French infantry column assemble and march away, and fifteen minutes later re-mounted his patrol and led it into the village.

Blascho Sancho consisted of a single street, in which Hanley captured four dragoons who had been cutting forage, and who were making for a house within a walled stable-yard, into which there was a single doorway. Henley shot open the door and had his men maintain a brisk fire down the passage leading to the stable to keep any inhabitants pinned down, but while giving instructions was shot at through the window of the house. Poking his pistol through the broken window, Hanley called upon its occupant to surrender, and out came the officer commanding the enemy detachment. Using one of the Germans as interpreter, Hanley told the officer to order his men to surrender or be burned out; whereupon they filed out and gave up their weapons, which Hanley's men smashed. An enemy sergeant and 26 dragoons were formed up in ranks four deep, leading their horses with stirrups across their saddles to frustrate escape; Hanley allowed the officer to ride, but kept hold of his reins. As they moved off a French colonel approached with his servant and two mules, and seeing so few British soldiers presumed they were the prisoners; he cheerily clapped Hanley's shoulder and said, 'Bon jour, Englishman'; whereupon Hanley thrust his pistol against the colonel's breast and drew the officer's sword.

Adding them to his column, Hanley pushed on quickly to tire the prisoners, who were beginning to mutter about the smallness of Hanley's party. By dusk they reached the village where they had halted earlier; Hanley put his prisoners in the church and refreshed them with bread and wine provided by the village mayor. In bright moonlight the march recommenced and eventually reached the 14th Light Dragoons' forward post, which was alarmed by the sight of so many long-tailed horses (i.e., clearly not British), so fired and fell back upon the main picquet, which came up at a gallop. When the identity of the patrol was established, the whole camp was roused to greet Hanley with cheers. Almost unprecedentedly, given that no officer was involved, the exploit was mentioned in official dispatches, and the patrol received not only the usual reward of £25 per captured horse, but on Wellington's instruction a further 12 dollars per man, 24 dollars for Hanley. He also received what was perhaps the most well-deserved regimental medal bestowed during the period, and after 34 years' service retired as a sergeant-major, still in the same regiment.[671]

The remainder of 1812 was not marked by such success. On 12 August Wellington made a triumphal entry into Madrid, but his siege of Burgos had to be abandoned for lack of resources and a French threat to the line of communication with Portugal. The retreat from Burgos was accompanied by privations as severe as on that to Corunna, but despite the losses there was no major battle. Although Madrid was re-possessed temporarily by King Joseph, French confidence had been severely dented and Wellington was ready to make the final drive against them.

The Peninsular War, 1813–14

To divert French resources, British forces had been allocated to operate against the east coast of Spain from mid-1812, but little progress was made until the spring of 1813, when command devolved upon Sir John Murray, an incompetent of whom Wellington wrote, 'he always appeared to me to want what is better than abilities, viz. sound sense. There is always some mistaken principle in what he does.'[672] Consequently, although Murray won an action at Castalla on 13 April 1813, his expedition to Tarragona had to withdraw with the loss of his precious siege-guns.

Wellington's advance began in late May, brilliantly out-manoeuvring the French and winning a crushing victory over the army of King Joseph and Marshal Jourdan at Vittoria on 21 June 1813, the rout of the French being so profound that they were able to extricate only one fieldpiece and one howitzer, of which the former was lost two days later. The Battle of Vittoria effectively settled the outcome of the Peninsular War, but was marred by a breakdown in discipline as the army fell upon the French baggage and treasury instead of conducting an effective pursuit. Wellington was duly scathing: 'We started with the army in the highest order, and up to the day of battle nothing could get on better; but that event has, as usual, totally annihilated all order and discipline. The soldiers of the army have got among them about a million sterling in money ... the night of the battle, instead of being passed in getting rest and food to prepare them for the pursuit of the following day, was passed by the soldiers in looking for plunder. The consequence was, that they were totally knocked up ... This is the consequence of the state of discipline of the British army. We may gain the greatest victories; but we shall do no good until we shall so far alter our system, as to force all ranks to perform their duty. The new regiments are, as usual, the worst of all.'[673]

As Wellington hinted, it was not only the 'vagabond soldiers' who plundered the French baggage; officers were equally to the fore, most notably those of the 14th Light Dragoons who took King Joseph's silver chamber-pot, which was used ever after as a punchbowl in the mess. Most famous, however, was the capture of Jourdan's baton of office, apparently originally found by Corporal Fox of the 18th Hussars, who removed the inscribed gold ends before the remainder was stolen from him. The main part found its way to Wellington, the gold ends being reunited some months later when Fox surrendered them to his commanding officer, Major James Hughes. Wellington sent the baton to the Prince Regent; in return, and to confirm his promotion to field marshal, the Prince sent Wellington a British baton: 'Your glorious conduct is beyond all human praise, and far above my reward; I know no language the world affords worthy to express it. I feel I have nothing left to say, but devoutly to offer up my prayers of gratitude to Providence, that it has in its omnipotent bounty blessed my country and myself with such a General. You have sent me, among the trophies of your unrivalled fame, the staff of a French Marshal; and I send you in return that of England. The British army will hail it with enthusiasm, while the whole universe will acknowledge these valorous efforts which had so imperiously called for it.'[674]

Wellington pushed on against what remained of the French forces in Spain, now unified under the command of Marshal Soult, who made great efforts to bar the Allies' path through the Pyrenees, which hinged upon the border fortresses of San Sebastian and Pamplona. Soult was able to achieve local superiority in his attacks at selected points along the Allied positions, and desperate fighting was necessary to repel them at Roncesvalles and Maya (25 July) and Sorauren (28–30 July). At Roncesvalles there occurred, virtually by accident, that rarest of events, a genuine bayonet-fight.

Near Roncesvalles Captain George Tovey of the 20th Foot led forward his company at double-quick time to clear away some French skirmishers. On reaching the edge of a plateau, the skirmishers having fled, Tovey met the head of the French 6ème *Léger* which, unseen, had just ascended the slope: 'my company absolutely paused in astonishment, for we were *face* to *face* with them; and, the French officers calling to us to *disarm*, I repeated "Bayonet away – bayonet away!" and, rushing headlong amongst them, we fairly turned them back into the descent of the hill; and such was the panic and confusion occasioned amongst them by our sudden onset, that this small party – for small it was compared to the French column – had time to regain the regiment ... The company, with which I was the only officer present on this occasion, did not amount to more than between seventy and eighty men, and we had eleven killed and fourteen wounded ... A powerful man by the name of Budworth returned with only the *blood-soiled* socket of the bayonet on his piece, and he declared he had *killed away* until his bayonet broke; and I am confident, from the reckless and intrepid nature of the man, that he had done so.'[674] John Kincaid described the action in less modest terms: 'The moment was fraught with disaster, when a gallant Centurion, a choice spirit of the old 20th, at once came forth in character ... in the sight of the whole division, he with his single company, with desperate and reckless charge, dashed into the head of a whole column of French infantry which had already gained the heights, overthrew them, and sent the whole mass rolling headlong and panic-stricken into the valley below! It was one of the most brilliant feats of the war. It gave his division time to form ...'[675]

The action at Sorauren was one of the most bitter of the war; as Wellington reported, 'I never saw such fighting ... it began on the 25th, and, excepting the 29th ... we had it every day till the 2nd. The battle of the 28th was fair *bludgeon* work.'[676] The Marquis de Chambray recorded a typical example of the 'reverse slope' tactic here, save for the absence of skirmishers:

'The English there occupied an elevated hill, of which the slope was rather steep ... a first line ... was deployed parallel with the crest ... and about fifty yards behind this crest. The first line could neither see the troops which were to climb the hill to attack it, nor be seen by them ...[they] were much less numerous than their assailants. The French division destined to attack was formed in close columns of divisions, and ascended the hill; it was not preceded by skirmishers, and the English had none either. From time to time the English officers came to examine at what point the French columns had arrived. As soon as they appeared, the English battalions fired, charged with the bayonet, and over-threw them, but did not pursue; on the contrary, after having remained some moments near the crest ... they retired in double quick time, at the command of their General, resumed their position, and gave three successive cheers. Nevertheless, the French division, of which the first ranks only had attained the plateau, astonished at being repulsed, almost without having fought, rallied immediately, and re-ascended the hill with great resolution ... The French columns debouched, as before, received a discharge of musketry, and were again charged and overthrown. The English battalions again resumed their position in double quick time, and repeated their cheers.'[677]

Captain Sempronius Stretton of the 40th on this occasion described the efficacy of the tactic even when adopted by an unsupported single unit. One of the French attacks on 28 July was delivered against a hill held by the 40th (numbering only one captain, nine subalterns and less than 400 men) and two Spanish battalions, which 'retired in the utmost confusion, and scattering themselves over the face of the mountain in our rear' upon the French attack. Assailed by almost 2,000 French infantry (three battalions of the 120ème *Ligne*, two of the 122ème), the 40th held on unsupported: 'As soon as the head of the attacking French column had reached the brow of the hill, and formed, a volley was fired by the 40th, and a charge of bayonets made which drove them down in the utmost confusion. Four times the enemy renewed the attack, and each time they were driven back at the point of the bayonet, leaving the 40th in final possession of the hill which they had so resolutely defended.'[678]

This account includes some interesting tactical observations: the 40th were formed some 80 yards from the top of the ascent, forming a 'killing ground' in their front; and contrary to the old theory that the French attempted to push their columnar attacks on to the very bayonets of the enemy, in this case it is obvious that they advanced in column and then deployed ('and formed' in Stretton's account above), as was probably generally the intention; and that rather than firing at the head of the column, the British waited until they were deploying before firing and bundling them back off the hill with a limited bayonet-charge. Evidently, despite the 40th's isolation, the terrain rendered impossible flank-attacks upon them; and other accounts note how each French assault became progressively more desperate, until the final attack, inspired by beating drums and the officers pushing the men forward, stopped about 25 yards from the crest before rolling back down the hill, unable to fight any more. The following day a French officer requested permission to remove his wounded, and admitted the attack had cost them several hundred casualties; the 40th's losses on the day were five officers and 124 other ranks, about 31 per cent of those involved, testimony to the desperate nature of the combat.

On 31 August San Sebastian was taken in a violent assault, in which the slaughter was so severe that a most unusual event was recorded by one officer: 'As fast as our men came up, they were knocked down by the dreadful fire from the defences which bore upon the breaches; and when a few got into them, they were unable to effect any thing from their weakness. In short, the carnage was so great, that the French themselves called out to our officers to draw the men off, and actually ceased firing upon them. Never was witnessed such heroism as on the part of our soldiery on this occasion ...'[679] Once again looting and rampage followed the storm, which George Gleig found 'truly shocking': dead, dying and drunk lying together indiscriminately, household goods thrown from windows in an orgy of destruction: 'Here you would see a drunken fellow whirling a string of watches round his head, and then dashing them against the wall ... the ceaseless hum of conversation, the occasional laugh and wild shout of intoxication, the pitiable cries or deep moans of the wounded, and the unintermitted roar of the flames, produced altogether such a concert as no man who listened to it can ever forget.'[680]

On the same day, a French attempt to relieve San Sebastian was repelled at San Marcial by Spanish troops, contrary to the opinion of their worth generally held by the army, and again proving the efficacy of the 'reverse slope' tactic. When asked for assistance, Wellington is said to have remarked that the Spanish were coping unaided, and that if British troops became involved they would receive the credit that was the Spaniards' due, perhaps acceptance of the fact that British observers, not unnaturally, concentrated upon the merits of their own army. At least one commentator attributed the good conduct of the Spanish to Wellington's proximity: 'The presence of this wonderful man inspires every one.'[681]

On 7 October Wellington forced the crossing of the River Bidassoa against outnumbered French defenders, at one point providing an example of the correct use of artillery support: 'Our brigade, which is the heavy 18 pounder brigade ... was ordered to take position on a small eminence which commanded the bridge and pass of the Bidassoa. The enemy were in great numbers on the opposite side of the Bidassoa, and appeared determined to make a great stand; they had fortified all the houses on that side, and had made loopholes in them for musquetry, which completely covered them from the fire of our infantry, and prevented the 5th division from crossing. In a very short time, however, from our position, we battered the place about their heads and the 5th division then crossed ... nothing could equal the bravery and intrepidity of our troops ... it was the grandest sight in the world to behold our men climbing up these steep hills, and when they had gained the top, clearing them of the enemy ... The French officers behaved nobly; we frequently saw them riding at the head of their columns, at a considerable distance, but the men would not advance, they tried to rally them repeatedly, but all in vain, they would not stand.' This writer observed Wellington at close range during the action, and 'he appeared in raptures during the whole of the battle',[682] an unusual description for a general usually described as calm and somewhat aloof.

On 9 November Wellington forced the French defences along the River Nivelle, allowing the army to escape the Pyrenean winter by establishing itself on the French side. Wellington took the greatest care not to offend the French civilian population in order to gain their co-operation, and consequently sent home all the Spanish save Morillo's division (in British pay and command), as 'I have not come to France to pillage; I have not had thousands of officers and soldiers killed and wounded for the remainder to plunder the French.'[683] Indeed, so well-behaved were the British troops in France, and so hated had become Napoleon's imposition of conscription, that Wellington's army received much better co-operation from the French civilians than did the French army: 'The peasants all rail loudly at Bonaparte, and offer us wine, and such other refreshments as they possess, and shew us, indeed, all the attention in their power.'[684]

On 10 December Soult attacked again at the River Nive, involving four days of heavy fighting before the French were repulsed. The attack at St. Pierre on 13 December produced some of the bitterest combat, the assault on the British 2nd Division highlighting the respective effects of good and bad battalion-commanders; and demonstrating that, as a consequence of the terrain, companies and detachments could operate in a semi-independent manner instead of battalions acting as unified bodies in the way often believed to have been universal. Although Rowland Hill was in overall command, the most serious combat was supervised by the divisional commander, Sir William Stewart, alias 'Auld Grog Willie' (from his issue of extra allowances of rum to his division).

The most serious attack was mounted by the French upon a hill in the centre of the British position; the terrain, interspersed with cottages and crofts, made movement in formation difficult, so that the forces of both sides resembled heavy skirmish-screens. The front line of Ashworth's Portuguese brigade began to fall back, so to reinforce them Stewart fed in elements of his first-line reserve, the brigade of Major-General Edward Barnes (1/50th, 1/71st, 1/92nd): first the light companies, then the remainder of the 71st, and then two companies of 92nd, each of which made local counter-attacks which only delayed the French advance. By sending half the 50th to bolster his right, Stewart retained only four companies of 50th and seven of the 92nd on top of the hill. At this juncture the quality of battalion-commanders became decisive.

The 1/71st was an excellent, experienced battalion, but had recently been inflicted with a new commander, Sir Nathaniel Peacocke, whom the brigade had already assessed as a tyrant off the battlefield and a coward on it. As the French advanced, Peacocke ordered his battalion to retire, leaving a gap in the centre of the British line, and took himself to the rear where he was found by Hill beating Portuguese ammunition-bearers, pretending to urge them forward while conveniently keeping himself out of danger. The last four companies of the 1/50th were needed to plug the gap, and there now occurred

another crisis on the right, where another undistinguished battalion commander, Bunbury of the 1/3rd, also withdrew his battalion. With all the efforts of
the brigade on the right thus needed to hold this position, the centre was left
without any chance of reinforcement, with just the seven remaining companies of the 1/92nd Highlanders. Their commander, however, was made of very
different material from Peacocke and Bunbury: John Cameron of Fassiefern, a
Highlander revered by his men in the manner of an old clan chief, a splendid
soldier but the sternest of disciplinarians, 'the very devil' in punishment of
dirty or drunken soldiers, according to one of his men.[685]

To halt French progress in the centre, Barnes launched this last reserve
in a charge down the hill, Cameron at the head. The fighting was so confused
that sources mention between two and four charges at this point; what is probably the earliest published account (*Edinburgh Evening Courant*, 22 January
1814) states that after the first charge, Cameron halted his men to draw breath,
when they were immediately assailed by fresh French troops: '"Then, my lads"
(said Colonel Cameron), "we must charge them again"', in course of which a
heavy fire killed Lieutenants Thomas Mitchell, Allan Macdonald and Duncan
McPherson, the latter while cheering on his company with bonnet in one hand
and broadsword in the other. So severe was the pressure that the 92nd had to
withdraw to their previous position, during which Cameron was pinned under
his dead horse. A corporal of the 92nd ran back and began to drag him clear,
only to be overtaken by the approaching French, one of whom seized the corporal around the neck until bayoneted by another 92nd man. As Cameron was
helped away, the corporal unfastened the saddle and removed it, remarking
that the French could have the dead horse but would not get the saddle upon
which Fassiefern sat![686] (His biography[687] attributes this to Cameron's foster-
brother, Ewan McMillan, who was certainly present; he served in the ranks of
the 92nd and it was in his arms that Cameron died at Quatre Bras.)

At this critical position, Hill in person led forward his last reserve, Le
Cor's Portuguese brigade; but before they could come into action, the survivors
of Barnes' brigade made their own counter-attack. Barnes went down,
wounded, and command passed to Charles Ashworth of the Portuguese, who
was himself hit shortly after. The 1/71st's shameful commander had gone to
the rear 'wounded' (a ball had passed through his coat-tails!), and as his
deputy, Major M. McKenzie, had been killed, the divisional commander Stewart personally led the battalion in a desperate charge, with what remained of
the 1/92nd, led by Cameron (now on foot), the Colours and their sole surviving piper, playing *Cogadh na sith* ('War or Peace'); as Napier wrote, 'how desperately did the fiftieth and Portuguese fight to give time for the ninety-second to
rally and reform ... how gloriously did that regiment come forth again to
charge with their colours flying and their national music playing as if going to
a review. This was to understand war. The man who in that moment and
immediately after a repulse thought of such military pomp was by nature a soldier.'[688] This attack was finally sufficient to persuade the French, who were
equally exhausted, to withdraw. Wellington arrived but declined to take command from Hill, saying that 'The battle is all your own.' Hill, indeed, received
the credit (and a joint of beef from the tradesmen of Shrewsbury as a reward!);
Bunbury was persuaded to sell his commission rather than face a court-martial,
and Peacocke and Colonel Duncan Macdonald of the 57th, who had also been

found wanting, were simply informed that the Prince Regent had no further need of their services.

Wellington consolidated his position preparatory to renewing his advance, and isolated actions continued. Contrasting with the often cordial relations between the advanced posts of the opposing armies, on the night of 16 January 1814, in front of Bayonne, there occurred an incidence of what in the First World War would be called a 'company raid'. The grenadier captain of the 11th Foot, Francis Gualey, decided to beat-up the French outpost in his front; for this he obtained official sanction from Beresford, so it would be unfair to ascribe this somewhat unfriendly spirit to the fact that Gualey was himself a Frenchman, though as an emigrant he might have more reason to feel antagonistic towards his French enemies. The French picquet, more than 200 strong, was stationed in a barn, behind a dry moat; Gualey's party was much smaller. Gualey sent forward Sergeant James Duffy and two grenadiers to deal with the outlying sentries; Duffy approached them by claiming to be a deserter, and both sentries were then bayoneted. Lieutenant William Dunkley and Sergeant Pike then jumped the moat and killed the inlying sentry, who was almost asleep; they then assisted the rest of the raiding-party to clamber in and out of the moat. Securing the Frenchmen's weapons, which were in a rack outside the barn, they took the whole lot prisoner, less six who were killed resisting; the officers were captured in an upstairs room, where they were entertaining a lady. The French arms and accoutrements were flung into the moat, and more than 200 prisoners were escorted to the British lines. For this unusual enterprise, Gualey received the brevet rank of major, but enjoyed it only briefly; he was mortally wounded at Toulouse, where Dunkley was killed.

As Wellington advanced towards Bayonne, the capture of an important hill at Garris on 15 February 1814 provided another rare occasion where bayonets were crossed. On that evening the 39th Foot advanced with shouldered arms at double-quick time up the hill, the musketry of the French defenders being aimed too high to take much effect save upon the mounted officers, all of whom, or their mounts, were hit; and to produce 'a singular effect' as the balls were heard to scythe through the trees on all sides of the advancing battalion. The crest was cleared and the 39th prepared to receive a counter-attack: 'Hitherto the regiment had reserved its fire, but at this point, immediately before the enemy closed, it opened upon him with great effect. Among those who was seen to fall was a French drummer, a very fine fellow, who was coming boldly on in front beating the charge. But the enemy, nothing daunted, still pressed on with great determination, until the bayonets, in many instances, were crossed ... Colonel the Hon. R. W. O 'Callaghan, whose horse had been shot from under him, and who was now fighting on foot at the head of the regiment, received one French bayonet at the breast, and another at the shin, at the same time ... Lieutenant Evans, the brave commander of the 60th Rifles, attached to the light companies of the brigade, personally grappled with a French captain, and they fell to the ground together. Evans was a small man, and no match for his antagonist; but he kept up the unequal contest, until a grenadier of the 39th, stepping forward to his assistance, the Frenchman was made prisoner. Among others, there were two privates of the regiment, of rather low stature, not well-looking, and so slovenly that everybody used to be down on them. These two men distinguished themselves greatly. One of them was so badly wounded as never afterwards to be able to rejoin the regiment.'[689] After repeated attacks the French gave way, and after more British troops came up, the pursuit continued into the night, involving a unique method of distinguishing friend from foe: 'they retreating and we advancing, the only way we could discover our enemy was by the feel of his hairy knapsack, and a sad discovery it proved to many of them'.[690]

Wellington again outwitted Soult by crossing the tidal estuary of the River Adour by assembling a pontoon-bridge of hired boats, and in the initial crossing an opportunity occurred for the Congreve rocket to prove its worth. A detachment of Foot Guards crossed the river, but before they could be reinforced some 2,000 French moved to evict them. A party of 40 artillerymen, carrying 160 rockets, was hurried across the river as the Guards were being driven back, 'and arrived at a proper and happy moment. The positions for two batteries of 20 rockets were directly taken up, and most part of them sent off rapidly after one another, at a distance of about 300 yards. The enemy gave way, and ran. Directly on this, the rocket party advanced on the left, in "double quick", occasionally firing a few to accelerate their flight. The light infantry of the Guards, rapidly advancing, regained the heights they had been driven from. The rocket battery still advanced beyond their front, and fired a few more rounds. The enemy ran most manfully ... Only three companies of the Guards were engaged, not more than 250 men, these and forty artillerymen, armed with rockets, put to flight 2,000 men ... I saw in one place seven Frenchmen killed and wounded by one rocket, and in another spot four ... Many of the men were dreadfully scorched by the fire of the rockets, and by the explosion of their cartouches as the rockets passed through the ranks.' Another witness remarked that the rockets alone saved the forward detachment of Guards; 'the second that was let off carried away the two legs of one man, set the knapsack of another on fire, and knocked about many more, throwing them into great confusion and wounding several. An old serjeant, whom we made prisoner, said, during all his service, he had not known what fear was before; but these machines were perfect devils, running up and down and picking out and destroying particular victims, as it were, in one place and then another. The rockets were discharged at the time when they produced the greatest effect, in a battery ten abreast.'[691]

Soult was defeated at Orthez on 27 February, and the final battle of the Peninsular War (save for a French sally from Bayonne four days later) was fought at Toulouse on 10 April, a position which the French relinquished after a stern defence. By dreadful irony, this was an unnecessary battle, for Napoleon had abdicated on 6 April, but the news had not reached the combatants. When it did, on 12 April, Wellington exhibited a rare display of emotion, snapping his fingers, spinning on his heels and crying 'Hurrah!'. More in character was his General Order to the army on 21 April:

'... the Commander of the Forces avails himself of the opportunity of returning the General Officers, Officers, and troops, his best thanks for their uniform discipline and gallantry in the field, and for their conciliating conduct towards the inhabitants of the country, which, almost in an equal degree with their discipline and gallantry in the field, have produced the fortunate circumstances that now hold forth to the world the prospect of genuine and permanent peace. The Commander of the Forces trusts that they will continue the same good conduct while it may be necessary to detain them in this country; and that they will leave it with a lasting reputation, not less creditable to their gallantry in the field than to their regularity and good conduct in quarters and in camp.'[692]

In as much as the Peninsular War was an important contributory cause towards Napoleon's defeat, and in the manner in which the army conducted itself throughout the war, its 'lasting reputation' as one of the finest armies ever fielded by Britain continues to endure.

The Netherlands, 1813–14

Other than the Peninsular War and the continuing presence in the Mediterranean, other operations included a small expedition to Swedish Pomerania, in collaboration with the continental allies, and the presence at Leipzig of a rocket troop (whose commander, Richard Bogue, was killed at that battle). In late 1813 a larger expedition landed in the Netherlands to aid in the liberation of that country, commanded by Sir Thomas Graham, and comprising mostly inexperienced 2nd battalions, with four battalions just returned from Pomerania. The most serious action was the assault of Bergen-op-Zoom on the night of 8 March 1814, a disaster largely because of the failure of officers commanding the attacking columns to carry out their orders. Having penetrated the defences, the columns were unco-ordinated and support was slow in arriving; even the column of Foot Guards was badly handled: 'The guards were drawn up, and prepared to fire by platoons, when they were ordered to throw out their priming and to charge. They advanced at the *pas de charge*, but they met nothing but showers of grape, canister-shot, and bullets. Almost all the brigade was laid prostrate ... in short, it was very like the Buenos Ayres business ...'[693] (To contemporary eyes, this comparison would be all that was needed to emphasize the mismanagement of the affair.) The attackers numbered about 3,950, of whom 381 were killed, 533 wounded, and 2,077 surrendered, a humiliation felt deeply by the army; yet not all were content to capitulate. When General Cooke surrendered his Guards, a Sergeant Townsend stepped from the ranks and said he would be damned if he would lay down his arms, and called upon any who would follow him. Thirteen did, and he led them to safety.

After so many years of tribulation, Napoleon's abdication was greeted with joy throughout the country. Among the celebrations in London to mark the 'Jubilee day in celebration of Peace' (1 August 1814) was a naval battle on the Serpentine, ending with the burning of the American fleet, and firework displays; that in Green Park depicted a castle which metamorphosed into the Temple of Concord, and that in St. James's Park accidentally burnt down the ornamental pagoda, with the death of two men. A Congreve rocket went astray and took off a spectator's calf, and at Green Park young Sadler the aeronaut took up his balloon, the Duke of Wellington dissuading a lady from accompanying him. This was further evidence of the Duke's good sense: Sadler had to bring down his balloon by slashing it with a knife, and it deposited him, somewhat precipitately, in Mucking Marshes, with no more than a slight sprain.

Much satisfaction was expressed at the fate of Napoleon, who exchanged his empire for the island of Elba:

'Little Nap Horner
Is up in a corner
Dreading his doleful doom;
He who gave, t'other day,
Whole kingdoms away,
Now is glad to get *Elba Room*.'[694]
Unfortunately, it was not quite the end of Little Nap Horner.

The War of 1812

The first major US attack on Canada was repelled at Queenston on 13 October 1812, in which the British commander, Major-General Isaac Brock, was killed; a leader of considerable skill, he had utilized his limited resources to defend the frontier and should be accorded much of the credit for resisting the attack, whereas the Governor-General at Quebec, Sir George Prevost, was a French-American of very limited ability. Despite some successes, American forces were unable to achieve much on the border, and at Chateauguay on 25 October 1813 an American contingent was defeated by Canadians, without the backing of any British regulars.

It was, perhaps, hardly surprising that the inhabitants of upper Canada should be eager to resist American incursions, and form reliable units of locally raised troops, as many were members of loyalist families who had fought for the king during the War of American Independence, and which had emigrated to Canada upon the conclusion of the war. Perhaps more unexpected was the loyalty of the French-speaking inhabitants of Lower Canada (now Quebec): that at a time when Britain was engaged in a bitter war against France, they should assist one English-speaking nation against another. In general, however, the French-Canadians were disapproving of the consequences of the French Revolution, and suspicious of the Americans. Hence there were French-speaking units in the Canadian forces, and even French titles, like that of the Canadian *Voltigeurs*, a regular corps on the establishment of the province of Lower Canada, formed by Charles-Michel de Salaberry of the 60th Foot, who commanded at Chateauguay.

After the conclusion of the war against Napoleon, large numbers of reinforcements were sent from Europe. On the eastern seaboard of the United States a British force won a victory at Bladensburg (24 August 1814) and captured Washington, after which the public buildings were burned, including the Capitol and White House, in retaliation for the American burning of York (now Toronto), the capital of Upper Canada, in April 1813. Much was made of the destruction wrought upon Washington, but most of the looting was ascribed to the 'knavish wretches about the town', and one American newspaper went so far as to remark that 'The British Army, it is no more than justice to say, preserved a moderation and discipline, with respect to private persons and property, unexampled in the annals of war.'[696]

However, the following British attack on Baltimore was repelled, and the British commander, Major-General Robert Ross, was mortally wounded.

The remaining action occurred in the south, where an expedition against New Orleans was commanded by Wellington's brother-in-law and Peninsula divisional commander, Sir Edward Pakenham. He landed on 13 December 1813 and was opposed by a force of American regulars and militia, commanded by the one American general of note, Andrew Jackson. Before the main engagement, the Americans made a nocturnal foray which involved another example of that rare occurrence, a hand-to-hand fight. As in other cases, this occurred basically by chance, when in the darkness part of the 85th Foot stumbled into the middle of an American unit, which first called out that they were friends, and then demanded that the 85th surrender. Only under such confusion were the two opposing bodies brought into contact, and what ensued was 'a most extraordinary struggle', in which 'not only were numerous bayonet wounds inflicted, but muskets were "clubbed", and men knocked down with their butt-ends! officers and privates were mixed "pell-mell" fighting, in every sense of the words, "hand-to-hand".'[697] Even the official dispatch stated that 'a more extraordinary conflict has perhaps never occurred, absolutely hand-to-hand both officers and men'.[698] Emphasizing how rare it was for a bayonet-fight to occur, George Gleig of the 85th, who participated, described it as 'a battle of which no language were competent to convey any distinct idea; because it was one to which the annals of modern warfare furnish no parallel. All order, all discipline were lost. Each officer, as he succeeded in collecting twenty or thirty men about him, plunged into the midst of the enemy's ranks, where it was fought hand to hand, bayonet to bayonet, and sabre to sabre.' The result left an indelible mark on him; he noted that although he had witnessed many battlefields, only here 'the most shocking and disgusting spectacles everywhere met my eyes ... wounds more disfiguring or more horrible I certainly never witnessed. A man shot through the head or heart lies as if he were in a deep slumber; insomuch that when you gaze upon him you experience little else than pity. But of these, many had met their deaths from bayonet wounds, sabre cuts, or heavy blows from the butt end of muskets; and the consequence was, that not only were the wounds themselves exceedingly frightful, but the very countenances of the dead exhibited the most savage and ghastly expressions ... such had been the deadly closeness of the strife, that in one or two places an English and American soldier might be seen with the bayonet of each fastened in the other's body.'[699]

On 8 January 1815 Pakenham made a frontal assault upon the American entrenchments at New Orleans, over land 'as flat as a bowling green'.[700] The Americans did not, as expected, give way; but held firm and beat off the attack with severe casualties, and negligible American loss. With Pakenham having been killed in the battle, a week later the British withdrew. Tragically, this celebrated defeat had been unnecessary, like Toulouse, for peace had been concluded at Ghent on 24 December 1814, but the news had not reached the combatants in time.

Much has been written on the reasons for the failure at New Orleans. One cause was undoubtedly the resolution of the Americans, and perhaps another the under-estimation of their abilities by the British, who did not in general rate the American troops very highly, as mentioned before. A British officer at Bladensburg wrote that 'for alacrity in quitting the field the Americans ... completely threw the Spaniards into the shade', and presented a common view by recording the reaction of a Negro slave whom the British freed: 'Ah! massa, we tink we you never git here, 'Merican talk so big! One Giniral say, "Come on, ye English cut-throat, red-coat rascals, and see how we'll sarve you!" but, by and by, dat gentleman be the bery fust to run away!'[701] This view was not borne out by experience, however, for although the opposition faced by the British was mixed, many American units could hardly be faulted. A French officer, commenting on the folly of the British attack at New Orleans, over rain-soaked terrain so slippery that even a man unencumbered by equipment would have had difficulty mounting the entrenchments, even had they not been defended, gave as his verdict: 'they were blinded by their pride'.[702]

Another cause of the failure was revealed by the court-martial of Captain the Hon. T. Mullins of the 2/44th, a brevet lieutenant-colonel and in command at the battle. (He was not the most senior of the regimental officers present, but Lieutenant-Colonel A. Brooke, having commanded the army before Baltimore after Ross's death, it was said apparently felt that a return to regimental duty would be demeaning.) The 2/44th, having come from the Mediterranean, were not in a high state of discipline, and were but a shadow of the brave 1st Battalion which had fought in the Peninsula. They were ordered to precede the attack, carrying ladders and fascines, but Mullins failed to ensure that the battalion could find them, and consequently was late in advancing. When they did start, they were seen straggling along in unsupervised parties, and when under fire some threw down their burdens and began to fire back, while others broke, 'running to the rear with fascines on their shoulders'. It was shortly after attempting to halt them, with cries of 'For shame! recollect you are British soldiers!'[703] that Pakenham was mortally wounded. His ADC, Major McDougall of the 85th, claimed that at no time did he see the 44th as a body, but only as scattered parties at the head, flanks and rear of the columns, which, he thought, was the reason the attack miscarried: that upon the advance the American fire was but a 'spit' insufficient to stop them, but without the ladders and fascines to penetrate the defences, the troops could only stand and be shot down until ordered to withdraw. A few of the ladder-carriers appear to have reached the entrenchments, for Lieutenant-Colonel Robert Renny of the 21st was killed inside the American position, but the foothold established by his party could not be exploited as by then the remainder of the force was already in retreat. Although the incapacity of the ladder-parties could not be held solely responsible for the failure of the attack, the action does demonstrate how an entire operation could be jeopardized by lack of resolution and leadership within one component part of an army.

However, despite the defeat and its heavy casualties, the British force regarded New Orleans in a very different light from the Americans, who hailed it as a triumph; as Cooper of the 7th remarked, the British saw it as merely a foolish attack against a strong position, and thus morale was quite unaffected. In the truce for burying the dead after the battle, he recorded an American who exclaimed, on seeing the rows of bodies, 'I never saw the like of that!' 'One of our party sneeringly said, "That's nowt, man; if you'd been wi' us in Spain, you would ha' seen summat far war!"'[704] which rather epitomizes the British soldiers' attitude to the entire American conflict.

The Hundred Days

Napoleon's return to France in 1815, and rapid re-assumption of power, led the British army into its final and climactic action of the period, the Waterloo campaign. The force Wellington led in this campaign, however, bore little resemblance to his magnificent Peninsula army, as even the British contingent included inexperienced units, and even those battalions with recent combat experience had numbers of newly enlisted men in their ranks. The remainder of the Allied army commanded by Wellington (itself only a portion of the forces with which Napoleon was faced in the 1815 campaign) comprised Netherlanders, Brunswickers and Hanoverian militia, few of whom were regarded as reliable; hence Wellington's famous remark concerning his 'infamous army'.

In some cases these opinions were justified, although some of the 'infamous' troops fought heroically, despite a British tendency to give them scant praise. A recent study[705] has suggested a rehabilitation of their reputation, but most British memorialists who were present supported Kincaid's opinion: 'We were, take us all in all, a very bad army. Our foreign auxiliaries, who constituted more than half our numerical strength, with some exceptions, were little better than a raw militia – a body without a soul, or like an inflated pillow, that gives to the touch, and resumes its shape again when the pressure ceases – not to mention the many who went clear out of the field, and were only seen while plundering our baggage in their retreat.'[706]

William Tomkinson presented the general opinion of the army by recounting 'the answer made by the Spanish General Alava to the Prince of Orange ... so nearly the truth that I mention it to point out the estimation in which they should be considered for their services on the 18th. Both General Alava and the prince had been for many years together on the Duke's staff in Spain. Question from the prince: "Well, Alava, what do you think your Spaniards would have done had they been present on this occasion?" Answer from Alava: "Your Highness, I do not think they would have run away, as your Belgians did, before the *first* shot was fired."'[707]

Although this was obviously an exaggeration, Tomkinson described a regiment in front of his own, 'not in the least cut up', but 'fancying the affair rather serious, and that if the enemy advanced any further (as their fears apprehended) they would have to oppose them', they began firing their muskets into the air and under the cover of the resulting clouds of smoke, began to steal away. Major Michael Childers of the 11th Light Dragoons rode up to stop them, and under this veiled threat and with Wellington's personal encouragement, they returned to their position, Childers moving a squadron immediately into their rear. 'That is right, that is right; keep them up' called Wellington as he rode off.[708]

Despite the fact that many ran off and others wavered, however, in general the 'unreliable' foreign troops held their ground under the most trying of circumstances, and (for example in the early stages of the battle of Quatre Bras) contributed materially to the French defeat. To reconcile these facts with the almost universal criticism they received from British observers, it is useful to recall the remarks of William Surtees already quoted in connection with the 1799 campaign: that even inexperienced or frightened soldiers might stand their ground if given the example of reliable units standing alongside them. As Wellington had deliberately integrated good with dubious units, so that the best qualities of the former would influence the latter, it may be that the example given to the 'unreliable' units was one of the major British contributions to the victory, in persuading to stand firm inexperienced men whose instinct for self-preservation and understandable terror would under other circumstances have led them to run.

The events of the Waterloo campaign are too familiar to require recapitulation; of how the Allies, initially surprised by the speed of Napoleon's advance, fought delaying actions on 16 June at Quatre Bras and (by Blücher's Prussian army) at Ligny; and how Wellington retired to the ridge of Mont St. Jean and on 18 June held off French attacks until Prussian arrival late in the day wrecked Napoleon's army, effectively ending the Napoleonic Wars. Some episodes, however, are worthy of mention.

Waterloo was not only the most decisive battle of the age but, even in the opinion of hardened Peninsula veterans, was the hardest-fought; Jonathan Leach noted that 'we had never before seen such determination displayed by the French', and wrote of their 'extraordinary perseverance and valour, and ... the vast efforts which they made for victory'.[709] This made the efforts all the more creditable, and to none was greater credit due than to the infantry who held the ridge of Mont St. Jean throughout the day, often under extreme pressure. The most famous episode was the resistance to the French cavalry attacks by the infantry in square, confirming the general invulnerability of the formation, one writer commenting that the squares were so intimidating that no truly determined effort was made to break them:

'... not in a single instance did [the French cavalry] preserve their order and come in a compact body against the ridges of bayonets; and even the best of these first charges, and the first were made in a more determined manner than those which followed, failed at a considerable distance from the infantry. The horsemen opened out and hedged away from every volley. Sometimes they even halted and turned before they had been fired at; sometimes, after receiving the fire of the standing ranks only. In this manner they flew from one square to another, receiving the fire of different squares as they passed; they flew (more frequently at a trot, however, than at a gallop) from one side of the square to another, receiving the fire of every face of the square. Some halted, shouted, and flourished their sabres; individuals, and small parties, here and there rode close up to the ranks. It is said that on some points they actually cut at the bayonets with their swords and fired their pistols at the officers ... The few that fell by the fire of the squares was also a matter of great astonishment to most of those officers present who allowed themselves to see with their own eyes, instead of seeing through the medium of subsequently published poems. Indeed, the ill-directed charges ... could not have continued so long and been so frequently renewed, had not the destroying power of the infantry been exceedingly small.'[710]

It is only fair to add that, under the sternest pressure, even the stalwart British infantry wavered at times, although they rallied rapidly. Most notable was probably the flight of Colin Halkett's brigade at Quatre Bras, which under threat of cavalry attack ran in a most disorganized manner into the cover of woodland, or as tactfully expressed by Frederick Pattison of the 33rd, retired 'in rather a precipitous manner'.[711]

An unusual feature of Waterloo was the expectation that no artillery would withdraw, even when about to be overrun, but would shelter in the nearest square and return to serve their guns as soon as each wave of cavalry had been beaten off. The fact that this did not always happen was probably the reason why Wellington appeared to ignore the service of the Royal Artillery, to the resentment of the members of that regiment. Wellington explained in a letter to Earl Mulgrave, Master-General of the Ordnance: 'To tell the truth, I was not very well pleased with the Artillery ... I had a right to expect that the officers and men of the artillery would do as I did, and as all the staff did, that is to take shelter in the Squares of the infantry ... But they did no such thing; they ran off the field entirely, taking with them limbers, ammunition, everything; and when in a few minutes, we had driven off the French cavalry, and could have made use of our artillery, we had no artillerymen to fire them...'[712]

This was not an accurate reflection upon the artillery in general (indeed, Wellington stated that 'The artillery, like others, behaved most gallantly'),[713] but his opinion may be explained by a number of cases of disobeying orders. Cavalié Mercer had his troop of Royal Horse Artillery continue to serve its guns throughout, lest their withdrawal to a square would so un-nerve the young Brunswickers in the vicinity that they would break and run; Rogers' battery lost a gun which was spiked by a panicky NCO, so that it had to be sent to the rear to have the spike drilled out; and the howitzer of Bolton's battery, having been mistakenly loaded with canister, had to be left behind later in the day to have the charge extracted. There were more serious cases, however; Lieutenant-Colonel Stephen Adye admitted that during the French cavalry attack, 'some of the Guns in confusion fell back on the road in their rear ... They afterwards resumed their original position nearby'.[714] The unit involved was apparently Sandham's battery, which withdrew without its commander's sanction.[715]

Another which withdrew was Sinclair's battery, but this on the orders of its commander, when charged by cuirassiers; one gun was abandoned, but recovered later in the day. Lieutenant John Wilson of the battery confirmed that before retiring their ammunition was 'nearly exhausted',[716] and that they returned when re-supplied. Conceivably one reason why Captain James Sinclair withdrew may be traced to his Peninsula career when, during his service as artillery adjutant of Hill's corps, some four Portuguese guns were lost at Maya. It may be that he was held culpable for this, as shortly after he was removed to become Hay's ADC, hardly a welcome transfer given the reputation of that general, and it is not impossible that having had his career impeded by the loss of one set of guns, he chose not to risk losing more, and thus disobeyed orders at Waterloo.[717] Whatever the case, it was probably incidents like these that resulted in Wellington's less than generous treatment of his gunners.

The final advance at Waterloo enabled William Tomkinson of the 16th Light Dragoons to give a graphic picture of cavalry charging broken infantry who, in their desperate attempts to escape death, clambered all over one another, forming piles of men: 'The enemy's infantry behind the hedge gave us a volley, and being close at them, and the hedge nothing more than some scattered bushes without a ditch, we made a rush and went into their column ... We completely succeeded, many of the infantry, immediately throwing down their arms and crowding together for safety. Many too ran away up the next rising ground. We were riding in all directions at parties attempting to make their escape, and in many instances had to cut down men who had taken up their arms after having in the first instance laid them down. From the appearance of the enemy lying together for safety, they were some yards in height, calling out, from the injury on one pressing upon another, and from the horses stamping upon them (on their legs). I had ridden after a man who took up his musket and fired at one of our men, and on his running to his comrades, my horse trod on them. (He had only one eye (Cyclops), and trod the heavier from not seeing them.) Lieutenant Beckwith, 16th, stood still and attempted to catch this man on his sword; he missed him, and nearly ran me through the body. I was following the man at a hand gallop. Captain Buchanan, of the 16th, was killed in the midst of their infantry. After some little delay in seeing they all surrendered, we proceeded in pursuit of the enemy's other scattered troops.'[718]

This battle, the final great carnage of the period, shocked even the most experienced Peninsula hands, whose emotions were described by John Kincaid of the 95th:

'I shall never forget the scene which the field of battle presented about seven in the evening. I felt weary and worn out, less from fatigue than anxiety. Our division, which had stood upwards of five thousand men at the commencement of the battle, had gradually dwindled down into a solitary line of skirmishers. The twenty-seventh regiment were literally lying dead, in square, a few yards behind us ... The smoke still hung so thick about us that we could see nothing. I walked a little way to each flank, to endeavour to get a glimpse of what was going on; but nothing met my eye except the mangled remains of men and horses, and I was obliged to return to my post as wise as I went. I had never yet heard of a battle in which everybody was killed; but this seemed likely to be an exception, as all were going by turns ... The field of battle, next morning, presented a frightful scene of carnage; it seemed as if the world had tumbled to pieces, and three-fourths of everything destroyed in the wreck. The ground running parallel to the front of where we had stood was so thickly strewed with fallen men and horses, that it was difficult to step clear of their bodies; many of the former still alive, and imploring assistance, which it was not in our power to bestow. The usual salutation on meeting an acquaintance of another regiment after an action was to ask who had been hit? but on this occasion it was "Who's alive?"'[719]

The end of the war meant, for the majority, an end of military service. Although for many the future was uncertain, bereft of the element of stability which military life engendered, however unpleasant its experiences might be, the end of 'wild war's deadly blast', 'the lines and tented field',[720] was welcomed by many:

'Adieu to every warlike scene,
Farewell the Soldier's martial mien;
No more shall the eternal sound
Of drums and fifes my thoughts confound;
No longer shall I view each blade,
With coat of red and black cockade,
To the parade, unwilling, stroll,
At call of morn and evening roll ...
Farewell – with happier scenes in view,
Such as my heart yet never knew,

265

And trusting that, ere life decline,
Some halcyon days may still be mine ...'[721]

For all too many of the rank and file, those 'halcyon days' were days of poverty, ill-health, starvation and neglect; but those whose circumstances were slightly more fortunate were able to make a more measured reflection upon their military careers. George Wood, whose health was severely impaired by his Peninsula service, regretted that unlike veterans of Waterloo, a 'mere party of pleasure' compared to the Peninsular War, he had no medal to commemorate his service, but was otherwise content: 'I have no longer different climes to contend with, nor hardships, storms, or dangers to encounter; and living ... at my own free will and pleasure, envying no man's wealth, but perfectly satisfied with the liberal allowance of Government for my trifling services, there is nothing that would induce me to quit this free State, but the honour of again serving my King and my Country.'[722]

There must have been many like George Gleig who found that army life in peacetime was unbearable, enthusiasm fading with the end of the war, and nothing which followed being its equal. He became a clergyman and found that in his new calling, if lacking the excitement and enjoyment of the old, 'at least there is more of calm and quiet gratification',[723] and, hanging his sabre to rust upon his wall, his change of situation allowed his faithful dog, his Peninsula companion-in-arms, to spend its latter years in comfort, lying in the sun upon his lawn, and perhaps, like its master, dreaming of the high days of youth spent in the light infantry.

As a final comment upon the experiences of the most humble of actors upon a great stage, Benjamin Harris of the 95th remarked that he learned 'the field of death and slaughter' was no bad place in which to judge men, and that his experience had taught him that the British soldier, given fair play, was unconquerable. For himself, he thought that his active service was the most enjoyable part of his life, and that as he looked back it seemed that only his sojourn in the Peninsula was worthy of remembrance. As he sat in his shoemaker's shop in Soho he recalled even the appearance of the regiments he had witnessed in battle, 'and comrades, long mouldered to dust, I see again performing the acts of heroes'.[724]

Appendices

1. POPULATION OF GREAT BRITAIN

	1801		1811	
	MALES	FEMALES	MALES	FEMALES
England	3,987,935	4,343,499	4,575,763	4,963,064
Wales	257,178	284,368	291,633	320,155
Scotland	734,581	864,487	826,191	979,497
Army and Navy	470,598	-	640,500	–

Inhabited houses in 1811:

England	1,678,106	occupied by	2,012,391 families
Wales	119,398	occupied by	129,756 families
Scotland	304,093	occupied by	402,068 families

Occupations, 1811:

	FAMILIES IN AGRICULTURE	FAMILIES IN TRADE AND MANUFACTURE
England	697,353	923,588
Wales	72,846	36,044
Scotland	125,799	169,417

(The remaining families were involved in neither agriculture nor trade and manufacturing.)

The most populous cities and towns in 1811:

London & Westminster	1,009,546	Plymouth	56,060
Edinburgh	102,987	Portsmouth	48,355
Glasgow	100,749	Norwich	37,256
Liverpool	94,376	Deptford and Greenwich	36,780
Birmingham	85,753	Paisley	36,722
Manchester	79,459	Sheffield	35,840
(19,114 more including Salford)		Nottingham	34,253
Bristol	76,433	Bath	31,496
Leeds and district	62,534		

2. MILITARY ADMINISTRATION:

Commander-in-Chief:
   Jeffrey, Lord Amherst, 1793–95
   Frederick, Duke of York, 1795-1809, 1811–27
   Sir David Dundas, Bt., 1809–11

Adjutant General:
   Lieutenant-General Sir William Fawcett, 1781–99
   Lieutenant-General Sir Harry Calvert, 1799–1820

Quartermaster General:
   Colonel George Morrison, 1761–96
   Sir David Dundas, Bt., 1796–1803
   Lieutenant-General Sir Robert Brownrigg, 1803–11
   Lieutenant-General Sir James Willoughby Gordon, Bt., 1811–51

Master-General of the Ordnance:
   Charles, 3rd Duke of Richmond, 1784–95
   Charles, 1st Marquess Cornwallis, 1795–1801

John, 2nd Earl of Chatham, 1801–6, 1807–10
Francis, 2nd Earl of Moira, 1806–7
Henry, 1st Earl of Mulgrave, 1810–18

3. FIELD MARSHALS OF THE BRITISH ARMY DURING THE WAR
with regimental colonelcies held during the war
(No field marshals existed before the outbreak of war.)

Date of creation

12 October 1793	Hon. Henry Seymour Conway (CinC, 1782-83); Royal Horse Guards, 1770–95
12 October 1793	HRH William Henry, Duke of Gloucester and Edinburgh; 1st Foot Guards, 1770–1805
12 October 1793	Sir George Howard (Governor of Royal Hospital 1768-95); 1st Dragoon Guards, 1779–96
10 February 1795	HRH Frederick Augustus, Duke of York and Albany; 2nd Foot Guards, 1784–1805, 1st Foot Guards, 1805-27; colonel-in-chief 60th Foot, 1797–1827
30 July 1796	John Campbell, 5th Duke of Argyll; 3rd Foot Guards, 1782–1806
30 July 1796	Jeffrey, 1st Lord Amherst; colonel-in-chief 60th Foot, 1768–97
30 July 1796	John Griffin, 4th Lord Howard de Walden; 4th Dragoons, 1788–97
30 July 1796	Studholme Hodgson; 11th Light Dragoons, 1789–98
30 July 1796	George, 1st Marquess Townshend (Governor of Royal Hospital 1795–96); 2nd Dragoon Guards, 1773–1807
30 July 1796	Lord Frederick Cavendish; 34th Foot 1760–97
30 July 1796	Charles Lennox, 3rd Duke of Richmond and Lennox; Royal Horse Guards, 1795–1806
5 September 1805	HRH Edward Augustus, Duke of Kent (CinC Gibraltar, 1802–19); 7th Foot, 1789-1801, 1st Foot, 1801–20
21 June 1813	Arthur Wellesley, 1st Duke of Wellington; 33rd Foot, 1806–12, Royal Horse Guards, 1813–27
26 November 1813	HRH Ernest Augustus, Duke of Cumberland; 15th Light Dragoons, 1801–27
26 November 1813	HRH Adolphus Frederick, Duke of Cambridge; 1st Foot Guards, 1805–50

(Wellington was the only one of these who held an active field command)

4. MILITARY EXPENSES

Although the 1803 Army Estimates (published 1802) were greatly exceeded upon the renewal of the war (almost £9 million in total instead of less than £5.8 million), they provide a comparison of expenditure on the various departments:

	Great Britain	Ireland
Guards, garrisons, etc.	£1,474,664 13s. 3d.	£848,035 7s.
Forces in plantations, etc.	£1,129,976 19s. 4d.	-
India forces	£518,653 11s. 4d.	-
Troops for recruiting ditto	£28,632 17s. 8d.	-
Recruiting and contingencies	£80,000	£93,341 7s.
General and Staff Officers	£35,063 0s. 5d.	£23,405 0s. 5d.
Officers	£120,719 11s. 3d.	£6,793 8s. 6d.
Subsistence to innkeepers	£155,000	£45,645 1s. 3d.
Half-pay	£297,000	£61,152 10s. 11d.
Half-pay American forces	£52,000	-
Half-pay Scotch Brigade	£1,000	-
Widows' pensions	£20,883 16s.	£6,000
Volunteer corps	£40,000	£59,169 4s. 8d.
Barrack Department	£293,667	£219,773 7s. 10d.
Foreign Corps	£159,672 1s. 11d.	-
Hospital contingencies	-	£18,461 10s. 10d.

The numbers of troops approved by the above included 66,574 Guards and garrisons, 37,778 in plantations, 22,814 India Forces, 546 troops for recruiting ditto, and 5,168 foreign corps. The India forces were financed separately, so their expenditure was deducted from the final totals.

Expenses for 1813 for British and Irish establishments combined:

Land forces (227,442 men)	£3,527,200
British forces, East Indies (28,009 men, counted under British expenses)	836,649
Recruiting service (533 men)	30,236
Militia (93,201 men)	3,082,490
Staff & garrisons	623,018
Full pay to supernumerary officers	32,088
Allowances to officers of public departments in Britain & Ireland	320,161
Half-pay officers	231,693
Pensioners of Chelsea & Kilmainham	581,550
Widows' pensions	58,114
Volunteers (68,000 men)	475,360
Local Militia (304,000 men)	636,623
Foreign corps (32,163 men)	1,205,642
Royal Military College	38,993
Royal Military Asylum	23,096
Allowances to retired chaplains	21,317
Medicines & hospital expenses	127,081
Compassionate list	30,055
Barrack Dept. of Ireland	460,583
Irish Commissariat Dept.	295,605
Superannuated allowances	15,964

(No Ordnance expenses are included in the above: the total for that department for 1813 was £3,404,527).

5. ARMY PAY, PER DIEM (1800)

	Cavalry	Fencible Cavalry Guards	Infantry	Militia, Fencible Infantry	Invalids
Colonel	32s. 10d.[1]	32s. 10d.[1]	22s. 6d.[2]	22s. 6d.	–
Lieutenant-Colonel	23s.	23s.	13s. 11d.	15s. 11d.	–
Major	23s.	23s.	14s. 1d.	14s. 1d.	–
Captain	14s. 7d.	14s. 7d.	9s. 5d.	9s. 5d.	9s. 5d.
Lieutenant	9s.	9s.	4s. 8d.[3]	4s. 8d.[3]	4s. 8d.
Cornet/Ensign	8s.	8s.	3s. 8d.[3]	3s. 8d.[3]	3s. 8d.
Adjutant[4]	5s.	5s.	4s.	4s.	–
Paymaster	15s.	15s.[5]	15s.	15s.[5]	–
Paymaster's clerk	–	2s. 2d.	–	1s. 6¾d.	–
Paymaster sergeant	2s. 11d.	2s. 11d.	1s. 6¾d.	1s. 6¾d.	–
Quartermaster	–	–	4s. 8d.[3]	4s. 8d.[3]	–
Surgeon	11s. 4d.	11s. 4d.[3]	9s. 5d.	9s. 5d.[3]	–
Assistant Surgeon	5s.	5s.[3]	5s.	5s.	–
Surgeon's mate	3s. 6d.	3s. 6d.	3s. 6d.	3s. 6d.[3]	–
Veterinary surgeon	8s.	8s.	–	–	–
Sergeant	2s. 11d.	2s. 11d.	1s. 6¾d.	1s. 6¾d.	1s. 6¾d.
Corporal	2s. 4½d.	2s. 4½d.	1s. 2¼d.	1s. 2¼d.	1s. 1¼d.
Trumpeter	2s. 4d.	2s. 4d.	–	–	–
Drummer	–	–	1s. 1¾d.	1s. 1¾d.	1s. 1¼d.
Fifer	–	–	1s. 1¾d.	1s. 1¾d.	–
Private	2s.	2s.	1s.	1s.	0s. 11¼d.

Pay for NCOs and men of the cavalry includes 9d. per diem for subsistence of a horse.

Notes:
1. Colonel's or commandant's pay was augmented by 1s. 2d. per diem per troop, plus 1s. 6d. per diem in lieu of one extra musician, in addition to that noted above.
2. Colonel's or commandant's pay was augmented by 6d. per company per diem, in addition to that noted above.

3. Plus an additional 1s. per diem to those not holding another commission.
4. In addition to pay as a subaltern.
5. Fencible paymasters had to hold an ordinary commission as well; if a subaltern their pay was made up to 15s. per diem, but if a captain it was 3s. 6d. per diem in addition to captain's pay.

6. OFFICERS' PAY, PER DIEM (1815)

	Life Guards	Royal Horse	Foot Guards	Cavalry	Infantry	Foot Artillery	Horse Artillery
Colonel	36s.	41s.	39s.	32s. 10d.	22s. 6d.	26s.	32s.
Lieutenant-Colonel	31s.	29s. 6d.	28s. 6d.	23s.	17s.	18s. 1d.	27s. 1d.
Major	26s.	27s.	24s. 6d.	19s. 3d.	16s.	16s. 11d.	22s. 11d.
Captain	16s.	21s. 6d.	16s. 6d.	14s. 7d.	10s. 6d.[1]	11s. 1d.[1]	16s. 1d.[1]
Lieutenant	11s.	15s. 6d.	7s. 10d.	9s.	6s. 6d.[2]	6s. 10d.[2]	9s. 10d.[2]
Cornet, Ensign, Second Lieutenant	8s. 6d.	14s. 6d.	5s. 10d.	8s.	5s. 3d.	5s. 7d.	–
Paymaster	–	–	–	15s.	15s.	–	–
Adjutant	13s.	10s.	10s.	10s.	8s. 6d.	8s. 6d.	10s. 6d.
Quartermaster	–	–	6s. 6d.	8s.[3]	6s. 6d.	7s. 10d.	10s. 10d.
Surgeon Major	–	–	20s.	–	–	–	–
Battalion Surgeon	–	–	12s.	–	–	–	–
Surgeon	12s.	12s.	–	11s. 4d.	11s. 4d.	11s. 4d.	–
Assistant Surgeon	8s. 6d.	8s. 6d.	7s. 6d.	8s. 6d.	7s. 6d.	7s. 6d.	–
Veterinary Surgeon	8s.	8s.	–	8s.	–	–	–

Notes:
1. Plus 2s. per diem if holding higher brevet rank.
2. Plus 1s. per diem if holding the rank for seven years or more.
3. Including 2s. per diem for maintenance of a horse.

Surgeons' pay increased to 14s. 1d. per diem after seven years' service in the line, and to 18s. 10d. per diem after twenty years; this also applied to artillery surgeons. Veterinary surgeons' pay in the cavalry increased to 10s. per diem after three years' service, to 12s. per diem after ten years, and to 13s. per diem after twenty years.

7. SUBSISTENCE ALLOWANCE FOR HOUSEHOLD TROOPS, PER DIEM (1800)

	Life Guards	Royal Horse Guards	Foot Guards
Colonel	27s.	14s. 6d.	17s. 6d.
Lieutenant-Colonel	23s. 3d.	6s.	9s.
Major	19s. 6d.	5s.	6s.
Captain	12s.	16s. 6d.	12s. 6d.
Lieutenant	8s. 3d.	11s. 6d.	6s.
Ensign/Cornet	7s. 3d.	11s. 6d.	4s. 6d.
Adjutant	8s. 3d.	4s. 6d.	3s.
Quartermaster	4s. 9d.	6s. 6d.	5s. 8d.
Surgeon	9s.	9s.	12s. 6d.
Assistant Surgeon	9s.	5s.	5s.
Veterinary surgeon	8s.	8s.	–
Solicitor	–	–	3s.
Sergeant	–	–	1s. 10¾d.
Corporal	3s. 9¼d.	3s. 0¼d.	1s. 4¾d.
Trumpeter	2s.	2s. 4d.	–
Kettle-drummer	2s.	2s. 6d.	–
Drum-major	–	–	1s.
Drummer	–	–	1s. 2¼d.
Hautbois	–	–	1s.
Private	3s. 2¼d.	2s. 5¼d.	1s. 1d.

(Other ranks' sum in the above includes 1s. 3d. per diem in the Life Guards and 9d. per diem in the RHG for subsistence of a horse; corporals in these regiments equated with sergeants in others. The allowance for field officers in the RHG was in addition to that as captain of a troop; presumably the allowance of a Foot Guards drum major and hautbois (musician) was in addition to that as a drummer.)

8. THE ARMY IN 1815

Regiments in order of seniority, with their colonels, whose rank is abbreviated as follows:
FM: field marshal; G: general; LG: lieutenant-general; MG: major-general; Col: colonel

Regt.	Colonel	Remarks
1st Life Guards	G. Charles, 3rd Earl Harrington	
2nd Life Guards	G. William, 1st Earl Cathcart	
Royal Horse Guards, Blue	FM. Arthur, 1st Duke of Wellington	
1st (King's) Dragoon Guards	G. Sir David Dundas	
2nd (Queen's) Dragoon Guards	LG. Sir Charles Craufurd	
3rd (Prince of Wales's) Dragoon Guards	G. Richard Vyse	
4th (Royal Irish) Dragoon Guards	MG. Sir Henry Fane	
5th (Princess Charlotte of Wales's) Dragoon Guards	G. Thomas Bland	'Princess Charlotte's' from 1804
6th Dragoon Guards (Carabiniers)	G. Henry, 2nd Earl Carhampton	
7th (Princess Royal's) Dragoon Guards	G. Richard Wilford	
1st (Royal) Dragoons	G. Thomas Garth	
2nd (Royal North British) Dragoons	G. Sir James Steuart	G. William, 5th Marquess of Lothian, colonel until 12 January 1815
3rd (King's Own) Dragoons	LG. William Cartwright	
4th (Queen's Own) Dragoons	LG. Francis Hugonin	
6th (Inniskilling) Dragoons	G. George, 11th Earl Pembroke	
7th (Queen's Own) Light Dragoons (Hussars)	LG. Henry, 1st Marquess of Anglesey	Hussars from 1806
8th (King's Royal Irish) Light Dragoons	G. Sir John Floyd, Bt.	
9th Light Dragoons	G. James, 2nd Earl Rosslyn	
10th (Prince of Wales's Own Royal) Light Dragoons (Hussars)	Prince Regent	Hussars from 1806; 'Royal' from 1811
11th Light Dragoons	LG. Lord William Bentinck	
12th (Prince of Wales's) Light Dragoons	LG. Sir William Payne, Bt.	Sir James Steuart colonel until 12 January 1815
13th Light Dragoons	LG. Hon. Sir Henry Grey	
14th (Duchess of York's Own) Light Dragoons	G. John, 7th Earl of Bridgwater	'Duchess's Own' from 1798
15th (King's) Light Dragoons (Hussars)	FM. Ernest, Duke of Cumberland	Hussars from 1806
16th (Queen's) Light Dragoons	G. William, 3rd Earl Harcourt	
17th Light Dragoons	G. Oliver de Lancey	
18th (King's) Light Dragoons (Hussars)	G. Charles, 1st Marquess of Drogheda	'King's' from 1807
19th Light Dragoons	MG. Sir John O. Vandeleur	
20th Light Dragoons	LG. Stapleton, Lord Combermere	'Jamaica Light Dragoons' to 1802
21st Light Dragoons	G. Banastre Tarleton	raised 1794
22nd Light Dragoons	G. Francis Gwyn	raised 1794 as 25th, 22nd from 1802
23rd Light Dragoons	MG. Sir George Anson	raised 1795 as 26th; 23rd from 1802
24th Light Dragoons	G. William Loftus	raised 1795 as 27th; 24th from 1802
25th Light Dragoons	LG. Lord Charles W. Stewart	raised 1795 as 29th; 25th from 1802

271

Regt.	Colonel	Remarks
1st Foot Guards	FM. Frederick, Duke of York	
2nd (Coldstream) Foot Guards	FM. Adolphus, Duke of Cambridge	
3rd Foot Guards	FM. William, Duke of Gloucester	
1st (Royal Scots)	FM. Edward, Duke of Kent	
2nd (Queen's Royal)	G. James Coates	
3rd (East Kent) or Buffs	G. Charles Leigh	
4th (King's Own)	G. John, 2nd Earl of Chatham	
5th (Northumberland)	LG. William Wynyard	
6th (1st Warwickshire)	G. Sir George Nugent, Bt.	
7th (Royal Fuzileers)	G. Sir Alured Clarke	
8th (King's)	G. Edmund Stevens	
9th (East Norfolk)	LG. Sir Robert Brownrigg	
10th (North Lincoln)	LG. Hon. Sir Thomas Maitland	
11th (North Devon)	G. Sir Charles Asgill, Bt.	
12th (East Suffolk)	G. Sir Charles Hastings, Bt.	
13th (1st Somersetshire)	G. Edward Morrison	
14th (Buckinghamshire)	LG. Sir Harry Calvert	'Bedfordshire' until 1809
15th (York East Riding)	LG. Sir Moore Disney	
16th (Bedfordshire)	LG. Sir George Prevost, Bt.	'Buckinghamshire' until 1809
17th (Leicestershire)	G. George Garth	
18th (Royal Irish)	G. John, Lord Hutchinson	
19th (1st York North Riding)	LG. Sir Hilgrove Turner	
20th (East Devonshire)	LG. Sir William Houston, Bt.	Sir John Stuart colonel until 5 April 1815
21st (Royal North British Fuzileers)	G. Hon. William Gordon	
22nd (Cheshire)	LG. Hon. Edward Finch	
23rd (Royal Welch Fuzileers)	G. Richard Grenville	
24th (2nd Warwickshire)	G. Sir David Baird	
25th (King's Own Borderers)	LG. Hon. Charles Fitzroy	'Sussex' until 1805
26th (Cameronians)	LG. George, 9th Earl Dalhousie	
27th (Enniskillen)	G. Francis, Earl of Moira	
28th (North Gloucestershire)	G. Robert Prescott	Hon. Sir Edward Paget colonel from 26 December 1815
29th (Worcestershire)	G. Gordon Forbes	
30th (Cambridgeshire)	G. Robert Manners	
31st (Huntingdonshire)	G. Henry, 1st Earl of Mulgrave	
32nd (Cornwall)	G. Alexander Campbell	
33rd (1st York West Riding)	LG. Sir John Sherbrooke	
34th (Cumberland)	G. Sir Eyre Coote	
35th (Sussex) 'Dorsetshire' until 1805	G. Charles, 4th Duke of Richmond	
36th (Herefordshire)	G. Hon. Henry St. John	
37th (North Hampshire)	LG. Sir Charles Green, Bt.	
38th (1st Staffordshire)	G. George, 3rd Earl Ludlow	
39th (Dorsetshire)	G. Nisbett Balfour	'East Middlesex' until 1807
40th (2nd Somersetshire)	G. Sir George Osborn, Bt.	
41st	LG. Josiah Champagne	
42nd (Royal Highland)	LG. George, Marquess of Huntly	
43rd (Monmouthshire Light Infantry)	G. Sir John Cradock	Lt. Inf. 1803
44th (East Essex)	G. John, 15th Earl of Suffolk	
45th (Nottinghamshire)	G. Frederick Lister	
46th (South Devonshire)	G. John Whyte	
47th (Lancashire)	LG. Hon. Sir Alexander Hope	
48th (Northamptonshire)	G. Lord Charles Fitzroy	

Regt.	Colonel	Remarks
49th (Hertfordshire)	G. Hon. Sir Alexander Maitland	
50th (West Kent)	G. Sir James Duff	
51st (2nd York West Riding) (Light Infantry)	G. William Morshead	Lt. Inf. from 1809
52nd (Oxfordshire Light Infantry)	LG. Sir Hildebrand Oakes, Bt.	Lt.Inf. from 1809
53rd (Shropshire)	LG. Hon. Sir John Abercromby	
54th (West Norfolk)	LG. James, 17th Lord Forbes	
55th (Westmorland)	LG. Sir William Clinton	
56th (West Essex)	G. Hon. Chapple Norton	
57th (West Middlesex)	G. Sir Hew Dalrymple	
58th (Rutlandshire)	G. Richard, 7th Earl of Cavan	
59th (2nd Nottinghamshire)	G. Alexander Ross	
60th (Royal American)	FM. Frederick, Duke of York (colonel–in–chief)	
61st (South Gloucestershire)	G. Sir George Hewett, Bt.	
62nd (Wiltshire)	G. Samuel Hulse	
63rd (West Suffolk)	G. Alexander, 6th Earl of Balcarres	
64th (2nd Staffordshire)	G. Henry Wynyard	
65th (2nd York North Riding)	LG. Thomas Grosvenor	
66th (Berkshire)	G. Oliver Nicolls	
67th (South Hampshire)	G. Sir William Keppel	
68th (Durham Light Infantry)	LG. Sir Henry Warde	Lt. Inf. from 1808
69th (South Lincolnshire)	G. Sir Cornelius Cuyler, Bt.	
70th (Glasgow Lowland)	LG. Hon. Sir Galbraith Lowry Cole	'Surrey' until 1812
71st (Highland Light Infantry)	G. Francis Dundas	'Glasgow Highland' 1808–10; Lt. Inf. from 1809
72nd (Highland)	LG. Rowland, Lord Hill	
73rd	G. George Harris	'Highland' until 1809
74th (Highland)	LG. James Montgomerie	
75th	G. Sir Robert Abercromby	'Highland' until 1809
76th	LG. Christopher Chowne	'Hindoostan Regt.' 1807–12
77th (East Middlesex)	LG. Sir Thomas Picton	Sir George Cooke colonel from 23 June 1815
78th (Highland) (Ross–shire Buffs)	LG. Sir Samuel Auchmuty	raised 1793
79th (Cameron Highlanders)	MG. Sir Alan Cameron	raised 1793; 'Cameronian Volunteers' until 1804
80th (Staffordshire Volunteers)	LG. Hon. Sir Edward Paget	raised 1793
81st	G. Henry Johnson	raised 1793; 'Loyal Lincoln Volunteers' 1793–94
82nd (Prince of Wales's Volunteers)	G. Henry Pigot	raised 1793
83rd	G. James Balfour	raised 1793
84th (York & Lancaster)	G. George Bernard	raised 1793; 'York & Lancaster' from 1809
85th (Bucks Volunteers) (Light Infantry)	G. Thomas Stanwix	raised 1793; Lt.Inf. from 1808
86th (Royal County Down)	G. Hon. Francis Needham	raised 1793; 'Leinster' 1809–12
87th (Prince of Wales's Own Irish)	LG. Sir John Doyle, Bt.	raised 1793; 'Prince of Wales's Irish' until 1811
88th (Connaught Rangers)	LG. William, Lord Beresford	raised 1793
89th	G. Albemarle, 9th Earl of Lindsey	raised 1794

Regt.	Colonel	Remarks
90th (Perthshire Volunteers)	LG. Thomas, 1st Lord Lynedoch	raised 1794
91st	LG. Duncan Campbell of Lochnell	raised 1794 as 98th; 91st from 1798; 'Argyllshire Highlanders' until 1809
92nd (Highland)	LG. John, Lord Niddery	raised 1798 as 100th; 92nd from 1798
93rd (Highland)	G. William Wemyss of Wemyss	raised 1800
94th (Scotch Brigade)	MG. Sir Charles Colville	formed 1685 but only brought into the line in 1802
95th Rifle Corps	G. Sir David Dundas, Bt. (colonel–in–chief)	raised 1800; not numbered until 1803
96th	G. George Don	raised 1798 as 2/52nd; 96th from 1802
97th (Queen's Own German)	LG. Sir Gordon Drummond	Queen's German Regt., ex–Minorca Regt., taken into line 1804
98th	Col. Sir J. Burke, Bt.	raised 1804
99th (Prince of Wales's Tipperary)	LG. Hon. M. Mathew	raised 1804; title granted 1811
100th (Prince Regent's County of Dublin)	Col. Sir F. J. Falkiner, Bt.	raised 1805; title granted 1812
101st (Duke of York's Irish)	Henry, Viscount Dillon	raised 1806
102nd	LG. Sir A. Gledstanes	New South Wales Corps taken into line 1808
103rd	LG. George Porter	9th Garrison Bn. taken into line 1808
104th	LG. M. Hunter	New Brunswick Fencibles taken into line 1810
Royal Staff Corps	MG. J. Brown	
1st West India Regiment	G. Lord Charles Somerset	
2nd West India Regiment	G. Sir George Beckwith	
3rd West India Regiment	LG. Sir John Murray, Bt.	
4th West India Regiment	LG. Sir James Leith	
5th West India Regiment	G. J. Despard	
6th West India Regiment	LG. Sir Miles Nightingall	
7th West India Regiment	LG. Isaac Gascoyne	
8th West India Regiment	LG. Sir Thomas Hislop, Bt.	
Royal African Corps	MG. Sir James Willoughby Gordon	
Royal York Rangers	LG. J. Fraser	
Royal West India Rangers	LG. Hon. Sir William Lumley	
York Chasseurs	MG. Hugh Gordon	
1st Ceylon Regiment	LG. Frederick Maitland	
2nd Ceylon Regiment	LG. Sir John Hamilton, Bt.	
3rd Ceylon Regiment	LG. William Thomas	
4th Ceylon Regiment	MG. John Wilson	
Cape Regiment	LG. G. Moncrieffe	
Bourbon Regiment	H. S. Keating	
1st Garrison Battalion	LG. H. Leighton	
2nd Garrison Battalion	MG. Sir Henry Torrens	
3rd Garrison Battalion	LG. John Hodgson	
2nd Royal Veteran Battalion	G. J. W. T. Watson	
3rd Royal Veteran Battalion	G. C. Mackenzie	
4th Royal Veteran Battalion	G. Lord Muncaster	
5th Royal Veteran Battalion	colonelcy vacant	
6th Royal Veteran Battalion	colonelcy vacant	

Regt.	Colonel	Remarks
7th Royal Veteran Battalion	MG. William Raymond	
8th Royal Veteran Battalion	Col. Alexander Mair	
Royal Newfoundland Fencibles	MG. Sir William Pringle	
Nova Scotia Fencibles	LG. F. A. Wetherall	
Canadian Fencibles	LG. Thomas Peter	
Glengarry Light Infantry Fencibles	MG. Edward Baynes	
New Brunswick Fencibles	LG. J. Coffin	
King's German Legion	FM. Adolphus, Duke of Cambridge (colonel–in–chief)	
K.G.L. 1st Light Dragoons	MG. Sir William Dornberg	
K.G.L. 2nd Light Dragoons	MG. Baron Veltheim	
K.G.L. 1st Hussars	LG. Charles, Baron Linsingen	
K.G.L. 2nd Hussars	MG. Victor, Baron Alten	
K.G.L. 3rd Hussars	Baron Arentsschildt	
K.G.L. 1st Light Battalion	MG. Baron C. Alten	
K.G.L. 2nd Light Battalion	MG. Sir Colin Halkett	
K.G.L. 1st Line Battalion	FM. Adolphus, Duke of Cambridge	
K.G.L. 2nd Line Battalion	MG. Baron Barsse	
K.G.L. 3rd Line Battalion	MG. Sir Harry de Hinuber	
K.G.L. 4th Line Battalion	MG. Baron Low	
K.G.L. 5th Line Battalion	Col. Baron Bussche (from 20 June 1815; vacant before)	
K.G.L. 6th Line Battalion	MG. A. Honstedt	
K.G.L. 7th Line Battalion	LG. Baron Drechsel	
K.G.L. 8th Line Battalion	MG. P. DuPlat	
K.G.L. Artillery	LG. Baron Decken	
De Roll's Regiment	MG. Francis, Baron Rottenburgh	
Meuron's Regiment	MG. Sir George Walker	
Watteville's Regiment	MG. L. de Watteville	
York Light Infantry Volunteers	LG. Sir Alexander Campbell, Bt.	
Royal Corsican Rangers	MG. Sir Hudson Lowe	
Sicilian Regiment	LG. Sir Ronald Ferguson	
Duke of York's Greek Light Infantry	MG. Sir John Oswald	
Foreign Veteran Battalion	Baron C. Decken	
Royal Regiment of Artillery	G. Henry, 1st Earl of Mulgrave	
Royal Engineers	G. Henry, 1st Earl of Mulgrave	

Glossary

This glossary includes contemporary military terms used in the British Army, but which might not be comprehensible with the use of a modern dictionary. Many French terms were used without anglicization, especially with regard to fortification; only some of the most common are included. (A wider glossary of foreign military terms can be found in the author's *Napoleonic Source Book*, London 1990.) Also included here are contemporary slang words and expressions, some exclusively military in usage and origin, and others emanating from civilian argot. Some examples of the former may only be found in contemporary memoirs, although for the lowest form of civilian slang, the 1811 revision of Grose's *Dictionary of the Vulgar Tongue* is most useful. Many colloquialisms must have been used for only a brief period and in a limited geographical area; the loaf styled a 'pampelonia', for example, presumably was known as such only in the region of the city from which its name was derived, and in the last stage of the Peninsular War. Anglicizations of foreign words, e.g. 'pong', would presumably only have been used among troops who had served in the country of its origin, as they do not seem to have passed into wider use in the way of 'char' (tea) or 'plonk' (*vin blanc*) from later periods.

abatis (or abbatis): breastwork or barricade constructed of trees and interwoven branches; from French *abattre*, to cut down.

Abram: 'to sham Abram' was to pretend sickness; see 'Belemite'.

accoutrement: a soldier's equipment, sometimes his clothing.

Act of Parliament: small beer, from the five pints of which a landlord was formerly obliged by law to provide each soldier billetted upon him.

agent: a functionary appointed by a unit's colonel or commandant, to keep the regimental accounts and to be responsible for the pay of officers and men, issuing the appropriate sum to the paymaster each month (for units stationed at home). A regimental agency was one of the few professions that disqualified its holder from sitting as a Member of Parliament.

aide-de-camp: junior staff officer, serving a general.

alarm post: in field or garrison, the place to which a unit marched or assembled in case of alarm.

Ambassador of Morocco: a shoemaker; from the supposed involvement of a shoemaker masquerading as the ambassador in the case of the Duke of York and Mary Ann Clarke.

ammunition: colloquial description for any item of issue equipment, e.g., 'ammunition boot'.

ammuzette: large-calibre musket or 'wall piece'.

approaches: siege-lines or trenches approaching the enemy defences.

apron: lead sheet, in two sizes: 'large', 12in x 10in, weighing 8¼ pounds; 'small', 6in x 4½in, weighing 1¾ pounds.

armed association: local volunteer corps.

articles: breeches (in plural; 'article' singular was a term for a wench).

August Allowances: system whereby volunteer corps were paid for 20 days' training per annum, in return for which they were required to serve in any part of the country in event of invasion.

bacon-bolters: colloquialism for grenadiers.

bad bargain: a useless soldier ('one of his Majesty's bad bargains').

baggage: colloquialism for women and children.

ball: musket-ball or musket-cartridge (as in 'ball-ammunition', 'thirty rounds ball', etc.).

bang-up: very fine (e.g., 'the Bang-up Locals' or Volunteers in Thomas Hardy).

banquette: firing-step behind a parapet.

barbette: a cannon fired *en barbette* over a parapet, without using an embrasure.

barker or barking-iron: a pistol (a barker was also a merchant who attracted customers by crying his wares).

bar shot: two half-roundshot connected by a bar, to act like chain-shot.

bastion: (i) a four-sided fortification; (ii) a similar-shaped lace loop on a uniform.

bât: pack or pack-saddle; orig. French but used in English to describe anything concerning baggage, provisions, etc., hence 'batman'. Sometimes pronounced 'bau', e.g., 'bau-men'.

battalion company: 'centre' company of infantry.

battalion guns: light fieldpieces attached to infantry.

battering train: siege train.

battery: orig. a gun-emplacement; later used to describe a 6- or 8-gun artillery company.

battery fascine: fascine 8 to 12 feet long, 10 to 12 inches thick.

belch: colloquialism for beer, from the flatulence caused by its consumption. (In civilian slang, a belcher was a coloured silk handkerchief).

Belemite: a malingerer (from the hospital at Belem, near Lisbon).

belly-box: cartridge-box worn on the front of the waist-belt (archaic).

Bengal lights: a carcass or illumination-firework composed of saltpetre, sulphur and red orpiment, which apparently burned with a bright blue light.

Bilboa: a sword, from a famous Spanish manufactory.

bishop: wine and water mixture.

bitch booby: a country wench, apparently a colloquialism exclusively military in use.

bivouac: although it could be employed in the modern sense of a camp in the open field, in the strictest sense the term described a camp at night in which the troops remained under arms, with only about one-third resting at any time.

black book: to be in the black book was to have been convicted of a crime; probably from regimental punishment-books having black covers.

black guard: a low or shabby person, said to originate from the beggars who congregated around Horse Guards and St. James's, offering to black the boots of soldiers for a small fee.

black hole: a guardhouse, or slang for gaol; from the concept of a windowless dungeon.

blacking-ball (or black-ball): blackening agent for equipment.

blackjack: orig. a jacked leather jug or drinking-vessel, later applied to a half-pint tin drinking-mug used on campaign.

black strap: wine, especially of Mediterranean origin; said to originate from a punishment used at Gibraltar.

bleeders: spurs.

blind: a construction used to conceal a besieger from the enemy, either a brushwood barricade, sandbags or gabions.

block-battery: a wooden floor for one or two cannon, to provide a solid and movable base for artillery.

block house: a fortified strongpoint; also slang for a prison.

bloody back: slang for a soldier, either from the red coat or perhaps from the punishment of flogging.

blue plum: a bullet; hence to 'take a blue plum' was to be wounded.

bog: 'Bog-land' = Ireland; a bogger or bog-trotter was slang for an Irishman; 'bog' also used as slang for a latrine.

bomb: mortar-shell; applied loosely to all explosive projectiles.

bombardier: junior NCO of artillery, orig. one trained to prepare explosive shells.

bonnet: triangular fortification in front of a ravelin.

boots: colloquialism for the youngest officer in a mess.

breaker: a small cask, used in boats to carry water, or for military use usually to carry rum.

breaking ground: commencing a siege.

breastplate: small metal badge worn on the shoulder-belt.

breastwork: protective parapet.

bricole: rope or strap for dragging a field-piece manually; a cannon fired *en bricole* when the shot struck a sloping revetment.

brigade: (i) tactical formation of two or more battalions or cavalry regiments; (ii) an artillery company.

brigade-major: brigade staff officer.

brigadier: a brigade-commander (an appointment, not a rank).

brimstone (contracted to 'brim'): an abandoned woman.

Brown Bess: nickname of the infantry musket, prob. orig. from the colour and 'buss', anglicization of German *buchse*, gun; or a term of endearment. 'To hug Brown Bess': to enlist or serve as a soldier. (In thieves' argot a 'bess' was a small crowbar used for forcing doors).

brown George: nickname for an issued loaf; also, an unpowdered wig. (A yellow George was a guinea).

budge barrel: powder barrel, usually with rope hoops so as not to strike sparks from metal bands, and a leather lining closed by a draw-string; orig. French *bouget*.

buffs: a soldier's belts, an abbreviation of 'buff-leather'; also semi-official title of the 3rd Foot.

bulldog: a pistol.

bumbo: mixture of brandy, water and sugar; vulgarly, a West Indian expression for a woman's private parts.

bumper: a full glass (as in the song *British Grenadiers*).

butcher's bill: colloquialism for casualty-returns.

Caçadore: Portuguese light infantry or rifleman (lit. 'hunter').

cadence: marching in step to a drum-beat; 'cadence-step', marching.

cagg: military slang for abstention from alcohol; 'to cagg' = 'to go on the wagon' in modern slang.

calfskin: slang for a drum (orig. 'calfskin fiddle').

calquing: tracing a map or plan by covering the back with black or red pigment and drawing over the lines to transfer the design on to a new sheet; term used by military engineers.

camisade: a nocturnal surprise attack; from Spanish *camisa*, a shirt, from the early practice of wearing a shirt over armour as a way of identifying friend from foe in the dark.

camp-colour: battalion marker-flag. 'Camp-colour-men' were soldiers who marched with the quartermaster to mark out the ground for each night's camp, the camp-colours being used to delineate this ground.

candlestick: slang for a bayonet ('camp-candlestick', from the ability to use the socket of a bayonet to hold a candle, the blade having been driven into the ground).

canister: artillery projectile of lead balls in a tin container; also 'case-shot'.

cannon-basket: a gabion.

cap: generic term for a military head-dress, especially a shako; in thieves' argot 'to cap' was to support another's story or to assist in cheating.

capsquare: metal plate securing the trunnions of a cannon-barrel to the carriage.

captain-lieutenant: commissioned rank, orig. the commander of the company nominally led by the battalion-commander, acting as captain but paid as lieutenant. From this came the slang use of 'captain-lieutenant' for any indefinable thing, or more specifically for the meat of an old calf, neither veal nor beef.

carbine: short cavalry musket.

carcass (or carcase): incendiary or illumination-shell; applied loosely to any illumination-device, e.g., a tar barrel.

carriage: wooden framework supporting a cannon-barrel.

carronade: large-calibre, short-range cannon, principally naval but also used on land; from Carron Ironworks, original place of manufacture.

cartel: agreement between opposing armies to exchange prisoners.

cascabel: knob at the 'sealed' end of a cannon-barrel.

casemate: chamber in a fortress wall.

case-shot: see 'canister'.

cassoon: small chest filled with gunpowder to act as a mine.

caterpillar: nickname for a soldier, said to derive from the Jacobite rebellion when a soldier was complimented as 'the pillar of the nation'. When the danger was passed and the soldier was slighted, he remarked that the civilian had previously called him the nation's pillar; the civilian replied that he must have meant 'caterpillar'!

cavalier: raised battery, usually inside a bastion.

centre company: infantry 'battalion company', called 'centre' from their position in a battalion when drawn up in line.

chain-shot: two roundshot connected by a chain, generally used at sea to destroy rigging.

chamade: signal by beat of drum or trumpet-call that a commander wished to confer with the enemy.

chandelier: wooden frame upon which fascines could be laid to cover men working in a trench.

chase: segment of cannon-barrel between chase-girdle and muzzle.

chausee-trap: a caltrop.

Chelsea: 'to get Chelsea' = to obtain a military pension.

cheval-de-frise: barricade made of beams or planks studded with spikes or blades.

Chinese light: illumination-shell composed of nitre, sulphur, antimony and orpiment.

chocolate: 'to give chocolate without sugar' was military slang for the act of reproving.

chosen man: lance-corporal (archaic, but used in the rifle corps).

clash-pans: cymbals.

clayes: hurdles used in fortification.

clinometer: instrument for measuring the gradient upon which a cannon stood.

club: hair-dressing of a short queue, sometimes folded back upon itself.

Coehorn (or Coehoorn): mortar, named after its designer.

cold burning: a minor punishment performed by soldiers on their fellows: pouring cold water over them.

coloured clothes: non-uniform or civilian dress.

common colour: the greenish-grey shade in which artillery carriages were painted.

company sergeant: artillery colour-sergeant.

condom (or cundum): in addition to the obvious definition, the term was used to describe a waterproof cover for a sword-scabbard, or the oilskin case for holding a regimental Colour.

conductor: commissariat assistant who supervised transport of stores; an artillery- or wagon-driver.

conversion: manoeuvre by which a unit changed its position so that its front was where its flank had been.

cool lady: female camp-follower or sutler-ess, especially one who sold liquor.

cork leg: artificial leg fitted with a foot and articulation.

counterscarp: slope or retaining-wall on outer side of ditch.

countersign: password given in answer to a challenge.

court-martial: in addition to the conventional use, the term also applied to any military court, even one which tried civilians, for example the prosecution of alleged rebels in the 1798 Irish rebellion.

covered way (or covert-way): infantry fire-step along a ditch.

cracker: slang for ammunition bread or biscuit; vulgarly, the backside.

crapaud: British nickname for French soldiers.

croaker: a complainer, pessimist or a person of gloomy disposition who was always predicting doom; from the croaking of a raven, supposedly an omen of ill-luck.

crocus: nickname for an army or navy surgeon.

croppy (or croppie): British nickname for an Irish rebel, presumably from the haircut ('crop' was a slang name for a Presbyterian for the same reason); 'crop-pyism' was support for the United Irishmen. A 'cropping drum' was an army drummer (especially of the Foot Guards) who earned money by beating a drum-call to celebrate a marriage. In non-slang usage, a crop was the cutting of a troop-horse's tail.

crowdy (or crowdie): term of Scots derivation to describe a mixture of oatmeal and water, or curdled milk made into a substance resembling cream-cheese.

crowsfoot: caltrop.

crusty: surly or bad-tempered.

Cumberland Gentlemen: nickname of the 34th Foot, from the select nature of their officers.

curler: in addition to the use of this word for a hairdressing implement, a curler was thieves' argot for a coin-clipper, the metal from which curled in the process.

curse of God: slang for a cockade, derivation unknown.

daddy-mammy: a drum-roll; presumably from this being the first thing taught to a drummer.

dead ground: a hollow or fold in terrain which would conceal troops from enemy fire.

dead man: an empty bottle (also 'dead marine' or 'marine officer'). Among bakers the term described a loaf falsely charged to a customer's account.

Death or Glory men: nickname for the Brunswick Oels Corps (from their skull and crossed bones badge).

defile: to reduce the frontage of a unit to enable it to pass through a narrow space or opening.

degen: a sword (slang, from German).

dehors: outworks some distance from the main defences of a fortification.

demijohn: a glass bottle encased in a wicker frame, with a large body and narrow neck; sometimes spelled 'demi-jean' at this period (from French *dame Jeanne*, 'dame Jane', originally presumably referring to the shape of a person).

demi-lune: a ravelin.

desagulier: (i) light fieldpiece, named after its designer; (ii) 'Desagulier's Instrument', a device for discovering imperfections inside a cannon-bore.

detachment (as in 'battalion of detachments'): composite unit formed of a number of small contingents.

devil carriage: four-wheeled wagon for the transportation of heavy ordnance.

Dirty Half-Hundred: nickname of the 50th Foot, from their number and black facings.

dispart: half the difference between the diameter of a gun-barrel at the base-ring and the swell at the muzzle; usually 1/56th of the length.

division: (i) a formation of one or two brigades; (ii) two companies of a battalion acting in concert; (iii) two fieldpieces with attendant vehicles. 'The Division' was the nickname of the Light Division in the Peninsular War.

dolphins: lifting-handles on a cannon-barrel.

dosser: basket in the form of a reversed sugar-loaf, carried on the shoulders, used to transport earth around a fortification.

doubling: not a double-march as in the modern sense, but to concentrate ranks or files into half the number, e.g., by making six files into three.

drab: a thick, strong, grey cloth; or an indeterminate, dull, grey-brown colour, perhaps originating from the colour of undyed wool. In low slang, a drab was a sluttish woman or cheap prostitute.

draft: system of breaking-up a unit, transferring its personnel to other regiments.

dragoon: 'medium' cavalry, orig. mounted infantry; from which in slang a dragoon was a man who followed two branches of his profession.

drawers: not in the more modern sense of undergarments, but a colloquialism for stockings.

drum: 'to pay the bill with a drum' was a slang expression for marching off, leaving debts unpaid (presumably as soldiers were wont to do upon hearing their drums beating). A 'drummer' was a horse that threw out its forelegs, like the flourish of drumsticks.

duck: a coarse fabric, sometimes a term applied to light sailcloth or sacking, used for clothing (from Dutch *doeck*, linen cloth).

dumpling: a short pistol; from the slang term for a short, squat person.

échauguette: a watch-tower; see *guérite*.

Eighteen Manoeuvres: the system of manoeuvre instituted by Dundas's manual.

embrasure: opening in a parapet to permit guns to fire through.

enceinte: fortress-wall or perimeter.

enfilade: fire upon the flank of a formation, raking its length.

Enthusiastics: nickname of the 4th Division of the Peninsular army, adopted after Wellington had referred to their enthusiastic conduct in the Pyrenees; prior to that they had been known as 'the Supporting Division'.

envelope: a continuous enceinte.

eprouvette: device for testing gunpowder.

esplanade: open space between a citadel and the nearest buildings.

evolutions: drill-movements.

expense magazine: small magazine placed near a battery.

facings: (i) coloured distinctions on a uniform, collar, lapels, cuffs, etc.; (ii) drill-movements.

faggot: a man hired at a muster to appear as a soldier.

family: colloquialism for the personal staff of a general.

fascine: bundle of brushwood used in fortification.

fearnought: a stout cloth (so as to fear no weather).

felloe (or felly): curved wooden segment forming part of the outer ring of a wheel.

Ferrara: common name for a Highland broadsword, from the many weapons which bore the maker's name of Andrea Ferrara.

Fighting Division: nickname for the 3rd Division of the Peninsular army.

file: a line of men ranged one behind another (hence 'rank and file'); in thieves' argot, a file was a pickpocket.

fire-ball: illumination-shell comprising rosin, sulphur, alum powder, starch, saltpetre, mealed powder and linseed oil.

firelock: flintlock musket.

firkin: unit of measure equal to one-quarter of a barrel, or 9 gallons; of butter, 56 pounds. (from Dutch *vierde*, fourth, with diminutive 'kin', i.e., *vierde-kin*).

fixed ammunition: artillery projectile with wooden 'sabot' affixed.

flank company: grenadiers and light infantry company of an infantry battalion, from their position on the flanks when the unit was assembled in line.

flash in the pan: a misfire, when the powder ignited in the priming-pan of a firearm but did not penetrate the touchhole to reach the charge in the barrel. In low slang a 'flash panney' was a brothel.

floating hell: slang for a prison-hulk.

fly: a wagon, especially one for the transportation of troops; from its rapid movement. 'Fly-slicers' was a nickname for the Life Guards, from their being observed on sentry duty, brushing away flies with their swords.

flying artillery: mobile horse artillery.

fogey: an invalid soldier, said to derive from French *fougueux*, fierce or fiery.

foot: infantry. 'Foot-wobbler' was an insulting description of infantry, usually applied by cavalrymen.

forlorn hope: advance storming-party, especially in attack on a breach; from Dutch *verloren hoop*, 'lost party' (also referred to simply as a 'forlorn'). From this it was used as a nickname for a gambler's final stake.

foreland: space between a rampart and a ditch, into which lumps of destroyed rampart might fall without filling the ditch.

former: wooden cylinder around which paper would be wrapped to produce a tubular cartridge.

fougasse (fougade, foucade): a small mine.

fourneau: the part of a mine in which powder was lodged.

fraises: stakes placed horizontally on the outward slope of a rampart to hinder escalade; also known as 'storm-poles'. 'To fraise' = to array a battalion behind a hedge of bayonets, as in a square.

frizzen: part of a musket-lock, from which the flint struck sparks.

fugelman: trained soldier who stood in front of the ranks during drill, from which the others took their time.

furlough: license to a soldier to be absent from duty, as when on leave.

fusilier (often spelled 'fuzileer'): orig. one armed with a fusil, a light musket, or one armed with a flintlock when the rest of the army still used matchlocks; by this period it was no more than a regimental title of the 7th, 21st and 23rd regiments of Foot.

gabion: earth-filled wicker basket used in fortification. For '*gabion farci*', see 'sap roller'.

gaiter-trousers: legwear of breeches and gaiters combined; also styled 'mosquito trousers'.

galloper: (i) light fieldpiece with shafts for a horse, obviating the use of a limber; (ii) an ADC or message-bearer; (iii) a blood horse.

garland: wooden framework used to keep roundshot in a neat pile.

gazon: earth sod with grass on, used to line a parapet, the grass ultimately growing into other gazons to make the rampart firmer.

general: the morning drum-beat warning the army to prepare to march.

Gentlemen's Sons: nickname of the 1st Division of the Peninsular army.

glacis: slope descending from a fortification.

Goddam: French nickname for British troops, from the British use of this expression; dates from the Hundred Years War.

grand division: tactical unit of two infantry companies.

grand-guard: guard of mounted or light troops posted about 1–1½ miles distant from a camp in the field.

grand rounds: main inspection of sentries, usually undertaken once a night.

Grasshoppers: French nickname for British rifle corps, from their green uniform.

graze: point at which a cannon-ball pitched; 'first graze', initial point of impact, from where it ricocheted.

grog: mixture of rum and water; named from Admiral Vernon, who introduced it, alias 'Old Grog', from his wearing grogram fabric.

guérite: sentry-box on a fortress rampart; loosely applied to any sentry-box.

gun: an artillery piece, generally unchambered (i.e., not a howitzer or mortar); in slang, to be 'in the gun' was to be intoxicated.

gunmetal: the alloy of which 'brass' guns were made, usually 8 to 10 or 12 parts tin to 100 parts copper.

halberd: common term for the sergeants' spontoon, even though a true halberd had an axe-head. 'To go to the halberds' = to be flogged (from being tied to a tripod of spontoons: see 'triangle'); 'to get a halberd' = to be promoted to sergeant; 'to have a halberd in the face' = to be an officer promoted from the ranks.

half-mounting: a soldier's smallclothes, consisting of one neck-cloth (stock from 1795), shirt, one pair of shoes and stockings.

Halkett's Green Germans: 7th Division

nickname for the Light Battalions of the King's German Legion, Peninsular War.

handicraft: one who practised his trade in a regiment, e.g., tailor, shoemaker, etc.

handspike: lever used to traverse a cannon.

hat company: 'battalion company', i.e., those wearing hats, not the fur caps or small caps of grenadiers and light infantry respectively.

haversack: fabric bag used for carrying provisions (from 'haver', oats).

helmet-cap: term usually applied to a fur-crested 'round hat' in imitation of a 'Tarleton' helmet.

hérisson: beam stuck with spikes, used as a *cheval de frise* for blocking a breach in a wall.

Holland: coarse, unbleached or brown-dyed linen, used for tropical clothing; 'Hollands' was gin.

housings: cavalry horse-furniture (holster-caps and shabraque).

howitzer: short-barrelled, chambered-bore cannon designed for high-angle fire.

hubbledeshuff: archaic military slang for confusedly or in an irregular manner, e.g., 'firing hubbledeshuff' = firing at will.

huzza!: a hurrah, stated to have been the national shout of the English, termed a cheer in the navy.

inexpressibles: slang for breeches.

insult: to 'insult' a fortification = to attack it.

Jack: a sailor ('Jack Tar'). A 'Jack Hatchway' was the nickname for an old-style, straight, stump-like artificial leg.

Jaggers: nickname of the 5/60th Foot, an anglicization of German *Jäger*, riflemen, from their predominantly German composition.

Japan: verb and noun, to make black and shiny by the use of lacquer.

Jingling Johnny: percussion musical instrument consisting of bells suspended from an ornamental pole.

Johnny Newcombe, or Johnny Raw: nickname for a new or inexperienced soldier.

Johnny Crapaud, or Jean Crapaud: nickname for the French, or a Frenchman.

Jolly: a marine.

Jonathan: nickname for Americans (sometimes 'Brother Jonathan'); originated in the War of American Independence, perhaps from Jonathan Trumbull.

June Allowances: terms under which volunteer corps were enrolled, giving pay for 85 days' training p.a. and requiring service within their military district.

kersey: coarse woollen cloth (possibly from Kersey in Suffolk).

kerseymere: fine twilled woollen cloth (corruption of 'cashmere' or 'cassimere').

kickshaws: French food (anglicization of *quelque chose*).

kidnapper: slang term for a crimp who inveigled recruits into the army.

klinket: small gate in a palisade, to permit sallies.

knapsack: infantry pack.

knock-me-down: strong ale.

laboratory: place where artillery technicians prepared cartridges, shells, etc.; in the field, a laboratory-tent.

lakh (or lac): a measure of rupees in India, 1 lakh = £100,000 sterling.

leg-bail: to 'give leg-bail' was to abscond leaving a debt unpaid.

levée en masse: mass-conscription; in Britain, styled levy en masse.

light bobs: colloquialism for light infantry; 'light bobbing' = light infantry service. 'Light troops' was a slang term for lice.

limber: two-wheeled carriage connecting a fieldpiece to its team of horses.

links: reins or leather straps used to fasten together a number of cavalry horses at a halt or bivouac, to prevent them straying.

linstock: pike to hold a slow-match, orig. 'linkstock'.

live lumber: nautical slang for troops being transported by sea.

lobster: a soldier, probably from the red coat, though applied during the English Civil War to cuirassiers, from their hard 'shell' (armour). 'To boil a lobster' was a colloquialism for a clergyman or religious person becoming a soldier, their black ecclesiastical clothing being exchanged for red.

lockspit: a small channel cut out by a spade to mark the place where a trench or fortification was to be dug.

lodgement: loosely, any inroad made in a fortification by an attacker; strictly, a lodgement was such a position hastily-fortified to guard against counter-attack.

lunette: (i) triangular fortification on or beyond a glacis; (ii) small fortification sited to one end of a ravelin.

madrier: long, robust plank used in field-works or temporary fortifications.

magazine: (i) storage-dump for munitions; (ii) container for cartridges carried by the soldier in addition to the ordinary cartridge-box.

mantlet: wooden screen, often wheeled, protecting diggers at the head of a sap.

Marching Division: nickname for the 6th Division of the Peninsular army.

marquis: large tent (now 'marquee').

match: impregnated burning-cord for igniting cannon, etc.

middlings: inferior grindings or refuse from wheat, sometimes used by fraudulent bakers for the production of ration bread.

mohair: contemptuous military colloquialism for a civilian, especially a tradesman, for their use of mohair-covered buttons instead of metal military buttons.

moonraker: nickname for a Wiltshire man, from the story of yokels who attempted to pull the moon's reflection out of a lake with a rake.

mosquioto trousers (or 'musquito'): see 'gaiter-trousers'.

Mother Shipton: tall 'round hat', named after a famous Yorkshire witch.

muff cap: colloquialism for a fur hussar busby.

Muscovy lantern: dark lantern used in camp at night to enable artillery technicians to prepare their stores.

music: regimental band.

musketoon: light musket.

muzzle droop: distortion of cannon-barrel caused by overheating.

nature: weight or classification of artillery piece.

necessaries: items of personal kit provided at the soldier's expense.

nightingale: a soldier who cried out when being flogged.

nose-bag: the feeding-bag of a horse; the expression 'to have a nose-bag in the face' was applied to an officer commissioned from the ranks.

Observing Division: nickname for the 2nd Division of the Peninsular army.

Old Trousers: British nickname for the French drum-call *Pas de charge* which heralded every attack; hence 'here comes Old Trousers' = the French are attacking.

outpost: an outlying picquet; scouting in general.

overslagh: verb of Dutch origin describing the equal sharing-out between a unit's officers of the duties of those on detached service.

Owls: nickname of the Brunswick Oels Corps in the Peninsular War (from 'Oels').

Pampalonia: loaf of bread two to three pounds in weight, used in the later Peninsular War; presumably named from the city.

parados: rearward parapet.

parallel: siege-trench running parallel to enemy fortifications.

parapet: wall or earthern bank on the forward edge of a fortification.

parish soldier: contemptuous term for a militiaman, adverting to a substitute hired by a parish in place of a ballotted man.

park: artillery reserve.

parleyvous; slang for the French language, or anything French.

parole: prisoner-of-war's promise not to escape or misbehave; or a password. A pass-parole was an order given at the head of a column and passed down it by word of mouth.

passage: a game with three dice popular among soldiers.

passe-volante; see 'faggot'.

patee: small, horseshoe-shaped earthwork fortification used to cover an exposed position or gate.

paterero: Spanish term for a huge type of mortar, generally projecting stones, used in the Peninsular War.

patlander: slang for an Irishman.

pear making: colloquialism for the practice of enlisting, taking the bounty and immediately deserting.

pickers: wire needles used for clearing a musket touch-hole.

picquet (sometimes spelled 'picket'): (i) an outpost or the men forming it; (ii) a sharpened length of wood or stake, from 6 inches to 6 feet long, used for tying horses to, fixing gabions in place, fastening down tents, etc.

piece: a cannon (orig. 'fieldpiece').

pigtail: colloquialism for plug of tobacco.

Pioneers: nickname of the 5th Division of the Peninsular army.

place of arms: enlargement of a covered way of a fortress where troops could be assembled for sorties.

plaster: greased patch used as wadding for loading a rifle.

poker: slang for a sword.

pomatum: hair-dressing of fine fat, lard or suet; like pomade.

pommel: the bulbous end of a sword-hilt; from this came the verb to pommel (or pummel), originally a beating with the pommel of a sword.

Pompadours: nickname of the 56th Foot, from their purple facings.

pong: slang for bread, an anglicized pronunciation of Portuguese *paõ*, bread; 'yellow pong' was bread made from Indian corn.

Pontius Pilate: nickname of the 1st Foot (from their claim to great antiquity) as being 'Pontius Pilate's guards'; in low slang a Pontius Pilate was a pawnbroker.

pop: nickname for a pistol (from the noise it made), although the verb 'to pop' = to pawn.

portfire: a holder for slow-match.

post: outpost, sentinel.

prepared ammunition: ball and propellant in a cartridge.

present: to 'present fire' = to take aim.

prime: to prime a gun was to fill the pan with powder; but adjective 'prime' = excellent.

principal: a ballotted militiaman serving in person, i.e., one who had not procured a substitute.

prog: colloquialism for food or provisions; 'to prog' = to forage.

prume: floating battery used to support amphibious landings; also 'praam' or 'pram', used to describe a coastal barge.

punk: slang for a soldier's female companion; in civilian use, a prostitute.

quadration: to quadrate a cannon was to mount it upon its carriage and check that the wheels were of equal height.

quarterguard: main guard provided by every battalion or regiment when encamped in the field.

quarters: accommodation for soldiers, either in barracks or by being billetted upon civilians. 'To quarter' or 'give quarter' = to accept surrender of a defeated enemy; alternatively, to allot part of the salary of an office-holder to another.

queue: (i) pigtail-hairstyle; (ii) tobacco plug shaped to resemble this.

quick-match: quick-burning match.

rag carrier: slang for an infantry ensign (the 'rag' being the Colour).

rag fair: slang for the inspection of a unit's necessaries and smallclothes.

rammer: the ramrod of a firearm or artillery piece; in slang, a rammer was a person's arm.

rampart: earthern or masonry wall forming the main part of a fortress defence.

random shot: strictly, an artillery term for a shot fired with the gun-barrel at 45° elevation upon a level plane.

ravelin: triangular detached fortification in front of a fortress wall.

ravenduck: a light fabric or fine, hempen sailcloth.

recruiting regiment: one formed to be split up immediately and the men drafted to other units.

redan: V-shaped fortification.

redoubt: detached fortification, or a redan placed in a bastion.

red rag: uniform dress (in civilian slang, the tongue).

redshank: colloquialism for a Highlander (from the bare legs below the kilt).

regimentals: items of uniform.

reinforces: strengthening-bands upon a cannon-barrel.

rejoicing fire: *feu de joie*. When a unit did not fire by volley but by a running fire from one end of a line to the other; upon the command 'begin', the files at the extreme right pulled their triggers; the file next to them pulled theirs when they saw the flash in the pan of the first file, and so on down the line.

relay horse: a spare draught-horse used by artillery, to be changed in a team to allow all to have a rest during a march, or to be used as additional power for marching uphill or over bad terrain.

Resurrection Men: nickname of the 3rd Foot after Albuera, when so many men returned to duty after wounds. (In civilian slang, 'resurrection men' were those who stole newly buried bodies and sold them for medical research and training).

retirade: in field fortification, a trench with a parapet; but used most commonly to describe a retrenchment within a defence-line.

retreat: evening drum-call to signal the end of the day's activity, and to order that sentries should challenge all comers until the beating of reveille next morning.

retrenchment: interior defences of a fortress, especially to cover a breach in the main defences.

returns: the turnings and angles of a trench; built to prevent enfilade fire from raking its entire length. (Also, collated statistics 'returned' by a unit to headquarters, with details of strength, equipment, etc.)

reversed colours: system by which musicians wore uniforms of the regimental facing-colour.

revetment: retaining-wall of a fortification.

ripons: colloquialism for spurs (from their manufacture in the town of Ripon).

Roast-and-Boiled: nickname for the Life Guards, from their consumption of abundant rations.

roller: neck-cloth.

round hat: squat top-hat with wide or upturned brim.

rounds: inspection of sentries.

rout: an order directing a march (from 'route').

ruffler: a beggar who pretended to be a crippled soldier or sailor.

rumbo: mixture of rum, water and sugar.

running-ball: a musket-charge without wadding.

sabot: wooden 'shoe' on 'fixed ammunition'.

saddle-sick: to be galled by riding.

saloop: drink composed of sassafras tea, milk and sugar; apparently a popular camp beverage.

salting-box: small box of mealed powder for sprinkling upon the fuze of a shell or mortar-bomb to assist its ignition.

sanky (or 'sank'): a tailor employed in making uniforms.

sap: narrow siege-trench. A 'sap roller' or 'gabion farci' was a gabion rolled in front of a sapper, to shield him from enemy fire. A 'sap faggot' was an 8in-thick fascine, three feet long.

saucissons: long, thin fascines (lit. 'sausages').

sauciss train: a powder-trail, sometimes laid along a pipe, to ignite a mine.

sconce: a malingerer, or one who avoided duty under the pretence of being ill.

Scotch Greys: slang for lice.

scour: to scour a line was to enfilade it at an exact right angle.

searcher: implement for detecting cracks inside a cannon-barrel.

sentinel: a sentry; also an archaic term for a private soldier.

serpent: (i) a leather-covered, bass wood-wind instrument of snake-like configuration; (ii) an ornamental, explosive firework.

sham fight: a field-day exercise.

sheepskin fiddler: slang for a drummer.

shell: (i) explosive projectile; (ii) shell-jacket, usually without sleeves; (iii) a light coffin.

shifting ballast: derogatory naval term for troops transported by sea.

sidearms: artillery tools, handspikes, rammers, etc.

skilly: thin, watery soup.

skulker: a soldier who feined illness to escape duty.

Slashers: nickname of the 28th Foot, supposedly invented by Colonel John Brown to compensate for the regiment's lack of a 'royal' title.

sling-cart: two-wheeled vehicle for the transportation of heavy ordnance or mortars.

slow-match: slow-burning match.

slug: misshapen bullet or lump of lead fired from a blunderbuss or musket; alternatively, a dram of liquor.

smabble: to kill in battle; or to loot the body of one killed (also 'snabble').

smallclothes: waistcoat, breeches and shirt.

smart money: compensation paid for an injury or loss of limb in battle; also, the fine paid by one wishing to leave the army after enlisting.

smasher: nickname for a carronade.

snapper: slang term for a pistol (from the snapping of the lock when fired).

snob: nickname for a shoemaker.

sod wad: turf packing for an artillery round.

soldier: in civilian slang, a red herring.

soldier's mawnd: a beggar pretending to be a crippled soldier.

spadroon: a light, straight-bladed sword.

spherical case: shrapnel shell.

spiking: method of rendering a cannon useless by hammering a metal spike into the touch-hole.

spit: slang for a sword; hence 'to spit' = to run through.

sponge: the reverse end of an artillery rammer, used to swab out the bore of a cannon to extinguish any burning fragments prior to the next load; in slang, a sponge was a great drinker. (Also spelled 'spunge'.)

spontoon: a short or half-pike as carried by infantry sergeants.

spread-eagle: a soldier tied to a triangle for flogging.

spring-spike: artillery-spike which expanded when inserted in the touch-hole of a cannon, requiring drilling to remove it.

squadron: cavalry regimental sub-unit, comprising two troops.

steel: a frizzen.

stick: slang term for a pistol.

stingo: strong beer or powerful liquor.

stirabout: stew or stock-pot.

stock: leather or fabric stock worn around the neck.

storm-poles: see 'fraises'.

stovepipe: cylindrical shako.

stuff: woollen cloth.

stuft gabion: a 'sap roller' or 'gabion farci', a gabion stuffed with wood and branches, rolled in front of engineers digging a trench, to shield them from enemy fire.

substitute: a militiaman paid to serve in place of a man selected by ballot.

suffocating pots: sulphur/nitre composition which when ignited was used to fumigate or cause distress to the enemy.

sugar-loaf: any tall, cylindrical head-dress.

Supporting Division: nickname of the 4th Division of the Peninsular army, until they were christened 'the Enthusiastics' in the Pyrenees.

Surprisers: nickname of the 2nd Division of the Peninsular army, after their actions at Arroyo dos Molinos.

sutler: a purveyor of drink and food to soldiers, usually in camp; in thieves' argot, one who stole small trinkets.

swad: nickname for a soldier (also 'swad-kin'); an early version of the later 'swaddy', sometimes rendered as 'squaddy'.

Sweeps: nickname of the 95th Rifles (from their dark-green uniform and black facings). In naval parlance, 'sweeps' were oars.

swipes: small beer; hence 'swipey', drunk.

swizzle: alcohol; in North America, a mixture of spruce beer, rum and sugar (in 1760 the 17th Foot had a Swizzle Club in that continent).

sword racket: alternative colloquialism for 'pear making': enlisting to receive a bounty and immediately deserting.

tail: slang term for a sword (from its appearance in silhouette, protruding behind the wearer); in low slang 'tail' was a term for a prostitute.

tame army: earlier nickname for the Trained Bands; archaic by this period but applied to militia.

Tarleton: fur-crested light dragoon helmet named after General Banastre Tarleton; a term not in use in British service at the time, but later.

tattoo: evening drum-call to signal troops to return to quarters, and for sutlers to close their booths; orig. 'tap-to', i.e., turn off the taps of the beer-barrels.

tenaille: small fortification in a ditch in front of a wall.

terreplein: wide upper part of a rampart.

thill cart: one with a thill or shaft.

tilter: nickname for a sword (from its appearance resembling the lance used in tilting-matches).

time-beater: percussion musician.

tin helmet: lightweight, tropical cavalry helmet.

toad-eater: slang for a flatterer or one who sought to ingratiate himself with his superiors.

toasting-iron: slang term for a sword.

toise: old French unit of measurement, 6.395 English feet, used for measuring fortifications.

tol: slang term for a sword (from Toledo, where fine blades were produced).

Tommy: slang for bread; 'brown Tommy' was that issued to the army, while 'white Tommy' or 'soft Tommy' was a naval term to distinguish bread from biscuit.

tompion: plug for the muzzle of a cannon.

town-major: assistant to a governor of a fortress or garrison, responsible for transmitting the governor's orders to the units forming the garrison (i.e., like a brigade-major); in seniority he ranked according to that held before his appointment, or otherwise as the most junior captain in the garrison.

Tow Row: nickname for a grenadier, probably from the chorus of the song *British Grenadiers*.

trench fascine: fascine four to nine inches thick, four to six feet long.

triangle: construction of three spontoons in a tripod, to which a man was tied for flogging; to 'go to the triangle' = to be flogged.

trucks: small, solid wheels for an artillery carriage.

trull: a soldier's female companion.

trunnions: lugs projecting from a cannon-barrel, securing it to the carriage.

Turkish music: musical instruments of oriental origin, e.g., 'Jingling Johnny', cymbals, tambourine, kettle-drum.

turn: to turn a fortification or outwork was to cut it off from reinforcement.

Unfortunate Gentlemen: nickname for the Household Cavalry, arising from a mid-18th century story of an officer, seeing some of them having difficulty bundling forage, asked who they were; to be answered, 'unfortunate gentlemen'.

unlaced: an 'unlaced' regiment was one in which the officers' uniforms had no metallic lace loops.

upright: a quart of beer to which a quartern (i.e., quarter-pint) of gin had been added. (This should not be confused with 'threepenny upright', slang for a low prostitute who dispensed her favours for that sum, standing against a wall).

utensils: the term describing the things with which a soldier had to be supplied when billetted upon an innkeeper: a bed with sheets, a pot, drinking-glass, dish, candle and a place at the fireside.

Valenciennes composition: incendiary mixture of saltpetre, sulphur, antimony and pitch, so called from its first use at the siege of that place.

vamps (or vampers): colloquialism for stockings. ('To vamp' was slang for the pawning or patching of old clothes.)

vedette: cavalry scout.

vent: touch-hole in a cannon-barrel; the 'ventsman' was the gunner who placed his thumb over the vent during the loading procedure.

Volunteers: (i) part-time, home-defence troops; (ii) aspirant officers serving in the ranks in the hope of obtaining a commission.

wad cutter: implement for cutting 'sod wads' for use as packing for artillery rounds.

wad hook: screw-ended shaft to extract unfired cartridges from a cannon.

wadmiltilt: waterproof tarpaulin made of woollen material, retaining the natural oils of the wool.

walking cornet: slang for an ensign of infantry.

wall-piece: large-calibre musket mounted upon a fortress-wall.

wantie: wagon-rope.

watch-coat: a greatcoat, named from these garments originally being issued only to sentries going on watch.

waterdeck: waterproof, painted canvas saddle-cover, large enough to cover the saddle and harness when placed on the ground.

water fascine: fascine six feet long, one or two feet thick, weighted with stones to make it sink into wet or marshy ground.

watering cap: cylindrical shako, usually with folding peak, worn by cavalry in undress.

wattle: hurdle used in fortification.

Wee Gees: nickname for the Corps of Drivers, Royal Artillery.

whiskers: colloquialism for facial hair, moustaches, etc.; occasionally used as a nickname for grenadiers, who sometimes wore moustaches (used, for example, in reference to the 36th Foot's grenadiers at Bangalore in 1791).

white cockade corps: French emigrant units in British pay but retaining allegiance to the French monarchy, signified by their use of white cockades.

white light: see 'Chinese light'.

wing: (i) shell-like epaulette; (ii) half an infantry battalion, or more loosely any element of a battalion greater in size than a company.

winter quarters: obviously the quarters in which an army rested in winter; but also used to describe the time between leaving camp and taking the field.

wolf-pit: cone-shaped pit, usually 6 feet deep and 4 to 5 feet wide at the top, used as an anti-personnel trap; often styled by its French name, *trou de loup*.

worm: corkscrew-device for extracting an unfired charge from a gun-barrel.

worn out: the usual description of a soldier no longer fit for active service.

yeomanry: volunteer cavalry, but applied in Ireland to volunteer infantry as well.

Young Eyes: nickname for light dragoons applied by the Foot Guards, presumably in respect of the comparative youth of their regiments, and perhaps having some connection with the Guards' nickname 'Old Eyes'.

zig-zags: approach-trenches in siege-works, from their configuration.

Bibliography

The following lists a small number of the works pertaining to the British Army during the French Revolutionary and Napoleonic Wars. Although many of the more important works are included, it is in no way comprehensive, and a wider listing is to be found in *Napoleonic Military History: A Bibliography*, ed. D. D. Horward, London 1986, in the section 'England at War, 1798-1815' by G. C. Bond.

General histories and the art of war

Alison, Sir Archibald. *History of Europe from the Commencement of the French Revolution to the Restoration of the Bourbons*, Edinburgh 1860 (still remains of interest, with useful statistical appendices).

Baines, E. *History of the Wars of the French Revolution*, London 1817 (interesting contemporary view).

Bryant, Sir Arthur. *The Age of Elegance 1812–22*, London 1950.

– *The Years of Endurance 1793–1802*, London 1942.

– *The Years of Victory 1802–12*, London 1944.

Chandler, D. G. *The Campaigns of Napoleon*, London 1967 (invaluable study of the Napoleonic art of war in general).

Duff, C. *Fire and Stone: The Science of Fortress Warfare 1660–1860*, Newton Abbot 1975.

Emsley, C. *British Society and the French Wars*, London 1979.

Griffith, P. *Forward into Battle: Fighting Tactics from Waterloo to Vietnam*, Chichester 1981.

Haythornthwaite, P. J. *The Napoleonic Source Book*, London 1990.

– *Weapons and Equipment of the Napoleonic Wars*, Poole 1979.

Hughes, Major-General B. P. *Firepower*, London 1974.

– *Open Fire: Artillery Tactics from Marlborough to Wellington*, Chichester 1983.

Rothenberg, G.E. *The Art of War in the Age of Napoleon*, London 1977.

Campaign histories

Austin, T. *Old Stick–Leg: Extracts from the Diaries of Major Thomas Austin*, ed. H. H. Austin, London 1926 (probably more appropriate to the 'memoirs' section, but is a rare account of the Netherlands campaign of 1813-14).

Batty, R. *An Historical Sketch of the Campaign of 1815*, London 1820, r/p London 1981.

– *Campaign of the Left Wing of the Allied Army in the Western Pyrenees*, London 1964 (collection of first-hand accounts).

Bunbury, Sir Henry. *Narratives of Some Passages in the Great War with France 1799–1810*, London 1854; r/p with intro. by Hon. Sir John Fortescue, London 1927 (1799 campaign in North Holland, Mediterranean 1805-10).

Caffrey, K. *The Lion and the Unicorn: the Anglo-American War 1812–15*, London 1978.

Cotton, E. *A Voice from Waterloo*, 9th enlarged edn. Brussels 1900.

Fletcher, I. *In Hell Before Daylight*, Tunbridge Wells 1984 (storm of Badajoz, 1812).

– *The Waters of Oblivion: The British Invasion of the Rio de la Plata 1806–07*, Tunbridge Wells 1991.

Gleig, G. *The Campaigns of the British Army at Washington and New Orleans*, London 1827, r/p with intro. by R. Reilly, Wakefield 1972.

Glover, M. *Britannia Sickens: Sir Arthur Wellesley and the Convention of Cintra*, London 1970.

– *The Peninsular War 1807–14: a Concise Military History*, Newton Abbot 1974.

– *Wellington's Peninsular Victories*, London 1963.

Hamilton-Williams, D. C. *Waterloo New Perspectives: The Great Battle Reappraised*, London 1993

Hibbert, C. *Corunna*, London 1961.

Howarth, D. *A Near Run Thing*, London 1968 (the Waterloo campaign).

Jones, J. T. *Journals of the Sieges undertaken*

by the Allies in Spain, London 1814.

Katcher, P. R. N. *The American War 1812–14*, London 1974.

Kelly, C. *The Memorable Battle of Waterloo*, London 1817 (an interesting early view).

Londonderry, Marquess of. *Narrative of the Peninsular War from 1808 to 1813*, London 1828.

Myatt, F. *British Sieges of the Peninsular War from 1808 to 1813*, Tunbridge Wells 1987.

Napier, W. F. P. *History of the War in the Peninsula*, London 1832-40 (the classic early history; the same author's *English Battles and Sieges in the Peninsula*, London 1855, r/p London 1990, is a condensed version, but with some new material).

Naylor, J. *Waterloo*, London 1960.

Oman, Sir Charles. *History of the War in the Peninsula*, Oxford 1902-30, r/p 1980 (still the standard work on the subject).

Pakenham, T. *The Year of Liberty: the great Irish Rebellion of 1798*, London 1969.

Siborne, H.T. (ed.). *The Waterloo Letters*, London 1891, r/p London 1983 (firsthand accounts by participants written in answer to questions posed by the editor's father).

Siborne, W. *The Waterloo Campaign*, London 1844 (classic early history, criticized but reflecting some contemporary views).

Weller, J. *Wellington at Waterloo*, London 1967.

– *Wellington in India*, London 1972.

– *Wellington in the Peninsula*, London 1962.

Wellington, 1st Duke of. *Dispatches of Field Marshal the Duke of Wellington*, ed. J. Gurwood, London 1834-8.

Supplementary Despatches and Memoranda of Field Marshal the Duke of Wellington, ed. 2nd Duke of Wellington, London 1858–72.

– *Wellington at War 1794–1815*, ed. A. Brett-James, London 1961 (selections from Wellington's correspondence).

The British Army

Barthorp, M. J. *British Cavalry Uniforms*, Poole 1984.

– *British Infantry Uniforms*, Poole 1982.

Blackmore, H. L. *British Military Firearms 1650–1850*, London 1961.

Brett-James, A. *Life in Wellington's Army*, London 1972.

Buckley, R. N. *Slaves in Red Coats: the British West India Regiments 1795–1815*,

New Haven and London 1979.

Fortescue, Hon. Sir John. *History of the British Army*, London 1899–1920.

– *The County Lieutenancies and the Army 1803–1814*, London 1909.

Fosten, B. *Wellington's Heavy Cavalry*, London 1982.

– *Wellington's Infantry, I* and *II*, London 1981–2.

– *Wellington's Light Cavalry*, London 1982.

Gates, D. *The British Light Infantry Arm 1790–1815*, London 1987.

Glover, M. *Wellington's Army in the Peninsula*, Newton Abbot 1977.

Glover, R. *Peninsular Preparation: the Reform of the British Army 1795–1809*, Cambridge 1963.

Guy, A.J. (ed.). *The Road to Waterloo: the British Army and the Struggle against Revolutionary and Napoleonic France 1793–1815*, London 1990.

Haythornthwaite, P. J. *British Infantry in the Napoleonic Wars*, London 1987.

– *Wellington's Military Machine*, Tunbridge Wells 1989.

– *Wellington's Specialist Troops*, London 1988.

Lawson, C. C. P. *History of the Uniforms of the British Army*, Vols. IV, London 1966, and V, London 1967.

Oman, Sir Charles. *Wellington's Army*, London 1912 (important companion to the same author's *History of the Peninsular War*).

Page, E. C. G. *Following the Drum: Women in Wellington's Wars*, London 1986.

Priest, G. *The Brown Bess Bayonet 1720–1860*, Norwich 1986.

Reid, S. *Wellington's Highlanders*, London 1992.

Rogers, H. C. B. *Wellington's Army*, London 1979.

Ward, S. G. P. *Wellington's Headquarters*, London 1957.

Wilkinson-Latham, R. *British Artillery on Land and Sea 1790–1820*, Newton Abbot 1973.

Wood, Sir Evelyn. *Cavalry in the Waterloo Campaign*, London 1895.

Regimental histories

Few regimental histories concentrate exclusively on the Napoleonic Wars, but the following are examples which do. An excellent bibliography is White, A.S. *A Bibliography of Regimental Histories of the British Army*, expanded edn., London 1988.

Beamish, L. *History of the King's German Legion*, Hanover 1832.

Caldwell, G., and Cooper, R. *Rifle Green at Waterloo*, 1990 (95th Rifles, including nominal rolls).

Greenhill Gardyne, Lieutenant-Colonel C. *The Life of a Regiment: the History of the Gordon Highlanders, Vol. I 1794–1816*, London 1901, r/p 1929.

Hofschröer, P. *The Hanoverian Army of the Napoleonic Wars*, London 1989 (includes King's German Legion).

Holme, N., and Kirby, E. L. *Medal Rolls, 23rd Foot, Royal Welch Fusiliers, Napoleonic Period*, Caernarfon and London 1978 (significant biographical analysis of a representative battalion).

Lagden, A., and Sly, J. *The 2/73rd at Waterloo*, Brightlingsea 1988 (another valuable biographical study of a typical battalion).

Leeke, Revd. W. *History of Lord Seaton's Regiment (the 52nd Light Infantry) at the Battle of Waterloo*, London 1866; and supplement to the same, London 1871.

Mackay Scobie, I. H. *An Old Highland Fencible Corps: the History of the Reay Fencible Highland Regiment of Foot, or Mackay's Highlanders, 1794–1802*, Edinburgh 1914.

Macintosh, H. B. *The Grant, Strathspey, or First Highland Fencible Regiment*, 1793-1799, Elgin 1934.

– *The Inverness Shire Highlanders, or 97th Regiment of Foot, 1794–1796*, Elgin 1926.

Mayne, Lieutenant-Colonel W., & Lillie, Captain. *Narrative of the Campaigns of the Loyal Lusitanian Legion*, London 1812, r/p Cambridge 1986.

Pivka, O. von. *Brunswick Troops 1809–15*, London 1985.

Verner, W. *History and Campaigns of the Rifle Brigade 1809–13*, London 1919 (the best 'Peninsular' regimental history).

– *The First British Rifle Corps*, London 1890.

'Home Front'

Abell, F. *Prisoners of War in Britain 1756 to 1815*, Oxford 1914.

Ashcroft, M. Y. *To Escape the Monster's Clutches*, Northallerton (defence against invasion in North Yorkshire).

Beckett, I. *Call to Arms: Buckingham's Citizen Soldiers*, Buckingham 1985.

Berry, R. P. *History of the Volunteer Infantry*, London and Huddersfield 1903.

Bloomfield, P. *Kent and the Napoleonic Wars*, Maidstone 1987.

Fox, K. O. *Making Life Possible*, Kineton 1982 (military aid to civil power).

Glover, R. *Britain at Bay*, London 1973 (defence against invasion).

Hanger, G. *Reflections on the Menaced Invasion*, London 1804, r/p 1972.

Hay, Colonel G. J. *An Epitomized History of the Militia, The 'Constitutional Force'*, London 1908, r/p Newport 1987.

Kinross, J. *Fishguard Fiasco*, Tenby 1974.

Knox, T. *Some account of the Proceedings that took place on the landing of the French near Fishguard*, London 1800.

Lennox, C. (Duke of Richmond). *Thoughts on the National Defence*, London 1804 (published anonymously).

Lloyd, P. A. *The French are coming: The Invasion Scare of 1803–05*, Tunbridge Wells 1991.

Longmate, N. *Island Fortress: the Defence of Great Britain 1603–1945*, London 1991.

Logue, K. J. *Popular Disturbances in Scotland 1780–1815*, Edinburgh 1979.

Maurice, Revd. J. W. *History of the French Invasion near Fishguard*, Fishguard 1911.

McAnally, Sir Henry. *The Irish Militia 1793–1816*, Dublin and London 1949.

Sebag-Montefiore, C. *A History of the Volunteer Forces*, London 1908.

Steppler, G. A. *Britons, To Arms! The Story of the British Volunteer Soldier*, Stroud 1992 (uses Leicestershire and Rutland to exemplify the whole).

Sutcliffe, S. *Martello Towers*, Newton Abbot 1972.

Walker, T. J. *The Depot for Prisoners at Norman Cross*, London 1913.

Wells, W. *Insurrection: The British Experience 1795–1803*, Gloucester 1983.

Werner, J. *We Laughed at Boney*, London n.d. (reactions to the invasion threat)

Biography

Abercromby, J. (later Lord Dunfermline). *Lieutenant–General Sir Ralph Abercromby, KB*, 1861.

Anglesey, 7th Marquess of. *One–Leg: the Life and Letters of Henry William Paget*, London 1961.

Aspinall-Oglander, C. *Freshly Remembered: The Story of Thomas Graham, Lord Lynedoch*, London 1956.

Blanco, R.L. *Wellington's Surgeon General: Sir James McGrigor*, Durham, N. Carolina, 1974.

Brownrigg, B. *The Life and Letters of Sir John Moore*, London 1921.

Craufurd, Revd. A. H. *General Craufurd and his Light Division*, r/p Cambridge 1987.

Fraser, Sir William, Bt. *Words on Wellington*, London 1889.

Glover, M. *Wellington as Military Commander*, London 1968 (much on the army in addition to Wellington's generalship).

Griffith, P. (ed.). *Wellington Commander: the Iron Duke's Generalship*, Chichester 1985.

Griffiths, A. J. *The Wellington Memorial*, London 1897.

James, L. *The Iron Duke: A Military Biography of Wellington*, London 1992.

Longford, Elizabeth Countess of. *Wellington: the Years of the Sword*, London 1969.

– *Wellington: Pillar of State*, London 1972.

Maurice, Sir J. F. *The Diary of Sir John Moore*, London 1904.

Maxwell, Sir Herbert. *Life of Wellington*, London 1899.

McGuffie, T. H. *Peninsular Cavalry General 1811–13*, London 1951 (Robert Ballard Long).

Moore Smith, G. C. *The Life of John Colborne, Field-Marshal Lord Seaton*, London 1903.

Myatt, F. *Peninsular General*, Newton Abbot 1980 (Sir Thomas Picton).

Oman, C. *Sir John Moore*, London 1953.

Parkinson, R. *Moore of Corunna*, London 1976.

Robinson, H. B. *Memoirs and Correspondence of Lt. Gen. Sir Thomas Picton*, London 1836.

Sidney, Revd. E. *The Life of Lord Hill*, London 1845.

Tefferteller, G. L. *The Surpriser*, Newark, New Jersey, 1983 (life of Lord Hill).

Thoumine, R. H. *Scientific Soldier: A Life of General Le Marchant*, London 1968.

Ward, S. G. P. *Wellington*, London 1963.

Memoirs

The following is but a selection of the most significant memoirs of the period; a larger bibliography appears as an appendix to Sir Charles Oman's *Wellington's Army*, but is restricted to the Peninsular War, and to those titles published before the appearance of Oman's work.

Blakeney, R. *A Boy in the Peninsular War*, ed. J. Sturgis, London 1899.

Cooper, J. S. *Rough Notes of Seven Campaigns in Portugal, Spain, France and America*, Carlisle 1869, r/p 1914.

Costello, E. *Memoirs of Edward Costello*, London 1857; r/p as *The Peninsular and Waterloo Campaigns: Edward Costello*, ed. A. Brett-James, London 1967.

Gleig, Revd. G. R. *The Subaltern*, Edinburgh 1872.

Grattan, W. *Adventures with the Connaught Rangers 1809–14*, London 1847; r/p ed. Sir Charles Oman 1902, r/p London 1989.

Harris, B. *The Recollections of Rifleman Harris*, ed. H. Curling, London 1848; r/p ed. C. Hibbert, London 1970. (The author is sometimes styled 'John Harris' as in the 1970 edn.; he was actually Benjamin Harris).

Kincaid, Sir John. *Adventures in the Rifle Brigade*, London 1830, and *Random Shots from a Rifleman*, London 1835; r/p in Maclaren's combined edn., London 1908.

Larpent, F. S. *The Private Journal of Judge-Advocate F. S. Larpent*, London 1853.

Lawrence, W. *The Autobiography of Sergeant William Lawrence*, ed. G. N. Bankes, London 1886, r/p Cambridge 1987.

Leach, J. *Rough Sketches in the Life of an Old Soldier*, London 1831, r/p London 1986.

Low, E. B. *With Napoleon at Waterloo*, ed. McK. MacBride, London 1911 (also contains accounts of Egypt and the Peninsula).

Mercer, C. *Journal of the Waterloo Campaign*, Edinburgh and London 1870.

Morris, T. *Recollections*, 1845, r/p as *The Napoleonic Wars: Thomas Morris*, ed. J. Selby, London 1967.

Neville, J. F. *Leisure Moments in the Camp and in the Guard-Room*, York 1812 (published under *nom-de-plume* of 'A Veteran British Officer').

Ompteda, Baron C. von. *In the King's German Legion: Memoirs of Baron Ompteda*, ed. L. von Ompteda, London 1894, r/p Cambridge 1987.

Sherer, M. *Recollections of the Peninsula*, London 1823 (published as 'by the Author of "Sketches of India"').

Shipp, J. *The Memoirs of John Shipp*; modern edn. pub. as *The Path of Glory*, ed. C. J. Stranks, London 1969.

Simmons, G. *A British Rifle Man*, ed. W. Verner, London 1899.

Smith, Sir Harry. *The Autobiography of Sir Harry Smith 1787–1819*, ed. G. C. Moore Smith, London 1910; an excellent modern biography is Lehmann, J. *Remember You are an Englishman*, London 1977.

Surtees, W. *Twenty-Five Years in the Rifle Brigade*, London 1833, r/p with intro. by L. V. Archer, London 1973.

Tomkinson, W. *The Diary of a Cavalry Officer in the Peninsula and Waterloo Campaign*, ed. J. Tomkinson, London 1895.

Warre, W. *Letters from the Peninsula 1808–12*, ed. Revd. E. Warre, London 1909.

Wheeler, W. *The Letters of Private Wheeler 1809–28*, ed. B. H. Liddell Hart, London 1951.

Wood, G. *The Subaltern Officer*, London 1825, r/p Cambridge 1986.

Manuals

The following is a selection of the many manuals and drill-books which appeared during the period, many published privately as elucidations of the official manuals.

Adye, R.W. *The Bombardier and Pocket Gunner*, 2nd rev. edn., London 1802.

Anon. *A Manual for Volunteer Corps of Cavalry*, London 1803.

– *A Manual for Volunteer Corps of Infantry*, London 1803.

– *An Elucidation of Several Parts of His Majesty's Regulations for the Formations and Movements of the Cavalry*, London 1808.

– *A Treatise on Military Finance*, London 1796.

– *General Regulations and Orders for the Army*, London 1811 (official publication).

– *Instructions and Regulations for the Formations and Movements of the Cavalry*, London 1801 (official publication).

– *Rules and Regulations for the Formation, Field–Exercise and Movements of His Majesty's Forces*, London 1792, rev. edn. 1798 (official publication: Sir David Dundas's drill).

– *The British Military Library or Journal, comprehending a Complete Body of Military Knowledge*, London 1799-1801.

– *The Military Mentor, being a Series of Letters recently written by a General Officer to his Son . . . calculated to unite the Characters and Accomplishments of the Gentleman and the Soldier*, London 1804.

Beaufoy, H. *Scloppetaria; or, Considerations on the Nature and Use of Rifled Barrel Guns*, London 1808, r/p Richmond 1971 (published under the *nom–de–plume* of 'A Corporal of Riflemen').

Cooper, Captain T. H. *A Practical Guide for the Light Infantry Officer*, London 1806, r/p London 1970.

Dickinson, Captain H. *Instructions for Forming a Regiment of Infantry for Parade of Exercise, together with the Eighteen Manoeuvres*, London 1798.

Gross, Baron. *Duties of an Officer in the Field, and Principally of Light Troops*, London 1801.

James, C. *The Regimental Companion; containing the Relative Duties of every Officer in the British Army*, London 1804.

Langley, T. *The Eighteen Manoeuvres for His Majesty's Infantry*, London 1794, r/p Hemel Hempstead 1988.

Manningham, C. *Military Lectures delivered to the Officers of the 95th (Rifle) Regiment at Shorn-Cliffe Barracks, Kent, during the Spring of 1803*, London 1803; r/p with intro. by W. Verner, 1897.

Riddell, Sir John, Bt. *Rules and Regulations for the Drill, or Instruction of the Recruit*, Kelso 1805 (typical abridgement of the full regulations, prepared for the use of a particular unit, in this case the 2nd Roxburghshire Volunteers).

Periodicals

Of early periodicals, probably the most significant is the *United Service Journal*, which contained many memoirs and comments by participants in the wars, and first published such works as those of Costello and Grattan. Much significant material can also be found in current periodicals, most notably in the *Journal of the Society for Army Historical Research*.

Chapter Notes

In the following, complete citations of sources are given only for the first occurrence of the source; subsequent references are abbreviated. The following abbreviations are also used:

BML *The British Military Library or Journal*, London 1799–1801.
EEC *Edinburgh Evening Courant.*
GM *The Gentleman's Magazine.*
JSAHR *Journal of the Society for Army Historical Research.*
LC *London Chronicle.*
MC *Morning Chronicle.*
USJ *United Service Journal.*
WD *Dispatches of Field Marshal the Duke of Wellington*, ed. J. Gurwood, London 1834–8.
WSD *Supplementary Despatches and Memoranda of Field Marshal the Duke of Wellington*, ed. 2nd Duke of Wellington, London 1858–72.

1. Leach, Lieutenant-Colonel J. *Rough Sketches of the Life of an Old Soldier*, London 1831, p. 399.
2. *GM*, supplement 1814, p. 691.
3. *MC*, 3 December 1798.
4. *Newcastle Courant*, 4 September 1813.
5. *Cobbett's Weekly Political Register*, 22 June 1811, col. 1546 (this publication unpaginated but columns numbered).
6. Ibid., 9 November 1811, col. 581.

7. *The News*, 30 July 1809.
8. *GM*, supplement 1806, p. 1193.
9. *GM*, April 1804, p. 333.
10. *The News*, 25 July 1809.
11. *GM*, 1807, p. iii.
12. The 15th Light Dragoons' Villers-en-Cauchies song; *BML*, I, p. 324.
13. Trenchard, J. *A Short History of Standing Armies in England*, London 1698, p. 1).
14. See Du Cane, E. F. 'The Peninsula and Waterloo: Memories of an Old Rifleman', in *Cornhill Magazine*, December 1897, p. 755. This article concerns the reminiscences of John Molloy, a first lieutenant of the 95th at Waterloo.
15. Yonge's reputation may not have been as bad as sometimes stated; see Steppler, G. A., 'The British Army on the Eve of War', in *The Road to Waterloo*, ed. A. J. Guy, London 1990, p. 12, and the references there cited.
16. *Biographical Sketch of Major-General John Fitzmaurice*, written by his son, Anghiari (Italy) 1908, p. 85.
17. Ibid., p. 15; named after Edward Bouverie Pusey, the Anglican divine whose theology was regarded as approaching Roman Catholicism.
18. Ward, Mrs. *Recollections of an Old Soldier*, 1849; originally published as *Recollections of an Old Soldier, by His Daughter*, *USJ*, 1840, II, p. 217 (Francis

Skelly Tidy, 14th Foot).
19. Sherer, M. *Recollections of the Peninsula, by the Author of Sketches in India*, London 1823, p. 145.
20. *GM*, February 1809, p. 164.
21. *GM*, May 1809, p. 458.
22. *GM*, July 1809, p. 673.
23. *The News*, 25 June 1809.
24. *The Military Mentor*, London 1804, II, p. 29.
25. Napier, George. *Passages in the Early Military Life of General Sir George T. Napier*, ed. General W. C. E. Napier, London 1884, p. 84.
26. *The Times*, 2 February 1814.
27. *GM*, November 1811, p. 488.
28. Arthur, Captain Sir G., Bt. *The Story of the Household Cavalry*, London 1909, II, p. 557.
29. *The News*, 3 August 1806.
30. 'On the Purchase and Sale of Commissions', in *BML*, II, p. 401.
31. Grattan, W. 'Reminiscences of a Subaltern' (published anonymously), in *USJ*, 1831, II, pp. 179–80; later published as *Adventures with the Connaught Rangers*, London 1847; r/p with introduction by Sir Charles Oman, London 1902.
32. *BML*, II, pp. 378–9.
33. Sherer, pp. 51–2.
34. *Newcastle Courant*, 4 September 1811.
35. *Report of Commissioners for Inquiring into Naval and Military Promotion and Retirement*, London

1840, p. xxi.

36. On the Army Estimates debate, 21 January 1795; *LC*, 22 January 1795.

37. Neville, J. F. *Leisure Moments in the Camp and Guard-Room*, York 1812, pp. 98–9 (published anonymously: by 'A Veteran British Officer').

38. *Report of Commissioners for Inquiring into Naval and Military Promotion and Retirement*, London 1840, pp. xlv–xlvi.

39. Bell, Sir George. *Rough Notes by an Old Soldier*, London 1867, I, p. 34.

40. *USJ*, 1834, II, p. 385.

41. Details are given in his biography: Ravenhill, W. 'The Honourable Robert Edward Clifford: Officer in Dillon's Regiment', in *JSAHR*, LXIX (1991), pp. 81–90.

42. *USJ*, 1834, I, p. 236.

43. Blakiston, J. *Twelve Years' Military Adventure in Three Quarters of the Globe*, London 1829, I, pp. 1–2.

44. Simmons, G. *A British Rifle Man: Journals and Correspondence of Major George Simmons, Rifle Brigade, during the Peninsular War and the Campaign of Waterloo*, ed. Lieutenant-Colonel W. Verner, London 1899, p.104.

45. References in this paragraph from Simmons, pp. 219, 232, 269, 307, 315.

46. Sherer, pp. 261–2.

47. Austin, T. *Old Stick-Leg: Extracts from the Diaries of Major Thomas Austin*, ed. Brigadier-General H. H. Austin, London 1926, p. 152.

48. Elers, G. *The Memoirs of George Elers*, ed. Lord Monson and G. Leveson-Gower, London 1903, p. 37.

49. Ibid., p. 88.

50. *GM*, May 1811, p. 474.

51. Wood, Captain G. *The Subaltern Officer: A Narrative*, London 1825, p. 11.

52. *GM*, supplement 1813 Vol. I, p. 671.

53. This story is recounted in Daniell, D. S. *Cap of Honour: The Story of the Gloucestershire Regiment*, London 1951, rev. edn. London 1975.

54. Hood, pp. 116–23.

55. Harris, B. *The Recollections of Rifleman Harris*, ed. Captain Curling, London 1848; 1970 London edn. ed. C. Hibberts, p. 67.

56. Dalton, C. *The Waterloo Roll Call*, London 1904, p. 178, quoting Butler, W. F. *A Narrative of the Historical Events connected with the Sixty-Ninth Regiment*, London 1870.

57. Author's possession.

58. See Page, J. V. *Intelligence Officer in the Peninsula*, Tunbridge Wells 1986, p. 211.

59. Bell, I, p. 137.

60. See Glover, M. 'The Purchase of Commissions: A Reappraisal', in *JSAHR*, LVIII (1980) p. 228.

61. *GM*, September 1809, p. 858.

62. Wood p. 58.

63. *GM*, August 1813, p. 196.

64. *BML*, I, p. 459.

65. Quoted in Maxwell, Sir Herbert, *The Life of Wellington*, London 1899, II, pp. 122–3.

66. Napier, William F. P. *History of the War in the Peninsula*, London 1832–40, IV, p. 360.

67. Ibid., p. 361. Napier is apparently in error in describing Freer as being aged nineteen at the time of his death, as is his obituary in *GM*, December 1813; it would appear that he was twenty. See Scarfe, N. *Letters from the Peninsula: The Freer Family Correspondence 1807–1814*, Leicester 1953, r/p from *Transactions of the Leicestershire Archaeological Society*,

XXIX.

68. Dalton, p. 39.

69. Tomkinson, Lieutenant-Colonel W. *The Diary of a Cavalry Officer in the Peninsular War and Waterloo Campaign*, ed. J. Tomkinson, London 1895, pp. 218–20.

70. Leach, pp. 112, 120–1.

71. *LC*, 15 April 1794.

72. General Order, 18 March 1803; quoted in *The True Briton*, 25 March 1803, in an attempt to demonstrate that the Horse Guards was providing 'effectual protection to Civil Society, from the licentiousness of Military Insubordination'.

73. Quoted in *The 85th King's Light Infantry*, ed. C. R. B. Barrett, London 1913, p. 72.

74. *GM*, December 1814, p. 578.

75. *GM*, October 1807, p. 974.

76. Graham, H. *Annals of the Yeomanry Cavalry of Wiltshire*, Liverpool 1886, p. 28.

77. The story of these officers is recounted in Ward, S. G. P., 'Three Watercolour Portraits', in *JSAHR*, LXVI (1988), pp. 68–9.

78. *GM*, supplement 1805, pp. 1223–4.

79. *GM*, April 1813, p. 360.

80. *GM*, May 1813, p. 489.

81. Napier, George, pp. 192–3.

82. By 'An Old British Half-Pay Officer', in *BML*, II, p. 244.

83. *The Star*, 12 August 1801.

84. *The News*, 21 May 1809.

85. *LC*, 21 November 1795.

86. 'Corporal Trim', 'Nocturnal Contemplations in Barham-Down Camp, 1795', in *GM*, June 1801, p. 549.

87. Quoted by Leetham, Lieutenant-Colonel Sir Arthur, 'Old Recruiting Posters', in *JSAHR*, I (1922), p. 120.

88. Morris, T. *Thomas Morris: The Napoleonic Wars*, ed. J. Selby, London 1967, p. 2.

89. *EEC*, 13 April 1812.

90. Mr. Hussey in the Army Estimates debate, 21 January 1795; *LC* 22 January 1795, p. 78.

91. Army Promotions debate, 21 January 1795; *LC*, 22 January 1795, p. 77.

92. 73rd Foot: Paine, J. 'Recruiting Poster: 73rd Regiment, 1813', in *JSAHR*, XXXI (1953), p. 184.

93. 7th and 14th Light Dragoons respectively; Leetham, in *JSAHR*, I, p. 119.

94. Midlothian Light Dragoons; ibid., pp. 119–20.

95. 'Notes Respecting the Recruiting of the Army During the Last and Present Century', in *USJ*, 1839, I, p. 528.

96. *Monthly Magazine*, September 1799, p. 671.

97. 'Reminiscences of a Light Dragoon', in *USJ*, 1840, II, p. 455.

98. *LC*, 6 January 1798.

99. Quoted in Mackintosh, H.B. *The Grant, Strathspey or First Highland Fencible Regiment 1793–1799*, Elgin 1934, p. 24; this work reproduces examples of the old and new attestation forms.

100. Marshall, H. 'On the Enlisting, Discharging, and Pensioning of Soldiers', in *USJ*, 1839, III, p. 269.

101. See Holme, N., and Kirby, Major E. L. *Medal Rolls 23rd Foot - Royal Welch Fusiliers, Napoleonic Period*, Caernarfon and London, 1978.

102. Marshall, in *USJ*, 1839, III, p. 271.

103. The full return can be found in Everett, Sir Henry, *The History of the Somerset Light Infantry (Prince Albert's)* *1685–1914*, London 1934, pp. 133–7.

104. Seton, Colonel Sir Bruce, Bt. 'Recruiting in Scotland 1793–94', in *JSAHR*, XI (1932), pp. 41–2.

105. *LC*, 9 January 1798.

106. Anon. *Journal of a Soldier of the 71st Highland Light Infantry 1806–1815*, Edinburgh 1822, p. 13; p. xiii in the 1975 London reprint, ed. C. Hibbert.

107. Harris, p. 5.

108. See Aspinall-Oglander, C. *Freshly Remembered: the Story of Thomas Graham, Lord Lynedoch*, London 1956, pp. 73–4.

109. *GM*, December 1807, p. 1173.

110. 'Review of the Military Establishments of Great Britain', in *USJ*, 1834, II, p. 53.

111. Moore Smith, G. C. *The Life of John Colborne, Field-Marshal Lord Seaton*, London 1903, p. 15.

112. Figures conflict, between 10,696 and 11,161; see Fortescue, Hon. Sir John *The County Lieutenancies and the Army*, London 1909, p. 147.

113. Haly, A. 'A Letter to Colonel Brownrigg', in *BML*, II, p. 267.

114. To Earl Bathurst, 2 July 1813, in *WD*, X, pp. 495–6.

115. Maxwell, II, p. 126.

116. General Order, 18 January 1810.

117. Speech of Lieutenant-Colonel Sir John Oswald, colonel of the 35th, to the regiment at Phoenix Park, Dublin, 21 July 1834, in *USJ*, 1834, III, p. 127.

118. Order book, 109th Foot, author's possession; 5 May 1795.

119. Ibid., 23 June 1795.

120. *GM*, April 1807, p. 380.

121. *GM*, April 1806, p. 480.

122. Author's possession.

124. *GM*, August 1803, pp. 729–30.

125. 'The Ploughman's Ditty, Being an Answer to that foolish Question, What Have the Poor to Lose?', in *GM*, supplement 1803, p. 1238.

126. Morley, S. *Memoirs of a Sergeant of the 5th Regiment*, Ashford, 1842, p. 40.

127. *MC*, 19 October 1798.

128. This subject is covered in Emsley, C. 'Political Disaffection and the British Army in 1792', in *Bulletin of the Institute of Historical Research* (University of London), XLVIII (1975), pp. 230–45.

129. Baker, Lieutenant-Colonel B. G. 'Old Cavalry Stations: Norwich', in *Cavalry Journal* XX (1930), p. 542; and repeated in the same author's *Old Cavalry Stations*, London 1934, p. 57.

130. Emsley, 'Political Disaffection', pp. 237–8, 245.

131. Lloyd-Verney, Colonel. *Records of the Infantry Militia Battalions of the County of Southampton*, London 1894, p. 232.

132. *GM*, February 1808, pp. 176–7.

133. *General Evening Post*, 20 December 1806.

134. 'Corporal Trim', 'Nocturnal Contemplations . . .', in *GM*, June 1801, p. 549.

135. Fuller statistics and examples can be found in Barrett, C. R. B., 'Early Cavalry Barracks in Great Britain', in *Cavalry Journal*, VII (1912), pp. 161–76.

136. House of Commons, 13 April 1812; *EEC* 18 April 1812.

137. Mr. Freemantle, House of Commons, 1 May 1812; *EEC* 7 May 1812.

138. Ibid.

139. Order book, 109th Foot, 19 March and 28 April 1795.

140. Adye, R. W. *Bombardier*

and Pocket Gunner, London 1802, p. 180; the previous schedule is from *BML*, I, p. 477.

141. Sinclair of Ulbster, Sir John, Bt. 'Hints respecting the State of the Camp at Aberdeen in 1795, with some Observations on Encampments in general', in *BML*, I, p. 182. The unit in question was the Rothsay & Caithness Fencibles.

142. 'Answers to Queries from Sir John Sinclair, respecting the Situation of a British Soldier of Infantry', in *BML*, I, p. 479.

143. *EEC*, 27 June 1814.

144. *EEC*, 29 September 1817.

145. Cooper, J. S. *Rough Notes of Seven Campaigns in Portugal, Spain, France and America*, rev. edn., Carlisle 1914, p. 157 (orig. pub. 1869).

146. *MC*, 17 October 1798.

147. Costello, E. *Edward Costello: the Peninsular and Waterloo Campaigns*, ed. A. Brett-James, London 1967, p. 71 (orig. pub. in *USJ* 1839–40, then as *Adventures of a Soldier, written by himself*, London 1852. This dialogue did not appear upon first publication, *USJ* 1839, II, p. 489).

148. Kincaid, Sir John. *Adventures in the Rifle Brigade*, London 1830, r/p with *Random Shots from a Rifleman* (London 1835) in Maclaren's combined edn., London 1908, p. 95.

149. Cooper, p. 88.

150. Wood, pp. 205–6.

151. Burrows, J. W. *The Essex Yeomanry*, Southend-on-Sea, 1925.

152. Nyren, J. *Nyren's Cricketer's Guide . . . With Sketches of the Cricketers of my Time*, ed. C. C. Clarke, London edn. 1888, p. 60 (orig. pub. 1849).

153. Turton, R. B. *History of the North York Militia*, Leeds 1907, p. 119.

154. Stanhope, 5th Earl. *Notes of Conversations with the Duke of Wellington*, London 1888, p. 14.

155. *An Accurate and Impartial Narrative of the War, by an Officer of the Guards*, London 1796, p. 2. (For the authorship of this work see Ward, S. G. P., 'Accurate and Impartial Narrative', in *JSAHR*, LXX (1992), pp. 211–23).

156. Ibid.

157. Surtees, W. *Twenty-Five Years in the Rifle Brigade*, ed. J. Surtees, Edinburgh and London 1833, p. 88.

158. William Napier, *War in the Peninsula*, 2nd edn., I, p. xxviii, expanding on original version in I, p. 472.

159. Cooper, p. 15.

160. *MC*, 3 December 1798.

161. *The News*, 23 November 1809.

162. *GM*, November 1802, p. 1060.

163. *LC*, 16 November 1797, p. 478.

164. Sherer, p. 70.

165. Ibid., p. 181.

166. Speech upon the presentation of Colours to the 93rd Highlanders at Canterbury, 7 October 1834; in *USJ* 1834, III, p. 413.

167. *General Orders in Wolfe's Army during the Expedition up the River St. Lawrence*; entry for 22 August 1759; pub. Literary and Historical Society of Quebec.

168. To Earl Bathurst, 2 July 1813; in *WD*, X, pp. 495–6.

169. *MC*, 8 June 1798.

170. *GM*, September 1807, p. 843.

171. Cooper, p. 14.

172. *MC*, 3 December 1798.

173. *Cobbett's Weekly Political Register*, 27 February 1811, cols. 485–6.

174. Ibid., 22 June 1811, cols. 1554–5.

175. Such attribution to Cobbett and Burdett is given, for example, in *Liverpool Mercury*, 3 July 1812.

176. Horse Guards circular, 25 March 1812.

177. *Cobbett's Weekly Political Register*, 13 June 1812, cols. 741–2.

178. Ibid., 22 June 1811, col. 1542.

179. *USJ*, 1834, II, p. 558.

180. Poulett Cameron, Lieutenant-Colonel G. 'Personal Adventures and Excursions in Georgia, Circassia, and Russia', in *USJ*, 1840, III, pp. 41–42.

181. Harris, p. 92.

182. Lawrence, W. *The Autobiography of Sergeant William Lawrence*, ed. G. N. Bankes, London 1886, pp. 48–50.

183. Grattan, p. 174.

184. Gleig, G. R. *The Subaltern*, Edinburgh and London 1872, p. 111.

185. *BML*, I, p. 480.

186. Order book 109th Foot, 9 May 1795.

187. 'Peninsula', 'Invidious Distinctions', in *USJ*, 1834, II, p. 412.

188. Mr. Pratt, 'Lines on the Royal Hospital . . .', in *GM*, April 1810, p. 356.

189. *GM*, October 1814, p. 390.

190. Creevey, T. *The Creevey Papers*, ed. J. Gore, London 1934, p. 404.

191. To Lord Liverpool, 9 April 1812, in *WD*, IX, pp. 52–3.

192. See Holme and Kirby, *op. cit.*; some confusion exists in the rolls reproduced in this excellent source, men being shown as enlisted from the volunteers instead of actually from the militia.

193. Kincaid, p. 99.

194. *MC*, 13 August 1798.

195. Lawrence, p. 210.

196. Murray, Sir H. *Memoir and Correspondence of the late Captain Arthur Stormont Murray*, 1859, p. 51.

197. *MC*, 10 September 1807.

198. For an excellent study of British military music of this period, see Winstock, L. *Songs and Music of the Redcoats*, London 1970.

199. *GM*, June 1801, pp. 491–2.

200. 'Corporal Trim', 'Nocturnal Contemplations . . .', in *GM*, June 1801, p. 549.

201. Lawrence, p. 193.

202. Wood, p. 224.

203. Grattan, p. 50.

204. *WD*, VIII, pp. 371–2.

205. Mainwaring, F. 'Four Years of a Soldier's Life', in *Colburn's United Service Magazine*, 1844, p. 517.

206. *Edinburgh Advertiser*, 14 May 1802.

207. 'Militaris', 'On the Equipment of the British Infantry', in *USJ*, 1831, II, p. 204.

208. Cooper, pp. 85–6.

209. Quoted in Colonel W. Knollys' introduction to *A Journal of the Russian Campaign in 1812*, Lieutenant-General De Fezensac, London 1852, p. xlix.

210. Hawley, General H. 'General Hawley's "Chaos"', ed. Revd. P. Sumner, in *JSAHR*, XXVI (1948), p. 93.

211. Cotton, E. *A Voice from Waterloo*, 9th edn. Brussels 1900, pp. 81–2.

212. *LC*, 21 April 1796.

213. MS account by an unknown sergeant of 1/2nd Foot Guards, author's possession.

214. Hanger, Colonel G. *To All Sportsmen*, London 1814, p. 205.

215. Bunbury, Sir Henry. *Narratives of Some Passages in the Great War with France 1799–1810*, London 1854; r/p with intro. by Hon. Sir John Fortescue, London 1927, p. 30.

216. Haly, in *BML*, II, pp. 268–9.

217. Geike, A. *Life of Sir Roderick Murchison Bart.*, London 1875, I, p. 33.

218. Harris, p. 17.

219. Kincaid, p. 276.

220. Chambray, Marquis de 'Reflections on the Infantry of Our Days', in *Philosophie de la Guerre*; translation from *USJ*, 1834, II, pp. 505–07.

221. 'The Campaign of Waterloo, Strategically Examined', in *USJ*, 1834, II, p. 477 (present author's italics).

222. 'Colonel Mitchell in Conclusion of the Bayonet Discussion', quoting William Napier, in *USJ*, 1840, I, p. 263.

223. Curling, H. 'The Bayonet' (quoting Benjamin Harris), in *USJ*, 1839, II, pp. 399–400.

224. Haly, in *BML*, II, p. 269.

225. *GM*, April 1811, p. 383.

226. 'CC', 'Weapons and comparative efficiency of Modern Infantry', in *USJ*, 1834, III, p. 397.

227. 'Fluellyn', 'The Lance and Bayonet', in *USJ*, 1839, I, pp. 391–2.

228. Gleig, *The Subaltern*, p. 100.

229. Guthrie, G.J. *Commentaries on the Surgery of War*, London 1853, p. 16.

230. 'Partial Account of the Action fought in North Holland . . . on the 2d of October, 1799', in *BML*, II, p. 112.

231. Lieutenant-Colonel Peter Serle to Lord Bolton, 30 March 1807; Lloyd-Verney, p. 223.

232. Kincaid, p. 8.

233. Simmons, p. 27.

234. *A Manual for Volunteer Corps of Infantry*, London 1803, pp. 30–3.

235. MS account of Talavera by unknown sergeant of 1/2nd Foot Guards, author's possession.

236. 'Green Feather', 'Out-Post Anecdotes', in *USJ*, 1840, I, p. 224.

237. Latour, Major A. Lacarrière, *Historical Memoir of the War in West Florida and Louisiana in 1814–15*, Philadelphia 1816, p. 161.

238. Shaw Kennedy, General Sir James. *Notes on the Battle of Waterloo*, London 1865, pp. 100–1.

239. Tomkinson, p. 280.

240. Ward, Mrs. (Tidy), in *USJ*, 1840, II, p. 477.

241. Grattan, in *USJ*, 1831, II, p. 181.

242. Mill, Major J. 'Service in Ireland, the Peninsula, New Orleans and Waterloo', ed. Captain W. Macdonald Mill, *United Service Magazine*, September 1870.

243. Gleig, *The Subaltern*, p. 184.

244. 'Halberd', 'Use of the Pike by Serjeants', in *USJ*, 1834, II, pp. 555–6.

245. *BML*, I, p. 486.

246. Ibid., p. 445.

247. Ward, Mrs. (Tidy), in *USJ*, 1840, II, p. 477.

248. Gleig, *The Subaltern*, p. 163.

249. 'The Campaign of Waterloo Strategically Examined', in *USJ*, 1834, II, p. 453.

250. Duke of York to Lord Cornwallis, 26 July 1788; *Correspondence of Charles, 1st Marquis Cornwallis*, ed. C. Ross, London 1859, I, p. 402.

251. *MC*, 9 August 1808.

252. *BML*, II, p. 231.

253. *The Statesman*, 7 January 1815.

254. Dispatch of Lieutenant-General Count Wallmoden, 20 September 1813; *London Gazette*, 7 October 1813.

255. 'On the Treatment of Horses in the English Cavalry', in *BML*, II, p. 401.

256. Gleig, *The Subaltern*, pp. 270–1.

257. 'An Officer of Dragoons', 'The British Cavalry on the Peninsula', in *USJ*, 1831, II, p. 61.

258. 'Reminiscences of a Light Dragoon', in *USJ*, 1840,

III, pp. 369–70.

259. 'The Campaign of Waterloo Strategically Examined', in *USJ*, 1834, II, p. 453.

260. *GM*, supplement 1811, I, p. 665.

261. Leach, p. 269.

262. 'Fluellyn', 'Calibre of the Infantry Musket', in *USJ*, 1840, II, p. 548.

263. 'Officer of Dragoons', *op. cit.*, p. 61.

264. *MC*, 16 July 1798.

265. *The News*, 19 November 1809.

266. *LC*, 3 May 1794, p. 420.

267. Tomkinson, p. 135.

268. The author is indebted to Dr. John Hall for this anecdote, from the MS account by Lieutenant George Sulivan, 1st Life Guards.

269. *The Trial of Colonel Quentin*, London 1814, p. 76.

270. Gordon, A. *A Cavalry Officer in the Corunna Campaign 1808–09*, ed. Colonel H. C. Wylly, London 1913, p. 107.

271. To Lord William Russell, 21 July 1826; quoted in Maxwell, II, pp. 138–9.

272. To Hill, 18 June 1812; *WD*, IX, p. 240.

273. Note by the translator, Ludlow Beamish, of *Lectures on the Tactics of Cavalry*, Count von Bismarck, 1827; London edn. p. 134.

274. Tomkinson, p. 135.

275. Mercer, General C. *Journal of the Waterloo Campaign*, Edinburgh and London 1870, I, p. 315.

276. Swabey, W. *Diary of Campaigns in the Peninsula*, orig. pub. in *Proceedings of the Royal Artillery Institution*, r/p London 1984, p. 176.

277. Adye, p. 163.

278. See Lagden, A., and Sly, J. *The 2/73rd at Waterloo*, Brightlingsea 1988, p. 50; this exemplary biographical study permits a comparison between service records and a well-known memoir (Thomas Morris), demonstrating the accuracy possible in works of autobiography, written from memory, years after the event.

279. Kincaid, p. 64.

280. *The Waterloo Letters*, ed. Major-General H. T. Siborne, London 1891, p. 240.

281. Adye, p. 27.

282. 'Laswarri and the Royal Irish Hussars', in *USJ* 1840, I p.469.

283. 'Practical Observations on the most advantageous Use of Artillery in Hilly Situations', in *BML*, II, p. 367.

284. Adye, p. 26.

285. *GM*, September 1814, p. 260.

286. *EEC*, 28 February 1814.

287. Gleig, *The Subaltern*, p. 291.

288. *EEC*, 20 January 1814.

289. Jones, Lieutenant-Colonel J. T., *Journals of the Sieges Undertaken by the Allies in Spain in the Years 1811 and 1812*, London 1814, p. 336.

290. Belmas, J., *Journaux des Sièges faits ou soutenus par les Français dans la Péninsule de 1807 à 1814*, Paris 1837, III, p. 728.

291. William Napier, *War in the Peninsula*, IV, p. 193.

292. 'Remarks on Military Bridges', in *USJ*, 1840, I, p. 388.

293. Sherer, p. 208.

294. Grattan, in *USJ*, 1831, II, p. 329.

295. Kincaid, p. 63.

296. Gleig, *The Subaltern*, p. 52.

297. Surtees, p. 149.

298. LeMesurier, H. *A System for the British Commissariat*, 1796; this in reprinted in Glover, R. *Peninsular Preparation: the Reform of the British Army 1795–1809*, Cambridge 1963.

299. To Beresford, 11 May 1811; *WD*, VII, p. 531.

300. 27 May 1811; *WD*, VII, pp. 599–600.

301. *Monthly Magazine*, January 1810, p. 647.

302. 15 July 1809; *WD*, IV, pp. 511–12.

303. 17 April 1810; *WD*, VI, p. 43.

304. Order book, 109th Foot, 16 August 1795.

305. Schaumann, A. E. F. *On the Road with Wellington*, ed. A. M. Ludovic, London 1924.

306. Gordon, p. 24.

307. 7 January 1812; *WD*, VIII, p. 514.

308. Memorandum to Commissary-General J. Bissett, Fletcher and Dickson, 1 January 1812; *WD*, VIII, pp. 500–1.

309. *GM*, June 1808, p. 548.

310. *GM*, July 1809, p. 671.

311. See Caldwell, G. J., and Cooper, R. B. E., *Rifle Green at Waterloo*, n.d., p. 133; this includes the rest of Norcott's suggestions.

312. Stewart's dispatch credits this action to a mixed detachment of 82nd and 71st, commanded by Major William Fitzgerald of the 82nd; the 71st were in a different division from the 82nd.

313. *GM*, January and March 1800, disputed his age between 82 and 87 years.

314. Kincaid, pp. 43–4.

315. Pickles, H. *Foundations*, Halifax 1933, p. 490.

316. Stevenson, J. *Twenty-One Years in the British Foot Guards*, London 1830.

317. Page, G. A., *The Soldier-Schoolmaster: A Brief Memoir of Christopher Ludlam*, Louth 1874, p. 12.

318. *Public Ledger*, 22 June 1807.

319. *John Bull*, 26 November 1821.

320. Morris, p. 14.

321. Gleig, *The Subaltern*, pp. 180–1.

322. Geike, I, pp. 35–6.

323. *BML*, I, p. 479.
324. MS, author's possession.
325. 'Flexible Grummet', 'Leaves from my Log-Book', in *USJ*, 1834, I, pp. 487–8.
326. Mayne, John. 'Mary Marton, A Ballad', in *GM*, February 1807, p. 156.
327. Bell, I, p. 74.
328. Gordon, pp. 171–2.
329. Gleig, *The Subaltern*, pp. 119–20.
330. Eaton, Mrs., *Waterloo Days*, quoted in De Lancey, M. *A Week at Waterloo* in June 1815, ed. B. R. Ward, London 1906, p. 107.
331. Leach, p. 370.
332. Lejeune, Baron. *Memoirs of Baron Lejeune*, trans. and ed. Mrs. Arthur Bell, London 1897, II, pp. 107–8.
333. Tomkinson, p. 188.
334. William Napier, *War in the Peninsula*, V, p. 181.
335. Ward, Mrs. (Tidy), in *USJ*, 1840, II, pp. 358–9.
336. The author is indebted to Dr. John Hall for reference to the memoirs of George Sulivan, 1st Life Guards.
337. Lawrence, p. 129.
338. 19 March 1813; *WD*, X, p. 209. Names are deleted in the published version to prevent embarrassment; but see Chambers, J. W. *The Elopement of Anna Ludovina Teixeira de Aguilar* . . .
339. Smith, H. *The Autobiography of Sir Harry Smith 1787–1819*, ed. G. C. Moore Smith, London 1910, pp. 73–4.
340. *The Times*, 2 August 1803.
341. *LC*, 10 December 1795.
342. De Lancey, p. 101.
343. Moises, H. 'On the Qualifications of Regiment Assistant Surgeons', in *BML*, I, p. 397.
344. Dispatch, 19 May 1798.
345. McGrigor, Dr. J. *A Letter to the Commissioners of Military Enquiry, in Reply to Animadversions of Dr. E. Nathaniel Bancroft, on their Fifth Report*, 1808.
346. Leach, p. 16.
347. *GM*, December 1809, p. 1174.
348. *GM*, July 1803, p. 696.
349. 'Colonel Hope's Instructions to the First Regiment of Edinburgh Volunteers', in *GM*, November 1803, pp. 1068–9.
350. Sinclair of Ulbster, in *BML*, I, p. 182.
351. Leach, p. 240.
352. The boot is illustrated in Foss, M. *The Royal Fusiliers*, London 1967, p. 59.
353. *GM*, July 1807, p. 676.
354. *GM*, October 1809, p. 987.
355. Simmons, pp. 79, 80.
356. Kincaid, p. 257.
357. 'The Campaign of Waterloo, Strategically Examined', in *USJ*, 1834, II, p. 468.
358. George Napier, pp. 156, 219–20.
359. *USJ*, 1840, I, p. 364; the later version is slightly changed (1967 edn., p. 156) in that he observed that during the operation the Englishman was chewing tobacco vigorously, and has him saying, 'take that, and stuff it down your throat . . .'.
360. Gleig, G. R. *The Campaigns of the British Army at Washington and New Orleans*, London 1847, pp. 161–2.
361. 9 June 1812; *WD*, IX, p. 224.
362. Simmons, pp. 86–7.
363. Cooper, p. 82.
364. 'Reminiscences of a Light Dragoon', in *USJ*, 1840, III, pp. 363–4.
365. De Lancey, pp. 90–1.
366. Leach, p. 58.
367. Simmons, p. 371.
368. *The Times*, 27 October 1814.
369. *EEC*, 14 February 1814.
370. Kincaid, p. 206.
371. Ibid., p. 285.
372. Swabey, p. 147.
373. *GM*, July 1809, p. 683.
374. *GM*, July 1800, p. 687.
375. *GM*, May 1800, p. 479.
376. Grattan, in *USJ*, 1831, II, p. 183; this is one passage not included in Oman's edition.
377. *LC*, 6 May 1795, p. 429.
378. Neville, p. 160.
379. 'A Fig for the Grand Buonaparte', in *GM*, supplement 1803, p. 1239.
380. *GM*, August 1800, p. 783.
381. *LC*, 6 May 1794, p. 429.
382. House of Commons, 9 May 1796; *LC*, 10 May 1796.
383. *GM*, June 1800, p. 579.
384. *True Briton*, 25 March 1803.
385. Hay, W. *Reminiscences under Wellington*, ed. Mrs. S. C. I. Wood, London 1901.
386. Bunbury, p. 205.
387. Anon., *Account of the Operations of the Corps under the Duke of Brunswick*, London 1810, p. 50.
388. Leach, p. 191.
389. Costello, p. 47.
390. To Bathurst, 18 August 1813; *WD*, XI, pp. 11–12.
391. Tomkinson, p. 72.
392. Mill.
393. Wilkie, Lieutenant-Colonel 'The British Colonies Considered as Military Posts', in *USJ*, 1840, III, p. 332.
394. Simmons, pp. 169–70.
395. 'An Account of the Portuguese Military Establishments', in *BML*, I, p. 213.
396. Griffiths, A. J. *The Wellington Memorial*, London 1897, p. 308.
397. Warre, Sir William, *Letters from the Peninsula*, ed. E. Warre, London 1909, pp. 239, 63, 78, 101.
398. To Lord Liverpool, 25 July 1813; *WD*, X, p. 569.
399. To Beresford, 9 February 1811; *WD*, VII, p. 239.
400. Jones, Colonel J. T.

'Memoranda relative to Lines thrown up to cover Lisbon in 1810', *Papers on Subjects connected with the Duties of the Corps of Royal Engineers*, III, London 1839, p. 28.

401. *EEC*, 24 November 1810.

402. D'Urban, B. *The Peninsula Journal of Major-General Sir Benjamin D'Urban*, ed. I. J. Rousseau, 1930, p. 153.

403. Blakiston, II, p. 336.

404. Leach, p. 275.

405. Cooper, p. 13.

406. Warre, p. 239.

407. Wellington to Torrens, 2 December 1811; *WD*, VIII, p. 417.

408. 17 September 1813; *WD*, XI, p. 117.

409. *EEC*, 24 August 1812.

410. 19 August 1813; *WD*, XI, p. 19.

411. 19 September 1813; *WD*, XI, pp. 121–2.

412. Sir George Airey on behalf of General Fox to Stuart, 23 October 1806; MS, author's possession.

413. *WD*, XI, p. 123.

414. *GM*, March 1807, p. 275.

415. *The News*, 6 November 1808.

416. Bunbury, p. 31.

417. Ibid., p. 28.

418. To Dundas, January 1801; quoted in Fortescue, Hon. Sir John, *History of the British Army*, London from 1899; IV, p. 810.

419. Bunbury, p. 122.

420. Kincaid, pp. 245–6.

421. Sherer, p. 151.

422. Tomkinson, p. 117.

423. Cooper, pp. 67–8.

424. *EEC*, 1 June 1812.

425. Kincaid, p. 36.

426. *GM*, May 1811, p. 487.

427. 'Sonnet to Lord Wellington', in *GM*, November 1810, p. 461.

428. *EEC*, 24 and 27 February 1812.

429. *EEC*, 16 May 1814.

430. To Bathurst, 23 August 1813; *WD*, XI, pp. 34–5.

431. To Liverpool, 9 April 1812; *WD*, IX, p. 52.

432. *WSD*, X, p. 219.

433. *WD*, VII, pp. 34–5.

434. To Liverpool, 2 January 1810; *WD*, V, p. 404.

435. Torrens to Wellington, quoted in Fortescue, *History of the British Army*, VII, p. 419.

436. To Torrens, 2 December 1811; *WD*, VIII, p. 417.

437. To Torrens, 4 October 1810; *WD*, VI, p. 485. The miscreant's name is omitted in the published correspondence but is identified as Major-General Lightburne; see Glover, M., *Wellington as Military Commander*, London 1968, p. 206.

438. Gordon, p. 99.

439. Ibid., p. 66.

440. Tomkinson, pp. 98–9.

441. Boutflower, C. *The Journal of an Army Surgeon during the Peninsular War*, privately published, n.d., p. 173.

442. Robinson, F. 'A Peninsula Brigadier', ed. C. T. Atkinson, in *JSAHR*, XXXIV (1956), p. 168.

443. Smith, p. 118.

444. To Colville, 5 February 1814; *WD*, XI, p. 500.

445. 15 May 1811; *WD*, VII, pp. 552–3.

446. To Major-General Alexander Campbell, 15 May 1811; *WD*, VII, p. 546.

447. *USJ*, 1834, II, p. 224.

448. To Torrens, 8 August 1813; *WD*, X, pp. 616–17.

449. To Liverpool, 2 January 1810; *WD*, V, p. 404.

450. *EEC*, 30 June 1814.

451. 'The Duke of Wellington', in *USJ* 1840, II, p. 156.

452. Maxwell, II, p. 93.

453. Timbs, J. *Wellingtonia: Anecdotes, Maxims and Characteristics of the Duke of Wellington*, London 1852, p. 60.

454. Glazebrook, Lieutenant T. K. *Lines Recited at the Mess of the Warrington Local Militia*, 5 June 1809, Warrington 1809.

455. Austin, p. 195.

456. 'Corporal Trim', 'Nocturnal Contemplations', in *GM*, June 1801, p. 549.

457. *Edinburgh Advertiser*, 11 June 1802.

458. *LC*, 21 November 1795.

459. Robertson, W. *History of Rochdale Past and Present*, 1887, p. 217.

460. Song of the Royal Cornwall Militia on going to Ireland in 1811; written by James Brydges-Willyams, their lieutenant-colonel from March 1807, to the traditional tune of *One and All*; the full version is in Winstock, L., *Songs and Music of the Redcoats*, London 1970, p. 130.

461. Pinks, W. J. *A History of Clerkenwell*, 1880, p. 133.

462. Rowlandson, T. *Loyal Volunteers of London & Environs*, London 1798; unpaginated, text to plate 70.

463. 'A Declaration and Resolutions of the Loyal Loughborough Volunteer Infantry', *Transactions of the Leicestershire Architectural and Archaeological Society*, 1899, pp. 380–1.

464. Rowlandson, plate 26.

465. Rowlandson, plate 48.

466. Quoted in Berry, R. P. *History of the Volunteer Infantry*, London and Huddersfield, 1903, p. 86.

467. These statistics taken from *Returns: Volunteers of the United Kingdom, Ordered by the House of Commons to be printed, 9th and 13th December 1803*, revised to February 1804; and see Haythornthwaite, P. J. 'The Volunteer Force 1803–04', in *JSAHR*, LXIV (1986), pp. 193–204.

468. Hart, Colonel C. J. *History of the 1st Volunteer Battalion Royal Warwickshire Regiment and its Predecessors*, Birmingham 1906, p. 52.

469. Lord Sheffield to Duke of Richmond, 24 July 1803; quoted in Sebag-Montefiore, C., *History of the Volunteer Forces*, London 1908, p. 264.
470. *Gore's General Advertiser*, 27 August 1805; quoted in Stephen, W. *History of the Queen's City of Edinburgh Rifle Volunteer Brigade*, London and Edinburgh 1881, p. 22.
471. *GM*, November 1803, p. 1068.
472. Rowlandson, plate 21.
473. *GM*, May 1800, pp. 490–1.
474. Quoted in Berry, p. 326.
475. Quoted in Hoskins, W. G. *Exeter Militia List 1803*, Chichester 1972, p. 51.
476. Bell, J. *Rhymes of Northern Bards*, Newcastle 1812, pp. 29–30.
477. *The Craven Muster Roll*, Northallerton 1976, pp. 141–3.
478. Regimental order, 18 October 1803.
479. 'Edinburgh About Sixty Years Ago', *The Leisure Hour*, No. 368 (13 January 1859).
480. Cox, Revd. C. J. 'Belper Regiment - Grenadiers', in *Journal of the Derbyshire Archaeological and Natural History Society*, XII (1890), p. 64.
481. Summers, J. W. *History of the Loyal Sunderland Volunteers*, Sunderland 1860, p. 8.
482. Grimshaw, N. *Observations on the Reply to a Statement of the Question respecting the Comparative Rank of the Two Corps of Preston Volunteer Infantry*, Preston 1805, p. 7.
483. Bacon, R. M. *Address to the Norwich Riflemen*, Norwich 1804, p. 2.
484. Mockett, J. *A Letter to Capt. Thomas Garrett commanding the Thanet Troop of Volunteer Yeomanry*, Canterbury 1810, pp. 17–18.

485. 'T.W.', in *Royal Military Chronicle*, April 1813, pp. 454–5.
486. *Cobbett's Weekly Political Register*, 22 June 1811, col. 1545.
487. *USJ*, 1840, I, p. 261.
488. *The News*, 3 August 1806.
489. Baines, E. *History of the Wars of the French Revolution*, London 1817, II, p. 204.
490. General Order, St. Helier, 2 June 1795.
491. *LC*, 11 August 1795.
492. *LC*, 10 December 1795.
493. Boutflower, p. 47.
494. *GM*, October 1800, p. 994.
495. *LC*, 21 November 1795.
496. *LC*, 3 December 1795.
497. Robertson, *History of Rochdale*, p. 218.
498. Leader, R. E. *Reminiscences of Old Sheffield, its Streets and People*, 1876, p. 280.
499. *LC*, 11 August 1795.
500. *LC*, 24 March 1796.
501. *GM*, June 1812, p. 570.
502. Ibid., pp. 582–3.
503. *EEC*, 7 May 1812.
504. *LC*, 23 July 1795.
505. *MC*, 25 September 1798.
506. *GM*, March 1804, p. 270.
507. 'B.T.', 'Tour to the Lakes of Cumberland and Westmorland', in *GM*, June 1805, p. 507.
508. *MC*, 29 October 1798.
509. Wood, p. 14.
510. Gordon, p. 201.
511. Carr, J. *Annals and Stories of Colne and Neighbourhood*, Colne 1878, p. 88.
512. Grattan, in *USJ*, I, p. 502.
513. 'Old Sub', 'Recollections of the Expedition to the Chesapeake and Against New Orleans', in *USJ*, 1840, I, p. 447.
514. Gleig, *Washington and New Orleans*, p. 32.
515. Tomkinson, pp. 220–1.
516. 'Old Sub', in *USJ*, 1840, I, p. 446.
517. Adye, p. 179.
518. *Monthly Magazine*, January 1810, p. 558.
519. *USJ*, 1834, II, p. 223.

520. Kincaid, p. 234.
521. Ibid., p. 102.
522. Ibid., p. 22.
523. Ibid., p. 23.
524. Cooper, p. 156.
525. Leach, p. 160.
526. Sherer, p. 59.
527. *Monthly Magazine*, January 1810, p. 560.
528. Gleig, *The Subaltern*, p. 107.
529. *Bell's Weekly Messenger*, 22 January 1804.
530. Kincaid, p. 17.
531. Surtees, p. 14.
532. Kincaid, pp. 196, 235.
533. Gleig, *The Subaltern*, p. 264.
534. *MC*, 17 December 1804.
535. Leach, p. 151.
536. Sherer, p. 349.
537. Gordon, p. 109.
538. Sherer, pp. 179, 142.
539. George Napier, p. 177.
540. 'Green Feather', in *USJ*, 1840, I, pp. 223–4.
541. *USJ*, 1840, II, p. 526.
542. Leach, p. 189.
543. Gleig, *The Subaltern*, p. 235.
544. Grattan, in *USJ*, 1834, I, p. 507.
545. Landmann, Colonel G. *Recollections of My Military Life*, London 1854, II, p. 293–5.
546. Leach, p. 97.
547. Simmons, pp. 179, 194.
548. Kincaid, p. 18.
549. Brotherton, T. *A Hawk at War: The Peninsular War Reminiscences of General Sir Thomas Brotherton*, ed. B. Perrett, Chippenham 1986, p. 77.
550. Grattan, p. 33.
551. Costello, in *USJ*, 1839, II, p. 223; the book version is slightly different (1967 edn., p. 58). The story was repeated in *USJ*, 1840, II, p. 215.
552. Austin, p. 28.
553. Hay, p. 163.
554. Sherer, p. 155.
555. Gleig, *The Subaltern*, pp. 48–9.
556. Wood, p. 15.
557. Simmons, pp. 193–4.
558. *GM*, May 1807, p. 481.

559. Kincaid, pp. 210–211.
560. Bunbury, p. 13.
561. 'History of His Majesty's late Fifth, or Royal Irish Regiment of Dragoons', in *BML*, II, p. 228.
562. 'G.H.', in *USJ*, 1834, I, p. 399; presumably either Lieutenant George Harrison, 79th, or Captain George Holmes, 92nd.
563. Mrs Ward (Tidy), in *USJ*, 1840, II, p. 477.
564. Wood, p. 55.
565. Kincaid, pp. 25, 173.
566. Sherer, pp. 219–21.
567. 'Failure of the Plan of Campaign of 1794, in Flanders', in *BML*, II, p. 235. This was apparently a common expression: Surtees heard it in 1799 (p. 15).
568. *BML*, I, p. 459.
569. On Talavera; *Monthly Magazine* November 1809, p. 354. 'E' may be Captain Evans, 2/24th, mortally wounded at Talavera.
570. Sherer, pp. 221–3.
571. 'Waterloo, the Day after the Battle', in *With Fife and Drum*, ed. A. H. Miles, London n.d., pp. 14–15.
572. George Napier, p. 96.
573. 'Statement of the Unfortunate Affair at El Hamet', in *USJ*, 1839, II, p. 234.
574. *EEC*, 30 May 1814.
575. Low, E. B. *With Napoleon at Waterloo*, ed. M. Macbride, London 1911, pp. 212, 219.
576. Tomkinson, p. 115.
577. *EEC*, 15 and 17 February 1812.
578. See Samson, Major J. L. R., 'Geordie Adams - A Promoted Rascal of the 42nd', in *Journal of the Orders and Medals Research Society*, 1984, pp. 249–51.
579. Surtees, p. 382.
580. *The Times*, 26 July 1814.
581. 'Old Sub', in *USJ*, 1840, II, pp. 182–3.

582. Robert Burns, *The Soldier's Return*.
583. Le Marchant, J. G. 'New Light on the Flanders Campaign of 1793: Contemporary Letters of Capt. J. G. Le Marchant', ed. Lieutenant-Colonel A. H. Burne, in *JSAHR*, XXX (1952), p. 117.
584. 'P.H.', 'The City Militia', in Goold Walker, G. *The Honourable Artillery Company 1537–1926*, London 1926, pp. 189–90.
585. 'Scotus', 'Interesting Particulars of the Revolution in Holland', in *GM*, supplement 1801, p. 1165.
586. Stanhope, p. 182.
587. Signed 'A White Man'; in *GM*, February 1803, p. 136.
588. H. Marshall, *Contributions to Statistics of the British Army*; orig. pub. in *Edinburgh Medical & Surgical Journal*, July 1835.
589. *GM*, February 1808, p. 178.
590. Ibid., April 1809, pp. 300–1.
591. Leach, p. 411.
592. See Buckley, R.N. *Slaves in Red Coats*, New Haven and London 1979, p. 68.
593. *USJ*, 1839, I, p. 372.
594. 'Old Sub', in *USJ*, 1840, II, p. 195.
595. See Browne, T. H. *The Napoleonic War Journal of Captain Thomas Henry Browne 1807–1816*, ed. R. N. Buckley, London 1987, p. 95.
596. 'Old Sub', in *USJ*, 1840, II, pp. 27–8.
597. The full story of Cochrane-Johnstone's roguery is recounted in Cochrane, A. *The Fighting Cochranes*, London 1983.
598. *An Act Concerning the Militia*, 9 December 1802.
599. *EEC*, 24 November 1810.
600. *GM*, supplement, 1813, I, pp. 612–13.
601. Report by the Chairman and Deputy-Chairman of the Company, quoted in

EEC, 13 April 1812.
602. *USJ*, 1839, III, p. 421.
603. To Colonel Stevenson, 17 August 1803; *WD*, II, p. 210.
604. Lake's dispatch, 12 September 1803.
605. *USJ*, 1839, III, p. 95.
606. Thorn, Major. *Memoirs of Gillespie*, 1816, p. 102.
607. Gillespie's own account is in *USJ*, 1840, II, pp. 559–60.
608. Blakiston, I, p. 295.
609. Ibid., I, p. 311.
610. General Order, 26 February 1798; see Fortescue, *History of the British Army*, IV, p. 573.
611. To Portland, 8 July 1798; see ibid., pp. 590–1.
612. *MC*, 6 September 1798.
613. *Monthly Magazine*, September 1799, pp. 592–3.
614. 'The Voices of the British Isles' (to the tune *Hearts of Oak*), *GM*, July 1803, p. 666.
615. *Monthly Magazine*, September 1799, p. 673.
616. Surtees, pp. 21, 26–7.
617. 'On the Invasion of Egypt by the French', in *GM*, September 1801, p. 839.
618. Proceedings of the Highland Society, *Cobbett's Weekly Political Register*, 25 December 1802, col. 804, quoting *The True Briton*, 25 February 1802.
619. *Cobbett's* ibid., col. 823.
620. *GM*, April 1809, p. 352.
621. *The Star*, 30 December 1801.
622. A facsimile is reproduced in 'More Considerations and Conclusions on the Material Available from the French Official Archives', J. A. Lochet, *Empires, Eagles & Lions*, Paris, Ontario, No. 60 (December 1981) pp. 4–5.
623. Bunbury, p. 160.
624. Ibid., p. 167.
625. Wilkie, *USJ*, 1840, III, p. 331.
626. Oswald's dispatch, 24 March; *London Gazette*, 23 June 1810.

627. *GM*, January 1808, p. 16.
628. *USJ*, 1840, II, p. 522.
629. Ibid., p. 523.
630. Croker, J. W. *The Croker Papers*, London 1884, I, pp. 12–13.
631. *USJ*, 1839, II, pp. 399–400.
632. *USJ*, 1839, III, p. 106.
633. Sherer, pp. 42–3.
634. *The News*, 6 November 1808.
635. *GM*, October 1808, p. 941.
636. *The News*, 6 November 1808.
637. Surtees, p. 92.
638. Simmons, p. 60.
639. Gordon, p. 166.
640. Poulett Cameron, in *USJ*, 1840, III, p. 32.
641. Hall, B. *Voyages and Travels of Captain Basil Hall R.N.*, London 1895, pp. 223, 227–8.
642. *GM*, February 1810, pp. 159–60.
643. Costello, in *USJ*, 1839, I, p. 237.
644. Warre, p. 74.
645. Moore Smith, p. 130.
646. *Monthly Magazine*, November 1810, pp. 351–2.
647. See Verner, Colonel W. *History and Campaigns of the Rifle Brigade*, London 1919, II, pp. 487–9.
648. Leach, p. 83.
649. MS account by unidentified sergeant of 1/2nd Foot Guards, author's possession.
650. *Monthly Magazine*, January 1810, p. 557.
651. Jones, *Memoranda relative to the Lines . . .*, p. 38.
652. Simmons, p. 54.
653. To W. Wellesley Pole, 4 October 1810; in *WSD*, VI, p. 607.
654. *EEC*, 5 November 1810.
655. *EEC*, 1 December 1810.
656. All quotations in this section are from Blakeney, R. *A Boy in the Peninsular War*, ed. J. Sturgis, London 1899, pp. 187–96.
657. *The Courier*, 19 April 1811.

658. Ibid., 25 April 1811.
659. Kincaid, pp. 237–8.
660. William Napier, *War in the Peninsula*, III, pp. 540–1.
661. Griffiths, pp. 307–8.
662. *WD*, VII, p. 400.
663. *The Courier*, 20 April 1811.
664. Sherer, pp. 197–8.
665. Kincaid, p. 66.
666. Grattan, p. 210.
667. To Hill, 12 June 1812; in *EEC*, 16 July 1812.
668. 'Epigram', in *GM*, November 1812, p. 472.
669. *EEC*, 24 August 1812.
670. Grattan, in *USJ*, 1834, II, pp. 182–3; in the original publication he mis-identified the French division as that of Foy. In the quotations which follow this error has been rectified, as in Oman's 1902 edn., pp. 242–6.
671. This account differs slightly from that published in *USJ*, 1840, III, pp. 382–4; additional details are taken from Hanley's MS account, written some twelve years earlier, for reference to which the author is indebted to Alan Harrison.
672. To Torrens, 8 August 1813; in *WD*, X, p. 616.
673. To Bathurst, 29 June 1813; in *WD*, X, p. 473.
674. Tovey, Lieutenant-Colonel G. 'Charge of a Company of the 20th at Roncesvalles', in *USJ*, 1839, III, p. 398.
675. Kincaid, Sir John. 'Captain Kincaid on the Bayonet', in *USJ*, 1839, III, p. 252. Kincaid was not an eye-witness but had the story from one of Tovey's brother-officers. Both accounts also appeared in Smyth, B. *History of the XX Regiment 1688–1888*, London 1889, pp. 406–9.
676. To Lord William Bentinck, 5 August 1813; in *WD*, X, p. 602.

677. Chambray, in *USJ*, 1834, III, p. 507.
678. Stretton, Colonel S. 'Anecdote of the 40th Regiment in the Pyrenees', in *USJ*, 1840, I, p. 308.
679. *GM*, August 1813, p. 179.
680. Gleig, *The Subaltern*, p. 55.
681. Robinson, in *JSAHR*, XXXIV, p. 169.
682. *Liverpool Mercury*, 21 January 1814.
683. To General Manuel Freyre, 14 November 1813; in *WD*, XI, p. 287; the original was written in French.
684. *EEC*, 11 April 1814.
685. Gardyne, C. G., *The Life of a Regiment*, 2nd edn. London 1929, I, p. 359.
686. The reported dialogue, in Gaelic, can be found in ibid., p. 323.
687. Clerk, Revd. A. *Memoir of Colonel John Cameron*, Glasgow 1858, p. 63.
688. William Napier, *War in the Peninsula*, VI, p. 409.
689. 'Garris', 'Take the Hill Before Dark', in *USJ*, 1839, III, p. 168.
690. 'Ghunzee', 'Take the Hill Before Dark', in *USJ*, 1840, III, p. 530.
691. *EEC*, 11 April 1814.
692. *WD*, XI, p. 668.
693. *EEC*, 21 March 1814.
694. 'J.M.E.', in *GM*, April 1814, p. 376.
695. *GM*, January 1810, p. 76.
696. *USJ*, 1840, II, pp. 26–7.
697. 'Old Sub', in *USJ*, 1840, II, p. 191.
698. Dispatch of Major-General John Keane, 26 December 1814; in *London Gazette*, 7 March 1815.
699. Gleig, *Washington and New Orleans*, pp. 154, 160.
700. Cooper, p. 143.
701. 'Old Sub', in *USJ*, 1840, I, pp. 454–5.
702. Latour, p. 161.
703. *USJ*, 1840, II, p. 343.
704. Cooper, p. 142.

705. Hamilton-Williams, D. C. *Waterloo: The Great Battle Reappraised*, London 1993.
706. Kincaid, p. 171.
707. Tomkinson, p. 295.
708. Ibid., p. 309.
709. Leach, pp. 393-4.
710. 'The Campaign of Waterloo, Strategically Examined', in *USJ*, 1834, II, p. 463.
711. Pattison, F. H. *Personal Recollections of the Waterloo Campaign*, Glasgow 1873, p. 8.
712. 21 December 1815; *WSD*, XIV, pp. 618–20.
713. Ibid.
714. *Waterloo Letters*, p. 226.
715. The author is indebted to the researches of David Hamilton-Williams for this fact.
716. *Waterloo Letters*, p. 240.
717. The author is indebted to the researches of Dr. John Hall for this information.
718. Tomkinson, pp. 312–13.
719. Kincaid, pp. 172–3.
720. Robert Burns, *The Soldier's Return*.
721. 'P.C.C.H.', 'Farewell to Minorca', in *GM*, supplement, 1802, p. 1209.
722. Wood, p. 247.
723. Gleig, *The Subaltern*, p. 363.
724. Harris, pp. 105–6.

Index